Lecture Notes in Computer Science 10749

Commenced Publication in 1973
Founding and Former Series Editors:
Gerhard Goos, Juris Hartmanis, and Jan van Leeuwen

More information about this series at http://www.springer.com/series/7412

Manoranjan Paul · Carlos Hitoshi
Qingming Huang (Eds.)

Image and Video Technology

8th Pacific-Rim Symposium, PSIVT 2017
Wuhan, China, November 20–24, 2017
Revised Selected Papers

 Springer

Editors
Manoranjan Paul
School of Computing and Mathematics
Charles Sturt University
Bathurst, NSW
Australia

Qingming Huang
University of Chinese Academy of Science
Beijing
China

Carlos Hitoshi
University of São Paulo
São Paulo
Brazil

ISSN 0302-9743   ISSN 1611-3349 (electronic)
Lecture Notes in Computer Science
ISBN 978-3-319-75785-8   ISBN 978-3-319-75786-5   (eBook)
https://doi.org/10.1007/978-3-319-75786-5

Library of Congress Control Number: 2018934319

LNCS Sublibrary: SL6 – Image Processing, Computer Vision, Pattern Recognition, and Graphics

Cover illustration: Yellow Crane Pagoda, Wuhan. Photo by Reinhard Klette, Auckland, New Zealand

Printed on acid-free paper

This Springer imprint is published by the registered company Springer International Publishing AG part of Springer Nature
The registered company address is: Gewerbestrasse 11, 6330 Cham, Switzerland

Preface

The Pacific-Rim Symposium on Image and Video Technology (PSIVT) 2017 took place in amazing Wuhan, China. Wuhan is a city that changes virtually every day: An extensive subway system and a more than 30-km-long walk- and bicycle way around the famous East Lake are just two of the very recent additions to Wuhan. Previous PSIVT symposiums were held in Taiwan, Chile, Japan, Singapore, South Korea, Mexico, and New Zealand; all host countries sharing a coastline with the Pacific Ocean.

The 2017 issue of PSIVT had four keynote speakers: Xiaoyi Jiang from the University of Münster, Germany, with his talk entitled "Biomedical Imaging: A Galisonian Perspective for Sciences," Shuicheng Yan from the National University of Singapore about "Deep Learning Towards On-Device Visual Analytics," Martin Constable from the Royal Melbourne Institute of the Arts, Vietnam, about "Color Contrast in the Aesthetic Image: An Examination of the Complex Ways That Color Contrast Manifests in Paintings," and Domingo Mery from the Pontificia Universidad Católica, Chile, with a talk entitled "Modern Computer Vision Techniques for X-ray Testing in Baggage Inspection." We thank all four keynote speakers for presenting wonderful talks that were informative, sometimes surprising, and altogether very much stimulating for those working in the addressed fields.

PSIVT 2017 attracted 197 submissions to the main conference and the five workshops taking place the day before the main conference. This volume contains all the accepted submissions presented at the main conference. Workshop papers are published in a separate LNCS volume. Each submission to the main conference was reviewed in full by at least three (and up to four) reviewers, before area chairs made recommendations and the three program co-chairs the final decision. In the main conference, 19 papers were accepted for oral presentation and 20 papers were accepted for poster presentation. The acceptance rate is 21% for oral presentations and 43% overall for the main conference. According to reviewing results we selected the three top-ranked accepted papers for the first oral session of the conference. An especially formed Award Committee decided for these three outstanding papers:

The best paper award went to Tao Rong, Rui Yang, and Ruoyu Yang from State Key Laboratory for Novel Software Technology, Nanjing University, China for the paper "Continuous Motion Recognition in Depth Camera Based on Recurrent Neural Networks and Grid-based Average Depth."

The best presentation paper award went to Ryo Furukawa, Masahito Naito, Daisuke Miyazaki, Masahi Baba, Shinsaku Hiura, Yoji Sanomura, Shinji Tanaka, and Hiroshi Kawasaki from Hiroshima City University, Japan, Hiroshima University Hospital, Japan, and Kyushu University, Japan, for the paper "Auto-Calibration Method for Active 3D Endoscope System Using Silhouette of Pattern Projector."

The best paper runner-up award went to Guangbin Wu, Weishan Chen, Wangmeng Zuo, and David Zhang from the State Key Laboratory of Robotics and System, Harbin

Institute of Technology, Harbin, China, for the paper "Unsupervised Domain Adaptation with Robust Deep Logistic Regression."

The social program of PSIVT 2017 included a banquet at the Xiongchu International Hotel, and a bus excursion to selected sites in Wuhan, followed by a stunning "survivors' party" in a nicely illuminated restaurant on the waters of the East Lake. These social events certainly also contributed to the success of the conference.

We thank our PSIVT 2017 sponsors, the National Engineering Research Center for E-learning, a joint institute of Central China Normal University and Wollongong University, and Wuhan Jingtian Electrical Co., Ltd.

We acknowledge the careful work of all reviewers and area chairs, the local Organizing Committee, especially the general chair, Xinguo Yu, and the head of the local committee, Chao Sun, both from Central China Normal University; we also thank this university for providing the conference venue. Of course, last but not least, we thank the PSIVT Steering Committee that was chaired during 2015–2017 by Reinhard Klette, Auckland University of Technology, New Zealand, for helpful support throughout the preparation of PSIVT 2017.

We thank the IAPR, the International Association for Pattern Recognition, for endorsing PSIVT 2017, and Springer's *Lecture Notes in Computer Science* team, especially Alfred Hofmann and Anna Kramer, for the efficient communication when submitting and finalizing this volume.

We look forward to seeing you all again at PSIVT 2019 in Sydney, Australia.

December 2017   Manoranjan Paul
                                                                            Carlos Hitoshi
                                                                          Qingming Huang

Organization

Hosted by

Central China Normal University, Wuhan, China

Honorary Chairs

Zhengyou Zhang	Microsoft, Redmond, USA
Reinhard Klette	Auckland University of Technology, New Zealand

General Chairs

Larry Davis	University of Maryland, USA
Antonio Robles-Kelly	NICTA, Australia
Xinguo Yu	Central China Normal University, China

Program Chairs

Qingming Huang	University of Chinese Academy of Sciences, China
Carlos Hitoshi	University of São Paulo, Brazil
Simon Lucey	CSIRO ICT Centre, Australia
Manoranjan Paul	Charles Sturt University, Australia

General Workshop Chairs

Shin'ichi Satoh	National Institute of Informatics, Japan
Chong-Wah Ngo	City University of Hong Kong, SAR China
Junsong Yuan	Nanyang Technological University, Singapore

Local Arrangements Chairs

Jingying Chen	Central China Normal University, China
Chao Sun	Central China Normal University, China

Demo/Exhibition Chairs

Tiziana D'Orazio	Institute for Signal and Image Processing, Italy
Wen-Huang Cheng	Research Center for Information Technology Innovation, Academia Sinica, Taiwan
Lingyu Duan	Peking University, China

Publicity Chairs

Yong Man Ro	Korea Advanced Institute of Science and Technology, South Korea
Jun-Wei Hsieh	National Taiwan Ocean University, Taiwan
Liyuan Li	Institute for Infocomm Research, Singapore
Hanqing Lu	National Laboratory of Pattern Recognition, CAS, China

Sponsorship Chairs

Bin He	Central China Normal University, China
Yue Wang	Institute of Information Technology, Singapore

Steering Committee

Chair

Reinhard Klette	Auckland University of Technology, New Zealand

Members

Akihiro Sugimoto	National Institute of Informatics, Japan
Xinguo YU	Central China Normal University, China
Kap Luk Chan	Nanyang Technological University, Singapore
Domingo Mery	Pontificia Universidad Católica, Chile
Yo-Sung Ho	Gwangju Institute of Science and Technology, South Korea
Wen-Nung Lie	National Chung Cheng University, Taiwan
Mariano Rivera	Centro de Investigación en Matemáticas, México

Area Chairs

Fay Huang	National Ilan University, Taiwan
Michael Cree	The University of Waikato, New Zealand
Nicolai Petkov	Groningen University, The Netherlands
Phil Bones	University of Canterbury, New Zealand
Li Chen	University of the DC, USA
Jian Cheng	Chinese Academy of Sciences, China
Uwe Franke	Daimler A. G., Germany
Hanseok Ko	Korea University, South Korea
Chilwoo Lee	Chonnam National University, South Korea
Wen-Nung Lie	National Chung Cheng University, Taiwan
Chia-Yen Chen	National University of Kaohsiung, Taiwan
Rick Millane	University of Canterbury, New Zealand
Takeshi Oishi	Tokyo University, Japan
Lei Qin	Chinese Academy of Sciences, China
Terence Sim	National University of Singapore, Singapore
Zhixun Su	Dalian University of Technology, China
Wei Qi Yan	Auckland University of Technology, New Zealand

Program Committee

Ajjen Joshi	Boston University, USA
Alex Carneiro	University of São Paulo, Brazil
Alexandre Morimitsu	University of Sao Paulo, Brazil
Andrew Kurauchi	University of São Paulo, Brazil
Antonio Diaz Tula	University of São Paulo, Brazil
Carlos Elmadjian	University of São Paulo, Brazil
Carlos Eduardo Thomaz	Centro Universitario da FEI, Brazil
Chang-Tsun Li	Charles Sturt University, Australia
Chia-Hung Yeh	National Sun Yat-sen University, Taiwan
Chih-Yang Lin Yuan	Ze University, Taiwan
Ching-Chun Huang	National Chung Cheng University, Taiwan
Chiung-Yao Fang	National Taiwan Normal University, Taiwan
D. M. Motiur Rahaman	Charles Sturt University, Australia
Darin O'Keeffe	Christchurch Hospital, New Zealand
Darko Brodic	University of Belgrade, Serbia
Deng-Yuan Huang	Dayeh University, Taiwan
Elham Saraee	Boston University, USA
Estephan Dazzi Wandekoken	Federal University of Espirito Santo, Brazil
Fabricio Martins Lopes	Federal University of Technology – Paraná, Brazil
Fay Huang	Ilan University, Taiwan
Filipe Costa	Federal University of Minas Gerais, Brazil
Flavio Coutinho	University of Sao Paulo, Brazil
Francisco Rodrigues	University of São Paulo, Brazil
Frank Borsato	Federal University of Technology – Parana, Brazil
Guo-Shiang Lin	Dayeh University, Taiwan
Guorong Li	Chinese Academy of Sciences, China
Hajime Nagahara	Osaka University, Japan
Harvey Ho	University of Auckland, New Zealand
Hélio Pedrini	University of Campinas, Brazil
Henrique Morimitsu	Inria – Grenoble, Switzerland
Hiroshi Kawasaki	Kyushu University, Japan
Igor Leonardo Oliveira Bastos	Universidade Federal da Bahia, Brazil
Jasmine Seng	Charles Sturt University, Australia
Jesús Mena-Chalco	Federal University of ABC, Brazil
Jian Sun	Xi'an Jiaotong University, China
Jiunn-Lin Wu	National Chung Hsing University, Taiwan
Junbiao Pang	Beijing University of Technology, China
Kar-Ann Toh	Yonsei University, Japan

Xiujuan Chai	ICT, Charles Sturt University, Australia
Xufeng Lin	Charles Sturt University, Australia
Yasushi Makihara	Osaka University, Japan
Yongkang Wong	National University of Singapore
Yongxi Lu	University of California San Diego, USA
Zhixun Su	Dalian University of Technology, China

Sponsors

National Engineering Research Centre for E-Learning
Central China Normal University Wollongong Joint Institute
IAPR
Wuhan Jingtian Electrical Co. Ltd.

Additional Reviewers

Hossain, Mohammad
Kashiwabara, Andre
Rahaman, D. M. Motiur
Rahman, Hamidur
Ren, Dongwei
Vicente, Fábio
Wang, Hao
Yang, Dong
Yu, Xiangyu
Zhang, Kai

Contents

Pattern Recognition and Applications

Image/Video Processing and Analysis

Multiset Canonical Correlation Analysis: Texture Feature Level Fusion of Multiple Descriptors for Intra-modal Palmprint Biometric Recognition

Raouia Mokni[1(✉)] [iD], Anis Mezghani[2], Hassen Drira[3], and Monji Kherallah[4]

[1] Faculty of Economics and Management of Sfax, University of Sfax, Sfax, Tunisia
raouia.mokni@gmail.com
[2] University of Sfax, Sfax, Tunisia
anis.mezghani@gmail.com
[3] Institut Mines-Télécom/Télécom Lille, CRIStAL (UMR CNRS 9189),
Lille, France
hassen.drira@telecom-lille.fr
[4] Faculty of Sciences of Sfax, University of Sfax,
Road Soukra Km 3, 3038 Sfax, Tunisia
monji.kherallah@fss.usf.tn

Abstract. This paper describes a novel intra-modal feature fusion for palmprint recognition based on fusing multiple descriptors to analyze the complex texture pattern. The main contribution lies in the combination of several texture features extracted by the Multi-descriptors, namely: Gabor Filters, Fractal Dimension and Gray Level Concurrence Matrix. This means to their effectiveness to confront the various challenges in terms of scales, position, direction and texture deformation of palmprint in unconstrained environments. The extracted Gabor filter-based texture features from the preprocessed palmprint images to be fused with the Fractal dimension-based-texture features and Gray Level Concurrence Matrix-based texture features using the Multiset Canonical Correlation Analysis method (MCCA). Realized experiments on three benchmark datasets prove that the proposed method surpasses other well-known state of the art methods and produces encouraging recognition rates by reaching 97.45% and 96.93% for the PolyU and IIT-Delhi Palmprint datasets.

Keywords: Palmprint · Texture analysis · Gabor Filters
Fractal Dimension · Gray Level Concurrence Matrix
Information fusion · Multiset Canonical Correlation Analysis (MCCA)

1 Introduction and related works

Human biometrics has become an area of tremendous importance and potential. By human biometrics we mean the use of physiological characteristics,

M. Paul et al. (Eds.): PSIVT 2017, LNCS 10749, pp. 3–16, 2018.
https://doi.org/10.1007/978-3-319-75786-5_1

of human body parts and their appearances, to identify individual human beings in the course of their daily activities. The appearances of body parts, especially in imaged data, have a large variability and are influenced by their texture patterns, colors, lighting environment, and so on. Therefore, the biometrics researchers have focused on body parts and images that try to minimize this variability within class (subjects) and maximize it across classes. This paper investigates the identification of the persons from one of the physical body parts, namely: Palmprint. Till now, more attention by many researchers has been paid to palmprint recognition systems thanks to its low cost, affordable materials, high recognition accuracy, etc. These systems have been grouped into two major ways: (1) Line-based structural approaches and (2) Texture-based global approaches.

Line-based structural approaches group essentially the principal lines [20], the wrinkles [4] and the ridges [5]. However, the major drawback of these approaches is the presence of the computation cost to extract its features, which means to a significant computational time. Unluckily, those features alone cannot provide satisfactory information to identify the person efficiently. Otherwise, texture-based global approaches incorporate the global information of images involving the texture. Various descriptors have been applied for analyzing the palmprint texture pattern, such as the Local Binary Pattern (LBP) [11], Fractal Dimension (FD) [7], Discrete cosine Transform (DCT) [2], Gabor Wavelets [28], Gabor filter (GF) [16], Gray Level Co-occurrence Matrix (GLCM) [19], etc.

Many researchers claim that they spend less effort on analyzing the texture information contrast the methods that are relied on analyzing the principal line shape information. Therefore, the accuracy of their recognition commonly relies on the reliability of the features.

In this paper, we propose a novel intra-modal feature fusion approach for palmprint identification based on fusing multiple-texture features extracted by different descriptors using the feature fusion level. For this end, Gabor filter, Fractal Dimension and Gray Level Co-occurrence Matrix descriptors are used to analyze the palmprint texture. Subsequently, we apply the dimensionality reduction technique based on the Principal Component Analysis in order to select the more discriminant feature. Then, we fuse these obtained features at feature fusion level relying on the Multiset Canonical Correlation Analysis method.

The reminder of this paper is structured as follows: In Sect. 2, the pipeline of the proposed intra-modal feature fusion approach and its modules are detailed. Experimental evaluation and comparison of the accuracy of our proposed approach with other state-of-the-art methods are presented in Sect. 3. Lastly, a conclusion and some perspectives are drawn in Sect. 4

2   Proposed Intra-modal Texture-Feature Fusion for Palmprint Identification

The pipeline of our suggested intra-modal feature fusion approach for palmprint identification summarizes the following modules: (1) Hand Acquisition

(2) Palmprint Preprocessing (3) Multiple-Texture-Feature Extraction (4) Feature Selection and Fusion (5) Matching and (6) Decision.

The whole modules of our proposed approach is depicted in Fig. 1.

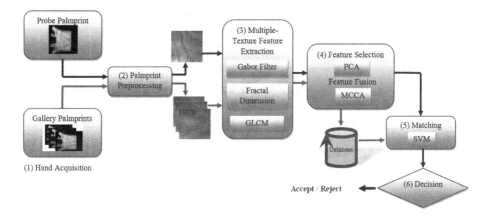

Fig. 1. Flowchart of our proposed intra-modal palmprint identification approach based on multiple-texture features

2.1 Palmprint Preprocessing

The palmprint preprocessing is a paramount module in the general biometric system. It is devoted for extracting the Region of interest (ROI) which has discriminatory and important features of recognition. This module includes three major steps, namely: Edge detection of the hand, Coordinate system Stabilization and ROI Preprocessing, which are described in detail in our previous work [23]. These steps are summarized in the following items:

- **(1) Edge detection of the hand:** This step aims to detect the hand contour in order that we can detect the finger-webs addressing to stabilize the ROI. To this end, we firstly converted the input hand image into binary image using an automatic thresholding technique such as the Otsu technique [24]. Then, we applied the Morphology operations incorporating the closing and the opening operations in order to surmount some identification problems, which are founded when the users place their hands in front of the camera with wearing accessories as the rings. Finally, we detected the contour of the hand and applied the smoothing filter.
- **(2) Coordinate System Stabilization:** In order to extract the ROI, it is necessary to stabilize the coordinate system. For this end, we start by adjusting the hand image with its edge and detecting its centroid as a reference point. Subsequently, we extract the finger-webs in order to obtain a stable coordinate system which enables us to extract and locate the ROI square.

– **(3) ROI Preprocessing:** After the ROI square extraction and localization, it is necessary to fix its size to $S \times S$ with $S = 128$ pixels and then rotate it to a vertical position. Lastly, we applied a low pass filter to enhance the quality of ROI in order to restrict the noise.

Figure 2 shows the original image, the edge detection of the hand, the stabilization of the coordinate system and the final extracted ROI of the palmprint.

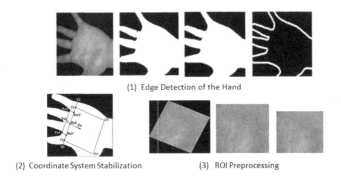

(1) Edge Detection of the Hand

(2) Coordinate System Stabilization   (3) ROI Preprocessing

Fig. 2. The Palmprint Preprocessing: (1) Edge detection of the hand, (2) Coordinate System Stabilization and (3) ROI Preprocessing

2.2 Multiple-Texture Feature Extraction

In this section, we provide a set of different features for every ROI palmprint image using multiple widely descriptors that better characterize the texture pattern in unconstrained environment, such as the Gabor Filter (GF) [18], the Fractal dimension (FD) [6] and the Gray Level Concurrence Matrix (GLCM) [12] descriptors. These different descriptors show its robustness to address the several challenges in terms of scales, position, direction and texture deformation of palmprint, that are produced when acquiring the images.

The Gabor Filter Descriptor. The Gabor Filter (GF) is one of the earliest and valuable frequency methods used to analyze the texture of the image. It has a huge variety in various pattern recognition applications [9,10,19]. The mainly advantage of GF focuses on their different challenging and variability concerning the rotation, position, translation, scale and lighting conditions of palmprint texture image in unconstrained environments. The Gabor filter is based on extracting directly the texture features from the Gray level images. In the spatial domain, a 2-D Gabor filter based in both frequency (scale) and orientation is a Gaussian kernel function modulated by a complex sinusoidal plane wave, defined as the following equation:

$$G(x,y) = \frac{\mu^2}{\Pi \times \gamma \times \eta} \exp\left(-\left(\frac{x'^2 + \gamma^2 \times y'^2}{2\sigma^2}\right)\right) \exp(j \times 2 \times \Pi \times \mu \times x' + \phi);$$

$$x' = x \cos \nu + y \sin \nu$$
$$y' = -(x \sin \nu + y \cos \nu)$$

$$(1)$$

Where μ represents the central frequencies (scale) of the sinusoidal plane wave and ν is the orientation of the normal to the parallel stripes of a Gabor function. σ is the standard deviation of the Gaussian envelope, ϕ is the phase offset and γ is the ratio of the spatial aspect that stipulates the ellipticity of the Gabor function support.

In our experimental evaluations, the palmprint image is convolved with $G = 40$ Gabor filters at five frequencies ($\mu = 5$) and eight orientations ($\nu = 8$), as illustrated in Fig. 3. We pursue to apply the same Gabor filters parameters suggested by Haghighat et al. [10] to build the feature vector. Thus, let us define that we calculated the vector dimension as:

$$FV_{GF} = ((S \times S) \times \mu \times \nu)/(d \times d) \qquad (2)$$

Where $S = 128$ pixels is the size of palmprint ROI image, $\mu = 5$ is the number of frequencies, $\nu = 8$ is the number of orientations and $d = 4$ is the factor of downsampling the features that is used to reduce the redundancy of the texture information producing by the correlation between the adjacent pixels in palmprint ROI image [10]. Therefore, the dimension of the feature vector is equal to $(128 \times 128 \times 40)/(4 \times 4) = 655,360/16 = 40,960$. In addition, this vector is normalized to zero mean and unit variance.

Fractal Dimension Descriptor. Fractal Dimension (FD) method is one of the effective methods used to extract the Model based texture features. It is considered as a widely applied descriptor, especially for analyzing the texture representation, in several fields like the signature recognition [30], palmprint recognition [7,22], writer identification [3], etc. A fractal object has a very complicate shape

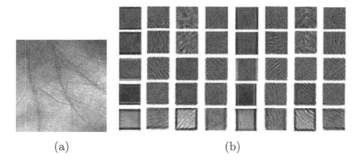

(a)   (b)

Fig. 3. (a) The extracted palmprint ROI. (b) The real part with applying the Gabor filter in five frequencies and eight orientations on the palmprint image.

which is a collection of different sub-objects recurring in different scales. Several methods are proposed to compute the fractal dimension like the Box Counting (BC), Differential Box Counting (DBC), Mass Radius (MR), Cumulative intersection (CI), etc. Among these methods, the BC is the deeply used method to estimate the fractal dimension and analyze the texture shape thanks to its utility to describe the interruption and complexity of the image texture. The ultimate principle of BC method focuses on converting the input image to binary image and then splitting it into a boxes number with several scales ϵ. After that, it is necessary to compute the number of boxes including the shape information $N(\epsilon)$ for each scale. Thus, the fractal dimension FD is obtained by a least squares regression method, as illustrated in the following equation:

$$FD = slop \frac{log(N(\epsilon))}{log(1/\epsilon)} \tag{3}$$

In our experiments, we proposed a method to provide the shape information in horizontal and vertical spaces of palmprint ROI image. In this case, we divided it, sequentially, into $r \times r$ sub regions equivalent squares. It is imminent that the value $r = 10$ is chosen after a set of experiments. For each sub-region, the fractal Dimension FD is calculated. Therefore, we obtained a sequence of FDs for the whole input palmprint ROI image presented by the following feature vector:

$$FV_{FD} = FD_1, FD_2, \ldots, FD_{(r \times r)} \tag{4}$$

Gray Level Concurrence Matrix Descriptor. The Co-occurrence Matrix (GLCM) is one of the robust statistical methods used to describe the image texture [19]. This method presents a matrix which contains valuable information about the statistical distribution of intensities and provides information about the relative position of neighborhood pixels of the analyzed image.

More specifically, let us have an image Img, of size $S \times S$, the GLCM matrix Gm can be defined by Riabaric et al. [25] as: $Gm(i, j, \delta, \theta)$, size $G \times G$, where the values of the pixels are quantized into G levels, contains at the position (i, j) a number of occurrences of a pair of pixels that are at the offset $\delta = 1, 2, 3, \ldots, etc$, (the offset δ is a distance between the interested neighborhood pixels) in the direction $\theta = 0°, 45°, 90°, 135°$ (θ is the angle between interested neighborhood pixels or the rotation angle of an offset), where one pixel has a gray-level value i and another pixel has a gray-level value j. In literature, Haralick described fourteen statistical Haralick features to normalize the gray level co-occurrence matrices [12]. In our empirical experiments, we applied only six of these features which are:

– Contrast:

$$f_1 = \sum_{n=0}^{G-1} n^2 \sum_{i=0}^{G-1} \sum_{j=0}^{G-1} Gm(i, j); \tag{5}$$
$$n = |i - j|$$

– Variance:

$$f_2 = \sum_{i=0}^{G-1} \sum_{j=0}^{G-1} (i - \mu)^2 Gm(i,j) \tag{6}$$

– Energy:

$$f_3 = \sum_{i=0}^{G-1} \sum_{j=0}^{G-1} Gm(i,j)^2 \tag{7}$$

– Entropy:

$$f_4 = \sum_{i=0}^{G-1} \sum_{j=0}^{G-1} Gm(i,j) \times \log(Gm(i,j)) \tag{8}$$

– Homogeneity or Inverse difference moment:

$$f_5 = \sum_{i=0}^{G-1} \sum_{j=0}^{G-1} \frac{Gm(i,j)}{1 + (i-j)^2} \tag{9}$$

Where Gm is GLCM matrix and G is Grey Scale value, μ is the mean value.
– Correlation:

$$f_6 = \sum_{i=0}^{G-1} \sum_{j=0}^{G-1} \frac{(i \times j) \times Gm(i,j) - (\mu_x \times \mu_y)}{\sigma_x \sigma_y} \tag{10}$$

Where Gm is GLCM matrix and G is Grey Scale value, μ_x, μ_y are the mean value and σ_x, σ_y are standard deviation along two axes X and Y.

In this work, we follow the same parameters proposed in our prior work [19] to construct the feature vector. So, the number of gray levels of palmprint ROI is $G = 256$. We have split each ROI into small 8×8 sub-images by a non-overlapping sliding window. For each ROI, we have obtained 64 sub-images. For each sub-image, the GLCMs matrices are calculated corresponding to four different values of direction with four different offset values mentioned above.

Hence, we have obtained 16 GLCMs (4 (offset value) × 4 (direction number)) for each sub-image. Then, we have calculated the six Haralick features for each GLCM. Therefore, the feature vector is calculated by the multiplication of the number of GLCMs for ROI image and the number of Haralick features, as follows:

$$VF_{GLCM} = (64 \times 16) \times 6 = 6144. \tag{11}$$

2.3   Feature Selection and Fusion

The fusion of different information in the biometric system has gained a great interest in various researchers teams. This fusion between the multiple descriptors will be improve the recognition accuracy. Indeed, it can occur in different ways for a recognition system, such as: Fusion at the data or feature level, Fusion at the score level and Fusion at the decision level.

Several prior researchers believe that the fusion at feature level way is considered to be more effective than the other ways by virtue of the capability of fusing the multiple sources of information to achieve a single feature set, that contains more efficient richer information than the fusion at the score and the decision levels [8,17]. Thus, the fusion at feature level is widely important to produce a substantial identification. There are many manners of the fusion at the feature level [29], namely: the Serial feature fusion and the Parallel feature fusion. The two fusion manners can ameliorate the accuracy of recognition of persons to some extent. However, neither of these fusion methods focused on the inherent correlations across multiple feature sets. Therefore, both of these fusion methods cannot reach tremendous feature fusion. To surmount this weakness, the Canonical Correlation Analysis (CCA) feature fusion method is conducted to extract the feature pairs describing the intrinsic relationship between two feature sets [21,26] and also the Multiset Canonical Correlation Analysis (MCCA) method is considered as a generalization of the CCA method and is proposed to be suitable for fusing more than two sets of features, as presented in our cases.

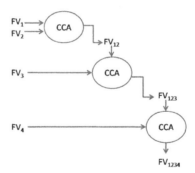

Fig. 4. Multiset Canonical Correlation Analysis method for 4 feature vectors with $rank(FV_1) > rank(FV_2) > rank(FV_3) > rank(FV_4)$

Therefore, the main principle of MCCA method is conducted by combining the first two feature vectors that have highest ranks using CCA method and then fusing the result with the next feature vector that has an utmost rank using CCA method, and so on. Figure 4 illustrates an example of the process of the MCCA method for four feature vectors with $rank(FV_1) > rank(FV_2) > rank(FV_3) > rank(FV_4)$. In this example, the first step of MCCA focuses on fusing FV_1 and FV_2, which have the highest ranks using CCA method. Then, FV_{12} is fused with the next highest rank feature vector FV_3 and finally, FV_4 is fused with FV_{123} using yet CCA method.

A Brief Background of Canonical Correlation Analysis Method. The Canonical Correlation Analysis method firstly implements a function of correlation criterion between two sets of feature vectors and secondly calculates the projection vector set of these two sets depending on the criterion. Finally, the fused canonical correlation features are extracted.

As defined in [21], given $X \in \mathbb{R}^{a \times n}$ and $Y \in \mathbb{R}^{b \times n}$ two matrices, where n is the number of samples, a is the dimensionality of the first feature set and b is the dimensionality of the second feature set.

Suppose that $M_{xx} \in \mathbb{R}^{a \times a}$ and $M_{yy} \in \mathbb{R}^{b \times b}$ present the within-sets covariance matrices of X and Y. Additionally, $M_{xy} \in \mathbb{R}^{a \times b}$ the matrix defines the between-set covariance matrix (where $M_{yx} = M_{xy}^T$). Hence, M includes all the information about the relationship between pairs of features, as defined follows:

$$M = \begin{pmatrix} M_{xx} & M_{xy} \\ M_{yx} & M_{yy} \end{pmatrix} = \begin{pmatrix} cov(x) & cov(x,y) \\ cov(y,x) & cov(y) \end{pmatrix} \tag{12}$$

Although the correlation between the two feature vector sets shows no coherent pattern, there exist huge difficulties to understand and analyze the association between multiple sets from this matrix [8,15,21]. For this purpose, the CCA method aims to find the linear combinations, $X^* = W_x^T X$ and $Y^* = W_y^T Y$, which maximize the pair-wise correlation through the two data sets. W_x and W_y are the transformation matrices which are establish by obtaining the following eigenvalue equations:

$$\begin{cases} M_{xx}^{-1} M_{xy} M_{yy}^{-1} M_{yx} \hat{W}_x = \xi^2 \hat{W}_x \\ M_{yy}^{-1} M_{yx} M_{xx}^{-1} M_{xy} \hat{W}_y = \xi^2 \hat{W}_y \end{cases} \tag{13}$$

Where, $\hat{W}_x$ and $\hat{W}_y$ are the eigenvectors and ξ^2 is the diagonal matrix of eigenvalues or squares of the canonical correlations. These two matrices W_x and W_y consist of the classed eigenvectors corresponding to the non-zero eigenvalues. $X^*, Y^* \in \mathbb{R}^{r \times n}$ are renown as canonical variates, note that r is the length of the projected feature vector, which presents the rank of the between-set covariance matrix M_{xy}, which is equal to the minimum rank of both input feature matrices, X and Y. Thus, $r = rank(M_{xy}) \leq (min(rank(X), rank(Y)))$ i.e. $r \leq rank(n, a, b)$ is the number of non-zero eigenvalues in each equation, that will be selected by the decrease order, $\tau_1 \geq \tau_2 \geq \tau_3 \ldots \geq \tau_r$.

In our experiments, in accordance by the suggested work by Sun et al. [26], the feature fusion is conducted either by summation or concatenation of these linear transformed feature vectors:

$$Z_{Sum} = X^* + Y^* = W_x^T X + W_y^T Y = \begin{pmatrix} W_x \\ W_y \end{pmatrix}^T \begin{pmatrix} X \\ Y \end{pmatrix} \tag{14}$$

Or

$$Z_{Concat} = \begin{pmatrix} X^* \\ Y^* \end{pmatrix} \begin{pmatrix} W_x^T X \\ W_y^T Y \end{pmatrix} = \begin{pmatrix} W_x & 0 \\ 0 & W_y \end{pmatrix}^T \begin{pmatrix} X \\ Y \end{pmatrix} \tag{15}$$

where Z_{Sum} and Z_{Concat} are named the Canonical Correlation Discriminant Features by summation and concatenation manners, respectively.

The CCA based fusion has a inconvenient which is focused in a Small Sample Size (SSS) issue. In the most applications, the number of samples n is habitually less than the number of features $(n < a)$ and $(n < b)$. In order to overcame this SSS problem, we proposed to reduce the dimensionality of the obtained feature vectors $(FV_{GF}, FV_{FD}$ and $FV_{GLCM})$ using Principal Component Analysis method (PCA) [14] and then applied the MCCA method incorporating for each fusion between two vectors the CCA method using the concatenation manner defined in Eq. 15 to fuse the different features vectors into a single feature vector.

2.4 Matching

Support Vector Machine (SVM) is a supervised classifier which is a vigorous statistical technique suggested by Vapnik [27]. This classifier has been widely intended to resolve the problems of discrimination, classification or regression in several applications. It is applied to determine an optimal separating hyper-plane or decision surface with the adaptation of a new corresponding technique to map the sample points into a high-dimensional feature space and categorized using a non-linear transformation, even when the data are linearly inseparable. The optimal hyper-plane is obtained by working out a quadratic programming problem relied on regularization parameters. This transformation was performed by kernel functions like Linear Kernel (LK), Radial Basis Function (RBF) and Polynomial Kernel (PK) which are exploited in this work in order to classify the query sample.

3   Experiments and Analyses

We performed our experimental researches fusing different texture information using MCCA method. The proposed approach was assessed over IIT-Delhi [13] and PolyU [1] databases. The results are discussed below.

3.1 Database Description

The IIT-New Delhi India campus provides a IIT-Delhi palmprint database that includes 2300 images acquired from 230 persons aged from 12–57 years. For each person, five samples have been collected from both left and right palms. These palmprint samples are captured in unconstrained environment with several challenges and variation in terms of position, scale, direction and texture deformation.

The Hong Kong Polytechnic University offered a PolyU-Palmprint database that contains 7752 images captured from 386 persons. Twenty samples of each palm were acquired in two separate sessions. Each session contains ten sample images. The average time interval between these sessions is two month. The samples collected during these two separate sessions acquired by two different cameras. This means that there exist a variation in terms of lighting between the first and second sessions, which leads to more difficulty in person's identification.

3.2   Experimental Evaluation

We evaluated the accuracy of our suggested approach over two benchmark databases described above. For the IIT-Delhi database, we arbitrarily singled three samples of each palm as gallery set and the remainder of samples as the probe set. On the other hand, we selected ten samples of each person from the first session of the PolyU database for the gallery set and ten samples from the second session were chosen for the probe set. This mixture between the samples collected in separate sessions is important in a real application.

In our experiments, we conducted the performance of our proposed intra-modal feature fusion using two different methods of fusion at feature levels, namely: Serial and MCCA methods. For more clearly, the Serial feature fusion is based on combining multiple feature vector sets into a single feature vector using a simple concatenation. We recall that before fusing the multiple features by MCCA method, we applied the dimensionality reduction based on PCA method in order to overcome the SSS problem. Likewise, when using Serial feature fusion method, we also used the PCA method for reducing the dimensionality of the final obtained vector. So, we reveal the experiment results of the Serial and MCCA feature fusion methods corresponding to several kernel functions of SVM classifier for IIT-Delhi and PolyU datasets in Table 1. It can be noticed that the recognition rates obtained by the SVM classifier with Radial Basis Kernel (RBF) outperforms other kernel functions results (LK and PK) for both datasets.

Table 1. The different results of our proposed intra-modal feature fusion approach based on both Serial and MCCA method evaluating over PolyU and IIT-Delhi databases.

RRs (%)	PolyU-database			IIT-Delhi-database		
	LK	RBF	PK	LK	RBF	PK
Serial + PCA	96.65	96.95	57.50	94.20	94.50	56.43
PCA + MCCA	97.20	**97.45**	60.55	96.88	**96.93**	57.03

Since we performed our experiments with both the MCCA and the Serial feature fusion methods, it is obvious that the performance of the MCCA feature fusion method surpasses the Serial feature fusion method for both databases.

4   Comparison with Other Works

Finally, we performed a comparison between our work and some of the earlier published works in literature, as Highlighted in Table 2. The protocols setting in terms of the sample classification between both the gallery set and the probe set used in these different experiments are the same, over IIT-Delhi dataset. Therefore, it is noted that we achieved a better RR of about 96.93% than both the presented works in [16, 20]. Despite all the experiments over PolyU database conducted by a mixture of two sessions, which leads to difficulty for individual's identification, this protocol is very significant in a real application. Noticeably, the result of our proposed method outperforms the totality of prior works results. For obtaining a fair comparison with the state-of the-art methods, we yet evaluated our method following the same evaluation protocols presented in the proposed works by [19,28]. Therefore, our proposed method provided yet the better performance 97.38% and 97.00% than these works, respectively. This brings to improved rates of about 0.83 % and 1.60 % to the results of these works ([19,28]).

Table 2. The comparison between our work and some of state of-the-art works. Protocols description: gallery set (G), probe set (P).

Approaches		Palmprint-databases (protocol setting)	RRs (%)
Method in [16]	Gabor filters	IIT-Delhi (3G/2P)	95.00
Method in [20]	FDBC+RF	IIT-Delhi (3G/2P)	95.80
Method in [19]	GLCM, Gabor Filters+GDA+SVM	PolyU (10G/5P)	96.55
Method in [2]	DCT, LDA+WSR	PolyU (2G/10P)	97.00
Method in [28]	2DGW+PCNN+SVM	PolyU (5G/10P)	95.40
The proposed method	GF+FD+GLCM+PCA+MCCA+SVM (RBF)	IIT-Delhi (3G/2P)	96.93
		PolyU (10G/10P)	97.45
		PolyU (10G/5P)	97.38
		PolyU (5G/10P)	97.00

. These achieved performance evaluating over two benchmark datasets demonstrate the effectiveness of our proposed method to the different existing challenges in unconstrained environment.

5   Conclusions and Perspectives

In this paper, we presented an intra-modal-texture feature fusion approach based on fusing multiple feature sets extracted from a texture representation. In fact, we combined different texture information extracted by multiple descriptors, like Gabor Filter, Fractal Dimension and Gray Level Concurrence Matrix descriptors which are invariant to different existing challenges. In fact, we proposed a feature fusion method such as the Multiset Canonical Correlation Analysis (MCCA) to fuse these obtained texture information incorporating the Principal Component Analysis (PCA) in order to reduce the feature dimensionality of each feature set. This proposed approach prove its robustness against different challenge attacks in unconstrained environment. The experimental results on the PolyU and IIT-Delhi databases demonstrate that our proposed approach surpasses the existing state-of-the-art methods. As future works, we plan to integrate a fusion between multiple representation of palmprint such as the texture and the principal line. We also pursue to assess our proposed approach with other biometric metrics in order to provide a palmprint verification system.

References

1. Polyu database. http://www4.comp.polyu.edu.hk/~biometrics/
2. Ahmad, M.I., Ilyas, M.Z., Ngadiran, R., Isa, M.N.M., Yaakob, S.N.: Palmprint recognition using local and global features. In: IWSSIP, pp. 79–82 (2014)
3. Chaabouni, A., Boubaker, H., Kherallah, M., Alimi, A.M., El Abed, H.: Fractal and multi-fractal for Arabic offline writer identification. In: 20th International Conference on Pattern Recognition, pp. 3793–3796. IEEE (2010)
4. Chen, J., Zhang, C., Rong, G.: Palmprint recognition using crease. In: 2001 Proceedings of International Conference on Image Processing, vol. 3, pp. 234–237. IEEE (2001)
5. Dai, J., Feng, J., Zhou, J.: Robust and efficient ridge-based palmprint matching. IEEE Trans. Pattern Anal. Mach. Intell. **34**(8), 1618–1632 (2012)
6. Fractals, M.B.L.O.: Forme, hasard et dimension. Flammarion, Paris (1975)
7. Guo, X., Zhou, W., Wang, Y.: Palmprint recognition algorithm with horizontally expanded blanket dimension. Neurocomputing **127**, 152–160 (2014)
8. Haghighat, M., Abdel-Mottaleb, M., Alhalabi, W.: Fully automatic face normalization and single sample face recognition in unconstrained environments. Expert Syst. Appl. **47**, 23–34 (2016)
9. Haghighat, M., Zonouz, S., Abdel-Mottaleb, M.: Identification using encrypted biometrics. In: Wilson, R., Hancock, E., Bors, A., Smith, W. (eds.) CAIP 2013. LNCS, vol. 8048, pp. 440–448. Springer, Heidelberg (2013). https://doi.org/10.1007/978-3-642-40246-3_55
10. Haghighat, M., Zonouz, S., Abdel-Mottaleb, M.: Cloudid: trustworthy cloud-based and cross-enterprise biometric identification. Expert Syst. Appl. **42**(21), 7905–7916 (2015)
11. Hammami, M., Jemaa, S.B., Ben-Abdallah, H.: Selection of discriminative subregions for palmprint recognition. Multimedia Tools Appl. **68**(3), 1023–1050 (2014)
12. Haralick, R.M.: Statistical and structural approaches to texture. Proc. IEEE **67**(5), 786–804 (1979)
13. IIT Delhi (IIoTD): IIT Delhi Touchless Palmprint Database (Version 1.0) (2014). http://web.iitd.ac.in/~ajaykr/Database_Palm.htm
14. Jollie, I.: Principal Component Analysis. Wiley, Hoboken (2002)
15. Krzanowski, W.: Principles of Multivariate Analysis: A User's Perspective. Clarendon, New York (1988)
16. Kumar, A., Shekhar, S.: Palmprint recognition using rank level fusion. In: 2010 17th IEEE International Conference on Image Processing (ICIP), pp. 3121–3124. IEEE (2010)
17. Latha, Y.M., Prasad, M.V.: Intramodal palmprint recognition using texture feature. Int. J. Intell. Syst. Des. Comput. **1**(1-2), 168–185 (2017)
18. Lee, T.S.: Image representation using 2D gabor wavelets. IEEE Trans. Pattern Anal. Mach. Intell. **18**(10), 959–971 (1996)

19. Mokni, R., Elleuch, M., Kherallah, M.: Biometric palmprint identification via efficient texture features fusion. In: International Joint Conference on Neural Networks, pp. 4857–4864 (2016)
20. Mokni, R., Drira, H., Kherallah, M.: Combining shape analysis and texture pattern for palmprint identification. Multimedia Tools Appl. **76**, 1–28 (2016). https://doi.org/10.1007/s11042-016-4088-5
21. Mokni, R., Drira, H., Kherallah, M.: Fusing multi-techniques based on LDA-CCA and their application in palmprint identification system. In: 2017 IEEE/ACS 14th International Conference on Computer Systems and Applications (AICCSA). IEEE (2017, in press)
22. Mokni, R., Kherallah, M.: Palmprint recognition through the fractal dimension estimation for texture analysis. Int. J. Biometr. **8**(3–4), 254–274 (2016)
23. Mokni, R., Zouari, R., Kherallah, M.: Pre-processing and extraction of the ROIs steps for palmprints recognition system. In: International Conference on Intelligent Systems Design and Applications, pp. 380–385 (2015)
24. Otsu, N.: A threshold selection method from gray-level histograms. Automatica **11**(285–296), 23–27 (1975)
25. Ribarić, S., Lopar, M.: Palmprint recognition based on local texture features. In: 9th International Conference on Machine Learning and Data Mining in Pattern Recognition, MLDM 2013, International Workshop on Intelligent Pattern Recognition and Applications, WIPRA 2013 (2013)
26. Sun, Q.S., Zeng, S.G., Liu, Y., Heng, P.A., Xia, D.S.: A new method of feature fusion and its application in image recognition. Pattern Recogn. **38**(12), 2437–2448 (2005)
27. Vapnik, V.: The Nature of Statistical Learning Theory. Springer Science & Business Media, New York (1995). https://doi.org/10.1007/978-1-4757-3264-1
28. Wang, X., Lei, L., Wang, M.: Palmprint verification based on 2D-gabor wavelet and pulse-coupled neural network. Knowl.-Based Syst. **27**, 451–455 (2012)
29. Yang, J.: Yang, J.y., Zhang, D., Lu, J.f.: Feature fusion: parallel strategy vs. serial strategy. Pattern Recogn. **36**(6), 1369–1381 (2003)
30. Zouari, R., Mokni, R., Kherallah, M.: Identification and verification system of offline handwritten signature using fractal approach. In: 1st International Image Processing, Applications and Systems Conference, pp. 1–4. IEEE (2014)

Complex-Valued Representation for RGB-D Object Recognition

Rim Trabelsi[1,2,3]($\boxtimes$), Issam Jabri[4], Farid Melgani[5], Fethi Smach[6],
Nicola Conci[5], and Ammar Bouallegue[2]

[1] Advanced Digital Sciences Center, Singapore, Singapore
rim.t@adsc.com.sg
[2] SysCom Laboratory, National Engineering School of Tunis,
University of Tunis El Manar, Tunis, Tunisia
[3] Hatem Bettaher IResCoMath Research Unit,
National Engineering School of Gabes, University of Gabes, Gabès, Tunisia
[4] College of Computer and Information Systems, Al Yamamah University,
· Riyadh, Kingdom of Saudi Arabia
[5] Department of Information Engineering and Computer Science,
University of Trento, Trento, Italy
[6] Profil Technology, 92120 Montrouge, France

Abstract. Object recognition methods usually tend to focus on single cues coming from traditional vision based systems but ignore to incorporate multi-modal data. With the advent of depth RGB-D sensors which provide synchronized multi-modal data with good quality, new opportunities have been emerged. In this paper, we make use of RGB and depth images to propose a new object recognition approach. Using a pixelwise scheme, we propose a novel method to describe RGB-D images with a complex-valued representation. By means of neural network, we introduce a new CVNN (Complex-Valued Neural Network) with RBF neurons. Different from many RGB-D features, the proposed approach is able to jointly use RGB and depth data within a unified end-to-end learning framework. Category and instance object recognition tasks are evaluated through experiments carried out on a large scale RGB-D object dataset. Results show that our method can efficiently recognize objects in RGB-D images and outperforms state-of-the-art approaches.

Keywords: RGB-D representation · Object recognition
Complex-valued neural networks · Multi-modal data

1 Introduction

Object recognition is technologically challenging and practically useful problem in computer vision area owing to its wide spectrum of potential applications. This task deals with classifying an object into one of several predefined categories in an image. Strong solutions have been proposed in controlled environment [1,2]. However, many issues still challenging until now with the presence

© Springer International Publishing AG, part of Springer Nature 2018
M. Paul et al. (Eds.): PSIVT 2017, LNCS 10749, pp. 17–27, 2018.
https://doi.org/10.1007/978-3-319-75786-5_2

of color camouflage, cluttered backgrounds, objects occlusion and uncontrolled illumination. Most of the proposed attempts rely on traditional vision systems specifically on appearance data and their features. Recently, the development of 3D cameras and depth sensors have created new opportunities to advance the state-of-the-art of this field. In fact, depth information is less affected by those challenging matters. Yet, the extraction of depth may be itself affected by other issues including illumination changes. For this reason, the joint use of these multi-modal information, i.e., appearance and depth, is very required to get robust features. With the advent of RGB-D sensors, depth maps can be extracted in real-time scenarios with good quality at low cost synchronized with RGB frames. Since the public release of RGB-D object dataset [3], a number of attempts have been made to recognize objects in RGB-D images [4–6]. Most of the proposed methods relied on region-based or holistic features that are combined in a trivial way from RGB and depth frames without joint fusion of the two modalities and ignores the particularity of depth maps and treat them the same way as appearance images.

In this paper, we propose to address the problem of object recognition in RGB-D images in a pixel-wise way. To this end, we introduced a new end-to-end strategy to classify images with a complex-valued representation. Inspired by the fact that point cloud, which corresponds to the mapping between RGB and depth images, could be easily seen as a complex-valued signal, we investigate complex-valued neural networks (CVNNs) to make use of both modalities in a joint way. Precisely, the main contributions of this paper are as follows. (i) A new RGB-D representation is proposed by projecting the real-valued data into the complex coordinate space where the depth is assumed as the imaginary part. (ii) Inspired by CVNNs [7,8], a new end-to-end approach is introduced to solve the object recognition task in a pixel-wise fashion using RBF networks. (iii) Since RBF networks have a single hidden layer, their prototype vectors are here constructed using a K-means clustering algorithm with an adaptive method in order to fit complex-valued data. (iv) Evaluation of the proposed approach is finally evaluated over a large scale RGB-D dataset and compared with state-of-the-art methods.

The remaining of the paper is organized as follows. After reviewing related work in Sect. 2, we present the proposed method for object recognition with complex-valued representation in Sect. 3. Evaluation of two object recognition tasks over a large scale RGB-D dataset and comparisons with other state-of-the-art methods are reported in Sect. 4. Finally, in Sect. 5, the main contributions of the proposed approach in this paper are summarized.

2   Related Work

In this section, we will briefly highlight connections and differences between our approach and existing works mainly RGB-D representations designed for object recognition and since CVNNs are not employed so far to solve the target task, we present here a summary about their fundamental advances.

RGB-D based Representations. Using the RGB-D object recognition dataset published in 2011 [3], Bo et al. [9] succeeded to propose a new descriptor, named kernel descriptors, which enabled the use of multi-modal data by generalizing a set of features based on kernels. Lai et al. [10] proposed an efficient hierarchical classification approach where all hierarchy levels of the objects were used to enhance classification as well as pose estimation with stochastical gradient descent. In [11], the proposed method extracted hierarchical features from RGB-D images without supervision using hierarchical matching pursuit extended from [12].

Along with these hand-crafted methods, a quite interesting endeavors tried to adapt the revolutionary deep Convolution Neural Networks (CNNs) to fit RGB-D data. For example, using ImageNet pre-trained models, [13] proposed an architecture composed of two separate CNNs, one for the RGB and the other for the "D". These two networks were combined with a late fusion network. An effective encoding to color space of depth images is proposed as well to fit model devoted to RGB images. Addressing objects detection problem, [5] come up with a new idea regarding the adaptation of depth information to the pre-trained color CNN model: the so-called HHA encoding. They extracted from depth image three channels at each pixel: horizontal disparity, height above ground, and the angle the pixels local surface normal makes with the inferred gravity direction. This representation has been intensively reused for further RGB-D tasks based CNN features.

Complex-Valued Neural Networks (CVNNs). In our daily lives, the large variety of information is dramatically increasing. It is hence expected to develop systems that process a wider range of information in more adaptive and effective ways just like human brain executes or better. So, this requires more suitable information's representations. In order to make use of data with different modalities, we can model a couple of related real-valued signal as a complex-valued signal. With application to our context, we will later make use of such representation with visual 2D and 3D data. To this end, CVNNs were extended from the classic neural networks that we call here Real-Valued Neural Networks (RVNNs). CVNNs deal with information belonging to the complex coordinate space with complex-valued parameters and variables. "In relation to physicality, neural functions including learning and self-organization are influenced by sensorimotor interfaces that connect the neural network with the environment" [14]; this characteristic is of great importance also in CVNNs. Thus, there exist certain situations where CVNNs are inevitably required or greatly effective. Fundamental contributions to CVNNs were done by the pioneer Akira Hirose: the author of the first-ever concept of fully complex neural networks [15] and continuous complex-valued backpropagation [16] as well as a detailed survey of the critical concepts of CVNNs [14,17]. Regarding the learning algorithms for CVNNs, we should mention here the contributions of Fiori [18] which consists of generalizing the Hebbian learning for complex-valued neurons with an original optimization method which fits well CVNNs [19].

3 Multi-modal Representation by Means of Complex-Valued Neural Network

3.1 Overview

In this section, we are going to present the new multi-modal data representation and learning approach CVNN based. Our main goal is to build a robust representation of the image content that combines the advantages of the two modalities, *i.e.*, RGB and depth, to achieve high classification accuracy.

To formalize this learning problem, we consider the following notation. Let $\mathbb{X} \subset \mathbb{C}^m$ ($\mathbb{C}^m$ is an m-dimensional complex coordinate space) be an input space and $\mathbb{L} = \{l_1, l_2, \cdots, l_n\}$ be a finite real set of class labels. An instance $z \in \mathbb{X}$, represented in terms of features vector of dimension m as $z = [z_i]_{\{1 \leq i \leq m\}}$, is associated with a label $l \in \mathbb{L}$.

Let us also assume $\mathbb{T} = \{(z_i, l_i)\}_{i \in \{1,2,...n\}}$ a training set of n instances where $z_i \in \mathbb{X}$ and $l_i \in \mathbb{L}$. The purpose of this scheme of learning is to build a multi-class classifier: $\mathbb{M} : \mathbb{X} \to \mathbb{L}$ that optimizes some evaluation functions. To this end an RBF (Radial Basis Function) CVNN classifier is introduced.

3.2 Complex-Valued RBF-Networks

Motivation. By definition, an RBF is a function which has built into it a distance criterion with respect to a center. In the context of neural networks, the RBF function succeeded to replace the sigmoid activation function in multi-layer perceptron networks. The RBF neurons constitute the hidden layer units characterized by a center. In case where this function corresponds to a Gaussian, the network is trained by deciding on the number of hidden units/prototype vectors there should be as well as their centers and their sharpness (standard deviation), and then training up the output layer. Owing to the shallow yet wide architecture, RBF networks are able to extract a sparse model representation from a given training set. Motivated by these advantages of RBF-RVNNs, we propose to make use of RBF network to deal with complex-valued configuration for object recognition in RGB-D images. In the literature, this intuition has been exploited in other signal processing approximation and different classification tasks as in [20].

Architecture. Now, let us assume an RBF neural network that we call here RBF-CVNN which possesses complex-valued configuration (inputs, weights, activation functions, etc.). The network is composed of three layers: input, hidden and output layer as shown in Fig. 1. The input layer is composed of m nodes, each has a couple of inputs (a_i, b_i). The functionality of this layer is to transform them into a complex values as $z_i(a_i, b_i) = a_i + \underline{j}b_i \; \forall \; i \in \{1, 2, \ldots, m\}$ where $\underline{j}$ is the imaginary unit, *i.e.*, the input prepared for the next layer is a complex-valued vector $z_i = (z_1, z_2, \cdots, z_m)^T$. In what follows, $z_i(a_i, b_i)$ will be denoted by z_i.

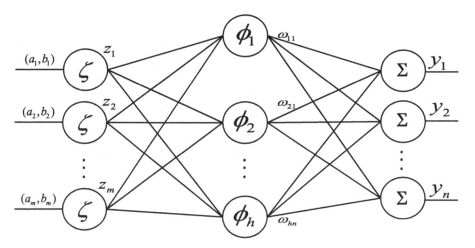

Fig. 1. Architecture of RBF-CVNN Network: composed of input, hidden and output layer (from left to right). The inputs of the network correspond to couples of real-valued numbers (a_i, b_i), the ζ function converts each couple to a complex-valued number z_i which will be fed into the hidden neurons where a transformation will take place with a complex-valued activation function ϕ. Those prototype vectors have been choose using a specific clustering method as described in Sect. 3.2. A fully complex-valued gradient descent learning algorithm is exploited in order to learn weights between the hidden layer and the output layer which correspond a label vector of n category scores.

As for the hidden layer, it corresponds to the complex activation function RBF-based, specifically a gaussian-like one, defined as follows:

$$\phi_j(z_i) = \exp(\frac{-j\|z_i - c_j\|^2}{2\sigma_j{}^2}) \tag{1}$$

where $\|.\|$ is the Euclidean distance, c_j is the center of the jth hidden node and σ_j its corresponding variance. This function is suitable for CVNNs since it satisfies the property considered in [20, 21] which states that the fully complex non-linear activation function have to be analytic and bounded almost everywhere.

Using an unsupervised fashion, for a given number of hidden node h which corresponds to the number of prototype vectors, K-means [22] is used to determine their corresponding centers and means (c_j and σ_j). The clustering is proceeded on the training set $\mathbb{T}$ using a specific setting. Instead of training K-means using couples of instance z_i and their corresponding label. To this end, a random instance is firstly chosen and assigned to the h neuron center. Then, for each element of the training set $\mathbb{T}$, the Euclidean distance is computed from each of the randomly chosen centers. Later, the instances of $\mathbb{T}$ are clustered into h clusters depending on the minimum of the computed distance, *i.e.*, with objective to find:

$$\arg\min\sum_{j=1}^{h}\sum_{z_i\in\mathbb{T}} d(z_i, c_j) \tag{2}$$

with

$$d(z_i, c_j) = \sqrt{(z_i - c_j)\overline{(z_i - c_j)}} \tag{3}$$

Next, the centers c_j are calculated as the mean of the instances belonging to each cluster. Once clustering is done, the distance between centers is checked and if it is less than the width of the cluster, those clusters will be joined together. This process is repeated until convergence, *i.e.*, until there is no changes of the values of c_j.

Regarding the output layer, it is constituted of n node, each one refereeing to the class label corresponding to the score of each category where the highest value is selected as the category. For a given instance/input vector z_i, the output vector Y is defined as $Y_i(z_i) = [y_k(z_i)]_{1 \leq k \leq n}$ where y_k are the score of z_i on the kth category/class is given by Eq. (4). Each neuron output y_k is connected to all the h prototype vectors.

$$\begin{aligned}
y_k(z_i) &= \sum_{j=1}^{h} \omega_{kj}\phi_j(z_i) \\
&= \sum_{j=1}^{h} (\mathrm{Re}(\omega_{kj})Re(\phi_j(z_i)) - Im(\omega_{kj})Im(\phi_j(z_i))) \\
&+ \underline{j}(\mathrm{Re}(\omega_{kj})Im(\phi_j(z_i)) + Im(\omega_{kj})Re(\phi_j(z_i)))
\end{aligned} \tag{4}$$

In Eq. (4), ω_{kj} is complex-valued weight which is learned by minimizing the sum-squared errors (E) defined as:

$$E = \frac{1}{2} \sum_{i=1}^{p} \|T_i - Y_i\|^2 = \frac{1}{2} \sum_{i=1}^{p} \sum_{k=1}^{n} \|t_k - y_k\|^2 \tag{5}$$

where $T_i = [t_k]_{1 \leq k \leq n}$ and t_k are the target corresponding to z_i on the kth class.

Using the fully complex-valued gradient descent learning algorithm proposed in [20], and according to Eq. (4), the update of output weights requires the differentiation of the E function with respect to ω_{kj} which allows us to obtain the following equation:

$$\frac{\partial E}{\partial \omega_{kj}} = -\overline{\phi}_j \frac{\partial E}{\partial y_k} \Leftrightarrow \Delta \omega_{kj} = \alpha \overline{\phi}_j \frac{\partial E}{\partial y_k} \tag{6}$$

where Δ is the delta rule, *i.e.*, a gradient descent learning rule for updating the weights here, α a complex-valued learning rate and $\overline{\phi}_j$ denotes the complex-conjugate of ϕ_j. Then, the update of the variance and the centers requires the differentiation of the E function with respect to the real and imaginary components of σ_j and c_j respectively, which allows us to write:

$$\Delta \sigma_j = \beta \overline{\phi}_j [\sum_{i=1}^{p} (\omega_{kj}^R \frac{\partial E}{\partial y_k^R} + \omega_{kj}^I \frac{\partial E}{\partial y_k^I})] \frac{\|z_i - c_j\|^2}{\sigma_j^3} \tag{7}$$

$$\Delta c_j = \gamma \overline{\phi}_j [\frac{1}{\sigma_j^2} \sum_{i=1}^{p} (\omega_{kj}^R \frac{\partial E}{\partial y_k^R} Re(z_i - c_j) + \underline{j}\omega_{kj}^I \frac{\partial E}{\partial y_k^I} Im(z_i - c_j))] \tag{8}$$

where β and γ are the learning rate parameters corresponding to σ_j and c_j respectively, ω_{kj}^R and ω_{kj}^I are the real and imaginary part of ω_{kj} respectively, Re and Im mean real and imaginary part respectively.

Thus, the fully complex-valued gradient descent learning algorithm allows us to update the parameters of our network ω, σ and c and correspond to each of them a learning rate parameter α, β and γ respectively.

3.3   Application to RGB-D Object Recognition

As reviewed earlier in the paper, significant advances have been made in quest of object recognition in RGB-D images, but much remains to be done, especially to improve the effective joint use of both modalities to take profit of their complementarities in a smarter way. To this end, we make use here of the proposed CVNN techniques explained above to define new solution using RGB-D images. RGB-D features have gained many computer vision tasks due to the complementarities between appearance and depth information. Here, we choose to investigate such type of data to enhance objects recognition using a joint pixel-wise classification strategy. Fusion between two different modes of data is done through complex-valued representation inspired by the fact that 3D point cloud, which corresponds to the mapping between RGB and depth images, could be easily seen as a complex-valued signal. Given a training set of n couples of RGB and depth images, we assume that each RGB-D image can be represented as a feature vector $z_i \in C_m$ in m dimensional space and assigned to a label l which corresponds to the instance category. Our objective is to obtain a robust description of z_i such that we can make use jointly of RGB and depth in an end-to-end classifier with higher accuracy. CVNN method is exploited with application to RGB-D object recognition using the same setting defined in Sect. 3.2.

4   Experimental Results

We evaluate our proposed RGB-D based CVNN approach using the large scale RGB-D object recognition dataset named "RGB-D Object Dataset" [3] with two evaluation settings: instance and category object recognition tasks. In fact, this dataset contains 41,877 images of common 300 household objects classified into 51 categories such as "Bowl", "Camera", "Hand towel", etc. Along with category labels, objects in this dataset are organized into instances: for example, the category "Food can" can be divided into physically unique instances like "Pepsi Can" and "Mountain Dew Can". RGB-D images were recorded in a multi-view scheme using Microsoft Kinect sensor (v.1) which provides RGB and depth images at a resolution of 640 × 480. To be aligned the practices used in the literature, we follow the same evaluation process used in [3]. For category recognition, it consists of leaving one object instance out from each category for testing, and train models on the remaining objects, i.e., 249 objects for training and 51 for testing at each trial. Reported results are obtained over a 10-fold cross validation procedure. As for instance recognition, we train models on images captured from 30° and 60° elevation angles, and test them on the images of the 45° angle. Samples from RGB-D object dataset are provided in Fig. 2.

For better comparison with state-of-the-art approaches, we consider several baseline methods. Firstly, in order to prove the efficiency of using both RGB and depth data in a unified framework, we compare the results of the RGB-D based methods with their single-mode based variants, *i.e.*, RGB and depth separately. Then, to show the robustness of our complex-valued representation through neural networks, we compare it to a real-valued representation by means of RVNNs, specifically with an RBF-RVNN. Also, we compared our proposal to the state-of-the-art approaches coming from handcrafted features detailed earlier in the related work section: kernel descriptors [9], hierarchical matching pursuit (HMP) [12] and its unsupervised variant (U-HMP) [11].

Results for the category and instance recognition tasks are reported in Tables 1 and 2, respectively. It is clear that the use of multi-modal data is outperforming all single-based methods except for the RVNN baseline method where combining RBG and depth data in a trivial way is performing worse than its variant of single-based cues. Recognition methods proposed in [9,11] outperform the proposed approach using single-based methods this is owing to their rich handcrafted feature and most important because our proposal is exclusively proposed to deal with RGB-D at once since its devoted to encapsulated RGB and depth in a unified way by means of complex-valued representation and using just a single data type will decrease its performance.

Regarding instance recognition, the best results is achieved by our proposal using RGB-D images and similarly to the above results our proposal is not able

Fig. 2. Examples of objects with different categories presented in the large scale RGB-D objects dataset.

Table 1. Results for the category recognition task and evaluation against state-of-the-art method with different modalities: RGB, depth and RGB-D.

Approach	Modality		
	RGB	Depth	RGB-D
Kernel descriptors [9]	80.7 ± 2.1	80.3 ± 2.9	86.5 ± 2.1
HMP [12]	74.7 ± 2.5	70.3 ± 2.2	82.1 ± 3.3
U-HMP [11]	**82.4 ± 3.1**	**81.2 ± 2.3**	87.5 ± 2.9
RVNN-baseline	76.8 ± 2.6	75.0 ± 3.0	71.8 ± 3.2
CVNN (ours)	78.1 ± 2.3	77.4 ± 2.6	**88.2 ± 2.4**

to cope with single-based modalities since it is designed for RGB-D data from the fine-grained information. It is notable here that depth data provides the worst results for all the approaches. This can be explained by the fact that objects belonging to the same category and different instances share in almost all the cases the same shape, however appearance in such cases will perform better.

Table 2. Results for the instance recognition task and evaluation against state-of-the-art method with different modalities: RGB, depth and RGB-D.

Approach	Modality		
	RGB	Depth	RGB-D
Kernel descriptors [9]	90.8	**54.7**	91.2
HMP [12]	75.8	39.8	78.9
U-HMP [11]	**92.1**	51.7	92.8
RVNN-baseline	83.7	50.9	69.2
CVNN (ours)	82.2	48.2	**95.5**

Finally, we can conclude that our RGB-D based representation is more robust for both instance and category tasks over the challenging large scale RGB-D dataset thanks to the complementarities between depth and appearance information and our fine-grained way of fusion and shows that it is able to deal with challenging images with texture-less items (like "bowls" or "apple") or shape-less items (like "cereal boxes" or "hand towel") captured under variation of viewpoint and variation of lighting conditions.

5   Conclusion

In this paper we addressed the problem of object recognition using multi-modal data. In contrast to majority of proposed recognition systems, we proposed a pixel-wise approach that fuse in early stage of learning process RGB and depth data using a novel complex-valued representation within an end-to-end learning framework. An RBF layer is exploited in an adaptive way to construct a new CVNN network. Evaluation over the challenging large scale RGBD dataset is performed using two object recognition tasks shows that our proposal outperforms state-of-the-art methods. Increasing the number of layers and going deeper with our learning technique is very challenging but might be interesting and left for future work.

Acknowledgements. This work was supported by the European Union funding through ALYSSA program (ERASMUS-MUNDUS action 2 lot 6) and by the research grant from Singapore Agency for Science, Technology and Research (A*STAR) through the ARAP program.

References

1. Andreopoulos, A., Tsotsos, J.K.: 50 years of object recognition: directions forward. Comput. Vis. Image Underst. **117**(8), 827–891 (2013)
2. Bucak, S.S., Jin, R., Jain, A.K.: Multiple kernel learning for visual object recognition: a review. IEEE Trans. Pattern Anal. Mach. Intell. **36**(7), 1354–1369 (2014)
3. Lai, K., Bo, L., Ren, X., Fox, D.: A large-scale hierarchical multi-view RGB-D object dataset. In: 2011 IEEE International Conference on Robotics and Automation (ICRA), pp. 1817–1824. IEEE (2011)
4. Held, D., Thrun, S., Savarese, S.: Robust single-view instance recognition. In: 2016 IEEE International Conference on Robotics and Automation (ICRA), pp. 2152–2159. IEEE (2016)
5. Gupta, S., Girshick, R., Arbeláez, P., Malik, J.: Learning rich features from RGB-D images for object detection and segmentation. In: Fleet, D., Pajdla, T., Schiele, B., Tuytelaars, T. (eds.) ECCV 2014. LNCS, vol. 8695, pp. 345–360. Springer, Cham (2014). https://doi.org/10.1007/978-3-319-10584-0_23
6. Li, X., Fang, M., Zhang, J.-J., Wu, J.: Learning coupled classifiers with RGB images for RGB-D object recognition. Pattern Recogn. **61**, 433–446 (2017)
7. Amin, M.F., Murase, K.: Single-layered complex-valued neural network for real-valued classification problems. Neurocomputing **72**(4), 945–955 (2009)
8. Savitha, R., Suresh, S., Sundararajan, N., Kim, H.J.: A fully complex-valued radial basis function classifier for real-valued classification problems. Neurocomputing **78**(1), 104–110 (2012)
9. Bo, L., Ren, X., Fox, D.: Depth kernel descriptors for object recognition. In: 2011 IEEE/RSJ International Conference on Intelligent Robots and Systems (IROS), pp. 821–826. IEEE (2011)
10. Lai, K., Bo, L., Ren, X., Fox, D.: A scalable tree-based approach for joint object and pose recognition. In: AAAI, vol. 1, p. 2 (2011)
11. Bo, L., Ren, X., Fox, D.: Unsupervised feature learning for RGB-D based object recognition. In: Desai, J., Dudek, G., Khatib, O., Kumar, V. (eds.) Experimental Robotics. Springer Tracts in Advanced Robotics, vol. 88, pp. 387–402. Springer, Heidelberg (2013). https://doi.org/10.1007/978-3-319-00065-7_27
12. Bo, L., Ren, X., Fox, D.: Hierarchical matching pursuit for image classification: architecture and fast algorithms. In: Advances in Neural Information Processing Systems, pp. 2115–2123 (2011)

13. Eitel, A., Springenberg, J.T., Spinello, L., Riedmiller, M., Burgard, W.: Multimodal deep learning for robust RGB-D object recognition. In: 2015 IEEE/RSJ International Conference on Intelligent Robots and Systems (IROS), pp. 681–687. IEEE (2015)
14. Hirose, A.: Complex-Valued Neural Networks. Springer Science & Business Media, Heidelberg (2006). https://doi.org/10.1007/978-3-642-27632-3
15. Hirose, A.: Dynamics of fully complex-valued neural networks. Electron. Lett. **28**(16), 1492–1494 (1992)
16. Hirose, A.: Continuous complex-valued back-propagation learning. Electron. Lett. **28**(20), 1854–1855 (1992)
17. Hirose, A.: Complex-Valued Neural Networks: Theories and Applications, vol. 5. World Scientific, Singapore (2003)
18. Fiori, S.: Nonlinear complex-valued extensions of Hebbian learning: an essay. Neural Comput. **17**(4), 779–838 (2005)
19. Fiori, S.: Learning by criterion optimization on a unitary unimodular matrix group. Int. J. Neural Syst. **18**(02), 87–103 (2008)
20. Savitha, R., Suresh, S., Sundararajan, N.: A fully complex-valued radial basis function network and its learning algorithm. Int. J. Neural Syst. **19**(04), 253–267 (2009)
21. Kim, T., Adali, T.: Fully complex multi-layer perceptron network for nonlinear signal processing. J. VLSI Sig. Process. Syst. Sig. Image Video Technol. **32**(1–2), 29–43 (2002)
22. Kanungo, T., Mount, D.M., Netanyahu, N.S., Piatko, C.D., Silverman, R., Wu, A.Y.: An efficient k-means clustering algorithm: analysis and implementation. IEEE Trans. Pattern Anal. Mach. Intell. **24**(7), 881–892 (2002)

Video Highlight Detection via Deep Ranking Modeling

Yifan Jiao[1], Xiaoshan Yang[2], Tianzhu Zhang[2], Shucheng Huang[1(✉)], and Changsheng Xu[2]

[1] School of Computer, Jiangsu University of Science and Technology,
Zhenjiang 212003, China
schuang2015@gmail.com
[2] National Laboratory of Pattern Recognition, Institute of Automation,
Chinese Academy of Sciences, Beijing 100190, China

Abstract. The video highlight detection task is to localize key elements (moments of user's major or special interest) in a video. Most of existing highlight detection approaches extract features from the video segment as a whole without considering the difference of local features both temporally and spatially. Due to the complexity of video content, this kind of mixed features will impact the final highlight prediction. In temporal extent, not all frames are worth watching because some of them only contain background of the environment without human or other moving objects. In spatial extent, it is similar that not all regions in each frame are highlights especially when there are lots of clutters in the background. To solve the above problem, we propose a novel attention model which can automatically localize the key elements in a video without any extra supervised annotations. Specifically, the proposed attention model produces attention weights of local regions along both the spatial and temporal dimensions of the video segment. The regions of key elements in the video will be strengthened with large weights. Thus more effective feature of the video segment is obtained to predict the highlight score. The proposed attention scheme can be easily integrated into a conventional end-to-end deep ranking model which aims to learn a deep neural network to compute the highlight score of each video segment. Extensive experimental results on the YouTube dataset demonstrate that the proposed approach achieves significant improvement over state-of-the-art methods.

Keywords: Video highlight detection · Attention model
Deep ranking

1 Introduction

With the enormous growth of wearable devices, social media websites (e.g., Flickr, YouTube, Facebook, and Google News) have been rapidly developed in recent years. On YouTube alone, 6000 min of videos are uploaded and 2 million minutes of videos are browsed per minute, which narrows the distance among people and makes them know everything around the world without leaving home.

M. Paul et al. (Eds.): PSIVT 2017, LNCS 10749, pp. 28–39, 2018.
https://doi.org/10.1007/978-3-319-75786-5_3

However, most of the existing videos on the Internet are user-generated. People upload original videos in a variety of time and places for different purposes, which makes most of videos vary in length from a few minutes to a few hours and be full of noise (e.g., severe camera motion, varied illumination conditions, cluttered background) [1,2]. It is a time-consuming and laborious job to browse, edit and index these redundant videos [3–5]. Therefore, highlight detection, which automatically produces the most informative parts of a full-length video [4], has been becoming increasingly important to alleviate this burden.

In recent years, because of its practical value, highlight detection has been extensively studied including two main directions. (1) The rule-based approaches [6–13]. This kind of approach generally utilizes heuristic rules to select a collection of frames. Some of them detect highlight by making full use of clear shot boundaries [10–13]. Other methods take advantage of the well defined structure of specific videos in comparison to other egocentric videos [6–9]. A long video can be divided into several components and only a few of them contain certain well defined highlights, such as the score event in soccer games and the hit moment in baseball games. Though the above methods are effective for highlight detection in specific videos (e.g. sports video), they may not generalize well to generic and unstructured videos. (2) The ranking-based approaches [4,14,15]. This kind of method treats the highlight detection as scoring each video segment in terms of visual importance and interestingness. The segments with higher scores will be selected as video highlights. Recently, Sun et al. [4] propose a ranking SVM model which outperforms the former approaches. More recently, the landscape of computer vision has been drastically altered and pushed forward through the adoption of a fast, scalable, end-to-end learning framework, the Convolutional Neural Network (CNN), which makes us see a cornucopia of CNN-based models achieving state-of-the-art results in classification, localization, semantic segmentation and action recognition tasks. Based on the Convolutional Neural Network, Yao et al. [15] propose a novel deep ranking model that employs deep learning techniques to learn the relationship between highlight and non-highlight video segments. Here, the relationship of video segments can characterize the relative preferences of all segments within a video and benefit video highlight detection.

However, most of the previous rule-based and ranking-based approaches extract the feature from the video segment as a whole without considering the difference of local features both temporally and spatially. Due to the complexity of the videos, this kind of mixed features will have an impact on the final highlight prediction. In temporal or spatial extent, not all frames or their regions are worth watching because some of them only contain background without human or other moving objects.

To solve the above problem, we propose a novel attention model to automatically localize the key elements in a video without any extra supervised annotations. Specifically, the proposed attention model produces attention weights of local regions along both the spatial and temporal dimensions of the video segment. The regions of key elements in the video will be strengthened with large weights. Thus we can obtain more accurate feature representations of the video segment to effectively predict the highlight score. The proposed attention scheme can be easily integrated into the conventional deep ranking model. Our method utilizes a two-stream pairwise end-to-end neural network, which aims to learn a function that can denote the highlight score of each video segment for highlight detection. The higher the score, the more highlighted the segment. Segments with higher scores can be selected as video highlights.

Compared with existing methods, the contributions of this paper can be concluded as follows.

1. We propose a novel attention scheme to localize the key elements in a video both spatially and temporally without any extra supervised annotations.
2. We propose an end-to-end highlight detection framework by integrating the attention scheme into deep ranking model as an attention module.
3. Extensive experimental results demonstrate that the proposed attention-based deep ranking model consistently and significantly outperforms existing methods.

The rest of the paper is organized as follows: We present the architecture of our end-to-end deep convolutional neural network in Sect. 2, while Sect. 3 describes the procedure and results of experiments. Finally, conclusion is followed in Sect. 4.

2   The Proposed Method

In this section, we first show the formulation of the highlight detection problem, and then introduce the architecture of our end-to-end deep convolutional neural network including feature module, attention module and ranking module.

2.1   Problem Formulation

Suppose we have a set of pairs Q, in which each pair (p_i, n_i) consists of a highlight video segment p_i and a non-highlight segment n_i. The video segment is comprised of N frames from a raw video. Our goal is to learn a function $f(\cdot)$ which can transform a video segment to the highlight score. This function needs to meet the requirement that the score of highlight segment is higher than the score of the non-highlight segment:

$$f(p_i) > f(n_i), \forall (p_i, n_i) \in Q \tag{1}$$

In this work, the function $f(\cdot)$ is practically a deep neural network which will be illustrated in Sect. 2.2. To achieve the above goal, we learn the function $f(\cdot)$ by minimizing the following loss function:

$$L = \frac{1}{|Q|} \sum_{(p_i, n_i) \in Q} L_Q(p_i, n_i) + \lambda ||\Theta||_F^2 \tag{2}$$

$$L_Q(p_i, n_i) = max(0, 1 - f(p_i) + f(n_i)), (p_i, n_i) \in Q. \tag{3}$$

Here, Θ contains all parameters of the function $f(\cdot)$. The λ is used to control the regularization item. $L_Q(p_i, n_i)$ denotes the contrastive constraint for each pair (p_i, n_i), which is inspired by [17, 18]. $|Q|$ is the number of pairs.

2.2   Network Architecture

The deep neural network $f(\cdot)$ introduced in Sect. 2.1 contains three main parts which are feature module, attention module and ranking module as shown in Fig. 1. The network can output the highlight score for any input video segment comprised of N frames. Firstly, the visual feature tensor with size $W \times H \times C$ will be extracted by the feature module for each of the frames in the segment. Then, all the N feature tensors (blue color in Fig. 1) will be input to the attention module which can produce the N attention weight tensors (red color in Fig. 1) which have same size as the feature tensors. By employing weighted aggregation between the visual feature tensor and attention weight tensor, the more effective C-dimension visual feature representation (green color in Fig. 1) is obtained. Finally, the ranking module will output the highlight value. Details of the feature module, the attention module and the ranking module will be illustrated as follows.

Feature Module. This module is comprised of 5 convolution layers and several pooling layers. The exact size of each layer is also shown in Fig. 1. For the jth

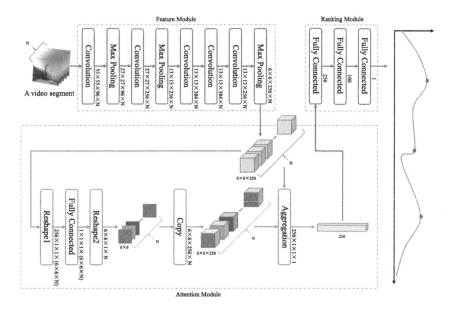

Fig. 1. The flowchart of the proposed end-to-end attention-based deep ranking neural network including three parts: feature module, attention module and ranking module. The input is a raw video segment consists of N frames. The function of attention module is to select the important local regions along spatial and temporal dimensions simultaneously. Then the ranking module predicts the highlight score. By assigning a highlight score to each segment, a highlight curve can be obtained for the full-length video. Next to each layer is the exact size of the output used in our implementation based on Caffe [16]. (Color figure online)

convolution layer, we denote its output as $h_j = s(\boldsymbol{w}_j * h_{j-1} + \boldsymbol{b}_j)$, $j \in \{1, ..., 5\}$. Here, $*$ denotes the convolutional operation, $\boldsymbol{w}_j$ and $\boldsymbol{b}_j$ are the convolutional kernel and bias. $s(\cdot) = max(0, \cdot)$ denotes the non-saturating nonlinearity activation function which is also used as the rectified linear units (ReLU) in [19]. We use $\boldsymbol{a} \in \mathbb{R}^{W \times H \times C \times N}$ to denote the final output of the feature module for all N frames in the input video segment.

Attention Module. This is the core module of our network which is a new and complicated attention scheme we designed. As we all know, given a raw video, not all regions in each frame are useful for highlight detection in spatial extent especially when there are lots of clutters in the background. It is similar in temporal extent that not all frames are worth watching because some frames just contain background of the environment without humans or other moving objects. Considering the aforementioned circumstance, the attention module aims to learn an attention function which can output positive attention weights of local regions along both the spatial and temporal dimensions of the video segment simultaneously.

This module mainly consists of two reshape layers, one fully connected layer, one copy layer and one aggregation layer which will be illustrated as follows.

– **Reshape1.** The output feature of the feature module is denoted as $\boldsymbol{a} \in \mathbb{R}^{W \times H \times C \times N}$ which contains the C feature maps with size $W \times H$ for each of the N frames in the video segment. Since the convolution layer retains the spatial information of the raw input frames and the feature map is always much smaller than the frame image, each element in the feature map corresponds to a specific local region in the original frame. All frame images can be implicitly divided into $W \times H$ regions and each of them corresponds to a specific C-dimensional feature vector in $\boldsymbol{a}$. We can decide whether a local region in the video frames is important for the highlight detection according to the corresponding C-dimensional visual feature.

To compute the attention weight based on the C-dimensional visual feature, we first need to transform the feature tensor $\boldsymbol{a}$ into a matrix so that the following computing of the attention weight can be easily carried out. Reshape1 layer is used to change the size of the feature tensor $\boldsymbol{a}$ from $W \times H \times C \times N$ to $C \times W \times H \times N$ first and then to a matrix $\boldsymbol{R} \in \mathbb{R}^{C \times (WHN)}$. More explicitly, we also can rewrite the matrix $\boldsymbol{R}$ as the following column vectors:

$$\boldsymbol{R} = [\boldsymbol{r}_1, ..., \boldsymbol{r}_2, ..., \boldsymbol{r}_{WHN}], \boldsymbol{r}_i \in \mathbb{R}^C \tag{4}$$

– **Fully Connected.** This layer in the attention module is designed to compute the attention weights of local regions along both the spatial and temporal dimensions of the video segment simultaneously. We denote the output of the Fully Connected layer as a vector $\alpha \in \mathbb{R}^{HWN}$ which can be computed as follows.

$$\alpha = \sigma(\boldsymbol{w}_\alpha^\top \boldsymbol{R} + b_\alpha) \tag{5}$$

Here, $\boldsymbol{w}_\alpha \in \mathbb{R}^C$ and b_α are the weight matrix and bias. $\boldsymbol{R}$ denotes the output from Reshape1 layer. $\sigma(\cdot)$ is the sigmoid function which is used to control the value of attention weight ranging from 0 to 1.

-   **Reshape2**. In the Reshape1 layer, we transform the feature tensor $\boldsymbol{a}$ of the video segment into the matrix $\boldsymbol{R}$ for the convenience of computing attention weight. Here, to match the attention weight vector α with $\boldsymbol{a}$ spatially and temporally, we transform it back into a tensor with size $W \times H \times N$.
-   **Copy**. In the previous Reshape2 layer, the attention weight α is transformed into a tensor with size $W \times H \times N$ which is still different from the size of the feature $\boldsymbol{a}$. In order to make them exactly the same, we adopt the Copy layer which transformations the size of α from $W \times H \times N$ to $W \times H \times C \times N$ by making C copies of the weight for each of the WH local regions. This means that, for each of the frames in the video segment, the attention weight tensor is comprised of C identical attention weight matrices of the size $W \times H$.
-   **Aggregation**. After obtaining the attention weight α of the video segment, we adopt the Aggregation layer to compute the C-dimensional output feature $\boldsymbol{z}$ of the attention module as

$$z_k = \sum_{l=1}^{N}\sum_{j=1}^{H}\sum_{i=1}^{W} a_{ijkl}\alpha_{ijkl}, \quad k = 1, ..., C \tag{6}$$

The two inner $\sum$ operations are the weighted aggregation spatially and the outer $\sum$ is the weighted aggregation temporally. It is worth noting that we also compute the output of the attention module by replacing $\sum$ in Eq. 6 with max. In the experiment, $\sum$ operation is simply implemented by average pooling while the max operation is implemented by max-pooling.

Through the attention weight α, the more important local regions in the video segment for highlight detection will be paid more attentions in the following ranking module.

Ranking Module. This module mainly consists of three fully connected layers (denoted by F with the number of neurons) which are $F256 - F100 - F1$. For the kth fully connected layer, we denote the output as $h_k = s(\boldsymbol{w}_k h_{k-1} + \boldsymbol{b}_k)$, $k \in \{1, ..., 3\}$. Here, $\boldsymbol{w}_k$ and $\boldsymbol{b}_k$ are the weight matrix and bias, respectively. For the activation function, the same rectified linear units $s(\cdot) = max(0, \cdot)$ as in the convolution layer of the feature module is adopted. The final output of the ranking module will be taken as the highlight score.

3   Experiments

In this section, we evaluate the performance of the proposed attention-based deep ranking model against several state-of-the-art methods on one public dataset [4].

3.1   Dataset

We evaluate the proposed algorithm on one public dataset. Details of this dataset are illustrated as follows.

YouTube dataset [4]. This dataset contains six normal activities: "gymnastics", "parkour", "skating", "skiing", "surfing" and "dog". Except "skiing" and "surfing" which include near 90 videos, for each domain, there are about 50 videos with various durations. The total time is about 1430 min, which is similar with the state-of-the-art large scale action recognition dataset [20]. This dataset is divided into training and test sets, and each of them covers the half of the videos. A raw video contains several segments and each segment is annotated on a three point ordinal scale: 1-highlight; 0-normal; -1-non-highlight. At the same time, each segment includes approximately 100 frames.

3.2   Baselines

We compare three variants of our method with three state-of-the-art baseline methods:

(1) **LR**, which is short for latent ranking [4]. This is a latent linear ranking SVM model which is trained with the harvested noisy data by introducing latent variables to accommodate variation of highlight selection. They use the EM-like self-paced model selection procedure to train the model effectively.

(2) **DCNN-A**, which stands for deep convolution neural network model [15]. This method uses a convolutional network to extract features and detect highlight by a ranking network. The extractor produces N vectors of a video segment consisting of N frames, each of which is a D-dimensional representation corresponding to one frame. For comparison, we use the average-pooling for the CNN feature representation before feeding into the ranking network with dimension from $D \times N$ to $D \times 1$ similar to the Aggregation layer in the attention module described in Sect. 2.2.

(3) **DCNN-M**, which is short for deep convolution neural network model [15]. The max-pooling operation similar to the Aggregation layer in the attention module described in Sect. 2.2 is applied on the features of a video segment.

(4) **Att-F-A** is our method with a fully connected layer to learn the attention weights and average-pooling operation for the features of a video segment both spatially and temporally in the attention module as described in Sect. 2.2.

(5) **Att-C-M** is our method with a convolution layer which just replaces the fully connected layer in the attention module described in Sect. 2.2 and shown in Fig. 1 to learn the attention weights and max-pooling operation for the features of a video segment both spatially and temporally in the attention module as described in Sect. 2.2.

(6) **Att-F-M** is our method with a fully connected layer to learn the attention weights and max-pooling operation for the features of a video segment both spatially and temporally in the attention module as described in Sect. 2.2.

The **DCNN-A** and **DCNN-M** methods are almost the same except the pooling operation before feeding into the ranking network. **DCNN-A** employs the average-pooling for the CNN feature extracted from the convolutional network while **DCNN-M** utilizes the max-pooling. The difference between **Att-F-A** and **Att-C-M** or **Att-F-M** is that **Att-C-M** or **Att-F-M** utilizes the max-pooling in the Aggregation layer in the attention module, while **Att-F-A** employs the average-pooling. In order to be more compact, two ways including convolution layer (**Att-C-M**) and fully connected layer (**Att-F-M**) based on the same algorithm and processing are both implemented to learn the attention weights in the attention module.

3.3 Implementation Details

Feature Representation. We initialize the parameters of the feature module in the proposed method according to AlexNet [19], and allow the parameters being fine-tuned. For each frame in an input video segment, the size of the output by the feature module is $6 \times 6 \times 256$. By employing a weighted aggregation between the visual feature tensor and attention weight tensor, the more effective feature representation is obtained for a video.

Evaluation Metrics. The pairwise accuracy Acc_v for the vth video is defined as

$$Acc_v = \frac{\sum\limits_{(p_i, n_i) \in \mathbf{Q}} [f(p_i) > f(n_i)]}{|Q|} \tag{7}$$

Where $[\cdot]$ is the Iverson bracket notation. $f(p_i)$ represents the final output score of a highlight segment, and $f(n_i)$ is the value of a non-highlight one. As described in Sect. 2.1, Q is the set of pairwise constraints for the vth video, and $|Q|$ is the number of pairs. The accuracy Acc_v is a normalized value ranging from 0 to 1. The higher the value, the more accurate the detection. We calculate the average precision of highlight detection for comparison with baseline methods.

Training Process. Since the data annotation on YouTube dataset [4] is not completely accurate in some videos, which means the segment annotated as highlight may be not correct in fact, it is a weak supervision dataset. We select a set of latent best highlighted segments iteratively using the EM-like approach as described in [4] to train the baseline methods.

3.4 Performance Comparison

Youtube dataset. Figure 2 summarizes the overall highlight detection results for different methods on YouTube dataset [4], and shows that our proposed approach significantly outperforms the state-of-the-art methods in all six domains on the public dataset based on the same evaluation metrics. In particular, the precision of "parkour" and "surfing" can achieve 0.75 and 0.78, which makes the considerable improvement over the compared methods, as they do not consider the region information in a frame spatially and the importance of each frame temporally. Instead, our approach outputs the attention weights to find the important regions and frames, which helps us obtain more accurate feature

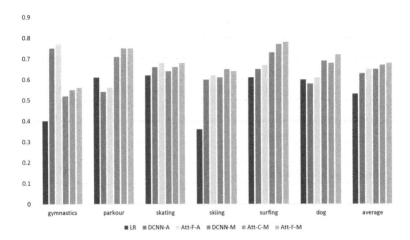

Fig. 2. Performance comparison between our attention-based ranking model and other baseline approaches. Our method shows better performance.

representation of videos for effective highlight detection. On average, the mean average precision of our attention-based model with **Att-F-M** can achieve 0.68, which makes the improvement over **LR**, **DCNN-A** and **DCNN-M** by 15%, 5% and 3% respectively.

In general, the result of max-pooling (**DCNN-M**, **Att-C-M**, **Att-F-M**) is better than that of average-pooling (**DCNN-A**, **Att-F-A**) in Fig. 2. The main reason may be that, compared with the average-pooling, the max-pooling is more likely to retain the feature of the most important local regions.

3.5   Visualization

Figure 3 shows several raw frames sampled in a segment and the corresponding heat maps of attention weight from YouTube dataset. The lighter the color, the bigger the weight. Therefore, the white regions in the heat map reflect that the corresponding regions in video frame contribute more for highlight detection than other regions. For instance, in the first ten frames selected from a segment of the parkour domain in Fig. 3, the boy is ready to run and another man is looking at him in the first frame, so the two white square regions in first heat map approximately describe the location of them, which means these regions are more important for highlight detection. When he runs approach to the tree, the white regions are moving as well in the second frame. He is jumping in the third frame, the white regions are also changing according to the location of the boy. It is similar for the rest seven frames that the white regions corresponding to the boy's movement are important for highlight detection spatially. The lightness of the ten heat maps are nearly the same, which means they are all important frames in this segment temporally. The heat maps of the first and second frames in the third group are lighter than the rest, which means they are more important than the other frames in the segment for highlight detection.

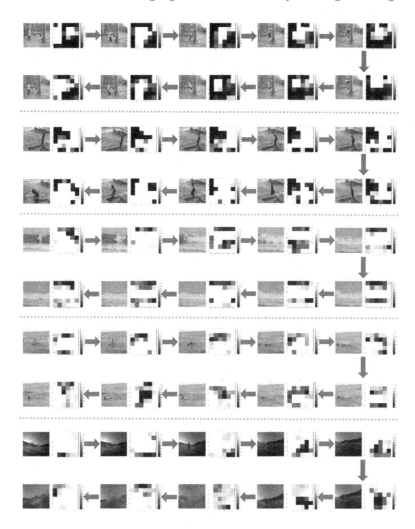

Fig. 3. Attention scores of each region of a frame in different video domains in [4]. We sample 10 frames from each raw video segment, and draw the heat map of attention weight in detail. The lighter the color, the bigger the weight. In particular, the regions that white color corresponds to are the most significant ones for highlight detection.

4   Conclusion

In this paper, we propose a novel attention-based deep ranking model to learn a function to output attention weights of local regions in the video segment along spatial and temporal dimensions simultaneously, which helps us obtain the more effective feature representation of interesting and significant components in videos for highlight detection. Extensive experiments show that our method performs better than state-of-the-art approaches on one public dataset.

In the future, we would like to develop a highlight-driven video summarization system based on our proposed attention-based model. We will also explore more comprehensive attention scheme to incorporate other useful information.

Acknowledgement. This work is supported in part by the National Natural Science Foundation of China under Grant 61432019, Grant 61572498, Grant 61532009, and Grant 61772244, the Key Research Program of Frontier Sciences, CAS, Grant NO. QYZDJ-SSW-JSC039, the Beijing Natural Science Foundation 4172062, and Postgraduate Research & Practice Innovation Program of Jiangsu Province, Grant NO. SJCX17_0599.

References

1. Liu, S., Wang, C.H., Qian, R.H., Yu, H., Bao, R.: Surveillance video parsing with single frame supervision. arXiv preprint arXiv:1611.09587 (2016)
2. Liu, S., Liang, X.D., Liu, L.Q., Shen, X.H., Yang, J.C., Xu, C.S., Lin, L., Cao, X.C., Yan, S.C.: Matching-CNN meets KNN: quasi-parametric human parsing. In: Proceedings of the IEEE Conference on Computer Vision and Pattern Recognition, pp. 1419–1427 (2015)
3. Zhang, T.Z., Liu, S., Ahuja, N., Yang, M.H., Ghanem, B.: Robust visual tracking via consistent low-rank sparse learning. Int. J. Comput. Vis. **111**(2), 171–190 (2015)
4. Sun, M., Farhadi, A., Seitz, S.: Ranking domain-specific highlights by analyzing edited videos. In: ECCV (2014)
5. Liu, S., Feng, J.S., Domokos, C., Xu, H., Huang, J.S., Hu, Z.Z., Yan, S.C.: Fashion parsing with weak color-category labels. IEEE Trans. Multimed. **16**(1), 253–265 (2014)
6. Rui, Y., Gupta, A., Acero, A.: Automatically extracting highlights for TV baseball programs. In: Proceedings of the 8th ACM International Conference on Multimedia 2000, Los Angeles, CA, USA, 30 October–3 November 2000, pp. 105–115 (2000)
7. Nepal, S., Srinivasan, U., Graham, J.R.: Automatic detection of goal segments in basketball videos. In: Proceedings of the 9th ACM International Conference on Multimedia 2001, Ottawa, Ontario, Canada, 30 September–5 October 2001, pp. 261–269 (2001)
8. Otsuka, I., Nakane, K., Divakaran, A., Hatanaka, K., Ogawa, M.: A highlight scene detection and video summarization system using audio feature for a personal video recorder. IEEE Trans. Consum. Electron. **51**(1), 112–116 (2005)
9. Tong, X.F., Liu, Q.S., Zhang, Y.F., Lu, H.Q.: Highlight ranking for sports video browsing. In: Proceedings of the 13th ACM International Conference on Multimedia, Singapore, 6–11 November 2005, pp. 519–522 (2005)
10. Ngo, C., Ma, Y.F., Zhang, H.J.: Video summarization and scene detection by graph modeling. IEEE Trans. Circuits Syst. Video Technol. **15**(2), 296–305 (2005)
11. Mundur, P., Rao, Y., Yesha, Y.: Keyframe-based video summarization using delaunay clustering. Int. J. Dig. Libr. **6**(2), 219–232 (2006)
12. Borth, D., Ulges, A., Schulze, C., Thomas, M.B.: Keyframe extraction for video tagging & summarization. In: Informatiktage 2008. Fachwissenschaftlicher Informatik-Kongress, 14–15 März 2008, B-IT Bonn-Aachen International Center for Information Technology in Bonn, pp. 45–48 (2008)

13. Qu, Z., Lin, L.D., Gao, T.F., Wang, Y.K.: An improved keyframe extraction method based on HSV colour space. JSW **8**(7), 1751–1758 (2013)
14. Lin, Y.L., Vlad, I.M., Winston, H.H.: Summarizing while recording: context-based highlight detection for egocentric videos. In: 2015 IEEE International Conference on Computer Vision Workshop, ICCV Workshops 2015, Santiago, Chile, 7–13 December 2015, pp. 443–451 (2015)
15. Yao, T., Mei, T., Rui, Y.: Highlight detection with pairwise deep ranking for first-person video summarization, pp. 982–990 (2016)
16. Jia, Y.Q., Shelhamer, E., Donahue, J., Karayev, S., Long, J., Ross, B.G., Guadarrama, S., Darrell, T.: Caffe: Convolutional architecture for fast feature embedding. CoRR, abs/1408.5093 (2014)
17. Yang, X.S., Zhang, T.Z., Xu, C.S., Yan, S.C., Hossain, M.S., Ghoneim, A.: Deep relative attributes. IEEE Trans. Multimed. **18**(9), 1832–1842 (2016)
18. Gao, J.Y., Zhang, T.Z., Yang, X.S., Xu, C.S.: Deep relative tracking. IEEE Trans. Image Process. **26**(4), 1845–1858 (2017)
19. Krizhevsky, A., Sutskever, I., Geoffrey, E.H.: ImageNet classification with deep convolutional neural networks. In: 26th Annual Conference on Neural Information Processing Systems, pp. 1106–1114 (2012)
20. Soomro, K., Zamir, A.R., Shah, M.: UCF101: a dataset of 101 human actions classes from videos in the wild. volume abs/1212.0402 (2012)

Ink-Jet Printer's Characterization by 3D Gradation Trajectories on an Equidistant Color Difference Basis

Oleg Milder[1] and Dmitry Tarasov[1,2]

[1] Institute of Radio-Engineering and IT, Ural Federal University,
Mira, 32, Ekaterinburg 620002, Russia
datarasov@yandex.ru
[2] Institute of Industrial Ecology UB RAS,
Kovalevskoy, 20, Ekaterinburg 620990, Russia

Abstract. We suggest using 3D gradation curves of CIE *Lab* space, which we call "gradation trajectories", as further development of common gradation curves. The trajectories are considered in terms of 3D curves of differential geometry. We offer the gradation trajectories, as well as their calculating method, as a powerful tool for ink-jet system characterization and further profile-making. In the work, we develop our method and apply it to ink-jet printer's characterization on a basis of equidistant color difference CIE *Lab* ΔE. We discuss the information that might be derived from the trajectories' analysis and show how they might me generally applicable.

Keywords: Gradation trajectories · Ink-jet · Characterization · Profile
Dot–gain

1 Introduction

In order to create images with faithfully reproduced colors on a given ink-jet printer system, it is essential to specify the color response the printer provides for a given selection of substrate (e.g. paper), inks types, and with given amounts of inks during the process of characterization.

The limitation of ink serves to doze the amount of ink that can be sent to the print head by the raster processor (RIP), and to reduce the desired or useful percentage of ink, which can often be less than 100%. Need of such a restriction caused by many factors, particularly the physics-chemical processes of interaction between inks and substrates, primarily for non- or weak-absorbing ones. When several dyes are being printed on top of each other, there is a limit on the amount of ink that can be applied to the substrate and on the previous color layer. When this technical restriction is ignored, the ink that stacks last will not properly attach to the previous layers, which will lead to dirty brown shades in the neutral tints. The ink will also not dry properly. This can cause set-off where the ink of a still wet substrate rubs off on whatever is stacked on top of it. In general, due to the printing process, the deposited ink surface coverage is larger than the nominal

© Springer International Publishing AG, part of Springer Nature 2018
M. Paul et al. (Eds.): PSIVT 2017, LNCS 10749, pp. 40–52, 2018.
https://doi.org/10.1007/978-3-319-75786-5_4

coverage, resulting in a physical dot-gain responsible for the ink spreading, which depends on the inks, on the substrate, and also on some other factors [1].

There is a systemic contradiction in the market. While manufacturers want to boost the ink usage, customers would like to reduce ink consumption with minimal impact on color quality. Sometimes, these limitations lead to loss in color. In any case, the problem of ink management is crucial. To solve this problem, manufacturers of image processing software and printing equipment recommend using different criteria, such as: visual evaluation by spreading or capillarity, numerical estimation of the optical density of color coordinates, etc.

Thanks to different color prediction models (CPMs) or reflectance prediction models (RPMs), the usage of inks can be substantially optimized especially in the case of current multi-colors printers. CPMs may help the image processing software to decide, which set of inks and how to select in order to print a certain color within a specific context. Such models need to account for both the interactions between the inks and the substrate and between the light and the halftone print, as well as the Fresnel reflections and light scattering. The lateral light scattering together with internal reflections at the interface between the substrate and the air are responsible for the optical dot gain effect.

1.1 Color Prediction Models

Today, a great deal of CPMs exists. The models take as their inputs a set of ink values and predict the resulting color in print, as specified by reflectance models or tristimulus values. *Empirical surface models* take into account superpositions of ink halftones. There, reflected or transmitted light is supposed to be a function of the effective colorants surface coverage or base patterns forming ink halftones. The models do not deal with the light propagation and fading within the print and only demonstrate the relationship between reflected light and surface coverages by colorants. *Physically inspired models* engage a more detailed analysis of light-print interaction based on mathematical prediction of how light paths within a halftone print go and what resulting fade is. *Ink spreading models* are designed to characterize the effective surface of a colorant/ink dot after it has been printed at a given nominal surface coverage. The difference between the effective and the nominal surface coverages is the physical dot gain, which show how much a colorant/ink dot spreads out. Ink spreading models accounting for ink spreading in all ink superposition conditions. They rely on ink spreading curves mapping nominal surface coverages to effective surface coverages for the surface coverages of single ink halftones, as well as ones superposed with single and two solid inks.

More complicated up-to-date CPMs deal with spread-based and light propagation probability, as well as light transportation. Moreover, the best accuracy in models reaches by implicating the hybridization. *Spectral reflection prediction models* (SRPM) are helpful in studying the impact of different factors influencing the range of printable colors (the inks, the substrate, the illumination conditions, and the halftones) and in creating printer characterization profiles for the purpose of color management [2]. The Kubelka–Munk model (1) is widely used to predict the properties of multiple layers of ink overlaid at a given location, given information about each constituent ink's reflectance and opacity [3].

$$\frac{K(\lambda)}{S(\lambda)} = \frac{(1 - R_\infty(\lambda))^2}{2R_\infty(\lambda)} \tag{1}$$

where K is absorption and S is scattering coefficients, R_∞ is the reflectance of an infinitely thick sample and the prediction of S and K from reflectance is made at a given wavelength λ. The formula (1) allows predicting the combined K and S coefficients for multiple inks:

$$K(\lambda) = K_B(\lambda) + \sum_{i=1}^{l} c_i K_i(\lambda) \tag{2}$$

where B refers to the substrate, l is the number of ink layers, c_i is the concentration and K_i is the absorption coefficient of the i-th layer. $S(\lambda)$ is computed analogously.

One of the first integrated CPM is the Neugebauer model, which predicts the CIE XYZ tristimulus values of a color halftone patch as the sum of the tristimulus values of their individual colorants [4]. Since the Neugebauer model does not take into account the lateral propagation of light within the paper and internal reflections at the paper-air interface, its predictions are considered inaccurate.

The most well-known SRPM among recent ones is the Yule–Nielsen modified spectral Neugebauer model (YNSN) where the Yule–Nielsen relationship applied to the spectral Neugebauer equations [5, 6].

$$R(\lambda) = \left(\sum_{i=1}^{p} w_i P_i(\lambda)^{\frac{1}{n}} \right)^n \tag{3}$$

where $R(\lambda)$ is the reflectance of a halftone pattern neighborhood that is optically integrated as it is being viewed, w_i is the relative area coverage of the i-th *Neugebauer primary* – P, n is the Yule-Nielsen non-linearity that accounts for optical dot gain.

The further enhancement of the model (EYNSN) accounts the ink spreading effect connected with the respective physical dot-gains of one ink halftone printed in different superposition conditions (single colorant and its combinations with 1–3 another colorants). The model uses multiple ink spreading curves (tone reproduction curves, TRC) to characterize the physical dot-gain of the ink halftones on substrate and in all solid ink superposition conditions [7]. Spectral reflection prediction models together with ink-spreading models accounting for physical dot-gain are able to predict reflectance spectra as a function of ink surface coverage for 3–4 inks [1, 8]. Minimization of difference metric between measured and predicted reflection spectrum for each superposition condition takes the effective ink surface coverage and the ink-spreading curve mapping nominal to effective surface coverage for each colorant.

1.2   Literature Review

Different CPMs have been successfully applied to color predictions in various contexts. Some studies inspired us to do the research into the development of this topic.

The work [9] devoted to calibrating the YNSN model with ink spreading curves derived from digitized RGB calibration patch images. Researchers carry out spectral predictions with the ink spreading curves calibrated by relying on RGB images of 36 C, M, and Y patches (without black channel). For calculating the ink spreading curves, 25%, 50%, and 75% nominal coverage are used in each superposition condition. In addition, for the broadband Yule–Nielsen equation [7, 10], they used the digitized RGB images of the paper white, the solid inks, and all the solid ink superposition. The model is tested on 729 patches comprising all nominal surface coverage combinations of 0%, 13%, 25%, 38%, 50%, 63%, 75%, 88%, and 100%. For the comparison, authors offer the prediction accuracies with the calibration of the ink spreading curves performed by spectral fits according to the YNSN model. As a reference, they consider also a single ink spreading function per ink obtained by computing the effective surface coverage of single ink halftones printed on paper. The prediction results demonstrate that the full ink-spreading model deduced from RGB images yields a better prediction accuracy than the classical single ink dot-gain relying on spectral fits. The full ink-spreading model relying on digitized RGB images shows a slightly lower accuracy compared with the one calibrated with measured reflection spectra.

Thus, authors reduce the effort of calibrating the YNSN model accounting for full ink spreading by computing the nominal to effective surface coverage curves from digitized RGB images instead of measured reflection spectra. For the calibration of the model by digitized RGB images, a user needs to measure only the reflection spectra of the solid colorant patches (for 3 inks: 8 patches) and digitize one sheet containing all calibration patches (for 3 inks: 44 patches). By using images instead of spectra, the prediction accuracy is not much affected. Tests are carried out with 729 color patches covering the complete gamut of the output device. In case of C, M, and Y ink, the mean CIE *Lab* ΔE_{94} difference between predicted and measured reflection spectra for calibration by spectral fits was 1.00. When calibrating with digitized RGB images, the mean prediction difference is CIE *Lab* $\Delta E_{94} = 1.29$.

Livens [11] describes multi-density ink calibration in a framework that includes ink limitation and characterization and proposes a technique called multiple characterization, which allows to achieve a predefined color response with respect to more than one quantity, by exploiting the additional degrees of freedom offered by similarly colored inks. The method aims to improve the visual uniformity. It is noted that the process of ink transition management must be under strict control since the transition between light and dark inks could result in some artefacts caused by too large amount of ink. However, a key characteristic of existing ink mixing solutions is that they define the mapping in a fixed way, independent of the calibration. The mapping is usually empirically optimized for a certain condition of the printer that might vary over time.

The author proposes to replace the fixed ink mixing by a calibrated ink mixing implies the multiple characterization, in which ink increments are computed that correspond to equal increments or decrements in the measured variable, however, the measured value implies a set of different solutions, corresponding with various ratios of light and dark inks. The choice is done by constructing a calibration that results in more uniform CIE *Lab* ΔE steps. The characterization covers only that pair of CIE *Lab* coordinates (*L, a, b*) which contributes much more to CIE *Lab* ΔE. In fact, the major contribution is made by the chromatic coordinate (*a, b*). In geometrical interpretation, with single and multi-density inks, a 1D trajectory is described in the 3D color space by varying the ink percentage.

The author suggests the characterization means dividing the trajectory into steps that correspond to an equal change in a measured variable. He also agrees that it is often useful or even necessary to set ink limitations in order to cut off areas that cause problems in characterization. However, there is no description of curves behavior and no suggestions how to manage ink limits.

In the work [12], the objective is to quantify the influence of ink-jet printer calibration and profile–making on the quality of color reproduction, in the context of fine art printing on a special paper compared with those obtained on a coated paper. The first step of the experiment is a fine setting of the printer, in order to stabilize the results. The second step is a complete printer characterization with profile-making, when different input parameters (total ink coverage, black ink limit, etc.) are adjusted. The performance of the color profiles is analyzed by color differences (CIE *Lab* ΔE), the volume of color gamut, and spectral characteristics of the printed colors. Then the profiles are edited and optimized in order to reduce the color differences.

The authors emphasize the importance of characterization because the tone increase value for ink-jet printing is generally larger than for the other printing processes. They also agree that the determination of the limit total area coverage (TAC) accepted by a paper is crucial in order to avoid problems such as poor ink drying and smudges, and indicate typical value of TAC for ink-jet on coated paper as 250%. Test-charts like IT8 7/3 are pointed to be a possible way for such a determination, as well as for obtaining the grey balance. ICC profiles are expected to be the overriding part of characterization.

During the TAC determination, the amount of ink supply is assessed visually, when for a limit of 280% there is a problem of ink migration towards the adjacent patches. Besides, there is a strong difference with the coated paper which accepts higher ink superimpositions. The best TAC (160%) is chosen by minimal CIE *Lab* ΔE variation. As a result, the work does not demonstrate a substantial scientific novelty, however, showed the typical way by which experts go when calibrate printing equipment.

The paper [13] is connected to ink consumption while achieve an accurate digital color reproduction by an ink-jet printer on different non-paper-substrates of POP display media. The assessments are done by measuring by a spectrophotometer raw characterization targets, which display color cast. The ink usage is determined in terms of amount of ink restriction. A characterization test target is used to exam the ink-jet hooking phenomena, i.e. the ink hue shifting associated with ink-jet printers. It is noted that the color shift happens in chromatic and neutral shadow areas of a print due to impurities in the ink-jet inks. For a particular substrate, a typical ink-jet hooking phenomenon (for C and M channels) is observed when printing with full ink load (see Fig. 1(a)).

It shows the hue angle of Cyan color begins to shift from a cyan blue to a contaminated cyan that turns purple because there is more red color in the cyan. The hue angle of magenta color shifts toward yellow. With further ink restriction (−16.25%), the ink-jet hooking is reduced, and ink distributed more evenly and correctly on the media (see Fig. 1(b)). At the same time, ink restriction reduces the size of the color gamut: 16.25% ink reduction cut down the size of color gamut about 9%. A similar effect is observed for another substrates. It is concluded that it is necessary to experiment with different characterization settings to achieve the right amount of ink distributed on the media. Each individual ink channel should be restricted just right after the color begins to change "hook" from the base primary color, while leaving extra color to extend the gamut for spot colors. Despite observation the phenomena, the author does not reveal the cause and offers only empirical estimates of ink reduction.

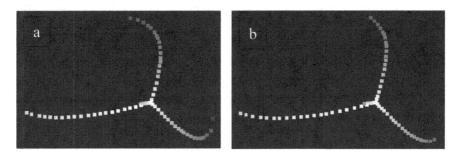

Fig. 1. Color hooking phenomena before (a) and after (b) ink reduction (Color figure online)

The described approach might be promising; however, it cannot be applied without correcting its shortcomings. The major one is the fact that in any case, some information about the color is lost when analyzing the projections on the *ab*-plane, without space considerations. For instance, yellow colorant do not tend to form "hook" on the *ab*-plane, but do it on the *Lb*-plane instead. Unfortunately, it is not reflected in figures, such as Fig. 1.

All mentioned approaches have their advantages as well as drawbacks, too. Majority of models are too complicated to be embedded in a real workflow without substantial development and adjustment that takes time. For instance, YNSN-based models are extremely critical to the selection of the parameter n. Generally accepted algorithms for its definition in the literature are not described. Usually it is suggested to carry out selection by brute force, which is utterly laborious. The empirical approach is more promising, however it requires a large number of printed tests for each pair of substrate-ink. Moreover, so far any complete model that predicts the behavior of ink in terms of its limited supply in inkjet printing has not been proposed.

Gradation scales and gradation-based techniques are known as an indispensable attribute of color printing systems settings [14, pp. 88–89]. At the same time, the authors expresses doubts about the rational use of these characteristics in digital printing technology. The main problem is the fact that using the gradation curves in conventional 2D embodiment significantly reduces the quantity and quality of information extracted from them. In the work [15], 3D gradation trajectories are introduced as a further development of the gradation curves approach. Implication the mathematical apparatus of differential geometry for gradation trajectories analysis in 3D CIE *L, a, b* space allows reveal their intrinsic features of curvature and torsion. The approach used is not a model in the full sense, since it does not use any a priori assumptions. It is only a description of the measurements results in the form of empirical functions.

These features are applied to define the ink limits in ink-jet printing systems and to create the empirical approach based on trajectories' curvature and torsion behavior analysis.

This work is devoted to further development of the proposed technique. We suggest using an equidistant CIE *Lab* ΔE color difference as a basement for ink-jet printers' characterization with help of 3D gradation trajectories. We offer a simple approach for such a characterization, which implies a small number of prints and rapid calculations.

2 Approach

The approach we describe as follows. Print specially developed test chart → Measure *Lab* coordinates of the chart with a spectrophotometer → Sorting data by color channels in order of increasing percentage of fill → Curve fitting by a polynomial of fourth degree → Curvature analysis, definition of the ink limitation point → Calculation of the arc length of a curve from 0 to the point corresponding to curvature's maximum → The curve is divided to segments based on the equal color difference → Print test chart to assess the result.

First, we introduce gradation trajectories. Let's a gradation trajectory is the locus of points in the CIE *Lab* space, which coordinates are consistent with the individual fields of measurement of the tone scale, arranged in ascending order of percentage of raster cells coverage in the layout of 0% (unsealed substrate) to 100% (dye). Tone scales generally comprise no more than two dozen of fields, i.e. in practice; the gradation trajectory is represented by a discrete set of points in CIE *Lab* space. Modern printing systems provide a color depth of at least 256 gradations (8 bits), i.e. color change characteristics (hue, saturation and brightness), as well as the color coordinates, might be assumed as a continuous function of the percentage (proportion) of raster cell filling. In other words, we can expect a nearly continuous change of color characteristics when filling percentage of a raster cell changes continuously.

If we took the percentage of raster cell filling as a parameter of a curve t, the gradation trajectory might be set by the parametric equations (4):

$$\begin{cases} t \in [0;\ 1] \\ L = c_{4L} \cdot t^4 + c_{3L} \cdot t^3 + c_{2L} \cdot t^2 + c_{1L} \cdot t + c_{0L} \\ a = c_{4a} \cdot t^4 + c_{3a} \cdot t^3 + c_{2a} \cdot t^2 + c_{1a} \cdot t + c_{0a} \\ b = c_{4b} \cdot t^4 + c_{3b} \cdot t^3 + c_{2b} \cdot t^2 + c_{1b} \cdot t + c_{0b} \end{cases} \tag{4}$$

where $c_{ij}(i = \overline{1,2,3,4};\ j = \overline{L,a,b}$ are some numerical coefficients, c_{0j} are *Lab*-coordinates of unsealed substrate. The interval of parameter t alteration is accepted from 0 (unsealed substrate) to 1 (100% dye).

Since we have agreed to assume the functions (1) to be continuous on the segment, then, according to the Weierstrass approximation theorem [16], their analytical form could be given by a polynomial of a certain extent. The theorem proves that if f is a continuous real-valued function on $[a,\ b]$, and if any $\varepsilon > 0$ is given, then there a polynomial p on $[a,\ b]$ such that $|f(x)-p(x)| < \varepsilon$ for all x in $[a,\ b]$ exists. In words, any continuous function on a closed and bounded interval can be uniformly approximated on

.

that interval by polynomials to any degree of accuracy. In our case, the polynomial of the fourth power is required to detect such features of a space curve as the curvature (κ) [17, p. 49], because in the process of calculating, the derivatives respect to a parameter up to the second power are used:

$$r = (a(t),\ b(t),\ L(t))$$
$$\kappa = \frac{|r' \times r''|}{|r'|^3} \tag{5}$$

Ink spreading on solid surfaces and penetration into porous matrices (coated and uncoated papers) describes by power-law exponents [18]. However, for coated papers polynomials of the fourth power give satisfactory approximation accuracy. In this case, approximation errors are less than measurement ones.

In order to define n equidistant points with respect to ink limitation we first need to evaluate trajectory's arc length of a curve S (6). Thus, we discover full tone increase corresponding to t increment, as well as t_x values corresponding to even tone segments (7).

$$S = \int_0^{t_{max}} dE_{94} \tag{6}$$

$$\int_0^{t_x} dE_{94} = \frac{S}{n} \tag{7}$$

3   Experimental Verification

For the experiment, we use the 4-color (CMYK) wide-format solvent ink-jet printer Mimaki CJV30-160BS. Print mode: 720×720 dpi, variable dot. Substrate: coated paper MediaPrint Gloss 150 g/m^2 as a weak-absorbent substrate. The measurement tools: spectrophotometer x-Rite iOne iSis + x-Rite ProfileMaker package.

Tone scales containing 20 bitmap fields are synthesized using a ChartGenerator/ MeasureTool in ProfileMaker design for the automatic iOne iSis (see Fig. 2, above). Sample scales are printed by "swastika" on the same sheet in order to average the results of scale measurement depending on the print direction and printing head movement in relation to the layout.

The results of the 4 measurements are averaged in ProfileMaker/MeasureTool and save as a text file, which then imports into MS Excel, where it stay out as a matrix of variables of dimension 21 (20 raster fields plus the unsealed substrate) $\times$ 4 (the proportion of a raster cell filling plus CIE *Lab* coordinates values). Measured data are divided into individual color channels. Matrix variables, which contained t, L, a, b data of each color patch as columns, are imported in MatLab, where they are carried out in further mathematical processing.

The approximation of dependences (4) by polynomials is implemented in MatLab package using the fit function. It is necessary to ensure a minimum cumulative CIE *Lab* ΔE_{76} [19] color difference between the theoretical trajectory and experimental points. The value of the total color difference CIE *Lab* ΔE_{76} of experimental points from the theoretical trajectory is 2–3 units. For comparison, the worst deviation from the average in the preparation of the experimental points was 3–6 color difference CIE *Lab* ΔE_{76} units. The obtained t_x values (7) are in fact the tone reproduction curves (TRC) points that are further implicated into raster image processor (RIP).

Final evaluation is done by preparation of a new arbitrary scale with 10% tone increase on a color channel (Fig. 2, below) that is further printed out and is measured.

Fig. 2. iOne iSis test charts to print: (above) tone chart for measurement (below) tone chart for evaluation

4   Results and Discussion

As for any other continuous space curve, the numerical factors such as curvature in terms of differential geometry can be defined at each point of the gradation trajectory. Figure 3 shows gradation trajectories for the Cyan and Yellow color channels (as for instance). The dots correspond to the tone scale fields variation, solid curve is an approximating gradation trajectory, a projection of the actual measurements on the *ab* chromaticity plane is shown at the bottom. Obviously, the points corresponding to an equal tone increase (+0.05) are located on the trajectory not equidistantly.

Figure 4 shows the dependencies of curvature on the part of tone. As can be seen, the curvature of the trajectory is different from zero in a narrow band of the range. The presence of local extrema points to a jerky change of hue while a raster cell is being filled. For the further calculations, the ink limits are set to 83.67% for the Cyan channel and to 85.17% for the Yellow channel .

Figure 4 shows a part of the curvature graph that is significantly different from zero. The maximum of curvature corresponds to the region of the sharpest bending of the gradation path, i.e. the sharpest change in color tone for the Cyan channel and the sharpest drop in brightness for the Yellow channel. These are the points that are chosen to limit the maximum ink supply for the specified color channels. In addition, this tone value is utilized as the upper limit of integration (t_{max}) in (6) for the further calculation.

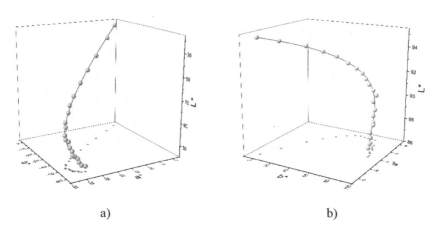

a)   b)

Fig. 3. Gradation trajectory for the (a) cyan and (b) yellow channels (Color figure online)

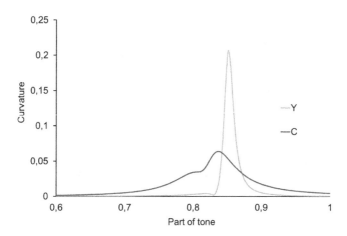

Fig. 4. Curvature values for the gradation trajectory depending on the part of tone (Color figure online)

Figure 5 shows *Lab*-coordinates of measured test patches, which correspond to 0.1 tone increment on the gradation trajectory after characterization for the Cyan and Yellow channels. The dots lie exactly on the calculated trajectory for both channels.

Arc lengths of curves of segments connecting neighbor dots are more equal than ones indicated in Fig. 3. This also is demonstrated in Fig. 6 where color differences that correspond to the related arc length seem to be the same.

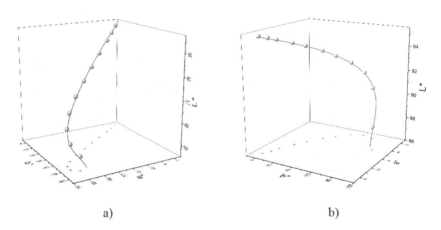

a)   b)

Fig. 5. Measured points on gradation trajectory after characterization for the (a) cyan and (b) yellow channels (Color figure online)

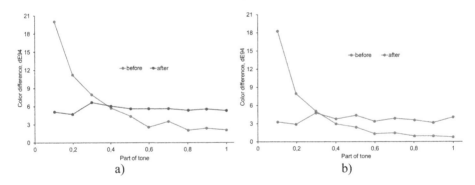

a)   b)

Fig. 6. CIE *Lab* ΔE_{94} color difference between patches, which correspond to 0.1 tone increment before and after characterization for the (a) cyan and (b) yellow channels (Color figure online)

5 Conclusion

A new three-dimensional interpretation of the gradation curves in CIE *Lab*-space is proposed. Gradation trajectories, as well as the method of their analytical description, are described. Gradational trajectories are conceived as continuous, bounded on the gradation range curves. In this connection, the apparatus of differential geometry of curves is applied to them, and the values of such parameters as curvature and arc length of a curve are calculated.

Gradation trajectories introduced by the described manner are the global features of ink-jet printing process that are depended on type of a substrate and properties of the ink only. They are not affected by rasterizing method, number of passes and measuring technique.

Recently, there was no sustainability criterion, which can be applied for certain specification of maximum percentage of the ink supply. Possible options for such a criterion might be a first maximum in the plot of gradation trajectory's curvature.

The arc length of a curve of the trajectory might be utilized as a powerful and fast-acting tool for ink-jet systems characterization.

Any limitation of ink supply and any method of characterization under the conditions of a tone scales print will give the family of the points belonging to the gradation trajectory. In other words, if the printing conditions mentioned are met, then regard-less of the selected ink supply limitations, the results of measurement of gradation scales will form a family of points on the gradation trajectories describing each color channel.

Since the described approach is not a model, the results cannot be compared to any CPM. The approach ensures reproduction of a given tint with accuracy to the quantization error. In the case of 8-bit color, the nearest of 256 possible halftones is selected. The further development of the approach implies introduction of 3D gradation surfaces as a method describing interconnection between two colorants, especially in the case of regular and light inks pairs.

References

1. Balasubramanian, R.: Optimization of the spectral Neugebauer model for printer characterization. J. Electron. Imaging **8**, 156–166 (1999)
2. Bala, R.: Device characterization. In: Sharma, G. (ed.) Digital Color Imaging Handbook, pp. 269–379. CRC Press, Boca Raton (2003)
3. Kubelka, P., Munk, F.: Ein Beitrag zur Optik der Farbanstriche. Zeitschrift für technische Physik **12**, 593–601 (1931). Germany
4. Neugebauer, H.E.J.: Die theoretischen Grundlagen des Mehrfarbendrucks. Zeinschrift fur Wissenschaftliche Photographie Photophysik Photochemie **36**, 36–73 (1937)
5. Yule, J.A.C., Nielsen, W.J.: The penetration of light into paper and its effect on halftone reproductions. In: Proceedings of TAGA Conference 1951, pp. 65–76. TAGA, Sewickley (1951)
6. Viggiano, J.A.S.: Modeling the color of multi-colored halftones. In: Proceedings of TAGA Conference 1990, pp. 44–62. TAGA, Sewickley (1990)
7. Hersch, R.D., Crété, F.: Improving the Yule–Nielsen modified spectral Neugebauer model by dot surface coverages depending on the ink superposition conditions. In: Proceedings of SPIE, vol. 5667, pp. 434–445 (2005)
8. Wyble, D.R., Berns, R.S.: A critical review of spectral models applied to binary color printing. Color Res. Appl. **25**, 4–19 (2000)
9. Garg, N.P., Singla, A.K., Hersch, R.D.: Calibrating the Yule–Nielsen modified spectral Neugebauer model with ink spreading curves derived from digitized RGB calibration patch images. J. Imaging Sci. Technol. **52**(4), 040908-1–040908-5 (2008)

10. Arney, J.S., Engeldrum, P.G., Zeng, H.: An expanded Murray-Davis model of tone reproduction in halftone imaging. J. Imaging Sci. Technol. **39**, 502–508 (1995)
11. Livens, S.: Optimisation of printer calibration in the case of multi density inks. In: Conference on Color in Graphics, Imaging, and Vision, CGIV 2002 Final Program and Proceedings, pp. 633–638 (2002)
12. Chagas, L., Blayo, A., Giraud, P.: Color Profile: methodology and influence on the performance of ink-jet color reproduction. In: IS&T's NIP20: 2004 International Conference on Digital Printing Technologies, pp. 655–659 (2004)
13. Wu, Y.-J.: Reducing ink-jet ink consumption with RIP software for POP display media. In: Digital Fabrication and Digital Printing: NIP30 Technical Program and Proceedings, pp. 108–111 (2014)
14. Kipphan, H.: Handbook of Print Media, p. 1207. Springer, Heidelberg (2001). https://doi.org/10.1007/978-3-540-29900-4
15. Milder, O.B., Tarasov, D.A., Titova, M.Y.: Inkjet printers linearization using 3D gradation curves. In: CEUR Workshop Proceedings. Proceedings of the 1st International Workshop on Radio Electronics & Information Technologies (REIT 2017), Yekaterinburg, Russia, 15 March 2017, vol. 1814, pp. 74–83 (2017)
16. Jeffreys, H., Jeffreys, B.S.: Weierstrass's Theorem on Approximation by Polynomials and Extension of Weierstrass's Approximation Theory, §14.08–14.081 in Methods of Mathematical Physics, 3rd edn, pp. 446–448. Cambridge University Press, Cambridge (1988)
17. Pogorelov, A.V.: Differential geometry. Noordhoff, 171p. (1959). (Translated from Russian)
18. Rosenholm, J.B.: Liquid spreading on solid surfaces and penetration into porous matrices: coated and uncoated papers. Adv. Colloid Interface Sci. **220**, 8–53 (2015)
19. Pauli, H.: Proposed extension of the CIE recommendation on "uniform color spaces, color difference equations, and metric color terms". J. Opt. Soc. Am. **66**, 866–867 (1976)

Gradation Surfaces as a Method for Multi-color Ink-Jet Printers Color Specifications Management

Oleg Milder[1] and Dmitry Tarasov[1,2](✉)

[1] Institute of Radio-Engineering and IT, Ural Federal University,
Mira, 32, Ekaterinburg 620002, Russia
datarasov@yandex.ru
[2] Institute of Industrial Ecology UB RAS,
Kovalevskoy, 20, Ekaterinburg 620990, Russia

Abstract. We offer 3D gradation surfaces as a further development of 3D gradation curves approach. The surfaces reflect the interaction between selected pair of colorants in CIE *Lab* space. The surfaces are strained on the gradation trajectories of selected colorants. They are considered in terms of 3D surfaces of differential geometry. Application of the method leads to increase the smoothness of the gradient in the pair. Geodesic lines of the surfaces are suggested to be gradation trajectories of binary colors impositions. In the work, we develop the approach and discuss mathematical methods of the surfaces' description as well as geodesic lines' estimation.

Keywords: Gradation surfaces · Ink-jet · Characterization · Geodesic lines

1 Introduction

Current multi-color printing systems require a special approach in characterization. Thanks to different color prediction models, the usage of inks can be substantially optimized especially in the case of current multi-color printers. The models may help the image processing software to decide, which set of basic colorants and how to select in order to print a certain color within a specific context. Such models need to account for both the interactions between the inks and the substrate and between the light and the halftone print, as well as the Fresnel reflections and light scattering.

Empirical surface models take into account superposition of ink halftones and do not deal with the light propagation and fading within the print. The models demonstrate the relationship between reflected light and surface coverages by colorants. Physically inspired models engage a more detailed analysis of light-print interaction based on mathematical prediction of how light paths go within a halftone print and what resulting fade is. Ink spreading models are developed to characterize the effective surface of an ink dot after it has been printed at a given nominal surface coverage compared to the effective surface coverage that forms the physical dot gain. The models accounting for ink spreading in all ink superposition conditions rely on ink spreading

© Springer International Publishing AG, part of Springer Nature 2018
M. Paul et al. (Eds.): PSIVT 2017, LNCS 10749, pp. 53–61, 2018.
https://doi.org/10.1007/978-3-319-75786-5_5

curves mapping nominal surface coverages to effective surface coverages for the surface coverages of single ink halftones, as well as ones superposed with one and two solid inks.

The further development of color prediction models deal with spread-based and light propagation and transportation probability. Spectral reflection prediction models study the impact of different factors influencing the range of printable colors (the inks, the substrate, the illumination conditions, and the halftones) and create printer characterization profiles for the purpose of color management [1]. These models together with ink-spreading models take into account physical dot gain and able to predict reflectance spectra as a function of ink surface coverage for 2–4 inks (binary and ternary color systems). The models uses multiple tone reproduction (ink spreading) curves (TRC) to characterize the physical dot gain of the ink halftones on the substrate and in all solid ink superposition conditions [2–4]. Different color prediction models have been successfully applied to color reproduction management in various contexts [5–9].

The major drawback of the mentioned models is the fact that all of them are computationally capacious, as n colorants require a solution of system of 2^n equations; therefore, they cannot be implicated into real workflow. The empirical approaches are more promising; however, they usually require a significant amount of print tests to do.

Gradation scales using for gradation curves building are known as an indispensable attribute of color printing systems settings [10, pp. 88–89]. Utilizing the gradation curves in a conventional 2D embodiment significantly reduces the quantity and quality of information extracted from them. Moreover, some information about the color is lost when analyzing the projections on the *ab*-plane, without space considerations.

In the work [11], 3D gradation trajectories are introduced as a further development of gradation curves. Implication the mathematical apparatus of differential geometry for gradation trajectories analysis in 3D CIE *Lab* space allows reveal their intrinsic features of curvature and torsion. These features are applied to define the ink limits in ink-jet printing systems and to create the empirical approach based on trajectories' curvature and torsion behavior analysis. This approach might be extended to the case of greater number of colorants.

In this work, we introduce 3D gradation surfaces as a practical tool for multi-color ink-jet systems characterization in the case of 2 colorants. The technique might help to predict the halftones of binaries even in the case of 2 colorants in one color channel (e.g. cyan/light-cyan) or colorants of complementary colors (e.g. Blue = Cyan + Magenta).

2 Approach

At first, we have to introduce a concept of gradation surfaces. The gradation trajectory of double overlapping is a surface constructed on the basis of gradation curves of two colorants. For the further work with these surfaces, we need to describe them analytically. The description of the curve by a polynomial of some degree is a part of the Matlab software functionality. All our models are built with help of Matlab package.

Let us consider the formation of color with the participation of a certain type of substrate and two colorants. Take as an example the pair of Cyan (n) and Magenta (*m*) inks. Each colorant is able to take a halftone value from 0 (pure substrate) to 1 (dye). Thus,

$$n \in [0; 1] \text{ for Cyan}$$
$$m \in [0; 1] \text{ for Magenta} \qquad (1)$$

In the case of continuous halftones, we obtain a square region of allowable recipes on the plane (*n*, *m*). In real print, a frequent grid occurs instead of a solid square. A color depth defines the number of gridlines (vertical and horizontal). Recent image processing systems provide color depth of at least 8 bit per channel; therefore, the grid is composed with $2^8 = 256$ lines. Such quantity of halftone values is considered enough for continuous halftone perception. Halftone recipes achievable within a given printing system are in grid nodes. This gives $2^{16} = 65536$ possible halftones of a chosen pair of colorants. Actually, the number of halftones is slightly less because a printing system characterization limits the ink supply at the expense of color depth. Nevertheless, this number is large enough to consider halftones as continuous. Each reproducible tone has its own recipe (*n*, *m*) and a set of *Lab*-coordinates. A smooth change in tone causes a smooth change of *Lab*-coordinates. This can be represented in (2), which describe smooth surfaces in *Lab*-space.

$$a = a(n, m); \quad b = b(n, m); \quad L = L(n, m) \qquad (2)$$

The Eq. (2) seems to be equal to equation of the surface in the Cartesian space [12]. Thus, a gradation surface is a locus of points in *Lab*-space that satisfies the system of conditions (1) and (2). Weather the printing system is preliminary characterized, it might me assumed that gradation trajectories of a single color channel effectively described by polynomials of the degree not higher than third (3). For *b* and *L* coordinates equations have the same type. Note, a_0, b_0, L_0 are the coordinates of the substrate.

$$a_{Cyan} = a_0 + \sum_{i=1}^{3} a_{Cyan,i} \cdot n^i$$
$$a_{Magenta} = a_0 + \sum_{i=1}^{3} a_{Magenta,i} \cdot m^i \qquad (3)$$

We designate a binary gradation surface as "stretched" on the gradation trajectories of generatrix pairs of colorants so that it contain them inside. In the system (2) it will be reflected as special cases, as for instance, the gradation trajectory Cyan is contained in the gradation surface of Blue tones (4).

$$a = a(n, 0); \quad b = b(n, 0); \quad L = L(n, 0) \qquad (4)$$

Weather gradation surface is stretched on the gradation trajectories then, taking into account (3), we can assume the explicit form of (2) is (5). For *b* and *L* coordinates equations have the same type. Note, a_0, b_0, L_0 are the coordinates of the substrate.

$$a_{Blue} = a_0 + \sum_{i=1}^{3} \sum_{j=0}^{i} a_{i-j,j} \cdot n^{i-j} \cdot m^j \qquad (5)$$

The required degree of the polynomial (third) was approved experimentally. The graph of the analytic surface (see Fig. 1) is deviated from the experimental data by a distance smaller than the measurement error of the spectrophotometer. A polynomial of the third degree was quite accurate, so the fourth-degree polynomial was superfluous.

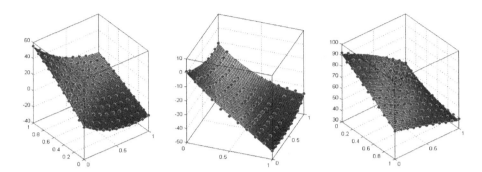

Fig. 1. Approximations of *Lab*-coordinates (2) by (5): left – *a*, central – *b*, right – *L*; dots are the measured values; colored surfaces are approximations (Color figure online)

At second, we have to introduce a concept of geodesic lines. Characterization of a printing machine is made by a uniform distribution of points along the gradation curve. Therefore, it would be logical to assume that this principle should also be adhered to in the case of a double halftone surface. But since the figure of double superimposition in color space is not a curve, but a surface, the points should be located evenly within the surface – at an equal distance from each other, as if by a grid. It is precisely this goal that an element of differential geometry, such as geodesic lines, perfectly fit. A geodesic line is an analog of a straight line on a plane for a surface, i.e. straight line, which, by the shortest path, connects two points on the surface. The basic property of a geodesic line: on any sufficiently small piece of surface through two points the only one arc of the geodesic line can be drawn, just as on a plane through two points the only one straight line do.

Surface geodesic lines are considered quite difficult. The following is an algorithm for finding out a geodesic in general form. In our case, we consider a regular piece of the surface *B* (blue) defined by vector Eq. (2). The first fundamental form of the surface *B* is the following (6):

$$
\begin{aligned}
dB^2 &= E(n,m)dn^2 + 2F(n,m)dndm + G(n,m)dm^2, \text{where} \\
E(n,m) &= \left(\frac{da}{dn}\right)^2 + \left(\frac{db}{dn}\right)^2 + \left(\frac{dL}{dn}\right)^2 \\
F(n,m) &= \frac{da}{dn}\frac{da}{dm} + \frac{db}{dn}\frac{db}{dm} + \frac{dL}{dn}\frac{dL}{dm} \\
G(n,m) &= \left(\frac{da}{dm}\right)^2 + \left(\frac{db}{dm}\right)^2 + \left(\frac{dL}{dm}\right)^2
\end{aligned}
\tag{6}
$$

A regular piece of the surface *B* with the first fundamental form is a two-dimensional Riemannian space referred to the coordinates (*n*, *m*). If we consider a surface as a Riemannian space, then vectors, tensors, scalar products, and covariant differentiation can be defined on it [13]. The three-index Christoffel symbols have the following form for the surface *B* (7):

$$\Gamma^1_{11} = \left\{ \begin{matrix} 1 \\ 1 & & 1 \end{matrix} \right\}_B = \frac{GE_n - 2FF_n + FE_m}{2(EG - F^2)}, \quad \Gamma^2_{11} = \left\{ \begin{matrix} 2 \\ 1 & & 1 \end{matrix} \right\}_B = \frac{-FE_n + 2EF_n - EE_m}{2(EG - F^2)},$$

$$\Gamma^1_{12} = \left\{ \begin{matrix} 1 \\ 1 & & 2 \end{matrix} \right\}_B = \left\{ \begin{matrix} 1 \\ 2 & & 1 \end{matrix} \right\}_B = \frac{GE_n - FG_m}{2(EG - F^2)}, \quad \Gamma^2_{12} = \left\{ \begin{matrix} 2 \\ 1 & & 2 \end{matrix} \right\}_B = \left\{ \begin{matrix} 2 \\ 2 & & 1 \end{matrix} \right\}_B = \frac{EG_n - FE_m}{2(EG - F^2)},$$

$$\Gamma^1_{22} = \left\{ \begin{matrix} 1 \\ 2 & & 2 \end{matrix} \right\}_B = \frac{-FG_m - 2GF_m - GG_n}{2(EG - F^2)}, \quad \Gamma^2_{22} = \left\{ \begin{matrix} 2 \\ 2 & & 2 \end{matrix} \right\}_B = \frac{EG_m - 2FF_m - FG_n}{2(EG - F^2)}.$$

$$(7)$$

For any geodesic $m = m(n)$, the corresponding function $m(n)$ satisfies the differential Eq. (8).

$$\frac{d^2 m}{dn^2} = \Gamma^1_{22_B} \left(\frac{dm}{dn} \right)^3 + \left[2\Gamma^1_{12_B} - \Gamma^2_{22_B} \right] \left(\frac{dm}{dn} \right)^2 + \left[\Gamma^1_{11_B} - 2\Gamma^2_{12_B} \right] \frac{dm}{dn} - \Gamma^2_{11_B} \quad (8)$$

The gradation trajectory of Blue color is the curve in the *Lab*-space containing two points $(n, m) = (0, 0)$ as pure substrate and $(n, m) = (1, 1)$ as binary dye. Moreover, this curve must lie on the surface of blue halftones B. Thus, the gradation trajectory of Blue color is the geodesic satisfying Eq. (8) with boundary conditions $m(0) = 0$, $m(1) = 1$ (Fig. 2).

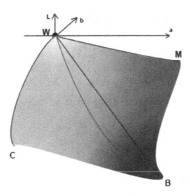

Fig. 2. The gradation surface of blue (B) halftones stretched on gradation trajectories of cyan and magenta (CM); red curve is a geodesic; black line is a nominal line of Blue color by recipe $C = M$; W is a white point (substrate) (Color figure online)

3   Experimental

For the experiment, we use the 4-color (CMYK) wide-format solvent ink-jet printer Mimaki CJV30-160BS. Print mode: 1440 × 1440 dpi, small dot. Substrate: coated paper FancyEmboss 110 g/m^2 as an absorbent substrate. The measurement tools: spectrophotometer x-Rite iOne iSis + x-Rite ProfileMaker package.

A halftone scale contains 14800 fields. The scale represents the multidimensional grid of test values. The total number of patches is 11 $(0, 0.1, 0.2...1)$ values per channel to the power of the number of colorants (four). They are synthesized using Argyll CMS and a TestChartGenerator in ProfileMaker for the automatic iOne iSis. Sample scales contain 5 sheets (see Fig. 3).

The results are saved as a text file, which then imports into MS Excel, where matrixes of variables of dimension 121 (120 raster fields plus the unsealed substrate) × 5 (the proportion of a raster cells n, m (Cyan + Magenta) plus CIE *Lab*-coordinates values) are detached. Matrix variables, which contained n, m, L, a, b data of each color patch as columns, are imported in MatLab, where they are carried out in further mathematical processing.

The proposed method of gradation surfaces is based on the interpolation of experimental data by polynomials of type (5). The approximation of dependences (2) by polynomials (5) is implemented in MatLab package using the fit function. Final evaluation is done by preparation of a new arbitrary scale with 5% tone increase on a color channel that is further printed out and measured (Fig. 5(b)).

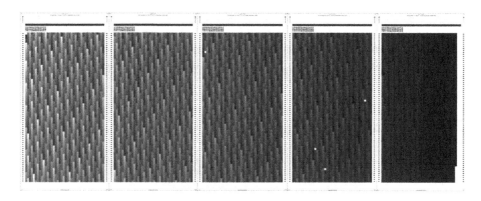

Fig. 3. iOne iSis halftone chart for measurement

4   Results and Discussion

The results of the measurement (L, a, b) of the extracted scale of 121 CM fields from the chart (Fig. 3) are shown in Fig. 4(a). Gradation surface and geodesics building is done in Matlab and shown in Fig. 4(b, c).

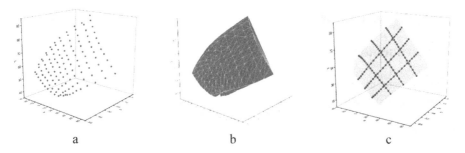

a   b   c

Fig. 4. Measurement of 121 CM CIE *Lab*-coordinates and gradation surface building: (a) measured points; (b) gradation surface stretched on the measured points; (c) geodesic lines corresponding to 25%, 50%, 75% of dye (Color figure online)

We can see that geodesics do not go along recipe lines. This means that the gradation line of Blue halftones do not correspond to the equivalent content of basic colorants (Cyan and Magenta) as it was supposed in (8) and Fig. 2. The calculated composition of colorants, which forms a Blue halftones line, is shown in Table 1 and Fig. 5(a).

Table 1. A blue halftones composition of cyan and magenta based on standard and geodesic recipes

Standard	C	5	10	15	20	25	30	35	40	45	50	55	60	65	70	75	80	85	90	95	100
	M	5	10	15	20	25	30	35	40	45	50	55	60	65	70	75	80	85	90	95	100
Geodesic	C	5	10	14	18	22	25	29	32	35	38	42	45	49	53	58	64	71	80	90	100
	M	7	14	20	26	32	38	43	49	54	59	63	68	72	77	81	85	89	93	96	100

We replaced the 5% tone increase arbitrary scale with one based on recipes correspond to intersection of geodesics (Fig. 5(b)). For instance, Table 1 represents the main diagonal of such a scale (Fig. 5(b), direction 1). We evaluated color difference between neighboring patches based on CIE ΔE_{94}. As additional assessment, we measured random directions on the scale (Fig. 5(b), directions 2–4). Distribution of the estimated CIE ΔE_{94} between the neighboring patches at various directions are shown in Fig. 6. The color differences CIE ΔE_{94} after a standard characterization are added for the comparison.

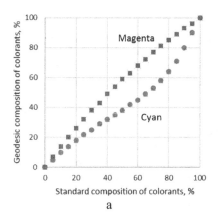
a

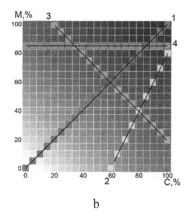
b

Fig. 5. Evaluation of color difference: (a) recipes of main diagonal of the arbitrary scale; (b) the scale of the binaries of cyan and magenta (CM) with marked equal-contrast scales 1, 2, 3 and 4

Figure 6 shows that when using geodesic characterization the scale becomes more equal-contrast in comparison to standard characterization. The dependence of the color difference on the pair number is described by a linear function. With the help of the coefficient of determination (R^2) we might ensure whether the dependence significant or not. After applying our algorithm, the R^2 decreased several times. This means that in the case of geodesic characterization, the dependence of CIE ΔE_{94} from the pair number disappears.

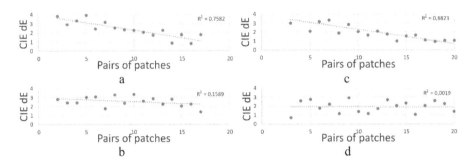

Fig. 6. CIE ΔE_{94} between the neighboring patches at various directions: (a) direction 3, standard characterization; (b) direction 3, geodesic characterization; (c) direction 4, standard characterization; (d) direction 4, geodesic characterization. Dotted lines are trends, R^2 are determination coefficients.

5 Conclusion

In this work, we introduced 3D gradation surfaces as a further development of 3D gradation curves and a practical tool for multi-color ink-jet printing systems characterization in the case of 2 colorants. They are described in terms of 3D surfaces of differential geometry. The surfaces are strained on the previously introduced gradation trajectories of selected colorants. The surfaces reflect the interaction between selected pair of colorants in CIE *Lab* space. The technique might help to predict the halftones of binaries in the case of 2 colorants. Geodesic lines of the surfaces are suggested to be gradation trajectories of binary colors impositions.

Experimental verification of the method shows significant improvement in the color contrast uniformity. Application of the method leads to increase the smoothness of the gradient in the colorants pair. This is confirmed by the CIE ΔE_{94} distribution analysis. In the case of geodesic characterization, the dependence of CIE ΔE_{94} from the gradation surface's location disappears.

We considered the approach based on pair of Cyan and Magenta colorants, however, it might be applied to any pair of colorants even in one color channel (e.g. Cyan/Light Cyan) or colorants of complementary colors (e.g. Red = Magenta + Yellow, Green = Cyan + Yellow). We suppose the approach to be expanded to the case of 3 colorants from one color segment (e.g. Magenta + Yellow + Orange), though this assumption requires additional studies.

References

1. Bala, R.: Device characterization. In: Sharma, G. (ed.) Digital Color Imaging Handbook, pp. 269–379. CRC Press, Boca Raton (2003)
2. Balasubramanian, R.: Optimization of the spectral Neugebauer model for printer characterization. J. Electron. Imaging **8**, 156–166 (1999)
3. Hersch, R.D., Crété, F.: Improving the Yule-Nielsen modified spectral Neugebauer model by dot surface coverages depending on the ink superposition conditions. In: Proceedings of SPIE, vol. 5667, pp. 434–445 (2005)
4. Wyble, D.R., Berns, R.S.: A critical review of spectral models applied to binary color printing. Color Res. Appl. **25**, 4–19 (2000)
5. Garg, N.P., Singla, A.K., Hersch, R.D.: Calibrating the Yule-Nielsen modified spectral Neugebauer model with ink spreading curves derived from digitized RGB calibration patch images. J. Imaging Sci. Technol. **52**(4), 040908–040908-5 (2008)
6. Arney, J.S., Engeldrum, P.G., Zeng, H.: An expanded Murray-Davis model of tone reproduction in halftone imaging. J. Imaging Sci. Technol. **39**, 502–508 (1995)
7. Livens, S.: Optimisation of printer calibration in the case of multi density inks. In: Conference on Color in Graphics, Imaging, and Vision, CGIV 2002 Final Program and Proceedings, pp. 633–638 (2002)
8. Chagas, L., Blayo, A., Giraud, P.: Color Profile: methodology and influence on the performance of ink-jet color reproduction. In: IS&T's NIP20: 2004 International Conference on Digital Printing Technologies, pp. 655–659 (2004)
9. Wu, Y.-J.: Reducing ink-jet ink consumption with RIP software for POP display media. In: Digital Fabrication and Digital Printing: NIP30 Technical Program and Proceedings, pp. 108–111 (2014)
10. Kipphan, H.: Handbook of Print Media, 1207 p. Springer, Heidelberg (2001). https://doi.org/10.1007/978-3-540-29900-4
11. Milder, O.B., Tarasov, D.A., Titova, M.Yu.: Inkjet printers linearization using 3D gradation curves. In: Proceedings of the 1st International Workshop on Radio Electronics and Information Technologies (REIT 2017). CEUR Workshop Proceedings, Yekaterinburg, Russia, 15 March 2017, vol. 1814, pp. 74–83 (2017)
12. Pogorelov, A.V.: Differential geometry. Noordhoff, 171 p. (1959). Translated from Russian
13. Korn, G.A., Korn, T.M.: Mathematical Handbook for Scientists and Engineers: Definitions, Theorems, and Formulas for Reference and Review, 1130 p. Courier Corporation, North Chelmsford (2000)

Multi-objective Visual Odometry

Hsiang-Jen Chien[1(✉)], Jr-Jiun Lin[2], Tang-Kai Yin[2], and Reinhard Klette[1]

[1] Department of Electrical and Electronic Engineering,
School of Engineering, Computer, and Mathematical Sciences,
Auckland University of Technology, Auckland, New Zealand
jchien@aut.ac.nz
[2] Department of Computer Science and Information Engineering,
National University of Kaohsiung, Kaohsiung, Taiwan

Abstract. Visual odometry (VO) has been extensively studied in the last decade. Despite a variety of implementation details, the proposed approaches share the same principle - a minimisation of a carefully chosen energy function. In this paper we review four commonly adopted energy models including perspective, epipolar, rigid, and photometric alignments, and propose a novel VO technique that unifies multiple objectives for outlier rejection and egomotion estimation to outperform mono-objective egomotion estimation. The experiments show an improvement above 50% is achievable by trading off 15% additional computational cost.

1 Introduction

Visual odometry (VO) uses an image sequence for calculating continuously egomotion of the camera. VO has been actively studied in the fields of computer vision, photogrammetry, or robotics. Egomotion estimation can be approached in a variety of ways. When dense depth data is available (e.g. from a ToF camera), the inter-frame pose can be derived by means of the alignment of 3D-to-3D structure correspondences. If the sensor also provides intensity images (e.g. an RGB-D camera), the pose can be estimated by minimising the photometric error when applied to perspectively warping the images. It is a more general case where 3D coordinates of sparse pixels are known only in the previous frame, where their locations need to be tracked in the next frame. Given such 3D-to-2D correspondences, egomotion is estimated by minimisation of the geodesic reprojection error.

In this paper we provide a review on adopted energy models of state-of-the-art VO methods. Based on these models, we propose a novel VO implementation that collaboratively uses multiple energy models to achieve more robust and accurate egomotion estimation. The rest of this paper is organised as follows. Section 2 gives a brief review on the recent development of VO techniques. In Sect. 3 we formulate VO as an energy minimisation problem. Section 4 walks through the energy models used by the state-of-the-art methods, based on which a unified framework is proposed in Sect. 5. Experimental results and discussions are given in Sect. 6, while Sect. 7 concludes this paper.

© Springer International Publishing AG, part of Springer Nature 2018
M. Paul et al. (Eds.): PSIVT 2017, LNCS 10749, pp. 62–74, 2018.
https://doi.org/10.1007/978-3-319-75786-5_6

2   Literature Review

In the last two decades, the development of VO has led to a separation into two different paths, namely appearance-based or feature-based techniques [1].

Appearance-based VO makes direct use of image intensities to minimise the photometric error between the perspective warping of a referenced frame and the image of a target frame. Early direct methods are influenced by optical flow estimation or *structure-from-motion* (SfM) techniques from the photogrammetry community [3,4]. After decades of oblivion, the direct methods have quickly become popular in the last few years, thanks to the advance of GPU computing and breakthroughs in the sparse *visual simultaneous localisation and mapping* (V-SLAM) domain [5,7–11].

In 2007 the first symbolic implementation of sparse direct VO is presented in the context of augmented reality [5], based on work published in 2001 [4]. In 2011 Davison et al. demonstrated a regularised photometric error function using the gradients of depth maps and intensity images to achieve accurate dense matching over multiple short-baseline movements [7]. For finding the optimal motion that minimises the regularised matching cost, the authors proposed a forward-compositional cost function.

A similar inverse compositional formulation is used in [8] during the iterative Gaussian minimisation over a photometric energy function derived from a number of 4×4 perspectively warped patches around the tracked key points. In [9] the error covariance is taken into account to build normalised photometric error terms. The uncertainty of each tracked key point is propagated by a Jacobian-based approximation, and continuously maintained following an update model that makes joint use of a dense depth map and its variance map. In the authors' follow-up work [10,11], the image gradient as well as the camera's photometric calibration are taken into account to revise the uncertainty estimation model for the photometric energy function.

Feature-based techniques, on the other side, keep tracking a set of distinctive scene points and derive the camera's egomotion from the correspondences established by descriptor matching. Approaches in this category have been dominating the development of VO since its early success on Mars [12]. The implementation on the Mars rovers uses a weighted 3D rigid point alignment model to optimise the estimation of rover's egomotion. In difference to the direct methods, feature correspondences are established in feature space.

In [13], robust outlier rejection is used to remove noisy correspondences. In [14], the observations of each tracked feature are integrated over time to yield more accurate state estimation. The technique is later generalised by [15]. A more recent work [16] demonstrates the feasibility of real-time feature extraction, matching, and pose estimation using oriented FAST key points and rotated BRIEF descriptors. The success of all these methods lies in the minimisation of the geodesic distances between observed feature locations and their predictions.

Few recent work attempts to fill in the gap between appearance-based and feature-based VO or V-SLAM. For example, Forster et al. deployed a reprojection minimisation technique, which is commonly used in feature-based VO, to refine the pose estimated from direct photometric alignment [8]. Another example is the bi-objective energy model used in [10] that takes into account not only a photometric error but also geodesic displacement. Such a trend has inspired this work to study the use of multiple objectives for egomotion estimation.

3 Visual Odometry

Historically, the estimation of a camera's egomotion relies on the tracking of some long-term key points, which are projections of distinctive scene points known as *landmarks*, and the minimisation of the deviation between their predicted locations and actual observations.

3.1 Theory

Let $P = (X, Y, Z)$ be the 3D coordinates of a landmark. Following the pinhole camera model, its projection (x, y) in the image plane is given by

$$\begin{pmatrix} x \\ y \\ 1 \end{pmatrix} \sim \begin{pmatrix} f_x & 0 & c_x & 0 \\ 0 & f_y & c_y & 0 \\ 0 & 0 & 1 & 0 \end{pmatrix} \begin{pmatrix} X \\ Y \\ Z \\ 1 \end{pmatrix} = (\mathbf{K}\, \mathbf{0}) \begin{pmatrix} X \\ Y \\ Z \\ 1 \end{pmatrix} \tag{1}$$

where the upper triangular matrix $\mathbf{K}$ is the *camera matrix* modelled by the intrinsic parameters of the camera including focal lengths f_x and f_y, and the image centre or principal point (c_x, c_y). By $\sim$ we denote projective equality (i.e. equality up to a scale).

As the camera moves, a new coordinate system is instantiated. The egomotion of the camera can then be modelled by a Euclidean transformation $\mathbf{T} \in \mathbb{SE}(3)$, from the previous frame to the new coordinate system, which consists of a rotation $\mathbf{R} \in \mathbb{SO}(3)$ and a translation component $\mathbf{t} \in \mathbb{R}^3$. If the landmark P remains stationary, its projection into the new camera position can be predicted by

$$\begin{pmatrix} x' \\ y' \\ 1 \end{pmatrix} \sim \mathbf{K}\, (\mathbf{R}\, \mathbf{t}) \begin{pmatrix} X \\ Y \\ Z \\ 1 \end{pmatrix} \tag{2}$$

The estimation of an unknown transformation $(\mathbf{R}\, \mathbf{t})$, given a set of 3D-to-2D correspondences $(X, Y, Z) \leftrightarrow (x', y')$, is known as the *perspective-from-n-points* (PnP) problem [18]. Such a problem has been extensively studied in the context of SfM or VO.

The implementation of visual odometry, however, is not limited to the use of 3D-to-2D point-to-point correspondences. For example, when dense depth data is available, one may alternatively use 3D-to-3D correspondences and replace Eq. (2) by a rigid alignment objective (see Sect. 4) to model the error of a motion hypothesis. In the monocular case, on the other hand, due to a lack of 3D data, a set of 2D-to-2D epipolar constraints is commonly used as the objective.

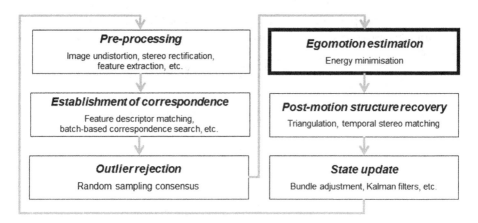

Fig. 1. General visual odometry model, with each stage annotated by related topics

Figure 1 shows the stages of a generalised visual odometry methodology in an abstract way, independent of the type of correspondences used. In such a general model, the egomotion estimation stage can be conceptualised as a general energy minimisation process.

3.2 Energy Minimisation Problem

As an energy minimisation problem, a residual function $\varphi(\mathbf{x}, \mathbf{y}; \xi) \in \mathbb{R}$ is defined for each established correspondence $\mathbf{x} \leftrightarrow \mathbf{y}$ to solve for egomotion. Note that $\mathbf{x}$ and $\mathbf{y}$ can be any entities of interest, and the residual is parametrised by twist coordinates $\xi \in \mathbb{R}^6$ which is the Lie-algebra entity minimally representing a Euclidean transform $\mathbf{T} = \exp_{\mathrm{se}(3)}(\xi) \in \mathbb{SE}(3)$. Note that two twists ξ and ξ' can be composited by the multiplication of their corresponding Euclidean transformation matrices

$$\xi \circ \xi' = \log_{\mathbb{SE}(3)} \left(\exp_{\mathrm{se}(3)}(\xi') \cdot \exp_{\mathrm{se}(3)}(\xi) \right) \tag{3}$$

where $\circ$ is the pose concatenation operator.

Individual residuals are further summarised as a scalar to be minimised. This is often done in the sum-of-squares form to achieve *maximum-likelihood estimation* (MLE) when the error distribution of residuals is believed to follow a Gaussian. Let $\Phi(\xi) = (\varphi_0, \varphi_1, ..., \varphi_{m-1})$ be an m-vector function instantiated from m correspondences; the optimal estimate of egomotion is found to be

$$\xi = \operatorname*{arg\,min}_{\hat{\xi} \in \mathbb{R}^6} (\|\Phi(\hat{\xi})\|_{\mathbf{\Sigma}}^2) \tag{4}$$

where $\|\cdot\|_{\mathbf{\Sigma}}^2$ is the squared Mahalanobis distance defined by $\mathbf{\Sigma}$, an $m \times m$ positive definite matrix denoting the error covariance over all the correspondences.

When the correspondences are believed to be established independently (as in most of the cases), $\mathbf{\Sigma}$ is simplified as a diagonal matrix. Equation (4) can then be rewritten as

$$\xi = \underset{\hat{\xi} \in \mathbb{R}^6}{\arg \min}(\sum_i w_i \, \|\varphi_i(\mathbf{x}_i, \mathbf{y}_i; \xi)\|^2) \tag{5}$$

where w_i is the inverse of the i-th diagonal entry in $\mathbf{\Sigma}$. An optimal estimate ξ, that minimises the weighted sum-of-squares, can be approached iteratively by

$$\xi_{k+1} = \Delta\xi_k \circ \xi_k \tag{6}$$

with the update computed using the Levenberg-Marquardt algorithm [19]:

$$\Delta\xi_k = (\mathbf{H} + \lambda \, \mathrm{diag}(\mathbf{H}))^{-1} \, \mathbf{J}^\top \Phi(\xi_k) \tag{7}$$

where $\lambda \in \mathbb{R}$ is the damping variable, and $\mathbf{H} = \mathbf{J}^\top \mathbf{W} \mathbf{J}$ is the Hessian matrix approximated by the weight matrix $\mathbf{W} = \mathrm{diag}(w_0, w_1, ..., w_{i-1})$ and the Jacobian

$$\mathbf{J}_{ij} = \frac{\partial \varphi_i}{\partial \xi_j}(\xi_k). \tag{8}$$

of Φ at ξ_k. The variable λ is adaptively adjusted to control the optimisation toward a Gauss-Newton-like process (when ξ is far from a local minimum), or a gradient-descent-like process (when ξ is closer to a local minimum.) All the energy functions considered in this work are minimised in this manner, with the Jacobian matrix numerically computed by first-order finite differentiations.

4   Energy Models in Visual Odometry

In this section we review three geodesic models and one photometric energy model, widely chosen in the literature.

4.1   Epipolar Alignment

Given an image point (x, y) in the current frame and $(\mathbf{R}, \mathbf{t})$ for the motion of the camera, the corresponding epipolar line can be obtained in the next frame identifying the search domain for the corresponding image point (x', y'). Such a 2D-to-2D point correspondence $(x, y) \leftrightarrow (x', y')$ is useful for evaluating the correctness of a motion hypothesis.

Let $(\hat{\mathbf{R}}, \hat{\mathbf{t}})$ be a hypothesis, and $(x, y) \leftrightarrow (x', y')$ be the projections of a static scene point. The back-projected rays through these image points have to be co-planar, leading to the well-known epipolar constraint

$$\mathbf{x'}^\top \mathbf{K}^{-\top} [\hat{\mathbf{t}}]_\times \hat{\mathbf{R}} \mathbf{K}^{-1} \mathbf{x} = 0 \tag{9}$$

where $[\hat{\mathbf{t}}]_\times$ is the skew-symmetric matrix form of vector $\mathbf{t}$, $\mathbf{K}$ is the camera matrix, and $\mathbf{x} = (x, y, 1)^\top$ are homogeneous coordinates of an image point in vector form.

In practice, the equality of Eq. (9) never holds, as a result of numerical computations, errors in correspondences, and the inaccuracy of the motion hypothesis. For the last factor, from a set of correspondences $\mathbf{x}_i \leftrightarrow \mathbf{x}'_i$ one may obtain the residual terms

$$\varphi_i(\mathbf{x}_i, \mathbf{x}'_i; \hat{\xi}) = \mathbf{x}'^\top_i \hat{\mathbf{F}} \mathbf{x}_i \tag{10}$$

where $\hat{\mathbf{F}} = \mathbf{K}^{-\top} [\hat{\mathbf{t}}]_\times \hat{\mathbf{R}} \mathbf{K}^{-1}$ is the fundamental matrix encoding the given epipolar geometry, and $(\hat{\mathbf{R}}, \hat{\mathbf{t}})$ is the motion hypothesis converted from $\hat{\xi}$.

The algebraic distances, however, are found biased as the image points far away from the epipole tend to be over-penalised. A geometrically meaningful modelling is to measure the shortest distance

$$\delta(\mathbf{x}', \mathbf{l}) = \frac{|\mathbf{x}'^\top \mathbf{F} \mathbf{x}|}{\sqrt{l_0^2 + l_1^2}} \tag{11}$$

between $\mathbf{x}'$ and the corresponding epipolar line $\mathbf{l} = \mathbf{F}\mathbf{x} = (l_0, l_1, l_2)^\top$, for a general correspondence $\mathbf{x} \leftrightarrow \mathbf{x}'$ and fundamental matrix $\mathbf{F}$. As the observation $\mathbf{x}'$ also introduces an epipolar constraint on $\mathbf{x}$, we have that

$$\delta(\mathbf{x}, \mathbf{l}') = \frac{|\mathbf{x}'^\top \mathbf{F} \mathbf{x}|}{\sqrt{l_0'^2 + l_1'^2}} \tag{12}$$

where $\mathbf{l}' = \mathbf{F}^\top \mathbf{x}'$ denotes the epipolar line in the first view.

By applying symmetric measurements on the point-epipolar line distances, the energy function defined by Eq. (10) is now revised as follows:

$$\varphi_i(\mathbf{x}_i, \mathbf{x}'_i; \hat{\xi}) = \delta^2(\mathbf{x}'_i, \hat{\mathbf{F}} \mathbf{x}_i) + \delta^2(\mathbf{x}_i, \hat{\mathbf{F}}^\top \mathbf{x}_i) \tag{13}$$

This yields geometric errors in pixel locations.

A noise-tolerant variant is to treat the correspondence $\mathbf{x} \leftrightarrow \mathbf{x}'$ as a deviation from the ground truth $\mathring{\mathbf{x}} \leftrightarrow \mathring{\mathbf{x}}'$. When the differences $\|\mathbf{x} - \mathring{\mathbf{x}}\|$ and $\|\mathbf{x}' - \mathring{\mathbf{x}}'\|$ are believed to be small, the sum of squared mutual geometric distances can be approximated by

$$\delta^2(\mathring{\mathbf{x}}, \mathring{\mathbf{l}}') + \delta^2(\mathring{\mathbf{x}}', \mathring{\mathbf{l}}) \approx \frac{(\mathbf{x}'^\top \mathbf{F} \mathbf{x})^2}{l_0^2 + l_1^2 + l_0'^2 + l_1'^2} \tag{14}$$

where $\mathring{\mathbf{l}} = \mathbf{F}\mathbf{x}$ and $\mathring{\mathbf{l}}' = \mathbf{F}^\top \mathbf{x}'$ are perfect epipolar lines [20]. This first-order approximation to the geometric error is known as the *Sampson distance* [20]. When such a metric is adopted for evaluating egomotion, Eq. (13) is formulated as follows:

$$\varphi_i(\mathbf{x}_i, \mathbf{x}'_i; \hat{\xi}) = \sum_i \frac{(\mathbf{x}'^\top_i \hat{\mathbf{F}} \mathbf{x}_i)^2}{(\hat{\mathbf{F}} \mathbf{x}_i)_0^2 + (\hat{\mathbf{F}} \mathbf{x}_i)_1^2 + (\hat{\mathbf{F}}^\top \mathbf{x}'_i)_0^2 + (\hat{\mathbf{F}}^\top \mathbf{x}'_i)_1^2} \tag{15}$$

As the computation of these epipolar errors only uses 2D correspondences, the energy model can be useful when 3D structures of a scene are not known (i.e. in case of monocular VO). A minimum linear solver, known as the *five-point method*, is credited to Nistér [21]. The absolute scale of $\mathbf{t}$, however, is not possible to be recovered without any reference in the 3D space.

4.2   Perspective Alignment

If the 3D location of a tracked feature is known in the current frame, and its 2D location is found in the next frame, then it is more reliable to use reprojection residuals [17]

$$\varphi_i(\mathbf{g}_i, \mathbf{x}'_i; \hat{\xi}) = \left\| \mathbf{x}'_i - \pi_{\mathbf{K}}(\hat{\mathbf{R}}\mathbf{g}_i + \hat{\mathbf{t}}) \right\|^2_{\mathbf{\Sigma}_i} \tag{16}$$

where $\mathbf{g}_i = (X_i, Y_i, Z_i)^\top$ is the current 3D location of the feature, $\mathbf{x}'_i = (x_i, y_i)^\top$ are the feature's image coordinates in the next frame, and $\pi_{\mathbf{K}} : \mathbb{R}^3 \to \mathbb{R}^2$ is the projection function that maps a 3D point into the 2D image coordinates using the camera matrix $\mathbf{K}$; $\mathbf{\Sigma}_i$ is the 2×2 error covariance matrix of the i-th correspondence. When the backward correspondences $\mathbf{g}'_i \leftrightarrow \mathbf{x}_i$ are known, Eq. (16) can be modelled in inverse mapping form as follows:

$$\varphi_i(\mathbf{g}'_i, \mathbf{x}_i; \hat{\xi}) = \left\| \mathbf{x}_i - \pi_{\mathbf{K}}\left(\hat{\mathbf{R}}^\top \left(\mathbf{g}'_i - \hat{\mathbf{t}} \right) \right) \right\|^2_{\mathbf{\Sigma}_i} \tag{17}$$

The geodesic reprojection error has been a widely adopted energy model in camera resectioning, including calibration, pose estimation, and bundle adjustment. Its closed-form linear solution has been extensively studied in the domain of *perspective-from-n-points* (PnP) problems. A popular solver is owed to an efficient algorithm worked out by Lepetit et al. [18]. A linear solution is usually iteratively refined using a derivative-based minimiser (e.g. a Gauss-Newton algorithm). It has been shown that the perspective alignment can be further regularised using the epipolar alignment to reduce the impact of noisy 3D measurements [22].

4.3   Rigid Alignment

If a dense depth map is available and the establishment of 3D point correspondences is straightforward, then a rigid alignment can also be used to measure the fitness of a motion hypothesis.

Given a set of 3D-to-3D correspondences $\mathbf{g}_i \leftrightarrow \mathbf{g}'_i$, where $\mathbf{g}_i = (X_i, Y_i, Z_i)^\top$ and $\mathbf{g}'_i = (X'_i, Y'_i, Z'_i)^\top$. The energy model is defined by

$$\varphi_i(\mathbf{g}_i, \mathbf{g}'_i; \hat{\mathbf{R}}, \hat{\mathbf{t}}) = \left\| g'_i - (\hat{\mathbf{R}}g_i + \hat{\mathbf{t}}) \right\|^2_{\mathbf{\Sigma}_i} \tag{18}$$

where $\mathbf{\Sigma}_i$ denotes the 3×3 error covariance matrix.

The formulation can be ill-behaved for far points if the 3D coordinates are derived from a disparity map, due to the non-linearity of disparity-to-depth conversion. It is therefore critical to model the covariance matrix properly. If 3D coordinates are obtained by using a two-view triangulation function $\tau : \mathbb{R}^2 \times \mathbb{R}^2 \to \mathbb{R}^3$, then the covariance matrix can be modelled as

$$\mathbf{\Sigma} = \mathbf{J}_\tau \begin{pmatrix} \mathbf{\Sigma}_{\mathbf{x}} & \mathbf{0} \\ \mathbf{0} & \mathbf{\Sigma}_{\mathbf{x}'} \end{pmatrix} \mathbf{J}_\tau^\top \tag{19}$$

where $\mathbf{\Sigma_x}$ and $\mathbf{\Sigma_{x'}}$ are the 2×2 error covariance matrices of image points $\mathbf{x} = (x, y)^\top$ and $\mathbf{x'} = (x', y')^\top$, respectively, and $\mathbf{J}_\tau$ is the 3×4 Jacobian matrix

$$\mathbf{J}_\tau = \left[\frac{\partial \tau}{\partial x}(\mathbf{x}, \mathbf{x'}) \; \frac{\partial \tau}{\partial y}(\mathbf{x}, \mathbf{x'}) \; \frac{\partial \tau}{\partial x'}(\mathbf{x}, \mathbf{x'}) \; \frac{\partial \tau}{\partial y'}(\mathbf{x}, \mathbf{x'}) \right] \tag{20}$$

with respect to correspondence $\mathbf{x} \leftrightarrow \mathbf{x'}$, used to triangulate $\mathbf{g} = (X, Y, Z)^\top$ [12].

Unlike the previous two alignment models, the rigid model has closed-form solutions that are guaranteed to minimise Eq. (18). A popular choice is based on the quaternion parametrization and *singular value decomposition* (SVD), as shown by Horn [23].

4.4   Photometric Alignment

If image correspondences $\mathbf{x} \leftrightarrow \mathbf{x'}$ are not available at all, one may perform direct photometric matching using a motion hypothesis. In this case, a matching residual is defined over intensity images I and I' as follows:

$$\varphi_i(\mathbf{x}_i, \mathbf{g}_i; \hat{\xi}) = I(\mathbf{x}_i) - I'[\pi_\mathbf{K}(\hat{\mathbf{R}}\mathbf{g}_i + \hat{\mathbf{t}})] \tag{21}$$

assuming that the 3D coordinates $\mathbf{g}_i = (X_i, Y_i, Z_i)$ of image point $\mathbf{x} = (x, y)$ are known. This is also known as *correspondence-free egomotion estimation*, and it is pervasively used by direct VO techniques. Equation (21) can be extended to use a block of pixels instead of single pixel intensities; in this case the subtraction needs be replaced by a proper metric, e.g. the *sum of absolute differences* (SAD).

The evaluation of Eq. (21) is computationally expensive compared to all the aforementioned geodesic criteria. It invokes a rigid transformation, a perspective transformation, and two image sub-sampling procedures. As the minimum of photometric errors can only be approached iteratively, such an expensive cost function will need to be invoked repeatedly for constructing numerically the Jacobian matrix. To ease the incurred burden, many direct methods adopt an inverse compositional form of the residual term [8]

$$\varphi_i^k(\mathbf{g}_i, \xi_k; \Delta \xi) = I \left[\pi_\mathbf{K} \left(\Delta \mathbf{T} \cdot \mathbf{g}_i \right) \right] - I' \left[\pi_\mathbf{K} \left(\mathbf{T}_k(\xi_k) \cdot \mathbf{g}_i \right) \right] \tag{22}$$

where $\Delta \mathbf{T} = \exp(\Delta \xi)$ and $\mathbf{T}_k = \exp(\xi_k)$. Along with the inverse form of

$$\xi_{k+1} = \Delta \xi_k^{-1} \circ \xi_k \tag{23}$$

the Jacobian of Φ can be written in the chained form

$$\frac{\partial \varphi}{\partial \Delta \xi}(\mathbf{g}_i, \xi_k) = \frac{\partial I}{\partial \mathbf{x}} \bigg|_{\mathbf{x} = \mathbf{x}_i} \cdot \frac{\partial \pi}{\partial \mathbf{g}} \bigg|_{\mathbf{g} = \mathbf{g}_i} \cdot \frac{\partial \mathbf{T}}{\partial \xi} \bigg|_{\xi = 0} \cdot \mathbf{g}_i \tag{24}$$

which is independent of the current motion hypothesis ξ_k.

The first term of Eq. (24) is the gradient of base image I at key point $\mathbf{x}_i$, which requires only one-time evaluation at the beginning of the minimisation procedure; the second and third term can be calculated symbolically, and the last term is constant, for each tracked key point.

5   Multi-objective Visual Odometry

In this section we describe a feature-based VO approach that uses multiple objectives to achieve egomotion estimation.

5.1   Feature Tracking

Given image I_k of new Frame k, a set of features is detected. Let $\mathcal{F}_k$ be the feature set, and $\nu(\chi)$ be the vector representation of a feature $\chi \in \mathcal{F}_k$. The tracking is performed by finding that feature $\chi' \in \mathcal{F}_{k-1}$ that minimises the distance $\delta\big(\nu(\chi) - \nu(\chi')\big)$, where the similarity metric δ can either be the Hamming distance if ν gives a binary string, or the L_2-norm in any other case.

We also carry out a symmetry check by performing backward feature matching. Any feature χ' is rejected that is not mapped to the original matcher χ. In addition to this check, ambiguity matches are also removed by checking the ratio of distances between (χ, χ') and (χ, χ'') where $\chi'' \in \mathcal{F}_{k-1}$ is the second best match of χ.

5.2   Construction of a Data Term

The tracked features (χ, χ') are then used to construct multiple sets of correspondences. Let $\rho_k(\chi)$ be the image coordinates of a feature observed in Frame k. The 2D-to-2D correspondences $\rho_{k-1}(\chi) \leftrightarrow \rho_k(\chi)$, where $\rho_k(\chi) = \rho_k(\chi')$ is set to the matched feature's location, are used to build the epipolar constraints, denoted by $\mathcal{M}_{\mathrm{EPI}}$. Let $\bar{g}_k(\chi)$ be the recursively filtered 3D coordinates of feature χ in Frame k. The correspondences $\bar{g}_{k-1}(\chi) \leftrightarrow \rho_k(\chi)$ are used to build the projection constraints, denoted by $\mathcal{M}_{\overrightarrow{\mathrm{RPE}}}$.

We also use the intensity-3D-intensity correspondences $I_{k-1}\big[\rho_{k-1}(\chi)\big] \leftrightarrow \bar{g}_{k-1}(\chi) \leftrightarrow I_k\big[\rho_k(\chi)\big]$ to instantiate a set of photometric constraints, denoted by $\mathcal{M}_{\mathrm{PHOTO}}$. Finally, if the measure $g_k(\chi)$ of a feature's 3D coordinates in the new Frame k is available (either from a disparity map, a LiDAR scan, or any other sources), we construct a set of 3D-to-3D constraints $\bar{g}_{k-1}(\chi) \leftrightarrow g_k(\chi)$, and have it denoted by $\mathcal{M}_{\mathrm{RIGID}}$. We also make use of constraints $g_k(\chi) \leftrightarrow \rho_{k-1}(\chi)$ to build backward reprojection constraints $\mathcal{M}_{\overleftarrow{\mathrm{RPE}}}$.

5.3   Outlier Rejection

All the constructed mappings $\mathcal{M}_{\mathrm{EPI}}$, $\mathcal{M}_{\overrightarrow{\mathrm{RPE}}}$, $\mathcal{M}_{\overleftarrow{\mathrm{RPE}}}$, $\mathcal{M}_{\mathrm{RIGID}}$, and $\mathcal{M}_{\mathrm{PHOTO}}$ are collaboratively used in a RANSAC process to remove outliers. First, at the estimation stage a minimum set of correspondences is randomly drawn from one of the five mappings. From the samples, an initial motion hypothesis $\bar{\xi}$ is solved by the closed-form solver associated with the chosen mapping. At the verification stage, the hypothesis is applied to each class.

By means of the appropriate energy model, introduced in Sect. 4, the data terms are evaluated and the inliers are found as the correspondences achieving an error below a pre-defined class-specific threshold. If the population of inliers, summed over all the classes, achieves a record high, the hypothesis is taken as the best model. Such a process goes until a stopping criterion is met.

The closed-form solver and associated energy model for each class are summarised in Table 1. Note that the $\mathcal{M}_{\mathrm{EPI}}$ class is excluded at the estimation stage, as the translation of estimated motion $\bar{\xi}$ does not have an absolute unit, prohibiting it from being used to evaluate data terms in other classes. The $\mathcal{M}_{\mathrm{PHOTO}}$ class is also excluded because there is no closed-form solver for the photometric alignment problem.

Table 1. Summary of data terms (read "Int.-to-int." as "Intensity-to-intensity")

	$\mathcal{M}_{\mathrm{EPI}}$	$\mathcal{M}_{\overrightarrow{\mathrm{RPE}}}, \mathcal{M}_{\overleftarrow{\mathrm{RPE}}}$	$\mathcal{M}_{\mathrm{RIGID}}$	$\mathcal{M}_{\mathrm{PHOTO}}$
Alignment	Epipolar	Perspective proj.	Rigid	Photometric
Correspondence	2D-to-2D	3D-to-2D	3D-to-3D	Int.-to-int.
Closed-form solution	Five-point [21]	EPnP [18]	SVD [23]	N/A
Closed-form data needed	5	6	4	N/A
Energy function	Φ_{EPI}	Φ_{RPE}	Φ_{RIGID}	Φ_{PHOTO}

5.4   Unified Energy Models

The best-fit model $\bar{\xi}$ from the RANSAC process serves as the initial guess at the non-linear optimisation stage over the integrated energy model

$$\Phi(\xi) = \Phi_{\mathrm{RPE}}(\xi) + \Phi_{\mathrm{EPI}}(\xi) + \Phi_{\mathrm{RIGID}}(\xi) + \Phi_{\mathrm{PHOTO}}(\xi) \qquad (25)$$

with each sub-objective instantiated from the inliers of the corresponding classes. Note that the combination does not use per-class weightings as the residuals are already normalised by the estimated error covariance, as discussed in Sect. 4. Function Φ is minimised using the iterative process described in Sect. 3.2.

6   Experiments

We selected a road scene from the KITTI benchmark suite [24] for evaluating the unified model. The vehicle had travelled 350 m in 188 frames. The VO implementation computes depth maps using OpenCV's SGBM functions and tracks SURF features through the image sequence. The images from the right camera are only used for disparity generation. The depth of a tracked feature is continuously integrated using a recursive Bayesian filter. No additional optimisation technique (e.g. bundle adjustment, lost feature recovery, or similar) has been deployed.

To test how each energy model affects the VO process, we tried all the possible combinations by enabling a subset of data terms among $\mathcal{M}_{\mathrm{EPI}}$, $\mathcal{M}_{\overrightarrow{\mathrm{RPE}}}$, $\mathcal{M}_{\mathrm{RIGID}}$ and $\mathcal{M}_{\mathrm{PHOTO}}$, for each test. Note that the forward-projection term $\mathcal{M}_{\overrightarrow{\mathrm{RPE}}}$ is

Table 2. Egomotion estimation drifts (%) of different energy model combinations. Letters B, P, R, and E, respectively, indicate the use of backward projection ($\mathcal{M}_{\overline{\text{RPE}}}$), photometric ($\mathcal{M}_{\text{PHOTO}}$), rigid ($\mathcal{M}_{\text{RIGID}}$), and epipolar ($\mathcal{M}_{\text{EPI}}$) alignment models. Maximum and minimum value in each column are in bold.

Model	Best	Worst	Mean	Std.	Model	Best	Worst	Mean	Std.
xxxx	4.97	5.54	5.21	0.27	Bxxx	**5.14**	5.99	5.41	0.34
xPxx	2.26	2.76	2.52	0.21	BPxx	1.99	2.50	2.23	0.21
xxRx	4.65	5.09	4.88	0.15	BxRx	5.10	**6.00**	**5.58**	**0.37**
xPRx	**1.84**	2.39	2.18	0.26	BPRx	1.96	2.56	**2.16**	0.26
xxxE	2.27	2.31	2.28	**0.01**	BxxE	2.21	**2.29**	2.24	0.03
xPxE	2.24	2.71	2.47	0.17	BPxE	2.17	2.48	2.31	0.11
xxRE	2.29	2.38	2.34	0.03	BxRE	2.18	2.31	2.24	0.05
xPRE	2.41	2.59	2.50	0.08	BPRE	2.21	2.40	2.33	0.08

always used as it is required to properly bootstrap the RANSAC process. This results in sixteen configurations. Due to the randomness introduced into the outlier-rejection stage, we carried out five trials for each configuration. Table 2 summarises motion drifts from eighty estimated trajectories.

In most cases, using additional energy model(s) significantly reduces the drift in estimated egomotion. Exceptions are observed in the cases of xxRx, Bxxx, and BxRx.

When the rigid alignment is solely imposed (xxRx), the drift only slightly reduces by 0.35%. A result, worse than the forward-projection-only baseline configuration (xxxx), is found in BxRx where it is simultaneously applied with the back-projection alignment model. A similar result is observed when the backward projection is used (Bxxx). The loss of accuracy can be due to the use of feature depths obtained in frame $t + 1$, where the recursive Bayesian filter has not been applied, as the egomotion from t to $t + 1$ is not yet estimated (see Fig. 1).

Interestingly the results show that, when the epipolar term is used with the forward projection model (xxxE), the VO process yields highly robust estimates with a very low standard deviation (0.01%). Such finding corresponds to the authors' previous work [22].

We further compared the baseline model with the best case, worst case, and the case using all energy models. Accumulated drifts are plotted in Fig. 2. In the best case the accuracy is improved by 58.3%, while by imposing all four energy models, this option achieves an improvement by 54.8%.

We also profiled the run-time of each test case. The processing time for each frame are 230 ms and 200 ms for the best case and the baseline implementation, respectively. This time measurement indicates that the introduction of additional energy terms only incurs 13% more computational cost, while an improvement of above 50% in terms of accuracy is attainable.

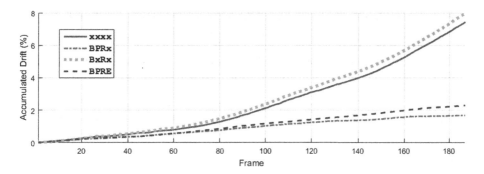

Fig. 2. Drift analysis of the best (BPRx), worst (BxRx), all-enabled (BPRE), and the baseline model (xxxx)

7   Conclusions

We reviewed four energy models, pervasively used in the context of VO, and formulated a unified model. Based on the model, our implementation deploys a multi-class RANSAC strategy to remove outliers with a proven enhanced robustness. Real-world experimental results show that, by taking into account multiple objectives, egomotion estimation is significantly improved over the traditional forward-projection model, at an affordable minor increase in computational costs.

In future work we test the proposed multi-modal VO technique in a wider range of road scenes. It is also interesting to study the interference between alignment models for the phenomena that the all-enabled combination does not achieve the best performance in the tested sequence.

References

1. Scaramuzza, D., Fraundorfer, F.: Visual odometry: part I - the first 30 years and fundamentals. IEEE Robot. Autom. Mag. **18**, 80–92 (2011)
2. Maimone, M., Cheng, Y., Matthies, L.: Two years of visual odometry on the Mars exploration rovers. J. Field Robot. **24**(3), 169–186 (2007)
3. Irani, M., Anandan, P.: All about direct methods. In: Proceedings of ICCV Workshop Vision Algorithms: Theory Practice, pp. 267–277 (1999)
4. Baker, S., Mathews, I.: Equivalence and efficiency of image alignment algorithms. In: Proceedings of International Conference on Computer Vision Pattern Recognition, vol. 1, pp. 1090–1097 (2001)
5. Klein, G., Murray, D.: Parallel tracking and mapping for small AR workspaces. In: Proceedings of International Symposium on Mixed Augmented Reality, pp. 1–10 (2007)
6. Davison, A., Reid, I., Molton, N., Stasse, O.: MonoSLAM: real-time single camera SLAM. IEEE Trans. Pattern Anal. Mach. Intell. **29**, 1052–1067 (2007)
7. Newcombe, R., Lovegrove, S., Davison, A.: DTAM: dense tracking and mapping in real-time. In: Proceedings of IEEE International Conference on Computer Vision, pp. 2320–2327 (2011)

8. Forster, C., Pizzoli, M., Scaramuzza, D.: SVO: fast semi-direct monocular visual odometry. In: Proceedings of IEEE International Conference on Robotics Automation, pp. 15–22 (2014)

9. Engel, J., Sturm, J., Cremers, D.: Semi-dense visual odometry for a monocular camera. In: Proceedings of IEEE International Conference on Computer Vision, pp. 1449–1456 (2013)

10. Engel, J., Schöps, T., Cremers, D.: LSD-SLAM: large-scale direct monocular SLAM. In: Fleet, D., Pajdla, T., Schiele, B., Tuytelaars, T. (eds.) ECCV 2014. LNCS, vol. 8690, pp. 834–849. Springer, Cham (2014). https://doi.org/10.1007/978-3-319-10605-2_54

11. Engel, J., Koltun, V., Cremers, D.: Direct sparse odometry. IEEE Trans. Pattern Anal. Mach. Intell. (99) (2017)

12. Maimone, M., Cheng, Y., Matthies, L.: Two years of visual odometry on the Mars exploration rovers. J. Field Robot. Special Issue Space Robot. Part I **24**, 169–186 (2007)

13. Kitt, B., Geiger, A., Lategahn, H.: Visual odometry based on stereo image sequences with RANSAC-based outlier rejection scheme. In: Proceedings of IEEE Intelligent Vehicles Symposium, pp. 486–492 (2010)

14. Badino, H., Yamamoto, A., Kanade, T.: Visual odometry by multi-frame feature integration. In: Proceedings of International ICCV Workshop Computer Vision Autonomous Driving (2013)

15. Chien, H.-J., Geng, H., Chen, C.-Y., Klette, R.: Multi-frame feature integration for multi-camera visual odometry. In: Bräunl, T., McCane, B., Rivera, M., Yu, X. (eds.) PSIVT 2015. LNCS, vol. 9431, pp. 27–37. Springer, Cham (2016). https://doi.org/10.1007/978-3-319-29451-3_3

16. Mur-Artal, R., Tardos, J.: ORB-SLAM2: an open-source SLAM system for monocular, stereo and RGB-D cameras. arXiv preprint arXiv:1610.06475 (2016)

17. Nister, D., Naroditsky, O., Bergen, J.: Visual odometry. In: Proceedings of International Conference on Computer Vision Pattern Recognition, pp. 652–659 (2004)

18. Lepetit, V., Moreno-Noguer, F., Fua, P.: EPnP: an accurate O(n) solution to the PnP problem. Int. J. Comput. Vis. **81**, 155–166 (2009)

19. Levenberg, K.A.: Method for the solution of certain non-linear problems in least squares. Q. Appl. Math. **2**, 164–168 (1944)

20. Hartley, R.I., Zisserman, A.: Multiple View Geometry in Computer Vision, 2nd edn. Cambridge University Press, Cambridge (2004)

21. Nister, D.: An efficient solution to the five-point relative pose problem. IEEE Trans. Pattern Anal. Mach. Intell. **26**(6), 756–777 (2004)

22. Chien, H.-J., Klette, R.: Regularised energy model for robust monocular egomotion estimation. In: Proceedings of International Joint Conference on Computer Vision Imaging Computer Graphics: Theory Applications, vol. 6, pp. 361–368 (2017)

23. Horn, B.: Closed-form solution of absolute orientation using unit quaternions. J. Opt. Soc. Am. A **4**, 629–642 (1987)

24. Geiger, A., Lenz, P., Stiller, C., Urtasun, R.: Vision meets robotics: the KITTI dataset. Int. J. Robot. Res. **32**(11), 1231–1237 (2013)

Visual Comparison Based on Multi-class Classification Model

Hanqin Shi[1,2] and Liang Tao[1(✉)]

[1] School of Computer Science and Technology,
Anhui University, Hefei 230601, China
taoliang@ahu.edu.cn
[2] School of Computer Science and Technology,
Huaibei Normal University, Huaibei 235000, China

'

Abstract. Visual comparison is that given two images, we can not only predict which one exhibits a particular visual attribute more than the other, but also predict whether a visual attribute of one image is equal to that of another image. Most existing methods for visual comparison relying on ranking Support Vector Machine (SVM) functions only distinguish which image in a pair exhibits an attribute more or less in test time. However, it is significant to distinguish which image in a pair exhibits an attribute more, less or equal in test time. To address this issue, we propose a multi-class classification model based on one-versus-one method for visual comparison, which can be formulated by learning mapping functions between any two different classes in image pairs. With regard to the mapping functions, we choose the linear regression functions. Experimental results on the three databases of UT-Zap50K-1, OSR and PubFig demonstrate the advantages of the proposed method.

Keywords: Visual comparison · Multi-class classification
Linear regression model · Ranking SVM · Relative attributes

1 Introduction

Visual comparison is a significant technique in computer vision, which is defined as that given two images and a special attribute, we can predict which one exhibits the attribute more, less or equal compared to the other. As is shown in Fig. 1, we could predict the relation of the right image pair according to prior relation of the left image pairs. Obviously, you are likely to conclude that given some indistinguishable image pairs there are meaningless to only predict the ordered results.

Attributes, which are visual properties describable in words, can capture anything from material properties ('plastic', 'wooden'), shapes ('pointy', 'round') to facial expressions ('serious', 'smiling'). Since their emergence, attributes have inspired a lot of work in image search [1–4], biometrics [5,6], and language based supervision for recognition [7–10]. Those attribute models are mainly

© Springer International Publishing AG, part of Springer Nature 2018
M. Paul et al. (Eds.): PSIVT 2017, LNCS 10749, pp. 75–86, 2018.
https://doi.org/10.1007/978-3-319-75786-5_7

Fig. 1. Visual comparison with attribute 'Smile'

divided into two forms: binary attributes and relative attributes. Whereas binary attributes are suitable only for clear-cut predicates, such as boxy, relative attributes can show 'real-valued' properties that inherently exhibit a series of strengths, such as 'comfort'. Relative attributes [8] were first proposed by learning the global ranking Support Vector Machine (SVM) functions, followed by much recent work for visual comparison based on ranking SVM functions [3,11–15]. With relative attributes, originally introduced in [8,16], images could be compared in terms of how strongly they exhibit a nameable visual property. Given an image pair, relative attributes could indicate which image in a pair exhibits an attribute more or less, while the Just Noticeable Differences (JND) method introduced in [15] could indicate one image in a pair exhibits an attribute equal or not to another image in test time. Now we propose a novel method to indicate which image in a pair exhibits an attribute more, less or equal in test time.

In order to obtain both the ordered pairs and equal pairs in test time for visual comparison, we propose one-versus-one multi-class classification with relative attributes by training the linear regression model for visual comparison, which can be formulated by learning a mapping function between a vector-formed feature input and a scalar-valued output.

Due to the wide existence of multi-class classification problems in different areas, many different methods have been developed to solve such problems. A wide variety of empirical studies have reported the decomposition and ensemble methods can increase the performance on multi-class classification problems. Most existing research shows that the design or selection of decomposition and ensemble strategies play an important role in the performance of decomposition and ensemble methods. With regard to decomposition strategies, One-vs-One (OVO) [17], One-vs-All (OVA) [18], and Error-Correcting Output Coding (ECOC) [19] are the most widely used. Due to the intrinsic of relative attribute, visual comparison with relative attribute could be casted into 3 class classification problem. Compared to OVA, OVO strategy is competent for the case the category number is pretty small.

The main contribution of this paper is the idea to learn OVO multi-class classification by linear regression for visual comparison, which to our knowledge has not been explored for visual comparison in any prior work. The other contribution is that we not only predict the ordered pairs but also predict equal pairs in test time. Tests on three challenging datasets show that the proposed approach obtains promising results for visual comparison.

2   Related Work

Comparing attributes has gained a lot of interest recently. The relative attributes approach learned a global linear ranking function for each attribute [8], which was extended to non-linear ranking functions in [20,21] by training a hierarchy of rankers and normalizing predictions at the leaf nodes. Aside from learning to rank formulations, researchers have applied the Elo rating system for biometrics [5], and a local learning method based on the ranking SVM [16] was proposed for fine-grained visual comparison. Most of the prior methods produce a ranking function based on SVM for each attributes, whereas we propose multi-class classification with relative attributes and produce a mapping function based on linear regression for each attribute in visual comparison. In contrast to the proposed approach, all those prior methods are only able to predict the ordered image pairs.

Regression is one of the critical techniques for visual attribute application. A number of computer vision problems such as human age estimation could be formulated as a regression problem by learning a mapping function between a high dimensional vector-formed feature input and a scalar-valued output [22–26]. A locally adjusted regression method [24] to search local regions for adjusting was proposed, and followed by bio-inspired features (BIF) for regression [25] in human age-estimation. Most of these regression methods have achieved better performance.

Besides, much prior work [8,16,21] predicting ordered image pairs in test time for visual comparison has been proposed in visual applications. JND method [15] proposed to identify equal image pairs in test time could predict ordered pairs according to the learned ranks of image pairs when the image pairs are not equal, but it cost a lot of time to compute the prior probability due to the local learning. Therefore, we propose a multi-class classification method to conduct visual comparison so that we can not only predict both ordered pairs and equal pairs in test time, but also can save a lot of computational time.

3   Approach

We use the OVO multi-class classification to conduct relative attributes for visual comparison, and apply linear regression to efficiently train the OVO models for visual comparison. In the following, we first introduce OVO multi-class classification for visual comparison, and then present the linear regression model to realize OVO multi-class classification for visual comparison.

3.1 OVO Multi-class Classification for Visual Comparison

Relative attributes are generally obtained from the ranking SVM functions for only predicting ordered pairs, while OVO multi-class classification are obtained from the regression model for predicting both ordered pairs and equal pairs in test time in visual comparison. The regression model will be introduced in the following section.

The Multi-class classification model aims at assigning a class label for each input observation. Given a training data set $\{(X_1, y_1), ..., (X_n, y_n)\}$, where $X_i \in R^r$ denotes the ith observation feature vector, and $y_i \in \{1, ..., K\}$ is the class label of the ith observation. It is a mapping function $f : X \rightarrow \{1, ..., K\}$ inferred from the labeled training data set through a training process. Therefore, visual comparison problem could be casted into the following multi-class classification problem. Given a certain attribute a_m and a set of images $I = \{u_i\}$, each of which is described by the image feature $u_i \in R^d$, and a set of image pairs $P_m = \{(s, t)\}$. P_m is a set of image pairs with attribute a_m and the corresponding class labels can be defined as $l_m \in \{1, 2, 3\}$. Among them, $l_m = 1$ or $l_m = 2$ denote that image s has the attribute a_m more or less than image t respectively, while $l_m = 3$ denotes image s has the attribute a_m as much as image t. We wish to learn a multi-class classification to successfully identify the relation between image s and image t given the attribute a_m. In particular, visual comparison could be categorized to 3 classes (more, less or equal) according to relations of image pairs. To this end, we define pairwise vector between image s and t as follows:

$$x_{st} = p(u_s, u_t), u_s, u_t \in I \tag{1}$$

where p is an entry-wise function that outputs a pairwise vector between u_s and u_t. Therefore, the multi-class training set for visual comparison can be represented as $\{(x, l_m)\}_{st}, \forall(s, t) \in P_m$.

The OVO [27] approach is to divide the multi-class problem with K classes into $C_2^K = K(K - 1)/2$ binary classification problems. One binary classifier is constructed for each binary classification problem for discriminating each pair of classes. Let the binary classifier that discriminates the classes of i and j be denoted by f_{ij}, the output of binary classifier f_{ij}, denoted by y_{ij}, is defined as follows.

$$y_{ij} = f_{ij}(x) \tag{2}$$

where $f_{ij}(.)$ is realized by linear regression introduced by the following section. More specifically, y_{ij} is the confidence score denoting that images pair x belongs to ith class, while $1 - y_{ij}$ is the confidence score denoting x belongs to jth class. The class selected by the weighted voting strategy for OVO is the class with the largest total confidence score from all binary classifiers and is defined as [18]:

$$class = \underset{i=1,...K}{argmax} \underset{1 \leq j \neq i \leq K}{\Sigma} (y_{ij}) \tag{3}$$

3.2   OVO by Linear Regression Model

Given the pairwise visual comparison training set $\{(x, l_m)\}$ and the attribute a_m, OVO multi-class classification is to train $N = K(K-1)/2$ binary classification functions by linear regression. Specifically, we select image pairs of class i and j to train linear regression model. Therefore, we need to learn the mapping relationship between x and l_m by a regression function for binary classification. Most existing relative attribute learning methods aim to establish a mapping by SVM. However linear ridge regression [28] is a classical statistical problem that aims to find a linear function that models the dependencies between vectors $\{x\}$ in R^r and label variables $\{l_m\}$ in R. In this paper, we learn the mapping by a multivariate linear ridge regression function, our goal is to learn N regression functions for each attribute:

$$f_{ij}(x_{st}) = w_m^T x_{st} + b_m, \forall (s,t) \in P'_m \quad and \quad P'_m \subset P_m \tag{4}$$

The objective functions by Ridge Regularization [29] can be written as:

$$min \quad \frac{1}{2}\|w_m\|_2^2 + C \sum_{(s,t)\in P'_m} loss(f_{ij}(x_{st}), l_m(x_{st})) \tag{5}$$

where the constant C is a balanced parameter between minimizing error function and regularization, and $loss(\cdot)$ denotes the loss function. To simplify the above objective functions without losing generality, quadratic loss function is considered as the loss function. The objective functions are then written as:

$$min \quad \frac{1}{2}\|w_m\|_2^2 + C \sum_{(s,t)\in P'_m} (l_m(x_{st}) - (w_m^T x_{st} + b_m))^2 \tag{6}$$

To further simplify the above objective functions, we set $z_k = x_{st}, N = |P'_m|$, and then the objective functions can be written as

$$min \quad \frac{1}{2}\|w_m\|_2^2 + C \sum_{k=1}^{N} (l_m(z_k) - (w_m^T z_k + b_m))^2 \tag{7}$$

where $z_k \in R^r$ is a training vector after the feature reduction, w_m is also a weight vector with r dimensions and $b_m \in R$ is a bias term respectively. The model parameters are estimated by solving an equality-constrained Quadratic Programming Problem, which has a closed-form global optimal solution as follows [6]:

$$\begin{bmatrix} w_m \\ b_m \end{bmatrix} = -(Q^T Q)^{-1} Q^T p \tag{8}$$

where positive semi-definite matrix Q and vector p are given by

$$Q = \begin{bmatrix} 2C\sum_{k=1}^{N} z_k z_k^T + E & 2C\sum_{k=1}^{N} z_k \\ 2C\sum_{k=1}^{N} z_k^T & 2CN \end{bmatrix} \tag{9}$$

$$p = \begin{bmatrix} -2C \sum_{k=1}^{N} l_m(z_k)z_k \\ -2C \sum_{k=1}^{N} l_m(z_k) \end{bmatrix} \tag{10}$$

where E is an identity matrix.

Therefore, given a test pair (s, t) and an attribute a_m, we can compute $x_{st} = p(u_s, u_t) = concat(u_s, u_t)$ and infer $y_{ij}(x_{st})$, and then we can obtain the class of the image pair by Eq. (3). At last we can predict image s exhibits the attribute a_m more, less or equal compared to image t through the obtained class label.

4   Experiments

To validate the advantages of the proposed method, we compare it with several state-of-the-art methods on three datasets: UT-Zap50K-1 [16], the Outdoor Scene Recognition dataset [30] (OSR), and a subset of the Public Figures faces dataset [31] (PubFig). All methods run for 10 random train/test splits on all pairs, in which we select 300 pairs for testing and the remaining for training. In all methods, we simply fix it at $C = 1$ and use the same labeled data as in [8], and then report the accuracy of the percentage of correctly pairs and macro-Average measure (maA) commonly used in evaluating performance on multi-class problems respectively. We will compare the following methods on the above datasets:

– JND [15]: The JND method which develops a Bayesian local learning strategy to infer whether images are indistinguishable or not for a given attribute. If the images are distinguishable, the ordered relation could be obtained by the learned ranks in pairs.
– RSVM + OVA: The method which develops a one-versus-all multi-class classification method by ranking svm (RSVM) for visual comparison.
– RSVM + OVO: The approach which develops a one-versus-one multi-class classification method by ranking svm (RSVM) for visual comparison.
– LRM + OVA: The one-versus-all method which develops a one-versus-all multi-class classification method by linear regression model (LRM) for visual comparison.
– LRM + OVO: The proposed approach which first develops a one-versus-one multi-class classification method by linear regression model (LRM) for visual comparison.

4.1   Experiments on Three Benchmark Datasets

Experiment on UT-Zap50K-1. UT-Zap50K-1 contains 50025 images with 4 attributes ('Open', 'Pointy', 'Sporty', 'Comfort') [16]. The image descriptors kindly provided by the authors of each dataset are 960-dim GIST and 30-bin Lab color histograms. We reduce their dimensionality to 30 with PCA to prevent overfitting. For a fair comparison, we take the same feature reduction as in the other methods. Table 1 demonstrates the test results of the proposed method compared to the other methods on UT-Zap50K-1.

Table 1. Accuracy of visual comparison tested on UT-Zap50K-1

Methods	Open	Pointy	Sporty	Comfort
JND [15]	70.88	66.13	63.90	65.83
RSVM + OVA	64.77	65.53	**67.98**	67.05
RSVM + OVO	66.03	65.93	67.55	67.52
LRM + OVA	70.77	69.28	67.52	69.70
LRM + OVO	**74.22**	**69.72**	67.08	**71.20**

Obviously as seen in Table 1, the accuracy of LRM is far higher than the accuracy of RSVM, which demonstrates the LRM has an advantage over the RSVM in visual comparison. This just validates RSVM method is not optimal because the model used in the method may be more sensitive to training samples. By the same token, the OVO method is superior to the OVA for most attributes in visual comparison. Only for the attribute 'Sporty' there are the approximate accuracy. More importantly, from the Table 1 we see the accuracy of LRM + OVO is far higher than that of JND [15], which shows the proposed method is more effective and significant for visual comparison.

The maA measure is another performance measure in multi-class problem, which is defined as follows [32]:

$$maA = \frac{1}{K} \sum_{i=1}^{K} \frac{n_{ii}}{n_i} \tag{11}$$

where n_{ij} denotes the number of observations of the i class which are predicted as the j class ($i = 1, ..., K, j = 1, ..., K$) and $n_i = \sum_{j=1}^{K} n_{ij}$.

Table 2 shows the maA measure on UT-Zap50K-1. Obviously, the proposed method outperforms the other methods in all attributes except the JND method. The maA mesure of the JND is a little more than that of the proposed method with attributes 'Pointy' and 'Sporty', but the accuracy of the proposed method is a lot more than that of the JND method. Therefore, the proposed method is still effective for visual comparison.

Table 2. The maA measure on UT-Zap50K-1

Methods	Open	Pointy	Sporty	Comfort
JND [15]	67.34	**69.67**	**63.95**	64.73
RSVM + OVA	59.20	58.47	62.73	58.33
RSVM + OVO	61.42	59.18	61.53	60.54
LRM + OVA	71.52	67.41	62.84	66.60
LRM + OVO	**73.47**	68.17	63.18	**67.95**

Experiment on OSR. The Outdoor Scene Recognition dataset [30] (OSR) consists of 2,688 images with 8 categories and 6 attributes ('natural', 'Open', 'perspective', 'size-large', 'diagonal-plane' and 'depth-close', the corresponding abbreviations are 'Natr', 'Open', 'Persp', 'LgSi', 'Diag' and 'ClsD'). The image pairs are those based on category-wise comparisons such that there are about over 20,000 pairs per attribute when we select 30 images in each category. Without loss of generality, we randomly select 1000 pairs used for training and 300 pairs for testing. Tables 3 and 4 respectively show the experimental accuracy and the maA measure on the OSR dataset for all attributes. Similar to the results on UT-Zap50K-1, the proposed method outperforms the other state-of-art methods on OSR. This just demonstrates both LRM and OVO are the effective approaches for visual comparison.

Table 3. Accuracy of visual comparison tested on OSR

Methods	Natr	Open	Persp	LgSi	Diag	ClsD
JND [15]	78.60	73.40	74.25	75.90	76.10	73.20
RSVM + OVA	71.85	68.90	73.10	73.15	73.80	64.15
RSVM + OVO	74.30	68.90	75.95	76.05	76.15	67.00
LRM + OVA	78.75	72.30	76.00	76.75	73.50	71.30
LRM + OVO	**81.25**	**74.75**	**78.25**	**77.90**	**76.40**	**79.60**

Table 4. The maA measure on OSR

Methods	Natr	Open	Persp	LgSi	Diag	ClsD
JND [15]	74.18	71.89	56.50	71.56	69.15	72.54
RSVM + OVA	68.35	67.11	58.37	66.08	63.37	65.16
RSVM + OVO	70.78	66.84	65.46	72.88	70.38	67.27
LRM + OVA	74.50	71.18	61.67	71.92	64.17	71.25
LRM + OVO	**78.53**	**73.72**	**67.98**	**74.54**	**71.34**	**80.18**

Experiment on PubFig. We select a subset of the Public Figures faces dataset [31] (PubFig), which includes 772 images with 8 categories and 11 attributes ('Masculine_looking', 'White', 'Young', 'Smiling', 'Chubby', 'Visible_Forehead', 'Bushy_Eyebrows', 'Narrow_Eyes', 'Pointy_Nose', 'Big_Lips', 'RoundFace', and the corresponding abbreviations are 'Male', 'White', 'Young', 'Smil', 'Chub', 'Foreh', 'Eyebrow', 'Eye', 'Nose', 'Lip', 'Face'). The method of generating the image pairs is similar to that on OSR. Tables 5 and 6 respectively report the experimental results on the accuracy comparison and the maA measure. Obviously, like the results on OSR, the proposed method almost achieves best results compared to the other methods for all attributes. This further validates the proposed method is an effective method for visual comparison.

Table 5. Accuracy of visual comparison tested on PubFig

Methods	Male	White	Young	Smil	Chub	Foreh
JND [15]	71.70	66.60	75.20	69.25	69.75	69.95
RSVM + OVA	72.20	65.25	74.40	69.50	69.65	66.35
RSVM + OVO	72.65	67.35	75.25	72.60	68.90	69.25
LRM + OVA	73.75	68.25	75.30	72.30	70.75	72.55
LRM + OVO	**74.05**	**70.80**	**75.95**	**74.95**	**71.50**	**77.10**
Methods	Eyebrow	Eye	Nose	Lip	Face	
JND [15]	69.60	70.20	61.70	73.30	74.95	
RSVM + OVA	68.90	69.25	61.25	72.60	75.05	
RSVM + OVO	68.80	69.80	65.55	72.30	**75.25**	
LRM + OVA	72.40	68.30	65.35	73.40	73.45	
LRM + OVO	**73.10**	**70.35**	**69.40**	**75.15**	75.05	

Table 6. The maA measure on PubFig

Methods	Male	White	Young	Smil	Chub	Foreh
JND [15]	52.78	46.90	58.02	58.16	54.85	65.35
RSVM + OVA	55.46	46.64	59.05	61.66	57.68	64.44
RSVM + OVO	58.79	53.09	**66.41**	68.74	60.01	67.18
LRM + OVA	53.29	47.31	59.80	65.33	54.62	73.06
LRM + OVO	**60.29**	**54.84**	65.51	**71.89**	**61.94**	**76.60**
Methods	Eyebrow	Eye	Nose	Lip	Face	
JND [15]	51.12	52.87	49.18	57.25	58.73	
RSVM + OVA	52.86	55.21	53.73	58.59	61.30	
RSVM + OVO	57.32	61.51	59.20	62.46	65.60	
LRM + OVA	55.21	54.36	56.64	60.10	56.54	
LRM + OVO	**61.92**	**62.29**	**62.52**	**66.42**	**65.81**	

Therefore, from experimental results on the above datasets, we can conclude that the proposed method is an effective method by applying one-versus-one multi-class classification and LRM for visual comparison.

4.2 Time Complexity Analysis

All algorithms are implemented by Matlab on a PC with an Intel i5-4670 CPU @3.40 GHz 3.40 GHz. Without loss of generality, Tables 7 and 8 respectively shows the train time and test time of the proposed method and JND method in a train/test split pairs on the UT-zap50k-1 dataset under the same setup. From these tables we can conclude that the proposed method significantly reduces the computational time compared to the JND method. For train time, the reason is that the JND is trained by RSVM which is solved by an optimized iterative approach, while the proposed method is realized by linear regression model which is solved by a closed form. For so much test time of the JND method, it is mainly because it is solved by a local learning strategy by finding K nearest pairs in order to obtain the prior probability of each test pair in test time and the method used to calculate the distance between the pairs is Information Theoretic Metric Learning (ITML) [33] method which is solved by an optimized iterative approach.

Table 7. Train time (s)

Methods	Time
JND [15]	1.7
LRM + OVO	0.018

Table 8. Test time (s)

Methods	Time
JND [15]	78.17
LRM + OVO	0.008

5   Conclusion

In this paper, we have proposed a novel visual comparison method, which applies one-versus-one multi-class classification method and linear regression model with relative attributes for visual comparison. The comprehensive experimental results on three benchmark datasets verified that the proposed method is an effective approach for visual comparison. Meanwhile, the proposed method can save a lot of computational time.

Acknowledgement. This study was funded by information assurance technology collaborative innovation center of anhui university.

References

1. Kumar, N., Belhumeur, P., Nayar, S.: FaceTracer: a search engine for large collections of images with faces. In: Forsyth, D., Torr, P., Zisserman, A. (eds.) ECCV 2008. LNCS, vol. 5305, pp. 340–353. Springer, Heidelberg (2008). https://doi.org/10.1007/978-3-540-88693-8_25
2. Siddiquie, B., Feris, R.S., Davis, L.S.: Image ranking and retrieval based on multi-attribute queries. In: IEEE Conference on Computer Vision and Pattern Recognition, pp. 801–808 (2011)

3. Kovashka, A., Parikh, D., Grauman, K.: Whittlesearch: image search with relative attribute feedback. In: IEEE Conference on Computer Vision and Pattern Recognition, pp. 2973–2980. IEEE (2012)
4. Kovashka, A., Grauman, K.: Attribute pivots for guiding relevance feedback in image search. In: IEEE Conference on International Conference on Computer Vision, pp. 297–304 (2013)
5. Reid, D.A., Nixon, M.S.: Using comparative human descriptions for soft biometrics. In: International Joint Conference on Biometrics, pp. 1–6 (2011)
6. Chen, K., Gong, S., Xiang, T., Loy, C.C.: Cumulative attribute space for age and crowd density estimation. In: IEEE Conference on Computer Vision and Pattern Recognition, pp. 2467–2474 (2013)
7. Lampert, C.H., Nickisch, H., Harmeling, S.: Learning to detect unseen object classes by between-class attribute transfer. In: IEEE Conference on Computer Vision and Pattern Recognition, pp. 951–958. IEEE (2009)
8. Parikh, D., Grauman, K.: Relative attributes. In: 2011 International Conference on Computer Vision, pp. 503–510. IEEE (2011)
9. Shrivastava, A., Singh, S., Gupta, A.: Constrained semi-supervised learning using attributes and comparative attributes. In: Fitzgibbon, A., Lazebnik, S., Perona, P., Sato, Y., Schmid, C. (eds.) ECCV 2012. LNCS, vol. 7574, pp. 369–383. Springer, Heidelberg (2012). https://doi.org/10.1007/978-3-642-33712-3_27
10. Biswas, A., Parikh, D.: Simultaneous active learning of classifiers and attributes via relative feedback. In: IEEE Conference on Computer Vision and Pattern Recognition, pp. 644–651 (2013)
11. Parkash, A., Parikh, D.: Attributes for classifier feedback. In: Fitzgibbon, A., Lazebnik, S., Perona, P., Sato, Y., Schmid, C. (eds.) ECCV 2012. LNCS, vol. 7574, pp. 354–368. Springer, Heidelberg (2012). https://doi.org/10.1007/978-3-642-33712-3_26
12. Liang, L., Grauman, K.: Beyond comparing image pairs: setwise active learning for relative attributes. In: Proceedings of the IEEE conference on Computer Vision and Pattern Recognition, pp. 208–215 (2014)
13. You, X., Wang, R., Tao, D.: Diverse expected gradient active learning for relative attributes. IEEE Trans. Image Process. 23(7), 3203–3217 (2014)
14. Qian, B., Wang, X., Cao, N., Jiang, Y.G., Davidson, I.: Learning multiple relative attributes with humans in the loop. IEEE Trans. Image Process. Publ. IEEE Signal Process. Soc. 23(12), 5573–5585 (2014)
15. Yu, A., Grauman, K.: Just noticeable differences in visual attributes. In: IEEE International Conference on Computer Vision, pp. 2416–2424 (2015)
16. Yu, A., Grauman, K.: Fine-grained visual comparisons with local learning. In: Proceedings of the IEEE Conference on Computer Vision and Pattern Recognition, pp. 192–199 (2014)
17. Sez, J.A., Galar, M., Luengo, J., Herrera, F.: Analyzing the presence of noise in multi-class problems: alleviating its influence with the one-vs-one decomposition. Knowl. Inf. Syst. 38(1), 179–206 (2014)
18. Hüllermeier, E., Vanderlooy, S.: Combining predictions in pairwise classification: an optimal adaptive voting strategy and its relation to weighted voting. Pattern Recogn. 43(1), 128–142 (2010)
19. Allwein, E.L., Schapire, R.E., Singer, Y.: Reducing multiclass to binary: a unifying approach for margin classifiers. In: Seventeenth International Conference on Machine Learning, pp. 9–16 (2000)

20. Li, S., Shan, S., Chen, X.: Relative forest for attribute prediction. In: Lee, K.M., Matsushita, Y., Rehg, J.M., Hu, Z. (eds.) ACCV 2012. LNCS, vol. 7724, pp. 316–327. Springer, Heidelberg (2013). https://doi.org/10.1007/978-3-642-37331-2_24
21. Li, S., Shan, S., Yan, S., Chen, X.: Relative forest for visual attribute prediction. IEEE Trans. Image Process. **25**(9), 1 (2016)
22. Yan, S., Wang, H., Tang, X., Huang, T.S.: Learning auto-structured regressor from uncertain nonnegative labels. In: IEEE Conference on International Conference on Computer Vision, no. 7, pp. 1–8 (2007)
23. Fu, Y., Huang, T.S.: Human age estimation with regression on discriminative aging manifold. IEEE Trans. Multimed. **10**(4), 578–584 (2008)
24. Guo, G., Fu, Y., Dyer, C.R., Huang, T.S.: Image-based human age estimation by manifold learning and locally adjusted robust regression. IEEE Trans. Image Process. **17**(7), 1178–1188 (2008)
25. Guo, G., Mu, G., Fu, Y., Huang, T.S.: Human age estimation using bio-inspired features. In: 2009 IEEE Conference on Computer Vision and Pattern Recognition, CVPR 2009, pp. 112–119 (2009)
26. Chan, A.B., Vasconcelos, N.: Counting people with low-level features and Bayesian regression. IEEE Trans. Image Process. **21**(4), 2160–2177 (2012)
27. Galar, M., Ndez, A., Barrenechea, E., Bustince, H., Herrera, F.: An overview of ensemble methods for binary classifiers in multi-class problems: experimental study on one-vs-one and one-vs-all schemes. Pattern Recogn. **44**(8), 1761–1776 (2011)
28. An, S., Liu, W., Venkatesh, S.: Face recognition using kernel ridge regression. In: IEEE Conference on Computer Vision and Pattern Recognition, CVPR 2007, pp. 1–7 (2007)
29. Haitovsky, Y.: On multivariate ridge regression. Biometrika **74**(3), 563–570 (1987)
30. Oliva, A., Torralba, A.: Modeling the shape of the scene: a holistic representation of the spatial envelope. Int. J. Comput. Vis. **42**(3), 145–175 (2001)
31. Kumar, N., Berg, A.C., Belhumeur, P.N., Nayar, S.K.: Attribute and simile classifiers for face verification. In: 2009 IEEE 12th International Conference on Computer Vision, pp. 365–372. IEEE (2009)
32. Zhou, L., Wang, Q., Fujita, H.: One versus one multi-class classification fusion using optimizing decision directed acyclic graph for predicting listing status of companies. Inf. Fusion **36**, 80–89 (2016)
33. Davis, J.V., Kulis, B., Jain, P., Sra, S., Dhillon, I.S.: Information-theoretic metric learning. In: International Conference on Machine Learning, pp. 209–216 (2007)

System Designs for Augmented Reality Based Ablation Probe Tracking

Hao Bo Yu and Harvey Ho[✉]

Auckland Bioengineering Institute, The University of Auckland,
70 Symonds Street, Auckland 1010, New Zealand
harvey.ho@auckland.ac.nz

Abstract. In this paper we present two Augmented Reality (AR) systems and associated algorithms to track and visualise a surgical ablation probe. The first system is based on the Kinect sensor while the second system makes use of a stereo-vision camera (OvrVision Pro) and a Head Mounted Display (HMD) device. Both systems utilise the fiducial markers on a custom-built rig attached to the ablation probe. We applied the first AR system to the navigation of a virtual liver, and the second AR system to the prediction of the 3D position of probe tip. The predication error for the tip was about 5–10 mm, with a computational speed of 10 FPS. In conclusion, two AR systems were designed and implemented with potential for further improvements to be applied in an actual clinical context.

Keywords: Augmented reality · Ablation probe · Computer vision
Virtual model

1 Introduction

Ablation is used to destroy liver tumours in-situ. It can be a primary curative option for small liver cancers (<3 cm) such as hepatocellular carcinomas and colorectal liver metastases, and is ideal for those that cannot undergo surgery. It can be performed percutaneously (under radiological guidance) or surgically (either laparoscopically or at open operation). The procedure involves the insertion of a gauge applicator into the tumour centre to destroy tumour cells using radiofrequency or microwave energy to generate heat. The placement accuracy of the probe tip is critical to ensure the destruction of the entire tumour whilst limiting damage to healthy cells. Current surgical ablation procedures typically use 2D ultrasound (US) images displayed on a monitor to guide the advancement of ablation probes. The US images are then compared with pre-surgical 3D CT, MRI images [1,2]. This practice poses challenges to a surgeon in interpreting the information from 2D images to guide the 3D positioning of the ablation probe [1,10], thus introduces errors due to *ad hoc* judgements of the location of the needle tip. Adding to the error are respiration and cardiac motion induced organ displacements and needle deflection [3,4].

© Springer International Publishing AG, part of Springer Nature 2018
M. Paul et al. (Eds.): PSIVT 2017, LNCS 10749, pp. 87–99, 2018.
https://doi.org/10.1007/978-3-319-75786-5_8

To address this problem, surgical navigation systems have been proposed to aid the prediction of 3D positions of the ablation probe. Some proposed solutions involve the use of robotic assistance [5,7]. Others use US images registered with pre-operational CT/MRI images [2]. In particular, CT images and intra-operative video are used to create an augmented reality (AR) guidance system [9]. While these all address some of the issues of the probe navigation problem, they each possess their own problems. These include the operator having to look away at a separate screen and/or the visualisation is only in 2D and still requires interpretation and mental processing to visualise the 3D position. This raises questions whether a head mounted displays (HMD) device could be utlised in this context. Indeed it was shown, as early as 2001 that AR system with HMD produced better results than traditional ablation ultrasound guided methods [10]. However, most HMD devices and their associated vision algorithms used in the surgical context are proprietary or in-house built, not based on consumer grade products.

The aim of this work is therefore to design and build an AR system using inexpensive, commercially available products. After testing the systems in simulated surgical scenes and phantoms we hope to gain insights of more sophisticated AR systems that are capable of yielding accurate and fast predication of probe positions to surgeons.

2   Methods

2.1   Camera Model

Regardless of camera systems to be used, the core of computer vision (CV) is to relate 2D image points and their corresponding 3D object points. This correspondence is built at first through the process of camera calibration, where the intrinsic, extrinsic and distortion parameters of a vision camera are found. Specifically, an AR scene setup requires the *projection* matrix P, which comprises of the *intrinsics* matrix (M), the *extrinsic* parameters $(R$ and $\overrightarrow{T})$ as:

$$P = M[R|\overrightarrow{T}]$$

The pixel coordinates can be related to the 3D coordinates by the extrinsic parameters as:

$$\begin{bmatrix} u \\ v \\ w \end{bmatrix} = [P] \begin{bmatrix} X \\ Y \\ Z \\ 1 \end{bmatrix} \tag{1}$$

where u, v are the pixel coordinates, w is associated with depth, X, Y, Z are the 3D coordinates of an object point. The problem we need to solve is the Perspective-n-Points (PnP) problem [8], and can be stated as: given a set of object points (3D) to image points (2D) pairs how to find a projection matrix, P, such that it satisfies Eq. (1) for all 3D to 2D pairs.

Different methods can be used to solve the PnP problem, including but not limited to, Levenberg-Marquart optimization, P3P, and EPnP methods [13]. The open source CV library OPENCV includes the CV::SOLVEPNP function that solves for the projection matrix P. Our methodology requires *intrinsic* values to be known beforehand, but methods such as Direct Linear Transformation (DLT) [8] solve for P without knowing the *intrinsic* parameters. However, knowing the *intrinsic* properties can reduce the number of correspondences required, for instance, in our probe navigation implementation only four correspondences were used.

2.2   Ablation Probe and Custom-Built Rig

The AR setup is based on an actual microwave ablation probe (Acculis Accu2i), which is used in the Auckland City Hospital, New Zealand for tissue ablation (Fig. 1a). The ablation probe's applicator, or the shaft, is the part inserted into

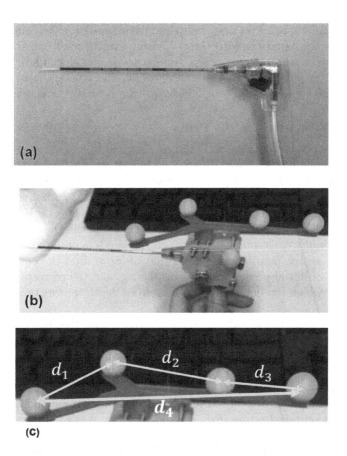

Fig. 1. (a) Accu2i ablation probe; (b) Removable rig designed for the probe; (c) Distances between individual fiducials for error estimation.

an organ, and heat released from the leading section of the probe serves the purpose of thermal coagulation. The probe is capable of ablating a tissue size of $4.5 \, \text{cm} \times 5.5 \, \text{cm}$ in $6 \, \text{min}$ (per Accu2i manual). Hence it is critical to accurately predict the location of the applicator, even when it is hidden, e.g., when it is inside a soft phantom. This is one of the challenges faced by surgeons, and the motivation of our work.

In order to monitor the movements of the probe, a rig system with fiducial markers was custom-designed and built (Fig. 1b). The rig was first designed in SolidWorks (Dassault Systemes) by taking measurements from the Accu2i ablation probe. The rig is designed to be removable, and has three screws that holds the probe firmly. The rig has three parts: a base in orange colour, a frame in red colour and fiducial markers (Fig. 1b). The red frame functions as a holder for the fiducial markers, and can be made in different shapes depending on users' need.

In terms of fiducial markers, two kinds of markers were used. Firstly RGB markers were used to complement the RGB stereo camera used. Secondly, the markers can be switched to retro-reflective (or self reflecting) markers suitable for an infra-red camera. RGB markers were used in this work for their simplicity and availability; it is compatible with the two vision system used, i.e. an OvrVision Pro based system and a Kinect-based system, to be introduced later.

Lastly, all rig parts including the base, frame, and markers were 3D printed except infra-red reflective markers, which are commercially available.

2.3 Pose Estimation for the Probe

The alignment of two sets of data cloud is a common problem in computer science. Three methods are commonly used, namely Principle Component Analysis (PCA), Singular Value Decomposition (SVD), and the Iterative Closest Point (ICP) methods [12]. In particular, ICP is a method that does not require correspondence between the initial and target data points [1]. However ICP is used for large data clouds, thus not suitable for our application. SVD and PCA, on the other hand, require correspondence between the two sets of data clouds. We use an exhaustive search method, similar to that of [6], to find the correspondence between a set of initial points, markers on the rig, and the corresponding set of target points, which are detected 3D points from depth sensors or stereo vision cameras.

Figure 2 explains the algorithm. On the left we have the *template* geometry ($\mathcal{V}$), with known relative distances between each of the nodes. On the right side, we have a set of nodes ($\mathcal{W}$) detected with vision systems. **Each *template* node in $\mathcal{V}$ needs to correspond to a *world* marker in $\mathcal{W}$, and this is the problem** we need to solve.

The *template* points are the *initial* points, and they correspond to the actual markers on the surgical probe (Fig. 1). A closed loop was used to connect template points, for instance $1 \to 2 \to 3 \to 1$, and the distance between each node i.e. the edge length in the loop can be determined. If $n = 3$ we have:

$$\mathcal{L} = \{l_1 = ||t_1 - t_2||, l_2 = ||t_2 - t_3||, l_3 = ||t_3 - t_1||\} \tag{2}$$

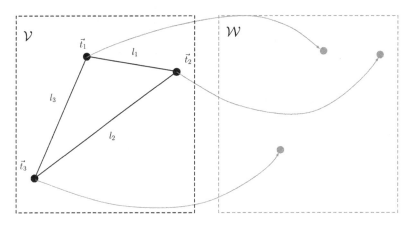

Fig. 2. This figure illustrates the correspondence problem. The left figure shows the template points $\mathcal{V} = \{t_1, t_2, t_3\}$. On the right, the three world points $\mathcal{W}$ detected by vision systems are represented by blue dots. (Color figure online)

After establishing the set of edge lengths $\mathcal{L}$, we move on to retrieve the 3D positions of the vertices from depth sensors.

Assuming the raw 3D position is unordered, $\mathcal{W}_{\text{unordered}} = \{\boldsymbol{p}_1, \boldsymbol{p}_3, \boldsymbol{p}_2\}$, all possible loops that can be formed by these points are listed in Eq. 3. For each scenario, $d_1, \ldots, d_3$ represents the distances between each node pair. Our goal now is to find which set of distances is the closest to the template distances $\mathcal{L}$.

$$
\begin{aligned}
loop_1 &:= p_1 \xrightarrow{d_1} p_2 \xrightarrow{d_2} p_3 \xrightarrow{d_3} p_1 \\
loop_2 &:= p_1 \xrightarrow{d_1} p_3 \xrightarrow{d_2} p_2 \xrightarrow{d_3} p_1 \\
loop_3 &:= p_2 \xrightarrow{d_1} p_1 \xrightarrow{d_2} p_3 \xrightarrow{d_3} p_2 \\
loop_4 &:= p_2 \xrightarrow{d_1} p_3 \xrightarrow{d_2} p_1 \xrightarrow{d_3} p_2 \\
loop_5 &:= p_3 \xrightarrow{d_1} p_1 \xrightarrow{d_2} p_2 \xrightarrow{d_3} p_3 \\
loop_6 &:= p_3 \xrightarrow{d_1} p_2 \xrightarrow{d_2} p_1 \xrightarrow{d_3} p_3
\end{aligned}
\tag{3}
$$

This is achieved by computing Eq. 4 for every loop from 1 to 6, where l_1, l_2, l_3 represents the template lengths. The loop that gives us the minimum value can be used to reorder $\mathcal{W}_{\text{unordered}}$.

$$
\|l_1 - d_1\| + \|l_2 - d_2\| + \|l_3 - d_3\|
\tag{4}
$$

For example, if $loop_5$ is the minimum to the above equation, then the ordered 3D point will be $\mathcal{W}_{\text{ordered}} = \{\boldsymbol{p}_3, \boldsymbol{p}_1, \boldsymbol{p}_2\}$. The above exhaustive algorithm was implemented for the case when $n = 4$. Once correspondence is established, SVD (in the PCL library [11]) was used to find the rotation $[R]$ and translation $[T]$ between the *template* points and the ordered 3D points $\mathcal{W}_{\text{ordered}}$, as detected by vision systems which were used in the work, as introduced below.

The idea behind the algorithm is explained by taking the number of data points $n = 3$, however the same concept applies to more data points.

2.4   Kinect-Based AR System

Kinect Sensors. The Kinect V2 sensor (Microsoft) was primarily aimed at the virtual 3D gaming community for the 3D gaming console XBox, however it is also used in scientific research, in particular in those areas that require depth information. The Kinect has a RGB *colour camera* with a resolution of 1920×1080 pixels, and an infra-red camera with a resolution of 512×424 pixels to capture depth information. The refresh rate for both cameras is 30 frames per second (FPS).

In a 3D virtual surgical guidance system, all elements important to surgeons during an ablation surgery need to be embodied, namely the organ, the probe, and the surgical world. In this system we used the depth sensor for the detection of the world or the environment, and the RGB sensor to detect fiducials and markers.

This process was achieved in three main steps. In the first step, 3D fiducials are detected by the Kinect. Next, the above exhaustive method and SVD are used to find the relative rotation $[R]$ and translation T between the *template* points and the 3D points detected from the Kinect. Thirdly the applicator is transformed with the same transformations (Fig. 3).

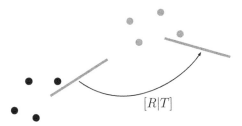

Fig. 3. Black dots represents the *template* points, and the green dots represents the 3D points retrieved from the Kinect. The blue line represents the applicator. (Color figure online)

Virtual Liver. Instead of applying the system in an actual surgical sense, we used a virtual liver model digitised from the Visible Human dataset, which contains the liver surface and the portal and hepatic veins (to be shown in Results). The virtual liver mesh was anchored to the AR scene by two ArUco markers shown in Fig. 4. All relevant geometries were then visualised in an OpenGL viewer environment allowing the user to rotate, pan, and zoom in the environment.

In the Kinect based system, the Kinect sensor was mounted on a tripod, and its location was fixed. The ArUco markers on the desk were also static, though they could be moved anywhere in the scene (Fig. 4). The moving element of the system is the probe and the rig attached to it. Next we introduced a HMD-based system where both the cameras and the probe are in motion in the scene, thus poses more challenges.

Fig. 4. Setup of Kinect-based system: The kinect was mounted on a tripod, from where this image was taken. Two ArUco markers, indicated by arrows, were used as fiducials to locate the virtual liver mesh in an AR scene. Note, the ArUco markers were different from the fiducials on the rig and they serve different purposes.

2.5   HMD and Stereo Vision-Based AR System

Stereo Vision Camera. The *OvrVision Pro* stereo camera system, shown in Fig. 5(a) is the product of the Wizapply company in Japan (www.ovrvision. com). It has two 1.8 MP cameras, with *optical* centres about 6 cm apart. This camera was originally designed for HMD-based AR applications. It possesses a large *barrel* distortion, and is corrected based on the principle that the corrected image is a function of the radial distance between the distorted points and the undistorted image centre r. This is achieved in the camera calibration process, which is explained in many texts and is not repeated here. We refer the interested reader to [13] for further reading. The result of the correction matrix for the OvrVision Pro camera is:

$$[M]_{\text{Left}} = \begin{bmatrix} 706.07 & 0 & 441.39 \\ 0 & 706.4 & 492.67 \\ 0 & 0 & 1 \end{bmatrix} [M]_{\text{Right}} = \begin{bmatrix} 703.31 & 0 & 482.2 \\ 0 & 703.19 & 477.62 \\ 0 & 0 & 1 \end{bmatrix} \quad (5)$$

The comparison with barrel effects of the OvrVision cameras before and after corrected is shown in Fig. 6.

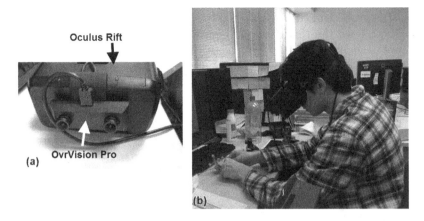

Fig. 5. Setup of the HMD-based AR environment: (a) An OvrVision Pro stereo vision camera is mounted on a Oculus Rift; (b) The AR scene is viewed from the Oculus goggles with real-time video stream captured by OvrVision. See Sect. 3.2 for an actual AR scene viewed from the goggles.

Fig. 6. Barrel effects of the stereo vision system is corrected.

Oculus Rift and OvrVision. To create an HMD-based AR environment, the OvrVision sensor was mounted on the Oculus Rift DK2, which is a virtual reality (VR) device used to visualise computer generated virtual environments by using stereoscopic displays. Oculus Rift itself does not have an interface to view the physical world. Rather, OvrVision was used to provide stereo-images and overlay them on the Oculus image frames. Indeed, the OvrVision Pro was designed for such purposes, and it has a mechanism for easy attachment on to the front of the Oculus DK2 (Fig. 5a).

Image fusion between the Oculus Rift and OvrVision begins by locating the ablation markers in 3D by using stereo-triangulation. Then, the exhaustive search method outlined above and the SVD method were used to find the transformation matrix $[R|T]$. This matrix is used to transform the applicator from its previous state to its new orientation.

Soft Phantom. A soft phantom was made from a gelatine powder (DAVIS Gelatine) combined with water at a concentration of 12% weight of gelatine. The size of the phantom is 150 mm × 150 mm × 100 mm. The phantom is placed inside a plastic box. Furthermore, a CharUco pattern (or chessboard + ArUco markers) [13] was placed over the gelatine phantom to create a virtual tissue block in the AR scene (to be shown in Results).

3   Results

The AR systems were run on a Intel i7-4790 CPU @ 3.60 GHz, RAM 32 GB, GPU 2 GB, with a NVIDIA 745 (OEM) GPU. The programming language is C++ in Visual Studio 2013.

3.1   Kinect-Based AR System

Figure 7 shows four screenshots of the 3D AR system in action. The purple cylinder represents the ablation applicator (the rig is currently not included). Figure 7(a) shows the relative position between the applicator and the virtual liver. The data cloud generated from the RF sensor is also visible in the background. Figure 7(b) is the close-up view, where the four white points represent the virtual fiducials whose transformation applies to the applicator as well. The blue points are the actual fiducals in the rig detected by the Kinect RGB camera.

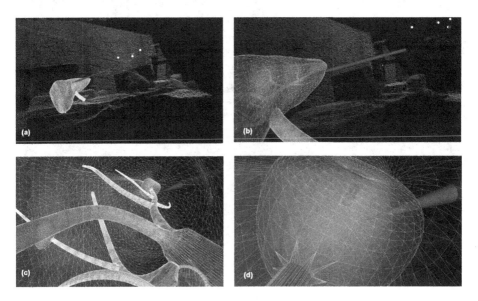

Fig. 7. Snapshots of the ablation visualisation system: (a) and (b) Relative position of the probe and the liver, and the environment as captured by Kinect; (c) The user is able to view inside of the liver, where the internal vessels geometry and tumour are visualised; (d) The virtual probe applicator approaches the tumour. (Color figure online)

The user is able to rotate, pan and zoom the applicator by using the mouse and keyboard. By doing so, the user is able to navigate within the liver mesh and visualise the geometries internally. In Fig. 7(d) the ablation tip can be seen inside of a tumour. This ablation visualiser system performed at 8–15 FPS. The tip of the applicator probe had an error of less than 10 mm.

3.2   HMD-Based AR System

The result of the HMD-based AR system is shown in Fig. 8. The left and right images are the video images viewed from the left and right lenses of the OvrVision stereo vision camera. The white line projected on the Oculus frames represents the ablation probe applicator, and the applicator tip is represented by a yellow circle. The virtual applicator follows the movements of the actual probe applicator (Fig. 8a). The CharUco described in Sect. 2.5 acts as landmarks for the virtual phantom, currently represented by a square wire frame (Fig. 8b).

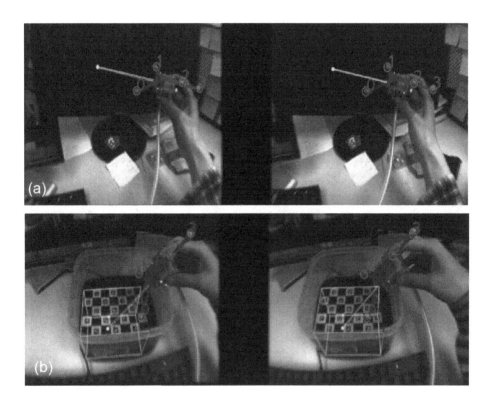

Fig. 8. Results of the HMD-based AR system: (a) The applicator is represented by a white line, the tip by a yellow circle; (b) The tip of the applicator and parts of the applicator is inserted into the phantom and is not visible, but by projecting the lines in Oculus HMD the 3D position of the tip becomes known to the user. (Color figure online)

Note that in Fig. 8(b) the probe was actually inserted into the phantom, i.e. the probe tip was invisible to cameras but was visible in the virtual AR scene to indicate the position of the applicator tip. This is exactly what we aimed to achieve, to inform surgeons where the tip reaches inside an organ.

3.3   Error Evaluation for the System

The error in the HMD-based system was evaluated in the following experiment. The distances between markers, $d_1, \ldots, d_4$ in Fig. 1(c), was compared with that computed from the stereo camera when the ablation probe was rotated and translated in space. The RMS errors (mm) and standard deviation (mm) are summarised in Table 1. These errors are slightly larger than literature [14], where they have achieved RMS values between -2 and 2 mm. Possible reasons include the OvrVision camera having a large lens distortion, and also possibly more camera calibrations are required. Future work should use stereo-vision systems with less *barrel* distortions.

Table 1. RMS error and standard deviation for measured distances.

	Dimension (mm)	RMS (mm)	Standard deviation (mm)
d_1	59	2.17	0.82
d_2	60	2.76	1.45
d_3	39	1.81	1.69
d_4	135	3.52	0.93

4   Discussion

The use of virtual reality and augmented reality in surgery is a growing area of research. They have been implemented in various ways including the projection of patient specific information from pre-operative scans onto the patient, or overlaying such information on live video footage which is displayed on a screen (for a brief review see [9]). Compared to VR applications, an AR application has an additional computation layer, which is to analyse a real-time video stream where a virtual model can be overlaid. This can cause computational bottlenecks if the AR system is not designed and implemented properly.

In this work, two different systems for the navigation and visualisation of ablation probes are presented. Four optical markers were used for both systems, with an exhaustive method to find correspondences between template points and corresponding 3D points. In the first system, the user was able to navigate in a 3D virtual organ. Through this system, a surgeon can have control over the 3D AR scene by using the keyboard and mouse to navigate to regions of interest, as illustrated in Fig. 7. However, such a 3D visualisation approach has its own drawbacks, including the operator has to look away at a separate screen. Moreover, several aspects need addressing. Firstly, the prediction error ($\sim$10 mm) of the applicator tip is rather large for such applications. This error was likely a result of the accumulation of errors from the individual markers because the tip is far from the marker arrangement, any small error from the markers is multiplied and passed to the tip. Secondly, the computation speed of 8 FPS is too slow for an actual clinical application.

In the second system, the HMD-based AR system overlay the virtual applicator onto the vision field, creating the illusion that the virtual object was "real" by providing spatial position of the tip to the user. After insertion of the applicator into the phantom, the portion inside of the gelatine becomes obstructed, but the applicator is augmented, allowing the user to see the occluded tip position. This system can be used as a core algorithm for an advanced ablation probe tracking system; for example, an integrated system with both preoperative CT/MRI data, and probe position relative to the patient, in real time. An ongoing work in our group is to use an abdominal biopsy phantom in conjunction with its corresponding MR images to create the AR scene.

Both proposed systems suffer from a high computation time thus further efforts are required to reduce the computation cost. For instance, retro-reflective markers can reduce the search space of the circle detection algorithm and increase the overall speed of the system. Lastly, a Finite Element solver can be added to update tumour positions accurately in order to mitigate for patient movements during surgery.

5   Conclusion

Two Augmented Reality based systems for microwave ablation probe were designed and implemented in this work. With further improvements on computational efficiency and rig design, the system has potential to be used in clinical scenarios for surgical training and probe navigation.

References

1. Jolesz, F. (ed.): Intraoperative Imaging and Image-Guided Therapy. Springer Science & Business Media, New York (2014). https://doi.org/10.1007/978-1-4614-7657-3
2. Ward, T., Goldman, R., Weintraub, J.: Electromagnetic navigation with multi-modality image fusion for image-guided percutaneous interventions. Tech. Vasc. Intervent. Radiol. **16**(3), 177–181 (2013)
3. Clifford, M., Banovac, F., Levy, E., Cleary, K.: Assessment of hepatic motion secondary to respiration for computer assisted interventions. Comput. Aided Surg. **7**(5), 291–299 (2002)
4. Abolhassani, N., Patel, R., Moallem, M.: Needle insertion into soft tissue: a survey. Med. Eng. Phy. **29**(4), 413–431 (2007)

5. Loser, M.H., Navab, N.: A new robotic system for visually controlled percutaneous interventions under CT fluoroscopy. In: Delp, S.L., DiGoia, A.M., Jaramaz, B. (eds.) MICCAI 2000. LNCS, vol. 1935, pp. 887–896. Springer, Heidelberg (2000). https://doi.org/10.1007/978-3-540-40899-4_92

6. Srikrishna, B.K., Musti, U., Heikkil, J.: Geometry based exhaustive line correspondence determination. In: 2016 IEEE International Conference on Robotics and Automation (ICRA), pp. 4341–4348. IEEE (2016)

7. Patriciu, A., Awad, M., Solomon, S.B., Choti, M., Mazilu, D., Kavoussi, L., Stoianovici, D.: Robotic assisted radio-frequency ablation of liver tumors – randomized patient study. In: Duncan, J.S., Gerig, G. (eds.) MICCAI 2005. LNCS, vol. 3750, pp. 526–533. Springer, Heidelberg (2005). https://doi.org/10.1007/11566489_65

8. Okuma, T., Sakaue, K., Takemura, H., Yokoya, N.: Real-time camera parameter estimation from images for a mixed reality system. In: Proceedings of the 2000 15th International Conference on Pattern Recognition, vol. 4, pp. 482–486. IEEE (2000)

9. Nicolau, S., Pennec, X., Soler, L., et al.: An augmented reality system for liver thermal ablation: design and evaluation on clinical cases. Med. Image Anal. **13**, 494–506 (2009)

10. Rosenthal, M., State, A., Lee, J., Hirota, G., Ackerman, J., Keller, K., Fuchs, H.: Augmented reality guidance for needle biopsies: an initial randomized, controlled trial in phantoms. Med. Image Anal. **6**(3), 313–320 (2002)

11. Rusu, R.B., Cousins, S.: 3D is here: point cloud library (PCL). In: 2011 IEEE International Conference on Robotics and automation (ICRA), pp. 1–4. IEEE (2011)

12. Kramer, J., Burrus, N., Echtler, F., Daniel, H.C., Parker, M.: Hacking the Kinect, vol. 268. Apress, New York (2012)

13. Forsyth, D., Ponce, J.: Computer Vision: A Modern Approach. Pearson, New York (2015)

14. Ren, H., Liu, W., Lim, A.: Marker-based surgical instrument tracking using dual kinect sensors. IEEE Trans. Autom. Sci. Eng. **11**(3), 921–924 (2014)

Using Sparse-Point Disparity Estimation and Spatial Propagation to Construct Dense Disparity Map for Stereo Endoscopic Images

Wen-Nung Lie[1]([⊠]), Hsi-Hung Huang[1], Shih-Wei Huang[2],
and Kai-Che Liu[3]

[1] Department of Electrical Engineering, National Chung Cheng University,
Chia-Yi, Taiwan, ROC
ieewnl@ccu.edu.tw
[2] Chang Bing Show Chwan Memorial Hospital, Lukang, Taiwan, ROC
[3] Medical Image Research Department,
Asian Institute of TeleSurgery/IRCAD-Taiwan, Lukang, Taiwan, ROC

Abstract. Disparity estimation for stereo endoscopic images is difficult due to their lack of distinct textures for matching. Many well-known algorithms fail in this kind of application to estimate a reliable dense disparity map. In this paper, we propose a strategy of using a sparse feature point set to estimate reliable disparity values, which are then propagated to other non-feature points to form the final dense disparity map. Our selected feature points include: SIFT, Canny-edge, Canny-edge-dilated, and grid points. The algorithms for disparity propagation are based on bilateral interpolation and refinement. Experiments show that our algorithm is successful in shaping the instruments in disparity map. This is helpful in 3D display for human perception. Disparity estimation for endoscopic images is still an open issue. Our preliminary result still presents some space for improvement.

Keywords: Minimally invasive surgery · Stereo matching · Sparse
Depth propagation

1 Introduction

In recent years, Minimally Invasive Surgery (MIS) has become a very important technology in medical operation. Compared to traditional surgical operations, MIS can reduce the wounds and shorten the patient's recovery time. However, the physicians need to be well-trained so that the operations could be accurate and safe. Traditionally, the physician holds the instruments for treatment, while looking at the LCD display in front of him/her which shows the video captured by the camera. Since the video is two-dimensional without depth perception, the physicians need to be skilled in operation so that the treatment is accurate and safe, without spending much time in achieving the parts of an organ that needs to be surged. Experiments through dual-eye stereo endoscope and 3D display have shown that 3D perception is capable of helping the surgeons in reducing the operation time by up to 50% relative to the traditional 2D endoscope (e.g., the famous Davinci surgical system has been equipped with a stereo endoscopic camera). However, the surgeons need to wear an IR-synchronized glasses so as to perceive the 3D effect. An autostereoscopic display (i.e., naked-eye 3D display) could release the surgeons from heavy glasses and make them more comfortable during surgical operations. This requires to provide depth information, which when accompanying with the texture (i.e., color) information, can be used to synthesize multiple novel views based on the well-known DIBR (Depth-Image-Based-Rendering) technique for 3D display.

Stereo matching (or disparity estimation) has been an important step in estimating depths of 3D points from two views (left and right) for computer vision applications. It can be categorized into local/window-based and global-based methods. In general, the global-based algorithms [1–6, 12, 14] minimizes an energy function, including data term and smooth term, to obtain optimal results through an iterative procedure. Though good depth quality can be obtained, the disadvantages are high complexity, considerable computation cost, and difficulty of hardware implementation. On the other hand, the local/window-based algorithms [7–9, 15–19] are easier to achieve, but less accurate than the global kind.

The simplest local approach to disparity estimation is the block matching procedure similar to motion estimation in video coding standards. However, the estimation result is too noisy to be used for practical applications. During block matching, the emphases are on the matching cost computation and the cost aggregation steps. Final disparity value for each pixel is determined based on the one with the minimally aggregated cost value. In order to reduce ambiguity, the matching costs are aggregated over a support window (often, a rectangle). A larger window size (e.g., over 35×35) often has better performance, but spending much time for computation. A fixed window often does not deal explicitly with uniform areas and repetitive patterns and ignores depth discontinuities. Hence, multiple windows are adopted in [16] for generating several depth candidates for each image pixel and a robust strategy is used for extracting high quality estimates from depth candidates. In [15], a new window-based method using varying support-weights to get accurate results at depth discontinuities as well as in homogeneous regions is proposed. The support-weights of the pixels in a given support window are computed based on color similarity and geometric proximity. However, their pixel-wise adaptive support-weight makes the computation a little more expensive than other area-based local methods. In [17], color segmentation technique is used to assist in finding a better matching window. This is beneficial in disparity estimation at depth discontinuity regions, but causes more complex computation. In [18], a multi-directional varying-scale polygon is used to approximate the spatially varying image structure around each image pixel, called locally adaptive polygon approximation (LAPA). LAPA still cannot accurately approximate the detailed image structure. Hence, the same authors continue to propose a cross-based support window approach [19], which leads to a superior performance than LAPA in approximating uniform color areas (whose pixels are supposed to have similar disparities) and presents hardware efficiency based on constant-time computation via integral images.

Endoscopic images in MIS are often captured within a distance of about 20 cm based on a point light source (e.g., laparoscopy). Compared to natural indoor/outdoor images, they are featured of: (1) possibly uneven lighting, (2) less and unclear texture on organ surfaces, (3) mirror-like reflection of the metal instrument, and (4) possible blur due to high instant motion of the camera or instrument. Figure 1 shows two examples of endoscopic images captured for a phantom and a pig living body, respectively.

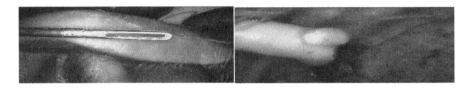

Fig. 1. Endoscopic images for (a) a phantom, (b) pig living body.

Due to the lack of significant textures for endoscopic images, stereo matching that estimates the disparity map faces a challenge, which is similar to the smoothness problem for traditional algorithms. That is, to estimate a dense disparity (depth) map, there would be a number of estimated disparities that have low confidence. In order to overcome this problem, we propose a strategy that traditional stereo matching is only applied to selected pixels that possesses high textures and might result in high confidence in disparity estimation. Disparities for pixels not selected are then obtained by spatially propagating the known disparities. Since the selected feature pixels are often sparse, the computation time for dense disparity map can be also reduced significantly.

The flowchart of our proposed disparity estimation algorithm based on sparse feature points is illustrated in Fig. 2. First of all, we define feature points that will be extracted for stereo matching. Different kinds of feature points are then estimated with disparities based on different algorithms. Finally, the estimated sparse disparities are spatially propagated to other non-estimated pixels to get a dense disparity (depth) map for 3D application (e.g., DIBR novel-view synthesis).

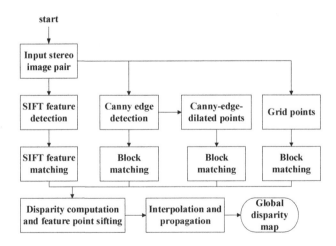

Fig. 2. Flowchart of proposed method.

2 Selection and Extraction of Feature Points for Disparity Estimation

The sparse feature points can be from four sources: (1) SIFT [10] feature points, (2) Canny edge points, (3) Canny-edge-dilated points, and (4) grid points, as shown in Table 1, where their methods for disparity estimation are also listed correspondingly.

Table 1. Feature points selected for disparity estimation in our system.

Feature point	Matching method
SIFT	SIFT descriptor
Canny edge	Block matching
Canny-edge-dilated	Block matching
Grid	Block matching

SIFT (Scale-Invariant Feature Transform) is well-known to act as good feature points in image registration applications. Points of high-strength in both the left and right views can be detected and their SIFT descriptors composed of 128-dimensional data are calculated for matching. Since the stereo views are often pre-calibrated to have horizontal epipolar lines, wrong matching can be easily removed. The disparity for paired SIFT feature points (one from left view and the other from right view) can be obtained from their displacement.

Since the number of SIFT feature points is often limited (only several hundreds), Canny edge points will constitute our main source of candidates for disparity estimation, as shown in Fig. 3.

Fig. 3. Result of Canny edge detection

In principle, Canny-edge points are located at boundaries between two depth planes. We need seeds at both planes (i.e., both sides of the boundaries) so that the respective depths (disparities) can be propagated throughout other portions. To overcome this problem, Canny-edge points are first expanded via two windows of different sizes. A differencing of these two expanded maps is conducted to obtain the Canny-edge-dilated points, as shown in Fig. 4.

Since it is possible that there does not exist any Canny-edge points in smooth areas, we generate grid points (as shown in Fig. 5) so that feature points for disparity

Fig. 4. Canny-edge-dilated points, (a) Canny-edge expanded by windows of 21 × 21 pixels, (b) Canny-edge expanded by windows of 19 × 19 pixels, (c) dilated result by differencing between (a) and (b).

estimation can be distributed more uniformly in the image. To optimize the performance, a neighborhood of each grid point which has the largest gradient over the window (e.g., 3 × 3) is selected to replace the corresponding grid point.

From Table 1, it can be seen that except the SIFT feature points, disparity estimation of all the other three kinds will resort to block matching. The window size in block matching here depends on the type of the feature points (see experiments).

To enhance the accuracy of our sparse disparities, random sample consensus (RANSAC) algorithm is used in each kind to eliminate false matching pairs based on homographic transform error. That is, only the sifted feature points are remained as seeds for spatial propagation.

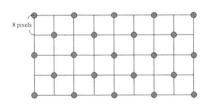

Fig. 5. Grid points

3 Spatial Propagation for Global Disparity Map

3.1 Iterative Interpolation by Bilateral Filtering

Since our disparity points are sparse, pixels of unknown disparity are first iteratively interpolated based on the known ones. They are then refined based on a criterion of global optimization. Bilateral filtering is used for interpolation in our system:

$$D(x,y) = \frac{\sum_{(x_i,y_i)\in N(x,y)} w(x_i,y_i)D(x_i,y_i)}{\sum_{(x_i,y_i)\in N(x,y)} w(x_i,y_i)} \tag{1}$$

$$w(x_i,y_i) = w_c(x_i,y_i)w_d(x_i,y_i) \tag{2}$$

$$w_c(x_i,y_i) = \exp\left(-\left(\frac{(I(x,y)-I(x_i,y_i))^2}{2\sigma_c^2}\right)\right) \tag{3}$$

$$w_d(x_i,y_i) = \exp\left(-\left(\frac{((x_i-x)^2-(y_i-y)^2)}{2\sigma_d^2}\right)\right) \tag{4}$$

where (x,y) is the pixel of unknown disparity, $D(x,y)$ is the estimated disparity, $N(x,y)$ is the neighborhood of (x,y), $w_c(x_i,y_i)$ is for color weighting, $w_d(x_i,y_i)$ is for distance weighting, $I(x,y)$ is the intensity at (x,y), σ_c and σ_d are parameters that determine the sharpness of the weighting function. Equations (1)–(4) are iteratively executed from the neighborhoods of the feature points until all pixels are interpolated. The result is as shown in Fig. 6.

Fig. 6. Disparity interpolation by bilateral filtering.

3.2 Global Refinement of Disparities

The interpolated disparities are adopted as the initial disparity map for refinement. By referring to [11], refinement is based on Eqs. (5) and (6):

$$D^t(x,y) = \frac{\sum_{(x_i,y_i)\in N(x,y)} w(x_i,y_i)c(x_i,y_i)D^{t-1}(x_i,y_i)}{\sum_{(x_i,y_i)\in N(x,y)} w(x_i,y_i)c(x_i,y_i)} \tag{5}$$

$$c^t(x, y) = \max_{(x_i, y_i) \in N(x,y)} w(x_i, y_i)\left(c^{t-1}(x_i, y_i)\right) \qquad (6)$$

where t represents the iteration number, $w(x_i, y_i)$ is the same as Eq. (2), $c(x_i, y_i)$ represents the confidence value for the disparity propagated from the neighboring point (x_i, y_i). Note that Eq. (5) is similar to Eq. (1), except the extra confidence term for each pixel, whose initial value is 1 for the feature points and $1/n$ for the interpolated points (n is the iteration number when the disparity is interpolated). The confidence terms will be updated according to the texture information. Normally, $N(x, y)$ is chosen as a 3×3 window (Fig. 7).

Fig. 7. Disparity map after global refinement.

4   Experimental Results

The stereo endoscopic images are captured by using KARL STORZ 3D System, as shown in Fig. 8. Three sets of images are captured from a phantom to simulate MIS environment and the 4th one is captured from a pig living body. The experiments are based on an Intel(R) Core(TM) i7-4790 3.60 GHz CPU with 16 GB memory, and Visual Studio C/C++ 2010 development platform.

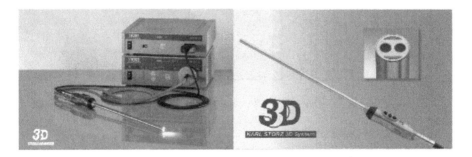

Fig. 8. The KARL STORZ 3D endoscope system.

The experiments are based on the following parameters: (1) minimum/maximum disparity = 0/300, (2) grid sampling = 8×8, (3) matching window size for Canny and Canny-edge-dilated points = 11×11, (4) matching window size for grid points = 31×31. The reasons that Canny-edge, Canny-edge-dilated, and grid points adopt different window sizes come from the following considerations: (1) Canny-edge and Canny-edge-dilated points might be located near depth boundaries, where the occlusion often influences the accuracy of block matching, so the window size is reduced accordingly, (2) grid points often possess less textures, so the window size is increased accordingly.

Figure 9 shows the matching results between the left and right views (for the first set of images) for four kinds of feature points. The feature points are colored in different color for easier discrimination. The number of matched pairs for them are 231, 18181, 11924, and 4996, respectively.

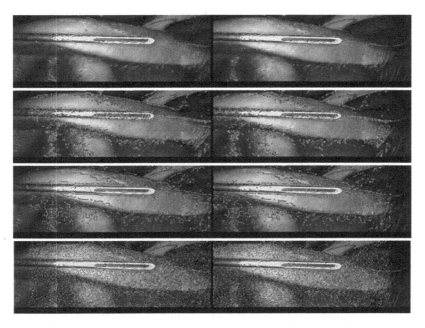

Fig. 9. Results of feature point matching between the left and right views.

We compare several methods in Fig. 10: (b) traditional block matching (BM), (c) cross-based method [19], (d) semi-global matching [13], and (e) proposed. In Fig. 10(b), (d), red pixels stand for disparity estimation that are considered unreliable. It is obvious that BM leads to noisy results, as expected. It is however surprised that the well-known r-sgm method [13] fails to estimate reliable disparities for endoscopic images. Over 80% of areas are considered unreliable and colored red! On the other hand, the popular cross-based matching method [19] also fails in estimating an accurate boundaries for the instrument. Our proposed algorithm, though still have space for improvement, is however capable of detecting the shape of the instrument.

Table 2 lists the numbers of the original and sifted feature points and their corresponding proportions for each test image set (the original image size is 1620×540 pixels). The average proportions before and after sifting are 7.065% and 3.15%, respectively, which are small enough to be helpful to reduce the overall computing time.

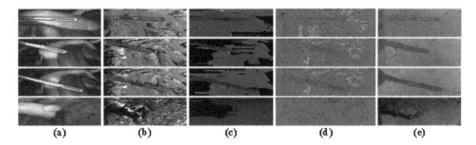

(a)   (b)   (c)   (d)   (e)

Fig. 10. Experimental results for endoscopic images. (a) Original images, (b) results of block matching, (c) results of [19], (d) results of [13], (e) results of our proposed algorithm. (Color figure online)

Table 2. Numbers and proportions of the feature points for 4 test image sets.

Image number	Original feature points	Sifted feature points	Proportion
Phantom 1	64784	35332	4.04%
Phantom 2	58269	26908	3.08%
Phantom 3	58420	25681	2.94%
Pig living body	65351	22518	2.57%

5 Conclusion

Due to the lack of distinct textures, it is difficult to estimate a correct and reliable disparity map for stereo endoscopic images. This paper proposes a strategy of estimating disparities based on a spare set of feature points, which is then spatially propagated to others to form a dense disparity map. We propose to define the sparse set of feature points to include: SIFT feature, Canny-edge, Canny-edge-dilated, and grid points. Their estimated disparities are then verified (sifted) to constitute the seeds for spatial propagation. Bilateral filtering is adopted for disparity interpolation first, whose results are then refined with information propagated from spatial neighbors.

Experiments show that many well-known algorithms fail in our endoscopic image sets, while our algorithm is successful in detecting the shape of the instruments. Disparity map estimation for endoscopic images is still an open issue for research. Our preliminary result still presents some space for improvement.

The future works will be on the selection of prominent feature points which are more suitable for reliable disparity estimation and propagation.

References

1. Boykov, Y., Veksler, O., Zabih, R.: Fast approximate energy minimization via graph cuts. IEEE Trans. Pattern Anal. Mach. Intell. **23**(11), 1222–1239, November 2001
2. Kolmogorov, V., Zabih, R.: Computing visual correspondence with occlusions via graph cuts. In: Proceedings of International Conference on Computer Vision, vol. II, pp. 508–515 (2001)

3. Hong, L., Chen, G.: Segment-based stereo matching using graph cuts. In: Proceedings of IEEE Conference on Computer Vision and Pattern Recognition, vol. I, pp. 74–81 (2004)
4. Sun, J., Zheng, N.-N., Shum, H.-Y.: Stereo matching using belief propagation. IEEE Trans. Pattern Anal. Mach. Intell. 25(7), 787–800, July 2003
5. Yang, Q., Wang, L., Yang, R., Stewenius, H., Nister, D.: Stereo matching with color-weighted correlation, hierarchical belief propagation and occlusion handling. In: Proceedings of IEEE Conference on Computer Vision and Pattern Recognition, June 2006
6. Klaus, A., Sormann, M., Karner, K.: Segment-based stereo matching using belief propagation and a self-adapting dissimilarity measure. In: Proceedings of International Conference on Pattern Recognition (2006)
7. Veksler, O.: Fast variable window for stereo correspondence using integral images. In: Proceedings of IEEE International Conference on Computer Vision and Pattern Recognition (CVPR), vol. 1, pp. 556–561 (2003)
8. Yuan, D., Cheng, F., Zhang, H.: Dense stereo matching based on edge constraint and variable windows. In: Proceedings of IEEE International Conference on Robotics and Biomimetics, pp. 1912–1917 (2011)
9. Qiu, M., Zhang, Y.: Feature guided multi-window area-based matching method for urban remote sensing stereo pairs. In: Proceedings of IEEE International Conference on Geoscience and Remote Sensing Symposium (IGARSS), pp. 1912–1917 (2011)
10. Lowe, D.: Distinctive image features from scale-invariant keypoints. Int. J. Comput. Vis. 2(60), 91–110 (2004)
11. Yan, X., Yang, Y., Er, G., Dai, Q.: Depth map generation for 2D-to-3D conversion by limited user inputs and depth propagation. In: Proceedings of IEEE International Conference the True Vision-Capture, Transmission and Display of 3D Video (3DTV-CON), pp. 1–4, May 2011
12. Rother, C., Blake, A., Kolmogorov, V.: Grabcut – interactive foreground extraction using iterated graph cuts. ACM Trans. Graph. 23(3), 309–314 (2004)
13. Spangenberg, R., Langner, T., Adfeldt, S., Rojas, R.: Large scale semi-global matching on the CPU. In: Proceedings of the IEEE Intelligent Vehicles Symposium Proceedings, pp. 195–201, June 2014
14. Yang, Q., Wang, L., Yang, R., Stewenius, H., Nister, D.: Stereo matching with color-weighted correlation, hierarchical belief propagation, and occlusion handling. IEEE Trans. Pattern Anal. Mach. Intell. (TPAMI) 31(3), 492–504 (2009)
15. Yoon, K., Kweon, I.: Adaptive support-weight approach for correspondence search. IEEE Trans. Pattern Anal. Mach. Intell. (TPAMI) 28, 650–656 (2006)
16. Boughorbel, F.: A new multiple-windows depth from stereo algorithm for 3D displays. In: Proceedings of IEEE International Conference on Capture, Transmission and Display of 3D Video (3DTV-CON), Kos Island, pp. 1–4, May 2007
17. Gerrits, M., Bekaert, P.: Local stereo matching with segmentation-based outlier rejection. In: Proceedings of IEEE International Conference on Computer and Robot Vision (CRV), New York, USA, p. 66, June 2006
18. Zhang, K., Lu, J., Lafruit, G.: Scalable stereo matching with locally adaptive polygon approximation. In: Prodings of IEEE International Conference on Image Processing (ICIP), pp. 313–316, October 2008
19. Zhang, K., Lu, J., Lafruit, G.: Cross-based local stereo matching using orthogonal integral images. IEEE Trans. Circuits Syst. Video Tech. 19(7), 1073–1079 (2009)

Globally Optimal Object Tracking with Complementary Use of Single Shot Multibox Detector and Fully Convolutional Network

Jinho Lee[✉], Brian Kenji Iwana, Shouta Ide, Hideaki Hayashi, and Seiichi Uchida

Kyushu University, Fukuoka, Japan
lee@human.ait.kyushu-u.ac.jp

Abstract. Object tracking is one of the most important but still difficult tasks in computer vision and pattern recognition. The main difficulties in the tracking task are appearance variation of target objects and occlusion. To deal with those difficulties, we propose a object tracking method combining Single Shot Multibox Detector (SSD), Fully Convolutional Network (FCN) and Dynamic Programming (DP). SSD and FCN provide a probability value of the target object which allows for appearance variation within each category. DP provides a globally optimal tracking path even with severe occlusions. Through several experiments, we confirmed that their combination realized a robust object tracking method. Also, in contrast to traditional trackers, initial position and a template of the target do not need to be specified. We show that the proposed method has a higher performance than the traditional trackers in tracking various single objects through video frames.

Keywords: Object tracking · Single Shot Multibox Detector
Fully Convolutional Network · Dynamic Programming

1 Introduction

Object tracking is defined as the problem of estimating the spatio-temporal trajectory of a target object in an image. Although it has been studied for many applications such as bio-image analysis, scene surveillance, autonomous vehicle control, etc., it is still a difficult problem. One difficulty comes from appearance variation. For example, for a general person tracking problem, we need to deal with various clothes, poses, and body shapes under various illumination condition. Traditional methods assume a predefined template of the target object and update it accordingly to any changes in appearance [1,2]. Another difficulty is occlusion. Traditional object tracking methods are often intolerant to severe occlusion [3–5].

In this paper, we propose a object tracking method robust to both of appearance variation and occlusion by using a complementary combination of Single

© Springer International Publishing AG, part of Springer Nature 2018
M. Paul et al. (Eds.): PSIVT 2017, LNCS 10749, pp. 110–122, 2018.
https://doi.org/10.1007/978-3-319-75786-5_10

Shot Multibox Detector (SSD) [6], Fully Convolutional Network (FCN) [7], and Dynamic Programming (DP) [8–10]. SSD and FCN are employed for tackling appearance variation. They have been proposed recently for object detection and they can provide a probability value of a target object for each category, such as person, car, and motorbike, given each bounding box or pixel respectively. Since SSD and FCN are types of CNNs, large amounts of training samples will make them robust to a variety of appearances.

To deal with occlusion, we utilized DP for global optimization of a target object's trajectory. DP is one of the most fundamental optimization techniques and has been used for obtaining a globally optimal tracking path. Since a slope constraint of DP prohibits the tracked position from moving steeply over all frames, it is possible to obtain a stable tracking path, regardless of occlusion.

It is very important to note the reason why we use the two CNN-based object detectors, SSD and FCN, in a complementary manner, is because they provide detection results in different ways. SSD provides an accurate detection result to a clear target object, however it is impossible to provide a detection result in an unstable situation such as occlusion. In contrast to SSD, FCN provides a result, regardless of any situation. Namely, combination of SSD and DP is useful to stable situation to obtain accurate result and it of FCN and DP is utilized in unstable situation to obtain any result.

It is also noteworthy that the proposed method requires neither the initial position nor the template of the target object. Traditional trackers may be sensitive to the template of the target object and the initialization in which the initial position of the target object is denoted on the first frame. However, the proposed method does not require either the template nor the initialization due to the synergy combining SSD, FCN, and DP.

The contributions of this paper are as follows. First, we show proposed method achieved the highest accuracy compared to the traditional trackers introduced in the Visual Tracker Benchmark [11]. Second, we confirm that the complementary use of the two CNN-based object detectors, SSD and FCN, are useful for tracking. Third, we confirm that the proposed method tackles appearance variation and occlusion through several experiments even without initialization, templates, and modifying parameters.

The remaining of this paper is organized as follows. In Sect. 2, we introduce related traditional tracking research. Section 3 elaborates on SSD, FCN, and DP and details the proposed method. In Sect. 4, we confirm that the proposed method is a robust tracker through several experiments and analyze the experimental results. Finally, Sect. 5 draws the conclusion.

2   Related Work

Object tracking is one of the important techniques in computer vision and has been actively studied for decades. Most object tracking algorithms are divided into two categories: generative and discriminative methods. Generative methods describe appearance of a target object using a generative model and search for

Table 1. Comparison between the proposed method and FCNT [29].

Tracker	Target	Template	Initialization	Path optimization	Offline/Online
Proposed	General	Unnecessary	Unnecessary	Globally optimal by DP	Offline
FCNT	Specific	Necessary	Necessary	Greedy	Online

the target object region that fits the model best. A number of generative model based algorithms have been proposed such as sparse representation [12,13], density estimation [14,15], and incremental subspace learning [16]. On contrary, discriminative methods build a model to distinguish a target object from the background. These tracking methods include P-N learning [17] and online boosting [18–20]. Even though these approaches are satisfactory in restricted situations, they have inherent limitations which include occlusion and appearance variation such as illumination changes, deformation etc.

To deal with limitations which traditional trackers can not tackle, recent trackers employ Convolutional Neural Networks (CNN) [21,22] and Deep Convolutional Neural Networks (DCNN) [23,24] by focusing on their powerful performance. A number of trackers using neural networks have been proposed such as human tracking, hand tracking, etc. [25–28]. Representative tracker using a neural network is a Fully Convolutional Network based Tracker (FCNT) [29] which also utilizes FCN. This method utilizes multi-level feature maps of a VGG network [30] to complement drastic appearance variation and distinguish a target object from its similar distracters. It selects discriminative feature maps and discards noisy ones, because the CNN features pretrained on ImageNet [23] are for distinguishing generic objects. Even though FCNT achieved a high accuracy compared to conventional trackers, initialization and templates are necessary to track a target object.

Table 1 shows the comparison of characteristics between the proposed method and FCNT. The main difference between the proposed method and FCNT is whether initialization and templates of a target object are necessary or not. Namely, FCNT can track only a specific target object with defined initial position and template. In contrast, it is possible to use the proposed method without them. The other difference is that FCNT uses a greedy tracking algorithm whereas the proposed method utilizes DP for globally optimal tracking. In Sect. 4.3, we will prove experimentally that the proposed method has superiority over FCNT.

3   The Proposed Method

3.1   Likelihood Maps by Single Shot Multibox Detector and Fully Convolutional Network

Figure 1 shows the pipeline of how to obtain a likelihood map from input image. In the proposed method, SSD and FCN are used for obtaining likelihood maps, each of which shows a two-dimensional probability distribution of a target object

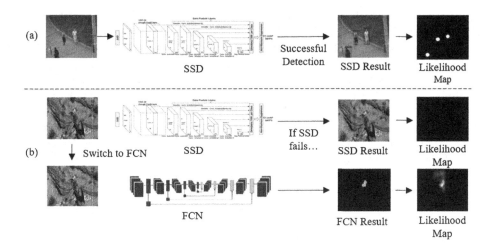

Fig. 1. Pipeline to generate a likelihood map from an input image: (a) shows the pipeline to generate a likelihood map by SSD. The likelihood map by SSD provides accurate probability values and positions of target objects when the targets are rather easy for detection. When SSD fails to detect the target, we switch to FCN and employ the likelihood map by FCN, as shown in (b). The likelihood map by FCN might include noisy probability values, compared to it by SSD.

position at a certain frame. A peak in a likelihood map at frame t suggests a candidate position of the target object at t. We will switch two likelihood maps according to the situation as shown in Fig. 1. This is because SSD and FCN shows different behaviors especially when object candidate detection is difficult, as follows.

SSD is based on VGG-16 network which includes 13 convolution layers and 3 pooling layers. It possesses supplementary two characteristics: convolutional predictors and multi-scale feature maps. The convolutional predictors generate a probability value for the presence of each object category in each default box and produce adjustments to the box to match the object shape. Additionally, the network combines predictions from multi-scale feature maps with different resolutions to handle objects of various sizes. We generate a likelihood map by setting a probability value, on the center position of resulting bounding box. Thus, likelihood maps obtained by SSD contain a very accurate probability value. However, when SSD fails to detect a target object, likelihood maps can not be obtained.

FCN is composed entirely of convolutional layers based on VGG-16 and trained end-to-end, pixels-to-pixels, for classification and segmentation. It takes input of arbitrary size and produces a correspondingly-sized likelihood map by up and down sampled pooling layers. The likelihood map by FCN might include noisy probability values by up and down sampled pooling layers. To obtain accurate positive response of a target object, links between the low-level fine layers and the high-level coarse layers are constructed. These are so called *skip connections* which combines information from fine layers and course layers. Even if we can obtain a more accurate likelihood map by *skip connections*, a likelihood map obtained by FCN still includes noisy probability values, compared to SSD.

Using both SSD and FCN to obtain a likelihood map increases the tracking accuracy. Although SSD is a detection method with high accuracy, it might not detect the target object in unstable situations such as occlusion, blurriness, and deformation, as shown in (b) of Fig. 1. If SSD fails to detect, we switch to FCN and obtain likelihood maps by FCN. The success and failure criteria of detection by SSD is whether the detected position exists within N pixels from the highest value position of the previous frame or not. FCN provides likelihood maps for all input images, regardless of unstable situation, even if they might include noisy probability values. Note that, as discussed later, even when both SSD and FCN cannot obtain likelihood values (e.g. when an object that has been tracked leaves the scene), DP complements the tracking path.

The other merit of using SSD and FCN is their computational efficiency. A naive method to obtain likelihood maps is to apply a CNN to a sliding window region of an input image. Using this method requires many forward calculations and can not deal with a target object of various sizes, because it accepts a fixed region size as input. However, both SSD and FCN accept the entire image and only require a single forward calculation with handling various sizes.

3.2 Global Path Optimization by Dynamic Programming

To apply DP to our method, we start by creating likelihood maps of each of the frames using SSD or FCN. Figure 2 shows the procedure to obtain the most optimal tracking path by DP. For each pixel on a likelihood map, we find the highest value within a given slope constraint of the previous frame which prohibits from

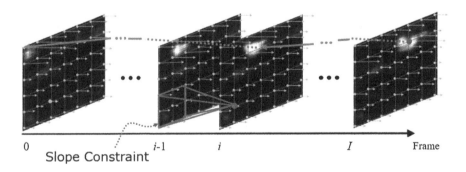

Fig. 2. The tracking path optimization in the proposed method: each frame is a likelihood map calculated by SSD or FCN and the green arrow suggests a probability value of a target object at each position. The blue rectangle is a slope constraint to restrict movement and the red plot is the position where the sum of probability values over the associated path is highest at the final frame. The orange arrows mean the most globally optimal tracking path obtained by back-tracking. (Color figure online)

moving steeply and create cumulative DP maps. This process is continued by iterating over all of the frames. Cumulative DP map $D^{(f)}$ is defined as:

$$D^{(f)}(x,y) = \max_{x-w_s \leq x \leq x+w_s, y-h_s \leq y \leq y+h_s} [D^{(f-1)}(x,y)] + L^{(f)}(x,y) \qquad (1)$$

where likelihood map is $L^{(f)}$, f is the number of frame and size of slope constraint is denoted as (w_s, h_s). We select the highest probability value on the final cumulative DP map. After that, DP searches for the most optimal tracking path by back-tracking along the highest probability value on each previous likelihood map. DP is a non-greedy algorithm to estimate the global optimal path in a sequence. Due to this, DP-based tracking is robust to occlusion, which degrades a tracking performance of greedy algorithms.

3.3 Synergies by Combining SSD, FCN, and DP

We propose combination of SSD, FCN, and DP as a robust object tracking method. The proposed method has not only advantage of robustness to appearance variation and occlusion, but also does not need to set a template, change initialization, or change parameters, even when appearance of a target object changes.

The proposed method does not need a template for object tracking. For traditional trackers, a template is necessary and needs to be updated when a target object changes. However, for the proposed method, it is unnecessary, under the condition that a category of a target object is trained sufficiently. Since, the proposed method can deal with appearance variation by learning numerous features of a target object, it also does not need to modify parameters even if appearance of a target object is changed. For traditional trackers, identifying the position of a target object on the first frame is important element to track. However, the proposed method can obtain the most globally optimal tracking path by back-tracking over all cumulative DP maps without any identifying the position.

4   Implementation and Experiments

4.1 Experimental Setup

We used the VOC2012 [31] dataset to train SSD and FCN on 20 categories. The training dataset has 11,530 images containing 27,450 ROI annotated objects and 6,929 segmentations. The categories are as follows: *person, bird, cat, cow, dog, horse, sheep, airplane, bicycle, boat, bus, car, motorbike, train, bottle, chair, dining table, potted plant, sofa and tv/monitor.*

To demonstrate that the proposed method can track a target object with a high accuracy, we evaluated the proposed method using sequences that have a target object in one of the 20 categories of VOC2012. Since the proposed method can detect only trained objects on the 20 categories, we selected 12 sequences for our experiments: *CarScale, Coke, Couple, Crossing, David3, Jogging1&2, MotorRolling, MountainBike, Walking1&2, Woman*. It is noteworthy that those sequences show various difficulties, such as illumination variation, scale variation, occlusion, fast motion, rotation, and low resolution.

The sequences were classified into two types, single-object sequences[1] and multi-object sequences[2]. Since the proposed method is designed to track a single object without initialization, single-object sequences are appropriate for performance evaluation. The proposed method, however, is still applicable to multi-object sequences by initialization. We therefore conducted two separated experiments, single-object sequences (without initialization) and multi-object sequences (with initialization). Moreover, we conducted two extra experiments. One is to compare the results using a likelihood map by both SSD and FCN, single SSD and single FCN. In th, we set N as 10, which is pixel number of the success and failure criteria to switch from SSD to FCN. The other is the comparison experiment between the proposed method and FCNT [29] which is a tracker using FCN, to demonstrate superiority of the proposed method than FCNT.

4.2   Evaluation Criterion

We evaluated the proposed method by comparing the precision which is established method in the Visual Tracker Benchmark [11]. The precision is defined as the percentage of frames whose estimated position is within a given threshold from a ground-truth. The distance between the estimated position and the manually labeled ground-truth is calculated by Euclidean distance. To show a performance efficiently, we conducted one-pass evaluation (OPE) that trackers run throughout a test sequence only one time and compare the precision of each of trackers.

4.3   Evaluation Results

Tracking methods can be divided into offline tracking such as the proposed method and online tracking. However, we compared the proposed method to online tracking methods in order to show the performance, because there is no comparable offline tracking methods which are released. We compared the proposed method to the top five traditional trackers introduced in the Visual Tracker Benchmark: Structured Output Tracking with Kernels (Struck) [32], a sparsity-based tracker (SCM) [33], P-N Learning tracker (TLD) [34], Context tracker (CXT) [35] and Visual Tracking Decomposition (VTD) [36].

Figure 3 shows all precision results including the proposed method without initialization and the traditional trackers with initialization. The score listed

---

[1] Single-object sequences contain *CarScale, Coke, Couple, Crossing, David3, Motor-Rolling, MountainBike, Walking1&2, Woman*.

[2] Multi-object sequences contain *CarScale, Coke, Couple, Crossing, David3, Jogging1&2, MotorRolling, MountainBike, Walking1&2, Woman*.

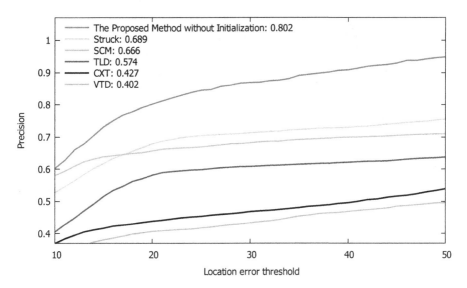

Fig. 3. Precision results for single-object sequences: We compared results of the proposed method without initialization and those of the traditional trackers with that by using single-object sequences. The precision is defined as the percentage of frames whose estimated position is within location error threshold. The permissible threshold distance is denoted as location error threshold. The score listed in the legend means the precision score at a threshold of 20 pixels. The proposed method possesses the higher performance for all thresholds and has no large deviation from ground-truth.

in the legend of Fig. 3 is the precision at a threshold of 20 pixels, since a 20 pixel threshold is the standard threshold for the Visual Tracker Benchmark. As shown in Fig. 3, we confirmed that the proposed method outperforms than the traditional trackers, even though the proposed method is not given the initial position of the object on the first frame. Since DP sets a slope constraint to prohibit tracked position from moving rapidly, the proposed method can track a target object with small deviation.

As we mentioned in Sect. 4.1, the proposed method is applicable to multi-object sequences by identifying a initial position of a target object. Figure 4 shows all results with initialization. For all thresholds, the proposed method possesses a higher performance compared to the traditional trackers. Through these results, when multi-objects even exist on the same frame, the proposed method can track a target object distinguishably by initialization. By comparing the results of Figs. 3 and 4, we also confirm that the precision of the proposed method with initialization is more accurate than that without initialization.

Figure 5 shows the precision results using likelihood maps by both SSD and FCN, a single SSD, and a single FCN, respectively, without initialization. The proposed method which utilizes both SSD and FCN has a higher performance than the others at a threshold of 20 pixels. Since the method using single SSD can not generate likelihood maps for all input images, the results by single SSD

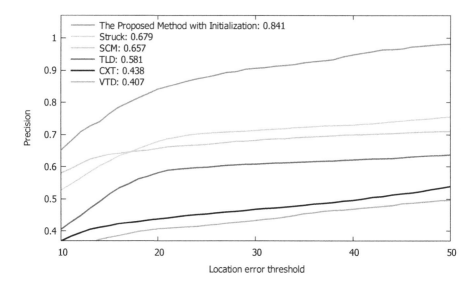

Fig. 4. Precision results for multi-object sequences: we summarized the all results with initialization by using multi-object sequences. The precision is defined as the percentage of frames whose estimated position is within location error threshold. The permissible threshold distance is denoted as location error threshold. The score listed in the legend means the precision score at a threshold of 20 pixels.

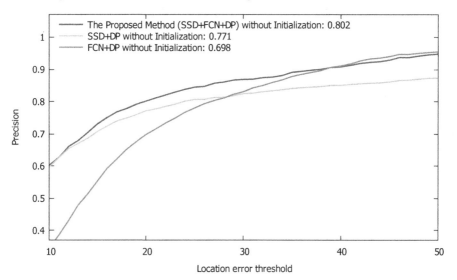

Fig. 5. Precision results according to how to generate a likelihood map: we compared the results using likelihood maps by both SSD and FCN, single SSD, and single FCN, without initialization. The precision is defined as the percentage of frames whose estimated position is within location error threshold. The permissible threshold distance is denoted as location error threshold. The score listed in the legend means the precision score at a threshold of 20 pixels. The proposed method which is using likelihood maps by both SSD and FCN, possesses a higher performance than the others.

Traditional trackers   The proposed method

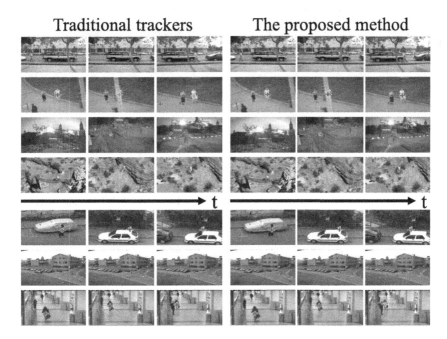

Fig. 6. Example results of the proposed method dealing with appearance variation and occlusion: the center of green and red '+' mean the ground-truth and the tracked position, respectively. Examples of left side are results of the top five traditional trackers introduced in the Visual Tracker Benchmark. Examples of right side are results of the proposed method. (Color figure online)

are worse than those by the proposed method. As shown in Fig. 5, the precision by single FCN ascends rapidly for low thresholds. When a target object is large enough, the method using single FCN might track the position which is far from the center position of a target object, because FCN does not always obtain the highest probability value which is close to center position of a target object. Due to this, the precision by single FCN is lower than the others for low thresholds.

Figure 6 shows examples of the proposed method dealing with appearance variation and occlusion. As shown in Fig. 6, although there are various target objects of same category in each sequence, the proposed method can track each target object without template and parameter modification. Also, we confirmed that the proposed method can track a occluded target object more stably, in contrast to the top five traditional trackers, because DP seeks the global optimal path over all frames. However, when target objects of same category appear with occlusion, such as the final sequence in Fig. 6, the proposed method does not know which object should track. Since the proposed method utilizes general features of same category during object tracking, we should add to specific features of a target object, when it tracks distinguishably.

We also observed the performance of FCNT [29] using the same sequences. It could achieve 0.951 and 0.945 precision for single-object and multi-object

FCNT   The proposed method

Fig. 7. Example results of FCNT and the proposed method to track the occluded target object.

sequences, respectively, at threshold of 20 pixels. It is, however, almost meaningless to compare this precision to ours. First of all, we should remember that FCNT needs a template and ours does not. In addition, FCNT needs initialization and ours does not. In fact, we can see that the proposed method without initialization has no severe degradation from comparison between Figs. 3 and 4. Furthermore, our DP-based method has theoretical superiority over FCNT at the robustness to occlusion, as shown in Fig. 7.

5   Conclusion

In this paper, we presented the object tracking method which combines SSD, FCN and DP. We confirmed that the proposed method is robust to appearance variation and occlusion through several experiments and achieved the highest accuracy compared to the traditional trackers in the Visual Tracker Benchmark. In contrast to traditional trackers, the proposed method can track the target object without initialization, modifying parameters, and templates as it synergizes the combination of SSD, FCN, and DP. However, the proposed method can be extended to tracking with multiple similar objects by using initialization. We confirmed that using both SSD and FCN is more stable to tracking than single SSD and single FCN as well.

We expect to use the proposed method in analysis field such as traffic analysis, bio-image analysis, etc. In future, we will connect SSD, FCN with network flows [37] to track multi-target objects simultaneously. To increase the tracking accuracy in situation when similar objects of same category appear with occlusion such as the last sequence in Fig. 6, we will apply Flownet [38], in order to utilize information of optical flow.

References

1. Lewis, J.P.: Fast template matching. In: Vision Interface vol. 95, no. 120123, pp. 15–19 (1995)
2. Okuma, K., Taleghani, A., de Freitas, N., Little, J.J., Lowe, D.G.: A boosted particle filter: multitarget detection and tracking. In: Pajdla, T., Matas, J. (eds.) ECCV 2004. LNCS, vol. 3021, pp. 28–39. Springer, Heidelberg (2004). https://doi.org/10.1007/978-3-540-24670-1_3

3. Comaniciu, D., Ramesh, V., Meer, P.: Real-time tracking of non-rigid objects using mean shift. Comput. Vis. Pattern Recogn. **2**, 142–149 (2000)
4. Zach, C., Gallup, D., Frahm, J.-M.: Fast gain-adaptive KLT tracking on the GPU. In: Computer Vision and Pattern Recognition, pp. 1–7 (2008)
5. He, W., Yamashita, T., Lu, H., Lao, S.: Surf tracking. In: IEEE 12th International Conference on Computer Vision, pp. 1586–1592 (2009)
6. Liu, W., Anguelov, D., Erhan, D., Szegedy, C., Reed, S., Fu, C.-Y., Berg, A.C.: SSD: single shot multibox detector. In: Leibe, B., Matas, J., Sebe, N., Welling, M. (eds.) ECCV 2016. LNCS, vol. 9905, pp. 21–37. Springer, Cham (2016). https://doi.org/10.1007/978-3-319-46448-0_2
7. Long, J., Shelhamer, E., Darrell, T.: Fully convolutional networks for semantic segmentation. In: Proceedings of IEEE Conference on Computer Vision and Pattern Recognition, pp. 3431–3440 (2015)
8. Uchida, S., Sakoe, H.: A monotonic and continuous two-dimensional warping based on dynamic programming. In: International Conference on Pattern Recognition, vol. 1, pp. 521–524 (1998)
9. Geiger, D., Gupta, A., Costa, L.A., Vlontzos, J.: Dynamic programming for detecting, tracking, and matching deformable contours. IEEE Trans. Pattern Anal. Mach. Intell. **17**(3), 294–302 (1995)
10. Arnold, J., Shaw, S.W., Pasternack, H.: Efficient target tracking using dynamic programming. IEEE Trans. Aerosp. Electron. Syst. **29**(1), 44–56 (1993)
11. Wu, Y., Lim, J., Yang, M.-H.: Online object tracking: a benchmark. In: Proceedings of IEEE Conference on Computer Vision and Pattern Recognition, pp. 2411–2418 (2013)
12. Mei, X., Ling, H.: Robust visual tracking using $l1$ minimization. In: IEEE 12th International Conference on Computer Vision, pp. 1436–1443 (2009)
13. Zhang, T., Ghanem, B., Liu, S., Ahuja, N.: Robust visual tracking via multi-task sparse learning. In: Computer Vision and Pattern Recognition (CVPR), pp. 2042–2049 (2012)
14. Han, B., Comaniciu, D., Zhu, Y., Davis, L.S.: Sequential kernel density approximation and its application to real-time visual tracking. IEEE Trans. Pattern Anal. Mach. Intell. **30**(7), 1186–1197 (2008)
15. Jepson, A.D., Fleet, D.J., El-Maraghi, T.F.: Robust online appearance models for visual tracking. IEEE Trans. Pattern Anal. Mach. Intell. **25**(10), 1296–1311 (2003)
16. Ross, D.A., Lim, J., Lin, R.-S., Yang, M.-H.: Incremental learning for robust visual tracking. Int. J. Comput. Vis. **77**(1), 125–141 (2008)
17. Kalal, Z., Mikolajczyk, K., Matas, J.: Tracking-learning detection. IEEE Trans. Pattern Anal. Mach. Intell. **34**(7), 1409–1422 (2012)
18. Grabner, H., Grabner, M., Bischof, H.: Real-time tracking via on-line boosting. In: BMVC, vol. 1, no. 5, p. 6 (2006)
19. Grabner, H., Leistner, C., Bischof, H.: Semi-supervised on-line boosting for robust tracking. In: Forsyth, D., Torr, P., Zisserman, A. (eds.) ECCV 2008. LNCS, vol. 5302, pp. 234–247. Springer, Heidelberg (2008). https://doi.org/10.1007/978-3-540-88682-2_19
20. Son, J., Jung, I., Park, K., Han, B.: Tracking-by segmentation with online gradient boosting decision tree. In: Proceedings of IEEE International Conference on Computer Vision, pp. 3056–3064 (2015)
21. Lawrence, S., Giles, C.L., Tsoi, A.C., Back, A.D.: Face recognition: a convolutional neural-network approach. IEEE Trans. Neural Netw. **8**(1), 98–113 (1997)

22. Ciresan, D.C., Meier, U., Gambardella, L.M., Schmidhuber, J.: Convolutional neural network committees for handwritten character classification. In: Document Analysis and Recognition (ICDAR), pp. 1135–1139 (2011)
23. Krizhevsky, A., Sutskever, I., Hinton, G.E.: ImageNet classification with deep convolutional neural networks. In: Advances in Neural Information Processing Systems, pp. 1097–1105 (2012)
24. Sainath, T.N., Mohamed, A.-R., Kingsbury, B., Ramabhadran, B.: Deep convolutional neural networks for LVCSR. In: Acoustics, Speech and Signal Processing (ICASSP), pp. 8614–8618 (2013)
25. Fan, J., Xu, W., Wu, Y., Gong, Y.: Human tracking using convolutional neural networks. IEEE Trans. Neural Netw. **21**(10), 1610–1623 (2010)
26. Maung, T.H.H.: Real-time hand tracking and gesture recognition system using neural networks. World Acad. Sci. Eng. Technol. **50**, 466–470 (2009)
27. Torricelli, D., Conforto, S., Schmid, M., D'Alessio, T.: A neural-based remote eye gaze tracker under natural head motion. Comput. Methods Prog. Biomed. **92**(1), 66–78 (2008)
28. Li, H., Li, Y., Porikli, F.: Robust online visual tracking with a single convolutional neural network. In: Asian Conference on Computer Vision, pp. 194–209 (2014)
29. Wang, L., Ouyang, W., Wang, X., Lu, H.: Visual tracking with fully convolutional networks. In: Proceedings of IEEE International Conference on Computer Vision, pp. 3119–3127 (2015)
30. Simonyan, K., Zisserman, A.: Very deep convolutional networks for large-scale image recognition. CoRR, abs/1409.1556 (2014)
31. Everingham, M., Eslami, S.M.A., Van Gool, L., Williams, C.K.I., Winn, J., Zisserman, A.: The Pascal visual object classes challenge: a retrospective. Int. J. Comput. Vis. **111**(1), 98–136 (2015)
32. Hare, S., Golodetz, S., Saffari, A., Vineet, V., Cheng, M.-M., Hicks, S.L., Torr, P.H.S.: Structured output tracking with kernels. IEEE Trans. Pattern Anal. Mach. Intell. **38**(10), 2096–2109 (2016)
33. Zhong, W., Lu, H., Yang, M.-H.: Robust object tracking via sparsity-based collaborative model. In: Proceedings of IEEE Conference on Computer Vision and Pattern Recognition, pp. 1838–1845 (2012)
34. Kalal, Z., Matas, J., Mikolajczyk, K.: P-N learning: bootstrapping binary classifiers by structural constraints. In: Proceedings of IEEE Conference on Computer Vision and Pattern Recognition, pp. 49–56 (2010)
35. Dinh, T.B., Vo, N., Medioni, G.: Context tracker: exploring supporters and distracters in unconstrained environments. In: Proceedings of IEEE Conference on Computer Vision and Pattern Recognition, pp. 1177–1184 (2011)
36. Kwon, J., Lee, K.M.: Visual tracking decomposition. In: Computer Vision and Pattern Recognition (CVPR), pp. 1269–1276 (2010)
37. Zhang, L., Li, Y., Nevatia, R.: Global data association for multi-object tracking using network flows. In: Computer Vision and Pattern Recognition, pp. 1–8 (2008)
38. Dosovitskiy, A., Fischer, P., Ilg, E., Hausser, P., Hazirbas, C., Golkov, V., van der Smagt, P., Cremers, D., Brox, T.: FlowNet: learning optical flow with convolutional networks. In: IEEE International Conference on Computer Vision, pp. 2758–2766 (2015)

Single Image Dehazing via Image Generating

Shengdong Zhang[1], Jian Yao[1(✉)], and Edel B. Garcia[2]

[1] School of Remote Sensing and Information Engineering,
Wuhan University, Wuhan, China
jian.yao@whu.edu.cn
[2] Advanced Technology Applications Center, Havana, Cuba
http://cvrs.whu.edu.cn/

Abstract. Outdoor images taken in bad weather conditions often suffer from poor visibility. However, single image haze removal is an ill-posed problem, because the number of the equations is smaller than the number of unknowns. In this paper, a deep learning-based method, called Dehaze CNN, is proposed to estimate a clear image patch from a hazy image patch, which can be used to reconstruct a haze-free image. Our method recovers a clear image by a learning model containing no hazy information. Our method also adopts Deep Convolution Neural Networks which takes the patch atom that can be used to generate hazy image patches and haze-free ones as the input and outputs the corresponding haze-free patch. Then we reconstruct a haze-free image from those patches. Finally, we remove the color distortion in the haze-free image via contextual regularization effectively. Experimental results show that the proposed method outperforms the state-of-the-art haze removal methods.

Keywords: Haze removal · Image restoration
Deep Convolution Neural Networks

1 Introduction

Outdoor scene images are often degraded because of the bad weather conditions, such as air particles, fog, haze and smoke, which reduce the visibility and quality of the images. The light received by the camera from an object in the distance is weakened along the line of sight. In addition, the receiving light is blended with the atmospheric light-the environment light reflected into the line of sight by air particles. The degraded images show low contrast and quality.

Haze removing or defogging is urgently needed in computer vision applications and commercial/computational photography due to its wide applications. However removing fog is a challenging problem due to that the fog is decided by the unknown depth information. This problem is ill-posed, because a single input image only provides three equations for a pixel, but there exists four unknown quantities. Therefore, a lot of methods have been proposed by using additional

© Springer International Publishing AG, part of Springer Nature 2018
M. Paul et al. (Eds.): PSIVT 2017, LNCS 10749, pp. 123–136, 2018.
https://doi.org/10.1007/978-3-319-75786-5_11

data or multiple images [1–3]. Tan and Oakley [1] removed the fog effect by taking multiple images of the same scene under the condition the depth of the scene is given. Schechner et al. [2] removed the haze by taking two or more images with different degrees of polarization. Kopf et al. [3] proposed a depth based method which requires user to input depth data or a 3D model of the scene. Further more, removing haze from single image is a more difficult case. But significant progress was made for single image haze removal in recent years. The series of methods rely on using stronger assumptions or priors. All these methods can be divided into two kind categories. The first is contrast-based, the second is statistical approaches. Fattal [4] proposed to remove haze from single image by explaining the image through a model that accounts for surface shading and the scene transmission. By assuming that the surface shading and medium transmission functions to be locally statistically uncorrelated, they solved the problem of a constant albedo and the airlight-albedo ambiguity, and recovered a haze free image. This method is physically sound and can generate a high quality results. However, it cannot deal with heavily hazy images very well and may lose efficacy in the cases of the assumption is false. He et al. [5] proposed a simple but effective method to remove the haze, which is based on the statistical observation of the dark channel, which is called dark channel prior and can be used to get a rough transmission map. In order to refine the transmission map, a time consuming matting was used to solve the unknown transmission region. He et al.'s results is high quality, but the time is very long, and maybe fail for some particular images. The first case is that the scene objects are similar to the air light and there no exists shadow in the image. The second case is that the image is physical invalid. Kratz and Nishino [6] found that scene albedo and depth have a natural ambiguity. They used novel probabilistic method (Factorial Markov Fandom Field) to solve this ambiguity, and treated the scene albedo and depth as independent latent layers. By using natural image and depth statistics as priors they could get a haze free image. Nishino et al. [7] introduced a novel Bayesian probabilistic method that jointly estimated the scene albedo and depth from a single foggy image by fully leveraging their latent statistical structures. Gibson and Nguyen [8] proposed a new dark channel prior for removing haze from the image. Unlike the dark-channel prior that assumes zero minimal value, the new prior searches for the darkest pixel average inside of each ellipsoid. Fattal [9] proposed to remove haze by using color-lines in natural images where pixels of small image patches typically show a one-dimensional distribution in RGB color space. He derived a local formation model that illustrates the color-lines in the context of hazy scenes and use it for solving the scene transmission. In contrast, by observing the haze free image and hazy image, Tan [10] found that the haze free images have higher contrast, so he removed haze from image by maximizing the local contrast of the result image and keeping the image smooth. The results are impressive but may not be physically sound. Tarel and Hautiere also proposed a contrast-based method in [11], and this method is computationally effective but it also has an assumption the transmission must be smooth except alone the edges regions with gradient jumps.

More recently, some learning based methods [12–15] had been proposed to remove haze from single image effectively. In [13], Tang et al. investigated the different haze-relevant feature of hazy image, and used best suitable feature combination to estimate a transmission map for a hazy image. In [12], Zhu et al. proposed a learning based method which considers the transmission as a linear combination of the saturation and brightness of pixels in a hazy image. They used a learning strategy to get the parameters of the model. The most related to our work is Cai et al.'s [14] and Ren et al.'s [15], which are also a deep learning-based method for estimating of transmission map. In [15], Ren et al. proposed a multi-scale deep convolutional neural networks to remove haze from single image. In contrast, our method estimates a haze-free image from hazy image directly. Compared with other learning-based methods, our network is much simpler and generates high quality results. Regarding the training data, Cai et al.'s method uniformly samples 10 random transmissions $t \in (0, 1)$ to generate 10 hazy patches for a clear image patch [14]. In contrast, our method simplifies the training data collection. By finding the common image atoms shared by hazy image patch and clear image patch, our method can generate one pair of image patch atom and clear image patch for a clear image patch.

The contribution of this paper is three-fold. First, we propose a deep convolutional neural networks to learn effective features from image patch atoms shared by hazy image patch and haze-free image patch for the estimation of an approximate clear image patch. Our goal is to estimate a clear image patch for image patch atom, which can provide a way to estimate a clear image directly from hazy image. Second, our work is the first to explore the relation between the hazy image patch and clear image patch. As shown in Sect. 2, we can see that a clear image patch will share a same image patch atom with hazy image patch, which can help us to train a network without hazy information to remove haze from the single image. Third, we can use the image patch atom by hazy image patch and haze-free image patch to simplify the preparation of the train data, we only need to consider the clear image and A, which also reduce the number of training data.

2   Image Patch Atom Generation

In this section, our goal is to find a image patch atom which can be used to generate hazy image patch and haze-free image patch.

2.1   Modeling of Hazy Images

Our model used in this paper is very similar to [16], which is widely used in computer graphics and computer vision, which also explains the formulation of the haze as follows:

$$\mathbf{I}(i,j) = J(i,j) \times t(i,j) + (1 - t(i,j)) \times A, \tag{1}$$

where $\mathbf{I}$ represents the hazy image, J represents the haze free image, A stands for the global atmospheric light, and t denotes the transmission describing the *probability* of the light that is not scattered and absorbed by air particle or mist and arrives at the camera. To remove haze from the hazy image is equal to solve the A and t from $\mathbf{I}$. The first term is called as direct attenuation and the second term is called as air light A contributions.

2.2 Proofing

Based on Eq. (1), we can derive the following equation:

$$\mathbf{I}(i,j) - A = (J(i,j) - A) \times t(i,j). \tag{2}$$

Generally, we can assume that pixels in a small image patch will share a same transmission, which is use widely in single image dehazing [5,9,17,18]. Based on this assumption, we assume that the transmission in a local patch is constant. We use $\tilde{t}(\mathbf{x})$ represents this transmission where $\mathbf{x}$ stands for (i,j). Then we use $(IA_1, \ldots, IA_n)$ and $(JA_1, \ldots, JA_n)$ to represent $\mathbf{I}(\mathbf{x}) - A$ and $J(\mathbf{x}) - A$, respectively.

We can normalize the hazy model in Eq. (1) as:

$$N(\mathbf{I}(\mathbf{x}) - A) = N((J(\mathbf{x}) - A) \times \tilde{t}(\mathbf{x})) = \frac{(J(\mathbf{x}) - A) \times t(\mathbf{x})}{\sqrt{\sum_{k=1}^{n}(JA_k \times \tilde{t}(\mathbf{x}))^2}}$$

$$= \frac{(J(\mathbf{x}) - A) \times t(\mathbf{x})}{\sqrt{\sum_{k=1}^{n} JA_k^2} \times \tilde{t}(\mathbf{x})} = \left(\frac{JA_1}{\sum_{k=1}^{n} JA_k^2}, \ldots, \frac{JA_n}{\sum_{k=1}^{n} JA_k^2} \right) = N(J(\mathbf{x}) - A). \tag{3}$$

According to the above equation, we can see that through a simple operation, a hazy image patch can be transferred to an image patch which can be used to generate the haze-free image patch. To the best of our knowledge, our work is the first study designed to explore the relation between the hazy image patch and the haze-free image patch. Because the hazy image patch and the haze-free image patch share same image patch atom, we can use the image patch atom to identify the haze-free image patch, the relation between image patch atom and the clear image patch can be learned via deep learning.

2.3 Validation

In this section, we conducted some experiments to validate our theory. In order to show the result visually, we chose to apply absolution and scale operation to common features. We chose to use 1000×1000 patch size for showing the result, which is not correct for dehazing. In our dehazing program we used the patch size 16×16, which is based on the assumption that pixels share same transmission value in a local image patch. In Fig. 1 we can see that our feature is determined by the A and the haze-free image patch, and one haze-free image patch will get the same image patch atom for all hazy image patches with the same A.

In this part, we also study the influence of A. In Fig. 2, we show the influence of A, and we can see the different values of A have different image patch atoms, and find that $A = (160, 160, 160)$ and $A = (200, 200, 200)$ have some similarity in the image patch atom.

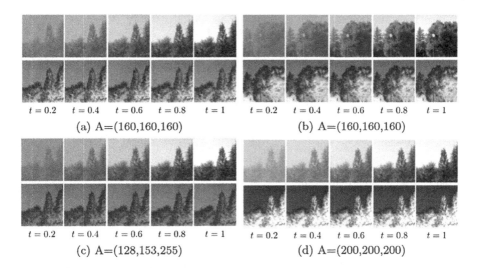

$t = 0.2$ $t = 0.4$ $t = 0.6$ $t = 0.8$ $t = 1$ $t = 0.2$ $t = 0.4$ $t = 0.6$ $t = 0.8$ $t = 1$

(a) A=(160,160,160)   (b) A=(160,160,160)

$t = 0.2$ $t = 0.4$ $t = 0.6$ $t = 0.8$ $t = 1$ $t = 0.2$ $t = 0.4$ $t = 0.6$ $t = 0.8$ $t = 1$

(c) A=(128,153,255)   (d) A=(200,200,200)

Fig. 1. The hazy image patches and their corresponding image patch atoms with different transmission and the global atmospheric lights.

(a)   (b)   (c)

Fig. 2. Comparison on the influence of A: (a) $A = (160, 160, 160)$; (b) $A = (128, 153, 255)$; (c) $A = (200, 200, 200)$.

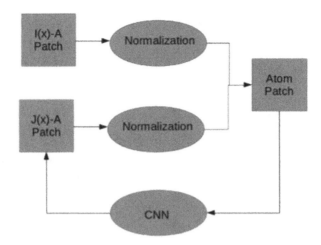

Fig. 3. The relation between the hazy image patch, the haze-free image patch and the corresponding image patch atom.

2.4   Motivation

Our patch image atom is inspired by the sparse coding, which uses dictionary to represent an image. In this paper, we use patch image atom to reconstruct a haze-free image. Sparse coding uses a linear combination of atoms to reconstruct an image. Different from traditional sparse coding, we use only one atom to reconstruct $J(\mathbf{x}) - A$. Our method learned a relation between the atom and haze-free image patch, we use this relation to reconstruct a haze-free image. In Fig. 3, we show the relation between the image hazy patch, image haze-free patch and image patch atom, and we can use the image patch atom to reconstruct the haze-free image patch.

3   Haze Removal

In this section, we describe our method how to use the image patch atom to remove haze from a single image. Our method consists of four essential steps: normalizing the hazy image, extracting patches from hazy image, estimating approximate clear image patches using Deep Convolution Neural Networks, removing color distortion and block artifacts (see Algorithm 1).

(1) Patch Extraction and Normalization: We estimate A using one of the previous methods [5,17] and define $\mathbf{I}_A$ as:

$$\mathbf{I}_A(\mathbf{x}) = \mathbf{I}(\mathbf{x}) - \mathbf{A}. \tag{4}$$

$$\mathbf{I}_A(\mathbf{x}) = ||\mathbf{I}_A(\mathbf{x})||. \tag{5}$$

In order to use the image patch atom described in Sect. 2, we need to extract patches from $\mathbf{I}_A$, and then normalize these patches. In our method, we set the

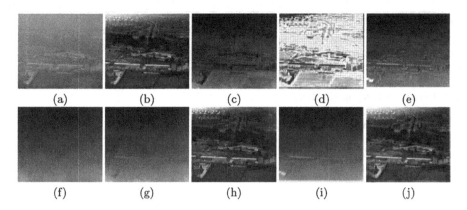

Fig. 4. Intermediate and final results of our method: (a) an input hazy image; (b) the output image; (c) the distance $r(\mathbf{x})$ of every pixel of the hazy image to the airlight; (d) the estimate distance $\tilde{r}(\mathbf{x})$; (e) the initial $\tilde{t}(\mathbf{x})$; (f) the final $t(\mathbf{x})$; (g) the guided filter output; (h) the dehazed result using transmission (g); (i) the contextual regularization output without guided filter; (j) the dehazed result using transmission (i).

patch size as 16×16 and the patches are non-overlapped. Then we normalize the patches, which will convert a hazy image patch into an image patch atom shared by the haze-free image patch and the hazy image patch.

(2) Estimating Initial Clear Patches: Based on the fact that weights sharing allows for relatively larger interactive range than other fully connected structures, we choose convolutional neural network (CNN) architecture. Our CNN architecture is very simple, which can be implemented easily. Our convolutional network architecture can be expressed as:

$$F^0(Y) = Y, \tag{6}$$

$$F^n(Y) = \max(W^n * F^{(n-1)}(Y) + B^n, 0), n = 1, 2, \tag{7}$$

$$F_W(Y) = W^n * F^{(n-1)}(Y) + B^n, n = 3, \tag{8}$$

where n represents the layers, which ranges from 1 to 3. Our convolutional network architecture consists of five layers and contains four hidden layers for convolution generation. For the bottom layer with index 0, which is the input layer and expressed by Eq. (6). In each intermediate layer, which is expressed by Eq. (7), represents a convolution process for the nodes in the convolution network regarding its neighbors. By convention, $*$ represents the convolution operation, W^n represents the convolution kernel and B^n is the bias. The top layer with $F_W(I)$ in Eq. (8) generates the initial clear patches from the network. Then we can get the initial clear image.

(3) Removing Color Distortion and Block Artifacts: Our estimated result may shift from the line formed by $\mathbf{I}(\mathbf{x})$ and $\mathbf{A}$. In order to recover a high quality result, we need to apply a regularization operation. Because we recover $\mathbf{J}(\mathbf{x}) - \mathbf{A}$ from the image patch atom, we can use this information and

---

Algorithm 1. Our proposed single image dehazing framework.

Input: The hazy image.

Output: The haze free image.

 1: Compute the atmospheric light A using Meng et al.'s method.

 2: $\mathbf{I}_A(\mathbf{x}) = \mathbf{I}(\mathbf{x}) - A$.

 3: Compute $r(\mathbf{x})$ using Eq. (10).

 4: Extract patches with the size 16×16 from $\mathbf{I}_A(\mathbf{x})$, normalizing each patch.

 5: Compute $\tilde{r}(\mathbf{x})$ using deep convolutional network.

 6: Compute transmission: $\tilde{t} = r(\mathbf{x})/r_J(\mathbf{x})$.

 7: Smooth transmission $\tilde{t}$ using guided filter.

 8: Get the final dehazing result using Eq. (11).

$\mathbf{I}_A(\mathbf{x})$ to recover the initial transmission of each pixel. Geometrically the hazy model 1 implies that in the RGB color space, the vector $\mathbf{I}(\mathbf{x})$, $\mathbf{J}(\mathbf{x})$, $\mathbf{A}$ is coplanar and the end points form a line. The transmission is the ratio of the two line segments [5]:

$$\tilde{t} = r(\mathbf{x})/\tilde{r}(\mathbf{x}), \tag{9}$$

where $r(\mathbf{x})$ represents the distance in the RGB space of every pixel in the hazy image to the airlight, and $\tilde{r}(\mathbf{x})$ represents the distance in the RGB space of our estimated clear pixel to the airlight. We define $r_J(\mathbf{x})$ as follows:

$$r_J(\mathbf{x}) = ||\tilde{\mathbf{J}}(\mathbf{x}) - A(\mathbf{x})||. \tag{10}$$

We can replace the $\tilde{r}(\mathbf{x})$ with $r_J(\mathbf{x})$ to get the initial transmission map $\tilde{t} = r(\mathbf{x})/r_J(\mathbf{x})$. Then we use the guided filter to get a smooth transmission map. We find that the result of the guided filter is not smooth enough, because our method may have some areas not are predicted, so we use the context regularization on the result of the guided filter. After that we get the final transmission map.

(4) Dehazing: Once the transmission map is estimated, we can recover the haze-free image using Eq. (1) as:

$$\mathbf{J}(\mathbf{x}) = \frac{\mathbf{I}(\mathbf{x}) - \mathbf{A}}{t(\mathbf{x})} + \mathbf{A}. \tag{11}$$

In Fig. 4, we show an example of our method, which is summarized in Algorithm 1. We find that for some images whose sizes can't be divided by 16, a contextual regularization needs to be applied to get a smooth transmission map.

In general, deep models [19] need a vast amount of labelled data to solve the parameters of the network. In this paper, we seek to find a way to reduce the number of training data. By intensive study of the hazy image patch and the haze-free image patch, we find that we can use a image patch atom to generate the haze-free image patch and the hazy image patch. We use this way to reduce the number of training data. For training of a network to remove haze from single input image, it is even more hard as the pairs of haze-free image and hazy image. We use the same assumptions [13] below. First, image content and medium transmission have no relation with each other. Second, the pixels in a local patch

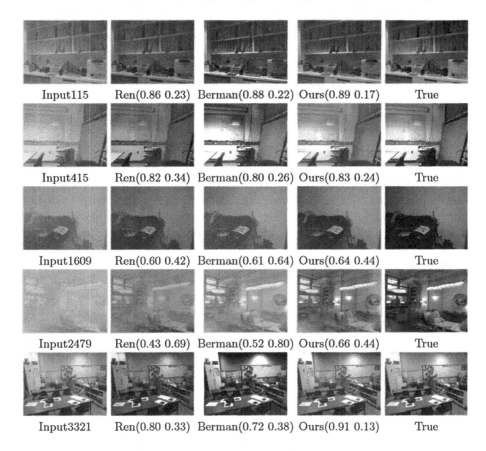

Fig. 5. Comparison on indoor hazy images. The number in left is SSIM value and the right is L1ERR.

have same transmission. According to these two assumptions, Cai et al. [14] assumed an arbitrary transmission for an individual haze-free image patch. For a haze-free image $\mathbf{J}^p$, Cai et al. [14] assumed $t \in (0,1]$, and generated a hazy image patch $\mathbf{I}^p$ according to the haze model $\mathbf{I}^p = t \times \mathbf{J}^p + (1-t) \times \mathbf{A}$. In contrast, according to the relation of haze-free image patch, hazy image patch and image patch atom, we generate a pair image patch atom and a haze-free image patch, because we eliminate the influence by normalization, we only need one pair of image patch atom and haze-free image patch for a haze-free image patch which is different from Cai et al.'s method. According to [14], they collected 10000 haze-free image patches from Internet. For a haze-free image patch, they uniformly sampled 10 random transmissions $t \in (0,1]$ to generate 10 hazy patches. So a training dataset containing 100000 image patches was generated. In contrast, our training data only needs one image patch atom for a haze-free image patch, so for a training dataset contains the same number of image patches, our dataset includes more diversity. Therefore, our method can get a better result than Cai et al.'s method.

Table 1. Quantitative comparison on indoor hazy images and outdoor hazy images. Red color indicates best result, and blue color indicates better.

Types	NR	GR
Outdoor	1.82E + 01	2.18E + 01
Indoor	1.57E + 03	1.60E + 03

4   Experimental Results

In this section, we evaluated our method on a large dataset containing both synthetic and natural images and compared our performance with state-of-art methods [5,9,14,15,18]. First, we show a comprehensive comparison with other state-of-the-art methods on indoor synthetic hazy images. Second, we show a comprehensive comparison with other state-of-the-art methods on outdoor synthetic hazy images. Third, we show a comprehensive comparison with other state-of-the-art methods on natural images. In this section, we used the $L1ERR = \frac{1}{N}\sum_{c \in R,G,B}|\mathbf{J}^c - \mathbf{G}^c|$ as metric, where $\mathbf{J}$ represents the dehazing result image and $\mathbf{G}$ denotes the ground truth image. In order to evaluate the dehazing methods, we generated an indoor hazy image dataset. This dataset is based on the indoor RGBD dataset [20], we used $\mathbf{A} = [0.78, 0.78, 0.78]$ and chose three values for β as $0.06, 0.3, 0.5$. The outdoor image dataset is obtained from [9].

4.1   Evaluation on Guided Filter

In this subsection, we show that our output of network have high quality. First, we do an operation of projection, which projects the pixel into the line form by $\mathbf{I}$ and $\mathbf{A}$, we denote this result as $\mathbf{NR}$. Then we apply a guided filter on $\tilde{t}$, and get a smooth transmission map, then use this transmission map to recover a haze-free image denoted as $\mathbf{GR}$.

As shown in Table 1, we can see that the guided filter will result in image degradation, but will improve the visual quality. The output of the network is more similar to the original image both for indoor images and outdoor ones. So our network result has contained enough information to recover a complete hazy free image. Due to that the guided filter reduces the performance of our method, we need to find a new method to reduce the halo and artifacts.

4.2   Tests on Synthetic Hazy Images

In this subsection, we compared our method with state-of-the-art methods on both indoor and outdoor synthetic hazy images. First, we compare our method with other state-of-the-art methods, and list the overall results. Second, we show some results on some images in Fattal's dataset and some images in our dataset.

An outdoor synthetic hazy image dataset was introduced by [9], which is available online. In order to evaluate the dehazing methods for indoor hazy

| Input | He et al. | Fattal | Berman et al. | Ours |

Fig. 6. Comparison on outdoor hazy images.

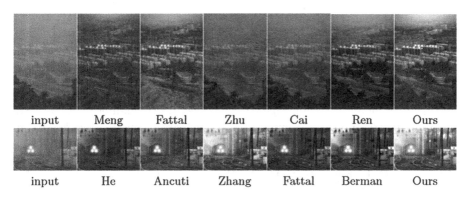

| input | Meng | Fattal | Zhu | Cai | Ren | Ours |

| input | He | Ancuti | Zhang | Fattal | Berman | Ours |

Fig. 7. Comparison on natural images: (Left) input images; (Right) our result. Middle columns display results obtained by several methods, since each paper reports results on a different set of images.

images, we generated an indoor hazy image dataset. This dataset is based on the indoor RGBD dataset [20], we used $\mathbf{A} = [0.78, 0.78, 0.78]$ and chose three values for β as $0.06, 0.3, 0.54$ to generate hazy images [15].

Indoor Hazy Images: In this part, we compared our method with Ren et al.'s [15] and Berman et al.'s [18]. The structural similarity (SSIM) image quality assessment index [21] was used to evaluate performance of the methods. The higher value of SSIM shows that the dehazing result is better. First, we show some results using SSIM and L1ERR. Second, we compared all images in our dataset using SSIM and L1ERR. For quantitative performance evaluation, we selected 5 images from our dataset, the results are shown in Fig. 5, from which we can find that Berman et al.'s [18] may overestimate the haze thickness in

Table 2. Quantitative comparison on our dataset. Red color indicates best result, and blue color indicates better.

Types	Ren et al.'s	Berman et al.'s	Ours
L1ERR	1.58E + 03	1.65E + 03	1.40E + 03
SSIM	3.12E + 03	3.19E + 03	3.24E + 03

Table 3. Quantitative comparison on road1. Red color indicates the best results and blue indicates the second.

Images	He et al.'s	Fattal's	Berman et al.'s	Ours
road1-D1	0.176	0.115	0.442	0.172
road1-D2	0.246	0.100	0.117	0.134
road1-D3	0.133	0.080	0.220	0.061
road1-S10	0.166	0.116	0.133	0.146
road1-S25	0.209	0.198	0.184	0.184
road1-S50	0.299	0.346	0.286	0.263
road1	0.146	0.098	0.117	0.134
road2	0.177	0.132	0.120	0.115

some slight regions in Input3321. Ren et al. [15] may underestimate the haze thickness in some heavy hazy regions. In contrast, our method can estimate the hazy thickness more reasonable than Ren et al.'s and Berman et al.'s. We also compared the overall results for our dataset, which are shown in Table 2. We can find that our method can get the best performance of all. We also tested and verified that our method can highest score for 1698 images using SSIM and 2106 highest score for 1698 images using L1ERR in 4347 images.

Outdoor Hazy Images: In this part, we also compared our method with some state-of-art methods [5,9,18] on some images in dataset. We show the qualitative result in Table 3. As we can see from the results, our method can get a very similar results to the ground truths in general and also can get highest quality result for particular image. In Fig. 6 we show some results on four hazy images, we can see our network output is very similar to haze-free image.

4.3   Quantitative Evaluation on Natural Images

In this subsection, we compared our method with state-of-the-art methods. As previously pointed by [5], the image after dehazing might look dim, since the scene radiance is usually not as bright as the airlight. For display, we performed a global linear contrast stretch on the output, clipping 0.5% of the pixel values both in the shadows and in the highlights.

Figure 7 compared our method with state-of-the-art methods [5,12,14,15,17, 22]. Some of the results are provided by Fattal [9], Berman et al. [18] and Cai et al. [14], which are online. We also obtained some results via the program provided by Ren et al. [15]. As shown in Fig. 7, Ancuti et al.'s method can't remove haze completely. He et al.'s method can yield an excellent result in general but lack some micro-contrast details when compared to [9] and ours. This is obvious in the zoomed-in buildings shown in Cityscape results, where in our result and [9] the windows are clearer than in [5]. We also find that the result of Ren et al.'s loss some details of tree in Cityscape. In contrast, our method can deal with this area well, our result shows much better details of tree. For "train" image, the result of Zhang and Yao [22] cannot deal with the boundary between segments well, which results in a lot of artifacts. The Ancuti's result can't remove haze completely from the hazy image. Fattal's and Berman's methods can't deal with tree areas well. In contrast, our method can deal with tree area well.

5   Conclusions

In this paper, we proposed a deep learning-based method for removing haze from single input image. First, we study the relation between the hazy image patch and haze-free image patch, and find that image patch atom can be used to generate hazy image patch and haze-free image patch, we use this relation to simple the preparation of training data. Second, we proposed a deep network to remove haze from single input image, and illustrated that our method can get a high quality and quantitative results. Third, we verified that the guided filter can reduce the halo and artifacts, but reduce the quality of dehazing result. Finally, we did an extensive evaluation of the method on different types of datasets that demonstrate its high accuracy. In order to improve our method we will extend our method by using haze-line as a regularization. Inspired by [18], we can use a few hundreds of distinct colors to represent an image, which will reduce the halo and artifacts.

Acknowledgments. This work was partially supported by the National Natural Science Foundation of China (Project No. 41571436), the Hubei Province Science and Technology Support Program, China (Project No. 2015BAA027), the National Natural Science Foundation of China under Grant 91438203, LIESMARS Special Research Funding, and the South Wisdom Valley Innovative Research Team Program.

References

1. Tan, K., Oakley, J.: Enhancement of color images in poor visibility conditions. In: IEEE International Conference on Image Processing, vol. 2, pp. 788–791. IEEE (2000)
2. Schechner, Y.Y., Narasimhan, S.G., Nayar, S.K.: Instant dehazing of images using polarization. In: IEEE Conference on Computer Vision and Pattern Recognition, vol. 1, pp. 325–332. IEEE (2001)
3. Kopf, J., Neubert, B., Chen, B., Cohen, M., Cohen-Or, D., Deussen, O., Uyttendaele, M., Lischinski, D.: Deep photo: model-based photograph enhancement and viewing. ACM Trans. Graph. (TOG) **27**, 116 (2008)

4. Fattal, R.: Single image dehazing. ACM Trans. Graph. (TOG) **27**, 1–9 (2008)
5. He, K., Sun, J., Tang, X.: Single image haze removal using dark channel prior. IEEE Trans. Pattern Anal. Mach. Intell. **33**, 2341–2353 (2011)
6. Kratz, L., Nishino, K.: Factorizing scene albedo and depth from a single foggy image. In: IEEE International Conference on Computer Vision, vol. 30, pp. 1701–1708 (2009)
7. Nishino, K., Kratz, L., Lombardi, S.: Bayesian defogging. Int. J. Comput. Vision **98**, 263–278 (2012)
8. Gibson, K.B., Nguyen, T.Q.: An analysis of single image defogging methods using a color ellipsoid framework. Eurasip J. Image Video Process. **2013**, 1–14 (2013)
9. Fattal, R.: Dehazing using color-lines. ACM Trans. Graph. (TOG) **34**, 13 (2014)
10. Tan, R.T.: Visibility in bad weather from a single image. In: IEEE Conference on Computer Vision and Pattern Recognition, pp. 1–8. IEEE (2008)
11. Tarel, J.P., Hautiere, N.: Fast visibility restoration from a single color or gray level image. In: IEEE International Conference on Computer Vision, pp. 2201–2208. IEEE (2009)
12. Zhu, Q., Mai, J., Shao, L.: A fast single image haze removal algorithm using color attenuation prior. IEEE Trans. Image Process. **24**, 3522–3533 (2015)
13. Tang, K., Yang, J., Wang, J.: Investigating haze-relevant features in a learning framework for image dehazing. In: IEEE Conference on Computer Vision and Pattern Recognition (CVPR), pp. 2995–3002. IEEE (2014)
14. Cai, B., Xu, X., Jia, K., Qing, C., Tao, D.: Dehazenet: an end-to-end system for single image haze removal. arXiv preprint arXiv:1601.07661 (2016)
15. Ren, W., Liu, S., Zhang, H., Pan, J., Cao, X., Yang, M.-H.: Single image dehazing via multi-scale convolutional neural networks. In: Leibe, B., Matas, J., Sebe, N., Welling, M. (eds.) ECCV 2016. LNCS, vol. 9906, pp. 154–169. Springer, Cham (2016). https://doi.org/10.1007/978-3-319-46475-6_10
16. Harald, K.: Theorie der horizontalen Sichtweite: Kontrast und Sichtweite, vol. 12. Keim & Nemnich, Munich (1924)
17. Meng, G., Wang, Y., Duan, J., Xiang, S., Pan, C.: Efficient image dehazing with boundary constraint and contextual regularization. In: IEEE International Conference on Computer Vision, pp. 617–624 (2013)
18. Berman, D., Treibitz, T., Avidan, S.: Non-local image dehazing. In: IEEE Conference on Computer Vision and Pattern Recognition (CVPR), pp. 1674–1682 (2016)
19. Krizhevsky, A., Sutskever, I., Hinton, G.E.: Imagenet classification with deep convolutional neural networks. In: Advances in neural information processing systems, pp. 1097–1105 (2012)
20. Silberman, N., Hoiem, D., Kohli, P., Fergus, R.: Indoor segmentation and support inference from RGBD images. In: Fitzgibbon, A., Lazebnik, S., Perona, P., Sato, Y., Schmid, C. (eds.) ECCV 2012. LNCS, vol. 7576, pp. 746–760. Springer, Heidelberg (2012). https://doi.org/10.1007/978-3-642-33715-4_54
21. Wang, Z., Bovik, A.C., Sheikh, H.R., Simoncelli, E.P.: Image quality assessment: from error visibility to structural similarity. IEEE Trans. Image Process. **13**, 600–612 (2004)
22. Zhang, S., Yao, J.: Single image dehazing using fixed points and nearest-neighbor regularization. In: Chen, C.-S., Lu, J., Ma, K.-K. (eds.) ACCV 2016. LNCS, vol. 10116, pp. 18–33. Springer, Cham (2017). https://doi.org/10.1007/978-3-319-54407-6_2

Automatic Brain Tumor Segmentation in Multispectral MRI Volumes Using a Random Forest Approach

Zoltán Kapás[1], László Lefkovits[1], David Iclănzan[1], Ágnes Győrfi[1],
Barna László Iantovics[2], Szidónia Lefkovits[2], Sándor Miklós Szilágyi[2],
and László Szilágyi[1,3(✉)]

[1] Computational Intelligence Research Group,
Sapientia - Hungarian Science University of Transylvania, Tîrgu Mureş, Romania
lalo@ms.sapientia.ro
[2] Department of Informatics, Petru Maior University, Tîrgu Mureş, Romania
[3] Department of Control Engineering and Information Technology,
Budapest University of Technology and Economics, Budapest, Hungary

Abstract. The development of automatic tumor detection and segmentation procedures enables the computers to preprocess huge sets of MRI records and draw the attention of medical staff upon suspected positive cases. This paper proposes a machine learning solution based on binary decision trees and random forest technique, trained to provide accurate segmentation of brain tumors from multispectral MRI volumes. The current version of our system was trained and tested using all 220 high-grade tumor volumes from the MICCAI BRATS 2016 database. Image records were preprocessed to attenuate the effect of relative intensities in the MRI data, and to extend the feature set with neighborhood information of each voxel. The output of the random forest is also validated for each voxel, according to labels given to neighbor voxels. The achieved accuracy is characterized by an overall mean Dice score of 80.1%, sensitivity 83.1%, and specificity 98.6%. The proposed method is likely to detect all gliomas of 2 cm diameter.

Keywords: Decision tree · Random forest · Machine learning
Image segmentation · Magnetic resonance imaging

1 Introduction

Early detection is the key of success in the treatment of tumors, it is utmost important as it can save human lives. The accurate segmentation, the separation

This work was supported in part by the Sapientia Institute for Research Programs (KPI). The work of B.L. Iantovics, S. Lefkovits, and S.M. Szilágyi was supported by UEFISCDI Romania through grant no. PN-III-P2-2.1-BG-2016-0343, contract no. 114BG/01.10.2016.

The work of Z. Kapás was additionally supported by the Szekely Forerunner Federation.

© Springer International Publishing AG, part of Springer Nature 2018
M. Paul et al. (Eds.): PSIVT 2017, LNCS 10749, pp. 137–149, 2018.
https://doi.org/10.1007/978-3-319-75786-5_12

of brain tumors from normal brain tissues is also essential, as it can assist the medical expert in the planning of treatment and intervention. The manual segmentation of tumors requires plenty of time even for a well-trained expert. The fully automated segmentation and quantitative analysis of tumors is thus a highly beneficial service. However, it is also a very challenging one, because of the high variety of anatomical structures and low contrast of current imaging techniques which make the difference between normal regions and the tumor hardly recognizable for the human eye [1].

Magnetic resonance imaging (MRI) is the preferred imaging device in brain tumor screening, due to its better contrast and relatively fine resolution. However, it also bears difficulties like the possible presence of intensity inhomogeneity [2], and the relative intensity values that vary from device to device and from patient to patient. The MICCAI Brain Tumor Segmentation Challenge, organized yearly since 2012, intensified the research in this topic and led to several important solutions, which are usually assisted by the use of prior information, and employ various image processing and pattern recognition methodologies. Asman and Landman [3] applied a non-parametric intensity analysis in combination with a segmentation based on multiple atlases. Ghanavati et al. [4] provided a solution using the AdaBoost classifier to distinguish tumor voxels from normal ones using features based on intensity, texture, and symmetry. Hamamci et al. [5] proposed a cellular automata driven method that produces segmentation based on level sets. Sachdeva et al. [6] deployed a content based active contour model relying on intensity and texture features extracted from the histogram and co-occurrence matrix of the MRI data. Njeh et al. [7] introduced a graph cut based solution that performs distribution matching, which is highly efficient because of using rather global than pixel wise information. Zhang et al. [8] proposed a support vector machine based procedure to follow the evolution of brain tumors over time. Tustison et al. [9] combined random forests with symmetry based features to segment brain tumors. Szilágyi et al. [10] provided a semi-supervised framework for the fuzzy c-means clustering algorithm to produce accurately segmented tumors. Kanas [11] combined a clustering based preprocessing with a multi-parametric random walker segmentation. Havaei et al. [12] developed an automatic brain tumor segmentation procedure based on deep neural networks that exploits both local and global contextual features simultaneously. Pereira et al. [13] proposed a convolutional neural network solution exploiting small kernels and successfully applied it for brain tumor segmentation. Menze et al. [14] combined a Gaussian mixture model with the expectation maximization (EM) algorithm to achieve an accurate segmentation. Another Gaussian mixture based accurate solution was given by Juan-Albarracín et al. [15]. Islam et al. [16] employed multifractional Brownian motion features to provide patient-independent characterization of tumor tissues and applied the AdaBoost algorithm for tissue segmentation. Shin et al. [17] proposed deep convolutional neural networks and successfully combined it with transfer learning. Huang et al. [18] provided a brain tumor segmentation framework employing local independent projection-based classification. For further information on current brain tumor segmentation techniques, there are available recent reviews [1,19].

In a previous paper [20] we have presented a preliminary study on the use of binary decision trees (BDT) in brain tumor detection and segmentation. We selected 13 multispectral MRI volumes from the MICCAI BRATS 2013 data set, performed the training of individual BDTs and ensembles with information taken from a subset of the volumes, and tested using the complementary subset of volumes. As a further development of our previous algorithm, in this paper we propose a random forest solution trained and tested using the whole high-grade tumor data set of MICCAI BRATS 2016 that includes 220 volumes. Our main goal in this paper is to accurately separate the whole tumor from the normal tissues in each volume. Separating further parts of the tumor based on the ground truth offered by MICCAI BRATS human experts, remains out of the scope of this study.

The rest of this paper is structured as follows: Sect. 2 gives details on the proposed methodology. Section 3 exhibits and discusses the achieved results. Finally, Sect. 4 concludes the investigation.

2 Materials and Methods

Our main goal was to establish a machine learning algorithm that accurately segments tumors in MRI volumes. This paper presents preliminary results obtained using the random forest technique, combined with a neighborhood-based post-processing. The algorithm is trained to separate the whole tumor from negative tissues. A block diagram of the proposed segmentation procedure is given in Fig. 1.

2.1 BRATS Data Sets

Brain tumor image data used in this work were obtained from the MICCAI 2016 Challenge on Multimodal Brain Tumor Segmentation [21]. The challenge database contains fully anonymized images originating from four institutions. The image database consists of multi-contrast MR scans of 280 glioma patient, out of which 220 have been acquired from high-grade and 60 from low-grade glioma patients. For each patient, multimodal (T1, T2, FLAIR, and post-Gadolinium T1) MR images are available. All volumes were linearly co-registered to the T1 contrast image, skull stripped, and interpolated to 1 mm isotropic resolution. Each record contains approximately 1.5 millions of true tissue voxels. All voxels are provided with annotation produced by human expert. Beside the four observed features of each voxel, there is a strong need to extend the feature vectors with further, computed features.

2.2 Histogram Normalization

Because of the nature of MRI sensors, intensity values in MRI records are relative, so we need to map the histogram of each volume onto a uniform scale. In this order, all intensity values underwent a linear transformation $x \rightarrow \alpha x + \beta$,

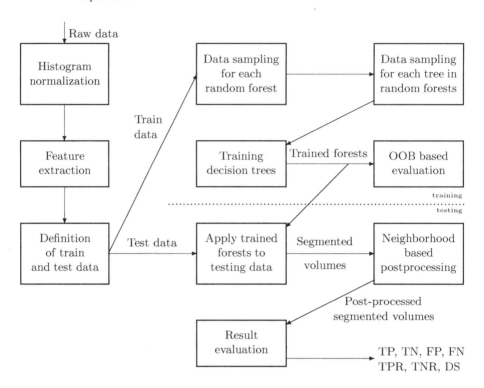

Fig. 1. Block diagram of the proposed method.

where parameters α and β were established separately for each volume and each feature, such a way that the 25-percentile and 75-percentile value became 600 and 800, respectively. Further on, a minimum and a maximum intensity barrier was set up at 200 and 1200, respectively.

2.3   Computed Features

Twelve computed features were added to the feature vector describing each voxel. For each of the four observed intensities (T1, T2, T1C, FLAIR), the minimum, the maximum, and the average value was extracted from the valid neighbors within the 26-neighborhood of the voxel. Neighbors were considered valid if they had nonzero observed intensity in the given channel. The 26-neighborhood of a voxel situated at coordinates (x_0, y_0, z_0) consists of all voxels whose (x, y, z) coordinated satisfy $|x - x_0| \leq 1$, $|y - y_0| \leq 1$, and $|z - z_0| \leq 1$.

2.4   Missing Data

Some voxels had zero valued observed features interpreted as a missing value. Voxels with more than one such value were excluded from further processing.

Those with a single zero value received an interpolated value from the neighborhood of the voxel. These voxels were not included in the main data processing.

2.5   Binary Decision Trees

Binary decision trees (BDT) can describe any hierarchy of crisp (non-fuzzy) two-way decisions [22]. Given an input data set of vectors $\mathbf{X} = \{x_1, x_2, \ldots, x_n\}$, where $x_i = [x_{i,1}, x_{i,2}, \ldots, x_{i,m}]^T$, a BDT can be employed to learn the classification that corresponds to any set of labels $\Lambda = \{\lambda_1, \lambda_2, \ldots, \lambda_n\}$. The classification learned by the BDT can be perfect if there are no identical training vectors with different labels, that is, $x_i = x_j$ implies $\lambda_i = \lambda_j$, $\forall i, j \in \{1, 2, \ldots, n\}$. The BDT is built during the learning process. Initially the tree consists of a single node, the root, which has to make a decision regarding all n input vectors. If not all n vectors have the same label, which is likely to be so, then the set of data is not homogeneous, there is a need for a separation. The decision will compare a single chosen feature, the one with index k $(1 \le k \le m)$, of the input vectors with a certain threshold α, and the comparison will separate the vectors into two subgroups: those with $x_{i,k} < \alpha$ $(i = 1 \ldots n)$, and those with $x_{i,k} \ge \alpha$ $(i = 1 \ldots n)$. The root will then have two child nodes, each corresponding to one of the possible outcomes of the above decision. The left child will further classify those n_1 input vectors, which satisfied the former condition, while the right child those n_2 ones that satisfied the latter condition. Obviously, we have $n_1 + n_2 = n$. For both child nodes, the procedure is the same as it was for the root. When at a certain point of the learning algorithm, all vectors being classified by a node have the same label λ_p, then the node is declared a leaf node, which is attributed to the class with index p. Another case when a node is declared leaf node is when all vectors to be separated by the node are identical, so there is no possible condition to separate the vectors. In this case, the label of the node is decided by the majority of labels, or if there is no majority, a label should be chosen from the present ones. In our application, this kind of rare leaves are labeled as tumor.

The separation of a finite set of data vectors always terminates in a finite number of steps. The maximum depth of the tree highly depends on the way of establishing the separation condition in each node. Our application uses an entropy based criterion to choose the separation condition. Whenever a node has to establish its separation criterion for a subset of vectors $\overline{\mathbf{X}} \subseteq \mathbf{X}$ containing $\overline{n}$ items with $1 < \overline{n} \le n$, the following algorithm is performed:

1. Find all those features which have at least 2 different values in $\overline{\mathbf{X}}$.
2. Find all different values for each feature and sort them in increasing order.
3. Set a threshold candidate at the middle of the distance between each consecutive pair of values for each feature.
4. Choose that feature and that threshold, for which the entropy-based criterion

$$E = \overline{n}_1 \log \frac{\overline{n}_1}{\overline{n}} + \overline{n}_2 \log \frac{\overline{n}_2}{\overline{n}} \tag{1}$$

gives the minimum value, where $\overline{n}_1$ $(\overline{n}_2)$ will be the cardinality of the subset of vectors $\overline{\mathbf{X}}_1$ $(\overline{\mathbf{X}}_2)$, for which the value of the tested feature is less than (greater or equal than) the tested threshold value.

After having the BDT trained, it can be applied for the classification of test data vectors. Any test vector is first fed to the root node, which according to the stored condition and the feature values of the vector, decides towards which child node to forward the vector. This strategy is followed then by the chosen child node, and the vector will be forwarded to a further child. The classification of a vector terminates at the moment when it is forwarded to a leaf node of the tree. The test vector will be attributed to the class indicated by the labeling of the reached leaf node.

2.6   The Random Forest

Binary decision trees (BDT) were trained to separate negative voxels from positive ones. In case of the BRATS high-grade tumor data set, we had a total number of 276 million negative and 24 million positive voxels. As a first step, randomly selected 90% of the negative voxels were eliminated and the remaining 10% kept for the training and testing process. Training data sets for various forests were created via random selection of negative and positive voxels, using the parameter p_N that stood for the ratio of negative pixels in each set. Any such learning data set contained voxels from volume records with either even or odd index, so that they can be tested on the complementary part of the records. Each training set consisted of $N_S = 10^6$ samples. Another parameter of each forest consisted in the number of trees n_T, which varied between 50 and 500. Each tree of a forest was trained with N_S/n_T samples that were randomly selected from the total number of voxels N_S assigned to the forest in question. Those samples that were not selected for the training of any tree in the forest, approximately 360,000 voxels, acted as out-of-bag (OOB) data and were used for primary testing, as recommended by Breiman in [23]. Testing on OOB data allowed us to preselect those forests that were likely to produce high accuracy, and discard those that were prone to more misclassifications. The best performing forests achieved 95–96% accuracy in labeling the OOB data.

All forests trained with data originating from volumes with even (odd) index were tested on all volumes indexed with odd (even) number. Forests were created using a great variety of parameter values (p_N and n_T). All 220 high-grade tumor volumes were fed to all valid forests, according to the rule that any trained forest was only tested on never seen data. Finally we established the parameter values that led to best overall accuracy.

2.7   Post-processing

A posterior relabeling scheme was implemented as follows. The input data of the post-processing step consisted in the labels provided by the random forest to all voxels in the volume. For each voxel, the number of tumor labeled neighbors

(ν_T) and the number of all neighbors (ν_{All}) were extracted, using a predefined cubic neighborhood. The final label of a voxel was set to tumor if and only if $\nu_T/\nu_{All} > \theta$. The overall optimal value of the threshold was established during the test and was found as $\theta = 0.4$.

2.8 Evaluation of Accuracy

We employed the Dice score (DS) as the main indicator of accuracy, defined as $DS = \frac{2 \times TP}{2 \times TP + FP + FN} \in [0, 1]$, where TP, FP, and FN stand for the number of true positives, false positives, and false negatives, respectively. Fine accuracy is reflected by DS values close to 1, but in this brain tumor segmentation problem, DS values around 0.94 are considered ideal [21], due to inter-rater differences that are present in the ground truth. Further on, the sensitivity (or true positive rate, TPR), and specificity (or true negative rate), defined as $TPR = \frac{TP}{TP+FN}$ and $TNR = \frac{TN}{TN+FP}$, were used as secondary accuracy indicators, where TN represents the number of true negatives.

3   Results and Discussion

All 220 high-grade tumor volumes from the BRATS 2016 were involved in the evaluation of the proposed methodology. Volumes with even (odd) index were tested on random forests trained only with data from odd (even) numbered volumes. Several random forests were trained, having the ratio of negative voxels p_N within their training data between 70% and 98%. Ratios lower than 70% led to too many false positives in case of any test volume.

For each of the test volumes, the ideal p_N ratio was identified. Which led to the highest Dice score. The histogram of these p_N values, presented in Fig. 2(a), shows us that the great majority of the volumes are best segmented for p_N ratios above 80%. Figure 2(b) exhibits the overall Dice score obtained for various values of the p_N ratio, and indicates that the highest overall Dice scores are obtained if $87\% \leq p_N \leq 89\%$. Choosing various values for the number of trees in each forest had little impact on accuracy. Best Dice scores were obtained in case of $n_T = 125$.

The proposed post-processing makes detected positive and negative regions more compact, it eliminates small isolated homogeneous regions that are either negative or positive, and thus improves the accuracy in case of a great majority of the test volumes via reducing the number false positives and false negatives. Table 1 shows the most important overall accuracy measures. The overall Dice score rises by 6%, while the median by almost 7%.

Figure 3 exhibits the main accuracy indicators for each individual volume, before and after post-processing. The indicator values were sorted in increasing order for better visibility. The final overall mean values for specificity and sensitivity are 98.6% and 83.1%, respectively. There is approximately 10% of the volumes that were segmented with lower accuracy, characterized by a Dice score

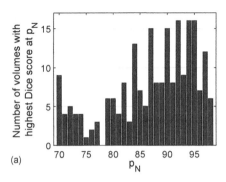 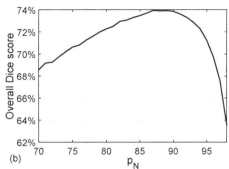

(a)   (b)

Fig. 2. Finding the overall best value for the ratio of negative voxels in the training data p_N: (a) histogram of ideal p_N values extracted for each of the 220 volumes tumor volumes; (b) the overall Dice score plotted against p_N. This figure reflects the case of $n_T = 125$ decision trees in the random forest, and the Dice scores obtained without post-processing.

Table 1. Main overall accuracy parameters

Dice scores	Average	Median	Above 80%	Above 85%	Above 90%
Without post-processing	73.9%	77.1%	99 of 220	61 of 220	24 of 220
With post-processing	80.1%	84.9%	139 of 220	109 of 220	60 of 220

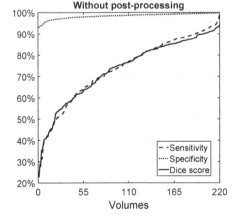 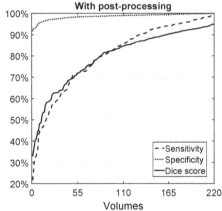

Fig. 3. Dice score, sensitivity, and specificity values obtained for all 220 high-grade tumor volumes in case of $n_T = 125$ and $p_N = 88\%$, sorted in increasing order. The result of the random forest is exhibited on the left side, while the graph on the right side shows the final result after post-processing. The specificity is well above 97% in case of most volumes, which is very important if we do not want to generate several false alerts. Sensitivity values are comparable with the Dice scores reported in Table 1: the overall mean and median sensitivity is approximately 83% and 86%, respectively, after post-processing.

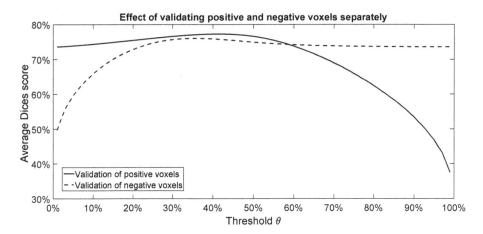

Fig. 4. The effect of post-processing on overall average Dice score: the neighborhood-based validation of positive and negative voxels was separately investigated. Overall Dice score is plotted against threshold θ. The overall Dice score without post-processing is visible at $\theta = 0\%$ of the graph indicating the positives and at $\theta = 100\%$ of the graph indicating the negatives. Both curves have wide ranges of θ that lead to improved overall Dice score.

below 60%, while almost two thirds of the volumes received a Dice score above the overall mean.

Figure 4 presents the separate effect of each component of the post-processing, namely validating the positive and negative voxels after classification. Both curves plot the achieved overall mean Dice score against threshold θ. In case of positive voxels, the mean Dice score rises together with θ and has a maximum somewhere around $\theta = 0.4$, and rapidly drops for higher values of the threshold. In case of negative voxels, the mean Dice score rapidly rises together with θ and has a maximum somewhere around $\theta = 0.35$, and slightly drops for higher values of the threshold. Both curves have wide ranges of the threshold θ that lead to improved overall Dice score. Our choice was to validate both positive and negative pixels using the threshold value $\theta = 0.4$.

Figure 5 presents the effect of the proposed post-processing. Figure 5(a) plots the individual Dice scores for each volume after post-processing vs. before post-processing, indicating that post-processing had a significant beneficial effect in a great majority of the cases, and only 6% of the volumes were slightly pushed toward worse accuracy. Figures 5(b) and (c) plot the individual Dice scores obtained for each volume vs. the size of the tumor, without post-processing and with post-processing, respectively. The identified linear trends show that the strongest effect of post-processing occurs in case of small tumors.

Figure 6 exhibits the segmentation result of 16 consecutive slices from a high-grade tumor volume. Most tumor pixels were accurately identified in this case, as we can only see a few false negatives beside the true positives indicated by

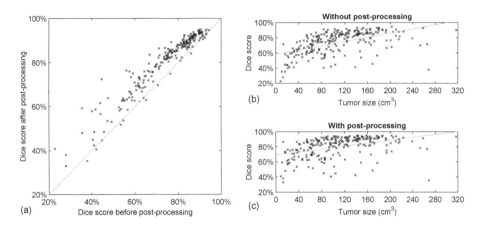

Fig. 5. The effect of post-processing in case of $n_T = 125$ and $p_N = 88\%$: (a) Dice scores after post-processing plotted against Dice scores without post-processing; (b) Dice scores without post-processing plotted against actual tumor size; (c) Dice scores after post-processing plotted against actual tumor size. The straight lines in (b) and (c) indicate the linear trend of Dice scores, extracted with linear regression.

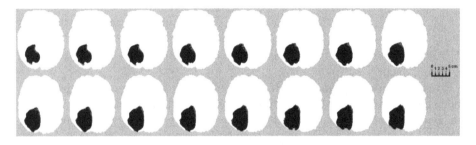

Fig. 6. Sixteen consecutive slices from an identified tumor. Black pixels represent true positives, red and blue ones stand for false positives and false negatives, respectively. The Dice score for this volume was 0.936. (Color figure online)

black pixels. This is one of the cases that were segmented with high accuracy. A worse, but still acceptable case is shown in Fig. 7.

The total runtime of the testing process, performed on a single volume ranges between 30 and 45 s, when executed on a single core of a PC with i7 processor running at 3.4 GHz frequency. Most operations can be easily implemented to run in parallel on all cores, making the processing even more efficient.

The overall mean Dice score above 80% allows us to detect the presence of the tumor in a great majority of cases. However, the accuracy indicators can be further improved the following ways:

1. Involving further morphological features into the feature vector, to collect much more information from the neighborhood of each pixel.

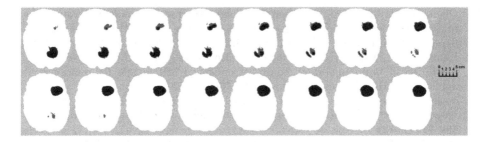

Fig. 7. Sixteen consecutive slices from an identified tumor. Black pixels represent true positives, red and blue ones stand for false positives and false negatives, respectively. The Dice score for this volume was 0.75 (Color figure online)

2. Including more sophisticated features, for example those obtained via wavelet transform, or employing fractal features.
3. Employing an effective feature selection scheme.
4. Implementing a more complex post-processing that investigates the contiguous ensembles of detected tumor voxels and discard small ones.

An objective comparison with existing methods enumerated in Sect. 1 is not an easily accomplishable task, as not all of them used the BRATS data set for evaluation, and even those which did, they did not evaluate all the 220 available volumes.

4   Conclusions

This paper we presented an automatic tumor detection and segmentation algorithm employing random forests of binary decision trees, in its preliminary stage of implementation. The proposed methodology already reliably detects tumors of 2 cm diameter. It is likely to obtain finer segmentation accuracy in the future via implementing some of the above mentioned further ideas. We will also concentrate on differentiating among the parts of the whole tumor (edema, tumor core, necrosis, active tumor), according to the grand truth provided by the BRATS data set.

References

1. Gordillo, N., Montseny, E., Sobrevilla, P.: State of the art survey on MRI brain tumor segmentation. Magn. Res. Imag. **31**, 1426–1438 (2013)
2. Vovk, U., Pernuš, F., Likar, B.: A review of methods for correction of intensity inhomogeneity in MRI. IEEE Trans. Med. Imag. **26**, 405–421 (2007)
3. Asman, A.J., Landman, B.A.: Out-of-atlas labeling: a multi-atlas approach to cancer segmentation. In: 9th IEEE International Symposium on Biomedical Imaging, pp. 1236–1239. IEEE Press, New York (2012)

4. Ghanavati, S., Li, J., Liu, T., Babyn, P.S., Doda, W., Lampropoulos, G.: Automatic brain tumor detection in magnetic resonance images. In: 9th IEEE International Symposium on Biomedical Imaging, pp. 574–577. IEEE Press, New York (2012)

5. Hamamci, A., Kucuk, N., Karamam, K., Engin, K., Unal, G.: Tumor-cut: segmentation of brain tumors on contranst enhanced MR images for radiosurgery applications. IEEE Trans. Med. Imag. **31**, 790–804 (2012)

6. Sachdeva, J., Kumar, V., Gupta, I., Khandelwal, N., Ahuja, C.K.: A novel content-based active contour model for brain tumor segmentation. Magn. Res. Imag. **30**, 694–715 (2012)

7. Njeh, I., Sallemi, L., Ben Ayed, I., Chtourou, K., Lehericy, S., Galanaud, D., Ben Hamida, A.: 3D multimodal MRI brain glioma tumor and edema segmentation: a graph cut distribution matching approach. Comput. Med. Imag. Graph. **40**, 108–119 (2015)

8. Zhang, N., Ruan, S., Lebonvallet, S., Liao, Q., Zhou, Y.: Kernel feature selection to fuse multi-spectral MRI images for brain tumor segmentation. Comput. Vis. Image Underst. **115**, 256–269 (2011)

9. Tustison, N.J., Shrinidhi, K.L., Wintermark, M., Durst, C.R., Kandel, B.M., Gee, J.C., Grossman, M.C., Avants, B.B.: Optimal symmetric multimodal templates and concatenated random forests for supervised brain tumor segmentation (simplified) with ANTsR. Neuroinformatics **13**, 209–225 (2015)

10. Szilágyi, L., Lefkovits, L., Iantovics, B., Iclănzan, D., Benyó, B.: Automatic brain tumor segmentation in multispectral MRI volumetric records. In: Arik, S., Huang, T., Lai, W.K., Liu, Q. (eds.) ICONIP 2015. LNCS, vol. 9492, pp. 174–181. Springer, Cham (2015). https://doi.org/10.1007/978-3-319-26561-2_21

11. Kanas, V.G., Zacharaki, E.I., Davatzikos, C., Sgarbas, K.N., Megalooikonomou, V.: A low cost approach for brain tumor segmentation based on intensity modeling and 3D random walker. Biomed. Sig. Process. Control **22**, 19–30 (2015)

12. Havaei, M., Davy, A., Warde-Farley, D., Biard, A., Courville, A., Bengio, Y., Pal, C., Jodoin, P.M., Larochelle, H.: Brain tumor segmentation with deep neural networks. Med. Image Anal. **35**, 18–31 (2017)

13. Pereira, S., Pinto, A., Alves, V., Silva, C.A.: Brain tumor segmentation using convolutional neural networks in MRI images. IEEE Trans. Med. Imag. **35**, 1240–1251 (2016)

14. Menze, B.H., van Leemput, K., Lashkari, D., Riklin-Raviv, T., Geremia, E., Alberts, E., et al.: A generative probabilistic model and discriminative extensions for brain lesion segmentation - with application to tumor and stroke. IEEE Trans. Med. Imag. **35**, 933–946 (2016)

15. Juan-Albarracín, J., Fuster-Garcia, E., Manjón, J.V., Robles, M., Aparici, F., Martí-Bonmatí, L., García Gómez, J.M.: Automated glioblastoma segmentation based on a multiparametric structured unsupervised classification. PLoS ONE **10**(5), e0125143 (2015)

16. Islam, A., Reza, S.M.S., Iftekharuddin, K.M.: Multifractal texture estimation for detection and segmentation of brain tumors. IEEE Trans. Biomed. Eng. **60**, 3204–3215 (2013)

17. Shin, H.C., Roth, H.R., Gao, M.C., Lu, L., Xu, Z.Y., Nogues, I., Yao, J.H., Mollura, D., Summers, R.M.: Deep convolutional neural networks for computer-aided detection: CNN architectures, dataset characteristics and transfer learning. IEEE Trans. Med. Imag. **35**(5), 1285–1298 (2016)

18. Huang, M.Y., Yang, W., Wu, Y., Jiang, J., Chen, W.F., Feng, Q.J.: Brain tumor segmentation based on local independent projection-based classification. IEEE Trans. Biomed. Eng. **61**(10), 2633–2645 (2014)

19. Iglesias, J.E., Sabuncu, M.R.: Multi-atlas segmentation of biomedical images: a survey. Med. Imag. Anal. **24**(1), 205–219 (2015)
20. Kapás, Z., Lefkovits, L., Szilágyi, L.: Automatic detection and segmentation of brain tumor using random forest approach. In: Torra, V., Narukawa, Y., Navarro-Arribas, G., Yañez, C. (eds.) MDAI 2016. LNCS (LNAI), vol. 9880, pp. 301–312. Springer, Cham (2016). https://doi.org/10.1007/978-3-319-45656-0_25
21. Menze, B.H., Jakab, A., Bauer, S., Kalpathy-Cramer, J., Farahani, K., Kirby, J., et al.: The multimodal brain tumor image segmentation benchmark (BRATS). IEEE Trans. Med. Imag. **34**, 1993–2024 (2015)
22. Akers, S.B.: Binary decision diagrams. IEEE Trans. Comput. **C–27**, 509–516 (1978)
23. Breiman, L.: Random forests. Mach. Learn. **45**, 5–32 (2001)

A New Scheme for QoE Management of Live Video Streaming in Cloud Environment

Dheyaa Jasim Kadhim[1]([✉]) [ID], Xinguo Yu[1], Saba Qasim Jabbar[2],
Yu Li[2], and Wenxing Luo[3]

[1] National Engineering Research Center for E-Learning, CCNU, Wuhan, China
dheyaajk@gmail.com
[2] Huazhong University of Science and Technology, Wuhan, China
[3] GuiZhou Vocational Technology College of Electronics and Information,
Kaili, China

Abstract. Live video streaming process consumes very large data storage and takes very long time, so it requires big data storage and computing infrastructures for implementation. Accordingly, the use of cloud computing is becoming a common practice solution for streaming service providers. This work proposes a new scheme to manage the quality of experience (QoE) for live video streaming viewers, aimed directly at cloud computing environments. This scheme proposes to make optimal usage of cloud computing resources and quality services to meet the quality of experience (QoE) requirements of the live video streaming viewers without considering another cost to the video service provider. We examine the user's quality of experience using dynamic adaptive streaming HTTP (DASH) technique. Then, we present and derive three important performance indicators which effect on viewer's QoE namely: startup delay, deadline time (time nulling including null duration and number of null time), and bit rate level variations. The simulation results show that the tested indication parameters do not need to access the service providers in order to manage QoE of viewers neither do not need to insert them into the video streaming client software to determine the user experience in live video streaming. So, we believe that our proposed scheme and the performance indicators that studied in our work can serve as useful and light-weight tools for live video streaming service provider to monitor and control their quality of services.

Keywords: Cloud computing · Live video streaming · QoE management
DASH

1 Introduction

Currently, to support high quality live streaming on different users' devices, video publishers must create multiple versions (i.e. different formats) of this video at their service providers. However, this method faces from hardware limitations and network bandwidth. In addition, this approach is not aware of the demands of viewers. This means that it can produce versions not requested by viewers. Thus, this approach has remained costly and ineffective [1]. Another approach is on-demand streaming video

© Springer International Publishing AG, part of Springer Nature 2018
M. Paul et al. (Eds.): PSIVT 2017, LNCS 10749, pp. 150–161, 2018.
https://doi.org/10.1007/978-3-319-75786-5_13

streaming, in this approach; the publisher creates only one copy of the video at its end. Live video can be broadcast to viewers as long as the devices are compatible with streaming format. Live video streaming is performed on demand when a new viewer joins in a compatible device format [2].

The provision and improvement of the live video streaming's infrastructure basically is required to meet the increasing global demands for video streaming but it is costly effective [3]. Therefore, the use of cloud services has become a common solution among all Internet service providers. As video streaming providers use cloud computing to host their services, they face challenges by assessing the quality of experience and designing unified strategies in this complex environment.

Live video viewers request to receive video without any delay. So we need to specify the display time as the last time (i.e. deadline) that the transcoding process can be completed for the video stream without any interruption. There is no value in converting the format of the video after its display time. This means that each transcoding task has an individual hard time limit. Consequently, for stable live video streaming, transcoding tasks that can't finish its processing must be dropped. In this research, we also need to specify a drop rate as a percentage of transcoded tasks because transcoding can't be completed during viewing times. To have maximal QoE (i.e. viewer satisfaction), we inquiry to minimize the drop rate of the video playback.

Previous work such as [4] shows that more than 40% of viewers watch only a few seconds of video streaming. So they assess the quality of the service provider depending on the initial delay that happens at the starting of the video streaming. So we need to determine the delay acquired by the user at the beginning of the stream as a startup delay. Under these situations, to have maximal QoE (i.e. viewer satisfaction), we inquiry to minimize the startup delay in video playback.

In this work, we will consider our objective problem is to maximize QoE of end users (i.e. viewers' satisfactions) with supposed constraints: minimizing the startup delay and the drop rate. Therefore, the challenge in this research is how to assign (i.e., management) transcoding tasks on cloud resources to satisfy the QoE requirements of live streams viewers without considering another cost to the video service provider.

So that our work is constituted from two stages: Firstly, we proposed a new QoE management scheme that will be useful for service providers to optimal usage of cloud resource without any additional cost. Our proposed scheme differs from previous works by using transcoding process for real time streaming using cloud resources to submit high video quality for many different video players. Secondly, this proposed scheme is experienced under three effective indicators (startup delay, deadline time and bit rate level variations), which it is also consider a new approach of monitoring and reviewing the user experience for live video streaming.

The work of this paper is organized as follows: Sect. 2 describes the main related works to our research approach, while Sect. 3 submits the detailed description of the proposed scheme architecture for QoE management of live video streaming. Section 4 will define and derive the three suggested QoE performance indicators of our proposed scheme. Section 5 shows the simulation results that will be drawn from our experiments to describe our proposed scheme. Finally, Sect. 6 will give the main conclusions are gained with this work.

2 Related Work

Video transcoding process consumes very large data storage and long time, so it requires big data storage and computing infrastructures for implementation. Accordingly, the use of cloud computing is becoming a common practice solution for streaming service providers. As a result, researchers have faced many challenges in leveraging cloud services.

The way in which videos are segmented plays an important role in transmitting and transcoding processes of video streaming. Authors of [5] describe how video segmentation technique can impact on the transcoding time seriously. While our work, the video is splitting into segments that contain a group of pictures (GOPs), and we will treat each GOP separately, so we can control and monitor transcoding time to improve the segmentation process. Authors of [6] suggested a scheduling and provision method with video on demand (VOD) approach in cloud, the purpose of this work was to ensure quality of service which is claimed by video viewers while minimizing the required cost of using cloud services. Our work is different from [6] by two main concepts: Firstly, we basically use live video streaming approach instead of VOD approach which means the transcoding time is definitely unknown. Secondly, at live video streaming, the GOP tasks will be dropped if they miss their final deadline times while at VOD must be completed even if they miss their final deadline times. This difference increases uncertainty in live video streams and makes their management a more challenging problem.

The provision and management of QoE in a cloud is currently an important research topic. Authors of [7] proposed a system to improve the provision and management of QoE using cloud resources, They studied the problem of cloud resource optimization based on quality indicators and proposed a multidimensional architecture where agents residing within the cloud used to monitor QoE. After that, these indicators can be used to update and manage the cloud resources. The current work is similar with [7] by the idea of monitoring QoE within the cloud but our work differs by the suggested modules that form our proposed scheme for QoE management as it will be shown in details in in Sect. 3 of this paper. Another work [8] deals with QoE assessment of cloud service providers. The authors of this work proposed a hierarchical model based on cloud provisioning subsets, output bandwidth, response time and latency, the use of the probability that the service could be successfully provided (i.e. the service is available and latency requirements are not violated) and the average time of service completion as QoE indicators. In our work we consider different QoE indicators for video quality assessment since we will present and derive three important performance indicators of QoE to reflect the live video streaming experience at viewer's side.

3 Proposed Scheme Description

We propose a new scheme of QoE management for live streaming using cloud services. An overview of this scheme architecture is presented in Fig. 1. The proposed scheme architecture shows the sequence of actions taken place when viewers request videos

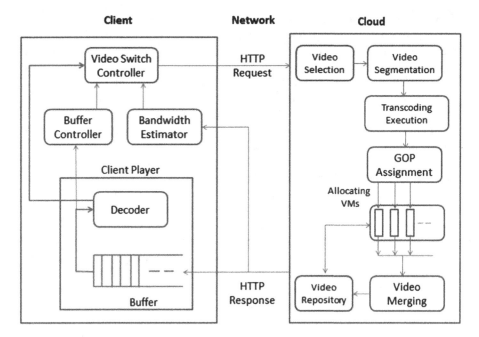

Fig. 1. Proposed scheme architecture

from a live streaming service provider. This proposed scheme architecture includes three main components, namely client, delivery network and server. The client side consists from the following key components:

- **Player buffer:** This buffer is used to store the received video frames from the server hosted in cloud.
- **Decoder:** It is used to decode the received video frames from the player buffer.
- **Buffer regulator:** It is used to control the player buffer length so it can avoid buffer underflow/overflow situations.
- **Bandwidth estimator:** It is used to estimate the available network bandwidth and requests the suitable segment to the server.

In the other side, the service provider side (Server) consists from the following main components and the cooperation of these components leads to cost-efficient and achieving QoS requirements for live streams within the cloud:

- **Video Selection:** The video selection is the process that the user may choose the video. This module may give all information about the video file. For example (video name, video format, video path and video size). At this module the user may select any video it does not affect with the video size.
- **Video Segmentation:** Live video is split into several groups of pictures (GOP) depending on coming video frames, which can then be independently transcoded. Each GOP has a specified deadline on the basis of the time of the first frame in that group.

- **Transcoding Execution:** At live video streaming, the execution time (transcoding process) of coming video frames (i.e. GOP tasks) can't be predicated. It is worth mentioning that this is a big difference of live streaming with the video on demand (VOD) where the video stream is processed several times. Thus, the execution time of each GOP task can be estimated based on previous implementation information.
- **GOP Assignment:** This module is responsible for assigning GOP functions to transcoding servers. The goal of this module is to meet the quality of service requirements for customers (in terms of minimum start delay and GOP drop rate for video streams) without additional cost is charged to video streaming provider.
- **Transcoding Virtual Machines (VMs):** VMs are assigned by the cloud service provider to handle GOP transcoding tasks. In this work, we assume that the default custom VMs are homogeneous. Each VM has a local queue where the required data is preloaded to GOPs before execution. When a free patch appears through the local queue of the virtual machine, a scheduler is assigned to set the GOP to the VM.
- **Video Merging:** The function of this merger is to put already transcoded GOPs in the right order and form live streams. Then, this video merger sends these live streams to corresponding viewers.
- **Video Repository:** This temporally pool to store the video after merging and to be served according to HTTP request. And this module can monitor the operation of the transcoding VMs in the streaming video structure directly, changing the size of the VM cluster to meet customer service quality requirements and reduce the cost incurred for the video service provider.

4   QoE Indicators of the Proposed Scheme

In this work, we propose the video segment duration is a fixed number of seconds, and if the client requests the high video rate, then it contains larger segment size (in bytes). When high video rate segment $R(t)$ is requested by the client and available bandwidth $B(t)$ is lower than the request video rate then the buffer is filled at the rate $B(t)/R(t) < 1$, and as the result the buffer decreases. If client continuously requests high video quality at a rate greater than network bandwidth, the buffer might be depleted as shown in Fig. 2. As a consequence, playback will freeze, and re-buffering event will occur, thus decreasing the client's QoE. However, if network bandwidth is always higher than the requested video rate, then client will never observe re-buffering events i.e. $B(t)/R(t) > 1$.

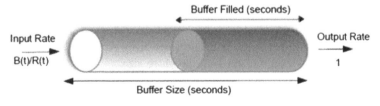

Fig. 2.   Video playback buffer

In live video streaming approach, the video is encoded into various bitrates. So, the player buffer length $q(t)$ can be modeled by using the following formula:

$$q(t) = \frac{B(t)}{R(t)} - d(t) \tag{1}$$

where $d(t)$ is the buffer draining rate, that can be expressed as given below:

$$d(t) = \begin{cases} 1 & playing \\ 0 & paused \end{cases} \tag{2}$$

where $B(t)$ represents the available network rate and $R(t)$ represents the received video level. The player buffer filling rate represents the number of seconds video are stored in the buffer per second. The term $d(t)$ is the draining rate which describes the number of seconds video are played per second.

In this work, we propose a scheme to manage QoE for live video streaming, generally there are many main quality influenced indicators for QoE performance. So that our proposed scheme for managing reviewers' QoE will consider three indication factors into account. These three indicators are startup delay, deadline time (including null time number and total duration) and bit rate level variation (the video quality and its fluctuation). However any QoE's model is a static and posterior model, which means it cannot be used for on-line and real-time service. While in our work, we derive this model into an iterative way for real-time QoE evaluation. This modification makes the QoE followed rate enhanced for on-line service possible.

First indication parameter is the startup delay which impacts directly to the QoE; this parameter is denoted by I_{SD}. According to [9], the factor α is defined as a threshold exists for viewers' impatience which is computed by linear regression. Before the segment i is requested, the already accumulating startup delay is $I_{SD(i-1)}$, if level j is selected for i, the startup delay will increase by $B_{i,j}/R(i)$. We modify the impact of startup delay in an iterative form as:

$$I_{SD(i,j)} = \alpha \left(I_{SD(i-1)} + \frac{B_{i,j}}{R(i)} \right), \quad q < q_{min} \tag{3}$$

The second indication parameter is the deadline time I_{DT} which it is the combination of the null time duration N_{DT} and null time numbers S_{DT}. If the client is in re-buffering state, requesting segment i will not introduce new null event but adding the null duration by $B_{i,j}/R(i)$. In order to evaluate the deadline indicators, we introduce a warning threshold $\acute{q}_{min} = \gamma q_{min} + (1 - \gamma)q_{max}$, $\gamma \in (0, 1)$ which is larger than q_{min} to indicate the upcoming deadline event. After download the segment i, then the buffer length becomes $q + \tau - B_{i,j}/R(i)$. And if the buffer length drops below q_{min}, a null event is assumed to occur, that increase S_{DT} by 1, and the N_{DT} is increased by the time cost to re-fill the buffer to q_{min} again. In such a situation, the client needs to download q_{min}/τ segments to resume palyback. Thus deadline threshold of current buffer length is:

$$T_{DT} = \acute{q}_{min} + \frac{B_{i,j}}{R(i)} - \tau \tag{4}$$

Combining the derivation above, the null number $S_{DT}(i, j)$ and null duration $N_{DT}(i, j)$ for the upcoming segment i with level j is:

$$S_{DT}(i,j) = \begin{cases} S_{DT}(i-1) + 1, & q_{min} < q < T_{DT} \\ S_{DT}(i-1), & otherwise \end{cases} \tag{5}$$

$$N_{DT}(i,j) = \begin{cases} N_{DT}(i-1) + \frac{B_{i,j}}{R(i)}, & q < q_{min} \\ N_{DT}(i-1) + \sum_{i+1}^{i+q_{min}/\tau} \frac{B_{i,j}}{R(i)}, & q_{min} < q < T_{DT} \\ N_{DT}(i-1), & otherwise \end{cases} \tag{6}$$

And according the relationship between the I_{DT}, N_{DT} and S_{DT} in [9], the influencing from deadline time can be obtained in expression (7) below:

$$I_{DT}(i,j) = aN_{DT}(i,j) + bS_{DT}(i,j) - c\sqrt{N_{DT}(i,j)S_{DT}(i,j)} \tag{7}$$

The cross-term in expression above is used to compensate the simultaneous effects of null duration and null time number, and the values of coefficients a,b and c in expression (7) are derived by linear regression [9].

The third indication parameter is level variation $I_{LV}(i, j)$. It is determined by quality factor $I_{quality}(i, j)$ as well as the switch factor $I_{switch}(i, j)$. Video Quality Metric (VQM) is described in details for frames quality assessment [10], while the value of VQM ranges in $(0, 1)$. The frames with the higher VQM are of the poorer qualities and definitions. The annoyance of the viewer increases exponentially as the streaming persistently stays at low quality level. So the quality factor is influenced by the distortion as expressed in the following equation:

$$I_{quality} = \sum_{i=1}^{M} VQM_{I(i)} e^{0.02\tau X(i)} / M \tag{8}$$

$I_{quality}$ is the weighted mean of the VQM of the M segments. The weight of each segment is given by the $e^{0.02\tau X(i)}$. The $X(i)$ stands for the number of continuous segments before i whose VQM is close to i's VQM, indicating that if the video remains in low quality, the QoE will be damaged exponentially. As for quality switch, facts are that viewers are much more sensitive to the switch-down than switch-up, so only the switch-down case is taken into consideration by a sign function:

$$I_{switch} = \frac{1}{M} \sum_{i=1}^{M} \left[(VQM_i - VQM_{i+1})^2 sign(VQM_{i+1} - VQM_i) \right] \tag{9}$$

However, the $I_{quality}$ and I_{switch} are calculated posteriorly in [9], in order to evaluate the QoE during the streaming service in real-time, the equations are modified into an iterative form for on-line service:

$$I_{quality}(i,j) = \left[(i-1)I_{quality} + VQM_j e^{k\tau X_i}\right]/i \tag{10}$$

$$I_{switch}(i,j) = \left[(i-1)I_{Switch}(i-1) + \left(VQM_j - VQM_{l(i-1)}\right)^2 sign\left(VQM_j - VQM_{l(i-1)}\right)\right]/i \tag{11}$$

And the total influence due to level variation is the weighted sum of $I_{quality}$ and I_{switch} according to the coefficients in [9]:

$$I_{LV}(i,j) = B_1 I_{quality}(i,j) + B_2 I_{switch}(i,j) \tag{12}$$

Where B_1 and B_2 coefficients are derived using linear regression technique.

The overall QoE metric is Q, which is a hundred-marked score, can be calculated from I_{LV}, I_{SD} and I_{DT}:

$$Q(i,j) = 100 - I_{SD}(i,j) - I_{DT}(i,j)$$
$$- I_{LV}(i,j) + 0.17 I_{SD}(i,j)\sqrt{I_{DT}(i,j) + I_{LV}(i,j)} + 0.31\sqrt{I_{ST}(i,j)I_{LV}(i,j)} \tag{13}$$

The coefficients and terms in expression (13) come from the regression of subjective test in [9]. We have developed a real-time QoE model; furthermore, it will be used as the guidance to select the bit-rate level.

5   Simulation Results

In this work, we studied the perceived video quality using DASH technology. We investigate three indication factors which impact on user perceived video quality (i.e. QoE): startup delay, null time (frame freezing), and bit rate level variations (frame quality fluctuations). Moreover, for each factor, we explore multiple dimensions that can have different effects on perceived quality. For example, in the case of the deadline time factor, while most previous research have studied how null duration correlates with user perceived quality, we also consider when the null times happen and how the nulls are distributed, since we believe they may also impact user experience. We design and conduct extensive subjective tests to study the impairments of the different dimensions of the three factors on user perceived video quality. We will describe the methodology to design the subjective tests, and present the results of the subjective tests. Based on the subjective tests, we derive impairment functions which can quantitatively measure the impairment of each factor on the user experience of any DASH video and also provides validation results.

The experiments for our simulation are done by using JAVA language, Net Beans 6.9.1 IDE and MySQL for database. Figure 3 below shows the follow diagram for the implementation of our proposed system which including main five modules (Video

Selection, Video Splitting, DASH Streaming Process, QoE Evaluation and Video Viewing Process). The video selection is the process that the user may choose the video; this module may give all information about the video file (i.e. video name, video format, video path and video size). In this module, the user may select any video it does not care about the video size. This process is a source process that the user may select the video and transmit the video. The video splitting process may split at based on video size and video duration, while the video may splitting at same frames the size does not vary, then the complete video may chunks at small components. The DASH streaming technique introduces an additional level of complexity for measuring perceived video quality (i.e. viewer's QoE), as it varies the video bit rate and quality. We investigate three factors which impact user perceived video quality (viewer's QoE): startup delay, null duration time (frame freezing), and bit rate level variations (frame quality fluctuations). Moreover, for each factor, we explore multiple dimensions that can have different effects on perceived quality. Finally, the Video viewing process shows the video merging process, the completed video may store into a destination folder that the user can view this video.

Fig. 3. Flow diagram of simulation implementation

Our experiments begin with testing 16 videos for different cases of simulation above. Firstly, we test videos number 1 to 5 by adding various length of startup delay in the beginning of streaming videos. Figure 4 below shows the relationship between the impairment subject and the startup delay for our tested videos from 1 to 5. So we can prove that this relationship between the average impairment subject and startup delay is linear as shown in figure below.

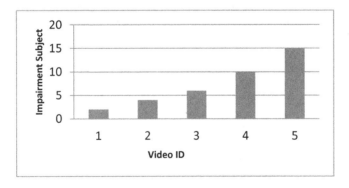

Fig. 4. Startup delay impairment effect

In second experiment, we test the videos from 6 to 16 to evaluate the second influenced parameter that it is the deadline time which is the combination of the null time duration and null time numbers. Figures 5 and 6 respectively show the average impairment values for tested videos (6–16), where null duration and null number are varied. From these two figures, we can note that when the null number is fixed, the subjective impairment value will increase consequently with null duration. While when the null duration is fixed, the subjective impairment value will not increase consequently with null number. However, we can observe that the impairment value is highest with the highest null number, which indicates that frequent nulls will cause big impairment on user experience.

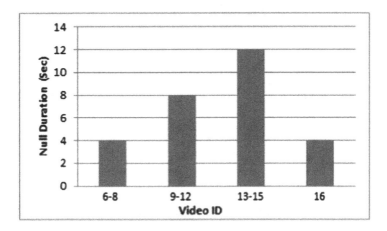

Fig. 5. Null duration in each tested videos

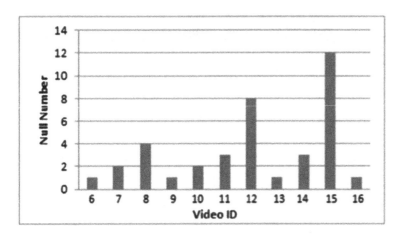

Fig. 6. Null time number in each tested videos

In another side, we examine the effect of level variation impairment factor on viewer's quality of experience, level variation impairment is the most complicated parameter to examine because it is difficult to describe and strip complex patterns of level fluctuations during each trace of the video session. As described in problem formulation section, there are three impact dimensions of this impairment parameter: average level of each video session, number of switches in each session, and average switch magnitude of each trace as shown in Figs. 7, 8 and 9 respectively. From these figures we can notice that the annoyance of the viewer increases exponentially as the streaming persistently stays at low quality level. We can also observe that the three

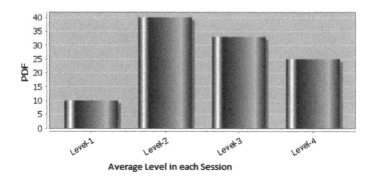

Fig. 7. Distribution of level variation in each session

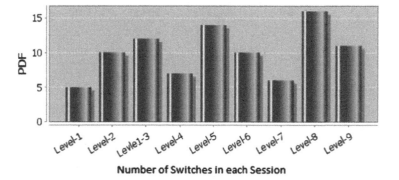

Fig. 8. Distribution of number of switches in each session

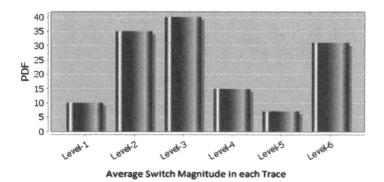

Fig. 9. Distribution of average switch magnitude in each session

impact dimensions will monotonically impact on user experience in a complicated way. Also we can notice that the annoyance of staying at a low level (low quality) will grow exponentially with the duration that the low level is maintained.

6 Conclusions

In this work we submitted a proposed QoE management scheme in cloud environment, and then we test this model under some subjective experiments to evaluate the QoE for viewers using three indication parameters for different DASH streaming videos. Based on the results from these evaluations, we can monitor and control the caused impairment by each one of these three indicators (startup delay, deadline time and bit rate level variation). The simulation results show that the tested indication parameters do not need to access the service providers in order to monitor QoE of viewers and neither any need to insert these indicators into the video streaming client software to determine the user experience in real time (live video streaming). We believe they can serve as useful and light-weight tools for live video streaming service provider to monitor and control their quality of service. Also our results prove that the cloud resources can satisfy the QoE requirements of live stream streaming viewers without considering another cost to the video service providers.

References

1. Hobfeld, T., Schatz, R., Varela, M., Timmerer, C.: Challenges of QoE management for cloud applications. IEEE Commun. Mag. **50**(4), 28–36 (2012)
2. De Cicco, L., Mascolo, S., Palmisano, V.: Feedback control for adaptive live video streaming. In: Proceedings of the Second Annual ACM Conference on Multimedia Systems, pp. 145–156. ACM (2011)
3. Vetro, A., Christopoulos, C., Sun, H.: Video transcoding architectures and techniques: an overview. IEEE Sig. Process. Mag. **20**(2), 18–29 (2003)
4. Cheng, X., Liu, J., Dale, C.: Understanding the characteristics of internet short video sharing: a YouTube-based measurement study. IEEE Trans. Multimed. **15**(5), 1184–1194 (2013)
5. Jokhio, F., Deneke, T., Lafond, S., Lilius, J.: Analysis of video segmentation for spatial resolution reduction video transcoding. In: International Symposium on Intelligent Signal Processing and Communications Systems (ISPACS), pp. 1–6. IEEE (2011)
6. Kafetzakis, E., Koumaras, H., Kourtis, M., Koumaras, V.: QoE4CLOUD: a QoE-driven multidimensional framework for cloud environments. In: International Conference on Telecommunications and Multimedia (TEMU), pp. 77–82. IEEE (2012)
7. Qian, H., Medhi, D., Trivedi, K.: A hierarchical model to evaluate quality of experience of online services hosted by cloud computing. In: International Symposium on Integrated Network Management (IM), pp. 105–111. IEEE (2011)
8. Wang, F., Liu, J., Chen, M.: CALMS: cloud-assisted live media streaming for globalized demands with time/region diversities. In: Proceedings of INFOCOM, pp. 199–207. IEEE (2012)
9. Liu, Y., Dey, S., Gillies, D., Ulupinar, F., Luby, M.: User experience modeling for DASH video. In: 20th International Workshop in Packet Video Workshop (PV), pp. 1–8. IEEE (2013)
10. Pinson, M.H., Wolf, S.: A new standardized method for objectively measuring video quality. IEEE Trans. Broadcast. **50**(3), 312–322 (2004)

Hybrid Adaptive Prediction Mechanisms with Multilayer Propagation Neural Network for Hyperspectral Image Compression

Rui Xiao[✉] and Manoranjan Paul

School of Computing and Mathematics, Charles Sturt University,
Bathurst, Australia
{rxiao,mpaul}@csu.edu.au

Abstract. Hyperspectral (HS) image is a three dimensional data image where the 3rd dimension carries the wealth of spectrum information. HS image compression is one of the areas that has attracted increasing attention for big data processing and analysis. HS data has its own distinguishing feature which differs with video because without motion, also different with a still image because of redundancy along the wavelength axis. The prediction based method is playing an important role in the compression and research area. Reflectance distribution of HS based on our analysis indicates that there is some nonlinear relationship in intra-band. The Multilayer Propagation Neural Networks (MLPNN) with backpropagation training are particularly well suited for addressing the approximation function. In this paper, an MLPNN based predictive image compression method is presented. We propose a hybrid Adaptive Prediction Mechanism (APM) with MLPNN model (APM-MLPNN). MLPNN is trained to predict the succeeding bands by using current band information. The purpose is to explore whether MLPNN can provide better image compression results in HS images. Besides, it uses less computation cost than a deep learning model so we can easily validate the model. We encoded the weights vector and the bias vector of MLPNN as well as the residuals. That is the only few bytes it then sends to the decoder side. The decoder will reconstruct a band by using the same structure of the network. We call it an MLPNN decoder. The MLPNN decoder does not need to be trained as the weights and biases have already been transmitted. We can easily reconstruct the succeeding bands by the MLPNN decoder. APM constrained the correction offset between the succeeding band and the current spectral band in order to prevent HS image being affected by large predictive biases. The performance of the proposed algorithm is verified by several HS images from Airborne Visible/Infrared Imaging Spectrometer (AVIRIS) reflectance dataset. MLPNN simulation results can improve prediction accuracy; reduce residual of intra-band with high compression ratio and relatively lower bitrates.

Keywords: Hyperspectral image · MLP neural network · BP neural network
Image coding · Data compression · Remote sensing · Inter-band prediction

© Springer International Publishing AG, part of Springer Nature 2018
M. Paul et al. (Eds.): PSIVT 2017, LNCS 10749, pp. 162–173, 2018.
https://doi.org/10.1007/978-3-319-75786-5_14

1 Introduction

HS image combines the power of digital imaging and spectroscopy. By using push broom-scanning mode, HS camera sensor scans objects line by line simultaneously in a narrow spectral band. Hence every pixel in the HS image contains a wide range of spectrum and can be used to characterize the objects in the scene with great precision and detail. HS images are beyond human vision ability, can provide moisture content, texture, reflectance and other external quality characteristics of diverse samples. This comes at a price that HS image has a big data set and high redundancy. The extensive implementation of HS imaging is well founded in both the civilian and military field, such as satellite/airborne based remote sensing (NASA's Airborne Visible/Infrared Imaging Spectrometer 2017), target detection (Cheng and Han 2016; Makki et al. 2017), safety and quality inspection, classification as well as quality control in food and agriculture, (Cheng et al. 2017; Park and Lu 2015) and lab applications etc. In Fig. 1, an example of an HS image, namely cuprite from NASA's AVIRIS dataset is shown. This HS image carries 224 contiguous channels with wavelengths from 0.4–2.5 μm. It shows that each pixel $P = (p_1, p_2, ... \ p_n)$ is represented as a vector with 224 elements. Because carrying wealthy spectral information, the HS image data becomes huge. Compression of HS image has gained increasing interest.

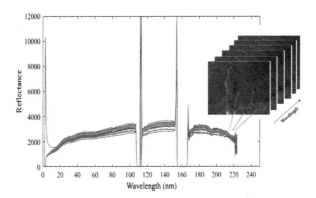

Fig. 1. An HS image, cuprite demonstrates reflectance values curve from randomly picked pixels.

HS image compression methods are different with traditional compression methods as spectral redundancy needs to be removed; it also distinguishes itself from videos as HS data has no motion. HS image has its unique structure, each pixel along the spectral axis is characterised by nonlinearity, continuity and similarity. Especially similarity trend in neighbouring bands of the spectrum can be extracted as learning samples to train a neural network.

Compression techniques can broadly be grouped into two main categories: lossless and lossy compression methods, depending on whether the original image can be precisely re-generated from the compression data (Motta et al. 2006). Or according to different compression technical characteristics, there is transform-based compression, prediction-based compression or vector quantization-based compression. Dictionary-based schemes such as Lempel-Ziv-Welch (LZW) compression algorithm are also prominent (King et al. 2014). Statistical-based schemes require distribution knowledge where the compression takes place based on the frequency of input characters. All these methods are based on lossless compression methods. The most well-known statistical-based algorithms are Huffman Coding (King et al. 2014) and Arithmetic Coding (Howard and Vitter 1992; Sasilal and Govindan 2013). Moreover, another type compression technique is based on LookUp Tables (LUT) (Aiazzi et al. 2009; Mielikainen and Toivanen 2008), which is also lossless type compression method. The LUT searches the previous band for a pixel equal to the current band in the same position called a predictor. The predictor is used as a key to search LUT to speed up the search process.

Transform-based technique, such as the Pairwise Orthogonal Transform (POT), also called multiple pairwise PCA (Amrani et al. 2016) is one of the spectral transforms that an image is transformed using multiple pairwise operations instead of a single transform. It overcomes the problem of KLT, such as bit depth expansion, lack of scalability and reduced memory requirements. (Shahriyar et al. 2016).

Prediction-based technique is an important research direction for compression coding. This type of method often uses a mathematical model to predict pixel values and encode only their prediction residuals (Conoscenti et al. 2016).

Zhao et al. (2016) and Zhu et al. (2015) introduce an algorithm based on intra-band prediction and inter-band fractal encoding. In this method, HS bands are partitioned into several Groups Of Bands (GOBs). The authors apply intra-band prediction to the first band then apply in each GOB. The hypothesis is that two blocks (8×8 pixels) located in the same position of adjacent HS bands are highly similar. There is no universal metric of GOB that is applicable to all HS image in different wavelengths. Moreover, in the experimental results (Zhao et al. 2016; Zhu et al. 2015) indicate that the algorithms get better compression performance at a low bit rate.

Rizzo et al. (2005) and Shen et al. (2017) use a two-stage predictor: one is an inter-band linear predictor, and the other based on least square predictor. The two stage predictor can remove redundancy form two directions, however, the computation cost is also relatively higher in this technique.

DPCM also is an important prediction approach. DPCM include a linear predictor and median filter. The predictor calculates the residual between the value of the current pixel and the predicted pixel. The residual normally has a smaller variance. It results in fewer bits for coding the image. An improved DPCM (Mielikainen and Huang 2012), named as C-DPCM, uses separated spectral clusters. The mean-square error inside each cluster is used to calculate the coefficients. All the pixels used to make the prediction have the same spatial location as the current pixel, and then the difference between the actual targeted value and the predicted value is encoded. This algorithm provides easy mathematical derivation and computational advantage. However, in many practical applications, this still shows an undesirable predictive result.

Paul et al. (2016) proposed a Gaussian mixture-based modelling to predict the succeeding band from current bands. The predicted band is then used as the additional reference band along with the previous band to apply on high efficiency video coding standard (HEVC). Using the number of Gaussian distributions and the initial parameters setting is vital for the result accuracy.

It is worth mentioning that the Consultative Committee for Space Data Systems (CCSDS) have published new compression standard for HS data (Multispectral and Standard 2012). The core predictor in CCSDS called "Fast Lossless (FL)" developed by the NASA Jet Propulsion Laboratory.

The artificial neural network based coding technique for image compression research is very active and fast development. Especially MLPNN with back propagation training algorithm is one of the most popular NN algorithms and have been used largely in image processing (AL-Allaf 2011; Faris et al. 2016).

In this paper, instead of using MLPNN directly applied to image compression coding, we try innovative MLPNN modelling by its excellent nonlinear approximation capability, finding the hidden relationships between the current band and the succeeding band to achieve high coding efficiency.

Encoding residue can compensate for the error between the predicted band and the previous band. The residue could be near to 0 if the predictor is able to reach an ideal result. On the contrary, bias could be huge. To avoid excessive bias, we use an APM. The procedure of applying quantization step in the encoder and decoder side are both same. In this way, we can save the amount of data that needs to be transmitted.

2   Methodology

The multilayer network can be used to approximate almost arbitrary curves if we have enough neurones in the hidden layers (Hagan et al. 1996). The neural network stores the specific information in the weights and biases of the network, which is equivalent to representing the original sample with a smaller data. This is actually a compression process.

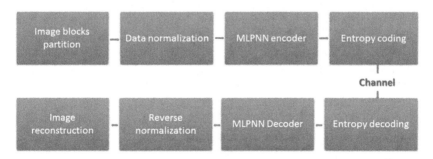

Fig. 2. A simplified prediction process by the proposed algorithm.

Figure 2 illustrates the prediction process of the proposed schema. The first band is encoded as lossless binary codes then transmitted to the decoder. The MLPNN will be trained on the encoder side and then send weights and biases to the decoder side. For each upcoming band, we need to train once. We have three data space, input data, target data and actual output data. A set of input-output data is generated for each pixel. The prediction process is an iterative process. Considering the first band as input data and the second band as the target output. The predicted band is actual output data of

MLPNN. Then the actual output band will be used as the input band for the next prediction process. That is to say, for the upcoming third band, the decoded 2nd band (after compensating the residual with the predicted 2nd band with help of decoded bias and weight) is used as the input. The actual third band is the training target. In the decoding site, we reconstruct the predicted band from the bias, weight and the previous band. Then the iterative process will continue until the last band has been trained and reconstructed at the decoder side. Firstly, we'll discuss training data space construction in the next section.

2.1   Image Data Pre-process

The data correlation among the neighbouring pixels and the current band l and the next $l + 1$ band are the basis for the proposed predicted coding technique. We will use MLPNN learning algorithm based feed forward neural network to predict l band then encoding the residual. The goal is to find the minimized value of mean square error (MSE) of surrounding bands.

Each band has been resizing to a 256×256 matrix and rescales to a range between [0, 1] that is MPLNN input and output expected values. Then the image was partitioned into 4×4 blocks and each block is converted to a $4^2 \times 1$ vector, e.g. input neuron numbers are 16. Each band converts to a 16×4096 matrix as seen Fig. 3.

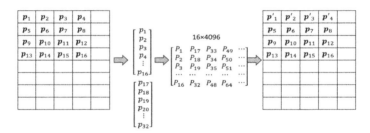

Fig. 3. Construction of input space. Input HS images are divided into 4×4 blocks of 256 pixels, and the each block is converted to a 16×1 vector. The input data is l band and the output will be predicted $l + 1$ band

2.2   Multilayer Neural Network Architecture

The MLPNN is a 16-10-16 architecture layer. This architecture network can be used as a function approximator. The objective is to find a function that map from the current band (input band) to approximate the reflectance value of the following band (target band). The input data will be a 16×4096 matrix of l band and the output will be predicted $l + 1$ band. We employed a transfer function tansig as hidden layer and the output layer is the linear function purelin. Using Purelin as output layer data there is no need for it to be normalised, however normalised data can speed up the convergence rate. In the multilayer networks the output of one layer becomes the input to the following layer. The advantage of this structure of network is it can be used as a nonlinear approximator and constrain the outputs of the network between 0 and 1. The network structure is illustrated at Fig. 4 below. The equations for the hidden layers $f^1(n)$ and output layer $f^2(n)$ is given at Eq. (1). Where x is the net input to a neuron.

$$f^1(x) = \frac{2}{1 + e^{-2x}} - 1 \text{ and } f^2(x) = x \tag{1}$$

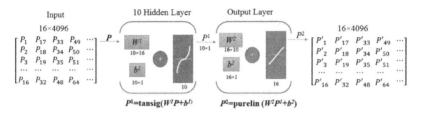

$$P^1 = \text{tansig}(W^1 P + b^1) \qquad P^2 = \text{purelin } (W^2 P^1 + b^2)$$

Fig. 4. MLPNN network structure is a 16-10-16 architecture layer. The tangent sigmoid transfer function is for the Hidden layers and linear function purelin is for the Output layers.

2.3   The Error Calculations and Weight Adjustments

The training process of MLPNN is basically tuning the values of the weights and biases of the network to approximate the expected value. The training process first is to propagate the input forward through the network and then propagate the sensitives backward through the network. First we need to choose some initial values for the weights and biases in the range from −1 and 1 before training the network. The initial values of weight bias were chosen randomly. Using above Eq. (1) to calculate input and output value of each layer respectively. The mean squared error E between the target P and the predictive value P' is defined as:

$$E = 1/M \sum_{i=1}^{M} (P_i - P'_i)^2 \tag{2}$$

Where M is the number of P. Then the weight vector W can be updated by

$$\Delta W = W_n - [J^T J + \mu I]^{-1} J^T E \tag{3}$$

Where I is the identity matrix, μ giving as learning rate, J is Jacobian Matrix can be written as

$$J(x) = \begin{bmatrix} \frac{\partial e_1(x)}{\partial x_1} & \frac{\partial e_1(x)}{\partial x_2} & \cdots & \frac{\partial e_1(x)}{\partial x_n} \\ \frac{\partial e_2(x)}{\partial x_1} & \frac{\partial e_2(x)}{\partial x_2} & \cdots & \frac{\partial e_2(x)}{\partial x_n} \\ \cdots & \cdots & \ddots & \vdots \\ \frac{\partial e_N(x)}{\partial x_1} & \frac{\partial e_N(x)}{\partial x_2} & \cdots & \frac{\partial e_N(x)}{\partial x_n} \end{bmatrix}. \tag{4}$$

Jacobian Matrix is easier to calculate, which don't need to calculate second-order partial derivatives Therefore we choose Levenberg-Marquardt (LM) algorithm as a training function. The LM generally is the fastest training function. It embraces the Gauss–Newton algorithm (GNA) and the method of gradient descent together.

2.4   Bands Reconstruction

We present a new idea, only need to encode the weights $\{W^1\}$ $\{W^2\}$ and biases $\{b^1\}$ $\{b^2\}$ then send to MLPNN decoder side. MLPNN decoder is the same structure network as encoder side. We only use the previous band P_{L-1} as an input band, substituted parameters $\{W^1\}$ $\{b^1\}$ and $\{W^2\}$ $\{b^2\}$ as shown in Fig. 4. the target band P_l can be calculated. For each 16×4096 band matrix, we got $n \times 16$ $\{W^1\}$ and $n \times 16$ $\{W^2\}$ matrix need to be encoded, n represents the number of hidden layers, e.g. each band with 65536 pixels, MLPNN model using 10 hidden layers will only need to encoded 10×16 $\{W^1\}$, 16×10 $\{W^2\}$ matrix, and 10×1 $\{b^1\}$, 16×1 $\{b^2\}$ vector. We process matrices by mapping minimum and maximum values to $[0, 255]$ data space then follow a lossless encoding algorithm. The compression ratio is therefore significantly improved. Let's see an example: a size of 256×256 image need to encode 65,536 pixels if only encode the weights $\{W\}$ and biases $\{b\}$, we need to encode two 16×10 matrixes for weights, 10×1 for the first bias and 16×1 for the second bias. Their values are from 0 to 255 after mapping. We also need to encode the maximum and minimum values of each matrix for mapping data. The experimental results reveal that the bit requirements for encoding the maximum, minimum, biases and weights are only 1% compared to that of encoding residuals.

2.5   Prediction Mechanisms

The predicted band result derived from the target values is further compensated in this step. The ultimate purpose of error-correction learning is bind the relative error between predicted band and the target band. The predicted band is approximated to the targeted band but is not identical, in some cases bias needs to be corrected.

Because the decoder has no original pixel information, refer to Conoscenti et al. (2016), using quantization step sizes in a predictive lossy compression that could reach a near-lossless compression ratio. We also encode quantization step. The process is an adaptive prediction mechanism.

O_l is the compensation value for lth band, $O_l = [P_l(1 + \lambda)] - P_l^R$ if the predicted pixel value is smaller than the targeted band pixel, in the case of the predicted pixel is bigger, set $O_l = [P_l(1 - \lambda)] - P_l^R$. In the decoder, O_l will be transmitted in the form of a short integer. This data will be read by the decoder. It is used to recalculate the image data after compensation $P_l^{\prime R} = P_l^R + O_l$ q_l is the quantization step size applied to that residual. P_l^R is the reconstructed pixel. λ represents maximum relative reconstruction error accepted.

3 Experiment Result

NASA's AVIRIS HS image dataset is used for our experiments. All of the experimental images have been resized to 256 × 256 for verification purpose. The numbers of neurones of input and output layers are 16. The maximum time of training is 1000. The training goal is set to 0.0001.

The validation of MLPNN model is obtained at the end of each training procedure. MSE gives the difference between observation and simulation.

The performance of training and testing plots the progress in Fig. 5 which indicated that the validation and test curves are very similar. The iteration at 219 Epochs performance reached the minimum MSE.

Figure 6 creates four regression plots for the training set (Train), the validation set (Validation), the test set (Test) and the entire dataset (All). It illustrates the obtained output, target and R-values. The correlation coefficient (R-value) between the outputs and the targets values is well fitted. R-values calculated for evaluating the trained MLPNN model. The reflectance values of pixels are plotted against the targets (circles). The dashed line in each plot represents the perfect result – outputs = targets. The solid line indicates the best linear fit. The R-value related to the training set is very close to 1, which indicates a very good fit. The R-value related to the test set is 0.99636, the training and validation results also show R values that are greater than 0.99.

Figure 7 is a demonstration of the compress results using band 101 ($l = 100$) of the HS image cuprite 1. Predicted $l + 1$ band is after prediction of the proposed method and the residual between the l and $l + 1$ neighbouring bands. The residual images calculate the prediction error between target and predicted $l + 1$ band, shown in its histogram. The figure are illustrated that the most of residual values are 0 which indicates the MLPNN approximator achieves good results, therefore, result in requiring less number of bits to encode.

Rate/distortion analysis is commonly used for evaluating different encoders which distortion is usually measured in terms of PSNR values. The performance of Fig. 8 shows rate distortion (RD) performance of four HS images Cuprite 1, Cuprite 2,

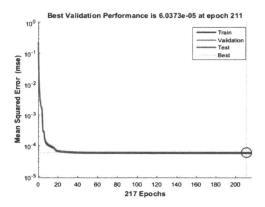

Fig. 5. The validation performance of the MLPNN model

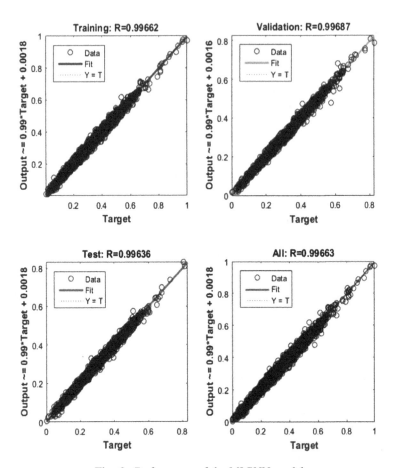

Fig. 6. Performance of the MLPNN model

Cuprite 3 and Cuprite 4 using the proposed MLPNN model, JP2 K, JPEG2 K-residual, JPEG, JPEG-residual encoder techniques. JP2 K is treating each band individually, encoding each band separately by using JPEG 2000 (JP2) image compression standard and coding system. JPEG is the similar method to deal with each band but using the JPEG standard. JP2K-residual and JPEG-residual are to calculate residual of current band and the previous band, then only encode residual instead of encoding each band by JP2 K or JPEG encoder. MLPNN model shows obvious advantages at low bit rate ranges as it only needs to encode weights and biases. APM is to ensure no bias bigger than the maximum accepted reconstruction error. Figure 7 is a demonstration of the compress results using band 101 ($l = 100$) of the HS image cuprite 1. Predicted $l + 1$ band is after prediction of the proposed method and the residual between the l and $l + 1$ neighbouring bands. The residual images calculate the prediction error between target and predicted $l + 1$ band, shown in its histogram. The figure are illustrated that the most of residual values are 0 which indicates the MLPNN approximator achieves good results, therefore, result in requiring less number of bits to encode.

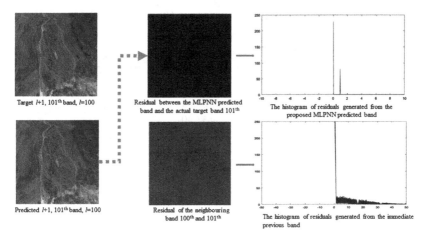

Fig. 7. A demonstration of HS image cuprite 1 compressed result by MLPNN model

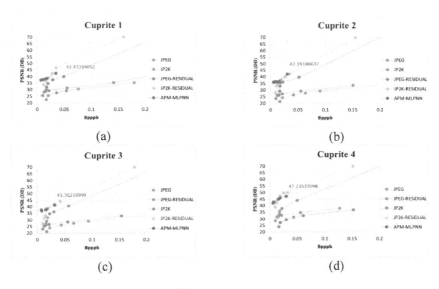

Fig. 8. Rate distortion performance of four Cuprite HS images using the proposed MLPNN model, JP2K (JPEG 2000), JP2K-residual (JPEG 2000-residual), JPEG, JPEG-residual encoder techniques.

Table 1 illustrates outstanding RD performance at Low bit rates 0.016 bpppb. Both JPEG2 K-residual and JPEG-residual are encoded based on the residuals between the target band P_{l+1} and the previous band P_l. Overall, APM-MLPNN model improved the compression rate with very low bit rate costs.

Table 1. Rate distortion performance of four Cuprite HS images encoded at low bit rates.

	Low bit rates 0.016 bpppb (30 PSNR or more)		
Images	JPEG-residual	JP2K-residual	APM-MLPNN
Cuprite 1	30.03	36.58	38.35
Cuprite 2	33.22	34.44	36.74
Cuprite 3	31.64	33.40	38.25
Cuprite 4	36.02	44.40	45.18

4 Conclusion

A hybrid APM with MLPNN model was implemented to predict the succeeding bands. We use the current band as a training data set, and the next band is the training target set in the encoder side. Each band is converted to a 16×4096 matrix. Our experimental result achieves better than JPEG and JPEG2 K according to RD performance metrics, PSNR at low bit rates where Bpppb range is from 0 to 0.05. The advance is significant.

The major advantage of this approach is that it only needs to use the binary entropy encoder to encode weights and bias; later in the decoder side the target band can be reconstructed by using transferred weights, bias, residual and the previous band information. Therefore, only a few bits of data need to be transferred. The obtained results were found to be quite satisfactory. The next challenge would be an improvement to reduce the computational time and implementation of deep learning neural networks to further improve the accuracy of the predictive model.

References

Aiazzi, B., Baronti, S., Alparone, L.: Lossless compression of hyperspectral images using multiband lookup tables. IEEE Signal Process. Lett. **16**, 481–484 (2009)

AL-Allaf, O.N.A.: Fast backpropagation neural network algorithm for reducing convergence time of BPNN image compression. In: 2011 International Conference on Information Technology and Multimedia (ICIM), pp. 1–6. IEEE (2011)

Amrani, N., Serra-Sagristà, J., Laparra, V., Marcellin, M.W., Malo, J.: Regression wavelet analysis for lossless coding of remote-sensing data. IEEE Trans. Geosci. Remote Sens. **54**, 5616–5627 (2016)

Cheng, G., Han, J.: A survey on object detection in optical remote sensing images. ISPRS J. Photogramm. Remote Sens. **117**, 11–28 (2016)

Cheng, J.-H., Nicolai, B., Sun, D.-W.: Hyperspectral imaging with multivariate analysis for technological parameters prediction and classification of muscle foods: a review. Meat Sci. **123**, 182–191 (2017)

Conoscenti, M., Coppola, R., Magli, E.: Constant SNR, rate control, and entropy coding for predictive lossy hyperspectral image compression. IEEE Trans. Geosci. Remote Sens. **54**, 7431–7441 (2016)

Faris, H., Aljarah, I., Mirjalili, S.: Training feedforward neural networks using multi-verse optimizer for binary classification problems. Appl. Intell. **45**, 322–332 (2016)

Hagan, M.T., Demuth, H.B., Beale, M.H.: Neural Network Design, vol. 3632. PWS Publishing Co., Boston (1996)

Howard, P.G., Vitter, J.S.: New methods for lossless image compression using arithmetic coding. Inf. Process. Manag. **28**, 765–779 (1992)

King, G.R.G., Seldev, C.C., Singh, N.A.: A novel compression technique for compound images using parallel Lempel-Ziv-Welch algorithm. Appl. Mech. Mater. **626**, 44 (2014)

Makki, I., Younes, R., Francis, C., Bianchi, T., Zucchetti, M.: A survey of landmine detection using hyperspectral imaging. ISPRS J. Photogramm. Remote Sens. **124**, 40–53 (2017)

Mielikainen, J., Huang, B.: Lossless compression of hyperspectral images using clustered linear prediction with adaptive prediction length. IEEE Geosci. Remote Sens. Lett. **9**, 1118–1121 (2012)

Mielikainen, J., Toivanen, P.: Lossless compression of hyperspectral images using a quantized index to lookup tables. IEEE Geosci. Remote Sens. Lett. **5**, 474–478 (2008)

Motta, G., Rizzo, F., Storer, J.A. (eds.): Hyperspectral Data Compression. Springer Science & Business Media, New York (2006). https://doi.org/10.1007/0-387-28600-4

Multispectral L, Standard HIC: CCSDS 123.0-B-1 Blue Book (2012)

NASA's Airborne Visible/Infrared Imaging Spectrometer (2017). https://aviris.jpl.nasa.gov/data/free_data.html

Park, B., Lu, R. (eds.): Hyperspectral Imaging Technology in Food and Agriculture. FES. Springer, New York (2015). https://doi.org/10.1007/978-1-4939-2836-1

Paul, M., Xiao, R., Gao, J., Bossomaier, T.: Reflectance prediction modelling for residual-based hyperspectral image coding. PLoS one **11**, e0161212 (2016)

Rizzo, F., Carpentieri, B., Motta, G., Storer, J.A.: Low-complexity lossless compression of hyperspectral imagery via linear prediction. IEEE Signal Process. Lett. **12**, 138–141 (2005)

Sasilal, L., Govindan, V.K.: Arithmetic coding-A reliable implementation. Int. J. Comput. Appl. **73** (2013)

Shahriyar, S., Paul, M., Murshed, M., Ali, M.: Lossless hyperspectral image compression using binary tree based decomposition. In: 2016 International Conference on Digital Image Computing: Techniques and Applications (DICTA), pp. 1–8. IEEE (2016)

Shen, H., Pan, W.D., Wu, D.: Predictive lossless compression of regions of interest in hyperspectral images with no-data regions. IEEE Trans. Geosci. Remote Sens. **55**, 173–182 (2017)

Zhao, D., Zhu, S., Wang, F.: Lossy hyperspectral image compression based on intra-band prediction and inter-band fractal encoding. Comput. Electr. Eng. **54**, 494–505 (2016)

Zhu, S., Zhao, D., Wang, F.: Hybrid prediction and fractal hyperspectral image compression. Math. Probl. Eng. **2015**, 10 (2015)

Secret Image Sharing for (k, k) Threshold Based on Chinese Remainder Theorem and Image Characteristics

Xuehu Yan[✉][iD], Yuliang Lu, Lintao Liu, Song Wan, Wanmeng Ding, and Hanlin Liu

National University of Defense Technology, Hefei 230037, China
publictiger@126.com

Abstract. Secret image sharing (SIS) based on Chinese remainder theorem (CRTSIS) has lower recovery computation complexity than Shamir's polynomial-based SIS. Most of existing CRTSIS schemes generally have the limitations of auxiliary encryption and lossy recovery, which are caused by that their ideas are borrowed from secret data sharing. According to image characteristics and CRT, in this paper we propose a CRTSIS method for (k, k) threshold, based on enlarging the grayscale image pixel values. Our method owns the advantages of no auxiliary encryption and lossless recovery for grayscale image. We perform experiments and analysis to illustrate our effectiveness.

Keywords: Secret image sharing · Chinese remainder theorem
Image characteristics · Lossless recovery

1 Introduction

Secret image sharing (SIS) scheme encodes the secret image into multiple noise-like shadow images i.e., shadows or shares, which are then assigned to multiple participants. The secret can be disclosed by sufficient shadow images while insufficient shadow images rebuild nothing about the secret. SIS may be applied in many scenarios, such as, authentication, watermarking, access control, information hiding, transmitting passwords, distributed storage and computing etc. To share grayscale image, there exist Shamir's polynomial-based method [5], Chinese remainder theorem-based SIS (CRTSIS) [1,10] and so on [9,11].

Shamir's polynomial-based SIS [5] encodes the secret image into the constant coefficient of a random $(k-1)$-degree polynomial to possess n shadow images, which are then as well assigned to n participants. The secret image can be disclosed with high-resolution making use of Lagrange interpolation by any k or more shadow images. Following Shamir's original scheme and using all the k coefficients of the polynomial to take secrets, Thien and Lin [7] decreased the shadow image size $1/k$ times to the original secret image. Inspired by Thien and

© Springer International Publishing AG, part of Springer Nature 2018
M. Paul et al. (Eds.): PSIVT 2017, LNCS 10749, pp. 174–181, 2018.
https://doi.org/10.1007/978-3-319-75786-5_15

Lin's research, some researchers [4,12] developed more Shamir's polynomial-based schemes to receive more features. Although Shamir's polynomial-based SIS only needs k shadow images for decoding the distortion-less secret image, it is in general lossy recovery with auxiliary encryption and high computation complexity. On account of the secret is decoded modulo 251 which is less than maximum pixel value 255, the recovery image will be lost when the pixel value of the secret image is larger than 251 so that Shamir's polynomial-based SIS owes a little bit of loss. Image encryption is usually utilized before sharing that results in auxiliary encryption. Because of Lagrange interpolations in the recovery phase, it needs $O(k \log^2 k)$ operations [1], i.e., complicated computations.

CRTSIS overall can achieve the advantages of lossless recovery, no auxiliary encryption and lower recovery computation complexity (the modular only $O(k)$ operations [1]), so that which is discussed by other researchers [2,3,6,8,10].

Related works of CRTSIS are analyzed as follows. Yan et al. firstly [10] discussed CRT in SIS, which may deduce a little information leakage and may be lossy. Shyu and Chen [6] put forward a threshold CRTSIS utilizing Mignotte's scheme based on pseudo random number generator which suffers from auxiliary encryption. Ulutas et al. [8] investigated a modified SIS using Asmuth Bloom's secret sharing scheme through dividing the grayscale image pixel values into more possible intervals. It fails to consider pixel value 2 times or more to the parameter, which may lead to lossy recovery. Chunqiang et al. [3] designated a CRTSIS employing the chaotic map which results in auxiliary encryption. Chuang et al. [2] gave a simple CRTSIS and examined (3, 5) threshold for RGB color images. Their method has the limitation of lossy or least significant bits pre-stored. In addition, their algorithm parameters condition is different from the adopted explicit parameters in the experiment. Finally, most existing CRTSIS schemes fail to provide applicable explicit parameters for the implementations based on the image characteristics. As a result, traditional CRTSIS methods overall suffer from auxiliary encryption, lossy recovery and ignoring the image characteristics, which are caused by that their ideas are borrowed from secret data sharing.

According to image characteristics and CRT, in this paper we propose a CRTSIS method for (k, k) threshold, through enlarging the grayscale image pixel values. Our method owns the benefits of no auxiliary encryption and lossless recovery for grayscale image. The contributions of this paper are that, according to the image characteristics, our (k, k) threshold CRTSIS for grayscale image is lossless recovery without auxiliary encryption. Furthermore, we provide explicit parameters for the implementations based on image pixel value range. We perform experiments and analysis to illustrate our effectiveness.

The rest of the paper is organized as follows. Section 2 introduces some basic requirements for the proposed method. In Sect. 3, our method is presented in detail. Section 4 is devoted to experimental results. Finally, Sect. 5 concludes this paper.

2 Preliminaries

In this section, we describe some preliminaries for our work. In (k, k) threshold SIS, the original secret image S is encrypted among k shadow images $SC_1, SC_2, \cdots SC_k$, and the decrypted secret image S' is reconstructed from k shadow images.

2.1 Chinese Remainder Theorem (CRT)

CRT has a long history. It motivates to solve a set of linear congruence equations.

A set of integers $m_i (i = 1, 2, \cdots, k)$ are chosen subject to $\gcd(m_i, m_j) = 1, i \neq j$. Then there exists only one solution $y \equiv \left(a_1 M_1 M_1^{-1} + a_2 M_2 M_2^{-1} + \cdots + a_k M_k M_k^{-1} \right) (\bmod\ M)$, $y \in [0, M-1]$ satisfying the following linear congruence equations.

$$
\begin{aligned}
y &\equiv a_1 \,(\bmod\ m_1) \\
y &\equiv a_2 \,(\bmod\ m_2) \\
&\cdots \\
y &\equiv a_{k-1} \,(\bmod\ m_{k-1}) \\
y &\equiv a_k \,(\bmod\ m_k)
\end{aligned}
\tag{1}
$$

where $M = \prod_{i=1}^{k} m_i$, $M_i = M/m_i$ and $M_i M_i^{-1} \equiv 1 \,(\bmod\ m_i)$.

$\gcd(m_i, m_j) = 1, i \neq j$ tells that every equation in Eq. (1) will not be eliminated by other equations.

We note that in $[0, M-1]$ there exists unique solution. If only the first $k-1$ equations in Eq. (1) are given, we can gain only one solution for the first $k-1$ equations in $[0, \prod_{i=1}^{k-1} m_i - 1]$, denoted as y_0. While in $[0, M-1]$, $y_0 + b \prod_{i=1}^{k-1} m_i$ for $b = 1, 2, \cdots, m_i - 1$ are the solutions as well satisfying the first $k-1$ equations in Eq. (1). Thus, there are another $m_i - 1$ solutions in $[\prod_{i=1}^{k-1} m_i - 1, M-1]$, other than unique one, which will be applied in the proposed method to get (k, k) threshold.

2.2 The Feature Analysis of Image

Image is different from pure data. The image consists of pixels, and there are some correlations between pixels as well, such as texture, edge, structure and other related information. As a result, SIS should scramble both the pixel values and the correlations between adjacent pixels.

The pixel value range of grayscale image is $[0, 255]$, which should be referred in the SIS design, such as, the secret pixel value is less than 256 and the shadow image pixel value is less than 256 as well. In addition, we know $m_i \leq 256$ in Eq. (1).

3   The Proposed CRTSIS Method for (k, k) Threshold

We present the proposed CRTSIS method for (k, k) threshold based on the secret image S outputting k shadow images $SC_1, SC_2, \cdots SC_k$ and corresponding private modular integers $m_1, m_2, \cdots m_k$. Our generation Steps are demonstrated in Algorithm 1. And the recovery Steps are given in Algorithm 2.

Algorithm 1. The proposed SIS CRTSIS method for (k, k) threshold

Input: The secret image S with size of $H \times W$.

Output: k shadow images $SC_1, SC_2, \cdots SC_k$ and corresponding private modular integers $m_1, m_2, \cdots m_k$.

Step 1: Select a set of integers $\{m_1, m_2, \cdots, m_k < 256\}$ subject to

$$\gcd(m_i, m_j) = 1, i \neq j.$$

Here we denote $M = \prod_{i=1}^{k} m_i$ and $N = \prod_{i=1}^{k-1} m_{n-i+1}$.

Step 2: For each position $(h, w) \in \{(h, w) | 1 \leq h \leq H, 1 \leq w \leq W\}$, repeat Steps 3-4 .

Step 3: Let $x = S(h, w)$. We have $0 \leq x < 256$.
Pick up a random integer A in $\left[\left\lceil \frac{N}{256} \right\rceil, \left\lfloor \frac{M}{256} - 1 \right\rfloor\right]$ and let $y = x + 256A$.

Step 4: Compute $a_i \equiv y \pmod{m_i}$ and let $SC_i(h, w) = a_i$ for $i = 1, 2, \cdots, k$.

Step 5: Output k shadow images $SC_1, SC_2, \cdots SC_k$ and their corresponding private modular integers $m_1, m_2, \cdots m_k$.

In Algorithm 1 and Algorithm 2, we remark that.

1. In Step 1 of our Algorithm 1, $\{m_1, m_2 \cdots, m_k < 256\}$ is due to shadow image pixel value range. We suggest that m_i is as large as possible so that the pixel values of shadow images will randomly lie in large range. $\gcd(m_i, m_j) = 1$ is issued to satisfy CRT conditions. The user may further restrict $\gcd(m_i, 256) = 1$ for $i = 1, 2, \cdots, k$ in specific applications.
2. From Step 3 of our Algorithm 1, A is randomly picked up from $\left[\left\lceil \frac{N}{256} \right\rceil, \left\lfloor \frac{M}{256} - 1 \right\rfloor\right]$, thus $N \leq y < M$ in order to obtain (k, k) threshold for y as explained in Sect. 2.1.
3. In Step 3 of Algorithm 1, since $0 \leq x < 256$ and Step 3 of Algorithm 2, we have x can be losslessly reconstructed for arbitrary $x \in [0, 255]$.
4. In Step 3 of Algorithm 1, A is randomly picked up for each x, therefore $y = x + Ap$ can enlarge x value in order to scramble both the pixel value and the correlations between adjacent pixels without auxiliary encryption.
5. In Step 3 of Algorithm 1, $y = x + Ap$ and $x < 256$ can determine only one x due to $x \equiv y \pmod{256}$.

4   Experimental Results and Analyses

In this section, experiments and analyses are realized to show the effectiveness of our method.

Algorithm 2. Secret image recovery of the proposed scheme.
Input:k shadow images $SC_1, SC_2, \cdots SC_k$, their corresponding private modular integers $m_1, m_2, \cdots m_k$.
Output: A $H \times W$ reconstructed secret image S'.
Step 1: For each position $(h, w) \in \{(h, w) | 1 \leq h \leq H, 1 \leq w \leq W\}$, repeat Steps 2-3. **Step 2:** Let $a_i = SC_i(h, w)$ for $i = 1, 2, \cdots, k$. To solve the following linear equations by the Chinese remainder theorem. $$\begin{aligned} y &\equiv a_1 \, (\mathrm{mod} \ m_1) \\ y &\equiv a_2 \, (\mathrm{mod} \ m_2) \\ &\cdots \\ y &\equiv a_{k-1} \, (\mathrm{mod} \ m_{k-1}) \\ y &\equiv a_k \, (\mathrm{mod} \ m_k) \end{aligned} \qquad (2)$$
Step 3: Compute $x \equiv y \, (\mathrm{mod} \ 256)$. Set $S'(h, w) = x$. **Step 4:** Output the reconstructed secret image S'.

Figure 1 demonstrates the experimental results for $(3, 3)$ threshold, where $m_1 = 253, m_2 = 254, m_3 = 255$ and the grayscale secret image is shown in Fig. 1(a). Figure 1(b–d) display the 3 shadow images SC_1, SC_2, SC_3, which are noise-like. Figure 1(e–h) indicate the reconstructed secret images by any 2 or 3 shadow images based on CRT, from which the recovered secret image from

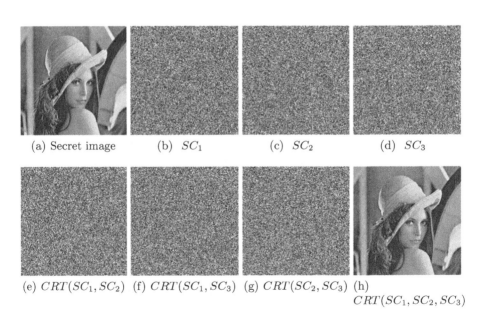

(a) Secret image   (b) SC_1 (c) SC_2 (d) SC_3

(e) $CRT(SC_1, SC_2)$ (f) $CRT(SC_1, SC_3)$ (g) $CRT(SC_2, SC_3)$ (h) $CRT(SC_1, SC_2, SC_3)$

Fig. 1. Experimental example of CRTSIS method for (k, k) threshold, where $k = 3$

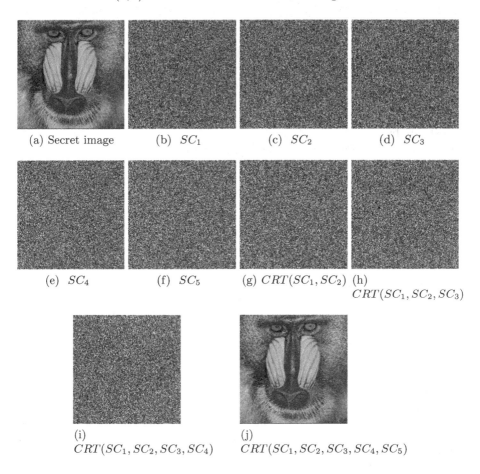

(a) Secret image   (b) SC_1 (c) SC_2 (d) SC_3

(e) SC_4 (f) SC_5 (g) $CRT(SC_1, SC_2)$ (h) $CRT(SC_1, SC_2, SC_3)$

(i) $CRT(SC_1, SC_2, SC_3, SC_4)$ (j) $CRT(SC_1, SC_2, SC_3, SC_4, SC_5)$

Fig. 2. Experimental example of CRTSIS method for (k,k) threshold, where $k = 5$

$k = 3$ shadow images is lossless by CRT due to $\sum_{h=1}^{H} \sum_{w=1}^{W} |S(h,w) - S'(h,w)| = 0$, where $S' = CRT(SC_1, SC_2, SC_3)$ indicates the recovered secret image from SC_1, SC_2, SC_3 by CRT. While any 2 shadow images give no clue about the secret.

The next example, we just give the results by the first tth shadow images for short.

Figure 2 denotes the experimental results for $(5,5)$ threshold, where $m_1 = 247, m_2 = 251, m_3 = 253, m_4 = 254, m_5 = 255$ and the grayscale secret image is exhibited in Fig. 2(a). Figure 2(b–f) show the 5 shadow images, which are also noise-like. Figure 2(g–j) demonstrate the reconstructed secret image with any $t\,(2 \leq t \leq 5)$ (taking the first t shadow images as an example) based on CRT recovery. When $t < 5$ shadow images are collected, there is no information of the secret image. In contrast, when 5 shadow images are given, the secret image is reconstructed losslessly by CRT.

Based on the above results we can see that:

- Since the shadow images are noise-like, the proposed method has no cross interference of secret image for single shadow image.
- When $t < k$ shadow images are obtained, there is no information of the secret image could be deduced, which shows the security of our scheme.
- When $t = k$ shadow images are given, the secret image will be reconstructed losslessly by CRT.
- CRTSIS method for (k, k) threshold is achieved.

In addition, due to no CRTSIS method for (k, k) threshold designed for image in the literature, we omit the comparisons.

5   Conclusion

In this paper, based on image characteristics and Chinese remainder theorem (CRT), we propose a CRTSIS method for (k, k) threshold, through enlarging the grayscale image pixel values. Our method realizes secure (k, k) threshold and lossless recovery for grayscale image without auxiliary encryption. Experimental results further show the effectiveness of our work, where explicit parameters for the implementations based on image pixel value range are presented. The proposed method may be extended to share color secret image based on color decomposition and color composition. (k, n) threshold extending will be our future work.

Acknowledgments. The authors would like to thank the anonymous reviewers for their valuable comments. This work is supported by the National Natural Science Foundation of China (Grant Number: 61602491).

References

1. Asmuth, C., Bloom, J.: A modular approach to key safeguarding. IEEE Trans. Inf. Theory **29**(2), 208–210 (1983)
2. Chuang, T.W., Chen, C.C., Chien, B.: Image sharing and recovering based on Chinese remainder theorem. In: International Symposium on Computer, Consumer and Control, pp. 817–820 (2016)
3. Chunqiang, H., Xiaofeng, L., Di, X.: Secret image sharing based on chaotic map and Chinese remainder theorem. Int. J. Wavelets Multiresolut. Inf. Process. **10**(3), 1250023 (2012). 18 p
4. Li, P., Yang, C.N., Kong, Q.: A novel two-in-one image secret sharing scheme based on perfect black visual cryptography. J. Real-Time Image Process. 1–10 (2016)
5. Shamir, A.: How to share a secret. Commun. ACM **22**(11), 612–613 (1979)
6. Shyu, S.J., Chen, Y.R.: Threshold secret image sharing by Chinese remainder theorem. In: IEEE Asia-Pacific Services Computing Conference, pp. 1332–1337 (2008)
7. Thien, C.C., Lin, J.C.: Secret image sharing. Comput. Graph. **26**(5), 765–770 (2002)

8. Ulutas, M., Nabiyev, V.V., Ulutas, G.: A new secret image sharing technique based on Asmuth Bloom's scheme. In: International Conference on Application of Information and Communication Technologies, AICT 2009, pp. 1–5 (2009)
9. Wang, G., Liu, F., Yan, W.Q.: Basic visual cryptography using braille. Int. J. Digit. Crime Forensics **8**(3), 85–93 (2016)
10. Yan, W., Ding, W., Dongxu, Q.: Image sharing based on chinese remainder theorem. J. North China Univ. Tech **12**(1), 6–9 (2000)
11. Yan, X., Lu, Y.: Progressive visual secret sharing for general access structure with multiple decryptions. Multimedia Tools Appl. **77**(2), 2653–2672 (2018)
12. Yang, C.N., Ciou, C.B.: Image secret sharing method with two-decoding-options: lossless recovery and previewing capability. Image Vis. Comput. **28**(12), 1600–1610 (2010)

Detection of Adulteration in Red Meat Species Using Hyperspectral Imaging

Mahmoud Al-Sarayreh[1](✉), Marlon M. Reis[2], Wei Qi Yan[1],
and Reinhard Klette[1](✉) (iD)

[1] School of Engineering, Computer and Mathematical Sciences,
Auckland University of Technology, Auckland, New Zealand
{malsaray,wyan,rklette}@aut.ac.nz
[2] AgResearch, Palmerston North, New Zealand
marlon.m.reis@agresearch.co.nz

Abstract. This paper reports the performance of hyperspectral imaging for detecting the adulteration in red-meat species. Line-scanning images are acquired from muscles of lamb, beef, or pork. We consider the states of fresh, frozen, or thawed meat. For each case, packing and unpacking the sample with a transparent bag is considered and evaluated. Meat muscles are defined either as a class of lamb, or as a class of beef or pork. For visualization purposes, fat regions are also considered. We investigate raw spectral features, normalized spectral features, and a combination of spectral and spatial features by using texture properties. Results show that adding texture features to normalized spectral features achieves the best performance, with a 92.8% overall classification accuracy independently of the state of the products. The resulting model provides a high and balanced sensitivity for all classes at all meat stages. The resulting model yields 94% and 90% average sensitivities for detecting lamb or the other meat type, respectively. This paper shows that hyperspectral imaging analysis provides a rapid, reliable, and non-destructive method for detecting the adulteration in red-meat products.

Keywords: Hyperspectral imaging · Spectral-spatial features
Meat classification · Meat processing · Adulteration detection

1 Introduction and Background

Adulteration of meat products is an important quality and safety factor of meat (e.g. the addition of another type of meat which may have a lower price compared to the original material).

Traditionally, meat quality and safety attributes are assessed using lab-based methods. Recently, spectroscopic measurements gain increased attention in the field of meat processing, providing optical properties of a single point on the sample surface and mapping those properties onto quality and safety attributes. Such properties can be defined by reflectance or absorbance of light at specific

M. Paul et al. (Eds.): PSIVT 2017, LNCS 10749, pp. 182–196, 2018.
https://doi.org/10.1007/978-3-319-75786-5_16

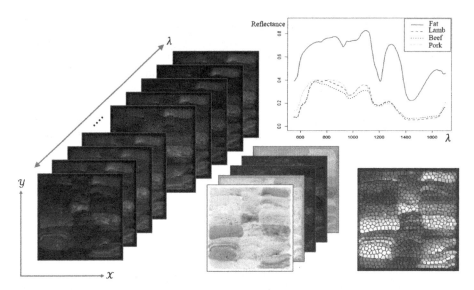

Fig. 1. *Left*: HSI image in spatial xy and spectral λ coordinates. *Upper right*: Spectral signatures of red-meat species. *Lower middle*: First five PCA-score images of an HSI image. *Lower right*: Superpixel segments of an HSI image

electromagnetic wavelengths [1,2]. The spectroscopic approach has disadvantages regarding the non-availability of spatial information, the non-inclusion of small-sized objects into the analysis, missing flexibility in measuring particular spectral information, and inability to generate distributions of attributes [3].

Conventional computer vision systems can be used to assess some meat attributes; they can also deal with the spatial information problem not solvable by single-point spectroscopy. Conventional computer vision systems do not provide multi-spectral information; a colour image provides only reflectance values for three particular energy distributions in the visible light (VIS) wavelengths range (identified as Blue, Green, and Red). The studies described in [4–6] show applications of colour images for the assessment of food quality.

Hyperspectral imaging (HSI) systems aim at a combination of advantages of spectroscopy (i.e. availability of spectral information) with benefits of conventional colour images (i.e. availability of spatial information). Figure 1, left, illustrates an HSI image in spectral [wavelength λ] and spatial [pixel locations (x, y)] coordinates forming a hypercube in this $xy\lambda$ space. Thus, a spectral imaging system is able to provide quality attributes for spectral information as well as spatial information for the localisation of those spectral data in the sample. Spectral imaging systems facilitate the visualization of objects and the chemical distribution of their components. In general, an HSI system collects information about external attributes (spatial information) and internal attributes (spectral information) as *spectral signatures* of materials. Figure 1, upper right, shows spectral signatures for four types of materials, namely lamb, beef, and pork muscles, and fat. Spatial and spectral information characterizes physical and chemical features of objects. In general, HSI systems are more reliable than conventional imaging systems or just using spectroscopy technology.

The rest of this paper is structured as follows. Section 2 provides an overview on related techniques for HSI classification and analysis. Section 3 describes the used data set and the used HSI system. Section 4 covers spectral analysis and pattern visualization. Section 5 describes our framework for classifying the red-meat species. After that, results and discussion are given in Sect. 6. Section 7 concludes.

2   Related Work

The classification of HSI data is the main task in many applications, such as in medical applications, remote sensing imagery, or, as considered here, in meat quality processing. In food and meat applications, HSI is considered as being a powerful tool for classifying or predicting attributes related to food quality. In [7], a linear model has been developed to classify the type of lamb muscles. The average of spectra for each sample was used to build a model. The results showed that HSI was able to define the type of muscles of lamb meat samples, while conventional RGB image analysis failed in performing this characterization.

[8] investigates an HSI system for the discrimination between three types of red-meat (lamb, pork, beef) using *partial least-squares discriminant analysis* (PLS-DA) as a supervised learning model for solving the classification problem. Results showed that PLS-DA performs well in cases of sample-based evaluation, but it provides a misclassification of pixels in cases of pixel-based evaluations. The misclassification of pixels results due to the model being built using the average spectrum of each sample; spatial features are ignored in this case. The system considers the spectral variation in the sample space only, without taking into account the spatial variation in pixel space. In fact, pixels of an HSI image are affected by the source light (light scattering or illumination effects).

In [9], PLS-DA was compared with soft *independent modelling of class analogy* (SIMCA) for the classification between lamb meat and other types (pork or beef). It was found that PLS-DA performed better than SIMCA, but the method's performance varied depending on the way samples were presented (i.e. vacuum packed or without packaging).

Understanding the balance between a variation of spectral information in sample space and the effect of light in pixel space, is a real challenge in building any learning model for classifying meat samples. This challenge needs to be addressed in the case of heterogeneous images. For example, detecting any adulteration in pre-packed rolling meat products is of significant importance. In this case, a pixel-wise (i.e. local) prediction is not only more practical but also more reliable than a sample-wise (i.e. global) prediction.

Building the classification model by using the average spectrum of each sample is a common way for collecting the spectral information for each material using an HSI system [7,8,11–13]. For reducing the effect of light scattering within one image, there are methods commonly used, such as spectral derivatives [8], *standard normal variates* (SNV) [12], or *multiplicative scatter correction* (MSC) [12].

In HSI systems, each pixel contributes to the spectral signature of a material. Thus, as a basic strategy, the use of a pixel as a sample of a material might produce a model invariant to local changes within an image. This methodology is commonly applied to hyperspectral imaging for remote sensing applications [10]. It is proposed due to a limitation in resources (i.e. in image data). Thus, taking a pixel as a sample, while considering different samples of material, provides a powerful model with the advantage of considering local changes within an image.

An HSI classification model that uses only spectral features may provide some useful (but not yet fully satisfying) results; in this case, the spatial information is ignored. Spatial features reflect the geometric or topologic structure of an objects interior. In addition, they also provide information about the local variation in spectral data for each pixel. Thus, also taking into account the spatial features requires a conversion of image data from a pixel-oriented into an object-oriented data structure, i.e. defined by image segments, where each segment is defined by some kind of uniformity in spatial information [14].

A method for spectral-spatial feature extraction in HSI applications is given by super-pixel identification. [15] uses *simple linear iterative clustering* (SLIC) to generate super-pixels of HSI images; the mean of spectral values in each super-pixel is used as an input for an SVM classification model. Then, a linear conditional random-field model is used to compute the final classification map. Following this method, an HSI image is converted into super-pixels based on spectral-spatial information; pixels in each super-pixel have "similar" spectral and spatial features.

Advantages of using super-pixels for extracting spectral features are as follows: (i) averaging over a super-pixel at each wavelength provides a stable spectral signature [15], (ii) a possibility of considering also spatial features [16] (e.g. as known from texture analysis or neighbourhood relationships), and (iii) a potential reduction of computation time in the analysis and prediction phases.

A combination between spectral and spatial features of HIS images are proposed in [16] using a multi-kernel composition of an SVM-RBF. Three types of features are used in this work: the spectrum for each pixel, the average of all pixels inside a generated super-pixel, and a weighted average of eight neighbours for each super-pixel. In [15,16], experimental results show that the use of super-pixels (or any other image segmentation method) for defining spectral features, potentially improves the performance of the fitted models. However, the use of super-pixels may also reduce the performance if extracted segments are inaccurate. For this reason, the segmentation is a critical step in HSI analysis. Ensemble classification rules, like the methods used in [15,16], may be more logical and efficient; decisions in these methods are a combination of spectral and spectral-spatial features.

In general, our study aims at exploring the robustness of hyperspectral imaging systems to discriminate between different types of red-meat muscles. The main contributions of this paper are as follows:

– Investigate the effects of realistic conditions on spectral appearance of fresh red-meat; studied conditions are (1) packing meat into a transparent bag, (2) meat frozen for six hours, and (3) thawing meat after being frozen.
– Develop a learning model to discriminate one type of meat muscle from the others (e.g. in case of adulteration), for example, identify lamb meat in difference to beef or pork with taking into consideration the conditions mentioned above.
– Develop a methodology to consider the local variation in both spectral and spatial features by using a method for super-pixel segmentation.
– Evaluate different types of spectral (e.g. normalization) and spatial (e.g. texture) feature extraction methods.

3   Data Set and HSI System

A collection of three red-meat species were procured from local supermarkets [9]. The total number of procured meat samples is 45, divided as follows: 17 samples of lamb muscle, 13 of beef, and 13 of pork. The samples were randomly partitioned into a calibration set of 30 samples (12 from lamb, 9 from beef, and 9 from pork). The remaining samples were used for evaluation. Pieces of each muscle type were extracted and put into designed *frames*. Figure 2 shows four of those frames, each having a specific muscle type in one of 4×4 cells.

Line-scanning HSI images were collected from these frames at five different *statuses*; a set of 20 HSI images was acquired for model calibration when the meat was (1) fresh, (2) freshly packed in a transparent bag, (3) frozen, (4) frozen and packed in a transparent bag, and (5) thawed (after being frozen) and unpacked. These statuses were investigated regarding their effect on the spectrum of red-meat muscles.

The HSI system, which was used in this work, provides a high spectral resolution of 4.9 nm, and it covers a wide range 547.8–1701.2 nm of wavelengths, thus 235 *bands* across the electromagnetic spectrum. The HSI acquisition system was set up, and the reflectance is calculated following [8,17]. The *reflectance* is computed as follows:

$$R = \frac{R_0 - D}{W - D} \tag{1}$$

This *calibrated* image reflectance R is obtained from the raw image irradiance R_0 by using the dark reference image D and the white reference image W. After reflectance calibration, the first and last five bands of the given 235 bands were removed due to the low SNR in these bands.

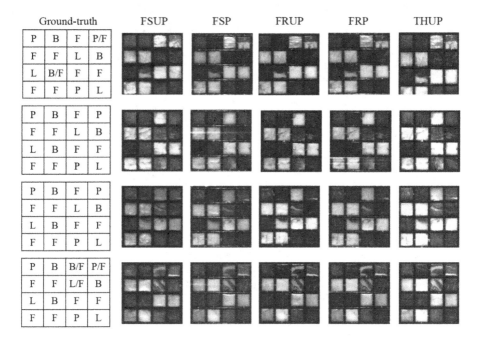

Fig. 2. Ground-truth and false-color images for frames 1 to 4 (*top to bottom*), where FSUP is short for *fresh red-meat unpacked*, FSP for *fresh packed*, FRUP for *frozen unpacked*, FRP for *frozen packed*, and THUP for *frozen-thawed unpacked*. In cells of ground truth, F is for *fat*, L for *lamb*, B for *beef*, and P for *pork*

4   Spectral Data Analysis and Visualization

For simulating the adulteration in red-meat products, we defined the following problem: Identify lamb muscles in difference to other muscles types (i.e. here beef or pork). Thus, the spectral properties of lamb meat are labelled as being one class (called LAMB), and we have another class spectral properties for both beef and pork (called OTHER). In addition, we also use a class FAT for visualization purposes.

When dealing with HSI images, a challenge is the dimensionality of the image data (their large size). The high dimensionality reflects negatively on data visualization and the analysis of this type of images. Agreeing with other authors [7,8,13], we also consider *principal component analysis* (PCA) as an appropriate model for dealing with the dimensionality of HSI images.

PCA can be used for proving and visualizing the separation between classes of different materials. PCA is used for reducing the dimension of HSI data, thus producing a limited number of images, called *score images*, sorted by eigenvalue magnitudes from *highest* to *lowest* score image (Recall: The highest score images represent the most important spectral information from the original spectral information.) For example, in [16], the first three score images were used as

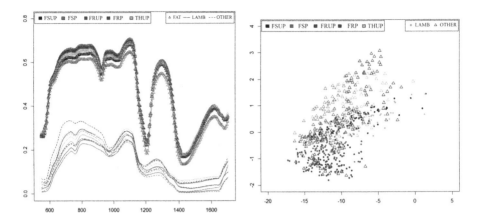

Fig. 3. PCA analysis. *Left*: Mean spectrum of each of the three classes for each of the five statuses; wavelengths between 547.8 nm and 1,701.2 nm versus reflectance values between 0 and 1. *Right*: Scatter plot for the LAMB and OTHER classes, showing 97.67% of the total variances of the original data; PCA 1 (97.3%) between −20 and +5 versus PCA 4 (0.37%) between −2 and +4

input for a segmentation model for segmenting an HSI image and for extracting spatial features from the resulting segments.

We used the data set as introduced in Sect. 3. The calibration subset was hand-labelled (ground truth) for manually defined image segments; the mean spectrum of each segment was used to represent this segment, for each class of the previously described set of HSI images. Then, PCA was applied on the extracted data set for two reasons: (1) for visualizing the patterns between the pre-defined classes (LAMB and OTHER), and (2) as a pre-processing step for extracting the spatial features from each image for each class.

Figure 3, left, shows the mean spectrum of each class at each status of meat. Clearly, this figure shows that there are significant differences in the mean spectrum for each class. For visually investigating the class separations, Fig. 3, right, shows the distribution of the data in the PCA space where the classes are subdivided into overlapping regions; "overlapping" comes from the data in frozen statuses.

5   Classification Framework

In general, a manual selection of pixels as samples, from each class, is impractical and inefficient for creating a robust learning model because no local changes are considered in this case. For this reason, we propose a super-pixel segmentation to convert the HSI image into a map of super-pixels. The pixels in each super-pixel share "similar" local spectral features. Also, super-pixels reflect local spatial features (e.g. similar texture) in the image.

Then, from each super-pixel we select a limited number of pixels to represent this super-pixel. In this work, the SLIC-superpixel algorithm of [19] is used to generate super-pixels of an HSI image. SLIC was originally proposed for colour images; it is based on measuring the similarity (using the Euclidean distance) in RGB or CIE-LAB space, combined with closeness of spatial coordinates.

Due to the high dimensionality of HSI images, we propose to use SLIC in the PCA space; we use the first (i.e. highest) five score images as input for SLIC; the Euclidean distance is used as similarity measure in the PCA space. Figure 1, lower middle, shows an example of five score images and (lower right) the resulting super-pixel segmentation of an HSI image. The resulting super-pixels are accurate, i.e. without any overlapping between different types of meat. As a classifier, an SVM-RBF algorithm was used for evaluating different types of features; it is also used for obtaining the final classification maps.

Extraction of spectral features. The resulting segmentation map is used for extracting samples (pixels) from each class. Considering all pixels in each segment requires high computing costs. For this reason, and for making the classes balanced, we use the *Kennard-Stone* (KS) algorithm [20] to select a subset of representative pixels. A challenge in HSI image data is the dependence of the reflectance values from the source light (light scattering). Transforming pixel values (a pixel value is a vector of reflectance values in the considered wavelength range) into a normalized version emphasizes the patterns between the spectral appearance of the classes, and also reduces the effect of the used lighting. By considering the pixel as a vector, there are two ways of normalization. Let $P(x, y) = [u_1, u_2, \ldots, u_n]^T$ be a pixel in an HSI image at location (x, y).

The first option is to simply convert the pixel-value vector into a unit vector by dividing the values by the L_2-norm $||P(x, y)||_2 = \sqrt{u_1^2 + u_2^2 + \ldots + u_n^2}$ of the vector:

$$P^\circ(x, y) = \frac{P(x, y)}{||P(x, y)||_2} = \left[\frac{u_1}{||P(x, y)||_2}, \frac{u_2}{||P(x, y)||_2}, \ldots, \frac{u_n}{||P(x, y)||_2} \right]^T \quad (2)$$

The second option for normalization is a *standard normal variation* (SNV). In this case, the expected value of pixel values is centred at zero by subtracting the mean μ of the vector values, and then scaled into a unit standard deviation by dividing by its standard deviation σ:

$$\overline{P}(x, y) = \left[\frac{u_1(x, y) - \mu_P}{\sigma_P}, \frac{u_2(x, y) - \mu_P}{\sigma_P}, \ldots, \frac{u_n(x, y) - \mu_P}{\sigma_P} \right]^T \quad (3)$$

Practically, an HSI camera is very sensitive to the lighting; typically measured spectral values have many spiking points. These spiking points affect the normalization transformation. The *Savitzky-Golay* (SG) algorithm [18] is used to reduce the effect of spiking points. The SG method smooths the spectral values by estimating the shape of a group of bands (defined by a window size) by multi-order polynomial fitting. Empirically, we set the window size to 9, with a 2nd-order polynomial fitting to estimate the shape of each pixel before the normalization transformation.

In general, HSI systems produce an enormous amount of spectral information. These cameras are designed to cover a large area of applications such as fruit sorting, medical applications, or, our case, meat processing. Practically, a lot of this information is redundant and not required to accomplish a particular task. Based on this fact, we use *recursive feature elimination* (RFE) [21,22] to select a set of "most significant" wavelengths for making a distinction between the lamb muscle and the other muscles. In the RFE procedure, we use a *random forest* (RF) algorithm to estimate the importance of each wavelength in this classification task. From our PCA analysis, we conclude that the reflectance of each class is strongly affected by the status of the meat. These changes in reflectance value affect the classification results and the importance of various wavelengths. Thus, in this case, we apply an RFE procedure on the data for each status individually (to estimate a set of the most significant wavelengths for each status). Then, a union of all sets is taken with removing any duplication.

Extraction of spectral-spatial features. Texture properties of an image are often used as spatial features in computer vision. A common model for extracting texture features is the *gray-level co-occurrence matrix* (GLCM); the GLCM supports a statistical methodology for analysing the spatial relationships of adjacent pixels by calculating how often a pair of pixels with the same intensity values occurs in an image; see, e.g., [14]. In [23], Haralick proposes a set of statistical features to represent spatial properties (texture properties) of an image. These features were extracted from the CLCM matrix. We use the following Haralick-features: *homogeneity, contrast, inverse difference moment* (IDM), *entropy, energy,* and *correlation*.

In the case of HSI images, extracting these features is demanding due to having many gray-level images (for wavelengths) inside the hypercube; it is hard to decide which wavelengths represent the texture of objects shown in an image. For dealing with this problem, we used the previous RFE analysis to select six wavelengths that have the highest importance (rank) resulting from the RF model. The selected wavelengths (all in nm) are as follows:

$$636.598, \ 646.456, \ 656.314, \ 932.338, \ 1134.43, \ \text{and} \ 1154.14$$

Figure 1, upper right, illustrates that these wavelengths are *logical*: at these wavelengths we have a significant difference between signatures of the considered different types of red-meat.

For computing the CLCM matrix, we use the SLIC segments by taking a window of 20×20 pixels centred in a super-pixel. The center of a super-pixel is defined as the first moment (centre of mass) of all pixels contained in this super-pixel. The selected window is masked by using value 0 to remove any pixel outside the segment border. For avoiding any effect caused by the masked pixels (i.e. the zeros) inside the window, the first row and first column of the CLCM are eliminated, and the selected wavelengths are normalized into the range of 1–255. After that, texture features are computed for each super-pixel at six wavelengths; the total number of the selected features is 36 features for each super-pixel. Then, these sets of features are added to the selected spectral features of pixels inside the considered super-pixel.

6   Experimental Results and Discussion

The data set, described in Sect. 3, is used to build the prediction model. First, the PCA was applied to each image. After that, the first five score images were used as input for the SLIC algorithm. The initial region size of each super-pixel was set to 100 pixels (i.e. 10×10). Then, the resulting segments are labelled by one of the classes (i.e. LAMB, OTHER, or FAT). By using the KS algorithm, from each super-pixel, we select a limited number of pixels (11 for lamb and 9 for the other cases) to represent the super-pixel. Then, a data set was built from these pixels.

We investigated the following feature vectors: *Raw spectral*, normalized spectrum by L_2 norm (L_2-*norm*), normalized spectrum by L_2 norm with texture (L_2-*norm-texture*), SNV normalization (*SNV-norm*), and SNV normalization with texture (*SNV-norm-texture*). In the case of raw spectral, raw reflectance features (by applying Eq. (1)) were considered, where the total number of features is 225, while in the normalization case, the raw spectral data were smoothed, then processed by applying Eq. (1), and then normalised using either P° as in Eq. (2) for the L_2-norm, or $\overline{P}$ as in Eq. (3) for the SNV-norm.

For reducing the dimensionality of the features, only optimal features (wavelengths) of the RF model were chosen (93 and 103 features for the L_2-norm and the SNV-norm, respectively). As described above, we select a set of 36 spatial features to represent the texture of each super-pixel. Thus, all the pixels which belong to the same super-pixel have the same spatial features. Then, these spatial features were added to the feature vectors in the case of L_2-norm and SNV-norm.

We use the SVM-RBF algorithm for performing classification. For model assessment, we use a 10-fold cross-validation with grid search [24] for hyper-parameter[1] selection. For evaluating the resulting models, a new set of samples (6 for lamb, 7 for beef, and 6 for pork) were evaluated and analyzed. In more detail, these samples were prepared and put in a private frame for imaging and simulating the situation of mixing different types of red-meat. Then, HSI images were captured for the meat at the following stages: two images for fresh meat (packed and unpacked), another two after having the meat frozen for six hours (packed and unpacked), and one image after thawing the frozen samples. The first column of Fig. 4 shows false color images of the HSI images which were used to evaluate the proposed features. The second column shows the selected regions for quantitative assessment (ground-truth). Some fat regions were eliminated from the assessment due to the fact that these regions are skinny fat, and this kind of fat was not considered during the model calibration.

---

[1] Hyper-parameters are parameters that are not directly learnt within estimators.

False color image Ground-truth Raw spectral L_2-norm L_2-norm - texture SNV-norm SNV-norm - texture

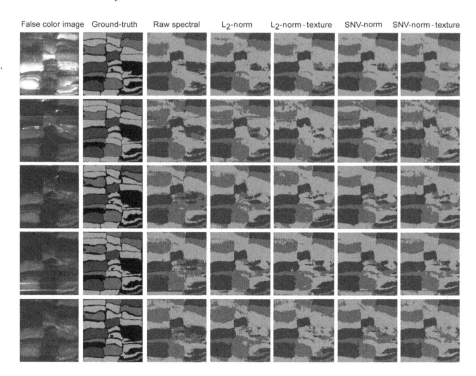

Fig. 4. Visualization results (classification maps) of the proposed feature vectors. The colors Red, Green, and Blue represent classes LAMB, OTHER (beef or pork), and FAT, respectively. *Top to bottom*: FSUP, FSP, FRUP, FRP; all four rows for HSI of fresh and frozen (packed and unpacked) red-meat, and, in the row at the bottom, THUP for HSI of fresh thawed unpacked red-meat (Color figure online)

The evaluation results show that HSI systems are robust tools for detecting the adulteration in red-meat products. Moreover, this robustness is invariant to the state of the products (e.g. fresh, packed, frozen, or frozen-thawed).

In case of sample-wise evaluation, visually, the proposed feature vector (SNV-norm-texture) provides a very accurate performance, where all samples of all types of meat are classified successfully. But a main objective of this paper was to evaluate the proposed features in a way of pixel-wise evaluation.

Table 1 shows pixel-wise quantitative performance results for each feature vector. In all cases, the proposed spectral normalization methods enhance the accuracy compared to a plain-spectral method.

The results show that raw spectral data are strongly affected by the state of the meat. The best overall accuracy was achieved for the state of fresh meat. However, the accuracy significantly decreased for the other statuses; this observation clearly appeared from our PCA analysis. The changes in accuracy document the need that other features need to be used. Our goal is to provide a model with a high stability between the sensitivity and precision of all classes.

Table 1. Performance evaluation of proposed features for different meat statuses

Status	Feature vector	Sensitivity			Precision			Overall accuracy
		Lamb	Other	Fat	Lamb	Other	Fat	
FSUP	Raw spectral	89.8	91.6	99.4	86.7	95.4	94.7	92.8
	L$_2$-norm	96.2	87.9	99.2	80.2	97.9	99.7	92.6
	L$_2$-norm-texture	92.9	92.2	98.9	85.3	96.4	99.4	93.9
	SNV-norm	96.1	94.4	99.8	92.3	98.1	96.2	96.1
	SNV-norm-texture	93.1	95.2	98.2	89.8	96.4	99.5	95.3
FSP	Raw spectral	93.4	70.8	99.8	62.4	97.4	92.8	83.3
	L$_2$-norm	95.1	67.2	98.3	58.1	96.2	98.9	81.5
	L$_2$-norm-texture	94.1	80.7	97.1	69.9	95.7	98.9	87.9
	SNV-norm	96.9	71.2	98.8	62.6	98.6	95.3	84.1
	SNV-norm-texture	96.1	84.9	96.6	74.8	97.2	98.7	90.3
FRUP	Raw spectral	96.1	75.3	99.9	66.4	97.9	96.5	86.3
	L$_2$-norm	97.4	78.2	99.8	70.8	98.5	94.6	88.1
	L$_2$-norm-texture	92.8	78.2	99.7	69.1	95.8	96.1	87.1
	SNV-norm	95.9	90.1	99.9	84.4	97.9	96.7	93.9
	SNV-norm-texture	93.6	88.6	99.7	81.2	96.8	97.4	92.5
FRP	Raw spectral	91.5	79.2	99.5	71.4	95.8	91.5	87.1
	L$_2$-norm	92.5	83.7	98.5	76.1	96.1	93.5	89.5
	L$_2$-norm-texture	86.8	85.5	98.3	76.7	93.1	94.3	88.9
	SNV-norm	91.3	89.1	99.4	82.6	96.1	94.6	92.1
	SNV-norm-texture	90.8	85.8	99.1	77.1	95.5	95.3	90.2
THUP	Raw spectral	95.1	77.4	99.2	68.5	97.4	93.6	86.8
	L$_2$-norm	97.8	71.8	98.5	61.7	97.9	99.3	84.4
	L$_2$-norm-texture	96.4	85.9	98.5	76.3	97.6	98.9	91.4
	SNV-norm	98.1	83.5	99.1	75.2	98.7	96.3	90.7
	SNV-norm-texture	96.6	93.6	98.4	87.7	97.9	99.1	95.5

Compared to raw spectral data, the enhancement given by the proposed method is even more obvious for the other meat states. For example, in case of FSP, the accuracy increased from 83.3% to 90.3%. In general, raw spectral features produced a non-stable model; for example, the sensitivity of classes (LAMB, and OTHER) significantly change from state to state. Also, there is a gap in the sensitivity of the classes at all the statuses except the FSUP status while normalizing the spectrum provides a more stable performance. The gap between the sensitivity of the classes is significantly reduced.

Table 2 shows the results (sensitivity, precision, and overall accuracy) on average for all meat statuses. On average, the SNV normalization outperforms the L$_2$ normalization where the mean overall accuracy of all meat statuses are 87.2% and 91.4% for L$_2$-norm and SNV-norm, respectively.

As expected, by adding spatial features (e.g. texture) we improve the accuracy and the stability of the proposed spectral normalization methods. In the case

Table 2. Performance evaluation on average of proposed features, independently of the state of the meat (i.e. summarising FSUP, FSP, FRUP, FRP, and THUP)

Feature vector	Sensitivity		Precision		Overall accuracy
	Lamb	Other	Lamb	Other	
Raw spectral	93.2	78.8	71.1	96.7	87.2
L$_2$-norm	95.8	77.8	69.4	97.3	87.3
L$_2$-norm-texture	92.6	84.6	75.5	95.7	89.8
SNV-norm	95.6	85.6	79.5	97.8	91.4
SNV-norm-texture	94.1	89.6	82.1	96.8	92.8

of the L$_2$-norm, the spatial features increase mean accuracy from 87.2% to 89.8%; in the case of SNV-norm, they increase mean accuracy from 91.3% to 92.8%.

By adding the spatial features we significantly improved the accuracy for meat statuses FSP and THUP. For example, in THUP, the accuracy jumped from 86.86% (raw spectral) to 95.5% (SNV-norm-texture), while there is no significant enhancement in the accuracy of statuses FSUP, FRUP, and FRP.

Also, adding texture reflects on the stability of the model; the gap in sensitivity and precision between the class LAMB and class OTHER decreases. This suggests that the model resulting from SNV with texture is the best and most efficient model in the set of considered models. Figure 4 shows the resulting classification map of each feature vector for each meat status. The last column shows results for the best-achieved accuracy which occurred when texture properties were added to the SNV-normalized spectral features.

7   Conclusions

Adulteration of red-meat products is a growing concern to the industry. This study investigates the use of HSI to detect adulteration independently of the state of the products (fresh, packed, frozen, or frozen and thawed). To achieve this goal, we investigated different types of spectral and spatial features. The quantitative performance analysis shows that SNV normalization with texture features produces a stable model, fairly invariant to the red-meat status with 92.8% average overall accuracy. The results show that packing the sample into a transparent bag did not affect the spectral response of that sample if it is packed tightly. Lamb meat is detected successfully without any misclassification of pieces with high sensitivity in the case of pixel-wise evaluation while the classification results of beef or pork are affected by the status of the meat, especially in the frozen status; here is space for improvements.

Acknowledgments. Authors appreciate funding by the AgResearch Core Fund and the Ministry of Business, Innovation and Employment, New Zealand. Authors also acknowledge conference support by Auckland University of Technology, the School of Engineering, Computer and Mathematical Sciences.

References

1. Bock, J., Connelly, R.: Innovative uses of near-infrared spectroscopy in food processing. J. Food Sci. **73**, 91–98 (2008)
2. Cen, H., He, Y.: Theory and application of near-infrared reflectance spectroscopy in determination of food quality. Trends Food Sci. Technol. **18**, 72–83 (2007)
3. Elmasry, G., Kamruzzaman, M., Sun, D.-W., Allen, P.: Principles and applications of hyperspectral imaging in quality evaluation of agro-food products: a review. Crit. Rev. Food Sci. Nutr. **52**, 999–1023 (2012)
4. Du, C., Sun, D.: Comparison of three methods for classification of pizza topping using different colour space transformations. J. Food Eng. **68**, 277–287 (2005)
5. Zheng, C., Sun, D., Zheng, L.: Recent developments and applications of image features for food quality evaluation and inspection: a review. Trends Food Sci. Technol. **17**, 642–655 (2006)
6. Wu, D., Sun, D.: Colour measurements by computer vision for food quality control: a review. Trends Food Sci. Technol. **29**, 5–20 (2013)
7. Kamruzzaman, M., Elmasry, G., Sun, D., Allen, P.: Application of NIR hyperspectral imaging for discrimination of lamb muscles. J. Food Eng. **104**, 332–340 (2012)
8. Kamruzzaman, M., Barbin, D., Elmasry, G., Sun, D., Allen, P.: Potential of hyperspectral imaging and pattern recognition for categorization and authentication of red meat. Innov. Food Sci. Emerg. Technol. **104**, 332–340 (2012)
9. Karrer, A., Stuart, A, Craigie, C., Taukiri, K., Reis, M.M.: Detection of adulteration in meat product using of hyperspectral imaging. In: Proceedings of Chemometrics Analytical Chemistry, p. 177 (2016)
10. Ghamisi, P., Couceiro, M., Benediktsson, J.: Integration of segmentation techniques for classification of hyperspectral images. IEEE Geosci. Remote Sens. Lett. **11**, 342–346 (2014)
11. Ropodi, A., Pavlidis, D., Moharebb, F., Panagou, E., Nychas, G.: Multispectral image analysis approach to detect adulteration of beef and pork in raw meats. Food Res. Int. **67**, 12–18 (2015)
12. Kamruzzaman, M., Makino, Y., Oshita, S.: Rapid and Non-destructive detection of chicken adulteration in minced beef using visible near-infrared hyperspectral imaging and machine learning. J. Food Eng. **170**, 8–15 (2016)
13. Sanz, J., Fernandes, A., Barrenechea, E., Silva, S., Santos, V., Goncalves, N., Paternain, D., Jurio, A., Melo-Pinto, P.: Lamb muscle discrimination using hyperspectral imaging comparison of various machine learning algorithms. J. Food Eng. **174**, 92–100 (2016)
14. Klette, K.: Concise Computer Vision. UTCS. Springer, London (2014). https://doi.org/10.1007/978-1-4471-6320-6
15. Hu, Y., Monteiro, S., Saber, E.: Super pixel based classification using conditional random fields for hyperspectral images. In: Proceedings of IEEE International Conference on Image Processing, pp. 2202–2205 (2016)
16. Fang, L., Li, S., Duan, W.: Classification of hyperspectral images by exploiting spectral-spatial information of superpixel via multiple kernels. IEEE Trans. Geosci. Remote Sens. **53**, 6663–6674 (2015)
17. Burger, J., Geladi, P.: Hyperspectral NIR image regression part I: calibration and correction. J. Chemom. **19**, 355–363 (2005)
18. Savitzky, A., Golay, M.: Smoothing and differentiation of data by simplified least squares procedures. Anal. Chem. **36**, 1627–1639 (1964)

19. Achanta, R., Shaji, A., Smith, K., Lucchi, A., Fua, P., Susstrunk, S.: SLIC super-pixels compared to state-of-the-art superpixel methods. IEEE Trans. Pattern Anal. Mach. Intell. **34**(11), 2274–2282 (2012)
20. Kennard, R., Stone, L.: Computer aided design of experiments. Technometrics **11**(1), 137–148 (1969)
21. Ambroise, C., McLachlan, G.: Selection bias in gene extraction on the basis of microarray gene-expression data. Proc. Natl. Acad. Sci. **99**(10), 6562–6566 (2002)
22. Svetnik, V., Liaw, A., Tong, C., Wang, T.: Application of Breiman's random forest to modeling structure-activity relationships of pharmaceutical molecules. In: Roli, F., Kittler, J., Windeatt, T. (eds.) MCS 2004. LNCS, vol. 3077, pp. 334–343. Springer, Heidelberg (2004). https://doi.org/10.1007/978-3-540-25966-4_33
23. Haralick, R.: Statistical and structural approaches to texture. Proc. IEEE **67**(5), 786–804 (1979)
24. Hsu, C.W., Chang, C.C., Lin, C.J.: A practical guide to support vector classification. Technical report, National Taiwan University (2003, last update 2016)

Pattern Recognition and Applications

Unsupervised Domain Adaptation with Robust Deep Logistic Regression

Guangbin Wu[1,3], Weishan Chen[1(✉)], Wangmeng Zuo[2], and David Zhang[3,4]

[1] State Key Laboratory of Robotics and System, Harbin Institute of Technology, Harbin, China
wuguangbin1230@outlook.com, cws@hit.edu.cn
[2] School of Computer Science and Technology, Harbin Institute of Technology, Harbin, China
cswmzuo@gmail.com
[3] Department of Computing, The Hong Kong Polytechnic University, Hong Kong, China
csdzhang@comp.polyu.edu.hk
[4] Harbin Institute of Technology Shenzhen Graduate School, Shenzhen, China

Abstract. The goal of unsupervised domain adaptation (UDA) is to eliminate the cross-domain discrepancy in probability distributions without the availability of labeled target samples during training. Even recent studies have revealed the benefit of deep convolutional features trained on a large set (e.g., ImageNet) in alleviating domain discrepancy. The transferability of features decreases as (i) the difference between the source and target domains increases, or (ii) the layers are toward the top layer. Therefore, even with deep features, domain adaptation remains necessary. In this paper, we treat UDA as a special case of semi-supervised learning, where the source samples are labeled while the target samples are unlabeled. Conventional semi-supervised learning methods, however, usually attain poor performance for UDA. Due to domain discrepancy, label noise generally is inevitable when using the classifiers trained on source classifier to predict target samples. Thus we deploy a robust deep logistic regression loss on the target samples, resulting in our RDLR model. In such a way, pseudo-labels are gradually assigned to unlabeled target samples according to their maximum classification scores during training. Extensive experiments show that our method yields the state-of-the-art results, demonstrating the effectiveness of robust logistic regression classifiers in UDA.

Keywords: Domain adaptation · Deep convolutional networks
Robust logistic regression · Semi-supervised learning

1 Introduction

In many computer vision and pattern recognition applications, it is generally assumed that the training and test samples are independent identically distributed (i.i.d.). This assumption, however, usually seldom hold true in most

© Springer International Publishing AG, part of Springer Nature 2018
M. Paul et al. (Eds.): PSIVT 2017, LNCS 10749, pp. 199–211, 2018.
https://doi.org/10.1007/978-3-319-75786-5_17

real-world scenarios, where the training and test data are collected with different sensors and at dissimilar scenarios [1–3], i.e. from different domains. Without loss of generality, we suppose the training data is from the source domain and the test data from the target domain. Thus, domain adaptation is introduced to learn a domain-invariant classifier from both target data and labeled source data [4,5].

Domain adaptation is a special kind of transfer learning method which aims at eliminating the distribution difference for two different but related domains [6,7]. According to the availability of labeled samples in target domain, there are three types of domain adaptation methods, i.e. supervised, semi-supervised, and unsupervised. In this work, we focus on unsupervised domain adaptation (UDA), where all the target samples are unlabeled during training.

For UDA, due to the unlabeled target samples, the classifier in general is trained by: (1) minimizing the classification loss on source data, and (2) reducing the discrepancy in distributions between source and target domains. By far, various classifiers, e.g., support vector machine (SVM) and logistic regression, have been deployed. A number of domain discrepancy metrics, such as maximum mean discrepancy (MMD) [5], distribution-matching embedding (DME) [8], and domain confusion [9], have also been presented.

With the progress in deep convolutional networks (CNNs), recent studies have shown that deep convolutional features trained on a large set (e.g., ImageNet) are beneficial in alleviating domain discrepancy [10]. Even so, as pointed out by Yosinski et al. [11], the transferability of features decreases along with the increase of the domain difference and the increase of layers toward the top layer. As a result, deep UDA methods have received considerable research interest in the last few years. In this paper, we present a semi-supervised learning (SSL) perspective for deep UDA. We note that most existing UDA methods [14,16–18] only consider the domain discrepancy and do not make full use of the unlabeled target samples in a SSL manner. Actually, UDA can also be treated as a special case of SSL, where the source samples are labeled while the target samples are unlabeled. Conventional SSL methods are based on the assumption that the labeled and unlabeled samples are i.i.d., which generally is not hold for UDA due to domain discrepancy. Thus, it remains a challenging issue to study for extending SSL to UDA.

To extend SSL to UDA, we propose a robust deep logistic regression (RDLR) model. Analogous to the SSL methods in [12,13], our RDLR alternates between (i) assigning pseudo-labels to target samples, and (ii) updating classifiers. Denote $\mathbf{D}_s = \{(\mathbf{x}_{s,i}, y_{s,i})\}_{i=1}^{N_s}$ and $\mathbf{D}_t = \{\mathbf{x}_{t,i}\}_{i=1}^{N_t}$ as the labeled source data and unlabeled target data in training.

We note that even the labels of source samples are known, label noise generally is inevitable in the pseudo-labels $\{\hat{y}_{t,i}\}_{j=1}^{N_t}$ when using the classifiers to predict target samples. Thus, we simply adopt the logistic loss $\mathcal{L}_s(\mathbf{W}; \mathbf{D}_s)$ on the source data. As to target data, we suggest to use the robust logistic regression loss to alleviate the adverse effect of labeling error. Specifically, the confidence of pseudo-label is assessed by considering two aspects: (i) the classification score, and (ii) the ratio between the first two maximum output values. Based on the confidence of pseudo-label, we divide the target samples into three groups, i.e. samples with high, medium, and low confidence. For each group, specific robust logistic regression loss is designed to improve the robustness against label noise.

Furthermore, we stack the robust logistic regression model upon the CNN architecture to utilize the discriminative ability and transferability of deep representation. As illustrated in Fig. 1, in forward propagation, we assign pseudo-label and confidence level for each target sample. According to the confidence level, specific robust logistic regression loss (e.g., ℓ_{TH}, ℓ_{TM}, or ℓ_{TL} in Fig. 1) is computed. In backward propagation, the model parameters are updated by minimizing the logistic loss on source samples and minimizing the specific robust logistic loss based on confidence level. Extensive experiments have been conducted to evaluate the proposed RDLR model on the Office-Caltech dataset and the Office-31 dataset [20]. The results show that RDLR is effective in handling label error and reducing domain discrepancy, and performs favorably in comparison with the state-of-the-art UDA methods.

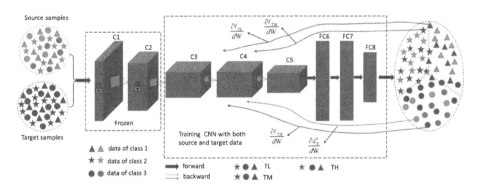

Fig. 1. The architecture of our proposed RDLR method based on Alexnet [19]. During training the model, the first two layer are frozen for avoiding overfitting, and other layers are optimized by both source and target data simultaneously. In forward propagation, pseudo labels are assigned for target samples which are divided into three groups: targets with high, medium and low confidence (TH, TM, TL). In backward propagation, the model parameters are updated by minimizing the logistic loss ($\mathcal{L}_s$) on source data and minimizing the specific robust logistic loss (ℓ_{TH}, ℓ_{TM}, or ℓ_{TL}) on target data.

To sum up, the contribution of this paper is three-fold:

1. We present a SSL perspective for UDA. To remedy the label error caused by domain discrepancy, we assess the confidence level of pseudo-labels for target samples, and suggest three specific robust logistic regression losses for them with high, medium, and low confidence, respectively.
2. By stacking robust logistic losses upon CNN, we propose a robust deep logistic regression (RDLR) model for UDA in a SSL manner. The back-propagation algorithm is then deployed to learn model parameters.

3. Experimental results on the Office-Caltech dataset and the Office-31 dataset validate the effectiveness of the proposed RDLR model in handling label error and reducing domain descrepancy. And RDLR can achieve the state-of-the-art results for UDA.

The remainder of this paper is organized as follows. Section 2 presents the model and learning algorithm of RDLR. Section 3 evaluates our RDLR method on standard UDA benchmarks datasets, i.e. Office-Caltech dataset and the Office-31 dataset. Section 4 analyzes the parameter sensitivity and feature visualization of the proposed RDLR method. Section 5 ends this paper by providing several concluding remarks.

2   Proposed Method

In this paper, the architecture of our unsupervised deep domain adaptation method is described in Fig. 1. This architecture is based on Alex network (AlexNet) [19] which is composed of an input layer, 5 convolutional layers from conv1 to conv5 (including pooling layers), 3 fully connected layers from fc6 to fc8 and an output layer. In our proposed model, the first two convolutional layers (conv1–conv2 layers) are frozen for learning general features and others layers are fine-tuned or trained to learn specific features for classification. During training our model progress, both source and target samples are taken as input data simultaneously, which is beneficial to fusing their knowledge in deep architecture and reducing the distribution divergency across two different domains.

2.1   Performing Pseudo Labels for Target Samples

For a training dataset $\mathbf{D} = \{(\mathbf{x}_n, y_n)\}_{n=1}^{N}$, the softmax logistic loss of a deep learning network is defined as function 1 which aims at optimizing parameters $\mathbf{W}$.

$$L(\mathbf{W}) = -\frac{1}{N} \sum_{n=1}^{N} \sum_{k=1}^{K} \delta(y_n = k) \log \frac{e^{z_{n,k}}}{\sum_{i=1}^{K} e^{z_{n,i}}} \tag{1}$$

where N is the number of training samples, K stands for the number of categories, $z_{n,k} = f(\mathbf{x}_n, y_n; \mathbf{W})$ denotes the k-th representation in the fully connected 8-th layer (fc8 layer) of Alex network, $\delta(\cdot)$ is the Kronecker delta function given by

$$\delta(y) = \begin{cases} 1; \text{ if } y = k \\ 0; \text{ if } y \neq k \end{cases} \tag{2}$$

The derivative about $z_{n,k}$ is given by function 3.

$$\frac{d(L(\mathbf{W}))}{dz_{n,k}} = -\frac{1}{N} \left(\delta(y_n = k) - \frac{e^{z_{n,k}}}{\sum_{i=1}^{K} e^{z_{n,i}}} \right) \tag{3}$$

During training the proposed model, we use stochastic gradient descent (SGD) approach to optimize the parameters $\mathbf{W}$ of deep neural network. The update progress of $z_{n,k}$ can be described as follows.

$$z_{n,k}^{p+1} \leftarrow z_{n,k}^p + \frac{\eta}{N}\left(\delta(y_n = k) - \frac{e^{z_{n,k}}}{\sum_{i=1}^K e^{z_{n,i}}}\right) \tag{4}$$

where η denotes learning rate and p stands for training epoch of deep neural network.

According to the function 4, the representation $z_{n,k}$ $(k = y_n)$ for a training sample $\{\mathbf{x}_n, y_n\}$ in fc8 layer of Alex network will increase relatively as the training epoch grows, while other representations $z_{n,k}$ $(k \neq y_n)$ decrease. In other word, the gap between the representation $z_{n,k}$ $(k = y_n)$ and other representations $z_{n,k}$ $(k \neq y_n)$ of an image sample is enlarged during optimizing the deep networks. Therefore, the values of $\{z_{n,1}, \cdots, z_{n,K}\}$ can be taken as the classification scores $\{\mathbf{s}_{n,1}, \cdots, \mathbf{s}_{n,K}\}$ and pseudo labels for target samples are set based on the maximum values of their classification scores $\{\mathbf{s}_{T,n,1}, \cdots, \mathbf{s}_{T,n,K}\}$.

Let $\mathbf{s}_{T,n,max}$ and $\mathbf{s}_{T,n,max2}$ be the first two maximum values among $\{\mathbf{s}_{T,n,1}, \cdots, \mathbf{s}_{T,n,K}\}$ of a target sample. According to the pseudo-label definition of target samples, we can deduce two inferences described as follows.

(1) For a set of target samples with same pseudo labels, they have a higher classification confidence to be classified into actual categories as the maximum classification scores $\mathbf{s}_{T,n,max}$ increase.

(2) For a target image sample, the ratio $\mu_{T,n}$ between the first two maximum classification scores $\mathbf{s}_{T,n,max}$ and $\mathbf{s}_{T,n,max2}$ suggests its noise level, which reflects the probability of classification accuracy. Hence, a target sample with a bigger ratio $\mu_{T,n}$ tends to have a higher classification confidence correspondingly.

2.2 Robust Deep Logistic Regression for Target Samples

Although, in Sect. 2.1, pseudo labels $\hat{\mathbf{Y}}_T$ of target samples are assigned according to their classification score, they can not be guaranteed to be true. It is rational that target samples whose pseudo labels correspond to their actual categories $\mathbf{Y}_T$ are in favor of training domain adaptation model, and vice versa. To learn a robust domain adaptation model, the target samples should be utilized based on their classification confidence during learning the parameters $\mathbf{W}$ with the fixed pseudo labels $\hat{\mathbf{Y}}$. We divide the target samples into three groups (samples with high, medium, and low classification confidence) and then construct robust logistic loss functions for them respectively.

Target samples with high classification confidence

The pseudo labels of this group target samples are correct with the highest probability. For reducing the disturbance by other classes, we just take the pseudo labels of target samples into consideration. And the logistic loss function can be given by

$$\ell_{TH}(\mathbf{W}) = -\frac{\alpha}{N_{TH}} \sum_{n=1}^{N_{TH}} \sum_{k=1}^K \delta(\hat{y}_{TH,n} = k) \log p(y_{TH,n} = \hat{y}_{TH,n} | \mathbf{x}_{TH,n}, \mathbf{W}) \tag{5}$$

where N_{TH} is the number of target samples with high classification score; α is the adaptive constant used to weight the target samples.

Target samples with medium classification confidence

Although the classification scores of these target samples are smaller than those mentioned above, their classification confidence is also high. Besides the pseudo labels, the ratio between the first two classification scores is taken into consideration. Their logistic loss function is described as

$$\ell_{TM}(\mathbf{W}) = -\frac{1}{N_{TM}} \sum_{n=1}^{N_{TM}} \gamma_n \sum_{k=1}^{K} \delta(\hat{y}_{TM,n} = k) \log p(y_{TM,n} = \hat{y}_{TM,n} | \mathbf{x}_{TM,n}, \mathbf{W})$$

(6)

where N_{TM} is the number of target samples with medium classification score; γ_n denotes adaptive parameter of n-th target sample depended on the ratio $\mu_{TM,n}$ between the first two maximum classification scores and $\gamma_n \leq \alpha$.

Target samples with lower classification confidence

In this part, the classification confidence of target samples is smaller than that of others. In order to learn a robust domain adaptation model, we take other classes into consideration besides the pseudo labels. Their logistic loss function is described as function 7.

$$\ell_{TL}(\mathbf{W}) = -\frac{1}{2N_{TL}} \sum_{n=1}^{N_{TL}} \sum_{k=1}^{K} \delta(\hat{y}_{T,n} = k)(\beta_1 \log p(y_{TL,n} = \hat{y}_{TL,n} | \mathbf{x}_{TL,n}, \mathbf{W}) +$$

$$\frac{\beta_2}{K-1} \sum_{j \neq \hat{y}_{TL,n}}^{K} \log p(y_{TL,n} = j | \mathbf{x}_{TL,n}, \mathbf{W}))$$

(7)

where $\beta_1 \geq \beta_2$, N_{TL} is the number of target samples with lower classification confidence.

The global objective function

Combining the objective functions mentioned above, we yield the global objective function for optimizing the parameters $\mathbf{W}$ which is described as function 8.

$$L_G(\mathbf{W}) = L_S(\mathbf{W}) + \lambda(\ell_{TH}(\mathbf{W}) + \ell_{TM}(\mathbf{W}) + \ell_{TL}(\mathbf{W}))$$ (8)

where $L_S(\mathbf{W}\}$ is the objective function for labeled source data, which is the same as function 1. The goal is to minimize the objective function $L_G(\mathbf{W})$ about parameters $\mathbf{W}$ of deep neural network. These parameters updated via SGD method in epoch $p+1$ are described as follows:

$$\mathbf{W}^{p+1} \leftarrow \mathbf{W}^p - \eta \frac{dL_G(\mathbf{W})}{d\mathbf{Z}} \cdot \frac{\partial \mathbf{Z}}{\partial \mathbf{W}}$$ (9)

where $\mathbf{Z}$ stands for the representation of target samples in the fc8 layer and η is the learning rate.

3 Experiments

To analyze the effectiveness of the proposed RDLR, we did some experiments on unsupervised adaptation problems over the Office-31 dataset [20] and the Office-Caltech dataset [14], which are standard domain adaptation datasets. Then we compared them with other state-of-the-art domain adaptation methods and found that our method was more effective in unlabeled target domains.

3.1 Setup

The Office-31 dataset used in our experiments is composed of three distinct domains: Amazon (A), Webcam (W) and DSLR (D). The images of Amazon were collected from www.amazon.com, and the images of Webcam and DSLR were taken by web camera and digital SLR camera respectively. Every these domains has 31 categories of common objections, such as tables, bottles, mugs and bags, which are used in a typical office/house environment. There are a total of 4110 images with an average of 16 images per category for DSLR, 90 images per category for Amazon, and 26 images per category for Webcam. The Office-Caltech dataset consists of 10 overlapping categories which are selected from the Office-31 dataset [20] (Amazon, Webcam and DSLR) and Caltech-256 (C) dataset [21]. In the corresponding domains, they have 958, 295, 157 and 1123 image samples respectively, with a total of 2,533 images. As these images were acquired in unconstrained settings with inconsistent lighting and backgrounds, they highlight the challenges for object recognition task and domain adaptation. Some images chosen from the Office-Caltech dataset are shown in Fig. 2.

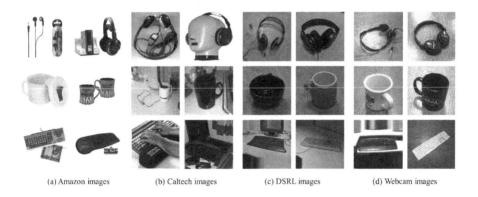

(a) Amazon images   (b) Caltech images   (c) DSRL images   (d) Webcam images

Fig. 2. Object images of Office-Caltech dataset

In our experiments, we minimally pre-processed the images to satisfy the AlexNet [19]: (1) All images were re-scaled to size 270 × 270 pixels; (2) Each pixel of an image was subtracted by its corresponding mean pixel of all source images, and then the results were divided by the maximum result value of all source images.

For all experiments, we initialized the deep CNN parameters from the convolutional layer 1 to the fully connect layer 7 using the pre-trained AlexNet [19] parameters which were downloaded from MatConvNet website [23]. As the low layers of the deep neural networks have a strong ability of learning general features and the high layers are good at extracting specific features contributing to the classification [11], we froze the first two convolutional layers, fine-tuned the conv4–conv5 layers and fully connected layers fc6–fc7, and trained the last layer fc8. The stochastic gradient descent (SGD) in our model was set by 0.9 momentum.

3.2 Evaluation

In domain adaptation experiments, we used the complete source data with labels as training data and the complete target samples without labels as test data for unsupervised problems. We made this decision primarily to have more training data per domain adaptation task, and also for the convenience of training the domain adaptation model [14]. Before training our proposed models, we firstly fine-tuned the initialized AlexNet only using the labeled source data until its classification ability did not improve on every domain of the Office-31 dataset and the Office-Caltech dataset. The learning rate in fine-tune process was set by 0.001. And the batch size was set by 128. The classification results of two datasets based on fine-tuned AlexNet are shown in the Tables 1 and 2.

Evaluation on Office-Caltech Dataset

While evaluating our models on Office-Caltech dataset, learning rate was set by 0.0001 at beginning which might be fine-tuned if the networks were not stable in the training period; $\lambda = 2$, $\alpha = 0.8$, $\beta_1 = 0.06$ and $\beta_2 = 0.04$. The value of the parameter γ_n is shown in function 10. These parameters will be analyzed in the following context.

$$\gamma_n = \begin{cases} 0; & \text{if } \mu_{TM,n} \in [1,11] \\ \alpha \cdot \mu_{TM,n}/22; & \text{if } \mu_{TM,n} \in (11,22] \\ \alpha; & \text{if } \quad \mu_{TM,n} > 22 \end{cases} \tag{10}$$

where $\mu_{TM,n}$ denotes the ratio between the first two maximum classification scores $s_{TM,n,max}$ and $s_{TM,n,max2}$ of n-th target sample with medium classification confidence.

In Table 1, RDLR0 denotes the unsupervised deep domain adaptation model trained by the target samples whose pseudo labels with high and medium classification confidence and RDLR1 stands for the proposed method optimized with all the target samples. Geodesic flow kernel (GFK) [14], transfer component analysis (TCA) [5], subspace alignment (SA) [15], and JCSL [3] are shallow transfer learning methods, and others, such as deep transfer learning (DTN) [22], DASH-N [18], AlexNet [19] and our methods RDLR0 and RDLR1, are based on deep learning.

Table 1. Classification accuracy (%) of unsupervised problems on the Office-Caltech

Methods	Database												
	A/C	A/D	A/W	C/A	C/D	C/W	D/A	D/C	D/W	W/A	W/C	W/D	Avg
GFK [14]	37.90	35.10	35.70	40.40	41.10	35.80	36.20	32.70	79.10	35.50	29.30	71.20	42.50
TCA [5]	40.07	34.39	35.25	45.82	35.67	30.51	31.42	32.06	86.44	28.81	29.92	85.99	43.03
SA [15]	35.30	37.60	38.60	39.00	39.60	36.80	38.00	32.40	83.60	37.40	32.30	80.30	44.24
JCSL [3]	42.60	42.50	47.60	44.30	46.50	46.50	41.30	35.10	74.20	43.10	36.10	66.20	47.17
DTN [22]	42.90	56.00	43.00	54.00	56.00	58.50	34.89	32.27	87.50	36.89	34.18	84.00	51,68
DASH-N [18]	54.90	–	75.50	71.60	81.40	–	68.90	–	77.10	70.40	50.20	–	68.75
AlexNet [19]	67.75	63.06	61.02	87.08	81.53	70.85	54.83	46.02	93.90	47.90	40.66	97.45	67.67
RDLR0	76.00	82.80	74.91	90.34	87.80	82.41	75.53	57.73	**98.30**	**76.05**	48.97	100.00	79.24
RDLR1	**78.46**	**84.81**	**75.25**	**90.86**	**89.17**	**84.41**	**77.73**	**65.06**	97.95	75.94	**53.26**	100.00	**81.08**

Table 2. Classification accuracy (%) on Office-31 dataset.

Methods	Database			
	W/D	D/W	A/W	Avg
TCA [5]	58.40	50.10	21.50	43.30
GFK [14]	63.10	49.70	19.70	44.20
DaNN [25]	74.30	70.50	35.20	60.00
DDC [16]	91.70	92.50	59.40	81.2
DLID [17]	84.92	68.93	26.13	59.99
DASH-N [18]	71.10	67.90	**60.60**	66.53
AlexNet [19]	95.00	93.50	38.49	75.66
RDLR0	98.39	96.60	51.59	82.06
RDLR1	**99.20**	**96.98**	51.44	**82.54**

The experimental results of these outstanding methods reported in their original papers are used to make comparison with the proposed models (RDLR0 and RDLR1). It is obvious that the transferable ability using deep learning significantly outperforms that of shallow models. Especially, our methods get excellent achievements on the unsupervised scenarios of the 12 across train/test splits, which improves about 11.57% for RDLR0 and 13.41% for RDLR1 on average, even more than 20% in some cases, compared with the AlexNet which just used the source data to train the classifier. Moreover, the classification performance of RDLR1 is better than that of RDLR0 in most of domain adaptation tasks.

Evaluation on Office-31 Dataset

In these group experiments, the adaptive parameters of our proposed model are the same as those used on Office-Caltech dataset. The Table 2 shows the classification results of some algorithms tested on the Office-31 dataset, where TCA [5], GFK [14] and domain adaptive neural networks (DaNN) [25] method are based on shallow transfer learning and others, such as DDC [16], DLID [17],

DASH-N [18], AlexNet [19] and our RDLR0 and RDLR1 methods, are based on deep learning. In contrast, our methods greatly outperform other compared methods, especially the RDLR1 whose average classification accuracy is higher about 7% than that of the baseline AlexNet algorithm on across domain adaptation tasks.

4 Analysis

Here we firstly analyze the sensitivity of parameters in our method. Then, according to the feature visualization, we prove that our method can reduce the distribution discrepancy between two different domains.

4.1 Parameter Sensitivity

During optimizing the proposed domain adaptation model, maximum classification scores and ratios between the first two maximum classification scores of target samples are always changing and the target samples for the three groups $\mathbf{X}_{TH}$, $\mathbf{X}_{TM}$, $\mathbf{X}_{TL}$ have to be reselected in each training epoch. So, the adaptive parameters α, γ, β_1 and β_2 weight different target samples. Considering γ depends on α which is reacted by parameters λ, β_1 and β_2 meanwhile, hence we just investigate the effects of parameters λ, β_1 and β_2 on across domain tasks.

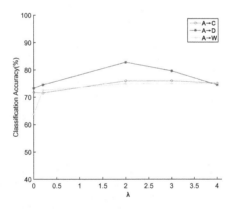

Fig. 3. Classification accuracy vs the parameter λ

Firstly, the parameter sensitivity of λ was evaluated while β_1 and β_2 were set to 0 and $\alpha = 0.8$. Its classification performance across domains was shown in Fig. 3 which indicated that all three domain adaptation tasks achieved highest classification accuracy when $\lambda = 2$. Then setting $\lambda = 2$, we tested the sensitivity of parameters β_1 and β_2 while one of them was fixed alternatively. According to their classification accuracy described in Fig. 4(a) and (b); when $\beta_1 = 0.06$ and $\beta_2 = 0.04$, the proposed domain adaptation model got the outstanding performance. Therefore, in our domain adaptation experiments, parameters were given by $\lambda = 2$, $\beta_1 = 0.06$ and $\beta_2 = 0.04$ while $\alpha = 0.8$.

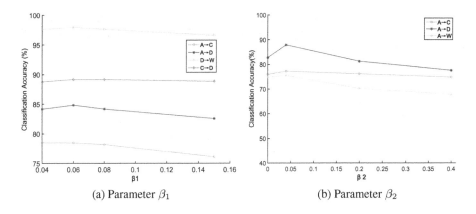

(a) Parameter β_1 (b) Parameter β_2

Fig. 4. Classification accuracy vs the β parameters

4.2   Feature Visualization

The proposed logistic loss function uses both source and target data simultaneously to train the domain adaptation model, so that their distribution discrepancy is reduced by fusing their knowledge together. In order to evaluate this theory, we used t-Distributed Stochastic Neighbor Embedding (t-SNE) approach [24] to visualize the representation features for the cross domain task D→W before and after domain adaptation (DA). Their features with 4096 dimension were extracted from the fc7 layer of AlexNet.

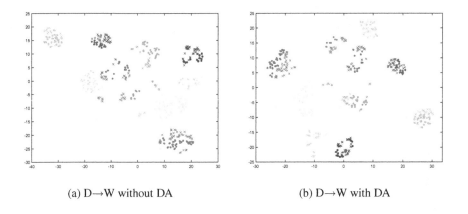

(a) D→W without DA   (b) D→W with DA

Fig. 5. Feature visualization

The feature visualization for the cross domain task is shown in Fig. 5 where points represent source samples and '×' denotes target samples. And different colors denote different categories of the cross domains. The Fig. 5(a) and (b) illustrate the representation features of across domain tasks before and after domain adaptation respectively. Compared with those without domain adaptation, the representation features extracted from our model tend to confuse together. It means that the distribution of target data is much more consistent with that of source data in our domain adaptation model.

5 Conclusion

In this paper, we proposed a novel method called RDLR, which used both source and target data to train an unsupervised deep domain adaptation model. During optimizing this model, target samples without labels were set to pseudo labels based on their maximum classification scores, and their robust logistic loss functions were built and weighted according to their classification confidence. By this method, the knowledge of source domain and target domain were learned simultaneously so that their knowledge fused together to decrease their distribution discrepancy and improve the domain adaptation ability.

On experimental evaluations, our method yielded the state of the art achievements on two benchmark databases. When we used all the unlabeled target samples to train the proposed domain adaptation model, the average classification accuracy improved more than 13% on the Office-Caltech dataset and nearly 7% on the Office-31 dataset for across domain tasks compared with the baseline method, AlexNet.

Acknowledgements. The work is partially supported by the GRF fund from the HKSAR Government, the central fund from Hong Kong Polytechnic University, the NSFC fund (61332011, 61671182, 50905040) and Shenzhen Fundamental Research fund (JCYJ20150403161923528, JCYJ20140508160910917). Besides, we gratefully acknowledge NVIDIA corporation providing the Tesla K40c GPU for our research.

References

1. Torralba, A., Efros, A.A.: Unbiased look at dataset bias. In: IEEE Computer Vision and Pattern Recognition (CVPR), pp. 1521–1528. IEEE (2011)
2. Shimodaira, H.: Improving predictive inference under covariate shift by weighting the log-likelihood function. J. Stat. Plann. Infer. **90**(2), 227–244 (2000)
3. Fernando, B., Tommasi, T., Tuytelaars, T.: Joint cross-domain classification and subspace learning for unsupervised adaptation. Pattern Recogn. Lett. **65**, 60–66 (2015)
4. Daumé III, H., Kumar, A., Saha, A.: Frustratingly easy semi-supervised domain adaptation. In: Proceedings of the 2010 Workshop on Domain Adaptation for Natural Language Processing, pp. 53–59. Association for Computational Linguistics (2010)
5. Pan, S.J., Tsang, I.W., Kwok, J.T., Yang, Q.: Domain adaptation via transfer component analysis. IEEE Trans. Neural Netw. **22**(2), 199–210 (2011)
6. Pan, S.J., Yang, Q.: A survey on transfer learning. IEEE Trans. Knowl. Data Eng. **22**(10), 1345–1359 (2010)
7. Ghosn, J., Bengio, Y.: Bias learning, knowledge sharing. IEEE Trans. Neural Netw. **14**(4), 748–765 (2003)

8. Baktashmotlagh, M., Harandi, M., Salzmann, M.: Distribution-matching embedding for visual domain adaptation. J. Mach. Learn. Res. **17**(1), 3760–3789 (2016)
9. Tzeng, E., Hoffman, J., Darrell, T., Saenko, K.: Simultaneous deep transfer across domains and tasks. In: Proceedings of the IEEE International Conference on Computer Vision (ICCV), pp. 4068–4076. IEEE (2015)
10. Donahue, J., Jia, Y., Vinyals, O., Hoffman, J., Zhang, N., Tzeng, E., Darrell, T.: DeCAF: a deep convolutional activation feature for generic visual recognition. In: International Conference on Machine Learning (ICML), pp. 647–655 (2014)
11. Yosinski, J., Clune, J., Bengio, Y., Lipson, H.: How transferable are features in deep neural networks? In: Advances in Neural Information Processing Systems, pp. 3320–3328 (2014)
12. Amini, M.-R., Gallinari, P.: The use of unlabeled data to improve supervised learning for text summarization. In: Proceedings of the 25th Annual International ACM SIGIR Conference on Research and Development in Information Retrieval (ACM), pp. 105–112 (2002)
13. Vapnik, V., Sterin, A.: On structural risk minimization or overall risk in a problem of pattern recognition. Autom. Remote Control **10**(3), 1495–1503 (1977)
14. Gong, B., Shi, Y., Sha, F., Grauman, K.: Geodesic flow kernel for unsupervised domain adaptation. In: IEEE Computer Vision and Pattern Recognition (CVPR), pp. 2066–2073. IEEE (2012)
15. Fernando, B., Habrard, A., Sebban, M., Tuytelaars, T.: Unsupervised visual domain adaptation using subspace alignment. In: IEEE Computer Vision and Pattern Recognition (CVPR), pp. 2960–2967. IEEE (2013)
16. Tzeng, E., Hoffman, J., Zhang, N., Saenko, K., Darrell, T.: Deep domain confusion: maximizing for domain invariance. arXiv preprint arXiv:1412.3474 (2014)
17. Chopra, S., Balakrishnan, S., Gopalan, R.: DLID: deep learning for domain adaptation by interpolating between domains. In: ICML Workshop on Challenges in Representation Learning, vol. 2, no. 6 (2013)
18. Nguyen, H.V., Ho, H.T., Patel, V.M., Chellappa, R.: DASH-N: joint hierarchical domain adaptation and feature learning. IEEE Trans. Image Process. **24**(12), 5479–5491 (2015)
19. Krizhevsky, A., Sutskever, I., Hinton, G.E.: Imagenet classification with deep convolutional neural networks. In: Advances in Neural Information Processing Systems, pp. 1097–1105 (2012)
20. Saenko, K., Kulis, B., Fritz, M., Darrell, T.: Adapting visual category models to new domains. In: Daniilidis, K., Maragos, P., Paragios, N. (eds.) ECCV 2010. LNCS, vol. 6314, pp. 213–226. Springer, Heidelberg (2010). https://doi.org/10.1007/978-3-642-15561-1_16
21. Griffin, G., Holub, A., Perona, P.: Caltech-256 object category dataset. California Institute of Technology (2007)
22. Zhang, X., Yu, F.X., Chang, S.-F., Wang, S.: Deep transfer network: unsupervised domain adaptation. arXiv preprint arXiv:1503.00591 (2015)
23. http://www.vlfeat.org/matconvnet/
24. Van, L., Maaten, D.: Accelerating t-SNE using tree-based algorithms. J. Mach. Learn. Res. **15**(1), 3221–3245 (2014)
25. Ghifary, M., Kleijn, W.B., Zhang, M.: Domain adaptive neural networks for object recognition. In: Pham, D.-N., Park, S.-B. (eds.) PRICAI 2014. LNCS (LNAI), vol. 8862, pp. 898–904. Springer, Cham (2014). https://doi.org/10.1007/978-3-319-13560-1_76

Continuous Motion Recognition in Depth Camera Based on Recurrent Neural Networks and Grid-based Average Depth

Tao Rong[1,2], Rui Yang[1,2], and Ruoyu Yang[1,2(✉)]

[1] State Key Laboratory for Novel Software Technology,
Nanjing University, Nanjing, China
raymond_rong@163.com, ryang@smail.nju.edu.cn, yangry@nju.edu.cn
[2] Department of Computer Science and Technology,
Nanjing University, Nanjing, China

Abstract. Inspired by the success of using RNN in some other fields, we propose to apply the RNN to recognize human motion based on depth data. RNN can directly model the depth sequence on the time axis, and learn the temporal information more naturally. For represent the skeleton and depth information in video, we use Orderlet features and Grid-based Average Depth (GbAD) proposed in this paper. Finally, we evaluate our models on the MSR 3D Online Action Dataset in comparison with the state-of-the-art methods. Experimental results show that the proposed models outperforms other ones.

1 Introduction

Most recognition methods are based on segmented video clips (each clip contains only one full action) to carry out training and testing. Because the most widely used benchmarks of depth camera data only provide with the segmented clips, some researchers [1] use the "simulation of continuous action video" to test their action segmentation methods. Nevertheless, MSR 3D Online Action Dataset [2] was proposed recently and has been used as a well-established benchmark in [3,4]. This dataset contains videos of complete natural individual daily activities and single clip contains more than one action type. In this paper, we will focus on the segmentation and recognition of real human motion depth data streams.

In order to use the powerful convolution neural network (CNN), [5] proposed the DMM-Pyramid and DMM-Cube features to organize the raw depth sequence into formats which can be accepted by convolution models. Experimental results show that the method is very robust in action recognition accuracy. However, CNN itself can not be modeled on the changes in time series. But recurrent neural network (RNN) [6] is able to model the samples automatically without destroying the temporal information.

Inspired by the success of using RNN in other related fields, we firstly try to utilize the RNN to recognize human motion based on depth data. We use single

© Springer International Publishing AG, part of Springer Nature 2018
M. Paul et al. (Eds.): PSIVT 2017, LNCS 10749, pp. 212–221, 2018.
https://doi.org/10.1007/978-3-319-75786-5_18

video frames as samples for training and testing, and achieve the recognition results of the entire video after temporal smoothness. Using single frames will cause that the number of samples increase exponentially. So we can't directly reuse the middle features which are accepted by CNN models. So we use Orderlet features and Grid-based Average Depth (GbAD) proposed in this paper.

Because action recognition is based on the single frame, action segmentation work is more convenient. Now we can get a probability distribution for each frame, which can also be regarded as a score for each action class. We follow the maximum sub array search method in [7], dynamic backward backtracking searching can help us to get the highest cumulative score of the action of the particular sub sequence, and ultimately to complete the segmentation.

The key contributions of this work can be summarized as follows:

1. We propose to apply the recurrent neural networks to recognize human motion based on depth data. RNN can directly model the depth sequence on the time axis, and learn the temporal information more naturally.
2. We propose the feature GbAD to roughly describe the shape of the hand. This feature is sufficient for our task.
3. We evaluate our models on the MSR 3D Online Action Dataset in comparison with the state-of-the-art methods. Experimental results show that the proposed models outperforms other ones.

2   Related Work

Li et al. [8] model the dynamics of the action by building an action graph and describe the salient postures by a bag-of-points (BOPs). It's an effective method which is similar to some traditional 2D silhouette-based action recognition methods. The method does not perform well in the cross subject test due to some significant variations in different subjects from MSR Action3D dataset.

Yang et al. [9] are motivated by the success of Histograms of Oriented Gradients (HOG) in human detection. They extract Multi-perspective HOG descriptors from DMM as representations of human actions. They also illustrate how many frames are sufficient to build DMM-HOG representation and give satisfactory experimental results on MSR Action3D dataset. Before that, they have proposed an EigenJoints-based action recognition system by using a NBNN classifier [10] with the same goal.

In order to deal with the problems of noise and occlusion in depth maps, Wang et al. extracts semi-local features called random occupancy pattern (ROP) features [11]. They propose a weighted sampling algorithm to reduce the computational cost and claim that their method performs better in accuracy and computationally efficiency than SVM trained by raw data. After that they further propose Local Occupancy Patterns (LOP) features [12] which are similar to ROP in some case and improve their results to some extent.

3   Recurrent Neural Networks

3.1   Brief Introduction of RNN

The purpose of recurrent neural network originally being proposed is to process sequence data, as well as some tasks that fully-connected network or convolutional neural network are difficult to deal with. For example, the analysis of the semantic meaning of a word in sentence is often judged by the words beside it, because they are not independent of each other. Similarly, in our judgment of the action category for the current frame, there is a chance to get a higher accuracy with the help of the information of previous frames. And RNN in such an situation is able to play its own advantages.

The RNN that we used in this paper is also known as Elman Network [13]. Vector $X(t)$ is concatenated with the feature vector $W(t)$ of the current frame and the output vector $S(t-1)$ of hidden layer in the last training step. The network contains three layers of input, hidden and output and is trained by the standard back propagation. The values are calculated by the following formula:

$$X(t) = [W(t)^T S(t-1)^T]^T$$

$$s_j(t) = f(\sum_i x_i(t) u_{ji})$$

$$y_k(t) = g(\sum_j s_j(t) v_{kj})$$

The cross entropy criterion is used to obtain an error vector at the output layer, which is then propagated to the hidden layer. A part of sampling data is used as a validation set. The training algorithm need to decide whether to terminate itself or adjust the learning rate according to the verification results on the validation set after each round of iteration. In our experiments, the training results generally tend to converge at the 200'th iteration. There is a problem that whether the back propagation is sufficient to train such a network especially when we assume that the current frame action label is affected by the previous frame data. It is difficult to determine how much useful information is retained in the hidden layer and the researchers have not yet figured out the problem. Which is also the future needs to continue to explore the solution of the problem. We think it need to be solved in the future.

3.2   Backpropagation Through Time

Backpropagation through time (BPTT) [14] can be seen as a simple extension of BP. The BPTT method, the deviation can be propagated within the specified time step, then the network will learn the temporal information of the specified range. The concrete implementation can be referred to [15].

In addition, Mikolov et al. [16] mentioned that it is generally required to train multiple networks with different initial weight or different number of units at the same time to merge in order to further enhance the power of RNN. In the experiment of this paper, we will also make a linear combination of multiple networks and observe the impact of it.

4   Orderlet Features and Grid-based Average Depth

In this paper, we mainly use the orderlet features and Grid-based Average Depth (GbAD) to describe the body skeletons and depth sequences of Kinect data. The orderlet features only reflect the relative relationship between the eigenvalues, so they are not sensitive to the small errors and the difference between the human body compared with the numerical features. The orderlet features are very suitable for use for skeleton data with much noise. In addition, orderlet feature can be applied to recognize the continuous action because we can extract it based on single frame data. Besides, we present GbAD as the descriptor of gesture. The descriptor GbAD roughly describes the shape of the hand.

4.1   Basic Skeleton Feature

In this section, we extract features based on single frame. For a given frame I_t, Skeleton node is defined as $S^t = s_1^t, s_2^t, \ldots, s_{N_s}^t$, where $s_i^t = (x_i^t, y_i^t, z_i^t)$ is the coordinate of the node i at the t't frame, $N_s = 20$ is the quantity of a single complete skeleton. Here we use the following three basic features:

– Euclidean distance between two nodes:

$$\lambda^{(1)} = ||s_i^t - s_j^t||,$$

– Simple node coordinate information:

$$\lambda^{(2)} = x_i^t \quad or \quad y_i^t \quad or \quad z_i^t,$$

– The position change of the node coordinates in a certain time step (Euclidean distance):

$$\lambda^{(3)} = ||s_i^t - s_j^{t-\Delta}||,$$

where Δ is the time step length.

We all know that there are many inherent instability in human movement. The same action performed by the same person may be different let alone by different people. Therefore, using these basic features of the original value is not robust. In this section the orderlet feature is used to deal with this problem.

As shown in Fig. 1, the absolute value of the distance between the two wrist joints (two green nodes) may be somewhat different at the beginning/ongoing/ending of the action. However, the its order of the length in all distance between each nodes is stable at all stages of the action.

We define a orderlet feature p with size n as:

$$p = (O_p, k)$$

$$O_p = [\lambda_{i_1}^f, \lambda_{i_2}^f, \ldots, \lambda_{i_n}^f]$$

Fig. 1. Skeleton orderlet (Color figure online)

where k is the index of minimum value in the vector O_p, f represents one of the three basic features. So for a given frame I^t, its value on orderlet p can be defined as:

$$v_p(I^t) = 1 : 0 \quad ? \quad \lambda_{i_k}^f \leq \lambda_{i_j}^f \quad for \quad all \quad \lambda_{i_j}^f \in O_p.$$

And for a given sequence v with T frames, its value on orderlet p can be defined as:

$$V_p(v) = \sum_{t=1}^{T} v_p(I^t)$$

4.2   Grid-based Average Depth

When we observe gestures in video, it is found that related skeleton information from Kinect is often deficient and inaccurate. That is to say, we can not describe gesture information only with skeleton information. So we present Grid-based Average Depth (GbAD) as the descriptor of gesture.

We divide the hand-related region into many grids. For each grid, we calculate the average depth value of all pixels in the grid. We arrangement the average depth values of grids and get the descriptor GbAD.

First, we know where wrists and elbows are with the skeleton information from Kinect, and we can infer where hands can be. That is to say, we can determine the hand-related regions in depth frame. Second, we divide the hand-related region into many grids. The rule about dividing is simple: for each hand-related region, we take wrist as the center point and make a semicircle, and the semicircle is divided into many grids along the radius and angle. Finally, for each grid, we calculate the average depth value of all pixels in the grid. The average depth values of grids are arrangemented as the descriptor GbAD. A example is shown in Fig. 2.

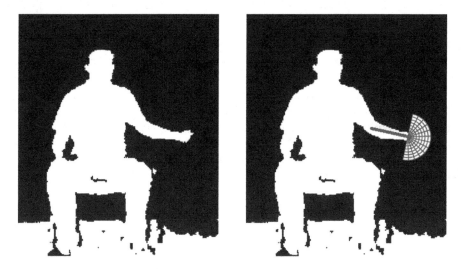

Fig. 2. GbAD. (A) A depth frame after preprocessing. (B) The depth frame with grids.

5   Online Motion Recognition

With the orderlet features, GbAD and RNN classification model, we have been able to recognize action on a single frame. But it is usually not reliable to judge a complete action by just one frame. So we use a time window to make a smooth operation of the single frame motion recognition of the whole video stream. Because the duration of action of different types will be different (there are also differences between different presentations), the size of the time window is hard to set, so we will use a window with dynamic time length. Firstly, we can get a probability distribution of each action class for each frame. Assuming the current frame t is recognized as action γ by our method and the probability is $P(\gamma, t)$. Here we denote that the positive score for the γ of frame t is $P(\gamma, t)$, the negative score is $P(\gamma, t) - 1$. Then we use the backtracking search to find a window w which can make the maximum accumulated score for the action γ.

Following the maximum subarray search method, we use dynamic programming to find the best comprehensive score of the current frame to a certain action label and avoid the backward search for each frame. The best comprehensive score of the current frame t can be defined as:

$$S(\gamma, t) = max(0, S(\gamma, t - 1) + P(\gamma, t)), t > 1$$

$$S(\gamma, 1) = P(\gamma, 1)$$

If the $S(\gamma, t)$ is less than 0 (or a specific threshold), its value will be reset to 0 and we believe that the current action is over and ready to start another action.

6 Experiment and Discussion

6.1 Dataset

MSR 3D Online Action Dataset is a dataset used to test the method of recognizing continuous human actions. It contains three forms of data (depth sequence, RGB video and human node coordinates). There are 7 action types in the dataset: Drinking, eating, using laptop, reading cellphone, making phone call, reading book, using remote. All of these actions are interactive movement of people and objects. The boundaries of the object in each frame are manually marked out in the dataset. But in order to get more general conclusions, we did not use these data in our experiments.

The dataset is designed to do three experiments:

- Same-environment action recognition
- Cross-environment action recognition
- Continuous action recognition.

6.2 Results

Same-environment action recognition. We first validate our approach based on the train/test set with the same background environment. The proportion of sample number of training set and test set is 1:1, and we used a 2 fold cross validation. As shown in Table 1, our experimental results are superior to other methods, which to a certain extent proved the effectiveness of our feature extraction method combined with RNN classification model. In order to prove the advantages of RNN, we used SVM/random forest to do the same experiment. As shown in Table 2, using the RNN classification model is far better than using the SVM/RF. It is also proved that RNN can preserve more motion information after modeling the temporal information. In the same case, we have made the comparison between the experimental results of a single network and a number of networks under the same experimental conditions. The details are shown in Table 3.

Table 1. Same-environment action recognition results

Method	Accuracy
Our method	**0.720**
Skeleton + LoP [12]	0.660
DSTIP + DCSF [17]	0.617
EigenJoints [10]	0.491
Yu et al. [2]	0.714

Table 2. Same-environment action recognition results compared with SVM/RF

Method	Accuracy
Our method	**0.720**
All features + SVM	0.667
All features + Random forest	0.630

Table 3. Same-environment action recognition results compared with different number of networks

Method	Accuracy
Single network	0.697
3 networks	0.712
5 networks	**0.720**
7 networks	0.697

Cross-environment action recognition. This experiment requires the recognition method to get much higher robustness and generalization ability. As shown in Table 4, most of the existing methods in this test have a rapid decline in accuracy. Our method did not perform as well as itself in the same-environment experiment. Compared with the traditional classifier, neural network is more prone to the problem of over-fitting (especially when the quantity of training samples is not very large). In the cross-environment action recognition experiment the problem will be more serious (i.e., poor generalization ability).

Table 4. Cross-environment action recognition results

Method	Accuracy
Our method	**0.607**
Yu et al. [2]	0.661
Skeleton + LoP [12]	0.598
DSTIP + DCSF [17]	0.215
EigenJoints [10]	0.357

Continuous action recognition. Different from the previous tests, here each sample contains multiple action. In addition to the 7 action types that were previously set in detail, there is a one more "background action" type, in fact, this type has no real sense but is just the connection between the various parts of the connection. The length of a single sample ranged from 30 s to 2 min where the proportion of "background action" is about 30%. Each frame of the sample is marked with an action label, but the dataset provider does not guarantee the accuracy of the motion boundary (in fact, it is difficult to unify the evaluation standard of human action segmentation) (Table 5).

Table 5. Continuous action recognition

Method	Accuracy
Our method	**0.569**
Yu et al. [2]	0.564
DSTIP + DCSF [17]	0.321
EigenJoints [10]	0.236

7   Conclusion

In this paper, we focus on the continuous motion recognition which has more practical application value. The proposed method is based on the single frame data and can be used for the recognition of real time video streams. We extract Orderlet features from the skeleton data, concerning about the relative relation between the eigen values but not their absolute values. Also we present GbAD as the descriptor of gestures. Then we utilize RNN to do the human action recognition work, taking advantage of self feedback and propagation in the time domain. We also train a number of networks which have different initial weights, the number of hidden cells and apply a linear combination to them to obtain better recognition accuracy.

Experiments performed on the benchmark dataset show that the method proposed in this paper is superior to some other existed methods. But the poor performance in the cross-environment experiment indicates that the generalization ability of the method is partly defective, which is the point where we hope to improve in the future.

Acknowledgment. This work was supported in part by the National Natural Science Foundation of China under Grant Nos. 61672273.

References

1. Yang, R., Yang, R.: Action segmentation and recognition based on depth HOG and probability distribution difference. In: Huang, D.-S., Bevilacqua, V., Premaratne, P. (eds.) ICIC 2014. LNCS, vol. 8588, pp. 753–763. Springer, Cham (2014). https://doi.org/10.1007/978-3-319-09333-8_82
2. Yu, G., Liu, Z., Yuan, J.: Discriminative orderlet mining for real-time recognition of human-object interaction. In: Cremers, D., Reid, I., Saito, H., Yang, M.-H. (eds.) ACCV 2014. LNCS, vol. 9007, pp. 50–65. Springer, Cham (2015). https://doi.org/10.1007/978-3-319-16814-2_4
3. Eum, H., Yoon, C., Lee, H., Park, M.: Continuous human action recognition using depth-MHI-HOG and a spotter model. Sensors **15**, 5197–5227 (2015)
4. Zhang, J., Li, W., Ogunbona, P.O., Wang, P., Tang, C.: RGB-D-based action recognition datasets: a survey (2016)

5. Yang, R., Yang, R.: DMM-pyramid based deep architectures for action recognition with depth cameras. In: Cremers, D., Reid, I., Saito, H., Yang, M.-H. (eds.) ACCV 2014. LNCS, vol. 9007, pp. 37–49. Springer, Cham (2015). https://doi.org/10.1007/978-3-319-16814-2_3

6. Mikolov, T., Karafiát, M., Burget, L., Cernocky, J., Khudanpur, S.: Recurrent neural network based language model. In: Conference of the International Speech Communication Association, INTERSPEECH 2010, Makuhari, Chiba, Japan, pp. 1045–1048, September 2010

7. Bentley, J.: Programming pearls: algorithm design techniques. Commun. ACM **27**, 865–873 (1984)

8. Li, W., Zhang, Z., Liu, Z.: Action recognition based on a bag of 3D points. In: 2010 IEEE Computer Society Conference on Computer Vision and Pattern Recognition Workshops (CVPRW), pp. 9–14 (2010)

9. Yang, X., Zhang, C., Tian, Y.L.: Recognizing actions using depth motion maps-based histograms of oriented gradients. In: ACM International Conference on Multimedia, pp. 1057–1060 (2012)

10. Yang, X., Tian, Y.L.: EigenJoints-based action recognition using Naive-Bayes-nearest-neighbor. Percept. Mot. Skills **38**, 14–19 (2012)

11. Wang, J., Liu, Z., Chorowski, J., Chen, Z., Wu, Y.: Robust 3D action recognition with random occupancy patterns. In: Fitzgibbon, A., Lazebnik, S., Perona, P., Sato, Y., Schmid, C. (eds.) ECCV 2012. LNCS, pp. 872–885. Springer, Heidelberg (2012). https://doi.org/10.1007/978-3-642-33709-3_62

12. Wang, J., Liu, Z., Wu, Y., Yuan, J.: Mining actionlet ensemble for action recognition with depth cameras. In: Computer Vision and Pattern Recognition, pp. 1290–1297 (2012)

13. Elman, J.L.: Finding structure in time. Cogn. Sci. **14**, 179–211 (1990)

14. Rumelhart, D.E., Hinton, G.E., Williams, R.J.: Learning internal representations by back-propagating errors, pp. 533–536 (2014)

15. Boden, M.: A guide to recurrent neural networks and backpropagation. Dallas Project Sics Technical Report T Sics (2001)

16. Mikolov, T., Kombrink, S., Burget, L., Cernocky, J.H.: Extensions of recurrent neural network language model. In: IEEE International Conference on Acoustics, pp. 5528–5531 (2011)

17. Xia, L., Aggarwal, J.K.: Spatio-temporal depth cuboid similarity feature for activity recognition using depth camera, vol. 9, pp. 2834–2841 (2013)

Auto-calibration Method for Active 3D Endoscope System Using Silhouette of Pattern Projector

Ryo Furukawa[1]([✉]), Masahito Naito[1], Daisuke Miyazaki[1], Masahi Baba[1],
Shinsaku Hiura[1], Yoji Sanomura[2], Shinji Tanaka[2], and Hiroshi Kawasaki[3]

[1] Hiroshima City University, Hiroshima, Japan
{ryo-f,miyazaki,baba,hiura}@hiroshima-cu.ac.jp,
naito@ime.infohiroshima-cu.ac.jp
[2] Hiroshima University Hospital, Hiroshima, Japan
{sanomura,colon}@hiroshima-cu.ac.jp
[3] Kyushu University, Fukuoka, Japan
kawasaki@ait.kyushu-u.ac.jp

Abstract. In this paper, we develop an active stereo system for endoscope which requires auto-calibration, because a micro pattern projector is inserted through the instrument channel during an operation and
cannot be fixed to the endoscope. For solution, a new auto-calibration
technique with full 6-DOF estimation of an active stereo system without any extra devices nor extra pattern projections is proposed. In the
technique, the pattern projector itself is simultaneously captured with a
target scene by an endoscope camera and the silhouette of the pattern
projector is used to conduct 2D-3D matching by using the knowledge of
the shape of the projector. In addition, the markers which is included
in the projection pattern are extracted and the distances from the closest epipolar lines are calculated as for the cost function. To enhance the
robustness of the reconstruction, we also propose a simple high dynamic
range (HDR) imaging system for an endoscope by alternating the input
power of the pattern projector ON and OFF to blink the pattern so that
exposure time will vary with beat frequency, realizing a virtual multi-
exposure camera. By applying our auto calibration technique with HDR
imaging system, we achieved a robust and accurate reconstruction of
tissue in metric 3D under practical operation of the endoscopic system,
such as reconstruction of the inside of a real stomach of a pig.

1 Introduction

In this paper, we develop an active stereo system for endoscope which requires
auto-calibration, because a micro pattern projector is inserted through the
instrument channel during an operation and cannot be fixed to the endoscope.

Auto-calibration is a basic, but yet an important research topic for computer
vision. Recently, auto-calibration is applied to active stereo systems and it has
been researched for two decades. In general, calibration process requires stable

© Springer International Publishing AG, part of Springer Nature 2018
M. Paul et al. (Eds.): PSIVT 2017, LNCS 10749, pp. 222–236, 2018.
https://doi.org/10.1007/978-3-319-75786-5_19

and sufficient number of correspondences, however, this requirement is hard to achieve for active stereo systems before calibration, because correspondences are only acquired after calibration; this is a typical chicken and egg problem. To solve the problem, additional devices, such as a spherical calibration tool with known size [1] or extra pattern projections, such as gray code are used [2]. Since it is not possible to install such extra devices nor extra patterns to endoscopes, it makes auto-calibration more difficult than ordinary case.

In this paper, we propose a new auto-calibration technique for an active stereo system with full 6-DOF estimation without any extra devices nor extra pattern projections. In our technique, a pattern projector itself is simultaneously captured by an endoscope camera as well as a target scene; note that simultaneous capture of the projector and the scene is not difficult for the endoscope camera because the field of view of the camera is usually extremely wide. In actual process, we extract the silhouette of the pattern projector and conduct 2D-3D matching by using the knowledge of the shape of the projector. In addition, we extract markers which are included in the pattern and calculate the distances from the epipolar lines as for the cost function; note that we just impose 9 markers into the pattern, which makes it possible to specify the markers in the captured images.

In the paper, we also propose a simple high dynamic range (HDR) imaging system for an endoscope. Usually HDR images are synthesized by using multiple-exposure images, however, it is impossible to precisely control the exposure of the camera frame by frame for commonly available endoscope systems. Therefore, we alternate the input power of the pattern projector ON and OFF to blink the pattern with certain frequency so that exposure time will be varied with beat frequency, realizing a virtual multi-exposure camera.

By applying our auto calibration technique to the HDR images which are efficiently captured by our proposed system, we can achieve a robust and accurate reconstruction of tissue in metric 3D under practical operation of the endoscope system. In the experiments, we show the effectiveness of our technique with several tests using the real system, and demonstrate the successful reconstruction of the inside of a real stomach of a pig.

2 Related Work

3D endoscopes based on binocular stereo are actively being researched at the present [3,4]. For the binocular stereo algorithm, which is a typical passive stereo technique, correspondence retrieval is essentially difficult, especially on textureless surfaces. To cope with textureless surfaces, techniques using Shape from Shading (SfS) have been proposed [5], however, the 3D reconstruction is only up-to-scale and it cannot be directly applied for measuring real sizes of 3D tissues.

An active stereo technique is a simple solution for the aforementioned problems. Using color-coding for the projected pattern is one solution [6, 7]. However, accurate classification of illumination colors on textured tissues may need careful adjustment. Some other vision techniques using special cameras being applied to endoscopes such as ToF sensors are proposed [8,9]. However, the resolution of ToF sensor is inevitably low [8] or the size is larger than those of RGB sensors and only applicable to laparoscope systems [9]. Recently, Furukawa et al. proposed a structured light system for endoscope [1,10,11], which allows users to update a common endoscope system without any reconfiguration.

In terms of auto-calibration, there is a long history for binocular stereo and many papers have been published so far and they are summarized in [12]. On the other hand, there is a few techniques for active stereo systems, especially for structured light systems [1,2,13–15]. The structured light system can be categorized into three, such as light sectioning method, temporally encoding method and spatially encoding method. An auto-calibration for light sectioning method estimates three unknown parameters for each laser sheet by using intersections of multiple lasers [13,14]. In terms of an auto-calibration for temporally encoding method, since the method usually assumes video projector, which can project an arbitrary pattern such as gray code, dense and accurate correspondences are easily retrieved and a calibration is efficiently achieved [2,15]. Unlike the temporally encoding method, spatially encoding method, which is used in our endoscope system, basically cannot change the pattern and has essential difficulty on retrieving correspondences, and thus, only few technique is proposed [1]. In the method [1], since the authors attached the projector to the head of the endoscope and only 2-DOF remains, they can use a special calibration tool with known size to estimate the remaining 4-DOF in advance. In our technique, we estimate full 6-DOF without any extra devices nor projections, and similar techniques has never been proposed yet with our best knowledge.

About HDR image synthesis, usually multiple-exposure images are assumed [16]. However, it is difficult to capture images with different exposures using video cameras. There are several techniques which achieve HDR synthesis and tone-mapping for video [17,18], however active lighting conditions are not considered. If a lighting condition can be precisely controlled with camera synchronization, multi-exposure images are easily retrieved, however, the system becomes complicated. In our system, instead of adopting such a complicated system, we simply alternate the input power to blink the pattern ON-and-OFF with no synchronization mechanism, and such an approach has never been published yet.

3 DOE-Based Laser Pattern Projector for Endoscopy

3.1 System Configuration

A projector-camera system is constructed by installing a micro pattern projector on a standard endoscope system as shown in Fig. 1(a). For our system, we used a FujiFilm VP-4450HD system coupled with a EG-590WR scope. The DOE-based laser pattern projector is inserted in the endoscope through the instrument channel, the projector protrudes slightly from the endoscope head and emits structured light. The light source of the projector is a green laser module with

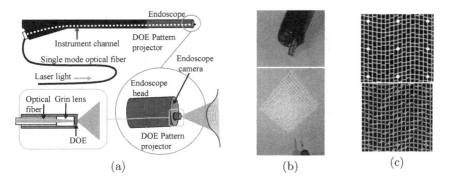

(a)　　　　　　　　　　　(b)　　　　　　　(c)

Fig. 1. System configuration: (a) System components. (b) DOE micro projector inserted though the instrument channel of an endoscope. (c) The projected pattern (top), and embedded codewords of S colored in red, L in blue, and R in green (bottom). S means edges of the left and the right sides have the same height, L means the left side is higher, and R means the right is higher. (Color figure online)

a wavelength of 517 nm. The laser light is transmitted through a single-mode optical fiber to the head of the DOE projector. The DOE generates the pattern through diffraction of the laser light.

Our system is based on active stereo method proposed by Furukawa *et al.* [11], in which a gap-based grid pattern is used for avoiding effect of subsurface scattering that is harmful for 3D reconstruction. Here, we describe the pattern and 3D reconnection method briefly.

The projected pattern consists of only line segments as shown in Fig. 1(c) (top). The vertical lines of pattern are all connected and straight, whereas the horizontal segments are designed in a way to leave a small variable vertical gap between adjacent horizontal segments and their intersections with the same vertical line. With this configuration, a higher-level ternary code emerges from the design with the following three codewords: S (the end-points of both sides have the same height), L (the end-point of the left side is higher), and R (the end-point of the left side is higher). The codes of the pattern of Fig. 1(c) (top) are shown by color in Fig. 1(c) (bottom).

3.2 3D Reconstruction

The source image is first geometrically corrected on the fish-eye lens distortion. Noises of the image are suppressed using Gaussian filters or median filters at the same time. The projected vertical and horizontal lines are detected in the undistorted image using the line detection algorithm from Sagawa *et al.* [19]. This method can detect projected parallel lines whose approximate directions are known, ignoring intersecting non-vertical lines, based on loopy belief propagation.

From the detected line patterns, grid-graph structure is constructed by detecting intersections between the horizontal and vertical lines. Then, each

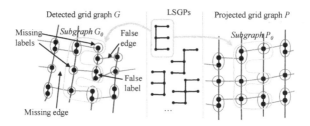

Fig. 2. Matching the detected grid graph and the projected pattern using LSGPs.

node is connected with its up, down, left, or right adjacent nodes by vertical or horizontal edges. Some horizontal edges might have a missing edge because of misdetection. In this case, the node will only have either a left or a right edge, which may be later matched by looking at other connectivity of the grid graph. Figure 11(f) shows examples of the detected vertical and horizontal patterns with estimated gap codes.

Let the detected grid-graph be G and let the grid-graph of the pattern in Fig. 1(c) be P. Note that graph G may lack some edges or have undesired false edges, missing labels or false labels of $S/L/R$ as shown in the left part of Fig. 2. To match G and P allowing topological errors, we exploit the notion of local sub-graph patterns (LSGPs). We define an LSGP to be a sub-graph of a grid-graph used as a template for matching common local topologies of G and P. In Fig. 2, the left part shows G, the right part shows P, and the middle part shows LSGPs. Given a dictionary of LSGPs, G may be matched to P robustly to missing or false edges. By providing multiple LSGPs and trying to match G and P using each of them, flexible matching can be realized. In our implementation, an LSGP is represented by a path that traces all of its edges. To merge all the matching results of LSGPs, voting scheme is used.

Once the correspondences of the captured image to the pattern is obtained, the points on the vertical and horizontal lines are reconstructed in 3D using a light-sectioning method.

4   Auto-calibration of the Projector Position

In this system, the target surface, which is projected by pattern projector, is captured by the endoscope camera. Since the head of the projector is not tightly fixed to the endoscope, the relative position between the projector head and the endoscope camera varies during endoscopic operations, such as bending the head. Since, for active stereo techniques, the position of the projector is an important parameter for 3D reconstruction, such unstable condition is problematic for robust and accurate shape measurement.

Furukawa et al. [1] modeled the relative position by 2-DOF rigid transformation, where projector translates along or rotates around the axis of the instrument channel (Fig. 3(a)). This 2-DOF model could be applied to our system if the pattern projector's outer diameter perfectly fitted to the inner diameter

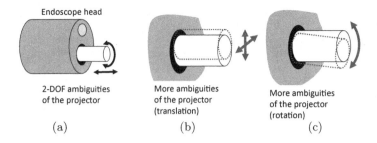

Endoscope head

2-DOF ambiguities
of the projector

(a)

More ambiguities
of the projector
(translation)

(b)

More ambiguities
of the projector
(rotation)

(c)

Fig. 3. Ambiguities of the projector. (a) 2-DOF ambiguity proposed in Furukawa *et al.*
[1]. (b), (c) More freedom that is not modeled in Furukawa *et al.* [1] caused by margin
between the projector and the instrument channel.

of the instrument channel. However, there should be some margin between the
projector and the channel in order for the projector to be inserted during the
endoscopic operations. Thus, in real situations, the projector have more freedom
to move beyond the 2-DOF model within the margin (Fig. 3(b), (c)).

Another limitation of the work of Furukawa *et al.* [1] is that they estimate
the projector's position by detecting a marker drawn on the projector from the
endoscope image. In real situations where endoscope image is captured in dark
environments, markers drawn on the projector are difficult to be detected from
the captured image.

In the proposed system, we use silhouette of the projector and the markers
embedded in the grid pattern projected onto the target surface. The silhouette
of the projector can be observed from the captured image, even if there are not
illumination except for the projected pattern. The markers in the grid pattern
can be also detected from the same image (see Fig. 11(d) for an example, where
the projector silhouette can be observed at the bottom of the image).

The actual process is as follows: From the input image captured for measurement, markers in the grid pattens (m_i) are detected. Also, several points
in the projector's silhouette (s_j) are also sampled (Fig. 4). The auto-calibration
is processed as an optimization of 6-DOF rigid transformation parameters that
represent projector's position, while using the 2-DOF freedom described in [1]
as 'soft' constraints. To achieve this, we divide the estimated 6 parameters into
2 sets of parameters: one set is for 2-DOF freedom described in [1] and the other
is for the rest 4 parameters. We regard the 2-DOF parameters (the former set)
as freely changing parameters, since they represent the motion of the pattern
projector that rotates around and translates along the axis of the instrument
channel, while we suppress the rest 4 parameters (the latter set) since they are
deviation from the 2-DOF freedom of [1]. Because of this 'soft' 2-DOF constraint,
the estimated projector position does not have scale ambiguity.

The optimized cost function is defined as follows:

1. The cost function takes 6 parameters $p_1, p_2, q_1, q_2, q_3, q_4$, representing the 3D
   position of the projector (rotation $\mathbf{R}$ and translation $\mathbf{t}$) relative to the endoscope camera, where p_1 and p_2 are 2-DOF parameters described in [1], and
   $q_1, \cdots, q_4$ represents the rest of the 6-DOF rigid transformation.

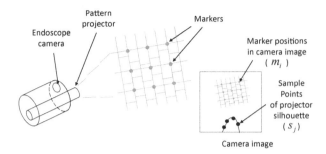

Fig. 4. Input points for auto-calibration of the projector.

2. For the markers m_i, the corresponding epipolar line is calculated, and the distance between m_i and the epipolar line is calculated as $g_i(p_1, p_2, q_1, q_2, q_3, q_4)$.
3. The virtual silhouette of the projector is rendered as a cylinder moved by the rigid transformation $\mathbf{R}$ and $\mathbf{t}$. From each s_j, the minimum distance from s_j to contours of the rendered silhouette is calculated as $h_j(p_1, p_2, q_1, q_2, q_3, q_4)$.
4. $\sum_i \{g_i(p_1, p_2, q_1, q_2, q_3, q_4)\}^2 + w_1 \sum_j \{h_j(p_1, p_2, q_1, q_2, q_3, q_4)\}^2 + w_2 \sum_{k=1}^{4}$ $(q_k)^2$ is calculated as the cost value, where w_1 is weight of the cost of silhouette fitting and w_2 is weight for the 'soft' constraints of the 2-DOF freedom [1], which suppress the parameters $q_1, \cdots, q_4$.

The cost function is optimized with respect to p_1, p_2, q_1, q_2, q_3 and q_4. In current implementation, selection of the marker position and sampling points on the silhouette contour are conducted manually for each frame in image sequences and auto-calibration should be conducted for each frame. Further automation for point selection will be our future work.

4.1   Details of Implementation

Generally, projectors and cameras can be described in the same model (*i.e.*, pinhole-camera model). The standard coordinates of 3D camera calibration is the camera coordinates, which is (x_c, y_c, z_c) in Fig. 5(a), where the origin is the optical center of the endoscope camera, and the z-axis goes through both the optical center and the principal point of the image plane. The projector coordinates can be also modeled similarly, as shown as (x_p, y_p, z_p) in Fig. 5(a). The relative position between the projector and the camera is described as the rigid transformation $(\mathbf{R}_{pc}, \mathbf{t}_{pc})$ between these two coordinates.

In the work of Furukawa *et al.* [1], this rigid transformation is defined by 2-DOF rigid transformation, which is a composition of rotation around the z-axis of the projector coordinates, and translation in parallel with the same axis. Let the two parameters be p_1 and p_2, and the rest 4-DOF of rigid transformation be $q_1, \cdots, q_4$, then the transformation from the projector-coordinates to the camera coordinates be described as

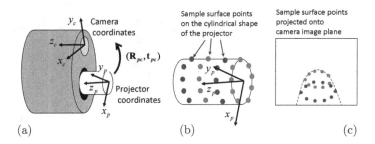

Fig. 5. (a) The camera/projector coordinates and rigid transformation $(\mathbf{R}_{pc}, \mathbf{t}_{pc})$. (b) Surface points on the cylinder-like projector shape. (c) Sample surface points projected onto the image plane of the camera.

$$
\begin{pmatrix} x_c \\ y_c \\ z_c \end{pmatrix} = \mathbf{R}_x(q_1)\,\mathbf{R}_y(q_2)\,\mathbf{R}_z(p_1) \begin{pmatrix} x_p \\ y_p \\ z_p \end{pmatrix} + \begin{pmatrix} q_3 \\ q_4 \\ p_2 \end{pmatrix} = \mathbf{R}_{pc} \begin{pmatrix} x_p \\ y_p \\ z_p \end{pmatrix} + \mathbf{t}_{pc} \quad (1)
$$

where $\mathbf{R}_x, \mathbf{R}_y$ and $\mathbf{R}_z$ rotations around x, y, and z-axis, respectively.

In calculation of the cost function, the silhouette of the cylinder-shaped projector is rendered using transformation (1). We project the 3D points onto the image plane and render a 2D convex hull of them (Fig. 5(b), (c)). In the cost function, the distances from the contours of the rendered virtual silhouette to sampled points on the imaged silhouette (s_j) should be calculated. To estimate these distances, we obtain Euclidean distance transformation from the convex hull using the OpenCV library and look-up the pixels of the distance transformation at the sampled points. Approximately, the point set on the surface of the projector can be modeled as a cylinder surface whose axis is the same as z-axis of the projector coordinates, and the cylindrical bottom is at the origin of the projector coordinates. However, the projector coordinates are defined from the geometry of optical projection, where the cylinder is the physical shape of the projector. Thus, the precise relative positional relationships between them are unknown, and the object coordinates of the cylinder shape and the projector coordinates have a small deviation as shown in Fig. 6(a). This deviation can be described as a rigid transformation $(\mathbf{R}_{op}, \mathbf{t}_{op})$ and can be calibrated in the following steps.

First, the pattern is projected onto a sphere with a known size, and image with the projected patterns and the projector silhouette is captured. Then, from the projected patterns, the relative position of the projector coordinates is estimated using the calibration method described in [10]. Then, the deviation between the object coordinates and the projector coordinates is estimated by fitting the virtual silhouette of the projector to the imaged silhouette points with respect to $(\mathbf{R}_{op}, \mathbf{t}_{op})$ using the similar method as the auto-calibration except that the epipolar constraints are not used.

The effect of calibration of $(\mathbf{R}_{op}, \mathbf{t}_{op})$ is shown in Figs. 6(b), (c) and (d). Figure 6(b) is not the image used for calibration of $(\mathbf{R}_{op}, \mathbf{t}_{op})$, so that we can

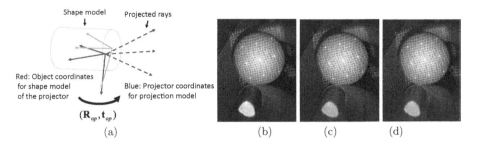

Fig. 6. (a) Projector coordinates and object coordinates of the projector shape rigid transformation $(\mathbf{R}_{op}, \mathbf{t}_{op})$ between them. (b) An image with calibration object. (c) Projector shape overlayed onto (b) without calibration of $(\mathbf{R}_{op}, \mathbf{t}_{op})$. (d) Projector shape overlayed onto (b) with calibration of $(\mathbf{R}_{op}, \mathbf{t}_{op})$.

validate the estimated $(\mathbf{R}_{op}, \mathbf{t}_{op})$. In Fig. 6(c), the virtual shape of the projector is not overlayed correctly onto the real image of the projector. In Fig. 6(d), the error between these shapes is drastically reduced.

5   HDR Synthesis Using Asynchronous Blinking Pattern

To synthesize HDR image, usually multiple-exposure images are required. However, it is not possible to capture such images with commonly available endoscopic systems. To solve the issue, we control the light source instead of the camera, *i.e.*, blinking the pattern. Note that we just switch the pattern ON-and-OFF periodically without synchronization mechanism.

Using just two levels of intensity for the projector are fine for synthesizing HDR images because we utilize 'beat' between the frequencies of the camera capturing and the projector illumination. Suppose n Hz for the camera and m Hz for the projector, then, beat frequency becomes $n - m$ Hz $(n > m)$. With ON-and-OFF switching signal, it makes half of exposure time, *i.e.*, $1/(2m)$ sec. for the projector, whereas we cannot control the shutter speed of the camera. Suppose the camera shutter speed to be α/n sec $(\alpha < 1)$, then the exposure time varies between $min(0, 1/(2m) + \alpha/n - 1/m)$ to $max(1/(2m), \alpha/n)$ as shown in Fig. 7. In our experiment, we set $n = 30$ and $m = 26$ and then the exposure time varies with 4 Hz and we can synthesize HDR using the 8 frames. Then, tone mapping is applied to the HDR images to make 8 bit images, which allows to use conventional image processing tools.

To synthesize HDR images, exposure times are supposed to be known, however, since the camera and the projector are not synchronized, it cannot be retrieved with our system. For solution, we estimate the exposure time only from captured image set. In our implementation, we simply average the intensity of the pattern excluding outliers with simple thresholding technique for each frame and use the ratio of the average as for the exposure time.

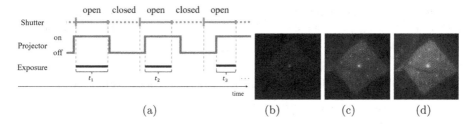

(a) (b) (c) (d)

Fig. 7. Acquiring multi-exposure images: (a) Timings of exposure time and pattern projection time (t_i represents an exposure time). (b)–(d): Multi-exposure images. One cycle of multi-exposure images includes about 8 images $I_1, I_2, \cdots, I_8$. I_1, I_3 and I_5 are shown here.

6 Experiments

6.1 Auto-calibration of the Projector Position

To confirm the accuracy of the proposed auto-calibration, we compare the results of auto-calibration and calibration based on known objects. As already explained, Fig. 6(b) shows an image with a sphere that can be used as a calibration object. Generally, calibration by using a known-shaped object such as sphere-based calibration [10] is supposed to be more accurate than auto-calibration which cannot use known-shaped objects. Thus, we compared the auto-calibration results with this data, assuming that [10] is the ground truth.

In the experiment, the image of Fig. 6(b) is calibrated by sphere-based calibration and auto-calibration. To show effectiveness of using silhouette of the pattern projector, the auto-calibration was tested with and without silhouette fitting cost function (*i.e.*, weight w_1 in the cost function was set to zero in the case without silhouette fitting). Figure 8(a) shows the results, in which 6 parameters of the translation and rotation are compared. The proposed method was more accurate than the method without silhouette fitting and par with calibration method based on a known-shaped object [10]. In Fig. 8(b), we can observe

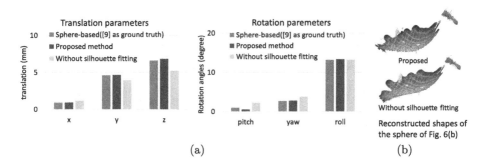

(a) (b)

Fig. 8. Comparison of the proposed method with sphere-based calibration [10] as ground truth and an auto-calibration without silhouette fitting of the pattern projector.

that the reconstructed sphere by the method without silhouette fitting was partially distorted, whereas the shape generated by the proposed method did not have such distortion.

6.2   Improvement Using HDR Image for 3D Reconstruction

To show effectiveness of the HDR image generation, we tested our algorithm using a human hand as the target object. We first captured images of the target surface which is projected by a blinking laser pattern projector. Although pattern is just illuminated bright and dark repeatedly, we could obtain an image sequence with different exposures. We have extracted 8 images of one multi-exposure cycle $I_1, I_2, \cdots I_8$. I_1, I_3, and I_5 are shown in Fig. 7.

Then, HDR image is created from the sequence, and then, tone-mapped for 3D reconstructed algorithm. The HDR image is shown in Fig. 9(b). The 3D reconstructed results with/without HDR algorithm are shown in Fig. 9(c) and (d). The numbers of reconstructed points for each frame and HDR image are shown in Fig. 10, proving that the area which was successfully reconstructed from the HDR image was larger than the results of any of the original input images. In Fig. 9, we can see that the regions around the brightest center marker

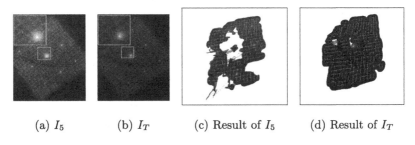

(a) I_5 (b) I_T (c) Result of I_5 (d) Result of I_T

Fig. 9. Comparison between the original and the tone-mapped HDR images. (a) I_5 from Fig. 7, which was most successfully reconstructed in images I_1 to I_8. (b) The tone-mapped HDR image generated from I_1 to I_8. (c) 3D reconstruction result of (a). (d) 3D reconstruction result of (b).

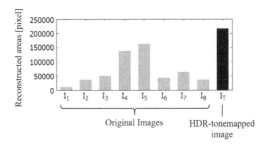

Fig. 10. Comparison of 3D reconstructed areas of original and tone-mapped HDR images.

were reconstructed in the result of I_T (HDR image), whereas, in the result of I_5 (note that I_5 was the most successfully reconstructed image from Fig. 10), the same regions were not reconstructed. In Fig. 9, we can also see that the noises in the source images are reduced in the tone-mapped HDR image, because multiple images are merged so that independent noises are suppressed.

6.3   3D Reconstruction Inside a Stomach of a Pig

To evaluate the system in more realistic conditions, we captured shapes inside a stomach of a pig, which is often used for evaluation purpose and a practice of an endoscopist. To evaluate the scales captured by the 3D endoscope, we first curved

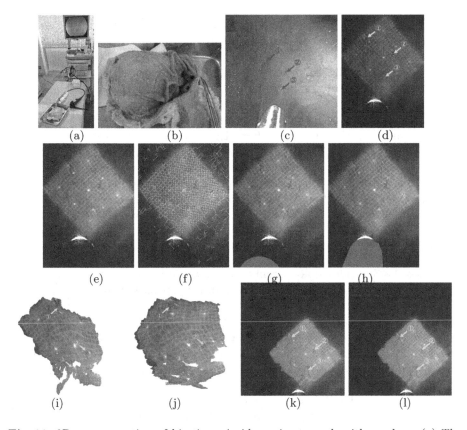

Fig. 11. 3D reconstruction of bio-tissue inside a pig stomach with markers. (a) The environment of the experiment. (b) The pig-stomach cut open after experiment session. (c) The appearance inside the stomach with marker positions. (d) The captured image with the pattern projected. (e) The HDR enhanced image. (f) The detected grid graph. (g), (h) Before and after the auto-calibration of the projector. The rendered projector positing is the read cylinder and the epipolar lines are pink line segments. (g) is before the auto-calibration and (h) is after the auto-calibration. (i), (j) Reconstructed 3D shape rendered from two different view points. (k), (l) Distance measurements between the two markers. Red regions are reconstructed areas. (Color figure online)

Table 1. Estimated distances between two markers on the surface inside a pig stomach

Marker IDs	Ground truth	Ground truth (expanded)	Our result
1 and 2	24.6 mm	29.4 mm	25.9 mm
2 and 3	14.2 mm	15.1 mm	13.9 mm

several markers on the surface of pig's stomach, then, reconstruct 3D shape of the entire surface. The distances between the two markers are estimated and compared to the ground truth, which is obtained by measuring the real distances between the markers after the measurement process; we cut and opened the stomach. Since the stomach was inflated while the endoscopy diagnosis, the ground truth distances that are actually measured were considered to be smaller than the estimated distances. To compensate such error, we also measure the ground truth distance while expanding the stomach surface manually.

Figure 11 shows the experimental situation and the results. Comparison between estimated results and ground truth are shown in Table 1. The precision was about 5.0% and 2.1% from the unexpanded ground truth. Considering the difference of measurement situation, we could conclude that the measurement was sufficiently accurate. In Fig. 11(g), (h), we also show the result of auto-calibration. In Fig. 11(g), which shows situation before auto-calibration, the rendered silhouette of the projector is different from the captured silhouette of Fig. 11(e). After auto-calibration, the projector position fits to the captured image, and the epipolar lines lie on the marker position as shown in Fig. 11(h).

7   Conclusion

We proposed a 3D endoscopic system based on an active stereo, where the micro laser pattern projector is inserted through an instrumental channel. Since there is a margin between the projector and the channel and the head of endoscope dynamically moves during an actual operation, the relative position of a camera and a projector is not fixed with respect to each other. For 3D reconstruction the relative position should be known, we propose an auto-calibration technique using the silhouette of the pattern projector. In addition, since the laser projector has a strong light intensity and dynamic range of the camera is not enough, we propose a new HDR image synthesis technique using a blinking modulation applied to the projector. The ability of the techniques were confirmed by intensive experiments using real endoscopic systems and demonstrated by reconstructing the 3D shape of the inside surface of a pig's stomach. Our future work is to construct the realtime system and use it to actual diagnosis and operations.

Acknowledgment. This work was supported in part by JSPS KAKENHI Grant No. 15H02779, 16H02849, MIC SCOPE 171507010 and MSR CORE12.

References

1. Furukawa, R., Masutani, R., Miyazaki, D., Baba, M., Hiura, S., Visentini-Scarzanella, M., Morinaga, H., Kawasaki, H., Sagawa, R.: 2-DOF auto-calibration for a 3D endoscope system based on active stereo. In: 2015 37th Annual International Conference of the IEEE Engineering in Medicine and Biology Society (EMBC), pp. 7937–7941, August 2015
2. Furukawa, R., Kawasaki, H.: Uncalibrated multiple image stereo system with arbitrarily movable camera and projector for wide range scanning. In: IEEE Conference on 3DIM, pp. 302–309 (2005)
3. Nagakura, T., Michida, T., Hirao, M., Kawahara, K., Yamada, K.: The study of three-dimensional measurement from an endoscopic images with stereo matching method. In: World Automation Congress, WAC 2006, pp. 1–4, July 2006
4. Stoyanov, D., Scarzanella, M.V., Pratt, P., Yang, G.-Z.: Real-time stereo reconstruction in robotically assisted minimally invasive surgery. In: Jiang, T., Navab, N., Pluim, J.P.W., Viergever, M.A. (eds.) MICCAI 2010. LNCS, vol. 6361, pp. 275–282. Springer, Heidelberg (2010). https://doi.org/10.1007/978-3-642-15705-9_34
5. Visentini-Scarzanella, M., Stoyanov, D., Yang, G.: Metric depth recovery from monocular images using shape-from-shading and specularities. In: ICIP, Orlando, USA, pp. 25–28 (2012)
6. Schmalz, C., Forster, F., Schick, A., Angelopoulou, E.: An endoscopic 3D scanner based on structured light. Med. Image Anal. **16**(5), 1063–1072 (2012)
7. Lin, J., Clancy, N.T., Elson, D.S.: An endoscopic structured light system using multispectral detection. Int. J. Comput. Assist. Radiol. Surg. **10**(12), 1941–1950 (2015)
8. Köhler, T., Haase, S., Bauer, S., Wasza, J., Kilgus, T., Maier-Hein, L., Feußner, H., Hornegger, J.: ToF meets RGB: novel multi-sensor super-resolution for hybrid 3-D endoscopy. In: Mori, K., Sakuma, I., Sato, Y., Barillot, C., Navab, N. (eds.) MICCAI 2013. LNCS, vol. 8149, pp. 139–146. Springer, Heidelberg (2013). https://doi.org/10.1007/978-3-642-40811-3_18
9. Penne, J., Schaller, C., Engelbrecht, R., Maier-Hein, L., Schmauss, B., Meinzer, H.P., Hornegger, J.: Laparoscopic quantitative 3D endoscopy for image guided surgery. In: Bildverarbeitung für die Medizin, pp. 16–20. Citeseer (2010)
10. Furukawa, R., Aoyama, M., Hiura, S., Aoki, H., Kominami, Y., Sanomura, Y., Yoshida, S., Tanaka, S., Sagawa, R., Kawasaki, H.: Calibration of a 3D endoscopic system based on active stereo method for shape measurement of biological tissues and specimen. In: EMBC, pp. 4991–4994 (2014)
11. Furukawa, R., Sanomura, Y., Tanaka, S., Yoshida, S., Sagawa, R., Visentini-Scarzanella, M., Kawasaki, H.: 3D endoscope system using doe projector. In: The 38th Annual International Conference of the IEEE Engineering in Medicine and Biology Society (EMBC 2016) (2016)
12. Forsyth, D., Ponce, J.: Computer Vision: A Modern Approach, 2nd edn. Pearson Education Inc., London (2011)
13. Furukawa, R., Kawasaki, H.: Self-calibration of multiple laser planes for 3D scene reconstruction. In: 3DPVT, pp. 200–207 (2006)
14. Furukawa, R., Kawasaki, H.: Laser range scanner based on self-calibration techniques using coplanarities and metric constraints. Comput. Vis. Image Underst. **113**(11), 1118–1129 (2009)

15. Yamazaki, S., Mochimaru, M., Kanade, T.: Simultaneous self-calibration of a projector and a camera using structured light. In: 2011 IEEE Computer Society Conference on Computer Vision and Pattern Recognition Workshops (CVPRW), pp. 60–67. IEEE (2011)
16. Debevec, P.E., Malik, J.: Recovering high dynamic range radiance maps from photographs. In: SIGGRAPH 2008, pp. 1–10. ACM, New York (2008)
17. Kalantari, N.K., Shechtman, E., Barnes, C., Darabi, S., Goldman, D.B., Sen, P.: Patch-based high dynamic range video. ACM Trans. Graph. **32**(6), 202–1 (2013)
18. Eilertsen, G., Mantiuk, R., Unger, J.: A comparative review of tone-mapping algorithms for high dynamic range video. In: Computer Graphics Forum, vol. 36, pp. 565–592. Wiley Online Library (2017)
19. Sagawa, R., Ota, Y., Yagi, Y., Furukawa, R., Asada, N., Kawasaki, H.: Dense 3D reconstruction method using a single pattern for fast moving object. In: ICCV (2009)

A Novel No-reference Subjective Quality Metric for Free Viewpoint Video Using Human Eye Movement

Pallab Kanti Podder[1]([⊠]), Manoranjan Paul[1], and Manzur Murshed[2]

[1] School of Computing and Mathematics,
Charles Sturt University, Bathurst, NSW 2795, Australia
{ppodder,mpaul}@csu.edu.au
[2] School of Information Technology,
Federation University Churchill, Churchill, VIC 3842, Australia
manzur.murshed@federation.edu.au

Abstract. The *free viewpoint video* (FVV) allows users to interactively control the viewpoint and generate new views of a dynamic scene from any 3D position for better 3D visual experience with depth perception. Multiview video coding exploits both texture and depth video information from various angles to encode a number of views to facilitate FVV. The usual practice for the single view or multiview quality assessment is characterized by evolving the objective quality assessment metrics due to their simplicity and real time applications such as the *peak signal-to-noise ratio* (PSNR) or the *structural similarity index* (SSIM). However, the PSNR or SSIM requires reference image for quality evaluation and could not be successfully employed in FVV as the new view in FVV does not have any reference view to compare with. Conversely, the widely used subjective estimator- *mean opinion score* (MOS) is often biased by the testing environment, viewers mode, domain knowledge, and many other factors that may actively influence on actual assessment. To address this limitation, in this work, we devise a no-reference subjective quality assessment metric by simply exploiting the pattern of human eye browsing on FVV. Over different quality contents of FVV, the participants eye-tracker recorded spatio-temporal gaze-data indicate more concentrated eye-traversing approach for relatively better quality. Thus, we calculate the *Length*, *Angle*, *Pupil-size*, and *Gaze-duration* features from the recorded gaze trajectory. The content and resolution invariant operation is carried out prior to synthesizing them using an adaptive weighted function to develop a new *quality metric using eye traversal* (QMET). Tested results reveal that the proposed QMET performs better than the SSIM and MOS in terms of assessing different aspects of coded video quality for a wide range of FVV contents.

Keywords: Eye-traversal · Eye-tracking · Free viewpoint video
Gaze-trajectory · HEVC · QMET · Quality assessment

© Springer International Publishing AG, part of Springer Nature 2018
M. Paul et al. (Eds.): PSIVT 2017, LNCS 10749, pp. 237–251, 2018.
https://doi.org/10.1007/978-3-319-75786-5_20

1 Introduction

The *video quality evaluation* (VQE) is a promising research area due to its wide range of applications in the development of various video coding algorithms [1]. The technical coding areas involved with the FVV are characterized by the view generation using *multiview video coding* (MVC) and the view synthesis. This process first goes through the image warping and then a hole filling technique e.g. the inverse mapping technique or spatial/temporal correlation as simple post processing filtering [2,3]. Since the synthesized view is generated at a virtual position between left and right views, there is no available reference frame for quality estimation of FVV [4]. Usually the quality estimation is performed in two ways: objective and subjective, where the former one is more widely used due to its simplicity, ease of use and having real-time applications. Thus, a good number of citable researches have been conducted based on the objective image quality estimation [5–7]. The quality estimation could be further categorized into full-reference (i.e. original videos as reference), reduced-reference (i.e. existence of partial signals as reference) and no-reference schemes. Among them, the applications of full-reference metrics such as the SSIM or PSNR have been restricted to the reference based situations only and these metrics lose their suitability in estimating different qualities of FVV where the reference frame is not available. To address the limitations of full-reference metrics, a number of no-reference based research works have recently come into the light for quality evaluation [8–10]. The introduced statistical metrics may not be suitable to some high quality ranges since the quality perception in these area is mostly due to perceptual *human visual system* (HVS) features, rather than to the statistics of the image [11]. However, different features of the HVS are not actively studied in the existing schemes. The authors in [12] performed the human cognition based quality assessment using eye-tracking and evolved more realistic ground truth visual saliency model to improve their algorithm. In fact, the eye-tracking has become a non-intrusive, affordable, and easy-to-use tool in human behavior research today. With very few exceptions, anything with a visual component can be eye tracked by simply employing the software based eye-tracking simulator [13]. Unlike objective quality evaluation, the subjective studies could yield valuable data to evaluate the performance of objective methods towards aiming the ultimate goal of matching human perception [14]. Thus, a number of quality assessment algorithms have been proposed which are closely related to the studies of human visual attention and cognition. The study in [15] introduced a no-reference framework using blur and blockiness metric to improve the performance of objective metric using eye-tracker data. The authors in [16] introduced a model to judge the video quality on the basis of psychological merits including- the pupil dilation and electroencephalogram signalling. Exploiting the eye gaze-data, Albanesi and Amadeo [17] generated a voting algorithm to develop a no-reference method. Using the scan path of eye movements, Tsai et al. [18] subjectively assessed the perceived image and its colour quality. Conversely, the widely used subjective testing scheme- the MOS [19,20] is often biased by a number of factors such as viewers mode, domain knowledge, testing environment, and many more which may actively influence the effectiveness of quality assessment process. Podder et al. [21] first introduced the subjective metric- QMET, however, their initial work is based on the single view video where the viewing angle is fixed for users. Moreover, their introduced approach highly depends on threshold selection for each feature and incur with the lack of proper correlation setting among features. The most importantly, their metric does not perform well in different contents and resolutions of the videos. The proposed method is a significantly extended version of their work where the major amendments include the employment of FVV i.e. in the no reference scenario, increasing number of features, better correlation analysis of features, performing content and resolution invariant operation on features, synthesizing them by an adaptive weighted function, comparing the new metric with PSNR, SSIM, and MOS, and eventually employing two widely used estimators the *Pearson Linear Correlation Coefficient* (PLCC) and *Spearman Rank-Order Correlation Coefficient* (SRCC) to justify the effectiveness of the proposed QMET for a range of FVV sequences.

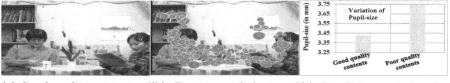

(a) Good quality contents of the *Newspaper* sequence (b) Eye-traversal for good quality contents (c) Pupil-size variation for different qualities

(d) Poor quality contents of the *Newspaper* sequence (e) Eye-traversal for poor quality contents (f) Gaze-duration variation for different qualities

Fig. 1. More concentrated eye-traversing approach is perceived for relatively better quality contents (e.g. *Newspaper* sequence image in (b)). The opposite is noticed in (e) for which the pupil-size sharply increases in (c), while the gaze event duration notably decreases in (f).

Let us first concentrate on Fig. 1 in which (a) and (d) represent a multiview video sequence namely *Newspaper* encoded as good and poor quality respectively, while (b) and (e) demonstrate the eye traversing approach of a viewer for good and poor quality image contents respectively. The tracked gaze plots indicate more concentrated eye-traversal for relatively better quality contents. Now if we determine *Length* (L) and *Angle* (A) features for the gaze plots, they could explicitly tell about the viewers pattern browsing (i.e. smooth or random as depicted in Fig. 1(b) and (e)). Then we discover that the quality variation effects on both *Pupil-size* (P) and *Gaze-duration* (T) variation presented in Fig. 1(c) and (f), thus, we calculate four cardinal features- L, A, P, and T for each *potential gaze plot* (PGP) from the gaze trajectory. The $PGPs$ in this test are defined by the fixations (i.e. visual gaze on a single location) and saccades (i.e. quick movement of eyes between two or more phases of fixations). The content and resolution invariant operations are then performed on the features and adaptively synthesized using a weighted function to develop the proposed QMET. The higher QMET score promises good quality video as the viewers could better capture its content information with smooth global browsing. Experimental results reveal that the quality evaluation carried out by the QMET could better perform compared to the objective metric SSIM, and the subjective estimator MOS. Since the eye tracker data could be easily captured today by directly employing the software based eye-tracking simulator (i.e. device itself is no longer required), the utility of the QMET could also be more flexible simple simulator generated data set.

2   Proposed Method

First of all, by employing the HEVC [22] reference software $HM15.0$ [23], different video quality segments were generated and then watched by a group of participants. The processed eye-tracker recorded data were analyzed using four quality correlation features, i.e. L, A, P, and T. The content and resolution invariant operations were carried out on the features and the features were synthesized by an adaptive weighted function to develop a new metric- QMET. The process diagram of the entire process is presented in Fig. 2, while the key steps are described in the succeeding sections.

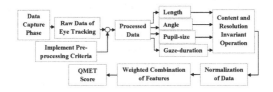

Fig. 2. Process diagram of the proposed QMET development.

2.1   Data Capture and Pre-processing

The participants (including males and females) who were recruited from the University had normal or corrected-to-normal vision and did not suffer from any medical condition to adversely influence our project [*ethical approval no. 2015/124*]. They fall within the 20–45 age band and are undergraduate/postgraduate students, PhD students, and lecturers of the University.

A number of multiview sequences which are used in this test comprise the resolution type of 1920×1088 and 1024×768 (detail to be found in [24]). To avoid the biasness, initially we use the gray scale components only and randomly vary the display order of the quality segments to the participants. We generate three different quality types of each video including *Excellent* (using *quantization parameter* $QP = 5$), *Fair* ($QP = 25$), and *Very-poor* ($QP = 50$). Calibration and a trial run was performed so that the participants feel comfort about the whole process. Upon their satisfaction, the Tobii eye tracker [25] was employed to record their eye movements. As the device recorded data at 60 HZ frequency and allocated frame rate was 30 (fps), each frame could accommodate two gaze points and a single whole video covered 9000 gaze plots having 1800 for each quality segment.

2.2 Features Correlation Analysis with Quality

The *Length* (*L*- in pixel) of the *ith* potential gaze plot is calculated using the *Euclidean distance* with respect to the $(i+1)th$ gaze plot, while the *Angle* (*A*- in degree) of the *ith* plot is calculated by using both the reference of its $(i-1)th$ and $(i+1)th$ values (where $i = 1, 2, \ldots,$ n and the values of L and A are not calculated for the *1st* and *nth* plots). The *pupil-size* (*P*- in mm) and *Gaze-duration* (*T*- in ms) for each *ith* plot are determined by averaging the values of left and right pupil size and the eye-tracker recorded timestamp data respectively by employing MATLAB R2012a (MathWorks Inc., Massachusetts, USA). The overall calculated results indicate that L, A, P features have a proportionate correlation, while the feature T has an inversely proportionate correlation with the video quality degradation as demonstrated in Fig. 3.

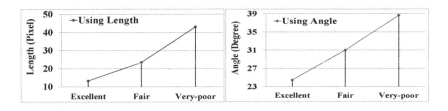

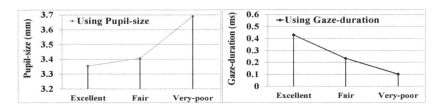

Fig. 3. The *Length* (*L*), *Angle* (*A*), and *Pupil-size* (*P*) features have a proportionate correlation, while the *Gaze-duration* (*T*) feature has an inversely proportionate correlation with quality degradation

This time, the contribution of each feature has been estimated in the context of segregating different quality contents. It is observed that no single feature could solely be the best representative in distinguishing different qualities. The individual $Q - score$ (i.e. the calculated pseudo score of the proposed QMET) of each feature is determined by exploiting the Eqs. (1)–(4), where Q1, Q2, Q3, and Q4 indicate the $Q - score$ for the individual feature L, A, P, and T respectively.

$$Q_1 = L^{\delta L} \tag{1}$$

$$Q_2 = A^{\varphi A} \tag{2}$$

$$Q_3 = (P/2)^{\gamma P} \tag{3}$$

$$Q_4 = \sqrt{2T}^{(\eta/\sqrt{2T})} \tag{4}$$

here, δ, φ, γ, and η are the weighting factors of L, A, P, and T features respectively. Let us briefly discuss the formation of equations to produce different $Q - scores$ using the power law where the relative change in one quantity results in a proportional change in the other quantity, i.e. one quantity varies as a power of another [26]. In our case, the relative value change of the features is unknown, and their corresponding reproduced $Q - score$ is unknown as well, however, whether they have proportionate or inversely proportionate relation is known. For example, lower L indicates higher quality and respective higher $Q - score$, but still, we do not know how much. Since the value change of L for each quality segment is not significant (e.g. 0.08 for *Excellent* and 0.12 for *Fair* and the maximum average does not exceed 0.50), it could be best represented only by its power representation as the smaller power with smaller base produces a higher score. This could eventually produce a clear score difference for different quality segments. The features L, A, and P work with power-weight multiplication, however, power-weight division for T similarly works here as it has as inversely proportionate relation with Q-score. The relationships are presented in Eqs. (1)–(4). The rationality of using the Q-score is to predict a better picture of the QMET performance change for various changes of L, A, P, and T within a sizable format that ranges from 0 to 1. Since L, A, P, and T features could jointly advice about how far, how much, how large, and how long respectively in the spatiotemporal domain, the features are synthesized by developing an adaptive weighted function equated as $Q = L^{\delta L} \times A^{\varphi A} \times (P/2)^{\gamma P} \times \sqrt{2T}^{(\eta/\sqrt{2T})}$. The purpose of this multiplication is to keep a persistent relation of L, A, P, and T features with the reproduced Q-score. As the normalized value of the features varies within the range 0 to 1 using Eqs. (1)–(4), their multiplication could better reproduce the ultimate score within the predefined limit. Note that the weight for δ, φ, γ, and η in the Eqs. (1)–(4) is fixed with 0.5 in this test. This is because we further calculate the slope at each point changing the quality (i.e. Excellent, Fair, and so on) and determine their average for a number of weights. Since the calculated average using weight 0.5 outperforms the other weight combinations, we fix it for the entire experiment to best distinguish different quality segments which is demonstrated in Fig. 4. The distribution of other combinations might work better; however, the tested results demonstrate a good correlation of QMET with other metrics.

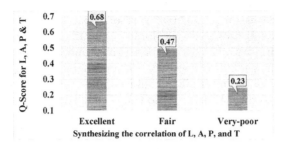

Fig. 4. The synthesizing operation using *Length*, *Angle*, *Pupil-size*, and *Gaze-duration* features could better distinguish different quality segments

2.3 Content and Resolution Invariant Operation on Features

Let us first consider the content (left in Fig. 5) and resolution (right in Fig. 5) based unprocessed L of two example sequences e.g. *Poznan_Street* and *Newspaper* presented in Fig. 5. The calculated variations between the highest and lowest values are 41.72% and 28.63% according to the contents and resolutions respectively. Now, the content invariant operation follows a number of steps. First, we figure out the L of the PGPs as mentioned in Sect. 2.2; Second, calculate the average of potential gaze plot (x) and (y) and entitle it by the centre coordinate $C(x,y)$; Third, with respect to $C(x,y)$, we calculate the Euclidean distance of all PGPs and sort the values of length by lowest to the highest order. The rationality of this ordering scheme is due to prioritize the foveal central concentration on pixels by partially avoiding the long surrounded parafoveal, or perifoveal fixations [27] that may incur even with attentive eye browsing; Fourth, to determine the object motion area, we take the average of first μ sorted values ($\mu = 75\%$ in this test since it could help the QMET in obtaining the highest score) which is the foreseen radius of captured affective region; Fifth, the radius is then employed as a divisor of calculated lengths for each potential gaze plots in the First step.

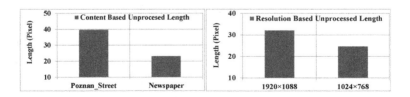

Fig. 5. The video content and resolution based unprocessed Length

Similar to the content based lengths, we also observe a stunning variation of 28.63% for different resolution based lengths in Fig. 5 (right). As a result, we exploit a number of multiplication factors (passively act as compensators) eventually to neutralize the impact of various size video resolutions displayed on the screen. For example, assuming 1024×768 resolution sequence as a reference, the unprocessed lengths of its higher and lower resolution sequences are multiplied by 0.75 and 1.25 respectively. Almost for all the sequences, since the eye-tracker recorded data demonstrates a good correlation among the highest to the lowest resolution videos, the multipliers could perform well in resolution invariant operation. The outcomes then turn into the normalized values ranging within 0 to 1. The resultant effect of content plus resolution invariant operation for L is revealed in the top-left of Fig. 6 which is undertaken for the final QMET scoring. Once the similar operations are performed on the features A, P, and T, the variation effects could be significantly minimized as illustrated in the top-right, bottom-left and bottom-right respectively as demonstrated in Fig. 6.

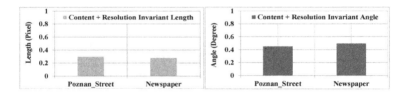

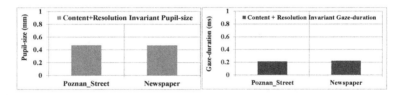

Fig. 6. The obtained values of L, A, P, and T (normalized) after performing the content and resolution invariant operation

2.4   The Development of QMET

If relatively lower values of L, A, and P, and higher values of T belong to a potential gaze plot, the QMET should produce relatively higher score. Thus, the QMET score is calculated for all PGPs of each *Excellent*, *Fair*, and *Very-poor* quality segment of the sequences by adaptively synthesizing the features as follows:

$$Q_{MET} = L^{\delta L} \times A^{\varphi A} \times (P/2)^{\gamma P} \times \sqrt{2T}^{(\eta/\sqrt{2T})} \tag{5}$$

where the weight for δ, φ, γ, and η is fixed with 0.5 in this experiment as stated earlier. In an unusual case, if the normalized values of L and A become 0 for 30 consecutive frames (as the frame rate is kept 30 in this test), then a mimicking operation is performed. The rationality of allocating such operation is due to handling the consecutive 0 s that may incur with the intentional eye fixation of participants to a certain PGP. Thus, the user data which have got stack over the frames are forcefully panelized by arbitrarily setting the value of $L = 0.1$ and $A = 0.1$. This operation is applicable only for the features L and A since P and T are still $! = 0$ then. Note that during this test, we did not experience such unusual situation and carried out no such operation.

3   Experimental Outcomes

The QMET evaluated maximum and minimum scores for each quality segment using two example sequences are presented in Fig. 7(a). For both sequences, the obtained score for the *Excellent* quality segment is the highest which gradually decreases with respect to the quality degradation and reaches its lowest for the *Very-poor* segment of quality. Compared to the *Newspaper*, the QMET score sharply decreases for the *Poznan_Street* sequence. This is because compared to its *Excellent* quality segment, the recorded supporting gaze data for the *Very-poor* quality incur with recurrent unsuitable feature values and produce a lower QMET score. Once we calculate the average score of each Max and Min for the individual quality segment, we notice that the average recognition of variation between the best and worst quality becomes 72.35% which indicate a clear quality distinguishing capability of the QMET.

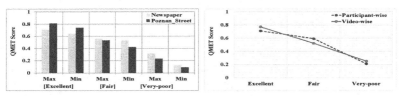

(a) Maximum (Max) to minimum (Min) QMET score at each quality segment using two test sequences

(b) The QMET score has a proportionate correlation to the coded video quality (person and video-basis)

Fig. 7. Different scoring orientations of QMET for a wide range of qualities (both the participant and video-basis)

Figure 7(b) revels the participant-wise and video-wise average QMET score for three different quality segments. The QMET could obtain the highest score i.e. 0.78 and 0.71 for the *Excellent* quality segment according to both the video and participant basis as the participants could better capture information from the best quality contents with smooth global browsing. Conversely, for the lowest scores i.e. 0.25 and 0.21 at *Very-poor* segment, participants in most cases do not succeed to capture content information due do its unpleasant quality and then immediately move to the next but still erroneous. As the number of such hits and miss browsing sharply increases with time, the quality score also decreases as plenty of inappropriate feature values incur with the scoring process. Therefore, for a sequence having really *Poor* to *Very-poor* quality, it becomes very unlikely to acquire higher quality score using the proposed QMET. This time, for better justifying the performance of QMET against the PSNR, SSIM, and the MOS using the FVV, two different quality segments (i.e. *Excellent* and *Very-poor*) have been taken into account. The calculated average score of four metrics for these segments are reported in Fig. 8(a)–(d). The obtained percentages of variations between the highest score (for *Excellent* quality segment) and the lowest score (for *Very-poor* quality segment) using PSNR, SSIM, QMET, and MOS are 57.39, 32.49, 78.51, and 69.71 as represented in Fig. 8(e). The outcomes indicate that the QMET estimated average quality segregation score outperforms the rest of the metrics. This is because viewers could better capture good quality synthesized video content with smooth global browsing. Conversely, the poorly reconstructed synthesized views incur with the localized edge reconstruction and crack like artifacts. Thus, the recorded gaze data of poor contents indicate participants haphazard means of browsing (being affected by unsuccessful attempts due to unpleasant quality) that could not meet the balanced feature correlation criteria and generate lower QMET score. Figure 8(f) indicates the maximum achievable difference (e.g. the difference between the highest score of *Excellent* quality and the lowest score of *Very-poor* quality segment) picked out by the four metrics where the MOS could outperform the other metrics. The *Very-poor* quality segment of some synthesized video (e.g. *Newspaper*) incur with an arbitrarily nominated lower score such as 0.05 (out of 1.0) which lead to such stunning variations. The calculated results for free viewpoint videos in Fig. 8 indicate that the improvement using the subjective assessment such as MOS could perform better than those of the objective metrics PSNR and SSIM. This is mostly due to the PSNR and SSIM do not find an available reference image to calculate the score in this regard. However, according to Fig. 8(e), the human visual perception based QMET could demonstrate relatively improved performance compared to the MOS in terms of segregating different aspects of coded video quality.

Now, two remarkable annotations: first, if different videos are coded using the same quality (e.g. QP = 5 for *Excellent*), the reproduced scores should have no stunning variations. Surprisingly, the PSNR discard this trend and almost for all quality segments, its variation reached the highest as illustrated in Fig. 9. Thus, it might lose its suitability for a wide range of free view video sequences. On the other side, for the *Very-Poor* quality segment, the participants perhaps give some arbitrary scores for which the MOS reaches its apex and its proficiency drops down in this regard. This example also requires the development of another subjective metric other than MOS for relatively fairer scoring. Although the QMET performs better than PSNR and MOS, the SSIM appears most stable for all segments. This is because the SSIM is a perception-based model that considers degradation in an image mainly by recognizing the change in structural information. To justify the second observation, i.e. even the same sequence

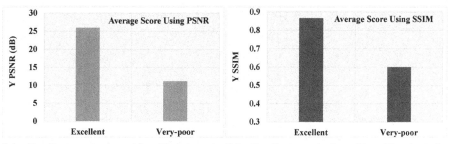

(a) Quality variation identification by PSNR

(b) Quality variation identification by SSIM

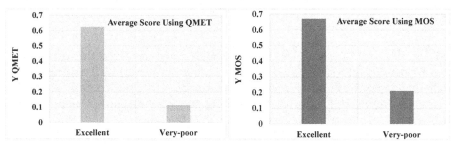

(c) Quality variation identification by QMET

(d) Quality variation identification by MOS

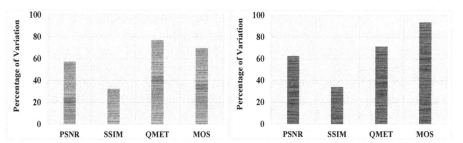

(e) Four metrics estimated average variations

(f) Four metrics assessed maximum variations

Fig. 8. In the figure, (a–d) reveal the average quality variation identification carried out by the PSNR, SSIM, QMET, and MOS for the *Excellent* and *Very-poor* quality segments of free viewpoint videos which is more explicitly presented in (e), while (f) indicates the maximum achievable difference (e.g. the difference between the highest score of *Excellent* quality and the lowest score of *Very-poor* quality segment) obtained by four metrics.

is coded with a range of qualities, the recognition of quality variation should be prominent which has been verified by employing two ranges of variations (*Excellent - Fair* and *Fair - Very-poor*) and reported in Fig. 10. For the first range of segments, all the metrics with free view video although perform in a similar manner, the QMET appears the most responsive in differentiating the range of

Fig. 9. The performance comparison of PSNR, SSIM, QMET, and MOS metrics on the *Excellent, Fair,* and *Very-poor* quality segment using FVV. Lower the calculated variation for a segment better the metric performance is presumed.

qualities. The SSIM tends to be the least responsive metric in this regard. For the second range of segments (i.e. *Fair - Very-poor*), the QMET and the MOS reach their apex to indicate their best performance in the context of quality segregation. Interestingly, for both range of segments, the subjective estimators perform relatively better compared to the objective ones.

For further performance estimation of four metrics, the calculated results for all videos used in this test are reported in Table 1 by implementing both the PLCC and SRCC's evaluation criteria. A good quality metric is expected to achieve higher values in both PLCC and SRCC [8]. According to both PLCC and SRCCs judgement, the QMET reveal the similar performance compared to the PSNR, however, it could obtain relatively higher score compared to the SSIM and MOS. In fact, the obtained results of the proposed metric are promising given the fact that no information about the reference image is available to the QMET for evaluating quality. Since the scoring pattern of four metrics are approximately similar in terms of distinguishing different quality contents as illustrated in Figs. 9 and 10, and Table 1, the proposed QMET could be well represented as a new member of the quality metric family and successfully employed

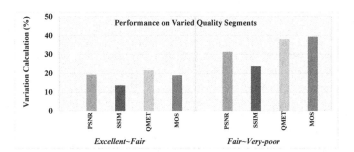

Fig. 10. The PSNR, SSIM, QMET, and MOS metrics recognized percentage of quality variation for a range of quality segment differences. Higher the calculated percentage of variation detection in segments [X–Y], better the metric performance is presumed.

as an impressive alternative to the subjective estimator MOS. It could also be employed to evaluate the effectiveness of using the objective metrics PSNR and SSIM since the QMET does not require any ground-truth reference for quality estimation.

Table 1. Average performance of four metrics according to both PLCC and SRCC's evaluation criteria.

Performance estimators	PSNR	SSIM	QMET	MOS
PLCC	0.68	0.63	0.69	0.68
SRCC	0.71	0.62	0.71	0.68

The potential application of QMET could be the evaluation of synthesized views reproduced by different FVV generation algorithms. A good number of contributions could be found in the literature which claim about the image quality improvement mostly depending on the objective metric PSNR, SSIM or the subjective estimator MOS. However, it is presented earlier that the subjective estimator MOS performs better than the objective metrics in most cases during evaluating the FVV quality. Since the proposed QMET is mostly correlated to the proximity of human cognition, its assessment process is presumed to be more neutral compared to the MOS. Moreover, since the view synthesis algorithms go through some post-processing phases such as inverse mapping or inpainting for crack filling, it is highly anticipated to obtain higher quality evaluation score using QMET especially for those algorithms successfully overcoming the crack filling artifacts.

4   Conclusion

In this work, a no-reference video quality assessment metric has been developed based on the free view video. The newly developed metric QMET could be an impressive substitute to the popularly used subjective estimator MOS for quality evaluation and comparison. In the metric generation process, the human perceptual eye- traversing nature on videos is exploited and discovered the patterns of *Length, Angle, Pupil-size,* and *Gaze-duration* features from the recorded gaze trajectory for varied video qualities. The content and resolution invariant operations are carried out prior to synthesizing them using an adaptive weighted function to develop the QMET. The experimental analysis reveal that the quality evaluation carried out by the QMET is mostly similar to the MOS and the reference required PSNR and SSIM in terms of assessing different aspects of quality contents. Eventually, the outcomes of four metrics have further been tested using the Pearson Linear Correlation Coefficient (PLCC) and Spearman Rank-Order Correlation Coefficients (SRCC) evaluation criteria which indicate that the QMET could relatively better perform compared to the MOS and the

SSIM for a wide range of free viewpoint video contents. Since the eye-tracker data could be easily captured nowadays by directly employing the software based eye-tracking simulator (i.e. device itself is no longer required), the utility of the QMET could also be more flexible using such simple simulator generated data set.

Acknowledgement. This work was supported in part by the Australian Research Council under Discovery Projects Grant DP130103670.

References

1. Gu, K., Zhai, G., Lin, W., Liu, M.: The analysis of image contrast: from quality assessment to automatic enhancement. IEEE Trans. Cybern. **46**(1), 284–297 (2016)
2. Rahaman, D.M., Paul, M.: Adaptive weighting between warped and learned foregrounds for view synthesize. In: 2017 IEEE International Conference on Multimedia and Expo Workshops (ICMEW), pp. 49–54. IEEE (2017)
3. Zhu, C., Li, S.: Depth image based view synthesis: new insights and perspectives on hole generation and filling. IEEE Trans. Broadcast. **62**(1), 82–93 (2016)
4. Battisti, F., Bosc, E., Carli, M., Le Callet, P., Perugia, S.: Objective image quality assessment of 3D synthesized views. Sig. Process.: Image Commun. **30**, 78–88 (2015)
5. Xu, M., Zhang, J., Ma, Y., Wang, Z.: A novel objective quality assessment method for perceptual video coding in conversational scenarios. In: 2014 IEEE Visual Communications and Image Processing Conference, pp. 29–32. IEEE (2014)
6. Gu, K., Liu, M., Zhai, G., Yang, X., Zhang, W.: Quality assessment considering viewing distance and image resolution. IEEE Trans. Broadcast. **61**(3), 520–531 (2015)
7. Liu, H., Klomp, N., Heynderickx, I.: A no-reference metric for perceived ringing artifacts in images. IEEE Trans. Circuits Syst. Video Technol. **20**(4), 529–539 (2010)
8. Fang, Y., Ma, K., Wang, Z., Lin, W., Fang, Z., Zhai, G.: No-reference quality assessment of contrast-distorted images based on natural scene statistics. IEEE Signal Process. Lett. **22**(7), 838–842 (2015)
9. Zhu, K., Li, C., Asari, V., Saupe, D.: No-reference video quality assessment based on artifact measurement and statistical analysis. IEEE Trans. Circuits Syst. Video Technol. **25**(4), 533–546 (2015)
10. Gu, K., Lin, W., Zhai, G., Yang, X., Zhang, W., Chen, C.W.: No-reference quality metric of contrast-distorted images based on information maximization. IEEE Trans. Cybern. **47**, 4559–4565 (2016)
11. Tourancheau, S., Autrusseau, F., Sazzad, Z.P., Horita, Y.: Impact of subjective dataset on the performance of image quality metrics. In: 2008 15th IEEE International Conference on Image Processing, ICIP 2008, pp. 365–368. IEEE (2008)
12. Liu, H., Heynderickx, I.: Visual attention in objective image quality assessment: based on eye-tracking data. IEEE Trans. Circuits Syst. Video Technol. **21**(7), 971–982 (2011)
13. Böhme, M., Dorr, M., Graw, M., Martinetz, T., Barth, E.: A software framework for simulating eye trackers. In: Proceedings of the 2008 Symposium on Eye Tracking Research and Applications, pp. 251–258. ACM (2008)

14. Seshadrinathan, K., Soundararajan, R., Bovik, A.C., Cormack, L.K.: Study of subjective and objective quality assessment of video. IEEE Trans. Image Process. **19**(6), 1427–1441 (2010)
15. Jia, L., Zhong, X., Tu, Y.: No-reference video quality assessment model based on eye tracking data. In: International Conference on Information, Electronics and Computer, pp. 97–100 (2014)
16. Arndt, S., Radun, J., Antons, J.N., Möller, S.: Using eye-tracking and correlates of brain activity to predict quality scores. In: 2014 Sixth International Workshop on Quality of Multimedia Experience (QoMEX), pp. 281–285. IEEE (2014)
17. Albanesi, M.G., Amadeo, R.: A new algorithm for objective video quality assessment on eye tracking data. In: 2014 International Conference on Computer Vision Theory and Applications (VISAPP), vol. 1, pp. 462–469. IEEE (2014)
18. Tsai, C.-M., Guan, S.-S., Tsai, W.-C.: Eye movements on assessing perceptual image quality. In: Zhou, J., Salvendy, G. (eds.) ITAP 2016. LNCS, vol. 9754, pp. 378–388. Springer, Cham (2016). https://doi.org/10.1007/978-3-319-39943-0_37
19. Ribeiro, F., Florencio, D., Nascimento, V.: Crowdsourcing subjective image quality evaluation. In: 2011 18th IEEE International Conference on Image Processing (ICIP), pp. 3097–3100. IEEE (2011)
20. Streijl, R.C., Winkler, S., Hands, D.S.: Mean opinion score (MOS) revisited: methods and applications, limitations and alternatives. Multimed. Syst. **22**(2), 213–227 (2016)
21. Podder, P.K., Paul, M., Murshed, M.: QMET: a new quality assessment metric for no-reference video coding by using human eye traversal. In: 2016 International Conference on Image and Vision Computing New Zealand (IVCNZ), pp. 1–6. IEEE (2016)
22. Bross, B., Han, W.J., Ohm, J.R., Sullivan, G.J., Wiegand T.: High efficiency video coding text specification draft 8. JTCVC- J1003, Sweden (2012)
23. Joint collaborative team on video coding (JCT-VC), HM software manual, CVS server. (http://hevc.kw.bbc.co.uk/svn/jctvc-hm/). Accessed Dec 2016
24. Podder, P.K., Paul, M., Rahaman, D.M., Murshed, M.: Improved depth coding for HEVC focusing on depth edge approximation. Sig. Process. Image Commun. **55**, 80–92 (2017)
25. Mulvey, F., Villanueva, A., Sliney, D., Lange, R., Cotmore, S., Donegan, M.: Exploration of safety issues in eyetracking (2008)
26. The basics of power law. https://en.wikipedia.org/wiki/power_law. Accessed Dec 2016
27. Salehin, M.M., Paul, M.: Human visual field based saliency prediction method using eye tracker data for video summarization. In: 2016 IEEE International Conference on Multimedia and Expo Workshops (ICMEW), pp. 1–6. IEEE (2016)

Research on Color Space Conversion Model from CMYK to CIE-LAB Based on GRNN

Xinyue Bao, Wangan Song, and Sheng Liu[⊠]

College of Computer Science and Technology, Huaibei Normal University,
Anhui 235000, China
Liusheng@chnu.edu.cn

Abstract. In order to reproduce color information accurately in cross media transmission, a color space conversion model from CMYK color space to CIE-LAB based on generalized regression neural network (GRNN) was proposed. According to the structure and mathematical model of GRNN neural network, the CMYK-LAB color space conversion model was established. By training sample and comparing the mean square error of the sample data, the distribution coefficients were determined, and CMYK- LAB color space conversion model based on GRNN was eventually obtained and the accuracy was tested. According to these data, sample data and test data was determined. The results showed that color space conversion from CMYK to CIE-LAB on GRNN had faster conversion speed and accuracy compared with the color space conversion method based on BP neural network, the demand on printing industry can be met.

Keywords: Color space conversion
Generalized regression neural network · CMYK · CIE-LAB
BP neural network

1 Introduction

Color reproduction is an important issue in the fields of information dissemination, image processing and machine vision. Especially each of equipment in printing process, such as scanner, digital camera, display device, image processing software, digital proofing machine, the color features are different, resulting in the same set of color signals was displayed inconsistently on different devices. Color management is to solve the problem of color conversion between devices in the process of image reproduction, so that the consistency of image color in the process of reproduction is guaranteed. The color space conversion process in printing was shown in Fig. 1. Color space conversion is an important part of color management, the key technology of color management is to realize the transformation of different color spaces to the target color space, and the results

© Springer International Publishing AG, part of Springer Nature 2018
M. Paul et al. (Eds.): PSIVT 2017, LNCS 10749, pp. 252–261, 2018.
https://doi.org/10.1007/978-3-319-75786-5_21

can be used for image screen detection, computer color matching, image separation, digital proofing, and image restoration and so on. The CIE-LAB color space is a color system independent of the device, and its gamut is greater than the gamut of GRB and CMYK, as showed in (a) of Fig. 1. By establishing a suitable CMYK to CIE-LAB color space conversion model to ensure the same color information in different devices in the process of copying color keep consistency. The CIE-LAB color space is the uniform color space, and the color difference can be detected by color difference formula, as showed in (b) of Fig. 1.

The study of artificial neural networks began in 1943, when psychologist McCulloch and mathematician Pitts proposed the M-P model [1]. As with the RBF network, GRNN had good function approximation performance. For its convenient network training, GRNN was widely used in control decision system [2], medical [3], image [4] and other fields of science and engineering. A control algorithm used the calculated values to correct the errors in the optical system [5]. In energy terms, the neural control-scheme was a powerful instrument for optimizing air conditioning setback scheduling based on external temperature records [6]. In chemistry and chemical engineering, parameter solution of dynamic model for deep bed filtration process was studied by Osmak [7]. In the latest literature, [8] proposed a novel dynamic Red, Green, Blue (RGB)-to-CMYK color conversion method, which utilized the weighted entropy to extract the pixels with filter response change dramatically.

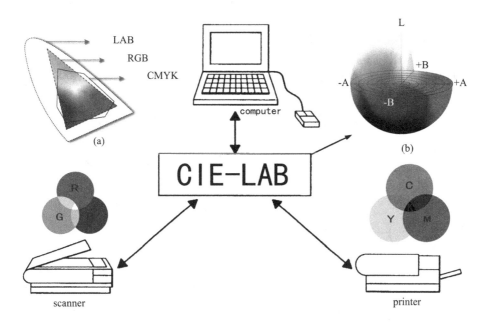

Fig. 1. Color space conversion model in printing process and color gamut in different color spaces (Color figure online)

Color space conversion method in the early stage mainly included data fitting method, look-up table and interpolation methods constructed by empirical ways [9], and the method of prism geometry linear interpolation [10,11]. In recent years, the artificial neural network method can effectively approximate the nonlinear relation between data sets. Color Space Conversion Based on RBF Neural Network [12] and the generalized regression neural network used as a model for the conversion of color space [13] was proposed, and the research involved the use of artificial neural networks to achieve faster and more accurate color conversion methods. Cao and Jing [13] proposed a CIE-LAB to CMYK color space conversion model based on GRNN, since there was no CMYK data in the previous color target, the target CMYK value needed to be obtained by professional printer, so the conversion accuracy was reduced. In this paper, color picker was used to acquire the value of target CMYK to reduce the conversion error, and the value of the target CIE-LAB obtained can be directly brought into the color difference formula, and a color space conversion model from CMYK to CIE-Lab based on GRNN was proposed. The results showed that a model of CMYK color space to CIE-LAB based on GRNN showed faster conversion speed and accuracy than BP neural network, the demand on printing industry can be met. Compared with RBF neural networks, GRNN had strong nonlinear mapping ability and learning speed, and the network converged to the optimal regression with more sample size. The unstable data can be processed by the network, and the excellent performance of the network when the sample was small (Fig. 2).

2   The Theoretical of GRNN

GRNN toke the sample data as a posteriori condition, performed the Parzen nonparametric estimation [14], and calculated the network output according to

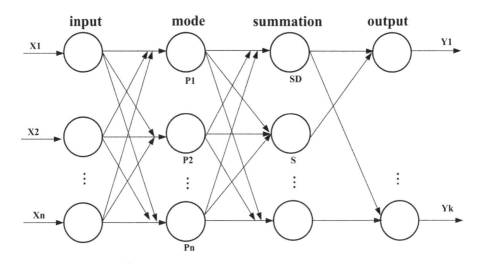

Fig. 2. Neural network structure

the maximum probability principle based on Nadaraya-Watson nonparametric kernel regression [15]. Although GRNN not need to set the model's form, the value of smoothing factor in the kernel function of the implicit regression unit had a great influence on the network. The theoretical basis of generalized regression neural network is nonlinear regression analysis, Let f (x, y) be a joint probability density of non-independent variable X and Y, to compute the regression analysis of Y relative to X is actually to compute the maximum probability value of Y. Let X is the observation value of the variable x, the value of conditional mean of the Y is relative to X:

$$E(y|X) = \widehat{y}(X) = \frac{\int\limits_{-\infty}^{+\infty} yf(x,y)dy}{\int\limits_{-\infty}^{+\infty} f(x,y)dy} \tag{1}$$

The generalized regression neural network has 4 layers: input, mode, summation and output. The model layer is hidden layer, the number of neurons is equal to the training sample capacity, and the transfer function of neuron is:

$$p_i = e^{-d(x_0 : x_i)} \tag{2}$$

In the formula (2), xi is the central vector of the kernel functions of each unit; the sum of output weights of each unit and the output of each unit of model layer were computed by summation layer, their transfer functions are:

$$s = \sum_{i=1}^{n} y_i p_i \tag{3}$$

$$s_D = \sum_{i=1}^{n} p_i \tag{4}$$

In the formula (3), yi is the weighted value of the weighted sum of each training sample. Finally, the output is calculated by the output layer, its formula is:

$$\widehat{y}(x_0) = S/SD \tag{5}$$

The number of output layer neurons was equal to the dimension of the output vector in the sample learning. In this paper, CMYK-CIE-LAB color space conversion model based on GRNN was eventually obtained and the accuracy was tested.

3   Data Acquisition and Normalization

The CIE-LAB data used in this paper came from the standard color target (IT8.7/2). In the experiment, because the standard color target IT8.7/2 had fewer color blocks, the blocks need not be pretreated and can be used in full IT8.7/2 color according to their color in order to be evenly divided into two parts, 132 pieces of color swatch and 24 pieces of Grayscale color block as modeling samples, 132 pieces of color swatch remaining as test samples. The accuracy of the color restoration model was evaluated by color difference between CIE-LAB and L0A0B0. Since the standard color target IT8.7/2 was the latest in the experiment, there was no fading due to the long duration, so the standard color of CIE CIE-LAB was used directly. The CMYK data used here for modeling was collected from the default Adobe workspace in the Abode Photoshop CS6 software, and the value of the CIE-LAB on the color target was manually converted to the value of the CMYK through the color picker. Figure 3 showed the color picker interface for manual conversion from CIE-LAB to CMYK. Since the data was converted manually one by one in color picker, considering the modeling accuracy, workload and sample data uniformity, so IT8.7/2 was adopted in this paper.

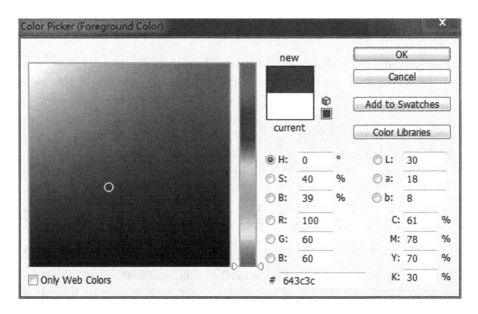

Fig. 3. The color picker interface in Abode Photoshop used for manual conversion from CIE-LAB to CMYK

The value of CMYK ranged from 0 to 1, A and B in LAB ranged from -128 to 127. Because the amplitude changed vary greatly, affected the training effect and increased the training time, so before training, the training data need to be normalized. According to the formula (6), the value of CIE-LAB was normalized to [0–1], the CMYK value of the simulation data was inverted normalized, and the normalized data was trained as the target data according to the formula (7). Normalization algorithm

$$x_i' = \frac{x_i - x_{\min}}{x_{\max} - x_{\min}} \tag{6}$$

Normalization algorithm

$$x_i = x_i'(x_{\max} - x_{\min}) + x_{\min} \tag{7}$$

4   Establishment and Verification of Color Space Conversion Model Based on GRNN

Matlab7.0 was used in color space conversion model programming. In Matlab environment, GRNN neural network creation function is: net = newgrnn (P, t, spread). For GRNN, when the training samples are determined, the corresponding network structure and the connection weights among the neurons are also determined, and the training of the network is actually only the process of determining the value of the scatter constant. The predictive performance of GRNN and the width of the base function around the center are influenced by the scatter constant values. As a general rule, the network function approximation accuracy increase with the decrease of spread, but with the decrease of spread approximation the smoothness of the curve was reduced; On the other hand, the smoothness of the curve increase with the increase of spread, but the approximation error is increase and the network accuracy is reduce. Therefore, the choice of spread dispersion constant is an important link in the network design, the performance of MSE function in Matlab is used to determine the dispersion constant value, the function is the mean square error function, and spread value calculation steps are listed as follows:

☐ Spread initial value was set.
☐ The training samples were back into the network simulation, then the training mean square error of network was obtained, then the test sample was substituted into network simulation, and the mean square error of the test sample was obtained. Finally, the training mean square error and the mean square error of the test sample were used as the training evaluation index of the network.
☐ The spread value was changed so that the scatter constant increased within a certain range of [a, b], and the previous step was repeated. Finding the spread that simultaneously satisfied the training mean variance of the network within the allowable range and the minimum variance of the variance in the test samples. The value of spread was used in the last generalized regression neural network. Sometimes it was difficult to find the best spread value at cycle time, and the range of spread needs to be reduced many times and the program was executed to determine the best spread.

4.1   Finding the Optimum Dispersion Constant

First, the value of spread was valued at 0.1, and the value of spread was increased by 0.1 each time until the spread equals 0.9. Then the value of spread was used as the abscissa, the value of mean square was as ordinate, Fig. 4 was established. The figure showed that when the value of spread was taken from 0.1 to 0.3, the value of MSE reached the minimum, then the value of spread started from 0.1, and each time increased by 0.01 until the value of spread was 0.3, and Fig. 5

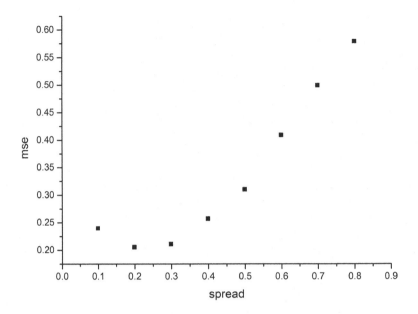

Fig. 4. Find the optimal dispersion constant between 0.1 and 0.9 based on GRNN

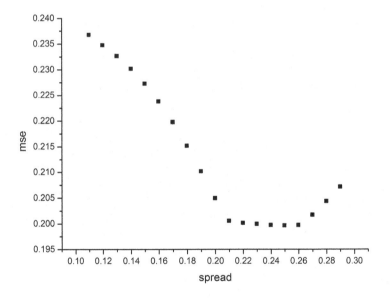

Fig. 5. Find the value of the optimal dispersion constant for the minimum mean square deviation based on GRNN

was established. In the prophase of test, sampling and conversion from CIE-LAB to CMYK were manual operation, the main time complexity of the whole method was to find the optimal spread. In this paper, we found the optimal spread through two cycles, the time complexity was O(n). As showed in Fig. 5, when the value of spread was 0.25, the value of the mean variance reached the minimum value of 0.1996.

4.2   Accuracy of Evaluation Model

After the optimal spread value was found, the modeling sample was tested by back generation and simulation experiments were carried out. The measured values of the detected samples were compared with the simulation values, and the difference were calculated (as calculated by formula $E = (L2 + a2 + b2)1/2$). The mental lightness L was taken as an abscissa, the absolute chromatic aberration E was used as ordinate, and Fig. 6 was established. When the GRNN neural network model was established, by using the function $(y = \text{sim}(net, test))$, the detection samples were brought into the trained GRNN neural network model, and the simulation results of the detection samples transformation were obtained based on the GRNN neural network. All the test data of absolute color difference was less than 6, and most of the data of the absolute color difference was less than or equal to 3 can be seen from Fig. 6. The model of color space transition from CMYK to CIE-LAB based on GRNN neural network was proved to have higher precision.

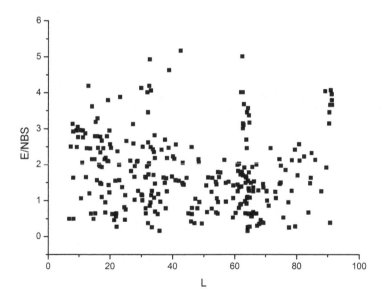

Fig. 6. Chromatic aberration of measured values and simulation values based on GRNN

5 Conclusions

In this paper, a color space conversion model from CMYK to CIE-LAB based on GRNN was implemented. The specific parameters of the network model were established through experiments, and the RGNN neural network was trained and simulated on the basis of normalization, and the good results were obtained, and the accuracy of the model was evaluated by measuring the sample data. The GRNN neural network was proved to play a good role in color space conversion. Because of the condition and time constraints, the modeling samples and detection samples were not selected optimally. In future experiments, ECI2002R color targets can be adopted in order to reduce chromatic aberration. The results show that a model of CMYK color space to CIE-LAB based on GRNN showed faster conversion speed and accuracy than BP neural network, the demand on printing industry can be met.

Acknowledgments. This work is supported by the Natural Science Fund for Colleges and Universities of Anhui Province (No. KJ2017ZD32) and the Innovation Fund for graduate students of Huaibei Normal University.

References

1. McCulloch, W., Pitts, W.: Logical calculus of the ideas immanent in nervous activity. Bull. Math. Biophys. **5**, 115–133 (1943)
2. Hansen, J.V., Meservy, R.D.: Learning experiments with genetic optimization of a generalized regression neural network. Decis. Support Syst. **18**(3–4), 317–325 (1996)
3. Anwar, T., Aung, Y.M., Jumaily, A.A.: The estimation of knee joint angle based on generalized regression neural network (GRNN). In: IEEE International Symposium on Robotics and Intelligent Sensors, pp. 208–213 (2016)
4. Alilou, V.K., Yaghmaee, F.: Application of GRNN neural network in non-texture image inpainting and restoration. Pattern Recogn. Lett. **62**(C), 24–31 (2015)
5. Kendrick, R.L., Acton, D.S., Duncan, A.L.: Phase-diversity wave-front sensor for imaging systems. Appl. Opt. **33**(27), 6533–6546 (1994)
6. Ben-Nakhi, A.E., Mahmoud, M.A.: Energy conservation in buildings through efficient A/C control using neural networks. Appl. Energy **73**(1), 5–23 (2002)
7. Osmak, S., Gosak, D., Glasnovic, A.: Dynamic mathematical model of deep bed filtration process. Comput. Chem. Eng. **21**(10), S763–S768 (1997)
8. Chen, Z.H., Wang, Z.Z., Sheng, B.: Dynamic RGB-to-CMYK conversion using visual contrast optimization. IET Image Process. **11**(7), 539–549 (2017)
9. Sharma, A., Gouch, M.P., Rughani, D.N.: Generation of an ICC profile from a proprietary style file. J. Imaging. Sci. **46**(1), 26–32 (2002)
10. Hu, J.L., Deng, J.B., Sui, M.X.: Color space conversion model from CMYK to CIE-LAB based on prism. In: International Conference on Granular Computing, pp. 235–238 (2009)
11. Hu, J., Deng, J., Zou, S.: A novel algorithm for color space conversion model from CMYK to CIE-LAB. J. Multimed. **5**(2), 159–166 (2010)
12. Cao, C.J., Liu, Q.J.: Study on color space conversion based on RBF neural network. J. Adv. Mater. Res. **174**, 28–31 (2011)

13. Cao, C., Jing, S.: Study on color space conversion between CMYK and CIE L*a*b* based on generalized regression neural network. In: International Conference on Computer Science and Software Engineering, pp. 275–277 (2008)

14. Specht, D.F.: A general regression neural network. IEEE Trans. Neural Netw. **2**(6), 568 (1991)

15. Hoti, F.: On estimation of a probability density function and mode. Ann. Math. Stat. **33**(3), 1065–1076 (2003)

GCP-SLAM: LSD-SLAM with Learning-Based Confidence Estimation

Aidi Feng[1], Weiqi Zhang[1], Zifei Yan[2], and Wangmeng Zuo[1(✉)] (iD)

[1] School of Computer Science and Technology, Harbin Institute of Technology,
No. 92 Xidazhi Street, Nangang District, Harbin 150001, China
for_further@163.com, weiqizhanghit@gmail.com, cswmzuo@gmail.com
[2] School of Mechatronics Engineering, Harbin Institute of Technology,
No. 92 Xidazhi Street, Nangang District, Harbin 150001, China
cszfyan@gmail.com

Abstract. Astonishing progress has been made in direct monocular SLAMs in the last few years. However, most direct methods, such as large-scale direct monocular SLAM (LSD-SLAM), usually have lower camera localization accuracy than feature-based methods. To tackle this issue, this paper suggests a novel LSD-SLAM model, i.e., GCP-SLAM, by incorporating with learning-based confidence estimation. A regression forest method is used to estimate confidence and select ground control points (GCPs). The estimated confidence and GCPs are then exploited for improving depth estimation and camera localization, respectively. Experiments show that GCP-SLAM is more reliable in tracking and relocalization than LSD-SLAM.

Keywords: Monocular SLAM · Ground control points (GCPs)
Localization · Random forest

1 Introduction

Monocular Simultaneous Localization and Mapping (SLAM) has received consistent attention in computer vision, robotics, and augmented reality for decades [1,2]. Based on whether feature observations are required to extract or not, there are two kinds of SLAMs, i.e., feature-based and direct ones. Early studies mainly focus on feature-based methods. Due to the amount of feature observations generally is very small, feature-based methods usually result in sparse reconstruction maps. In contrast, direct methods estimate the camera localization and the map by only using image intensity information. Compared with feature-based methods, direct methods can circumvent the tedious local feature detection and perform more robust, especially in the scenario with little textures and structures. As a result, monocular SLAM has recently witnessed a shift towards direct methods for tracking and reconstruction.

One representative direct method is Large-Scale Direct Monocular SLAM (LSD-SLAM) [3], which mainly includes three components: direct image alignment based tracking, filtering-based depth map estimation, and incorporation

© Springer International Publishing AG, part of Springer Nature 2018
M. Paul et al. (Eds.): PSIVT 2017, LNCS 10749, pp. 262–275, 2018.
https://doi.org/10.1007/978-3-319-75786-5_22

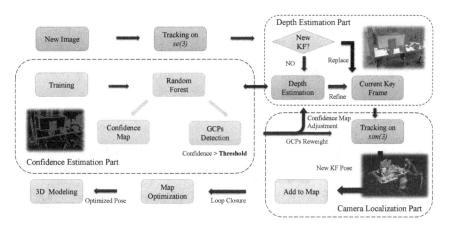

Fig. 1. Outline of GCP-SLAM pipeline, showing steps performed by depth estimation part, confidence estimation part and camera localization part.

into global map. Despite its success, LSD-SLAM is limited in camera localization accuracy. In LSD-SLAM, the camera pose optimization is based on the pixel intensities. This makes it computationally impracticable to adopt bundle adjustment (BA) [4], which is known to be the optimal method for camera localization. By far, the camera localization accuracy of LSD-SLAM is still lower than several state-of-the-art feature-based methods, such as ORB-SLAM [5] and Parallel Tracking and Mapping (PTAM) [6]. Moreover, even all pixel intensities have been utilized, LSD-SLAM actually relies on pixels with nonvanishing gradient in the estimation.

In this work, we develop a GCP-SLAM to improve the accuracy and completeness of LSD-SLAM. As illustrated in Fig. 1, our GCP-SLAM is composed of six major modules, i.e., camera tracking, keyframe selection, depth estimation, confidence estimation, camera localization, local and global mapping. The confidence estimation module is presented in Fig. 2, where random forests are used to predict the confidence. Besides raw image features, we also adopt depth-aware features for confidence modeling. A set of pixels with high confidence is selected as the ground control points (GCPs). We argue that one possible factor to affect the camera localization accuracy is that LSD-SLAM assigns the same confidence to all the pixels. Thus, to improve camera localization accuracy, we increase the weight of GCPs to alleviate the adverse effect caused by unreliable pixels. We also integrate the estimated confidence into depth estimation. Experiments show that GCP-SLAM is more reliable in tracking and localization.

The contribution of this work is as follows: To improve camera localization accuracy, a regression forest method is suggested to learn confidence estimation for monocular SLAM, where both image and depth-aware features are adopted for confidence modeling. The confidence estimation results are applied to depth estimation for improving the quality of depth map. By selecting a set of pixels with high confidence as GCPs, we provide an improved camera localization method by increasing the weight of GCPs in direct image alignment.

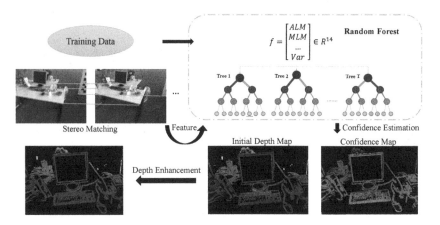

Fig. 2. Overview of the confidence estimation part.

The remainder of the paper is organized as follows. Section 2 provides a brief review on SLAM and learning based confidence estimation. Section 3 presents our confidence estimation method together with its application in camera localization and depth estimation. Section 4 reports the experimental results. Finally, Sect. 5 concludes the paper and discusses the limitation of our method.

2   Related Work

2.1   Feature Based and Direct Monocular SLAMs

Most earlier real-time monocular SLAMs are based on sparse interest points. One of the earliest real time methods proposed by Chiuso et al. [7] is based on the casual scheme of structure from motion (SFM). Davison et al. [8] proposed a real-time system, i.e., MonoSLAM, to create a sparse map under a probabilistic framework. PTAM [6] is the first real-time monocular SLAM algorithms by separating localization and mapping into two threads. Recently, Mur-Artal et al. [5] proposed a high performance monocular SLAM, i.e., ORB-SLAM, based on ORB features. Bags of words place recognition and covisibility graph are adopted in ORB-SLAM to improve the robustness of camera localization and loop detection.

Recently, direct methods have shown great success in monocular SLAM [3,9], and exhibited impressive results in scene reconstructions. Instead of sparse interest points, direct methods use all intensities for camera localization and are robust for textureless scenes. Newcombe et al. [9] develop a Dense Tracking and Mapping (DTAM) system for real-time tracking and reconstruction of small-scale scene. Besides DTAM, several other dense monocular SLAMs have also been proposed [10–12]. Engel et al. [3] suggest a LSD-SLAM algorithm for building real-time semi-dense maps of large scale scene, where OpenFABMAP [13] is utilized for loop closure. Unfortunately, while feature-based BA can obtain optimized camera localization accuracy, direct methods generally minimize the photometric error based on pixel intensities, and cannot achieve state-of-the-art localization performance.

2.2   Confidence Estimation in Stereo Matching

Learning-based confidence estimation has been adopted in stereo matching and camera relocalization [14,15], but it has not been employed in monocular SLAM. In [14], a random forest is built on eight features to predict the correctness of stereo correspondence and to detect the GCPs, which are chosen for further optimization using MRF to minimize energy function. In [15], two regression forests are deployed, where one is adopted to select features and the other is used to predict the confidence of matching. The prediction results are used in matching procedure to adjust the matching cost after rescaling. For camera relocalization, the candidate locations together with the uncertainty associated with each prediction is modeled as mixtures of anisotropic 3D Gaussians, and can be predicted by regression forests [16]. Unlike [14–16], we apply learning-based confidence estimation for camera localization, depth estimation in the monocular SLAM framework.

3   Monocular SLAM with Confidence Estimation

3.1   Method Overview

GCP-SLAM extends the LSD-SLAM framework, which continuously tracks pose of frames, maintains a pose graph of keyframes, and a semi-dense inverse depth distance map for each keyframe. In camera tracking, we utilize the random forest model trained offline to predict the confidence of estimation on keyframes. The GCPs are selected according to the predicted results. The major modules of our framework are summarized as follows:

(i) $\mathfrak{se}(3)$ **tracking & $\mathfrak{sim}(3)$ tracking:** After a new camera frame is captured, its rigid-body pose relative to the keyframe is tracked. The keyframe pose graph is maintained by alignment on $\mathfrak{sim}(3)$ with two differently scaled keyframes. GCPs are incorporated with optimization in the pose estimation part.

(ii) **Keyframe selection:** A new keyframe is created from the most recent tracked image if the camera moves far away, according to a weighted combination of relative distance and angle to the current keyframe.

(iii) **Depth map estimation:** When a keyframe is identified, an inverse depth map is initialized by stereo matching with a reference non-keyframe or propagated from the existing keyframe. The depth map is enhanced by several non-keyframes in the reference frame list before the next keyframe arrives according to the estimated confidence map.

(iv) **Confidence estimation:** A random forest regression model is trained offline with features corresponding to stereo matching and images information for predicting the confidence of depth estimation.

(v) **Pose-graph optimization and loop closure:** The system continuously performs pose graph optimization between all keyframes and also detects large-scale loop closure after adding new keyframe. A reciprocal tracking is applied to avoid inserting false loop closure for semi-dense modeling.

(vi) **Semi-dense 3D mapping:** After each optimization of pose-graph, an accumulated semi-dense pointclouds is generated based on the depth map and camera pose of keyframes.

3.2 Confidence Estimation

In LSD-SLAM, line search stereo matching is utilized to create new depth and update depth for keyframe (here depth means the inverse depth [17]). Depth estimation accuracy impacts not only on tracking procedure, but also on the quality of reconstruction of 3D model. To enhance the depth map, confidence estimation model can be applied to find whether the creation or the update of depth is reasonable. If the estimation is of high accuracy, the current depth will be considered. Otherwise, it will be discarded. With this procedure, the precision of depth information can be effectively improved.

In our confidence estimation model, we utilize some of the features mentioned in [14,15] and other features calculated from color map and depth map. Due to the real-time requirement, the features should be efficient to compute and the number of features should be as small as possible. We construct a regression type of random forest for more precise depth confidence prediction. Here we use features $f = (f_1, f_2, \cdots, f_{14})$, where $f_1 \sim f_7$ are calculated from stereo matching:

Distance from Border (DB) [14]. The distance of a pixel from its nearest image border.

Cost [14]. Minimum matching cost in line stereo matching. We use the square root of cost value while stereo matching is in square form.

Maximum Margin (MMN) [14]. The difference between the two smallest cost values (c_1 and c_2) of a pixel.

Winner Margin (WMN) [15]. Normalization of the difference between the two smallest local minima.

Attainable Maximum Likelihood (AML) [14]. This feature can be obtained by first subtracting the minimum cost from all cost values, and then converting the cost curve into a probability density function.

The Maximum Likelihood Measure (MLM) [15]. This feature is also obtained by converting the cost curve into a probability density function for disparity. Instead of subtracting the minimum cost, we assume that the cost follows a normal distribution and the disparity prior is uniform.

The Negative Entropy Measure (NEM) [15]. The negative entropy is used as a confidence measure.

Please refer to [14,15] for detailed information. The features $f_8 \sim f_{14}$ are calculated from the information of depth map and color map. The geometric error and photometric error are used as f_8 and f_9. The difference between estimation by current reference frame and last reference frame is used as f_{10}. The variance of depth is used as f_{11}. The gradient of pixel in color image and the second order gradient are used for f_{12} and f_{13}. f_{14} is the depth of the pixel itself. We exclude the left-right difference (LRD) because it needs stereo matching procedure that costs time. We also exclude the distance from discontinuity (DD) and some other features which are unable to calculate due to the discontinuity of pixels with depth. With features $f = (f_1, f_2, \cdots, f_{14})$, we train a regression-based random forest for confidence estimation. After training, the prediction can serve as an estimation of confidence map, which can be employed to enhance camera localization and depth estimation.

The estimated confidence map is then used to improve depth estimation. For better selection of accurate depth estimation points, we adopt different thresholds for creation and updating. The creation of depth will be improved during the updating, and thus we obtain more available points to the most. But for updating, we should adopt more strict rule to enhance the depth estimation. Our prediction results are shown in Sect. 4, which validates the effectiveness of our method.

3.3 sim(3) Tracking Based on GCPs

GCPs are defined as the pixels with reliable depth estimation and can be used to enhance tracking and mapping results. According to our confidence estimation model, we choose a threshold to select GCPs including the smallest fraction of wrong depth estimation in the set. It is set to 0.7 based on experiments and will be discussed in Sect. 4. 3D pose estimation in LSD-SLAM is computed by minimizing the variance-normalized photometric error. To solve the problem, a weighted Gauss-Newton optimization algorithm is utilized. For robustness, a weighted matrix is computed which down-weights the large residuals. Moreover, we argue that the pixel with high confidence, i.e., the GCPs, should be up-weighted and benefit pose estimation.

For detection of scale-drift, LSD-SLAM proposes a novel method to do image alignment on sim(3), which aligns two differently scaled keyframes. Despite the photometric residual r_p, depth residual r_d is incorporated that penalized deviations in inverse depth. The overall objective function minimizing the variance-normalized photometric and depth error is given as follows:

$$E\left(\boldsymbol{\xi}_{ji}\right) = \sum_{\mathbf{p}\in\Omega_{D_i}} \left\| \frac{r_p^2\left(\mathbf{p},\boldsymbol{\xi}_{ji}\right)}{\sigma_{r_p(\mathbf{p},\boldsymbol{\xi}_{ji})}^2} + \frac{r_d^2\left(\mathbf{p},\boldsymbol{\xi}_{ji}\right)}{\sigma_{r_d(\mathbf{p},\boldsymbol{\xi}_{ji})}^2} \right\|_{\delta} \tag{1}$$

where $\|\cdot\|_{\delta}$ denotes the Huber norm, and $\boldsymbol{\xi}$ denotes the camera pose. The photometric residual r_p and the variance $\sigma_{r_p}^2$ are defined as,

$$r_p\left(\mathbf{p},\boldsymbol{\xi}_{ji}\right) = I_i\left(\mathbf{p}\right) - I_j\left(w\left(\mathbf{p}, D_i(\mathbf{p}), \boldsymbol{\xi}_{ji}\right)\right) \tag{2}$$

$$\sigma_{r_p(\mathbf{p},\boldsymbol{\xi}_{ji})}^2 = 2\sigma_I^2 + \left(\frac{r_p\left(\mathbf{p},\boldsymbol{\xi}_{ji}\right)}{D_i\left(\mathbf{p}\right)}\right)^2 V_i\left(\mathbf{p}\right) \tag{3}$$

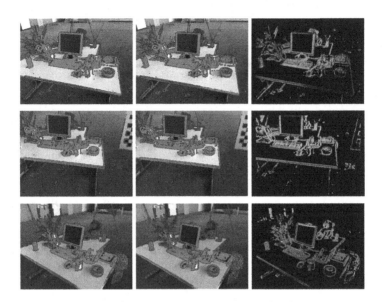

Fig. 3. Confidence estimation of TUM RGB-D datasets. Left: color-coded groundtruth semi-dense depth map. Middle: color-coded semi-dense depth map in LSD-SLAM. Right: confidence map projected to 0-255. (Color figure online)

The depth residual and its variance are computed as,

$$r_d\left(\mathbf{p}, \boldsymbol{\xi}_{ji}\right) = [\mathbf{p}']_3 - D_j\left([\mathbf{p}']_{1,2}\right) \tag{4}$$

$$\sigma^2_{r_d(\mathbf{p},\boldsymbol{\xi}_{ji})} = \left(\frac{r_d\left(\mathbf{p},\boldsymbol{\xi}_{ji}\right)}{D_j\left([\mathbf{p}]_{1,2}\right)}\right)^2 V_j\left([\mathbf{p}]_{1,2}\right)$$
$$+ \left(\frac{r_d\left(\mathbf{p},\boldsymbol{\xi}_{ji}\right)}{D_i\left(\mathbf{p}\right)}\right)^2 V_i\left(\mathbf{p}\right) \tag{5}$$

where $\mathbf{p}'$ denotes the transformed point. Considering what mentioned above, we up-weight the residuals of points which are selected as GCPs for $\mathfrak{sim}(3)$ estimation. In each iteration, we solve for a left-multiplied increment,

$$\delta\boldsymbol{\xi}^n = -\left(\mathbf{J}^{\mathrm{T}}\mathbf{W}_C\mathbf{J}\right)^{-1}\mathbf{J}^{\mathrm{T}}\mathbf{W}_C r \tag{6}$$

where r is the stacked residual vector and $\mathbf{W}_C$ is the diagonal weighted matrix which down-weights large residuals with low confidence and up-weights the large residuals with high confidence.

To sum up, by incorporating GCPs into $\mathfrak{sim}(3)$ tracking, better camera localization accuracy can be attained. Note that confidence estimation is based on efficient features and is performed only on keyframes. We can build an improved LSD-SLAM system running in real-time on CPU.

4   Experiments

We evaluate our GCP-SLAM on the TUM RGB-D datasets [18], which contains several long and challenging trajectories with camera rotation, motion blur and rolling shutter artifacts. We implement GCP-SLAM, where we incorporate confidence estimation into camera tracking and depth estimation. All the experiments are executed in a PC with 8 Intel Cores Xeon E3-1230 V2 CPU (3.3 GHz) and 32 GB RAM. Our GCP-SLAM can be run in real time in CPU. In this section, we first evaluate the performance of confidence estimation, and then evaluate our GCP-SLAM on TUM RGB-D in terms of depth estimation and motion tracking.

4.1   Evaluation on Confidence Estimation

We use pairs of images from each of the sequence $fr2\_desk$, $fr2\_xyz$ and $fr1\_xyz$, which contain about 1,000,000 pixels, to train the confidence estimation model. The numbers of reliable depth and unreliable depth are nearly balanced for $fr2\_desk$, while most of the depth value is unreliable for $fr1\_xyz$ and reliable for $fr2\_xyz$. In the training stage, we adopt the 14 features introduced in Sect. 3, and assign the label y to each sample according to ground truth.

Specifically, the code from the website of the TUM RGB-D dataset is exploited to align color images and the depth images. The difference between estimated depth and ground truth is mapped to the value $prediction \in [0, 1]$. Here a pixel is treated as a reliable depth estimation and can be selected as a GCP when $prediction > 0.7$, an inaccurate depth estimation when $0.7 \geq prediction \geq 0.4$, and an incorrect depth estimation when $prediction < 0.4$. Figure 4 shows the importance of features for confidence estimation. One can see that the cost, MMN, AML, MLM, the difference of depth and the depth value are more important for 3 datasets, while the other eight features have the similar contributions to confidence estimation.

To analyze the estimation performance of various confidence threshold, we use the sparsification curve and its area under curve (AUC) value shown in

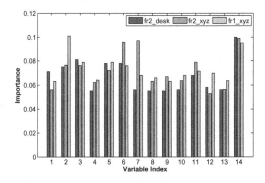

Fig. 4. The importance of each feature used in training the confidence estimation model.

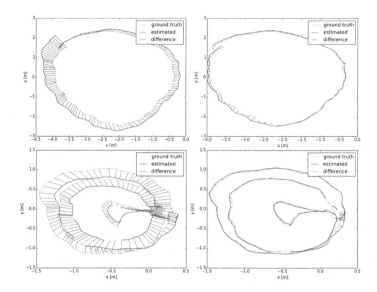

Fig. 5. $fr3\_nostructure\_texture\_near$ and $fr2\_dishes$ sequences from the TUM RGB-D dataset. Left: Keyframe trajectories of LSD-SLAM. Right: Keyframe trajectories of our method.

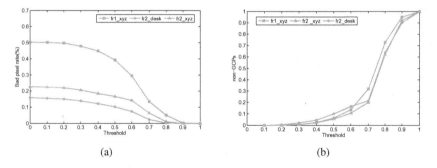

(a)   (b)

Fig. 6. (a) Comparison of sparsification curves for selected datasets. (b) Non-GCPs density with different threshold for selected datasets.

Fig. 6(a). The sparsification curve draws the change of bad pixel rates while removing least confident pixels from the depth map. After training, we test on different pairs of images on the sequence $fr2\_desk$, $fr2\_xyz$ and $fr1\_xyz$. According to the results in Fig. 6(a) and (b), the pixel can be selected as a GCP when $prediction > 0.7$ to obtain the highest possible density of GCPs while excluding most wrong depth estimation.

After training, we test the learned model on all keyframes of five other sequences, i.e., $fr1\_xyz$, $fr2\_xyz$, $fr2\_deskwp$, $fr3\_sithalf$, and $fr3\_sitxyz$ by excluding the ones that return error in stereo matching. Table 1 reports the prediction accuracy of our random forest model on the test set. The first and

Table 1. Prediction accuracy of GCPs using our depth confidence estimation model. Threshold is set to 0.7 to balance the density and accuracy of GCPs. The first and third column correspond to correct classification. The second and fourth column correspond to misclassficaiton.

Datasets	Reliable depth		Unreliable depth	
	$prediction > 0.7$	$prediction \leq 0.7$	$prediction \leq 0.7$	$prediction > 0.7$
fr1_xyz	6,561,645	2,338,623	25,72,890	575,845
fr2_xyz	12,920,669	1,417,387	11,170,000	2,484,462
fr2_desk	20,591,387	4,686,548	2,655,680	160,108
fr2_deskwp	15,180,134	4,305,554	10,805,695	1,266,768
fr3_sithalf	1,137,471	81,181	2,101,169	157,178
fr3_sitxyz	6,406,993	1,357,164	2,072,123	119,684
Average	81.64%		89.92%	

Table 2. The prediction time per frame and TPR results for different number of trees.

# of trees	20	25	30	35	40
Times (ms)	132.0	180.5	241.4	291.8	376.9
Results (%)	81.45	81.53	81.56	81.57	81.58

third column correspond to accurate prediction, while the second and fourth to inaccurate prediction. We show raw pixel numbers for these sequences and the prediction accuracy in the last row. Table 2 shows the effect on the number of trees N on the prediction accuracy and run time for confidence estimation. One can see that the number of trees N is linearly correlated with the run time for prediction, and has little effect to the prediction accuracy when N is higher than 30. Therefore, we set $N = 30$ to train our model for the tradeoff between run time and prediction accuracy.

4.2   Evaluation on GCP-SLAM

We evaluate our GCP-SLAM on the TUM RGB-D datasets. Figure 3 shows the original depth map estimated in LSD-SLAM and the corresponding confidence map as well as the groundtruth. The colored semi-dense depth map overlaid with frame and the predicted confidence map show that the unreliable depth value can be detected by our model, thus verify the credibility for confidence estimation using our model. Table 3 gives the results of absolute trajectory RMSE (cm), and for comparison we also show respective results from LSD-SLAM, direct dense visual SLAM (DVO-SLAM) [19] and feature-based RGB-D SLAM (RGBD-SLAM) [20].

The keyframe trajectories are aligned using a similarity transformation [21] for our methods, the original LSD-SLAM, DVO-SLAM and RGBD-SLAM despite the scale. The localization error results showed in Table 3 are the median

Table 3. Keyframe localization error on the TUM RGB-D benchmark, measured as absolute trajectory RMSE(cm). Trajectories from RGBD-SLAM are taken from the benchmark website and only available for $fr1$ and $fr2$ sequences. '-' denotes no available data.

Datasets	GCP-SLAM			LSD-SLAM	DVO-SLAM	RGBD-SLAM
	Depth	sim(3)	Depth & sim(3)			
fr1_xyz	1.6	4.0	**1.5**	6.0	1.16	1.34
fr1_desk	33.4	31.0	**30.1**	39.2	2.10	2.58
fr1_floor	39.4	31.9	**27.1**	34.2	5.50	9.00
fr2_xyz	1.11	**0.84**	0.86	1.23	1.18	2.61
fr2_deskwp	6.16	4.65	**4.43**	31.73	-	6.85
fr3_sitxyz	6.03	6.53	**6.01**	6.94	-	-
fr3_longoff	35.2	30.4	**28.5**	36.9	3.50	-

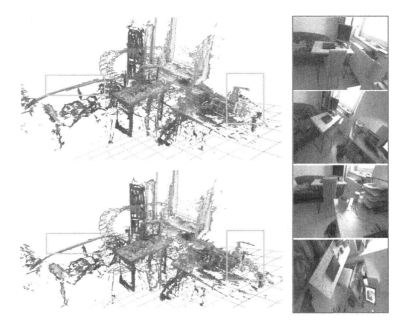

Fig. 7. Accumulated pointclouds of LSDroom sequence. Top: LSD-SLAM thresholded with maximum variance. Bottom: our method thresholded with confidence value.

over 5 executions in each sequence. From Table 3, our method significantly improves the accuracy of pose estimation in LSD-SLAM. On some sequences such as $fr1\_xyz$, $fr2\_xyz$ and $fr2\_deskwp$, our GCP-SLAM is even comparable or better than the RGBD-based SLAMs. Besides, according to the experiment, we find that setting the depth threshold to 0.4 for long sequence datasets and 0.2 for short sequence datasets stabilize the localization error results. The original LSD-SLAM fails on the same sequence occasionally (tracking lost at totally

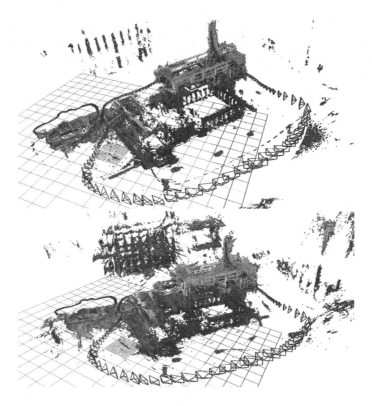

Fig. 8. Accumulated pointclouds of GCPs for LSD-machine sequence with different maximum variance.

different frame [22]), and differ greatly for different runs. But for our method the results are more stable and consistent. The keyframe trajectories of LSD-SLAM and our GCP-SLAM on long sequence with loop in one run are illustrated in Fig. 5, which shows that reliable motion tracking also improves efficiency on loop closure. Besides, the results of pointclouds in Fig. 7 show the reconstruction results of LSD-SLAM and our method on LSD-room sequence thresholded by the same maximum variance. From Fig. 8 which includes pointclouds of a big outdoor scene, we can see that the pointclouds thresholded by the estimated confidence is more effective than only thresholded by maximum variance, while the later includes more noise when the reconstruction becomes more dense.

5   Conclusion

We proposed a GCPs based monocular SLAM method, which tracks the motion of camera on both $\mathfrak{se}(3)$ and $\mathfrak{sim}(3)$ and gets more reliable results. In contrast to LSD-SLAM, it detected GCPs for improving camera localization and depth estimation using a trained random forest model. We experimentally showed that our confidence estimation model is reliable, and the integration of SLAM with confidence prediction via learning method is a promising direction to improve the depth estimation and traditional direct motion tracking. In future, deep learning method will be investigated in confidence estimation and depth estimation using large number of training data to further improve the efficiency of GCP-SLAM based on the traditional method.

References

1. Mahmoud, N., Grasa, Ó.G., Nicolau, S.A., Doignon, C., Soler, L., Marescaux, J., Montiel, J.M.M.: On-patient see-through augmented reality based on visual SLAM. Int. J. Comput. Assist. Radiol. Surg. **12**(1), 1–11 (2017)
2. Yuan, W., Li, Z., Su, C.Y.: RGB-D sensor-based visual SLAM for localization and navigation of indoor mobile robot. In: International Conference on Advanced Robotics and Mechatronics (ICARM), pp. 82–87 (2016)
3. Engel, J., Schöps, T., Cremers, D.: LSD-SLAM: large-scale direct monocular SLAM. In: Fleet, D., Pajdla, T., Schiele, B., Tuytelaars, T. (eds.) ECCV 2014. LNCS, vol. 8690, pp. 834–849. Springer, Cham (2014). https://doi.org/10.1007/978-3-319-10605-2_54
4. Triggs, B., McLauchlan, P.F., Hartley, R.I., Fitzgibbon, A.W.: Bundle adjustment — a modern synthesis. In: Triggs, B., Zisserman, A., Szeliski, R. (eds.) IWVA 1999. LNCS, vol. 1883, pp. 298–372. Springer, Heidelberg (2000). https://doi.org/10.1007/3-540-44480-7_21
5. Mur-Artal, R., Montiel, J.M.M., Tardos, J.D.: ORB-SLAM: a versatile and accurate monocular SLAM system. IEEE Trans. Robot. **31**(5), 1147–1163 (2015)
6. Klein, G., Murray, D.: Parallel tracking and mapping for small AR workspaces. In: 6th IEEE and ACM International Symposium on Mixed and Augmented Reality (ISMAR), pp. 225–234 (2007)
7. Chiuso, A., Favaro, P., Jin, H., Soatto, S.: Structure from motion causally integrated over time. IEEE Trans. Pattern Anal. Mach. Intell. **24**(4), 523–535 (2002)
8. Davison, A.J., Reid, I.D., Molton, N.D., Stasse, O.: MonoSLAM: real-time single camera SLAM. IEEE Trans. Pattern Anal. Mach. Intell. **29**(6), 1052–1067 (2007)
9. Newcombe, R.A., Lovegrove, S.J., Davison, A.J.: DTAM: dense tracking and mapping in real-time. In: International Conference on Computer Vision, pp. 2320–2327 (2011)
10. Newcombe, R.A., Davison, A.J.: Live dense reconstruction with a single moving camera. In: IEEE Conference on Computer Vision and Pattern Recognition (CVPR), pp. 1498–1505 (2010)
11. Pizzoli, M., Forster, C., Scaramuzza, D.: REMODE: probabilistic, monocular dense reconstruction in real time. In: IEEE International Conference on Robotics and Automation (ICRA), pp. 2609–2616 (2014)
12. Stühmer, J., Gumhold, S., Cremers, D.: Real-time dense geometry from a handheld camera. In: Goesele, M., Roth, S., Kuijper, A., Schiele, B., Schindler, K. (eds.) DAGM 2010. LNCS, vol. 6376, pp. 11–20. Springer, Heidelberg (2010). https://doi.org/10.1007/978-3-642-15986-2_2
13. Glover, A., Maddern, W., Warren, M., Reid, S., Milford, M., Wyeth, G.: Open-FABMAP: an open source toolbox for appearance-based loop closure detection. In: IEEE International Conference on Robotics and Automation (ICRA), pp. 4730–4735 (2012)

14. Spyropoulos, A., Komodakis, N., Mordohai, P.: Learning to detect ground control points for improving the accuracy of stereo matching. In: IEEE Conference on Computer Vision and Pattern Recognition (CVPR), pp. 1621–1628 (2014)
15. Park, M.G., Yoon, K.J.: Leveraging stereo matching with learning-based confidence measures. In: IEEE Conference on Computer Vision and Pattern Recognition (CVPR), pp. 101–109 (2015)
16. Valentin, J., Niebner, M., Shotton, J., Fitzgibbon, A., Izadi, S., Torr, P.H.: Exploiting uncertainty in regression forests for accurate camera relocalization. In: IEEE Conference on Computer Vision and Pattern Recognition (CVPR), pp. 4400–4408 (2015)
17. Civera, J., Davison, A.J., Montiel, J.M.: Inverse depth parametrization for monocular SLAM. IEEE Trans. Robot. **24**(5), 932–945 (2008)
18. Sturm, J., Engelhard, N., Endres, F., Burgard, W., Cremers, D.: A benchmark for the evaluation of RGB-D SLAM systems. In: IEEE/RSJ International Conference on Intelligent Robots and Systems, pp. 573–580 (2012)
19. Kerl, C., Sturm, J., Cremers, D.: Dense visual SLAM for RGB-D cameras. In: IEEE/RSJ International Conference on Intelligent Robots and Systems, pp. 2100–2106 (2013)
20. Endres, F., Hess, J., Engelhard, N., Sturm, J., Cremers, D., Burgard, W.: An evaluation of the RGB-D SLAM system. In: IEEE International Conference on Robotics and Automation (ICRA), pp. 1691–1696 (2012)
21. Nießner, M., Zollhöfer, M., Izadi, S., Stamminger, M.: Real-time 3D reconstruction at scale using voxel hashing. ACM Trans. Graph. (TOG) **32**(6), 169 (2013)
22. Huletski, A., Kartashov, D., Krinkin, K.: Evaluation of the modern visual SLAM methods. In: Social Media and Web Search FRUCT Conference on Artificial Intelligence and Natural Language and Information Extraction (AINL-ISMW FRUCT), pp. 19–25 (2015)

Layer-Wise Weight Decay for Deep Neural Networks

Masato Ishii$^{(\boxtimes)}$ and Atsushi Sato

NEC Data Science Research Laboratories, Kawasaki, Japan
`m-ishii@nd.jp.nec.com`

Abstract. In this paper, we propose layer-wise weight decay for efficient training of deep neural networks. Our method sets different values of the weight-decay coefficients layer by layer so that the ratio of the scale of back-propagated gradients and that of the weight decay is constant throughout the network. By utilizing such a setting, we can avoid under or over-fitting and train all layers properly without having to tune the coefficients layer by layer. Experimental results show that our method can enhance the performance of existing deep neural networks without any change of network models.

1 Introduction

In many machine learning methods, regularization plays an important role in helping achieve better performance by avoiding over-fitting. In deep learning, three kinds of regularization are typically utilized: drop-out [15], data augmentation [8], and weight decay. In drop-out, units are randomly ignored during training; it is known for providing a strong and effective regularization. In data augmentation, training data is increased by conducting subtle transformations to the original training data; it can be seen as a regularization based on a prior knowledge in which what kind of transformation has no effect on the label information of the training data. Weight decay is derived from L_2 regularization over trainable weights. In this paper, we focus on weight decay, as it is the most traditional and widely used method.

Compared with drop-out and data augmentation, weight decay has not been as extensively studied recently. This is probably because L_2 regularization has been quite common in the field of machine learning for several decades now. There are only a few works that allow different values of weight-decay coefficients for individual layers. In [1], it is recommended to treat the input layer and the output layer differently when setting the coefficients, but no specific method to set them is described. In Bayesian optimization [12,13], different values are set for the weight-decay coefficients through the optimization process, but this requires trial and error, which results in high computational cost. In this work, we propose a specific method to set layer-wise weight-decay coefficients without any trial-and-error process. We formulate it so that it regularizes all layers of the network with the same rate during training. While some recent studies [6,16] have shown

© Springer International Publishing AG, part of Springer Nature 2018
M. Paul et al. (Eds.): PSIVT 2017, LNCS 10749, pp. 276–289, 2018.
https://doi.org/10.1007/978-3-319-75786-5_23

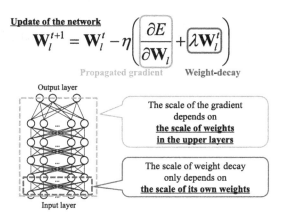

Fig. 1. The problem with using constant coefficient of weight decay. The scale of the back-propagated gradient depends on the scale of the weights in the upper layers, while the scale of weight decay depends only on the scale of its own weight. The ratio between the two is thus different for each layer, which results in over-fitting or under-fitting depending on the layer.

that updating all layers with the same rate leads to better performance of DNNs, they ignore the regularization of the network such as weight decay. In contrast, we focus on the weight decay to regularize the network effectively.

Weight-decay regularization reduces the L_2 norm of connection weights in a network by adding it to an object function. Before adding, the norm is multiplied by a pre-determined coefficient. Tuning this coefficient is important when it comes to training the network properly because a very small coefficient leads to over-fitting while a very large coefficient leads to under-fitting. Although it is possible to set different coefficients layer by layer, many existing works set the same coefficient for all layers, probably because treating all layers equally is intuitively plausible, and also because it avoids tremendous computational costs required to tune each coefficient manually. However, ultimately this approach is unreasonable because it ignores the relationship between back-propagated gradient and weight decay. In typical training methods, the network is updated by both the gradient and the weight decay, as shown in Fig. 1. Let us focus on the update of the first trainable layer denoted by the blue broken line. As indicated by the red broken line, the scale of the gradient depends on the scale of weights in the upper layers due to back-propagation. In contrast, the scale of the weight decay depends only on the scale of its own weight, as indicated by the blue broken line in the figure. The ratio between both of these is different for each layer, which leads to over-fitting on some layers or under-fitting on others. Therefore, we need to balance the scale of the gradient and that of the weight decay.

In this work, we propose layer-wise weight decay for efficient training of deep neural networks. Our method sets different values of the weight-decay coefficients layer by layer so that the ratio between the scale of back-propagated gradients and that of weight decay is constant through the network. By utilizing this setting, we can train all layers properly without having to tune the coefficients layer by layer. Experimental results show that our method can enhance the performance of existing deep neural networks without any change of network models.

2   Proposed Method

2.1   Overview

In deep learning, a stochastic gradient descent method (SGD) based on back-propagation is often used to train a neural network. In SGD, connection weights in the network are updated as follows:

$$\mathbf{W}_l^{t+1} = \mathbf{W}_l^t - \eta \left(\frac{\partial E}{\partial \mathbf{W}_l} \Big|_{\mathbf{w}_l^t} + \lambda \mathbf{W}_l^t \right), \tag{1}$$

where $\mathbf{W}_l^t$ represents the connection weights in the l-th layer ($l = 1, ..., L$) of the network after the t-th update, η is a learning rate, E is an object function to be minimized (e.g. multinomial logistic loss), and λ is a weight-decay coefficient that represents strength of regularization. $\mathbf{W}_l^t$ is used for feed-forward calculation and back-propagation at the l-th layer as shown in Fig. 2. The update value in Eq. (1) consists of the gradient term $\frac{\partial E}{\partial \mathbf{W}_l}$ and the regularization term $\lambda \mathbf{W}_l^t$. The gradient is calculated by back-propagation and its scale therefore depends on the scale of $\mathbf{W}_k^t (k > l)$. In contrast, the scale of the weight decay depends only on $\mathbf{W}_l^t$. Consequently, the ratio between the scale of the gradient and that of the weight decay is different for each layer. If we use the same value of λ for all layers, it would be too strong or too weak for some of the certain layers, thus resulting in over-fitting or under-fitting of the network. To avoid this problem, we utilize layer-wise weight decay so that the ratio between the scale of the gradient and that of the weight decay is constant throughout the network:

$$\mathbf{W}_l^{t+1} = \mathbf{W}_l^t - \eta \left(\frac{\partial E}{\partial \mathbf{W}_l} \Big|_{\mathbf{w}_l^t} + \lambda_l \mathbf{W}_l^t \right), \tag{2}$$

$$\lambda_l = \frac{\text{scale}(\frac{\partial E}{\partial \mathbf{W}_l})}{\text{scale}(\mathbf{W}_l)} \lambda, \tag{3}$$

where λ_l ($l = 1, ..., L$) is a layer-wise coefficient of weight decay and scale($*$) represents a function that calculates the scale of a vector or matrix. How to implement scale($*$) is described in the following subsections. Except for setting the layer-wise weight decay, the network is trained in our method the same as it is in existing methods. This means that our method can be applied to the wide range of existing networks used in various pattern recognition tasks.

In the remainder of this section, we discuss two methods to calculate λ_l: a data-dependent method and a data-independent method. Since λ_l depends on $\frac{\partial E}{\partial \mathbf{W}_l}$, directly calculating λ_l requires training data; this is the data-dependent method. However, there are two problems if we use data-dependent λ_l: first, it

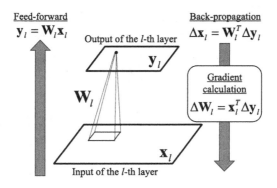

Fig. 2. Feed-forward calculation and back-propagation on the l-th layer.

somewhat increases the computational cost in the training process because we have to calculate λ_l for each update of the network, and second, the training process cannot guarantee its convergence due to frequent changes of the objective function stemming from the variable coefficient of the weight decay. To resolve these problems, we derive data-independent λ_l by approximating Eq. (3) at the initial network. In this method, λ_l is calculated with the initial network and is fixed during training.

2.2 Data-Dependent Layer-Wise Weight Decay

In this subsection, we directly calculate λ_l in Eq. (3) for each update of the network during training. We define scale($*$) as scale($\mathbf{W}$) := ave $(|\mathbf{W}|)$, where ave($*$) represents a function that calculates an average over all elements of a matrix. We utilize the average of the absolute values of the elements, as this can be efficiently calculated on a GPU by using cuBLAS. As stated in the previous section, coefficients that are too variable would affect the optimization performance, so to alleviate this problem, we set the upper and lower bounds of λ_l as

$$\lambda_l = \max\left(\rho_{min}, \min\left(\rho_{max}, \frac{\text{scale}(\frac{\partial E}{\partial \mathbf{W}_l})}{\text{scale}(\mathbf{W}_l)}\right)\right)\lambda, \quad (4)$$

where $\rho_{max}\lambda$ and $\rho_{min}\lambda$ are the upper and lower bounds of λ_l, respectively. We implemented this calculation of λ_l on *Caffe* [5] setting $\rho_{max} = 1$ and $\rho_{min} = 10^{-4}$, and found that it increases the calculation cost in the training process by about 20%.

2.3 Data-Independent Layer-Wise Weight Decay

In this subsection, we derive how to calculate λ_l at the initial network before training without training data. When initializing the network, $\mathbf{W}$ is typically set to have zero mean, so we can naturally define scale($*$) as scale($\mathbf{W}$) := std($\mathbf{W}$), where std($*$) represents a function that calculates a standard deviation over all elements of a vector or matrix. By substituting it into Eq. (3), we obtain the following equation:

$$\lambda_l = \frac{\text{std}(\frac{\partial E}{\partial \mathbf{W}_l})}{\text{std}(\mathbf{W}_l)} \lambda. \tag{5}$$

To calculate λ_l in Eq. (5), we have to estimate $\text{std}(\frac{\partial E}{\partial \mathbf{W}_l})$ and $\text{std}(\mathbf{W}_l)$ in the initial network. Since $\text{std}(\mathbf{W}_l)$ depends on how to initialize the network and is easy to obtain, the estimation of $\text{std}(\frac{\partial E}{\partial \mathbf{W}_l})$ is mainly described in this subsection. For simplicity, we describe $\frac{\partial E}{\partial *}$ as $\Delta *$ (e.g., $\Delta \mathbf{W}_l = \frac{\partial E}{\partial \mathbf{W}_l}$) below.

As shown in Fig. 2, let $\mathbf{x}_l$ and $\mathbf{y}_l$ respectively denote the input and output values of the l-th layer. Note that $\mathbf{y}_l$ equals $\mathbf{x}_{l+1}$. As in [3], for simplicity we assume that an identity function is used as an activation function, but our work can be easily extended to the case of ReLU by using [4]'s work. Under this assumption, we can describe feed-forward calculation and back-propagation on the l-th layer as follows:

$$\text{Feed-forward calculation: } \mathbf{y}_l = \mathbf{W}_l \mathbf{x}_l \tag{6}$$

$$\text{Back-propagation: } \Delta \mathbf{x}_l = \mathbf{W}_l^T \Delta \mathbf{y}_l \tag{7}$$

$$\Delta \mathbf{W}_l = \mathbf{x}_l^T \Delta \mathbf{y}_l. \tag{8}$$

According to the back-propagation, we can obtain the following equation:

$$\text{var}(\Delta \mathbf{W}_l) = \text{var}\left(\mathbf{x}_l^T \Delta \mathbf{y}_l\right) = \text{var}(\mathbf{x}_l)\text{var}(\Delta \mathbf{y}_l), \tag{9}$$

where $\text{var}(*)$ is a function to calculate variance over all elements of a matrix or vector. Here, we assume that $\mathbf{x}_l$ and $\Delta \mathbf{y}_l$ are mutually independent and that their means are zero. We will treat $\text{var}(\mathbf{x}_l)$ as a constant value, since recent initialization methods [3,4] induce it as a constant through the network. In contrast, $\text{var}(\Delta \mathbf{y}_l)$ can be calculated as

$$\text{var}(\Delta \mathbf{y}_l) = \text{var}(\Delta \mathbf{x}_{l+1}) = M_{l+1}\text{var}(\mathbf{W}_{l+1})\text{var}(\Delta \mathbf{y}_{l+1}) \quad (\because \text{back-prop})$$
$$= \beta_{l+1}\text{var}(\Delta \mathbf{y}_{l+1}), \text{ where } \beta_k = M_k\text{var}(\mathbf{W}_k). \tag{10}$$

M_k is the number of connections between an input unit of the k-th layer and all output units of the k-th layer. By definition, β_k represents the ratio between variances of the back-propagated gradients of two consecutive layers. By applying Eq. (10) to itself iteratively, we obtain

$$\text{var}(\Delta \mathbf{y}_l) = \left(\prod_{k=l+1}^{L} \beta_k\right) \text{var}(\Delta \mathbf{y}_L) = \gamma_l \cdot \text{var}(\Delta \mathbf{y}_L), \tag{11}$$

$$\text{where } \gamma_l = \begin{cases} \prod_{k=l+1}^{L} \beta_k & (l = 1, ..., L-1) \\ 1 & (l = L) \end{cases} \tag{12}$$

By substituting Eq. (11) into Eq. (9), $\text{var}(\Delta \mathbf{W}_l)$ can be deformed as

$$\text{var}(\Delta \mathbf{W}_l) = \text{var}(\mathbf{x}_l) \cdot \gamma_l \text{var}(\Delta \mathbf{y}_L) = C \cdot \gamma_l, \tag{13}$$

where C equals $\mathrm{var}(\mathbf{x}_l)\mathrm{var}(\Delta\mathbf{y}_L)$, which can be treated as a constant value because we have assumed that $\mathrm{var}(\mathbf{x}_l)$ is constant. By substituting Eq. (13) into Eq. (5), we can obtain

$$\lambda_l = \frac{\mathrm{std}(\Delta\mathbf{W}_l)}{\mathrm{std}(\mathbf{W}_l)}\lambda = \sqrt{\frac{\mathrm{var}(\Delta\mathbf{W}_l)}{\mathrm{var}(\mathbf{W}_l)}}\lambda = \sqrt{\frac{C\cdot\gamma_l}{\mathrm{var}(\mathbf{W}_l)}}\lambda. \tag{14}$$

Since the above equation contains two constant values (C and λ), we deform the equation by utilizing λ_L as a base coefficient of weight decay.

$$\lambda_l = \lambda_L\cdot\frac{\lambda_l}{\lambda_L} = \lambda_L\cdot\frac{\sqrt{\frac{C\cdot\gamma_l}{\mathrm{var}(\mathbf{W}_l)}}\lambda}{\sqrt{\frac{C\cdot\gamma_L}{\mathrm{var}(\mathbf{W}_L)}}\lambda} = \lambda_L\sqrt{\frac{\mathrm{var}(\mathbf{W}_L)}{\mathrm{var}(\mathbf{W}_l)}}\gamma_l \quad (\because \mathrm{Eq.}(12)). \tag{15}$$

Using Eq. (15), we can calculate λ_l for each layer in the initial network without training data, because we have assumed constant $\mathrm{var}(\mathbf{x}_l)$ and eliminate it from Eq. (14) by considering the ratio between λ_l and λ_L. Strength of regularization over the network can be adjusted by setting λ_L.

2.4 Effects of Drop-Out

In this section, we show that drop-out does not affect the layer-wise weight decay in Eq. (15). Since it is obvious that drop-out does not affect the scale of the weight decay, we focus instead on the scale of the gradient, which is represented by $\mathrm{var}(\mathbf{x}_l)$ and $\mathrm{var}(\Delta\mathbf{y}_l)$, as shown in Eq. (9). If the hidden nodes at the l-th layer are dropped out with probability p, $\mathrm{var}(\Delta\mathbf{y}_l)$ in Eq. (10) is modified as follows:

$$\mathrm{var}(\Delta\mathbf{y}_l) = (1-p)M_{l+1}\mathrm{var}(\mathbf{W}_{l+1})\mathrm{var}(\Delta\mathbf{y}_{l+1}^*), \tag{16}$$

where $\mathbf{y}_l^*$ denotes the output values of the l-th layer with drop-out. Since the dropped hidden values are treated as zero and the remaining hidden values are multiplied by $1/(1-p)$, we can deform $\mathrm{var}(\Delta\mathbf{y}_{l+1}^*)$ as shown below:

$$\mathrm{var}(\Delta\mathbf{y}_{l+1}^*) = \mathrm{ave}\left(\left(\Delta\mathbf{y}_{l+1}^*\right)^2\right)$$
$$= (1-p)\cdot\mathrm{ave}\left(\left(\frac{1}{1-p}\Delta\mathbf{y}_{l+1}\right)^2\right) + p\cdot\mathrm{ave}\left(0^2\right)$$
$$= \frac{1}{1-p}\mathrm{ave}\left(\left(\Delta\mathbf{y}_{l+1}\right)^2\right) = \frac{1}{1-p}\mathrm{var}\left(\Delta\mathbf{y}_{l+1}\right) \tag{17}$$

By substituting Eq. (17) into Eq. (16), we can obtain the same equation as Eq. (10), thus indicating that drop-out does not affect $\mathrm{var}(\Delta\mathbf{y}_l)$. Since $\mathrm{var}(\mathbf{x}_l)$ is not affected due to the multiplication of the hidden values, drop-out has no effect on the scale of the gradient. Therefore, we can ignore drop-out when calculating the layer-wise weight decay.

2.5 Effects of Pooling Layer

In Sect. 2.3, we consider only convolution or fully-connected layers that have trainable weights, but pooling layers are also utilized in many cases. Although the pooling layer does not have a large effect on $\text{var}(\mathbf{x}_l)$, it actually does affect $\text{var}(\Delta \mathbf{y}_l)$. Therefore, β_l in Eq. (10) should be also defined in the pooling layer. In this section, we define β_l in a max-pooling layer and an average-pooling layer. Let p and s denote pooling size and stride size, respectively.

Max-pooling. In the max-pooling layer, the maximum input value in a local area is propagated feed-forward, and only the corresponding unit receives $\Delta \mathbf{x}_l$ in the back-propagation while the $\Delta \mathbf{x}_l$ of the other units in the local area is set to zero. Therefore, if we assume the mean of $\Delta \mathbf{x}_l$ is zero, $\text{var}(\Delta \mathbf{x}_l)$ is scaled to $1/s^2$ in the back-propagation, which means that β_l in the max-pooling layer should be set to $1/s^2$. As p becomes larger than s, the proportion of the units that receive $\Delta \mathbf{x}_l$ becomes small, but we ignore this effect and utilize the above definition anyway for simplicity. This problem will be addressed in future work.

Average-pooling. In contrast to max-pooling, all units in an average-pooling layer receive $\Delta \mathbf{x}_l$. However, $\Delta \mathbf{x}_l$ is scaled by a factor of M_l/N_l in the back-propagation, as each unit in $\mathbf{x}_l$ is connected to M_l units in $\mathbf{y}_l$ with a weight of $1/N_l$. Therefore, β_l in the average-pooling layer should be set to $(M_l/N_l)^2$. For example, when $p = s$, N_l equals p^2, and M_l equals 1, so β_l should be set to $1/p^4$.

2.6 Rescaling Invariance of Layer-Wise Weight Decay

To theoretically validate our method, we will show that our layer-wise weight decay is invariant for layer-wise rescaling of the network. The rescaling of the network [11], also known as reparameterization [2], is a transformation by rescaling the connection weights without any change of the function computed by the network. Such rescaling can be easily derived if we use some kinds of activation function f, such as an identity function or ReLU, that satisfy $f(\alpha x) = \alpha f(x)$ for any positive scalar α. Figure 3 shows an example of layer-wise rescaling, which is one of the simplest rescaling. When we rescale $\mathbf{W}_{l-1}$ to $\alpha \mathbf{W}_{l-1}$ and $\mathbf{W}_l$ to $\frac{1}{\alpha} \mathbf{W}_l$, the value of $\mathbf{x}_{l+1}$ does not change. Since the rescaling does not affect the functionality of the network, it should not affect the update of the network in the training process, either. If the rescaling affects the update, it means that how the network is to be updated depends highly upon the scale of each weight, which results in instability of the training process. We will show that the strength of the regularization is affected by the rescaling if constant weight decay is used but is invariant if our layer-wise weight decay is used. Note that we focus on the balance between the gradient and the weight decay, which is in contrast to the existing works [2, 11] that focus on only the scale of the gradient.

Suppose the network is rescaled as shown in Fig. 3. Since any layer-wise rescaling can be represented by the combination of this kind of rescaling, studying this rescaling is enough to show rescaling invariance in the proposed method.

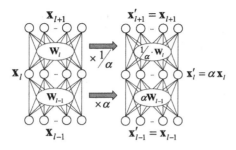

Fig. 3. Layer-wise rescaling of the network.

Let $\mathbf{x}'_l$ and $\mathbf{W}'_l$ denote the input values and connection weights of the l-th layer after the rescaling, respectively. Here, we can derive $\Delta\mathbf{W}'_{l-1}$ and $\Delta\mathbf{W}'_l$ as

$$\Delta\mathbf{W}'_{l-1} = \mathbf{x}'^T_{l-1}\Delta\mathbf{y}'_{l-1} = \mathbf{x}^T_{l-1}\left(\frac{1}{\alpha}\Delta\mathbf{y}_{l-1}\right) = \frac{1}{\alpha}\Delta\mathbf{W}_{l-1}, \tag{18}$$

$$\Delta\mathbf{W}'_l = \mathbf{x}'^T_l\Delta\mathbf{y}'_l = \alpha\mathbf{x}^T_l\Delta\mathbf{y}_l = \alpha\Delta\mathbf{W}_l. \tag{19}$$

By substituting the above equations into Eq. (1), we can obtain the update values of the rescaled network in the case of constant weight decay:

$$\Delta\mathbf{W}'_{l-1} + \lambda\mathbf{W}'_{l-1} = \frac{1}{\alpha}\Delta\mathbf{W}_{l-1} + \lambda\alpha\mathbf{W}_{l-1}, \tag{20}$$

$$\Delta\mathbf{W}'_l + \lambda\mathbf{W}_l = \alpha\Delta\mathbf{W}_l + \frac{\lambda}{\alpha}\mathbf{W}_l. \tag{21}$$

If α is large, the weight-decay term is dominant in the update of $\mathbf{W}_{l-1}$, and in contrast, the gradient term is dominant in the update of $\mathbf{W}_l$. This indicates that the rescaling affects the strength of the weight decay. In contrast, in the case of the layer-wise weight decay, the values of the weight-decay coefficients will be changed by the rescaling as follows:

$$\lambda'_{l-1} = \frac{\text{scale}(\Delta\mathbf{W}'_{l-1})}{\text{scale}(\mathbf{W}'_{l-1})}\lambda = \frac{\frac{1}{\alpha}\text{scale}(\Delta\mathbf{W}_{l-1})}{\alpha\,\text{scale}(\mathbf{W}_{l-1})} = \frac{\lambda_{l-1}}{\alpha^2}, \tag{22}$$

$$\lambda'_l = \frac{\text{scale}(\Delta\mathbf{W}'_l)}{\text{scale}(\mathbf{W}'_l)}\lambda = \frac{\alpha\,\text{scale}(\Delta\mathbf{W}_l)}{\frac{1}{\alpha}\text{scale}(\mathbf{W}_l)} = \alpha^2\lambda_l. \tag{23}$$

Using them, we can derive the update values of the rescaled network in the case of layer-wise weight decay:

$$\Delta\mathbf{W}'_{l-1} + \lambda'_{l-1}\mathbf{W}'_{l-1} = \frac{1}{\alpha}\Delta\mathbf{W}_{l-1} + \frac{\lambda_{l-1}}{\alpha^2}\alpha\mathbf{W}_{l-1}$$

$$= \frac{1}{\alpha}\left(\mathbf{W}_{l-1} + \lambda_{l-1}\mathbf{W}_{l-1}\right) \propto \mathbf{W}_{l-1} + \lambda_{l-1}\mathbf{W}_{l-1}, \tag{24}$$

$$\Delta\mathbf{W}'_l + \lambda'_l\mathbf{W}'_l = \alpha\Delta\mathbf{W}_l + \frac{\alpha^2\lambda_l}{\alpha}\mathbf{W}_l$$

$$= \alpha\left(\Delta\mathbf{W}_l + \lambda_l\mathbf{W}_l\right) \propto \Delta\mathbf{W}_l + \lambda_l\mathbf{W}_l. \tag{25}$$

These equations indicate that the strength of the weight decay is rescaling invariant in our method. This invariance stems from the sufficient consideration of the scale of the gradients that is affected by the scale of the weights in the upper layers. Although the scale of the update should be compensated by the adaptive learning rate or some other sophisticated optimization method, we can conclude that our layer-wise weight decay makes the training of the network invariant against rescaling.

3   Experiments

To evaluate the performance of our method, we conducted experiments on the MNIST [9] and CIFAR-10 [7] datasets, both of which are widely used to benchmark deep learning methods. We compared our layer-wise weight decay with the constant weight decay that is utilized in many existing methods. We set various values of the coefficients for training and evaluated the performance of the trained networks. SGD with a momentum was used for training the networks, and the momentum value was set to 0.9. No data augmentation was performed. Xavier initialization [3] was used to initialize the networks. We trained each network five times with different random initializations and examined their average test error rates.

3.1   Classification Performance

CIFAR-10. The CIFAR-10 dataset includes 32×32 color images that have ten classes. There are 50,000 training images and 10,000 test images. All images are preprocessed by a global contrast normalization and ZCA whitening, which are typically utilized in this benchmark. We used a conlutional neural network in [14]; its architecture is described in Table 1. Note that this network has already achieved superior results for the CIFAR-10 task in [14]. The initial learning rate was set to 0.01 and was multiplied by a fixed multiplier of 0.1 after 100,000, 125,000, and 150,000 iterations. The network was trained for a total of 175,000 iterations. We applied drop-out to the input layer as well as after each pooling layer. The drop-out ratio was 20% at the input and 50% otherwise.

Figure 4 shows test error rates by the network trained with our layer-wise weight decay and that with constant weight decay. A horizontal axis represents λ_L, which is the weight-decay coefficient in the last layer of the initial network and should be tuned for the training of the network to achieve the best performance. At the best setting of the coefficient, our method successfully reduces the error from 9.71% to 9.28%. This is because the proposed method can regularize the network more effectively. Note that λ_L at the best performance becomes higher by adopting our method. As shown in Table 1, λ_l in our method is relatively high at the upper layers; in other words, constant weight decay insufficiently regularizes the upper layers. By adopting layer-wise weight decay, the upper layers are sufficiently regularized, which results in the better performance of the network, as shown in Fig. 4.

Table 1. Architecture of the network for CIFAR-10

Type	Filter size/Stride/ No. of filters	Output size	Layer-wise λ_l (data-independent)
Input		$32 \times 32 \times 3$	
Convolution + ReLU	$3 \times 3/1/96$	$32 \times 32 \times 96$	$0.030\lambda_L$
Convolution + ReLU	$3 \times 3/1/96$	$32 \times 32 \times 96$	$0.171\lambda_L$
Max-pooling	$3 \times 3/2/1$	$16 \times 16 \times 96$	
Convolution + ReLU	$3 \times 3/1/192$	$16 \times 16 \times 192$	$0.242\lambda_L$
Convolution + ReLU	$3 \times 3/1/192$	$16 \times 16 \times 192$	$0.342\lambda_L$
Max-pooling	$3 \times 3/2/1$	$8 \times 8 \times 192$	
Convolution + ReLU	$3 \times 3/1/192$	$8 \times 8 \times 192$	$0.685\lambda_L$
Convolution + ReLU	$1 \times 1/1/192$	$8 \times 8 \times 192$	$0.228\lambda_L$
Convolution + ReLU	$1 \times 1/1/10$	$8 \times 8 \times 10$	λ_L
Average-pooling	$8 \times 8/1/1$	$1 \times 1 \times 10$	
Output		$1 \times 1 \times 10$	

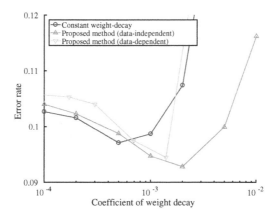

Fig. 4. Experimental result on CIFAR-10.

MNIST. The MNIST dataset includes 28×28 gray-scale images that have ten classes. There are 60,000 training images and 10,000 test images. All images are preprocessed by scaling the range of intensity to be from zero to one. We used the same network as that used in the *Caffe* example, which is based on LeNet [9]. Its architecture is described in Table 2. The initial learning rate was set to 0.01 and was multiplied by $(1 + 0.0001 \cdot t)^{-0.75}$ during training for gradual reduction. The network was trained for a total of 100,000 iterations. Drop-out was not applied to the network.

Figure 5 shows test error rates by the networks. As in the case with CIFAR-10, the proposed method achieved better performance than constant weight decay. Since the performance for MNIST is somewhat saturated, the improvement is relatively small compared with that on CIFAR-10.

Table 2. Architecture of the network for MNIST

Type	Filter size/Stride/ No. of filters	Output size	Layer-wise λ_l (data-independent)
Input		$28 \times 28 \times 1$	
Convolution	$5 \times 5/1/20$	$24 \times 24 \times 20$	$0.0099\lambda_L$
Max-pooling	$2 \times 2/2/1$	$12 \times 12 \times 20$	
Convolution	$5 \times 5/1/50$	$8 \times 8 \times 50$	$0.056\lambda_L$
Max-pooling	$2 \times 2/2/1$	$4 \times 4 \times 50$	
Fully-connected + ReLU	$1/1/500$	$1 \times 1 \times 500$	$0.18\lambda_L$
Fully-connected	$1/1/10$	$1 \times 1 \times 10$	λ_L
Output		$1 \times 1 \times 10$	

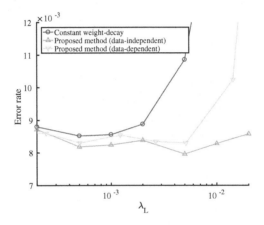

Fig. 5. Experimental result on MNIST

3.2 Transferability

In the second experiment, we evaluated the transferability of DNNs. Since training a DNN from scratch often requires a huge amount of training data and extremely high computational cost, fine-tuning an existing network that is pre-trained for other related tasks would be a good choice in many cases. This is called transfer learning, and transferability, which is the potential of the pre-trained network to show high performance after fine-tuning, is quite important when utilizing DNNs. For our experiments with transfer learning, we divided the MNIST dataset into two datasets: one with even-number patterns and one with odd-number patterns. We pre-trained the network with the first dataset and fine-tuned it with the second. We varied the amount of training data in the fine-tuning by random sampling from the second dataset and then evaluated the performance of the fine-tuned network. The network model is same as that in Sect. 3.1 except for the number of units in the last layer. In the pre-training

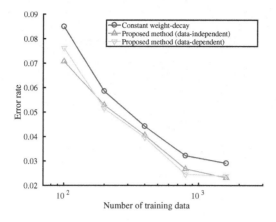

Fig. 6. Performance of the fine-tuned networks.

of the network, the learning rate and the number of iterations is set to be the same as that in Sect. 3.1. In the fine-tuning, we fixed the learning rate to 0.001 and set the number of iterations to 10,000. Weight decay was not utilized in the fine-tuning so as to fairly evaluate the transferability of the pre-trained networks.

Figure 6 shows test error rates by the fine-tuned networks. We tuned the weight-decay coefficient for each method and show the best performances in this figure. The error rates of all methods decrease along with an increase in the amount of training data, and those of the proposed methods are substantially smaller than those of the constant weight decay in all cases. As noted in Sect. 3.1, the upper layers of the network were sufficiently regularized in the proposed method. This leads to an acceleration of the training of the lower layers, which results in high transferability of the network.

3.3   Effects of Batch Normalization

The most recent network often conducts batch-normalization (BN) process [10] that normalizes hidden values within mini-batch. Due to the normalization, BN may alleviate the scale-imbalance problem tackled in this paper. However, we can expect that our method can also enhance the performance of such network because it does not consider the balance between the gradient and the regularization. Although BN violates some assumptions in our method, we tried to apply our method to the network with BN. We added BN layers just after each convolutional layer in the network shown in Table 1. Using this new network, we conducted almost same experiment with that in Sect. 3.1 and evaluated its performance. Since adopting BN allows for a larger learning rate, the initial learning rate was changed to 0.1. Figure 7 shows test error rates by the trained networks. The proposed method achieved slightly better performance (8.65%) than constant weight decay (8.88%). This result shows the similar tendency with the results in Sect. 3.1. It indicates that BN is not so effective for the scale-imbalance problem, and our method can also enhance the performance of such network.

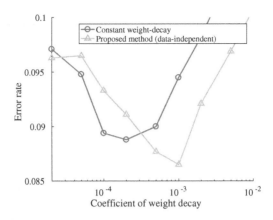

Fig. 7. Experimental result on CIFAR-10 with batch normalization.

4   Conclusion

In this paper, we proposed layer-wise weight decay for training deep neural networks. In our method, the weight-decay coefficient is set layer by layer to balance the scale of weight decay with that of back-propagated gradients. By adopting such a setting, every layer is properly regularized, which results in a better performance of the trained network. Experimental results show that our method can enhance the performance of existing networks, even state-of-the-art ones. Our method can be applied to a wide range of existing deep neural networks, and future work will thus include an evaluation of our method on various types of network.

References

1. Bengio, Y.: Practical recommendations for gradient-based training of deep architectures. In: Montavon, G., Orr, G.B., Müller, K.-R. (eds.) Neural Networks: Tricks of the Trade. LNCS, vol. 7700, pp. 437–478. Springer, Heidelberg (2012). https://doi.org/10.1007/978-3-642-35289-8_26
2. Desjardins, G., Simonyan, K., Pascanu, R., Kavukcuoglu, K.: Natural neural networks. In: Advances in Neural Information Processing Systems (2015)
3. Glorot, X., Bengio, Y.: Understanding the difficulty of training deep feedforward neural networks. In: International Conference on Artificial Intelligence and Statistics (2010)
4. He, K., Zhang, X., Ren, S., Sun, J.: Delving deep into rectifiers: surpassing human-level performance on imagenet classification. In: IEEE International Conference on Computer Vision (2015)
5. Jia, Y., Shelhamer, E., Donahue, J., Karayev, S., Long, J.: Caffe: convolutional architecture for fast feature embedding. arXiv:1408.5093 (2014)
6. Krähenbühl, P., et al.: Data-dependent initializations of convolutional neural networks. In: International Conference on Learning Representations (2016)

7. Krizhevsky, A., Hinton, G.: Learning multiple layers of features from tiny images. Technical report, University of Toronto 10 (2009)
8. Krizhevsky, A., Sutskever, I., Hinton, G.E.: Imagenet classification with deep convolutional neural networks. In: Advances in Neural Information Processing Systems (2012)
9. LeCun, Y., Bottou, L., Bengio, Y., Haffner, P.: Gradient-based learning applied to document recognition. IEEE **86**(11), 2278–2324 (1998)
10. Loffe, S., Szegedy, C.: Batch normalization: accelerating deep network training by reducing internal covariate shift. In: International Conference on Machine Learning, pp. 448–456 (2015)
11. Neyshabur, B., Salakhutdinov, R., Srebro, N.: Path-SGD: path-normalized optimization in deep neural networks. In: Advances in Neural Information Processing Systems (2015)
12. Shahriari, B., Bouchard-Cote, A., de Freitas, N.: Unbounded Bayesian optimization via regularization. In: International Conference on Artificial Intelligence and Statistics (2016)
13. Snoek, J., Rippel, O., Swersky, K., Kiros, R., Satish, N., Sundaram, N., Patwary, M., Prabhat, M., Adams, R.: Scalable Bayesian optimization using deep neural networks. In: International Conference on Machine Learning (2015)
14. Springenberg, J.T., Dosovitskiy, A., Brox, T., Riedmiller, M.: Striving for simplicity: the all convolutional net. In: International Conference on Learning Reprensentation (Workshop Track) (2015)
15. Srivastava, N., Hinton, G., Krizhevsky, A., Sutskever, I., Salakhutdinov, R.: Dropout: a simple way to prevent neural networks from overfitting. J. Mach. Learn. Res. **15**(1), 1929–1958 (2014)
16. Yosinski, J., Clune, J., Bengio, Y., Lipson, H.: How transferable are features in deep neural networks? In: Advances in Neural Information Processing Systems (2014)

Adaptive Dehaze Method for Aerial Image Processing

Rong-qin Xu, Sheng-hua Zhong[✉], Gaoyang Tang, Jiaxin Wu,
and Yingying Zhu

College of Computer Science and Software Engineering, Shenzhen University,
Shenzhen, People's Republic of China
{xurongqin,2150230510,jiaxin.wu}@email.szu.edu.cn,
{csshzhong,zhuyy}@szu.edu.cn

Abstract. Remote sensing images or images collected by unmanned aerial vehicles in the hazy weather are easily interfered by scattering effect generated by atmospheric particulate matter. The terrible interference will not only lead to the images quality seriously degraded, but also result in a bad effect on the process of images feature extraction and images feature matching. In this paper, by proposing an effective adaptive dehaze method, we compare the statistical results of feature detection and matching based on Scale-invariant feature transform (SIFT) detector and descriptor before and after haze removal. And we also provide the comparisons of image stitching task. The experimental results show that, after the haze removal is implemented on hazy images, more SIFT feature keypoints and SIFT matching keypoints will be extracted, which is also beneficial to images stitching. Moreover, the proposed adaptive method performs better than the original dehaze method.

Keywords: Adaptive haze removal · SIFT detector and descriptor
Image matching · Image stitching · Kernel graph cuts · Random walk

1 Introduction

The digital image stitching technology has become a hot research field nowadays. It deals with remote sensing images collected by satellites or planes as well as aerial images collected by UAV (unmanned aerial vehicles). Aerial image processing [1,2] is the key process in image stitching technology. At present, the image registration method based on the extracted image features is the main tendency in the field of image stitching. The core of the method is to find all of the matching feature point pairs by measuring similarity between each of the two images. Therefore, how to effectively extract more distinguished features from aerial images is very important.

Although there are not many existing work try to explore the feature detection, extraction and matching in aerial images, lots of algorithms are proposed to detect and extract features from other types of natural images, such as Harris

© Springer International Publishing AG, part of Springer Nature 2018
M. Paul et al. (Eds.): PSIVT 2017, LNCS 10749, pp. 290–301, 2018.
https://doi.org/10.1007/978-3-319-75786-5_24

algorithm [3], Canny algorithm, SIFT algorithm [9,10], S-SIFT algorithm [11], V-SIFT algorithm [12] and so on. Among them, the SIFT algorithm has the advantage of maintaining invariance for the cases of image scaling, translation, rotation and even affine transformation. Unfortunately, aerial images have obvious different characters and properties with other types of natural images. The scattering effect generated by the atmospheric particulate matter will easily interfere with the fidelity and contrast of aerial images, leading to the loss or the degradation of the features from aerial images.

In view of these limitations, in recent years, many haze removal models and techniques are proposed to alleviate the influences from haze. Tan [5] removes the haze by maximizing the local contrast of the restored images. Fatal [6] estimates the albedo of the scene and then infers the medium transmission. Besides, in 2009, He et al. [7,8] put forward a new kind of prior rule called dark channel prior, which will directly evaluate the transmission information of light in the haze and then remove the haze from a single input image. This effective method of removing haze can both maximally retain the feature information of the original image and adjust the overall color brightness of the image and keep the color unchanged. Unfortunately, their methods do not consider the differences in image properties between different image regions.

In this paper, we propose a novel adaptive dehaze method to adaptively estimate the optimal patch size in different regions of aerial images and remove the image haze under this consideration. We are the first to use a series of experiments to evaluate the proposed image dehaze method on aerial images. In experiments, we collect two aerial image datasets, including the images obtained by unmanned aerial vehicle, and the satellite images from Google Earth [19]. In each dataset, by using the proposed adaptive dehaze method, we obtain better performance on feature detection, image matching, and image stitching.

2   Adaptive Dehaze Method

2.1   Image Haze Removal

The key part of the famous haze removal method proposed by He et al. is they propose a new prior dark channel prior [7,8], to estimate the transmission directly from a hazy image. Simplify, the dark channel prior means that in most of the non-sky patches, at least one color channel has very low intensity at some pixels. In other words, the minimum intensity in such a patch should have a very low value. And due to the additive airlight, a hazy image is brighter than its haze-free version in where the transmission is low. So the dark channel of these images will have higher intensity in regions with denser haze. According to haze removal approach proposed by He et al., a haze-free image can be recovered from a widely used model:

$$\mathbf{J}(x) = \frac{\mathbf{I}(x) - \mathbf{A}}{\max(t(x), t_0)} + \mathbf{A} \tag{1}$$

where the scene radiance $\mathbf{J}(x)$ is a haze-free image, $\mathbf{I}(x)$ is a haze image, $\mathbf{A}$ is the global atmospheric light, t is the medium transmission describing the portion of the light that is not scattered and reaches the camera and t_0 is a lower bound to restrict the transmission $t(x)$. Then, we can estimate the transmission $t(x)$ simply by

$$t(x) = 1 - \omega \min_{y \in \Omega(x)} \left(\min_c \frac{I^c(y)}{A^c} \right) \qquad (2)$$

where I^c is a color channel of $\mathbf{I}$, ω is a constant parameter to keep a very small amount of haze for the distant objects on images, and $\Omega(x)$ is a local patch centered at x. A key parameter in haze removal algorithm is the patch size x_n, which is the length of $\Omega(x)$ in Eq. (2). In this famous haze removal algorithm, the patch size is always fixed to be 15. In our paper, we propose a novel method to adaptively remove the haze effects in different image conditions.

2.2   Image Segmentation Using Kernel Graph Cuts

In our preliminary experiments, we already found that the effects of image haze removal are different in sky and non-sky regions. Therefore, in order to obtain the optimal patch size for the sky and non-sky regions respectively, we segment the hazy images into sky and non-sky regions using Kernel Graph Cuts. Based on Boykov's model [13], Salah [14] proposed a fully automated kernel graph cuts model, which can divide a single image into several regions unsupervisedly. In Salah's algorithm [14], the energy equation of the simplified kernel-induced distance segmentation model is defined as follows,

$$E(\{\mu_l\}, \delta) = \sum_{l \in L} \sum_{p \in R_l} J_K(I_p, \mu_l) + \alpha \sum_{\{p,q\} \in D} r(\delta(p), \delta(q)) \qquad (3)$$

where J_K is the kernel function, $l \in L$ is the number of the regions to be divided, L is the total number of regions and μ_l is the parameter of the unsupervised multi-parameter Graph cuts algorithm. δ is the penalty for each pixel marked as foreground or background. $l \in R_l$ is a pixel that belongs to a segmented region. $r(\delta(p), \delta(q))$ is the smooth term in neighborhood D. The first term on the right side of the Eq. (3) is the data item, the second term is the smoothing term. α is the positive coefficient, which is used to adjust the weight of the data item and the smoothing item.

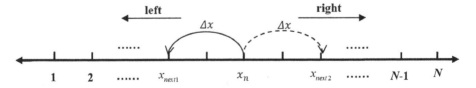

Fig. 1. Illustration of one-dimensional discrete random walk. Initially a particle is placed at x_n. The black arrows marked "left" and "right" indicate two different jumping directions.

2.3   Adaptively Obtain Optimal Patch Size Using Random Walk

After the image segmentation, we could use brute force method to obtain the optimal patch size of the sky region and the non-sky region individually on the training images. At the optimal patch size, we believe that both sky regions and non-sky regions will be extracted more keypoints after haze removal than fixed patch size. However, using exhaustive method to find the optimal patch size is a time-consuming work. Therefore, in order to make our approach efficiently, we are supposed to obtain optimal patch size effectively. Based on previous research, random walks are stochastic processes formed by successive summation of independent, identically distributed random variables and are one of the most studied topics in probability theory [15]. So, in our method, we try to find out the optimal patch size using the random walk algorithm. More specifically, we regard the procedure of searching for optimal patch size as a one-dimensional discrete random walk problem [16].

Algorithm 1. Obtain Optimal Patch Size using Random Walk

Input:

A training set with M segmented images.

Integer T specifying number of iteration.

p_{left}, p_{right} specifying probability of turning forwards left or right direction respectively.

Initialize:

$times(x_n) = 0$ for all $x_n \in (1, N)$.

$p_{left} = p_{right} = 0.5$.

Randomly generated initial patch size x_n.

Do for $t = 1, 2, ..., T$:

1. Calculate the average number $Y_n : Y_n = \sum_{i=1}^{M} \varphi_n(i)/M$, where $\varphi_n(i)$ is the number of detected keypoints of the i-th segmented image when the value of patch size is x_n.

2. Obtain next patch size: $x_{next} = \begin{cases} x_n + \Delta x, \text{when it jumps to the right} \\ x_n - \Delta x, \text{when it jumps to the left} \end{cases}$

   where Δx is jumping step ($\Delta x \in (1, N)$). The jumping direction is purely depended on p_{left} and p_{right}.

3. Update current average number: $Y_{current} = \max(Y_{current}, Y_{next})$.

4. Record last jumping direction and define jumping probability: $p_{left} \leftarrow p$ and $p_{right} \leftarrow 1 - p_{left}$. And the probability p is defined as:

$$p = \begin{cases} k, & \text{last direction is left} \\ 1 - k, & \text{last direction is right} \end{cases} (0.5 < k < 1)$$

5. Count jumping times $times(x_n)$ when it jumps to patch size x_n : $times(x_n) = times(x_n) + 1$.

Output: The optimal patch size $x_{optimal}$ where $times(x_{optical}) = \max(times(x_n))$.

As shown in Fig. 1, a particle on a one-dimensional lattice jumps from one site to an adjacent site at random with a probability p_{right} to the right and p_{left} to the left. The algorithm to obtain optimal patch size using discrete random walk is shown in Algorithm 1. In Algorithm 1, the particle jumps in the same direction as previous jump with the probability k ($0.5 < k < 1$) and the change the jump direction with the probability $1 - k$. This probability does not create preferred direction.

3   Experiments

3.1   Experimental Setting

In this part, to validate the performance of our proposed method, experiments are carried out on two sets of hazy images. The first dataset UAV is collected by our group. This data set includes 55 images obtained by the unmanned aerial vehicles. The original resolution of these images is 4000×3000. The second dataset GE is collected from Google Earth [19], which provides us a series of satellite images from all over the world. This dataset has 100 images totally, is collected from four different cities that were seriously suffering from heavy haze. In addition, the resolution of the images is 800×500 and the overlap part between images pairs is between 20% and 50%. In Table 1, we demonstrate some basic information about these four different cities.

Table 1. Specific information about four different cities in the second dataset GE

City	Longitude	Latitude	Date
Beijing	16°23′22.15″E	39°55′22.88″N	Oct 18th, 2014
Guangzhou	113°19′12.16″E	23°06′52.54″N	Oct 12th, 2015
New Delhi	78°02′32.15″E	27°10′30.01″N	Mar 15th, 2014
Karachi	67°10′21.2″E	24°53′48.63″N	Apr 6th, 2015

In each dataset, we conduct the following three experiments: keypoint detection, keypoint matching and image stitching [17]. We use the OpenCV toolbox provided by Rob Hess from Oregon State University [18]. All the experiments were carried out on an Intel(R) Core(TM) 2.6 GHz PC running under Windows 10 operating system with 16.0 GB RAM.

3.2   Experiments on GE Dataset

In the experiments on GE dataset, we keep the original resolution 800×500 of images to test the performance of keypoint detection and matching. Firstly, we test the keypoint detection performance based on SIFT detector on 100 collected images. In Table 2, we show the number of keypoints detected by SIFT detector before and after haze removal. From Table 2, it is obviously that the number of keypoints increases dramatically by 262.04% on average. In Fig. 2, we show this improvement in keypoint detection task. Apparently, more keypoints will be detected after haze removal, especially those aerial images with heavy haze.

Table 2. The average number of detected keypoints before and after haze removal

Before haze removal	After haze removal	Increment
980	3548	262.04%

In this part, we combine 100 images into 160 pairs. Then, we evaluate the keypoint matching performance based on SIFT descriptors in 160 image pairs. In Table 3, we provide the number of matching keypoints of SIFT descriptors in the case of before and after haze removal. From this table, the average number of matching keypoints will increase about 177.89% without RANSAC [4]. With RANSAC, this average number increases about 178.20%. In Fig. 3, we demonstrate a group of example images of the keypoint matching task.

Table 3. Average number of matched keypoints based on SIFT descriptors before and after haze removal

	Before haze removal	After haze removal	Increment
Without RANSAC	305	848	177.89%
With RANSAC	292	812	178.20%

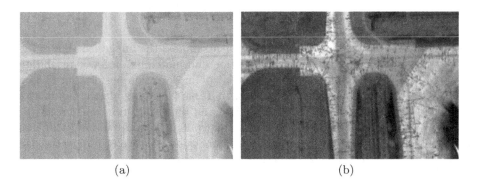

(a)　　　　　　　　　　　　　　　　(b)

Fig. 2. A group of example images in the keypoint detection task. (a) Before the haze removal, 35 keypoints are detected. (b) After the haze removal, 2048 keypoints are detected.

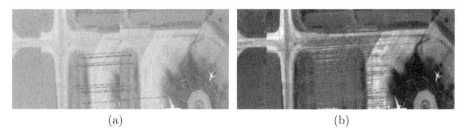

(a)   (b)

Fig. 3. A group of example images in the keypoint matching task (with RANSAC). (a) Before the haze removal, 19 keypoint pairs are matched. (b) After the haze removal, 744 keypoint pairs are matched.

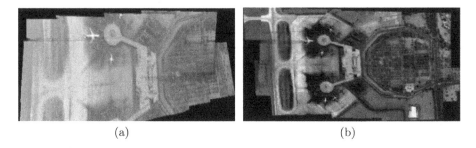

(a)   (b)

Fig. 4. A group of example images in the image stitching task. (a) is the result before haze removal, and (b) is the result after haze removal.

In this part, we use 25 images to do the image stitching task. And the resolution of each image is 400×250. In Fig. 4, we demonstrate the result of image stitching task on two cases. Compared with the results without haze removal, our methods based on haze removal helps us to obtain better stitching results.

3.3   Experiments on UAV Dataset

In the experiments on UAV dataset, we down-sampled the images to 1000×750 to test the performance of keypoint detection and matching on lower resolution image. In this part, we firstly evaluate the keypoint detection performance based on SIFT detector on 55 collected images. In Table 4, we provide the number of keypoints detected by SIFT detector before and after haze removal. From this table, we could find the number of detected keypoints increase about 10.25% on average. This improvement shows the haze removal is effective to reduce the bad effect of haze in the keypoint detection task.

Table 4. The average number of detected keypoints before and after haze removal

Before haze removal	After haze removal	Increment
4138	4562	10.25%

In Fig. 5, we demonstrate a group of example images in the keypoint detection task. From the comparisons of this group, we can easily find that most of newly detected keypoints are located in the regions that are badly influenced by haze. In hazy image, the buildings in a distant view (shown in the black box) cannot be distinguished clearly. And it also has a bad influence on the keypoint detection. After we utilize the algorithm of haze removal, more keypoints could be detected in these regions.

(a)   (b)

Fig. 5. A group of example images in the keypoint detection task. (a) Before the haze removal, 2773 keypoints are detected. (b) After the haze removal, 3453 keypoints are detected.

Table 5. Average number of matched keypoints based on SIFT descriptors before and after haze removal

	Before haze removal	After haze removal	Increment
Without RANSAC	447	464	3.80%
With RANSAC	261	275	5.36%

Based on the geographic position of the collected images, we divide the collected images into seven groups. In the image matching experiment, we could combine 55 images into 167 aerial image pairs. In each pair, the overlap part is not less than 20%. In this part, we evaluate the keypoint matching performance based on SIFT descriptors in 167 pairs. In Table 5, we provide the number of matching keypoints of SIFT descriptors in the case of before and after haze removal. From this table, we could find the average number of matched keypoints will increase about 3.80% without RANSAC method. With RANSAC, this average number increases about 5.36%. This improvement also evidences that the haze removal is effective to reduce the bad influence of haze in the task of keypoint matching.

(a)   (b)

Fig. 6. A group of example images in the keypoint matching task (with RANSAC). (a) Before the haze removal, 147 keypoint pairs are matched. (b) After the haze removal, 179 keypoint pairs are matched.

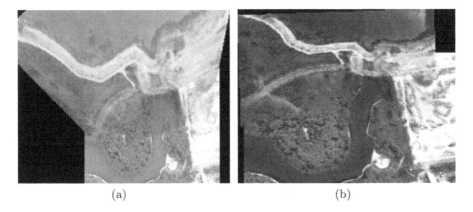

(a)   (b)

Fig. 7. A group of example images in the image stitching task. (a) is the result before haze removal, and (b) is the result after haze removal.

In Fig. 6, we demonstrate a group of example images of the keypoint matching task. Similar with our previous results in the keypoint detection task, after the haze removal, we could obtain more matched keypoints, especially for the buildings in a distant review. These results evidence the effectiveness of the algorithms for haze removal in hazy aerial images.

Figure 7 shows the results of image stitching task on one sample image. We use four images to do image stitching task, the resolution of each image is 200 × 150. Compared with the results without haze removal, our method based on haze removal helps us to obtain better mosaicking results.

3.4   Adaptive Haze Removal

In this section, we apply our proposed method to obtain optimal patch size for both sky region and non-sky region individually. And we will evaluate the effectiveness of our method as well. Firstly, we divide UAV dataset into two subsets which are named as UAV-Training and UAV-Testing respectively. The UAV-Training subset, as a training set, contains 35 images. And UAV-Testing subset, as a testing set, contains 20 images. Secondly, to obtain the optimal patch size, we conduct the training on the images of UAV-Training using Algorithm 1 described in Sect. 2.3. Thirdly, to evaluate the effectiveness of our proposed method, we test the learnt model on UAV-Testing. Besides, all images in UAV-Training and UAV-Testing are down-sampled to 1000×750.

We use our adaptive method to obtain the optimal patch size for sky and non-sky region. In image segmentation, to segment a single image into two consecutive regions, the parameter L in Eq. (3) is set to 2 and the parameter α in Eq. (3) is set to 10. In random walk method, the step size Δx is 2, the maximum patch size N is 100, and the iteration times T is set to be 100. Besides, the value of probability k is set to 0.9. In Fig. 8, we could obtain the optimal patch size for sky region is 34 and the optimal patch size for non-sky region 40. These results obtained by our adaptive method are also consistent with the results of the exhaustive method.

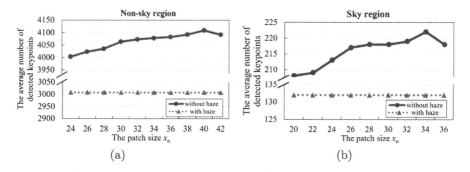

Fig. 8. (a) The obtained candidate optimal patch sizes x_n and their corresponding average numbers Y_n of detected keypoints on the non-sky region. (b) The obtained candidate optimal patch sizes x_n and their corresponding average numbers Y_n of detected keypoints on the sky region.

In this part, we test our adaptive model on UAV-Testing subset as well as GE dataset. The optimal patch size obtained by our adaptive model, for non-sky region is 40 and the optimal patch size for sky region is 34. As we known, in He's method, the patch size is fixed to be 15 [7,8] for all images or regions. In Table 6, we provide the results of keypoint detection and matching (with RANSAC) for different methods, including: the method without haze removal (without haze removal), the proposed method based on fixed patch size (fixed method), and the proposed adaptive method (adaptive method). Based on these results, we could find our adaptive method performs better than others.

Table 6. Comparisons among methods of without haze removal, fixed method and adaptive method.

	UAV-testing subset		
	Without haze removal	Fixed method	Adaptive method
AVE_KP	4229	4611	**4765**
AVE_KPM	258	277	**282**
	GE dataset		
	Without haze removal	Fixed Method	Adaptive method
AVE_KP	980	3548	**3738**
AVE_KPM	292	812	**844**

Note: "AVE_KP" and "AVE_KPM" are respectively the average numbers of detected keypoints and matched keypoints

4 Conclusion

Images of outdoor scenes are usually degraded by the haze in the atmosphere. This kind of degraded images loses the contrast and color, which is possible to have a bad effect of detecting, describing, and matching image local features, or some related image applications. In this paper, we try to explore the performance based on haze removal technique using dark channel prior for aerial image obtained by the unmanned aerial vehicle. In our paper, we propose a novel method to adaptively remove the haze effects in different image conditions. We did experiments on two self-constructed datasets based on scale-invariant feature transform for keypoints detection, keypoints matching, and image stitching. Our results evidence that the haze removal is effective to decrease the bad effect of haze in these tasks. The adaptive method also demonstrates better performance than fixed one. Future work will be explored from two aspects. The first direction is to test the performance of other local feature detectors and descriptors. The second direction is to propose new real-time haze removal models for aerial images obtained by the unmanned aerial vehicles.

Acknowledgments. This work was supported by the National Natural Science Foundation of China (No. 61502311, 61602314), the Natural Science Foundation of Guangdong Province (No. 2016A030310053, 2016A030313043), the Shenzhen high-level overseas talents program, and the Tencent "Rhinoceros Bird" - Scientific Research Foundation for Young Teachers of Shenzhen University.

References

1. Patel, P.M., Shah, V.M.: Image registration techniques: a comprehensive survey. Int. J. Innov. Res. Dev. (2014)
2. Lee, J.N., Kwak, K.C.: A trends analysis of image processing in unmanned aerial vehicle. Int. J. Comput. Inf. Sci. Eng. **8**(2), 2–5 (2014)

3. Harris, C.: A combined corner and edge detector. In: Proceedings of the Alvey Vision Conference, no. 3, pp. 147–151 (1988)
4. Shuang, D., Cai, H., Yang, Y.: Analysis of image stitching error based on scale invariant feature transform and random sample consensus. In: International Conference on Fuzzy Systems and Knowledge Discovery, pp. 1883–1887. IEEE (2016)
5. Tan, R.T.: Visibility in bad weather from a single image. In: IEEE Conference on Computer Vision and Pattern Recognition, CVPR 2008, pp. 1–8. IEEE (2008)
6. Fattal, R.: Single image dehazing. ACM Trans. Graph. (TOG) **27**(3), 72 (2008)
7. He, K., Sun, J., Tang, X.: Single image haze removal using dark channel prior. In: IEEE Conference on Computer Vision and Pattern Recognition, CVPR 2009, pp. 1956–1963. IEEE (2009)
8. He, K., Sun, J., Tang, X.: Single image haze removal using dark channel prior. IEEE Trans. Pattern Anal. Mach. Intell. **33**(12), 2341–2353 (2011)
9. Lowe, D.G.: Object recognition from local scale-invariant features. In: Proceedings of the 7th IEEE International Conference on Computer Vision, pp. 1150–1157 (1999)
10. Lowe, D.G.: Distinctive image features from scale-invariant key points. Int. J. Comput. Vis. **60**(2), 91–110 (2004)
11. Zhong, S.H., Liu, Y., Wu, G.: S-SIFT: a shorter SIFT without least discriminability visual orientation. In: IEEE/WIC/ACM International Conferences on Web Intelligence and Intelligent Agent Technology, pp. 669–672. IEEE (2013)
12. Zhong, S.H., Liu, Y., Chen, Q.C.: Visual orientation inhomogeneity based scale-invariant feature transform. Expert Syst. Appl. **42**(13), 5658–5667 (2015)
13. Boykov, Y., Funka-Lea, G.: Graph cuts and efficient N-D image segmentation. Int. J. Comput. Vis. **70**(2), 109–131 (2006)
14. Salah, M.B., Mitiche, A., Ayed, I.B.: Multiregion image segmentation by parametric kernel graph cuts. IEEE Trans. Image Process. **20**(2), 545–557 (2011)
15. Lawler, G.F., Limic, V.: Random Walk: A Modern Introduction. Cambridge University Press, Cambridge (2010)
16. Ibe, O.C.: One-dimensional random walk. In: Elements of Random Walk and Diffusion Processes, pp. 44–102. Wiley, Hoboken (2013)
17. Fathima, A.A., Karthik, R., Vaidehi, V.: Image stitching with combined moment invariants and sift features. Procedia Comput. Sci. **19**, 420–427 (2013)
18. Rob Hess. http://blogs.oregonstate.edu/hess/
19. Google Earth. https://www.google.com/earth/

Efficient GPU Implementation
of Informed-Filters for Fast Computation

Takuro Oki[1(✉)] and Ryusuke Miyamoto[2]

[1] Department of Computer Science, Graduate School of Science and Technology,
Meiji University, Tokyo, Kanagawa 2148571, Japan
o_tkr@cs.meiji.ac.jp
[2] Department of Computer Science, School of Science and Technology,
Meiji University, Tokyo, Kanagawa 2148571, Japan
miya@cs.meiji.ac.jp

Abstract. Human detection is an important task for several practical applications that require high-speed processing with good detection accuracy. This paper proposes a high-speed implementation of Informed-Filtersthat shows excellent accuracy in human detection. Our implementation reduces memory access during feature calculation and realizes efficient computation on an NVIDIA GPU where a thread is allocated to a detection sub-window. Experimental results using top-view images considering surveillance from UAVs showed that the processing speed was about 100 fps for 2560×1352 images on an NVIDIA 980Ti GPU, whereas it was 5.4 fps on an Intel Xeon 2.30 GHz CPU.

1 Introduction

Vital sensing during exercise on the basis of multi-hop sensor networks is useful for preventing sudden unwellness and for improving the effectiveness of training [1]. To realize such sensor networks, a novel routing scheme is indispensable because conventional schemes that use RSSI or GPS cannot account for the high density and moving speed of sensor nodes attached to humans doing exercise. The target applications of these sensor networks are not limited to only one kind of exercise but include several kinds of exercises as shown in Fig. 3. Therefore, vital sensor networks should work well for several node densities and moving speeds.

To enable the effective routing useful for such multi-hop networks, the authors are trying to realize Image Assisted Routing where the locations of sensor nodes are determined with visual information obtained from several cameras mounted on unmanned aerial vehicles (UAVs). An overview of the Image Assisted Routing is shown in Fig. 4. Remarkable advances in object detection and tracking enable accurate localization of humans wearing vital sensors; however, real-time processing of the localization on embedded systems has not been achieved yet. The huge computation requirements are an especially significant problem in the implementation of human detection on embedded systems.

© Springer International Publishing AG, part of Springer Nature 2018
M. Paul et al. (Eds.): PSIVT 2017, LNCS 10749, pp. 302–313, 2018.
https://doi.org/10.1007/978-3-319-75786-5_25

Several schemes aim to quickly compute object detection [2,3]. The authors are taking several approaches toward realizing accurate and high-speed object detection [4–8]. However, the classification accuracy of [2] is insufficient for human detection, and [3] requires stixel images obtained from a stereo camera that is not used in generic scene and especially in aerial images that are used in our project. Moreover, the classification accuracy of [3] is worse than Informed-Filters [9] that exhibit state-of-the-art classification accuracy in human detection. A novel approach [10,11] for object detection that does not use exhaustive search on the basis of sliding windows has been developed. [10,11] show good accuracy for multi-class object detection; however, the accuracy of one-class object detection for human target is not sufficient. Therefore, the authors are trying to speed-up Informed-Filters-based human detection by using an NVIDIA GPU.

GPU implementation of Informed-Filtersis more difficult than that of Intergral channel features [12] and Aggregate channel features [13] because feature computation of Informed-Filtersis more complex than that of intergral channel features and aggregate channel features, which use simple rectangular features as shown in Fig. 1; integral images can drastically reduce computation time in these schemes. In Informed-Filters, ternary features as shown in Fig. 2 are used to improve classification accuracy considering the complicated shapes of detection targets but feature computation using ternary features requires data to be accessed more frequently to generated integral images than intergral channel features and aggregate channel features. To solve this problem, a novel and parallel implementation that reduces the number of data access to pixels for feature computation and parallel implementation by using an NVIDIA GPU is shown. Our implementation reduces branch divergence and minimizes data transfer between a CPU and a GPU to achieve high speed processing without deteriorating of detection accuracy.

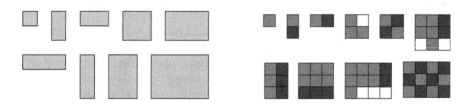

Fig. 1. Square features   **Fig. 2.** Ternary features

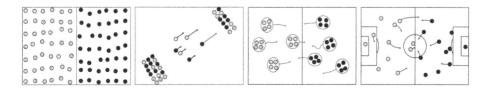

Fig. 3. Several kinds of motion patterns during exercise

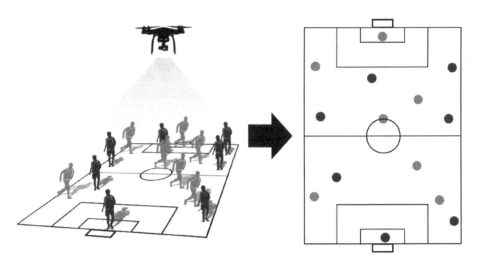

Fig. 4. Concept of image assisted routing

2 How to Reduce the Frequency of Data Access in the Informed-Filters

This section analyzes the processing flow of Informed-Filtersand shows how to reduce the frequency of data access in feature computation on the basis of an appropriate division of rectangular features that is much more efficient than intergral channel features and aggregate channel features.

2.1 The Frequency of Data Access During Feature Computation

In the Informed-Filters, a strong classifier is constructed with many decision trees from weak classifiers selected by boosting. These decision trees calculate the score for classification using rectangular features called filters as shown in Fig. 2. The types and locations of these filters composed of cells are determined at the training process by boosting. A cell is a unit rectangle and has a label assigned from $\{+1, -1, 0\}$. In the Informed-Filters, a feature F corresponding to a filter is computed by the following equation:

$$F = \sum_{i=0}^{n} L(cell_i) \cdot I(cell_i), \tag{1}$$

where n, $I(cell_i)$, and $L(cell_i)$ mean the number of cells included in the filter, the sum of pixels included in a $cell_i$, and a label assigned to a $cell_i$, respectively.

Equation (1) shows that feature computation requires frequent data access to pixels. A straightforward implementation of this computation needs $width \times height \times n$ read operations from pixels when the size of a cell is $width \times height$.

The number of read operations is still $4 \times n$ even if integral images are used in feature computation; this is about n times as large as the number of read operations used in intergral channel features or aggregate channel features.

2.2 Reduction of Read Operations in Feature Calculation by Filter Division

To reduce the number of read operations for feature calculation in Informed-Filters, the authors decided to divide a filter into several rectangles whose sizes are as large as possible: this division minimizes the number of divided regions. Using this division, the sizes of rectangles are larger than the sizes of cells, and the number of read operations can be reduced. In the proposed dividing scheme, first cells included in a filter are merged to a composite rectangle according to their labels, and then the generated composite rectangle is divided into several rectangles while minimizing the number of divisions. In the proposed scheme, this division is performed by [14], whose procedure can be summarized as follows:

Phase 1. Obtain degenerate chords from a composite rectangle and divide the composite rectangle according to the degenerate chords,
Phase 2. store vertices in a divided region clockwise,
Phase 3. scan the stored vertices and sort all horizontal line segments in descending order about $y-$coordinate, and
Phase 4. divide a composite rectangle by the most appropriate pattern selected from Fig. 6.

These operations are detailed in the rest of this subsection.

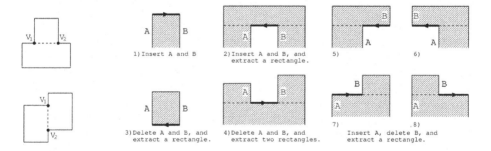

Fig. 5. Degenerate chords   **Fig. 6.** Pattern

Phase 1. This operation obtains degenerate chords that minimize the number of divisions from a composite rectangle. A degenerate chord is a line segment included in a composite rectangle whose both endpoints are recessed points having the same $x-$coordinate or $y-$coordinate. Figure 5 shows examples of degenerate chords as dashed lines where V_1 and V_2 are recessed points. If a composite rectangle has any degenerate chords, the composite rectangle is divided into several rectangles with no degenerate chords. After this division, a minimum division of the composite rectangle can be obtained by a minimum division of the rectangles generated by this division. In this operation, appropriate degenerate chords must be selected because a minimum division of the composite rectangle is not obtained if the selected degenerate chords are dependent as shown in [14].

A problem in obtaining a maximum independent set of degenerate chords can be represented by a bipartite graph $G(V_d, E)$ that is composed of line segments generated from endpoints of overlapping degenerate chords. V_d and E show a set of degenerate chords and line segments generated from endpoints of overlapping degenerate chords, respectively. A maximum independent set of vertices V_d' shows a maximum set that does not have any common edges among vertices included in the set. Therefore, the maximum set is equal to a maximum set of dependent degenerate chords. A maximum independent set of vertices can be computed by the following equation(Gallai) using a minimum vertex cover $MinV_{cover}$ obtained from maximum matching M' of a bipartite graph G(König)

$$V_d' = V_d - MinV_{cover} \tag{2}$$

Phase 2. In this operation, vertices included in a composite rectangular are scanned as internal regions and are located at the left side of the edge between the current and the next vertices. This scan order is represented by the word "clockwise".

Phase 3. In this operation, a scanning direction for a line segment is stored. Sorted horizontal line segments are stored in YList according to $y-$coordinate, and vertical line segments are stored in XList whose initial state is empty according to $x-$coordinate.

Phase 4. The following operations are applied to a line segment H obtained from YList. One pattern is selected from eight patterns shown in Fig. 6 considering the direction of the line segment H and the number of line segments included in XList that includes both endpoints of H. After this classification, some operations corresponding to the selected type are executed as shown in Fig. 6, and division is applied to a composite rectangle if possible. The above operations are applied to all horizontal line segments.

3   GPU Implementation of the Informed-Filters

This section explains how to apply parallel processing to Informed-Filtersusing a GPU, the effect of the soft cascade structure, and the improvement of memory access for high-speed processing.

3.1   Parallel Implementation Strategy on a GPU

Both search windows and weak classifiers can be computed in parallel in the case of detection by exhaustive search on the basis of sliding windows: parallel processing based on multiple weak classifiers has higher parallelism than multiple search windows. However, we cannot focus only on parallelism that is expected to perform well because the frequency of memory access and branch divergence that is caused when different branch operations are required in a warp are more important than parallelism itself in an implementation using CUDA [15] with an NVIDIA GPU.

If multiple weak classifiers of a strong classifier constructed by Informed-Filtersare computed in parallel, a block that is assigned to a streaming multiprocessor in a GPU handles a sub-window extracted from an input image, and each thread that is a smaller computational unit included in a block computes features independently using a weak classifier as shown in Fig. 7. In this case, branch divergence occurs frequently because a branch direction of a weak classifier depends on input data and on branch directions being generally different from each other.

Consequently, the authors use a parallel implementation for search windows as shown in Fig. 8, where a thread is allocated to the computation of a search window. In this implementation, the computation amount allocated to a thread is larger, but there is no branch divergence caused by the computation of a weak classifier composed of a decision tree. To improve the computation speed, the efficient scheme for feature calculation proposed in the previous section is used in addition to the window-based parallel implementation.

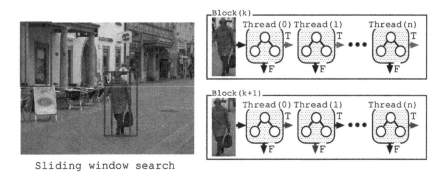

Sliding window search

Fig. 7. Block per window

3.2   Effect of the Soft Cascade Structure

A strong classifier used in this research has a soft cascade structure as shown in Fig. 9. This structure enables fast computation without deterioration in detection accuracy: an input sub-window that does not obviously include a detection

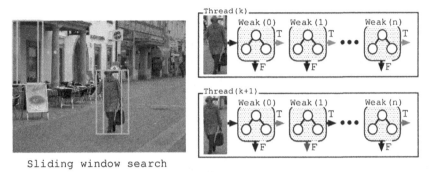

Sliding window search

Fig. 8. Thread per window

target is rejected at an early stage when the accumulated score given by each weak classifier becomes lower than a threshold that is determined prior during the training process. Our implementation may cause branch divergence because some sub-windows are rejected in early stages, but others should be checked by the subsequent stages. Here the branch divergence means a rejection of an input sub-window, and the computation of the thread becomes unnecessary, but the efficiency of parallel execution becomes lower. However, the effect of early rejection by the soft cascade structure is powerful for object detection by a sliding window search because the number of sub-windows not including a target object is much larger than the number of sub-windows including a target object. Therefore, the soft cascade structure of a strong classifier is used in our implementation.

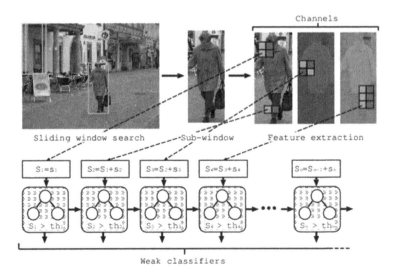

Fig. 9. Softcascade structure

3.3   Memory Access Improvement by the Constant Memory

The implementation described above executes feature computation using the same weak classifier at different threads that are computed in parallel. This operation causes many simultaneous requests to data corresponding to a weak classifier that may decrease the computation speed. To solve this problem, data that retain weak classifiers are stored to the constant memory, which is specially designed cache memory: the constant cache enables high-speed simultaneous accesses from multiple threads. In addition, our implementation is carefully designed to reduce the memory access by using broadcasting of the constant memory that enables simultaneous data transfer between memory and threads in half of a warp: the frequency of data transfer can be reduced to $\frac{1}{16}$ in the best case scenario.

3.4   Efficient Data Transfer Between a CPU and a GPU

Data transfer between a host CPU and a GPU requires huge overhead. Therefore, this kind of operation should be reduced for fast computation. A simple implementation causes images to be copied several times from a CPU to a GPU owing to the multiple channel images used in Informed-Filters. To avoid the increase in data transferred between a CPU and a GPU, only a feature image as shown in Fig. 10 that is generated from multiple channel images is transferred per input image in our implementation.

Fig. 10. Multiple channel images

4   Evaluation

This section evaluates the detection accuracy and the processing speed of the proposed implementation.

4.1   Experimental Conditions

In the evaluation, images as shown in Fig. 11 whose resolution were 2560×1352 were used. In the test images, several humans are located on the field and move appropriately. These images are created using sophisticated three dimensional computer graphics with human models and a field model to generate arbitrary views, where the human positions are determined by actual data obtained from an actual sports scene. Top view images were used because occlusions by other targets can be easily reduced in our project.

To construct a strong classifier, 200 weak classifiers composed of a decision tree whose depth were one was selected using 884 types of filters by Informed-Filters.

The specifications of the computer used to measure the processing speed is shown in Table 1.

Table 1. Computer specifications.

OS	Linux(Ubuntu 16.04)
CPU	Intel(R) Xeon(R) CPU E5-2697 v4 @ 2.30 GHz
Memory	128 GB, DDR4
GPU	GeForce GTX 980 Ti

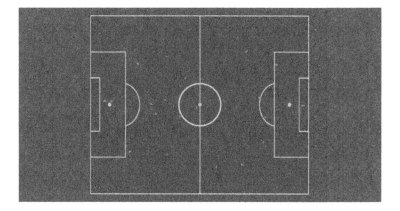

Fig. 11. Test data.

4.2 Detection Accuracy

Figure 12 shows the Detection Error Trade-off (DET) curves plotted using a miss rate and a false positive per image. These results show that the parallel implementation on a GPU can detect target humans the same as the sequential implementation on a CPU.

4.3 Processing Speed

To evaluate the processing speed, the average time consumed for the detection of an image was measured using 3000 test images. Table 2 shows the average processing speed by the parallel implementation on a GPU and the CPU implementation. These results show that the processing speed was about 18.58 times faster if parallel implementation on a GPU was applied. Then, Figs. 13 and 14 show the actual processing time for each test image. According to these results, the processing speed is stably faster if input images are changed.

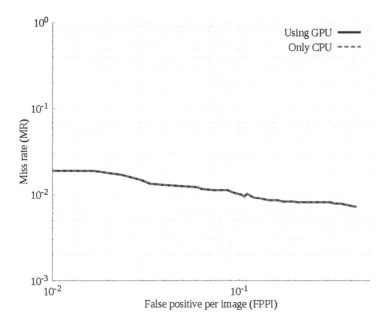

Fig. 12. DET curves.

Table 2. Processing speed.

	GPU	Only CPU
Average time	10.46 ms	186.54 ms

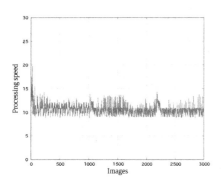

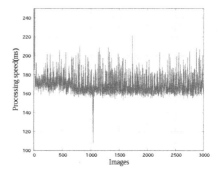

Fig. 13. Execution time for 3000 images by a GPU.

Fig. 14. Execution time for 3000 images by a CPU.

5   Conclusion

This paper proposed the parallel implementation of Informed-Filterson a GPU in order to realize real-time and accurate detection of humans in top view images captured from a camera mounted on a UAV. In our implementation, first computational costs caused by the huge number of read operations required for feature computation using filters composed of cells are reduced. To achieve this reduction, a minimum division for a composite rectangle is applied for filters used in the feature computation. Using this modification, the frequency of memory access to pixels was about 50% that of the straightforward implementation. In the GPU implementation, the authors decide to allocated a thread to a subwindow to reduce branch divergence during feature calculation; this approach seemed more suitable than others when the soft cascade structure was applied with the parallel implementation. In addition to the parallel implementation, appropriate use of the constant memory and a reduction in data transfer between a CPU and a GPU were applied in our implementation. Consequently, the processing speed of human detection in 2560×1532 top view images considering surveillance from UAVs was about 100 frames per second, whereas sequential implementation on a CPU processed at only about 5.4 frames per second.

Acknowledgment. The research results have been achieved thanks to "Research and development of Innovative Network Technologies to Create the Future", the Commissioned Research of National Institute of Information and Communications Technology (NICT), JAPAN.

References

1. Hara, S., Yomo, H., Miyamoto, R., Kawamoto, Y., Okuhata, H., Kawabata, T., Nakamura, H.: Challenges in real-time vital signs monitoring for persons during exercises. Int. J. Wirel. Inf. Netw. **24**(2), 91–108 (2017)
2. Oro, D., Fernández, C., Rodríguez, S.J., Martorell, X., Hernando, J.: Real-time GPU-based face detection in HD video sequences. In: Proceedings of IEEE International Conference on Computer Vision, pp. 530–537 (2011)
3. Benenson, R., Mathias, M., Timofte, R., Van Gool, L.J.: Pedestrian detection at 100 frames per second. In: Proceedings of IEEE Conference on Computer Vision Pattern Recognition, pp. 2903–2910 (2012)
4. Miyamoto, R., Oki, T.: Soccer player detection with only color features selected using informed Haar-like features. In: Blanc-Talon, J., Distante, C., Philips, W., Popescu, D., Scheunders, P. (eds.) ACIVS 2016. LNCS, vol. 10016, pp. 238–249. Springer, Cham (2016). https://doi.org/10.1007/978-3-319-48680-2_22
5. Hiromoto, M., Sugano, H., Miyamoto, R.: Partially parallel architecture for AdaBoost-based detection with Haar-like features. Proc. IEEE Trans. Circ. Syst. Video Technol. **19**, 41–52 (2009)
6. Hiromoto, M., Miyamoto, R.: Hardware architecture for high-accuracy real-time pedestrian detection with CoHOG features. In: Proceedings of IEEE International Conference on Computer Vision Workshops, pp. 894–899 (2009)

7. Hiromoto, M., Miyamoto, R.: Cascade classifier using divided CoHOG features for rapid Pedestrian detection. In: Fritz, M., Schiele, B., Piater, J.H. (eds.) ICVS 2009. LNCS, vol. 5815, pp. 53–62. Springer, Heidelberg (2009). https://doi.org/10.1007/978-3-642-04667-4_6

8. Yu, J., Miyamoto, R., Onoye, T.: Fast pedestrian detection using a soft-cascade of the CoHOG-based classier: how to speed-up SVM classiers based on multiple-instance pruning. IEEE Trans. Image Process. **22**, 4752–4761 (2013)

9. Zhang, S., Benenson, R., Schiele, B.: Filtered channel features for Pedestrian detection. In: Proceedings of IEEE Conference on Computer Vision Pattern Recognition, pp. 1751–1760 (2015)

10. Redmon, J., Divvala, S.K., Girshick, R.B., Farhadi, A.: You only look once: unified, real-time object detection. In: Proceedings of IEEE Conference on Computer Vision Pattern Recognition, pp. 779–788 (2016)

11. Redmon, J., Farhadi, A.: YOLO9000: better, faster, stronger. In: Proceedings of IEEE Conference on Computer Vision Pattern Recognition, pp. 6517–6525 (2017)

12. Dollár, P., Tu, Z., Perona, P., Belongie, S.J.: Integral channel features. In: Proceedings of British Machine Vision Conference, pp. 1–11 (2009)

13. Nam, W., Dollár, P., Joon, H.H.: Local decorrelation for improved pedestrian detection. In: Proceedings of Advances in Neural Information Processing Systems, pp. 424–432 (2014)

14. Ohtsuki, T., Sato, M., Tachibana, M., Torii, S.: Minimum partitioning of rectilinear regions. IPSJ J. **24**, 647–653 (1983)

15. NVIDIA Corporation: nVidia CUDA Programming Guide. http://docs.nvidia.com/cuda/

Automatic Problem Understanding
from Circuit Schematics

Xinguo Yu[1], Pengpeng Jian[1], Bin He[1(✉)], Gang Zhao[2],
and Meng Xia[1]

[1] National Engineering Research Center for E-Learning,
Central China Normal University, Wuhan, China
{xgyu,hebin}@mail.ccnu.edu.cn,
{jianpengpeng,xiameng}@mails.ccnu.edu.cn
[2] School of Educational Information Technology,
Central China Normal University, Wuhan, China
zhaogang@mail.ccnu.edu.cn

Abstract. This paper presents an algorithm for understanding problems from circuit schematics in exercise problems in physics at secondary school. This paper models the problem understanding as a problem of extracting a set of relations that can be used to solve problems with enough information. The challenges lie in not only analyzing the circuit schematics but also extracting the proper relations for a given exercise problem. To face these challenges a novel approach is proposed to detect circuit nodes with their current flows to extract the current equations for nodes. And the other novel approach is proposed to extract voltage equations of independent loops. The proposed approach was tested with a dataset collected from the text books and the exam papers for the students at secondary schools. Experimental results show that the effect of recognition and analysis we designed delivers promising result, and our approach can be adapted to more complex electrical circuit analysis.

Keywords: Circuit schematic · Symbols recognition · Problem understanding
Extract equations

1 Introduction

The analysis and understanding of circuit schematic is the necessary way to solve circuit problems for secondary school students, but it is a challenge for machine to not only analyze the circuit schematics but also extract the proper relations for a given circuit problem. To face this challenge, this paper proposes to extract enough information for problem understanding by using circuit schematic diagram analysis. In general, a circuit problem is provided as a text in natural language together with circuit schematic, and a correct answer must be provided, typically in the form of an answering list with circuit equations, reasoning processes and answers. Equations are often extracted from the analysis of circuit schematic, such as voltage and current relationship (shorted for VCR) is extracted from the identification of resistance components, node current equations can be obtained by analyzing nodes together with their current flows and so on.

© Springer International Publishing AG, part of Springer Nature 2018
M. Paul et al. (Eds.): PSIVT 2017, LNCS 10749, pp. 314–325, 2018.
https://doi.org/10.1007/978-3-319-75786-5_26

The task of circuit schematic analysis has received growing interest in recent years [1, 2]. One of the more interesting phenomenon of this research is that it combines visual question answering, web-based learning and intelligent tutoring system [4–6]. Symbolic analysis of linear circuit networks is the backbone of the design of electronic and systems [3]. The main task of this method is to obtain several algebraic expressions for corresponding specified circuit network functions. What's more, for the correctness of algebraic expressions, the validation method of symbolic expressions using both sets of control variables simultaneously was presented in [1]. However, this method is useful for linear networks, but for more complex networks (i.e., complicated circuit) it needs further optimization. Web-based approach [4] is another type of circuit analysis method that it stored a set of previously derived expressions into a database, and when an input is coming, the method will compare it with stored expressions. Whereas if the input is creative or unusual that several different solution paths could be exist, then obtaining a set of required equations from the database is a time-consuming work.

Another approach is based upon the introduction of a set of new variables (symbols) [5, 6]. By introducing appropriate nodes and loops, either a set of node voltages or a suitable set of loop currents can be used for forming Kirchhoff's voltage laws equations or Kirchhoff's current laws equations. But one of the challenge is that how to get the appropriate circuit nodes with the directions of current flows all around themselves automatically by machine, such as the node 1 and its current flows (I_2, I_4, I_5) in Fig. 1(a), and the other challenge is how to obtain independent loops, such as m1, m2 and m3 in Fig. 1(a).

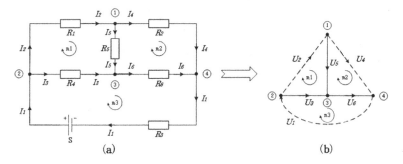

Fig. 1. Circuit schematic example

In this paper, a novel approach is presented to extract symbolic equations automatically by detecting circuit elements (i.e., components, nodes). The recognition of circuit elements by machine is the basic work for our approach. In order to detect the nodes with their current flows, the algorithm of node detection, LSD [10, 13] and the method of connectivity traversal will be orderly used. In the respect of extracting voltage equations of independent loops, a novel approach of simplifying the system of whole loop voltage's homogeneous linear equations is proposed. It is then show how this can be achieved to cover all circuit schematic and forming circuit equations corresponding to the physical quantities.

The remaining sections of this paper are organized as follows. In the following section, the analytical approach for circuit schematic is explained in detail. Section 3 deals with the elements recognition of circuit schematic by using image processing methods. In Sect. 4, detailed understanding procedure of circuit schematic is demonstrated with an auto-identifying algorithm. In Sect. 5, results of an actual test experiments are shown and discussed. Finally, in Sect. 6, conclusions are presented.

2 Analytical Approach of Circuit Schematic

The analytical approach focus on the recognition and analysis of circuit schematic. The section of circuit schematic recognition is to identify the elements of circuit schematic (i.e., components, nodes and so on), and the circuit schematic analysis section is used to obtain equations by analyzing two types of constraints (i.e., topology constraint and component constraint). The answers of circuit schematic problem are quantified by solving two kinds of simultaneous equations.

2.1 The Recognition of Circuit Elements

As soon as the circuit schematic is loaded into the system, three kings of fundamental recognition for circuit elements will be executed through a series of circuit schematic recognition algorithms: the tesseract OCR engine [12] is used to locate and recognize the characters and numbers of circuit labels, the approach of SVM [7, 11] is used to recognize circuit components, the approach of improved line segment detector (short for LSD) algorithm and nodes detection algorithm are used to obtain circuit nodes with their current flows. Then, a set of circuit labels, components (i.e., resistor, light, ammeter, voltmeter and so on) and nodes are identified. For each element symbol, the required properties are stored in a table.

2.2 Two Kinds of Constraints

The running state of circuit is determined by the components of circuit and the interconnection of each component. To summarize the analysis content of circuit schematic, two types of constraints should be understood clearly.

Component Constraint

Component constraint is determined by the nature of circuit elements, i.e. resistance, capacitor, inductance and power supply, so getting the properties of these four elements is the basis of circuit analysis. Besides, voltmeter and ammeter are tools for auxiliary measurement, and some appliances are the deformation of circuit elements, such as the light bulb is a resistive load. As is known to all, current, voltage and power are the basic quantities of physics analysis, however, power is the product of voltage and current. So, the essential thing for the single circuit element is to master the voltage and current relationship (short for VCR). With component constraint, VCR equations will be obtained by Ohm's law or other variant of Ohm's law.

Topology Constraint

Topology constraint is determined by the structure of circuit schematic and Kirchhoff's law is used to analyze the operation law of electricity in the circuit structure. Kirchhoff's current law (short for KCL) implies that: The algebraic sum of currents in a network of conductors meeting at a point is zero. Recalling that current is a signed (positive or negative) quantity reflecting direction towards or away from a node, this principle can be stated as: $\sum_{k=1}^{n} I_k = 0$.

Here, n is the total number of branches with currents flowing towards or away from the node. For example, the circuit node 1 and its current flows (I_2, I_4, I_5) is shown in Fig. 1(a), and the equation $I_2 - I_4 - I_5 = 0$ will be written by KCL.

Kirchhoff's voltage law (short for KVL) implies that: The directed sum of the electrical potential differences (voltage) around any closed network is zero, and it can be described as: $\sum_{k=1}^{n} V_k = 0$.

Here, n is the total number of voltages measured. For example, the circuit loop (mesh) m1 and its specified direction is shown in Fig. 1(b), and the equation $U_2 + U_5 - U_3 = 0$ will be written by KVL.

By analyzing topology constraint, two sets of equations will be obtained by KCL and KVL.

2.3   The Procedure of Analysis for Circuit Schematic

In general, the behavior of a circuit network is often governed by three sets of equations: VCR equations, KCL equations and KVL equations. Because of the topology constraint of KCL and KVL is adopted in the analysis of circuit nodes and loops, and the component constraint has been well embedded in the VCR theorems such as Ohm's law, so we only consider the circuit elements (i.e. Resistance and power supply), independent nodes and independent loops of a circuit schematic. The overall implementation procedure of analytical approach for circuit schematic are summarized as follows.

Procedure I: Analytical Approach of Circuit Schematic

Input: a physics problem text with corresponding circuit schematic.
Output: the recognition and analysis process for circuit schematic.
Step 1: circuit symbols recognition and screening of circuit components for VCR equations.
Step 2: circuit branch lines detection and circuit nodes detection.
Step 3: connectivity traversal based on circuit nodes to judge and set the reference directions of branch currents and detour directions of independent loops.
Step 4: independent nodes detection and extract node current equations by KCL.
Step 5: independent loops detection and extract loop voltage equations by KVL.

---

3   Circuit Schematic Recognition

3.1   The Recognition of Circuit Components

Circuit components are the basic elements of circuit schematic, whose properties contain more information on circuit understanding (i.e., current, voltage or VCR information). The goal of the detection algorithm is to recognize the components and line-linking in a circuit schematic. In particular, this algorithm strives to obtain VCR equations by analyzing circuit schematic in a digital document, which includes textual question stems and circuit schematics. Through the preprocessing, content representations (i.e., PDF images and circuit schematics) are rapidly extracted from a given digital document by using method [8, 14]. In addition, a segmentation process approach [15] is implemented to separate the textual and non-textual components in a diagram and circuit region is located by a convex bounding operation of non-text classes. In the framework, the textual and circuit schematic content of a document will be processed by our algorithms.

Circuit Labels Recognition

There are two kinds of circuit labels: the label outside the component (i.e., the label "R_1" and "S" in Fig. 1(a)) and the label inside the component (i.e., the label "A" of an ammeter) which is a part of the component. Initially, both circuit labels will be located and recognized by our method and the recognized labels inside the component is needed to populate back to the diagram.

First, the tesseract OCR engine [12] is adopted to locate and recognize the characters and numbers of circuit labels. Only clusters have a structure of "C", "Cn" and "Cnn" will be accepted as a valid label, in which "C" stands for character and "n" for number. Recording all the candidate labels and their locations in a table named T_{label}. Second, characters and number belonging to voltmeter, ammeter and motor are pushed back to the diagram, i.e. the character of "V" and "A" will be drawn back to diagram and they still in T_{label} as an accepted label. Besides, in order to avoid destroying the original image feature of circuit, we calculate a bounding rectangle for each of them and copy the pixel value of each rectangle from the source figure to the circuit schematic, instead of redrawing these characters.

Components Recognition

There are more than thirteen types of circuit components in physics at secondary school, and six most commonly used components are chosen as the target of recognition. What's more, a classification approach SVM was used to recognize the components of circuit schematic.

Component symbols segmentation is an important work that seriously affect the accuracy of recognition. In a circuit schematic, symbols are usually presented between two collinear segments. Based on this regularity, the gaps between two collinear segments are collected and the bounding rectangles G are calculated, and then removing blank rectangles in G which contain no symbols by contours analyzing. The process of symbols location and recognition are shown in Fig. 2.

Due to battery(s) symbol contains two or more separate connective component (i.e., Fig. 2(a)), a joint model is used for accurate battery symbols segmentation. In this

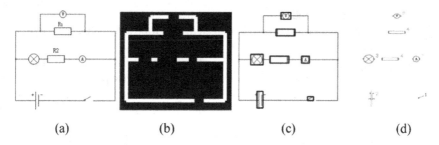

Fig. 2. Symbols location and recognition. (a) Input image (b) Overstriking mask of segment gaps (c) Bounding box on contours (d) Recognition results

model, we analyze the connectivity of each set of online segments and generate a default bounding box between two online segments. Then a combination operating is implemented on results of contour segmentation on gaps and all default boxes. The final segmentation results are shown in Fig. 2(c).

The corresponding sub-figure defined by box r in Fig. 2(c) is considered as a candidate circuit symbols and is resized to 32 * 32. Then the sub-figure is reshaped to a size of 1 * 1024 row vector which is used as the input of SVM classifier for training and prediction. A recognized sub-figure located by r is defined as a 3-element row vector *symbol* stored in a vector S:

$$symbol = (typeID, label, r)$$

Where, *label* is the corresponding label found in T_{label} according to the position correlation, *TypeID* denotes the symbol type obtained by SVM prediction. The final components recognition results are shown in Fig. 2(d).

3.2   Node Detection Algorithm of Circuit Schematic

According to KCL, choosing an arbitrary circuit node, the sum of currents flowing into the node is equal to the sum of currents flowing out of the node or equivalently, so the goal of this section is to detect the whole nodes of a circuit schematic. As soon as the circuit nodes are detected, a set of KCL equations for each nodes is obtained. In this subsection, we briefly describe the branch lines detection and nodes detection in a circuit schematic.

Branch Lines Detection
The main work in this section is to detect the short lines from circuit diagram. Symbols are connected by vertical and horizontal short lines, while some short lines are part of symbols. In reality, only connecting lines are remained by the approach of detection, which is based on LSD [10, 13]. Salient segments are removed and short segments are merged to amend the defects by a set of optimization processes.

There are three possible defects in the lines detected from a diagram by applying LSD algorithm: (1) a visually line segment may be detected as a series of unconnected parallel short ones, (2) a line in the figure is detected as some disconnected short segments, (3) the start or end points of a sub-circuit and the turning points of two connective segments cannot be accurately detected. The following sub steps are used to amend the defects.

To solve these problems, a set of optimization processes is performed. For each segment, we first find out all co-line segments as a segment group, then remove those segments far away from others and finally merge the remained segments into a new longer one. The distance between endpoints of two different segments is used for segments grouping. For example, in stage of grouping, put seed segment l_{vi} selected from L_v into a new group G_{vi}, add all co-line segments l_{vj} into G_{vi} if $dist(l_{vi}, l_{vj}) < \tau_v$, and remove l_{vj} from L_v. Where, τ_v is a pre-specified distance tolerance, $dist(l_{vi}, l_{vj})$ is the Euler distance. In stage of short segments merging, pair (l_{vi}, l_{vj}) is replaced by a new segment l'_{vi} when $co(l_{vi}, l_{vj}) > \delta_v$, where $co(\ ,\ )$ is the overlapping ratio on Y axis of (l_{vi}, l_{vj}), δ_v is a pre-specified tolerance. Put l'_{vi} into L'_v. Same strategies are used to merge short segments in L_h into L'_h.

On phase of gap detection, adjacency collinear segments are merged, and gaps between two collinear segments are detected. The graph in the bounding area of each gap is probably a circuit component symbol. Pairs of parallel segments which are part of the resistor and the battery may also be detected in clusters L'_v and L'_h. These pairs are removed before the operation of segments merging and gap detecting.

Circuit Nodes Detection

In the circuit topology, fork nodes denote the starting and ending of a parallel connection. Degree analyzing is applied to identify fork nodes from all intersection nodes in this step. Before degree analyzing, circuit will be converted to a connected graph $G_{connected}$ by combination of the position of row symbols vector S and segments clusters L'_v and L'_h.

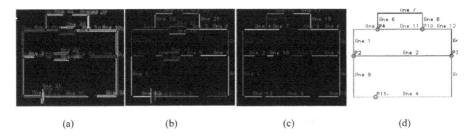

(a)   (b)   (c)   (d)

Fig. 3. Branch lines and nodes detection. (a) Segments detection (b) Sallient segments removing (c) Resistor and power symbol location (d) Recognize circuit structure and fork nodes

Two types of intersection nodes, including turning node and fork node, exist in the circuit. Degree analyzing is implemented in this step to identify fork node. The degree of a node d is defined by the number of segments connected. For each intersection node $n_i (1 \leq i \leq N)$, count the numbers of adjacency segments $degree(n_i)$. If $degree(n_i) \geq 3$, then node n_i is marked as a fork node. The battery position in the diagram is treated as the start and end point of the circuit, which is marked a fork node n_0. The process of branch lines and nodes detection is shown in Fig. 3.

4 Circuit Schematic Analysis

After the segmentation and connection analyzing, symbols are recognized (Fig. 2(d)) and fork nodes are obtained (Fig. 3(d)). In this section, the extraction method of independent node current equations and independent loop voltage equations based on circuit schematic diagram analysis is proposed. Before the extraction, a node connection traversal algorithm is introduced to find the available paths among fork nodes and to get the directions such as current directions and voltage directions all around fork nodes.

4.1 Connectivity Traversal Based on Circuit Nodes

Connection traversal described in this section is a special kind traversal which uses depth first algorithm for traversing and searching a max length connective path in the connected graph $G_{connected}$ in the first main path searching phase followed by a shortest path traversal in the sub path searching phase. Before vertex traversing, the connective segments between two adjacency fork nodes are linked and marked as an edge of the circuit graph.

Different with traditional DFS in graph theory, not all nodes are visited in one traversal path and some special strategies are defined as follows:

Strategy 1. The main path start from n_0 and end with n_0.
Strategy 2. The main path contains the maximum number of fork nodes.
Strategy 3. No repeated nodes in main path.
Strategy 4. No repeated edges in main path.
Strategy 5. The beginning and end nodes of each sub path are from the main path or sub path traversed.

For each adjacency fork node pair (n_i, n_j), $0 \leq i \neq j \leq N$, the edge from n_i to n_j is marked as $s_i = \{l_p\}$, where l_p is the segments between n_i and n_j.

The algorithm begins with vertex n_0, it then iteratively transitions from the current vertex to an adjacent, unvisited vertex, until it can no longer find an unexplored vertex to transition to from its current location. Then, the algorithm backtracks along previously visited vertices, until it finds a vertex connected to yet more uncharted territory. It will then proceed down the new path as it had before, backtracking as it encounters dead-ends, and ending only when the algorithm has backtracked past the vertex n_0 from the very first step.

Then, a sub path m_{i+1} is defined as a shortest path walking along the unvisited edges between each pair of visited node in the path set $M = \{m_0, \cdots, m_i\}$. The searching starts from m_0, for each node n_k in m_0, find the shortest sub path starting with n_k and put it to M. Do searching process for each path in M until these is no new path can be found.

4.2 Independent Node Identification

A well-known fundamental set of independent loop currents may be obtained by considering an arbitrary spanning tree and linking in each of the remaining edges (branches) of the circuit's graph [1]. If each circuit node is identified by a specific circuit symbol, any node current equations in the circuit schematic can be obtain by the topology constraint of KCL. This is a general method to form node current equations, but the problem is how to get independent nodes with their equations.

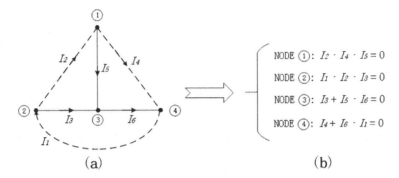

NODE ①: $I_2 \cdot I_4 \cdot I_5 = 0$

NODE ②: $I_1 \cdot I_2 \cdot I_3 = 0$

NODE ③: $I_3 + I_5 \cdot I_6 = 0$

NODE ④: $I_4 + I_6 \cdot I_1 = 0$

(a)   (b)

Fig. 4. Circuit nodes analysis

In order to clarify the analysis of circuit nodes, the simplified circuit schematic in Fig. 4 is used. The six branches describing the connection of the circuit are associated with four circuit nodes in Fig. 4(a). For the currents, a straightforward choice is to choose an arbitrary node as a reference and to analyze the current flows all around this node. Any node current equations in the network can be obtained by KCL as shown in Fig. 4(b). However, the four node current equations in the example are obviously linear dependent because of anyone equation can be derived by other three equations. In the process of solving, independent nodes or linear independent equations are required, so the method is simply remove any circuit node with its current equation.

4.3   Independent Circuit Loops Detection

For the voltages, an effective way is to find circuit loops that corresponding loop voltage equations can be written by KVL in topology constraint. In the process of connectivity traversal based on circuit nodes, the whole circuit loops can automatically be detected with voltage directions. Then, any different voltages in the circuit network will be involved by the relation of circuit loop voltages.

The proposed approach can be demonstrated through an example. The structure of circuit schematic Fig. 1(a) is shown in Fig. 5(a) and is asked to extract loop voltage equations. With connectivity traversal for circuit schematic, seven circuit loops were detected in Fig. 5(b). Corresponding to these loops, seven loop voltage equations can be obtained by KVL. It may prove to be more elegant to extract loop voltage equations, but some dependent loops were also extracted such as LOOP 6 contained LOOP 5 and LOOP 7 in Fig. 5(b). If linear dependent equations are present in equations group, the process of solving equations may drop into an endless loop. So a method of extracting independent loops by simplifying the system of homogeneous linear equations is proposed in Fig. 6.

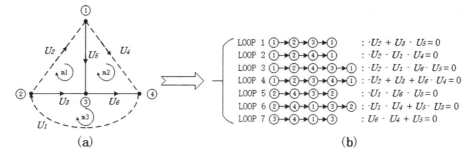

Fig. 5. Circuit loops analysis

$$
\begin{aligned}
&\cdot U_2 + U_3 \cdot U_5 = 0 \\
&\cdot U_2 \cdot U_1 \cdot U_4 = 0 \\
&\cdot U_2 \cdot U_1 \cdot U_6 \cdot U_5 = 0 \\
&\cdot U_2 + U_3 + U_6 \cdot U_4 = 0 \\
&\cdot U_1 \cdot U_6 \cdot U_3 = 0 \\
&\cdot U_1 \cdot U_4 + U_5 \cdot U_3 = 0 \\
&U_6 \cdot U_4 + U_5 = 0
\end{aligned}
$$

(a)

$$
\begin{pmatrix}
0 & -1 & 1 & 0 & -1 & 0 \\
-1 & -1 & 0 & -1 & 0 & 0 \\
-1 & -1 & 0 & 0 & -1 & -1 \\
0 & -1 & 1 & -1 & 0 & 1 \\
-1 & 0 & -1 & 0 & 0 & -1 \\
-1 & 0 & -1 & -1 & 1 & 0 \\
0 & 0 & 0 & -1 & 1 & 1
\end{pmatrix}
$$

(b)

$\sim$

$$
\begin{pmatrix}
1 & 0 & 1 & 0 & 0 & 1 \\
0 & 1 & -1 & 0 & 1 & 0 \\
0 & 0 & 0 & 1 & -1 & -1 \\
0 & 0 & 0 & 0 & 0 & 0 \\
0 & 0 & 0 & 0 & 0 & 0 \\
0 & 0 & 0 & 0 & 0 & 0 \\
0 & 0 & 0 & 0 & 0 & 0
\end{pmatrix}
$$

(b)

$$
\begin{aligned}
&U_1 + U_3 + U_6 = 0 \\
&U_2 \cdot U_3 + U_5 = 0 \\
&U_4 \cdot U_5 \cdot U_6 = 0
\end{aligned}
$$

(c)

Fig. 6. Independent circuit loops detection

A set of homogeneous linear equations is shown in Fig. 6(a), and the target is to extract independent loops such as m_1, m_2 and m_3 in Fig. 5(a). Our work is to extract the coefficients of the set of homogeneous linear equations that forming a coefficient matrix, and then simplifying the coefficient matrix to the simplest, which is shown in Fig. 6(b). Through simplification, the independent loops can be detected and the voltage equations of independent loops can also be written in Fig. 6(c).

5   Experiments

5.1   Experiment Setup

Dataset: The dataset contains 145 circuit schematics in physics at secondary school, which were collected from the textbook of secondary school and the academic test for the junior high school students. There are six kinds of components such as resistor, slide resistor, light, ammeter, voltmeter and power supply in circuit schematic will be recognized by our approach. The statistics of these components in dataset are shown in Table 1.

Table 1. Statistics on the dataset of experiment

	#CS	#R	#SR	#L	#A	#V	#S
Total	145	180	67	138	96	76	145

Note: #CS = Circuit schematic,
#R = Resistor, #SR = Slide resistor,
#L = Light, #A = Ammeter, #V = Voltmeter,
#S = Power supply.

5.2   Experimental Results

To test the generality and practicability of our approach, we have made experiments on the prepared dataset and part of the results are shown in Table 2.

Table 2. Part of experimental results

No.	1	2	3	460	3100	3740	3750	3820	3890	3930
N_s	7	6	6	6	6	6	5	6	6	5
N_f	5	2	2	5	5	4	2	2	4	2
T	85.45	97.97	81.8	53.08	69.19	57.28	59.81	86.42	61.45	67.52

N_s: the number of symbols recognized, N_f: the number of fork node calculated, T: processing time (ms).

Table 2 shows a part of our experimental results. More circuit schematics and corresponding results are available in http://pan.baidu.com/s/1kUKwcV9. In the experiment, our approach in the identification of circuit symbols has got a good performance that almost all the results are correct. The method of circuit node detection is also meet the design requirements. At the same time, we count the time of processing in Table 2 that indicates our approach is a time-saving work.

6   Conclusions

This paper has presented an algorithm for understanding the physics problems at secondary school by extracting the relations from circuit schematics. The algorithm first recognizes the circuit schematics, and then it extracts an enough set of relations. The main contributions of the paper are multiple. The first one is that it proposes the concept of independent node and the method to identity this type of nodes form a given circuit schematics. The second one is that it proposes the concept of independent loop and the method to identity this type of loops from a given circuit schematics. The third one is that it shows that the set of relations extracted from independent nodes and independent loops from a given circuit schematics are enough for solving the given problem. The experimental results show that the proposed algorithm is very promising in solving the concerning type of exercise problems.

Two of more jobs can be done in the future based on the results of this paper. We first can study how to use the deep learning algorithm to extract relations. Then we can do research on extracting relations from more complex circuit schematics.

Acknowledgment. This work has been supported by the project "Research on interactive virtual exhibition technology for Tujia Nationality's Brocade Culture" (No. 2015BAK27B02) under the National Science & Technology Supporting Program during the Twelfth Five-year Plan Period granted by the Ministry of Science and Technology of China.

References

1. Weyten, L., Rombouts, P., Catteau, B., De Bock, M.: Validation of symbolic expressions in circuit analysis e-learning. IEEE Trans. Educ. **54**, 564–568 (2011)
2. Ozogul, G., Johnson, A.M., Moreno, R., Reisslein, M.: Technological literacy learning with cumulative and stepwise integration of equations into electrical circuit diagrams. IEEE Trans. Educ. **55**, 480–487 (2012)
3. Huelsman, L.P.: Symbolic analysis-a tool for teaching undergraduate circuit theory. IEEE Trans. Educ. **39**, 243–250 (1996)
4. Weyten, L., Rombouts, P., De Maeyer, J.: Web-based trainer for electrical circuit analysis. IEEE Trans. Educ. **52**, 185–189 (2009)
5. Reisslein, J., Johnson, A.M., Reisslein, M.: Color coding of circuit quantities in introductory circuit analysis instruction. IEEE Trans. Educ. **58**, 7–14 (2015)
6. Johnson, A.M., Butcher, K.R., Ozogul, G., Reisslein, M.: Introductory circuit analysis learning from abstract and contextualized circuit representations: effects of diagram labels. IEEE Trans. Educ. **57**, 160–168 (2014)
7. Chang, C.-C., Lin, C.-J.: LIBSVM: a library for support vector machines. ACM Trans. Intell. Syst. Technol. (TIST), **2**, 27 (2011)
8. Chiu, P., Chen, F., Denoue, L.: Picture detection in document page images. In: Proceedings of the 10th ACM Symposium on Document Engineering, pp. 211–214. ACM (2010)
9. Mandal, P.D.S., Bhowmick, P., Chanda, B.: Topological simplification of electrical circuits by super-component analysis. In: 2015 13th International Conference on Document Analysis and Recognition (ICDAR), pp. 211–215. IEEE (2015)
10. Von Gioi, R.G., Jakubowicz, J., Morel, J.-M., Randall, G.: LSD: a fast line segment detector with a false detection control. IEEE Trans. Pattern Anal. Mach. Intell. **32**, 722–732 (2010)
11. Schölkopf, B., Smola, A.J., Williamson, R.C., Bartlett, P.L.: New support vector algorithms. Neural Comput. **12**, 1207–1245 (2000)
12. Smith, R.: An overview of the tesseract OCR engine. In: 2007 Ninth International Conference on Document Analysis and Recognition, ICDAR 2007, pp. 629–633. IEEE (2007)
13. Wang, H.-Y., Pan, D.-L., Xia, D.-S.: A fast algorithm for two-dimensional Otsu adaptive threshold algorithm. Acta Automatica Sinica **33**, 968–971 (2007)
14. Xu, C., Tang, Z., Tao, X., Shi, C.: Graphic composite segmentation for PDF documents with complex layouts. In: Proceedings of SPIE Document Recognition and Retrieval XX, p. 8658 (2013)
15. Zirari, F., Ennaji, A., Nicolas, S., Mammass, D.: A simple text/graphic separation method for document image segmentation. In: 2013 ACS International Conference on Computer Systems and Applications (AICCSA), pp. 1–4. IEEE (2013)

Feature Similarity and Frequency-Based Weighted Visual Words Codebook Learning Scheme for Human Action Recognition

Saima Nazir[1], Muhammad Haroon Yousaf[1(✉)], and Sergio A. Velastin[2]

[1] University of Engineering and Technology Taxila, Taxila, Pakistan
saima_nazir_91@yahoo.com, haroon.yousaf@uettaxila.edu.pk
[2] Universidad Carlos III de Madrid, Madrid, Spain
sergio.velastin@ieee.org

Abstract. Human action recognition has become a popular field for computer vision researchers in the recent decade. This paper presents a human action recognition scheme based on a textual information concept inspired by document retrieval systems. Videos are represented using a commonly used local feature representation. In addition, we formulate a new weighted class specific dictionary learning scheme to reflect the importance of visual words for a particular action class. Weighted class specific dictionary learning enriches the scheme to learn a sparse representation for a particular action class. To evaluate our scheme on realistic and complex scenarios, we have tested it on UCF Sports and UCF11 benchmark datasets. This paper reports experimental results that outperform recent state-of-the-art methods for the UCF Sports and the UCF11 dataset i.e. 98.93% and 93.88% in terms of average accuracy respectively. To the best of our knowledge, this contribution is first to apply a weighted class specific dictionary learning method on realistic human action recognition datasets.

Keywords: Human action recognition · Bag of visual words
Spatio-temporal features · UCF Sports

1 Introduction

Human action recognition is an emerging research area in computer vision, aiming at automatic classification of action present in a video. It has numerous applications such as intelligent surveillance systems, video search and retrieval, video indexing and human-computer interaction. Regardless of its popularity, it is one of the challenging problems in computer vision. Challenges include inter and intra class variation, changing viewpoint, cluttered background, camera motion etc. The low quality and high dimension of video data typically add difficulty to develop efficient and robust human action recognition algorithm.

© Springer International Publishing AG, part of Springer Nature 2018
M. Paul et al. (Eds.): PSIVT 2017, LNCS 10749, pp. 326–336, 2018.
https://doi.org/10.1007/978-3-319-75786-5_27

Spatio-temporal features are extensively used for recognizing human actions [2,11,18,20] and have gained the state-of-the-art recognition performance on many challenging action recognition datasets. These approaches do not need to detect human body, rather they treat the action volume as a rigid 3D-object and extract appropriate features to describe the patterns of each 3D volume. They are robust to illumination changes, background clutter, and noise [20].

The Bag of visual words (BoVW) approach along with local features representation and its variations [15,20] have have proved to be effective for human action recognition especially for realistic datasets and it is popular due to its simplicity and computational efficiency. BoVW approach for human action recognition consists of four steps in general i.e. feature representation, codebook generation, feature encoding, and action classification. In each step, many efforts have been made for improvement.

Many local features representation approaches has been presented in literature [16]. Popular feature detectors include Dense Trajectories [23], STIPs [5] etc. and feature descriptors includes 3D SIFT [19], MBH [23], HOF [6], HOG for action representation. For visual word codebook generation, k-mean is a popular approach used for providing a partition for local descriptors in local feature space [4]. For feature encoding many methods are available for effective and efficient representation (Peng et al. [16] for detail study).

How to make decision in each step to obtain the best variation of BoVW for action recognition still remains unknown and needs to be extensively explored. In this work, we present a scheme to recognize human action using weighted visual word codebook learning. The work is based on our preliminary work [13], where general bag of visual words approach has been evaluated for recognizing human action in realistic and complex scenarios using spatio-temporal features.

Our previous work shows that performance can be significantly improved in complex and realistic scenarios by incorporating spatio-temporal domain information to represent an action in form of visual features. We have used the state-of-the art space time interest point detector and descriptor to capture the maximum possible information to represent an action. It represents video by utilizing characteristic shape and motion, independent of space time shifts. No prior segmentation like individual segmentation is needed for this approach. Our method is general and shows better results on different type of human action recognition datasets. We have also performed comparison with the state-of-art result for three different human action recognition datasets i.e. KTH, UCF Sports and Hollywood2.

We extend our proposed model from [13] and learn a concatenated weighted class specific dictionary. The proposed scheme assigns weights to each visual word with respect to its feature similarity and occurrence frequency *within* its action class so as t have a more efficient representation of an action class. For evaluation, we analyze our method on human action recognition benchmark datasets and show that our model outperforms the traditional bag-of-words approach.

The rest of paper is organized as follows. In Sect. 2 we describe our proposed weighted visual word codebook learning scheme. We introduce the weighting mechanism used for weight assignment by incorporating the importance of each visual word with respect to its feature similarity and occurrence frequency within its action class. In Sect. 3 we evaluate the importance of each parameter for our proposed approach and also compares our work with recent state-of-the-art methods. Section 4 presents the main conclusions and state the potential future direction for the proposed scheme.

2 Human Action Recognition Using Weighted Visual Words Codebook

Figure 1 provides an overview of the proposed scheme used for recognition of human action using weighted visual words codebook. Firstly, features are represented using a local feature representation approach followed by learning a weighted class specific dictionary. Feature encoding is performed to represent each input video using the histogram of weighted visual words. Finally, this histogram representation for training videos is used to train a supervised classifier. Similarly, during the testing phase, feature representation is obtained for unlabeled videos and quantized using the weighted codebook generated during the training phase. Feature encoding is performed to obtain a histogram of weighted visual words for testing videos and passed to trained classifier to obtain action labels. These processes are explained in more detail in the following sub-sections.

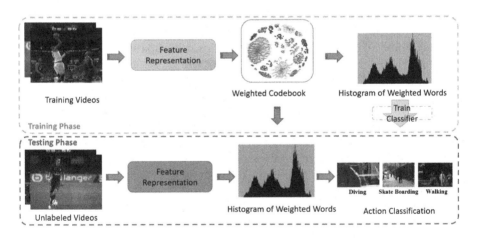

Fig. 1. Human action recognition using weighted visual words codebook scheme.

2.1 Feature Representation

A variety of feature representation methods exists for video representation. As proposed in [12], we use the popular 3D Harris interest point detector [5] to detect well-localized interest points in the spatio-temporal domain. These detected interest points are represented as $P = \{P_i \,|\, P_i \in (x, y, t)^n{}_{i=1}\}$. Detected interest points are shown (in space domain only) in Fig. 2. Further, we used the 3D SIFT descriptor [19] to describe these detected spatio-temporal interest points. 3D SIFT provides robustness to noise and orientation by encoding information in both space and time domains. Here feature vector is represented as $F = \{f_i\}^n{}_{i=1}$.

Fig. 2. Few detected space time interest points on example videos for UCF Sports dataset.

2.2   Weighted Class Specific Dictionary Learning

In the next step, we learn a weighted class specific dictionary which is discriminative enough to differentiate between each action class, by considering the relevance of each visual word within its action class. Consider the feature representation of an action class grouped together as $PF_l = \{P_i, F_i\}^{n_l}{}_{i=1}$, where n_l is the total no. of features l action class. We applied the popular k-means clustering algorithm [4] for the feature set PF_l and divide it into k clusters. Each cluster center is associated with a visual word. We formulated a weighting scheme for previously learned class specific dictionary based on a textual information concept. According to this concept words with high frequency describes a document better while the words occurrence frequency also depends on the length of a document [21]. Based on this concept, we assign a weight parameter WW_x to each visual word, μ_x (see below) is used to measure the similarity of a particular visual word with its action class. As a result, weight is calculated as

$$Weight(w_x) = \mu_x + WW_x \tag{1}$$

where μ_x is defined as

$$\mu_x = \frac{K(Fw_x, F_l)}{||wp_x - P_l||^2} \tag{2}$$

$K(Fw_x, F_l)$ is the cosine similarity measure between feature description of visual word w_x and set of feature vector F_l for class l. μ_x becomes low for the words that are too far and high for the words that are too close because of the distance value for wp_x and P_l, resulting in providing insignificant information in both cases. In such case we can ignore the value of μ_x.

In Eq. 8. WW_x provide an additional parameter to highlight the importance of a visual word within its action class according to its occurrence frequency.

We emphasize the visual words with high frequency by normalizing their occurrence frequency with the sum of visual words occurrence frequency in a particular action class. WW_x is defined as

$$WW_x = \frac{freq(w_x)}{\sum_{i=1}^{k} freq(w_i)} \tag{3}$$

Figure 3 shows the weighted visual words assigned to each action class for the UCF Sports action dataset using a graphical representation. There are a few action classes that have high weighted visual words representation e.g. Golf Swing, Riding Horse, Skate Boarding, Walking and Running as compared to other action classes. On the other hand, some action classes from the same dataset have less weighted visual words e.g. Lifting, Swing bench and Swing side. This weighted visual representation is highly dependent on the feature similarity of each visual word as well as its occurrence frequency within its relevant action class. Action classes with the high-weighted visual words representation tend to have more similar and high-frequency visual words representation with respect to other action classes.

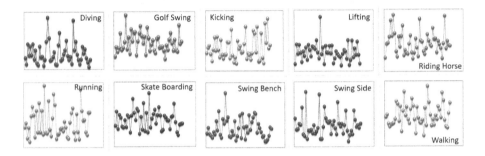

Fig. 3. Weighted visual words representation for UCF Sports dataset

2.3 Feature Encoding

In this step, the main focus is encoding feature representation for each video using weighted visual word codebook. Let $Feat = \{f_1, f_3, f_3, ..., f_z\}$ represents the features for each video. For each feature fm the codebook word wj can be viewed as function of f and is defined as:

$$A(f) = \begin{cases} Weight(w_j), & \arg\min_j ||f_m - w_j||_2 \\ 0, & otherwise \end{cases} \tag{4}$$

Each feature vector votes for only its nearest codebook word. The weighted occurrence of the votes are stored in histogram for each video.

2.4 Action Classification

For action classification, we used the popular supervised support vector machine (SVM) classification algorithm as proposed in [12]. SVMs is the state-of-the-art large margin classifier, which has recently gain popularity for human action recognition. We used a multi-class non-linear support vector machine trained using *c-1* binary SVM and *ordinal* coding design scheme. SVM used Gaussian kernel for learning which is defined as:

$$G(x_1, x_2) = exp(||x_1 - x_2||^2) \tag{5}$$

3 Performance Evaluation and Results

To test our scheme, we performed a number of experiments on publicly available datasets i.e. UCF Sports and UCF11. All experiments were carried out on an Intel Core i7-6500U CPU with 2.50 Ghz, and the proposed scheme was implemented in MATLAB 2015R(a).

3.1 Human Action Recognition Datasets

UCF Sports contains sports action videos captured in realistic environments. It contains 10 sports actions e.g. walking, diving, kicking, horseback riding etc. Sample frames from UCF Sports action dataset are shown in Fig. 4. It contains 150 video clips and the total duration of videos is 958 s. The average duration of action clips have great similarities across different classes, therefore it would not affect the performance of our proposed scheme. UCF Sports action videos have a large number of intra and inter-class variation typical of many real life environments. We used leave one out cross validation method as proposed in [17].

Fig. 4. Sample frames from the UCF Sports actions sequences.

UCF11, previously known as YouTube action dataset, is captured in realistic environments with large variation in viewpoints, backgrounds, camera motions, object appearances and poses. Sample frames from UCF11 action dataset are shown in Fig. 5. It contains 11 action categories and, for each action class, video clips are grouped into 25 groups each containing at least 4 video clips. Each group shares some similar features, like similar environment, same actor and similar viewpoints. As proposed by Rodriguez et al. [17], Leave One Group Out evaluation method is used for evaluation purposes.

Fig. 5. Sample frames from the UCF11 actions sequences.

3.2   Parameter Evaluation and Discussion

For constructing a class-specific dictionary, we performed k-means clustering using different no. of visual words for each action class. As shown in Table 1 accuracy and computational time increase with respect to an increase in the number of visual words till $k = 300$.

For evaluation of the weighted visual scheme, we performed different experiments and evaluated our approach on UCF Sports datasets. We studied the impact of both parameters used for weight assignment. As discussed in Sect. 2, the proposed weight is dependent on two different parameters and is defined as:

$$Weight(w_x) = \mu_x + WW_x \tag{6}$$

Table 1 shows the result of evaluation of effect of each individual parameter for UCF Sports dataset. By defining weight as:

$$Weight(w_x) = \mu_x \tag{7}$$

average accuracy is 97.5%. Here μ_x shows the feature similarity based importance of each visual words within its action class. The accuracy for second parameter is 96.5%. For which weight is defined as:

$$Weight(w_x) = WW_x \tag{8}$$

Here WW_x emphasize the importance of a visual word within its action class according to its occurrence frequency. This shows that both parameter have significant contribution in assigning the relevant weights to visual words representation. Finally, we evaluated our approach by combining both parameters and observed that it results in improved performance as compared to using only one parameter. We have also presented the performance of proposed scheme with $Weight(w_x) = 1$ to compare the effectiveness of proposed weighting scheme. Result shows that the proposed weighting scheme outperforms the base framework.

Table 1. Weighted visual words codebook parameter evaluation for UCF Sports dataset.

Weight's parameter	Accuracy
$Weight(w_x) = 1$	96.15%
$Weight(w_x) = \mu_x$	97.50%
$Weight(w_x) = WW_x$	96.50%
$Weight(w_x) = \mu_x + WWx$	**98.93%**

Figure 6(a) shows the performance of our scheme on the UCF sports dataset in the form of confusion matrix. Slight confusion between 'kicking' action class and a few other action classes is observed. Kicking is confused with Riding Horse, Running and Swing Side actions. Figure 6(b) shows confusion between a few action classes for the UCF11 dataset. As both datasets are captured in realistic scenarios some unwanted action in the background can mislead a classifier.

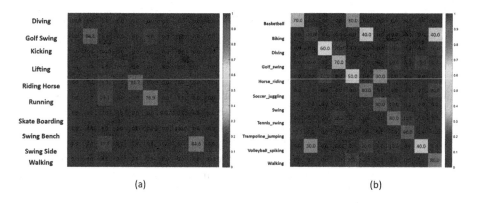

(a)   (b)

Fig. 6. Confusion matrix for UCF Sports and UCF11 datasets.

3.3   Comparison with State-of-the-Art Methods

Table 2 shows the comparison of our scheme with few recent approaches for human action recognition for UCF Sports and UCF11 datasets. Our proposed

Table 2. Comparison with state-of-the-arts methods for UCF-Sports and UCF11 Dataset.

Dataset	Paper	Method	Results
UCF Sports	**Our**	Weighted class specific dictionary learning scheme	**98.93%**
	[14]	Multi region two stream R-CNN	95.74%
	[1]	Bag of visual words	90.90%
	[23]	Dense trajectories and motion boundary descriptor	88.00%
	[3]	CNN + rank pooling	87.20%
	[9]	hk-means and TF-IDF scoring based vocabulary construction	78.40%
	[7]	Independent sub space analysis	86.50%
UCF11	**Our**	Weighted class specific dictionary learning scheme	**93.88%**
	[22]	Dense trajectories	84.20%
	[24]	Motion boundaries and dense trajectories	91.30%
	[10]	Tenser motion descriptor	75.40%
	[8]	Bag of visual words	71.20%

scheme outperforms other mentioned methods in term of average accuracy. We significantly improve the recognition performance for UCF Sports dataset presented in Peng and Schmid [14] by approximately 3%. Our scheme also showed significant improvement when compares with recent bag of visual words approach presented by Abdulmunem et al. in [1]. They have used saliency guided 3D SIFT-HOOF (SGSH) feature for feature representation. Performance is improved by around 3% for UCF Sports and for UCF11, we significantly improve the results presented in [24] by around 2%.

4   Conclusion and Future Work

In this paper, we enhance the performance of traditional bag of visual words approach for human action recognition. We have used local feature representation approach to represent complex action in realistic scenarios. Then, we exploit the importance of visual words for a particular action class. Our scheme is based on the concept of textual information present for document retrieval systems. We learned a class specific dictionary, further we assigned weight to each visual words based on its similarity with the respective action class and its occurrence frequency. Lastly, we have used these visual words weights to encode each videos. Our results showed improved performance for human action recognition in realistic and complex scenarios.

Future work includes several research directions. We can exploit the use of convolutional neural network instead for representing videos with handcrafted features such SIFT, HOF, 3D Harris etc. We can also improve the performance of bag of visual words by incorporating the neighboring information in a spatio-temporal grid for assigning weight to each visual word. Finally, the proposed scheme can be extended to work in complex and realistic scenarios i.e. Hollywood2 dataset.

Acknowledgements. Sergio A Velastin acknowledges funding by the Universidad Carlos III de Madrid, the European Unions Seventh Framework Programme for research, technological development and demonstration under grant agreement n 600371, el Ministerio de Econom y Competitividad (COFUND2013-51509) and Banco Santander. Authors also acknowledges support from the Directorate of ASR and TD, University of Engineering and Technology Taxila, Pakistan.

References

1. Abdulmunem, A., Lai, Y., Sun, X.: Saliency guided local and global descriptors for effective action recognition. Comput. Vis. Media **2**(1), 97–106 (2016)
2. Dollár, P., Rabaud, V., Cottrell, G., Belongie, S.: Behavior recognition via sparse spatio-temporal features. In: 2005 2nd Joint IEEE International Workshop on Visual Surveillance and Performance Evaluation of Tracking and Surveillance, pp. 65–72. IEEE (2005)
3. Fernando, B., Gould, S.: Learning end-to-end video classification with rank-pooling. In: Proceedings of the International Conference on Machine Learning (ICML) (2016)
4. Jain, A.K.: Data clustering: 50 years beyond K-means. Pattern Recognit. Lett. **31**(8), 651–666 (2010)
5. Laptev, I., Lindeberg, T.: Space-time interest points. In: proceedings of 9th IEEE International Conference on Computer Vision, Nice, France, pp. 432–439 (2003)
6. Laptev, I., Marszalek, M., Schmid, C., Rozenfeld, B.: Learning realistic human actions from movies. In: 2008 IEEE Conference on Computer Vision and Pattern Recognition, CVPR 2008, pp. 1–8. IEEE (2008)
7. Le, Q.V., Zou, W.Y., Yeung, S.Y., Ng, A.Y.: Learning hierarchical invariant spatio-temporal features for action recognition with independent subspace analysis. In: 2011 IEEE Conference on Computer Vision and Pattern Recognition (CVPR), pp. 3361–3368. IEEE (2011)
8. Liu, J., Luo, J., Shah, M.: Recognizing realistic actions from videos in the wild. In: 2009 IEEE Conference on Computer Vision and Pattern Recognition, CVPR 2009, pp. 1996–2003. IEEE (2009)
9. Markatopoulou, F., Moumtzidou, A., Tzelepis, C., Avgerinakis, K., Gkalelis, N., Vrochidis, S., Mezaris, V., Kompatsiaris, I.: ITI-CERTH participation to TRECVID 2013. In: TRECVID 2013 Workshop, Gaithersburg (2013)
10. Mota, V.F., Souza, J.I., Araújo, A.D.A., Vieira, M.B.: Combining orientation tensors for human action recognition. In: 2013 26th SIBGRAPI-Conference on Graphics, Patterns and Images (SIBGRAPI), pp. 328–333. IEEE (2013)
11. Murthy, O., Goecke, R.: Ordered trajectories for large scale human action recognition. In: Proceedings of the IEEE International Conference on Computer Vision Workshops, pp. 412–419 (2013)
12. Nazir, S., Haroon, M., Velastin, S.A.: Inter and intra class correlation analysis (IICCA) for human action recognition in realistic scenarios. In: International Conference of Pattern Recognition Systems (ICPRS) (2017, to appear)
13. Nazir, S., Haroon Yousaf, M., Velastin, S.A.: Evaluating bag of visual features (BoVF) approach using spatio temporal features for action recognition. In: Computer and Electrical Engineering (2017, submitted)
14. Peng, X., Schmid, C.: Multi-region two-stream R-CNN for action detection. In: Leibe, B., Matas, J., Sebe, N., Welling, M. (eds.) ECCV 2016 Part IV. LNCS, vol. 9908, pp. 744–759. Springer, Cham (2016). https://doi.org/10.1007/978-3-319-46493-0_45

15. Peng, X., Wang, L., Cai, Z., Qiao, Y., Peng, Q.: Hybrid super vector with improved dense trajectories for action recognition. In: ICCV Workshops, vol. 13 (2013)
16. Peng, X., Wang, L., Wang, X., Qiao, Y.: Bag of visual words and fusion methods for action recognition: comprehensive study and good practice. Comput. Vis. Image Underst. **150**, 109–125 (2016)
17. Rodriguez, M.D., Ahmed, J., Shah, M.: Action mach a spatio-temporal maximum average correlation height filter for action recognition. In: 2008 IEEE Conference on Computer Vision and Pattern Recognition, CVPR 2008, pp. 1–8. IEEE (2008)
18. Schuldt, C., Laptev, I., Caputo, B.: Recognizing human actions: a local SVM approach. In: Proceedings of the 17th International Conference on Pattern Recognition, ICPR 2004, vol. 3, pp. 32–36. IEEE (2004)
19. Scovanner, P., Ali, S., Shah, M.: A 3-dimensional sift descriptor and its application to action recognition. In: Proceedings of the 15th ACM International Conference on Multimedia, pp. 357–360. ACM (2007)
20. Sun, J., Wu, X., Yan, S., Cheong, L.-F., Chua, T.-S., Li, J.: Hierarchical spatio-temporal context modeling for action recognition. In: 2009 IEEE Conference on Computer Vision and Pattern Recognition, CVPR 2009, pp. 2004–2011. IEEE (2009)
21. Tirilly, P., Claveau, V., Gros, P.: A review of weighting schemes for bag of visual words image retrieval. Research report PI 1927, p. 47 (2009)
22. Wang, H., Kläser, A., Schmid, C., Liu, C.-L.: Action recognition by dense trajectories. In: 2011 IEEE Conference on Computer Vision and Pattern Recognition (CVPR), pp. 3169–3176. IEEE (2011)
23. Wang, H., Kläser, A., Schmid, C., Liu, C.-L.: Dense trajectories and motion boundary descriptors for action recognition. Int. J. Comput. Vis. **103**(1), 60–79 (2013)
24. Yadav, G.K., Shukla, P., Sethfi, A.: Action recognition using interest points capturing differential motion information. In: 2016 IEEE International Conference on Acoustics, Speech and Signal Processing (ICASSP), pp. 1881–1885. IEEE (2016)

A Critical Review of the Trifocal Tensor Estimation

Laura F. Julià[(✉)] and Pascal Monasse

LIGM (UMR 8049), École des Ponts, UPE, Champs-sur-Marne, France
{laura.fernandez-julia,pascal.monasse}@enpc.fr

Abstract. We explore the advantages offered by the trifocal tensor in the pose estimation of a triplet of cameras as opposed to computing the relative poses pair by pair with the fundamental matrix. Theoretically, the trilinearities characterize uniquely three corresponding image points in a tighter way than the three epipolar equations and this translates in an increasing accuracy. However, we show that this initial improvement is not enough to have a remarkable impact on the pose estimation after bundle adjustment, and the use of the fundamental matrix with image triplets remains relevant.

Keywords: Trifocal tensor · Fundamental matrix · Pose estimation

1 Introduction

The study of cameras and images has been a prominent subject since the beginning of computer vision, one of the main focus being the pose estimation and 3D reconstruction. Based on the perspective projection induced by pinhole cameras, there are constraints between the space points and their projections onto the images. Taking two images, the triangulation of the space points is possible from their projections when the poses are known. Eliminating 3D points from this model, the fundamental matrix is an algebraic operator encoding the relation between corresponding image points, which gives a way to infer the relative orientations and positions of a pair of camera viewpoints.

The natural extension is to consider three views and analyze the constraints between points to find a similar operator. The solution is the trifocal tensor; the algebraic constraints relating three corresponding image points are known as trilinearities. It was shown that a general multi-view matrix can be found for n views, but that the relations given by these n views depend only on the constraints involving two or three views at a time [6]. Theoretically, no extra geometric information about three views comes from considering additional views at once. Therefore, multi-view structure from motion pipelines always rely on initial view pairs [7,14,15] or triplets [4,8].

The conventional wisdom advocates the use of the trifocal tensor with a triplet of views rather than taking pairs and the fundamental matrix. We question this assumption with a study of the trifocal tensor and its performance

© Springer International Publishing AG, part of Springer Nature 2018
M. Paul et al. (Eds.): PSIVT 2017, LNCS 10749, pp. 337–349, 2018.
https://doi.org/10.1007/978-3-319-75786-5_28

against the fundamental matrix. In Sect. 2 we present its definition and parameterizations and in Sect. 3 its estimation and pose estimation. The experiments to quantitatively measure its performance are in Sect. 4. We finally conclude in Sect. 5 that the advantages of the trifocal tensor are marginal and not sufficient to consider it superior to the fundamental matrix.

2   The Trifocal Tensor

Throughout the paper, the following notation is used: vectors are represented by lowercase (v), matrices by uppercase (M) and tensors by uppercase bold ($\mathbf{T}$). The 3×3 matrix form of the cross product on the left by a 3-vector v is denoted by $[v]_\times$, i.e., $[v]_\times w = v \times w$. For a vector v, we note $\|v\|$ its L^2 norm, and for a matrix or tensor the L^2 norm of the vector built from its coefficients. For a matrix M, $\|M\|$ is knwon as the Frobenius norm, and for a tensor $\mathbf{T}$ it represents, analogously, the square root of the sum of the squares of all its elements, $\|\mathbf{T}\| := \sqrt{\sum_{i,j,k}(T_i^{jk})^2}$. Finally, we note $|M|$ the determinant of a matrix M.

2.1   Definition

The **Trifocal Tensor** (TFT) associated to three views is a $3 \times 3 \times 3$ tensor $\mathbf{T} = [T_1, T_2, T_3]$ usually defined for three canonical projective cameras $P_1 = (Id_3|0)$, $P_2 = (A|a_4)$, $P_3 = (B|b_4)$ with each slice T_i the 3×3 matrix

$$T_i = a_i b_4^\top - a_4 b_i^\top, \tag{1}$$

where a_i and b_i are the columns of A and B. A more general definition for non canonical cameras can be found in [3].

The TFT has 27 parameters, is unique up-to-scale for any 3-view configuration and invariant by projectivity. Still, the degrees of freedom of a set of three projective cameras up-to-projectivity is 18 [3]. Hence, the parameters of the trifocal tensor must satisfy some constraints reducing the 8 remaining degrees of freedom of the trifocal tensor. However, the missing constraints are not obvious nor easily derivable. Section 2.3 presents several minimal parameterizations and constraints developed over the years.

2.2   Trilinearities

At its origin, the TFT is derived from the relation between the projections of the same 3D line in the three images. Other incidence relations can be found for this tensor, in particular, the following equation for triplets of corresponding image points x_1, x_2, x_3 (in homogeneous coordinates) is satisfied:

$$[x_2]_\times \left(\sum_i (x_1)_i T_i \right) [x_3]_\times = 0_{3\times3}. \tag{2}$$

Among the 9 scalar equations in (2), only 4 are linearly independent. They are linear on the trifocal tensor parameters and trilinear on the image coordinates.

Considering the views pairwise, the incidence relations given by the fundamental matrices for the same corresponding triplet x_1, x_2, x_3 are a set of 3 equations linear on the fundamental matrices parameters and bilinear on the image points

$$x_2^\top F_{21} x_1 = 0, \qquad x_3^\top F_{31} x_1 = 0, \qquad x_3^\top F_{32} x_2 = 0. \tag{3}$$

The involved fundamental matrices are

$$F_{21} = [a_4]_\times A, \qquad F_{31} = [b_4]_\times B, \qquad F_{32} = [b_4 - BA^{-1}a_4]_\times BA^{-1}. \tag{4}$$

2.3 Minimal Parameterizations and Constraints

Many possible minimal characterizations for the trifocal tensor have been proposed in the literature [1,2,10–13,17]. We chose to focus on four representative ones that can be efficiently implemented in the pose estimation process.

Ressl. The minimal parameterization of the trifocal tensor proposed by Ressl in his thesis [13] is based on algebraic constraints of the correlation slices. It involves 20 parameters and 2 constraints. With this parameterization it is possible to completely characterize the trifocal tensor for three views. The three matrices of the trifocal tensor T_i can be parameterized in the following minimal form:

$$T_i = \left[s_i, \, v s_i + m_i e_{31}, \, w s_i + n_i e_{31} \right]^\top \quad i = 1, 2, 3 \tag{5}$$

where $s_i \in \mathbb{R}^3$ are such that $\left\| (s_1 \ s_2 \ s_3) \right\| = 1$, $e_{31} \in \mathbb{R}^3$ with $\|e_{31}\| = 1$, and $v, w, m_i, n_i \in \mathbb{R}$.

This parameterization is directly related to the epipoles since $e_{31} = b_4$ corresponds to the epipole, projection of the first camera center in the third image, and the epipole in the second image $e_{21} = a_4$ is proportional to $(1, v, w)^\top$. It is also related to an equivalent parameterization of three canonical projective matrices.

Nordberg. The trifocal tensor can also be parameterized by three 3×3 orthogonal matrices U, V and W that transform the original tensor into a sparse one, $\tilde{\mathbf{T}}$, with only 10 non-zero parameters up-to-scale [10]:

$$\tilde{\mathbf{T}} = \mathbf{T}(U \otimes V \otimes W) \quad \Rightarrow \quad \mathbf{T} = \tilde{\mathbf{T}}(U^\top \otimes V^\top \otimes W^\top) \tag{6}$$

where the tensor operation corresponds to the matrix operation on the slices $\tilde{T}_i = V^\top (\sum_m U_{m,i} T_m) W$. The scale can be fixed by imposing $\|\tilde{\mathbf{T}}\| = 1$. For canonical cameras, such orthogonal matrices can be computed as:

$$U_0 = (A^{-1}a_4, \, [A^{-1}a_4]_\times^2 B^{-1}b_4, \, [A^{-1}a_4]_\times B^{-1}b_4), \quad U = U_0(U_0^\top U_0)^{-\frac{1}{2}} \tag{7}$$

$$V_0 = (a_4, \, [a_4]_\times AB^{-1}b_4, \, [a_4]_\times^2 AB^{-1}b_4), \quad V = V_0(V_0^\top V_0)^{-\frac{1}{2}} \tag{8}$$

$$W_0 = (b_4, \, [b_4]_\times BA^{-1}a_4, \, [b_4]_\times^2 BA^{-1}a_4), \quad W = W_0(W_0^\top W_0)^{-\frac{1}{2}} \tag{9}$$

and each one can be parameterized by 3 parameters. Therefore, the trifocal tensor $\mathbf{T}$ is parameterized in this case by a total of 19 parameters and one constraint fixing the scale of $\hat{\mathbf{T}}$.

A main disadvantage of this specific parameterization is that the matrices U_0, V_0 and W_0 become singular when the three camera centers are collinear and, therefore, no orthogonal matrix can be computed from them. It is then a parameterization only valid for non-collinear centers.

Faugeras and Papadopoulo. In [2] a set of 12 algebraic equations are presented as sufficient constraints to characterize a trifocal tensor. It consists of 3 constraints of degree 3 corresponding to the determinant of the slices being zero, $|T_i| = 0$ for $i \in \{1, 2, 3\}$, and 9 more constraints of degree 6 combining several determinants of the elements of $\mathbf{T}$, for $j_1, j_2, k_1, k_2 \in \{1, 2, 3\}$ with $j_1 \neq j_2$, $k_1 \neq k_2$

$$|t^{j_1 k_1}\; t^{j_1 k_2}\; t^{j_2 k_2}|\,|t^{j_1 k_1}\; t^{j_2 k_1}\; t^{j_2 k_2}|-$$
$$|t^{j_2 k_1}\; t^{j_1 k_2}\; t^{j_2 k_2}|\,|t^{j_1 k_1}\; t^{j_2 k_2}\; t^{j_1 k_2}| = 0 \qquad (10)$$

where t^{jk} represents the vector $\left(T_1^{jk}, T_2^{jk}, T_3^{jk}\right)^{\top}$.

This set is not minimal since only 9 constraints should be enough for the characterization of a valid trifocal tensor. The authors give an outline of how to obtain a minimal parameterization using the constraints that requires to solve a polynomial of degree 2, thus giving two possible tensors. We considered best to use the minimization of the constraints instead of the minimal parameters for a more straightforward implementation.

Ponce and Hebert $\varPi$ Matrices. A completely different approach to characterize the 3-view model has been explored in [12]. Through the study on the incidence of three lines on space, a set of three matrices (related to the principal lines) that give constraints on the correspondence of three image points can be defined. These matrices have a total of 27 parameters and play a role similar to the TFT. Given three cameras with non-collinear centers and three image points x_1, x_2, x_3 there exist three 4×3 matrices up-to-scale $\varPi_i = (\pi_{1i}, \pi_{2i}, \pi_{3i}, \pi_{4i})^{\top}$ with $\pi_{ii} = (0\; 0\; 0)^{\top}$ and verifying:

$$x_1^{\top}(\pi_{41}\pi_{32}^{\top} - \pi_{31}\pi_{42}^{\top})x_2 = 0 \qquad (11)$$
$$x_1^{\top}(\pi_{41}\pi_{23}^{\top} - \pi_{21}\pi_{43}^{\top})x_3 = 0 \qquad (12)$$
$$x_2^{\top}(\pi_{42}\pi_{13}^{\top} - \pi_{12}\pi_{43}^{\top})x_3 = 0 \qquad (13)$$
$$(\pi_{21}^{\top}x_1)(\pi_{32}^{\top}x_2)(\pi_{13}^{\top}x_3) = (\pi_{31}^{\top}x_1)(\pi_{12}^{\top}x_2)(\pi_{23}^{\top}x_3) \qquad (14)$$

if, and only if, the x_i form a triplet of corresponding points. Ponce and Hebert propose the 6 homogeneous constraints:

$$\pi_{21}^1 = \pi_{32}^2 = \pi_{13}^3 = 0, \quad \pi_{31}^2 = \pi_{41}^3, \quad \pi_{12}^3 = \pi_{42}^1, \quad \pi_{23}^1 = \pi_{43}^2 \qquad (15)$$

that can be achieved by a projective transformation of the space. This reduces the parameters to 21 and with 3 norm constraints on the matrices, $\|\Pi_i\| = 1$, the minimal representation is attained.

Just like with the trilinearities (2) in the trifocal tensor case, these parameters give 4 equations describing the incidence relation for image points. Here, (11) to (13) are bilinear on the points and completely equivalent to the epipolar equations given by the fundamental matrices. Equation (14) is trilinear on the image points and it is key to the characterization of the correspondence of three points, which the fundamental matrices fail to achieve when one of the points lies on the line joining two epipoles. This is precisely the geometric contribution of taking three views instead of individual pairs to the characterization of matches.

Similarly to the parameterization of the trifocal tensor by Nordberg, the main drawback of the Π matrices is that they are only valid for non-collinear camera centers. For collinear camera centers, Ponce and Hebert [12] also proposed equivalent matrices with one extra trilinear constraint.

3   Pose Estimation

From a trifocal tensor **T** we can extract the epipoles, projections of the first camera center in the second and third images. The epipole e_{31} can be computed as the common intersection of the lines represented by the right null-vectors of T_1, T_2 and T_3. Analogously, the epipole e_{21} can be computed as the common intersection of the lines represented by the left null-vectors of T_1, T_2 and T_3. Then the fundamental matrices can be computed:

$$\begin{aligned} F_{21} &= [e_{21}]_\times [T_1 e_{31}, T_2 e_{31}, T_3 e_{31}], \\ F_{31} &= [e_{31}]_\times [T_1^\top e_{21}, T_2^\top e_{21}, T_3^\top e_{21}]. \end{aligned} \tag{16}$$

From the fundamental matrices and the calibration matrices K_i, the essential matrices can be obtained as $[t_{ij}]_\times R_{ij} = E_{ij} = K_i^\top F_{ij} K_j$, from which the relative orientations (R_{21}, t_{21}) and (R_{31}, t_{31}) can be retrieved by the singular value decomposition of E_{21} and E_{31}, each translation vector being up to unknown scale. The overall scale is fixed by setting $\|t_{21}\| = 1$ and the relative scale λ of t_{31} can be computed by using a triangulation of the space points $\{X^n\}_n$ from the projections in the first two cameras and minimizing the algebraic error with respect to the third image:

$$\arg\min_{\lambda \in \mathbb{R}} \sum_{n=1}^{N} \left\| x_3^n \times \left(K_3 (R_{31} X^n + \lambda \frac{t_{31}}{\|t_{31}\|}) \right) \right\|^2, \tag{17}$$

which admits a closed form solution.

So either from the trifocal tensor or the fundamental matrices, we have a way to compute the camera poses.

3.1 Linear Estimation of the Trifocal Tensor

The TFT can be estimated from a linear system given by the trilinearities of (2). From each triplet we get 9 equations linear on the parameters of the tensor, from which only 4 are linearly independent. At least 7 correspondences are needed to solve the linear system if we also impose $\|\mathbf{T}\| = 1$. If more triplets are available, a solution minimizing the algebraic error can be found by SVD. The resulting trifocal tensor will not necessarily be a valid tensor. To fix it, we can compute a valid trifocal tensor in the following way: extract the epipoles e_{21} and e_{31}, find matrices A and B that minimize (1) (resulting in linear systems), and finally compute a valid tensor.

Analogously, following the classical "normalized 8-point algorithm" specified in [3], the fundamental matrices can be computed linearly from the epipolar Eq. (3) and valid matrices can be found by imposing rank deficiency using SVD.

3.2 Optimization with Minimal Parameterization

Section 2.3 detailed four ways to parameterize minimally the 3-view model. All parameterizations involve non-linear constraints, so to be able to estimate the parameters an initialization is necessary. The linear solution from Sect. 3.1 can be used as an initial guess to estimate the different initial minimal parameterizations. Once the correct parameters of the initial model have been found they can be optimized by reinforcing the constraints and minimizing the Gold standard error (maximum likelihood estimator) with the Gauss-Helmert algorithm [9]. This algorithm finds a local optimum of the constrained least-square problem

$$\arg \min_{x,p} \|x - x_0\|^2 \qquad \text{s.t. } f(x,p) = 0, \qquad g(p) = 0 \qquad (18)$$

by linearizing at each iteration the constraints f and g. The variables in vector x_0 are the observations, in p the parameters to optimize and in x the variables fitting the model, i.e., verifying f.

In the 3-view or 2-view models, the observations x_0 correspond to the matching image points and the main constraints f are the trilinearities and epipolar equations. In Table 1 the parameters and constraints to use for each minimal parameterization are summarized, as well as the ones to use to optimize a fundamental matrix.

3.3 Optimization with Bundle Adjustment

A common last step in pose estimation is a refinement of the orientations by Bundle Adjustment. It minimizes the square reprojection error over the possible cameras orientations and space points: For N correspondences and $M = 3$ cameras,

$$\min_{\{R_j, t_j\}_j, \{X^i\}_i} \epsilon^2 \qquad \epsilon^2 = \sum_{i=1}^{N} \sum_{j=1}^{M} d(x_j^i, K_j(R_j X^i + t_j))^2, \qquad (19)$$

Table 1. Parameters and constraints to use in the Gauss-Helmert algorithm for the different minimal parameterizations of the 3-view model and the 2-view model.

Parameterization	p	#	f	g	#
Ressl	s_i, m_i, n_i e_{31}, v, w	20	(2)	$\|(s_1, s_2, s_3)\| = 1$, $\|e_{31}\| = 1$	2
Nordberg	$\tilde{\mathbf{T}}, U, V, W$	19	(2)	$\|\tilde{\mathbf{T}}\| = 1$	1
Faug.-Papad.	$\mathbf{T}$	27	(2)	$|T_i| = 0$, (10)	12
Ponce-Hebert	Π_i	21	(11)–(14)	$\|\Pi_i\| = 1$	3
Fundamental	F_{21}	9	(3)	$\|F_{21}\| = 1, |F_{21}| = 0$	2

with x_j^i the homogeneous coordinates of the observed image point. The distance d is the Euclidean distance of points expressed in homogeneous coordinates:

$$d\left((x, y, z)^\top, (t, u, v)^\top\right)^2 = \left(\frac{x}{z} - \frac{t}{v}\right)^2 + \left(\frac{y}{z} - \frac{u}{v}\right)^2. \tag{20}$$

The optimization can be carried out by the Levenberg-Marquardt algorithm [5].

4 Experiments and Discussion

We implemented and evaluated the results of the pose estimation for synthetic and real data using the trifocal tensor and also using the fundamental matrix.[1] In the first case, we compute the tensor linearly (TFT-L) and applying a Gauss-Helmert optimization with the minimal parameterizations of Ressl (TFT-R), Nordberg (TFT-N), Faugeras and Papadopoulo (TFT-FP) and Ponce and Hebert (TFT-PH). For the fundamental matrix we compute it linearly (F-L) and with a Gauss-Helmert optimization (F-O). One last result is represented for the minimum found by the bundle adjustment (BA) initialized by any of the other methods. Indeed, we found that all the initializations gave the same final pose after the minimization in almost all our experiments, an important observation of our tests that we discuss later.

4.1 Synthetic Data

We tested the trifocal tensor and the fundamental matrix pose estimation on synthetic data for different configurations. The standard scene for our experiments is composed of a set of space points contained in a cube of side 400 mm centered at the world's origin (see Fig. 1). Points are projected onto three views and Gaussian noise is added to the image points with $\sigma = 1$ pixel, if not stated otherwise. A sample of 12 points is used for the computations of the different

---

[1] The MATLAB code to reproduce these experiments is available at the GitHub repository https://github.com/LauraFJulia/TFT_vs_Fund.git.

models. The image size is 1800×1200 pixels, corresponding to a $36\,mm \times 24\,mm$ sensor and the focal length is set to $50\,mm$. The cameras all point at the origin. Results are averaged over 20 simulations of data.

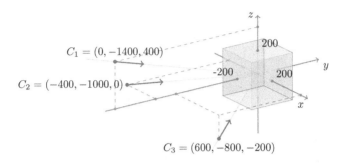

Fig. 1. Synthetic data.

The angular error in the estimated rotations and translation directions against Gaussian noise level added to the data points is shown in Fig. 2. The experiments reveal that the pose estimation based on the trifocal tensor is consistently more accurate than the fundamental matrix pose estimation. All different methods optimizing the trifocal tensor with a minimal parameterization manage to improve the initial linear solution and end up in the same minimum. In the same way, the optimization of the fundamental matrix decreases the error of the linear solution. All these improvements, while clear, have no consequence on the minimum found by the bundle adjustment, which is reached even when initialized by the simplest method (F-L). Also in Fig. 2, a plot of the

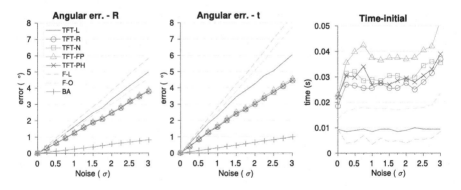

Fig. 2. Average errors for rotations (-R) on the left, for translation directions (-t) on the center, and computational time on the right, when varying the Gaussian noise added to the image points.

computational time spent on each initial estimation is shown.[2] As expected, linear methods (TFT-L, F-L) are faster than methods involving optimization, since the former are prerequisites for initialization of the latter. However, from the latter group, the fastest one is F-O, which involves two consecutive optimizations for two fundamental matrices.

Figure 3 tests the effect of changing the number of corresponding points used for the pose estimation. It shows how the fundamental matrix is much more affected by using a minimal set of correspondences than any trifocal tensor estimators but TFT-FP. The Faugeras-Papadopoulo minimal parameterization not only fails to improve the pose given by the linear estimation of the tensor for the minimal set of 7 correspondences but it returns a much worse estimation. For initial sets of more than 7 triplets, however, it performs as well as the other TFT methods. For sets with more than 15 triplets, all models start to stabilize. On the time plot in Fig. 3 we can see that linear methods maintain a constant computation time while optimization methods increase linearly with the number of initial points used.

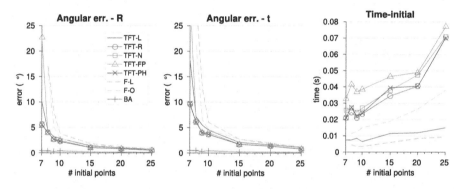

Fig. 3. Average angular errors for rotations (-R) on the left, for translation directions (-t) on the center, and computational time on the right, when the number of corresponding points is varied.

Long focal lengths are known to make difficult the camera pose estimation with the fundamental matrix. We studied the effect of increasing the focal length of our synthetic scene (while also proportionally getting the cameras farther away from the point cloud and from each other). Figure 4a shows that even if all methods get worse results in a similar way, the methods based on the fundamental matrix have an unstable higher increase of iterations for the bundle adjustment to converge after $f = 200$ mm. Still, the final estimation remains the same, whatever the initialization method.

In all these experiments, all TFT-based methods generally give the exact same results, showing the equivalence of all parameterizations. However, there is a degenerate case specific for the Ponce-Hebert and Nordberg parameterizations:

---

[2] Based on the MATLAB code run on an Intel Xeon E5-2643 CPU at 3.3 GHz with 192 GB of RAM.

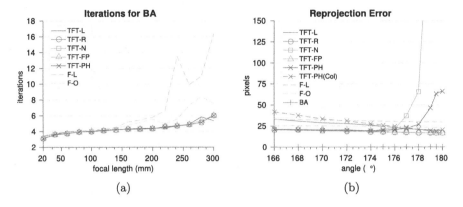

Fig. 4. On the left (a), average number of iterations needed in bundle adjustment to reach a minimum for different focal lengths. On the right (b), average reprojection error of the pose estimation when making camera centers collinear.

collinear camera centers. Alongside all the previously presented methods, we implemented and tested the collinear parameterization of the Π_i matrices given by Ponce and Hebert (TFT-PH(Col)). We tested all methods gradually moving the camera centers of the scene in order to make them align. The measure of collinearity is the angle $\widehat{C_2 C_1 C_3}$ (180° when collinear). Figure 4b shows the reprojection error, that is the error minimized in (19), with the estimated poses, for 100 points not used in the estimation. The results show an increasing accuracy on the collinear method, starting to be comparable to the others at 176°, the same point where the non-collinear parameterizations suffer a jump on the error, much greater for TFT-N than for TFT-PH. After 178° the initial poses given by the non-collinear parameterizations are no longer able to find the right minimum through bundle adjustment.

Based on these results and the instability of the Faugeras-Papadopoulo parameterization with a minimal set of initial points, the trifocal tensor parameterization of Ressl seems to be the most robust to degenerate scenes and the most recommended for pose estimation using the TFT.

4.2   Real Datasets

To evaluate the performance of these methods in real settings, we chose to use two scenes from the EPFL dense multi-view stereo test image datasets [16] that come with a reliable ground truth. These datasets consist of images of size 3072×2048 pixels taken with a 35 mm equivalent focal length. The first scene is the fountain-P11 dataset which has 11 images. We tested 70 of the possible image triplets and the averages of the results are shown in Table 2. The second scene is the Herz-Jesu-P8 dataset which consists of 8 images, from which we tested 50 possible image triplets. The averages of the obtained errors are shown in Table 3. For each triplet of images and method tested, the pose estimation is computed from a set of $N_{init} = 100$ triplets of correspondences chosen randomly from the total N inlier correspondences. The bundle adjustment optimization is carried out using a subset of $N_{BA} = 50$ correspondences from the initial set. The reprojection error, $\sqrt{\epsilon^2/(M\,N)}$ in (19), is evaluated on all N inliers.

Table 2. Average results over 70 triplets of images (one such triplet is shown) from the EPFL fountain-P11 dataset.

	repr. error (px)	R error (°)	t error (°)	init. time (s)	iter. BA
TFT-L	2.395	0.125	0.405	0.063	3.81
TFT-R	2.047	0.116	0.400	2.037	3.83
TFT-N	2.133	0.133	0.403	1.896	3.86
TFT-FP	2.365	0.119	0.403	2.063	3.84
TFT-PH	2.122	0.117	0.401	1.824	3.84
F-L	1.967	0.115	0.372	0.043	3.77
F-O	1.953	0.113	0.366	0.908	3.80
BA	0.281	0.064	0.074		

Table 3. Average results over 50 triplets of images from the EPFL Herz-Jesu-P8 dataset.

	repr. error (px)	R error (°)	t error (°)	init. time (s)	iter. BA
TFT-L	4.806	0.459	0.871	0.062	4.06
TFT-R	3.479	0.397	0.668	1.591	4.00
TFT-N	4.093	0.540	0.692	1.480	4.04
TFT-FP	4.506	0.446	0.833	1.887	4.06
TFT-PH	4.306	0.421	0.672	1.249	4.00
F-L	3.762	0.414	0.772	0.040	4.00
F-O	3.650	0.420	0.765	0.858	4.02
BA	0.372	0.063	0.068		

On the one hand, the results confirm that Ressl's parameterization is the most robust and better performing of all TFT-based methods getting the smallest error in all metrics. On the other hand, Nordberg's parameterization fails to improve the linear estimation since it gets a higher angular error in rotation. This might be due to the near-collinearity of some triplets (2 triplets in fountain-P11 and 4 in Herz-Jesu-P8 have a maximum angle between camera centers greater than 175°) which can cause great instability in the pose estimation of this methods as seen in the synthetic experiments (Fig. 4b).

We also notice how the fundamental-based methods get comparable results or even outperform the TFT-based methods in both datasets. What is more, they achieve it with less initial computation time and a similar average number of iterations to converge to the minimum in the bundle adjustment (two last columns of Tables 2 and 3).

In fact, all methods manage to reach the same minimum in the bundle adjustment optimization with around 4 iterations on average. The difference between the errors corresponding to the optimum reached and the errors from any method is much greater than the difference in the errors of the optimization-based methods and the linear methods. Therefore, one can conclude that the advantage of using an optimization to reinforce the constraints or minimal parameterization of the model before carrying out a bundle adjustment is negligible. The other lesson is that the bundle adjustment, even if performed with a small subsets of points for reduced computation time, is highly beneficial according to all error metrics.

Although not all known parameterizations of the trifocal tensor were covered by our tests, they all involve non-linear constraints admitting no closed form solution. As a consequence, they require also an initialization phase through the linear estimation of Sect. 3.1 and the possible initial benefits in terms of reduced error are likely to be erased by the bundle adjustment; the extra computation time would not make them advantageous alternatives to the standard fundamental matrix computation.

5   Conclusion

We reviewed methods of estimation of trifocal tensor and of the pose of three views. Compared with the pose estimation obtained by the fundamental matrices from the pairs of views, our experiments show that the trifocal tensor does not offer enough improvement to be considered the preferred choice. By its simplicity and lower computation time, the recommended option is to consider only pairwise constraints through the fundamental matrix, provided some bundle adjustment is used at the end (which is also highly recommended, as it can routinely decrease the error by a significant factor). In other words, the only usage of points viewed in image triplets, in the initialization phase of that approach, is to determine the relative scales of translations. Still, it would be interesting to study whether the use of the trifocal tensor improves results when $n > 3$ views are considered. However, in such a multi-view stereo pipeline, the way the image pairs and triplets are integrated is likely to have a preponderant importance. This research brought also another issue to our attention: observing that the bundle adjustment optimization is able to reach a correct minimum, even when starting from a far initial position, motivates us to study in future work the possible extended local convexity of the minimized energy.

References

1. Canterakis, N.: A minimal set of constraints for the trifocal tensor. In: Vernon, D. (ed.) ECCV 2000. LNCS, vol. 1842, pp. 84–99. Springer, Heidelberg (2000). https://doi.org/10.1007/3-540-45054-8_6
2. Faugeras, O., Papadopoulo, T.: A nonlinear method for estimating the projective geometry of 3 views. In: Sixth International Conference on Computer Vision (IEEE), pp. 477–484 (1998). https://doi.org/10.1109/ICCV.1998.710761

3. Hartley, R.I., Zisserman, A.: Multiple View Geometry in Computer Vision, 2nd edn. Cambridge University Press, Cambridge (2004). ISBN 0521540518

4. Havlena, M., Torii, A., Knopp, J., Pajdla, T.: Randomized structure from motion based on atomic 3D models from camera triplets. In: 2009 IEEE Conference on Computer Vision and Pattern Recognition, pp. 2874–2881 (2009). https://doi.org/10.1109/CVPR.2009.5206677

5. Levenberg, K.: A method for the solution of certain non-linear problems in least squares. Q. Appl. Math. **2**(2), 164–168 (1944). http://www.jstor.org/stable/43633451

6. Ma, Y., Huang, K., Vidal, R., Košecká, J., Sastry, S.: Rank conditions on the multiple-view matrix. Int. J. Comput. Vis. **59**(2), 115–137 (2004). https://doi.org/10.1023/B:VISI.0000022286.53224.3d

7. Moulon, P., Monasse, P., Marlet, R.: Adaptive structure from motion with a *Contrario* model estimation. In: Lee, K.M., Matsushita, Y., Rehg, J.M., Hu, Z. (eds.) ACCV 2012. LNCS, vol. 7727, pp. 257–270. Springer, Heidelberg (2013). https://doi.org/10.1007/978-3-642-37447-0_20

8. Moulon, P., Monasse, P., Marlet, R.: Global fusion of relative motions for robust, accurate and scalable structure from motion. In: Proceedings of the IEEE International Conference on Computer Vision, pp. 3248–3255 (2013)

9. Neitzel, F.: Generalization of total least-squares on example of unweighted and weighted 2D similarity transformation. J. Geod. **84**(12), 751–762 (2010)

10. Nordberg, K.: A minimal parameterization of the trifocal tensor. In: 2009 IEEE Conference on Computer Vision and Pattern Recognition, pp. 1224–1230 (2009). https://doi.org/10.1109/CVPR.2009.5206829

11. Papadopoulo, T., Faugeras, O.: A new characterization of the trifocal tensor. In: Burkhardt, H., Neumann, B. (eds.) ECCV 1998. LNCS, vol. 1406, pp. 109–123. Springer, Heidelberg (1998). https://doi.org/10.1007/BFb0055662

12. Ponce, J., Hebert, M.: Trinocular geometry revisited. In: 2014 IEEE Conference on Computer Vision and Pattern Recognition, pp. 17–24 (2014). https://doi.org/10.1109/CVPR.2014.10

13. Ressl, C.: A minimal set of constraints and a minimal parameterization for the trifocal tensor. In: The International Archives of the Photogrammetry, Remote Sensing and Spatial Information Sciences, Part 3A, vol. XXXIV. ISPRS-Comm. III Symposium, Graz, 9, p. 13 (2002)

14. Schönberger, J.L., Frahm, J.M.: Structure-from-motion revisited. In: IEEE Conference on Computer Vision and Pattern Recognition (CVPR) (2016)

15. Snavely, N.: Bundler: structure from motion for unordered image collections (2010). https://www.cs.cornell.edu/~snavely/bundler/

16. Strecha, C., von Hansen, W., Gool, L.V., Fua, P., Thoennessen, U.: On benchmarking camera calibration and multi-view stereo for high resolution imagery. In: 2008 IEEE Conference on Computer Vision and Pattern Recognition, pp. 1–8 (2008). https://doi.org/10.1109/CVPR.2008.4587706

17. Torr, P., Zisserman, A.: Robust parameterization and computation of the trifocal tensor. Image Vis. Comput. **15**, 591–605 (1997)

Deep Learning-Based Improved Object Recognition in Warehouses

Syeda Fouzia[1(✉)], Mark Bell[2], and Reinhard Klette[1]

[1] School of Electrical and Computer Engineering,
Auckland University of Technology, Auckland, New Zealand
syeda.fouzia@aut.ac.nz
[2] Crown Lift Trucks Ltd., Auckland, New Zealand
mark.bell@crown.com

Abstract. Research migrates in recent years from model-based object detection and classification to data-driven approaches. With the efficiency improvement of computational resources, improved acquisition systems, and bulks of data for training, deep learning models have found their way to accurate object category classification. Deep convolution nets have an inherent ability to extract features automatically and are used for accurate category classification. This paper has three parts. First, we extract moving foregrounds by using a mixture-of-Gaussians technique. Next, we aim at improving the quality of object foreground based on a pixel saliency map. Third, the obtained improved foreground is assigned labels using a pre-trained deep learning detector. Altogether, the paper proposes a way for improved video-based object detection and classification for logistics in warehouses.

1 Introduction

Various model-based methods for object detection have been proposed, such as feature-based [20], appearance-based [8], or motion-based [37]. A selection of the best technique for any specified application is relative; it depends on the extent of hardware resources or the scope of the targeted task.

Much of the progress achieved for detecting and classifying objects of interest is made by the development of robust image descriptors such as SIFT [20] or hand-crafted low-level features such as *histogram of oriented gradients* (HOG) [6], bag-of-features representations [4], or deformable part models [8], feature pooling [22], classic classifiers such as Support Vector Machine (SVM) [5] and random forests [2].

Recently, due to efficient computational resources and ease of data availability, data driven approaches have found their way. Deep learning is a form of representation learning. A computer is fed with large amounts of raw data and it finds out the features needed for detection, based on learning [25,26]. Deep convolutional neural nets, proposed by Krizhevsky et al. [17], have achieved tremendous success on bigger benchmark datasets, such as ImageNet. ImageNet

© Springer International Publishing AG, part of Springer Nature 2018
M. Paul et al. (Eds.): PSIVT 2017, LNCS 10749, pp. 350–365, 2018.
https://doi.org/10.1007/978-3-319-75786-5_29

is a dataset of over 15 million labeled high-resolution images belonging to roughly 22,000 categories. It took between five and six days on two GTX 580 3 GB GPUs to train a network with ImageNet dataset. Some modern object recognition models [18,19,32] have millions of parameters and may take some weeks to be fully trained. Hence, traditional deep learning models need a huge amount of training data for training and resources, such as multiple GPUs.

The reported research is motivated by tasks of improved object detection and classification. We also aim at using deep learning for improved recognition accuracy. We target our research towards logistics handling warehouses in our case. As per our observations, these particular indoor scenes come with the following environmental challenges:

1. There are multiple moving objects. We have recordings with pedestrians and forklift trucks moving inside a warehouse.
2. Color contrast between background and foreground is very marginal, most of the time.
3. Multiple occlusions are likely; the environment is semi-cluttered.
4. There are parked forklifts (stationery objects) in some areas.
5. Changes in loads occur frequently for racks in the background; typically these changes are gradual.
6. Illumination changes are also gradual. Warehouse indoor data have usually only a few low-illumination areas.
7. There are entries and exits of vehicles into a scene.
8. People are considered to be part of the background if they are static or moving only slightly.

A typical warehouse is a busy place. With many industrial pick and pack processes going on, we need accurate localization of occluded moving targets, to be used for precise visual surveillance. Also, moving foreground extraction is an essential requirement for object recognition surveillance tasks in computer vision. Thus, we need an indoor adaptive algorithm which can handle lighting changes, repetitive motions from clutter, and long-term scene changes inside a warehouse. See Fig. 1 for few typical warehouse scenes from our recordings.

First, we selected background subtraction, which is well suited for moving targets as in our case. We follow [27] where each pixel value is modelled as a *mixture of Gaussians* (MOG). By this means we can determine whether or not a pixel is part of the background. This supports an effective approach for separating background from foreground.

Second, we need to improve extracted foregrounds as they are not yet accurate. See Figs. 2, 3, 4, 5, 6 and 7. Due to a low background pixel recovery rate and a slow adaptation to scene changes when using the traditional MOG algorithm, foreground quality is not yet fair. We extracted salient pixels using a local contrast method [36], based on a visual saliency map. A pixel-wise saliency map, for each frame, is used to improve the corresponding foreground obtained by the MOG background extraction.

Fig. 1. Warehouse scenes from recorded videos

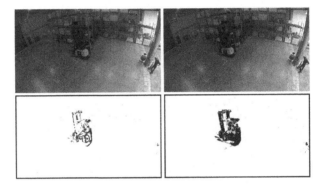

Fig. 2. Forklift crossing low illumination area. Foreground results in bottom left and right images, after applying MOG. The pedestrians at the right are detected poorly due to a more static posture

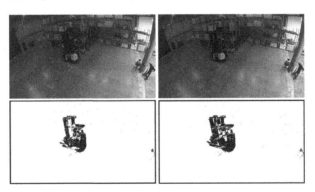

Fig. 3. A forklift crossing low illumination area. Frame 15 and Frame 20 foreground results in bottom left and right images, after applying MOG. Very slow recovery of background pixels have made the area of forklift foreground bigger than actual

Fig. 4. Scenario of three pedestrians standing inside warehouse. Starting from bottom extreme left, foreground is somewhat distorted. Some foreground pixels from previous frames are still there. For bottom middle, one of the pedestrian, who is more static, is poorly detected in foreground

Fig. 5. MOG results in a sudden camera movement scenario. A pedestrian is detected at the left, standing static in a warehouse scene. Due to variance changes in pixels due to camera motion, most of the background pixels appeared as foreground pixels. See upper right, bottom right, and left images

Third, we want to label the detected foreground. We can repurpose features, extracted from a pre-trained deep convolution neural network, for new object category recognition specific to our application [7]. This technique is called *transfer learning*. We transferred the learned features from a pre-trained model (i.e. *Google Inception Model*) for new category classification which are forklifts and pedestrians in a typical warehouse scenario [17,29].

The structure of the paper is as follows. Section 3 reports about the first step of foreground extraction. Section 4 explains the MOG- based foreground quality improvement achieved by computing pixel saliency map. Section 5 illustrates the use of a pre-trained deep-learning architecture model, for foreground category recognition. Section 6 concludes.

Fig. 6. A scenario in which three pedestrians and a forklift are detected. One of the three pedestrians is not detected in the bottom right-most result. This pedestrian was having a slightly static posture, so became part of the background pixels

Fig. 7. MOG results for occluded pedestrians. Two occluded pedestrians shown with clustered white pixels

2   Related Work

Deep convolution architectures, employing automatic feature learning and classification, are being researched in recent years. Out of many options, *convolutional neural networks* (CNNs), *region-based CNNs* (R-CNNs), or later versions are frequently explored. An R-CNN is a three-stage pipeline process. Features are extracted for every object proposal in an image and are being cached. A *support vector machine* (SVM) is used as object detector, replacing the *softmax classifier*. In the third stage of training, *bbox regressors* are learned [10]. *Spatial pyramid pooling networks* (SPPnets) were introduced to speed up R-CNNs by sharing the computation burden [14]. This is also a multi-stage process which computes a convolutional feature map for the whole input image and then classifies each object proposal, using a feature vector extracted from the shared feature map.

Fast R-CNNs use single-stage training and a multi-task loss for better detection accuracy and speed. Training can update all the layers of the network at once, and no feature caching is required [11]. These nets still used selective search for region generation; now removed in *faster R-CNNs* came. A cost-free *region proposal network* (RPN) was employed which predicted potential object bounds and an object score at each position in the faster R-CNN. This RPN, integrated with fast RCNN, was trained to share features across layers [24].

Inspired by this work we propose a pipeline for object detection. We use the Gaussian mixture model for possible objectness search in warehouse scenes and improve the foreground quality based on pixel saliency. Once achieved, we use a pre-trained CNN architecture for category label assignment for forklifts and pedestrians.

3   Gaussian Mixture Model for Foreground Extraction

The Gaussian mixture model is a natural choice for our analysis (i.e. for extracting moving targets out of a mostly stationery background). Mixture models are probabilistic models which assume that underlying pixels belong to a particular mixture distribution. To make the model more robust to lighting variations, and to handle multiple surfaces occurring in the view frustum of particular pixels, the mixture models need to be adaptive.

Basics of Gaussian Mixture Models. The values of particular pixels are modelled as a *mixture of adaptive Gaussian distributions*. A pixel process of a pixel (x, y, X) has the history of its previous t values, say from Frame 1 to Frame t. This can be represented by the set $\{X_1, \ldots, X_i, \ldots, X_t\}$, where $1 \leq i \leq t$.

The probability density function of the univariate Gaussian or normal distribution is given by

$$G(X, \mu, \sigma) = \frac{1}{\sigma\sqrt{2\pi}} \exp\left\{-\frac{1}{2}\left(\frac{X-\mu}{\sigma}\right)^2\right\} \tag{1}$$

for $-\infty < X < \infty$, where μ is the mean and $\sigma^2 > 0$ is the variance.

The probability of observing a specific mixture component at Frame t is given by products of *probability density functions* with their weight. For more than one density function, we have a multivariate case, such as

$$P(X_t) = \sum_{i=1}^{k} w_{i,t} \cdot G(X_t, \mu_{i,t}, \sigma_{i,t}) \tag{2}$$

Here, $w_{i,t}$ is the weight of the i_{th} Gaussian distribution at Frame t.

Aiming at a probabilistic model for separating the *background pixels* from the *foreground* by looking on the distributions, [27] proposed an update of the background model as follows:

(1) *Constructing adaptive mixture of multi-modal Gaussians per pixel.* The number of Gaussian components depends on the environmental complexity one wants to model. In a typical warehouse indoor environment, we observed relatively minor contrast in colors and brightness. Outdoor scenes have different conditions. Following [27], we also keep $k = 3$. Targeting RGB images, we also assume that all three RGB channels have the same σ^2, thus defining a 3×3 covariance matrix $\Sigma_{i,t}$ being the product of a variance with the unit matrix.

(2) *Method for updating the Gaussian parameters.* For every new pixel state for the next frame, we check whether it lies $X_t \leq 2.5$ standard deviations from the mean; we label it *matched* in this case. We update weight, mean, and variance as per the following update equations:

$$w_{i,t} = (1 - \alpha) \cdot w_{i,t-1} + \alpha \cdot M_{i,t} \tag{3}$$

$$\mu_{i,t} = (1 - \rho) \cdot \mu_{i,t-1} + \rho \cdot X_t \tag{4}$$

$$\sigma_{i,t}^2 = (1 - \rho) \cdot \sigma_{i,t-1}^2$$
$$+ \rho(X_t - \mu_{i,t})^\top (X_t - \mu_{i,t}) \tag{5}$$

where $\rho = \alpha \cdot P(X_t | \mu_{i,t-1}, \Sigma_{i,t-1})$, $0 < \alpha < 1$ is a selected learning rate, and $M_{i,t}$ equals 1 for a model which is matched, and equals 0 for other models.

If the ith Gaussian is marked as *unmatched*, we decrease its initial weight as per below equation:

$$w_{i,t} = (1 - \alpha) \cdot w_{i,t-1} \tag{6}$$

If all the k Gaussians in the mixture model, for pixel value X_t, are not matched to the pixel, we mark that specific pixel as a *foreground pixel*. If this is the case, then we find the Gaussian distribution with the lowest weight in the mixture and set its mean equal to X_t. We also adjust the corresponding variance to a higher value, and lower the weight of this distribution.

(3) *Heuristics for determining the background.* For finding the background distributions, we rearrange the distributions in descending order by w/σ. We add up the corresponding weights of the Gaussians in this order, till the final sum is greater than a pre-set threshold T. We set $T = 0.9$ in our case. We observe that there are fewer salient or moving objects, and more background portions in the frames.

Recent Variants for Addressing Challenges. Gaussian mixture models have been an active field of research since two decades. Many variants have been introduced for dealing with various challenges when dealing with "real time moving target detection". *Shadow elimination* has been a major subject. Foregrounds obtained by an MOG technique have shadow pixels as part of the foreground. Much work has been targeted towards shadow elimination, for example [9,31,34,35]. Shadow detection in color space is considered in [9,16]. For the detection of *slowly moving objects*, see [9]. Challenges arise when these objects are incorporated into the background due to less variance.

Adaptation of algorithms to scene changes. This is very important and controlled to some extent by learning rate and parameter selection, see [12,16,37]. *Background recovery rate improvement* is also studied in [34] for solving real-time surveillance issues. To incorporate abandoned objects for surveillance applications, *abandoned/removed object detection* is also throughly researched in [31].

Update to learning equations. This involves controlling the scene changes and slowly or fast moving objects, see [12,21,37]. *Learning rates* and their significance for incorporating scene changes is studied in [33]. The *number of Gaussian components or modes* depends on scene complexity and pixels modes [37]. For run-time improvements, to adapt MOG to real time, see [34,37]. *Initialization of parameters* is very important for initialization of an MOG model [34]. Parameter analysis and setting as per scenario is dealt with in [35].

Dirichlet-Gaussian distribution. [13] use a Dirichlet process and a Gaussian mixture model to estimate a per-pixel background distribution, which is followed by probabilistic regularization. This work was able to accurately model dynamic backgrounds.

Neighborhood correlation, to update the parameters of MOG [21], is also found effective. Importance of spatial information other than temporal one, for detecting accurate foregrounds [33,34], was able to improve the foreground quality. For using other cues such as intensity and texture, for better foregrounds, see [31]. This approach was not able to deal with resultant holes in foreground masks.

Qualitative Analysis for a Standard MOG Approach. As can be seen in the update equations above, α is the first learning rate. It needs to be adjusted as per the scenario conditions. To incorporate slowly moving objects and large homogeneously colored objects, we kept α small. For scenarios which are changing quickly, it needs to be larger to adapt to the scene. ρ is the second learning rate. Usually it is assigned a much smaller value than α. But, as per our trial experimentation, the use of the second learning rate increases the required computation time. Initial mean and variance are adjusted as per the scenario results. The thresholds are the same (value 0.9) for all the experiments.

We applied the mixture of Gaussian algorithm [27] with the following parameter setting: $\alpha = 0.001$ ranging to 0.79, $\rho = 0.00001$, threshold $T = 0.9$, the number of Gaussian components $k = 3$. We obtained our results by using Matlab 2017a.

For lower alpha values, slowly moving objects are detected with good quality foreground, but for higher values, results are not good for the same object. MOG cannot deal with sudden illumination changes and camera movements. This is as shown in Fig. 5. With passage of time, the variance decreases for more stable pixels. If the variance becomes too small, then even camera noise is marked as foreground pixel that effects the foreground quality. Bigger objects, uniform in color or slowly moving, are sometimes incorporated into background for a few frames. In conclusion, our extensive experiments, here illustrated by a few examples, lead to the conclusion: *We need some improvement in foreground detection, which makes it more robust to the mentioned challenges.*

4   Pixel Saliency for Foreground Improvement

Due to the stated observations above, we improved MOG-based foreground detection using a *saliency map-based foreground extraction scheme.*

We observed that pixel-based *saliency map* values, generated by the method of [36], can be useful for improving the average foreground quality obtained from the MOG method. It was computationally fast. It took 0.5 s or less per frame to compute a saliency map.

Visual saliency maps are able to mark salient pixels in the images and have good results with occluded objects in warehouse scenes. Different visual cues, such as compactness or uniqueness, are used to detect salient pixels in images [3]. Uniqueness-based methods are further split into *local* and *global* contrast methods. Most uniqueness-based methods use low-level features such as color, direction, or intensity to determine the contrast between image regions and their surrounding pixels.

Compactness-based methods use the variance of spatial features. Salient pixels tend to have a small spatial variance in the image space. The background is distributed on the whole image space and tends to have high spatial variance. Since single visual cue-based salient region detection methods have few limitations in detecting accurate salient pixels, different cues can be combined to make a composite framework [23]. Some methods are based on this approach, but the selection of visual cues depends on context.

Compared with the global contrast method, the local contrast is a relatively better cue to be combined with the compactness cue. Local contrast methods are able to identify the foreground region [15], but they have a limitation that they identify visible object boundaries rather than all the area. This effect can be minimized by propagation of saliency information based on diffusion [15].

To construct the pixel saliency map for the image, we converted it into a superpixel representation for constructing a resultant graph. We used SLIC [1] for an abstract graph representation of an image. Each superpixel, generated by SLIC, corresponds to some node. There are three parameters used in here: The number N of superpixel nodes used in SLIC, σ^2 which controls the fall-off rate of the exponential function, and α which balances the fitting constraints of manifold ranking algorithms. We experimentally set the parameters to $N = 200$, $\sigma^2 = 0.1$, and $\alpha = 0.99$ for experimentation. Next, the two saliency maps are computed based on the compactness visual cue and local contrast [36].

The resulting saliency maps are propagated using a diffusion process and the constructed graph later. Thus, a pixel-wise saliency map is generated from two computed maps. This pixel-wise saliency map for the specific frame is binary thresholded. We apply logical operations between salient binary thresholded pixels and moving pixels from MOG. Finally, some morphological processing is used to generate improved foreground masks.

See Figs. 8 and 9, for the improvement in foregrounds, as per the proposed improvement foreground strategy. It can be seen that foreground is better in quality with less redundant pixels from the background, as part of foreground. See Fig. 8. Fewer foreground holes are present in Fig. 9.

Fig. 8. Occluded forklift, foreground improvement based on pixel saliency, without morphological improvement

Fig. 9. Improved foreground based on pixel saliency. One of the pedestrians is missed, due to poor visibility both in MOG result and its saliency map

5   Deep Learning for Object Classification

After obtaining our improved foregrounds based on pixel saliency, we aim at classification. We use a pre-trained model of Google's Inception v3 [29] and retrain the top layer, for new categories.

We aim at overcoming the deficiency of the training data and limitations of computation time or resources by adapting a classifier, trained for other categories, to our dataset.

Basics and a Pre-trained Network. Deep *convolution neural nets* (CNNs) are able to learn rich feature representations. They have a reduced number of parameters and connections compared to the same-sized feed-forward networks. This characteristics make it easier to train and test them. They have successfully been used to categorize images and activities or tasks once trained with excess of data samples.

We can use a pre-trained convolutional deep learning model for classification tasks of new categories. We can retrain final or more layers of this model, and adapt it to our new categories and to the limited dataset available to us. This approach is called *transfer learning*. We select a pre-trained model architecture, replace the top layer by a new layer, and adapt the newly added layer to our own data classification task. We selected Google's Inception v3 Architecture model for moving object classification in warehouse scenes into two categories, either forklift or pedestrian.

Google's Inception v3 [29] is an architecture that provides a good-performance network with relatively low computational costs. To measure the classification accuracy, there are two main measurements used in the deep learning literature [29]; this is the top-5 error rate and the top-1 error rate. They measures the rate at which the architecture fails to include the correct class in the top-5 and the top-1 output, respectively.

Inception v3 achieved a 5.6% top-5 error rate, and a 21.2% top-1 error rate. Another famous architecture model, i.e., AlexNet [17] achieved a top-5 error rate of 15.3% and Inception (Google Net) [28] achieved 6.67% in the same category. Thus we selected the Inception v3 model architecture, pre-trained on ImageNet. We added a new Softmax and fully connected layer for training, and re-trained it in Tensor Flow 1.0 in the Ubuntu operating system. We re-train the model for classifying our two object categories. The top layer receives as input a 2,048-dimensional vector for each image. Since the Softmax layer contains two labels, this corresponds to learning 4,098 model parameters, corresponding to the learned biases and weights.

Training, Validation and Testing. We prepared our training data set containing 4,000 images, for two object categories of forklifts and pedestrians. We limited the training data to these two categories. Inception network rescales images to 299×299 size. So these are the input-width and input-height flags for the images. Most of the data we processed are from recorded video clips inside of a selected warehouse, showing different scenarios. Testing, validation percentages can be set by adjusting their flags in the script. We will use default values for these i.e. 80

First, a calculation of *transfer-values* is performed, for each of the images, arranged in training, testing, and validation sets. 'Transfer value' is the term we use for the output feature values, at the layer just before the final top layer. We used these feature values to differentiate the objects for new categories [7]. Since each image is reused many times during training and calculation, the transfer-values are being cached (stored on disk), to be reused repeatedly for training, validation, and testing [30]. Once the transfer value computation is complete, the actual training of the top layer of the network begins, for new labels, and for each image.

We have 4,000 training steps. Each step chooses ten images at random from the training set, finds their transfer values from the cache, and feeds them into the final layer to get predictions for the category. Those predictions are then compared against the actual labels, i.e. pedestrians or forklift, to update the top

Table 1. Results after 4,000 training iterations

Accuracy (in percent)	4,000 steps
Training	98
Validation	96
Cross entropy	0.12
Test	99.5

layer's weights through the *back-propagation process*. We obtain the following metrics for each training epoch.

The *training accuracy* shows what percentage of the images, we used in the present training batch, was labeled correctly with the true class.

The *validation accuracy* is the percentage on a randomly-selected set of images from a different data set, which are not present in the training set. If the training accuracy is very good, but the validation accuracy is not, that means that the network is *over fitting* to training data, and we need more training samples for network generalization.

The *cross entropy* is a loss function which evaluates how well the learning process for the model is executing. The training's objective is to make the loss as small as possible. If it is growing lower with each *epoch*, we assume that learning is progressing satisfactory.

As the process continues, we also observe an improvement in accuracy, i.e. in *test accuracy*, the evaluation which is run on a group of images which are kept separate from the training and validation images. This test accuracy is the best estimate of how well the trained model will work for a specified new classification task. This accuracy is based on the percentage of the images in the test set, that is given the correct label after the model is fully trained. We achieved very good testing accuracy of 99.5% after 4,000 training iterations.

Results. See below Table 1 for training, validation and test accuracy after 4,000 training iterations. Cross entropy is also listed.

We tested on images that the model has not been trained for, to check how does it generalize to unseen forklift and pedestrian images. See Figs. 10 and 11 for the category % assignment by the model. Figures illustrate our general finding that the model predicts the class with acceptable test accuracy for unseen images. For dependency upon number of training steps, see Table 2.

Hyper-Parameters. We have kept the hyper-parameters constant throughout training and testing, with learning rate 0.01. We have edited the hyper-parameter and *print misclassified test images*, to print the evaluation metrics for 20 training iterations for simplicity. These metrics are, true positive (TR), true negative (TN), false positive (FP), and false negative (FN). We define them as follows in our warehouse scenario: TP is the number of images categorized as forklifts in testing, TN is the number of images categorized as pedestrians in testing, FP is the number of images categorized as forklifts, although they were pedestrians in real, and FN is the number of images categorized as pedestrians, although they were forklifts in real.

Fig. 10. Model test accuracy for forklift test images. Upper left: 99.92, upper right: 86.8, bottom left: 46.1, and bottom right: 71.76

Fig. 11. Model test accuracy for pedestrian test images. Upper left: 86.7, upper right: 89.23, bottom left: 86.26, and bottom right: 99.5

Table 2. Evaluation metrics for 10 and 20 training steps

Evaluation metrics	10 steps	20 steps
True positive	197	200
False positive	1	2
True negative	217	217
False negative	1	8
Precision	99.5	99
Recall	94.7	96.2
f1	97	97.6
Accuracy	97.2	97.7

6   Conclusions

For detecting and classifying objects in warehouse scenes, we proposed a refinement of a standard MOG method by subsequent use of saliency maps, and the application of a CNN for the final step of object classification for the detected foreground segments.

Using the Inception pre-trained model, with only top-layer re-training, we achieved 99.5 classification accuracy for the specified task. The model is not able to generalize well for the test images of forklift models for which we have a relatively small number of training images only in our dataset. This can be seen in the bottom-left of Fig. 10 where a forklift is misclassified. Hence limitation in the current study is the availability of more training data. The current study is based on 4,000 labelled images.

We found that pixel saliency values have the potential to improve MOG-based foreground extraction. This also affects the learning rate selection for background or foreground pixels updates. We expect that this can help to further improve MOG-based real-time video surveillance in general.

References

1. Achanta, R., Shaji, A., Smith, K., Lucchi, A., Fua, P., Sasstrunk, S.: SLIC superpixels compared to state-of-the-art superpixel methods. IEEE Trans. Pattern Anal. Mach. Intell. **34**(11), 2274–2282 (2012)
2. Breiman, L., Cutler, A.: Random Forests (2004)
3. Cheng, M.M., Mitra, N.J., Huang, X., Torr, P.H., Hu, S.M.: Global contrast based salient region detection. IEEE Trans. Pattern Anal. Mach. Intell. **37**(3), 569–582 (2015)
4. Csurka, G., et al.: Visual categorization with bags of keypoints. Workshop Stat. Learn. Comput. Vis. **1**, 1–22 (2004)
5. Chang, C.C., Lin, C.: LIBSVM: a library for support vector machines. ACM Trans. Intell. Syst. Technol. **2**(3), 27 (2011)
6. Dalal, N., Triggs, B.: Histograms of oriented gradients for human detection. Proc. Comput. Vis. Pattern Recognit. **1**, 886–893 (2005)
7. Donahue, J., Jia, Y., Vinyals, O., Hoffman, J., Zhang, N., Tzeng, E., Darrell, T.: DeCAF: a deep convolutional activation feature for generic visual recognition. In: Proceedings of the International Conference on Machine Learning, pp. 647–655 (2014)
8. Felzenszwalb, P.F., et al.: Object detection with discriminatively trained part-based models. IEEE Trans. Pattern Anal. Mach. Intell. **32**(9), 1627–1645 (2010)
9. Friedman, N., Russell, S.: Image segmentation in video sequences: a probabilistic approach. In: Proceedings of the Conference on Uncertainty in Artificial Intelligence, pp. 175–181 (1997)
10. Girshick, R., Donahue, J., Darrell, T., Malik, J.: Rich feature hierarchies for accurate object detection and semantic segmentation. In: IEEE Conference on Computer Vision Pattern Recognition, pp. 580–587 (2014)
11. Girshick, R., Fast R-CNN. In: IEEE International Conference on Computer Vision, pp. 1440–1448 (2015)

12. Guo, D.J., Zhe-Ming, L., Hao, L.: Multi-channel adaptive mixture background model for real-time tracking. J. Inf. Hiding Multimed. Sig. Process. **7**, 216–221 (2016)
13. Haines, T.S.F., Xiang, T.: Background subtraction with Dirichlet processes. In: Fitzgibbon, A., Lazebnik, S., Perona, P., Sato, Y., Schmid, C. (eds.) ECCV 2012 Part IV. LNCS, vol. 7575, pp. 99–113. Springer, Heidelberg (2012). https://doi.org/10.1007/978-3-642-33765-9_8
14. He, K., Zhang, X., Ren, S., Sun, J.: Spatial pyramid pooling in deep convolutional networks for visual recognition. In: Fleet, D., Pajdla, T., Schiele, B., Tuytelaars, T. (eds.) ECCV 2014 Part III. LNCS, vol. 8691, pp. 346–361. Springer, Cham (2014). https://doi.org/10.1007/978-3-319-10578-9_23
15. Hou, X., Zhang, L.: Saliency detection: a spectral residual approach. In: Proceedings of the IEEE Conference on Computer Vision Pattern Recognition, pp. 1–8 (2007)
16. KaewTraKulPong, P., Bowden, R.: An improved adaptive background mixture model for real time tracking with shadow detection. In: Remagnino, P., Jones, G.A., Paragios, N., Regazzoni, C.S. (eds.) Video-Based Surveillance Systems, pp. 135–144. Springer, Boston (2002). https://doi.org/10.1007/978-1-4615-0913-4_11
17. Krizhevsky, A., Sutskever, I., Hinton, G.E.: ImageNet classification with deep convolutional neural networks. In: Proceedings of the Advances Neural Information Processing Systems, pp. 1097–1105 (2012)
18. LeCun, Y., Yoshua, B., Geoffrey, H.: Deep learning. Nature **521**, 436–444 (2015)
19. Lee, H., Grosse, R., Ranganath, R., Ng, A.Y.: Convolutional deep belief networks for scalable unsupervised learning of hierarchical representations. In: Proceedings of the International Conference on Machine Learning, pp. 609–616 (2009)
20. Lowe, D.G.: Distinctive image features from scale-invariant keypoints. Int. J. Comput. Vis. **60**(2), 91–110 (2004)
21. Panda, D.K., Meher, S.: A Gaussian mixture model with Gaussian weight learning rate and foreground detection using neighbourhood correlation. In: Proceedings of the IEEE Asia Pacific Conference on Postgraduate Research Microelectronics, pp. 158–163 (2013)
22. Perronnin, F., Sánchez, J., Mensink, T.: Improving the fisher Kernel for large-scale image classification. In: Daniilidis, K., Maragos, P., Paragios, N. (eds.) ECCV 2010 Part IV. LNCS, vol. 6314, pp. 143–156. Springer, Heidelberg (2010). https://doi.org/10.1007/978-3-642-15561-1_11
23. Perazzi, F., Krahenbuhl, P., Pritch, Y., Hornung, A.: Saliency filters, contrast based filtering for salient region detection. In: Proceedings of the IEEE Conference on Computing Vision Pattern Recognition, pp. 733–740 (2012)
24. Ren, S., He, K., Girshick, R., Sun, J.: Faster R-CNN: towards real-time object detection with region proposal networks. In: Proceedings of the Advances Neural Inform processing systems, pp. 91–99 (2015)
25. Sermanet, P., Kavukcuoglu, K., Chintala, S.C., Le-Cun, Y.: Pedestrian detection with unsupervised multi-stage feature learning. In: Proceedings of the IEEE Conference on Computer Vision Pattern Recognition, pp. 3626–3633 (2013)
26. Sohn, K., Zhou, G., Lee, C., Lee, H.: Learning and selecting features jointly with point-wise gated Boltzmann machines. In: Proceedings of the International Conference on Machine Learning, pp. 217–225 (2013)
27. Stauffer, C., Grimson, W.E.L.: Adaptive background mixture models for real-time tracking. Proc. IEEE Comput. Vis. Pattern Recognit. **2**, 246–252 (1999)

28. Szegedy, C., Liu, W., Jia, Y., Sermanet, P., Reed, S., Anguelov, D., Erhan, D., Vanhoucke, V., Rabinovich, A.: Going deeper with convolutions. In: Proceedings of the IEEE Conference Computer Vision Pattern Recognition, pp. 1–9 (2015)

29. Szegedy, C., Vanhoucke, V., Ioffe, S., Shlens, J., Wojna, Z.: Rethinking the inception architecture for computer vision. In: Proceedings of the IEEE Conference on Computer Vision Pattern Recognition, pp. 2818–2826 (2016)

30. TensorFlow: how to retrain inception's final layer for new categories. www.tensorflow.org/tutorials/. Accessed 26 July 2017

31. Tian, Y.L., Lu, M., Hampapur, A.: Robust and efficient foreground analysis for real-time video surveillance. Proc. IEEE Conf. Comput. Vis. Pattern Recognit. **1**, 1182–1187 (2005)

32. Wu, Y., Liu, Y., Li, J., Liu, H., and Hu, X.: Traffic sign detection based on convolutional neural networks. In: Proceedings of the International Joint Conference on Neural Networks, pp. 1–7 (2013)

33. Xia, Y., Hu, R., Wang, Z., Lu, T.: Moving foreground detection based on spatio-temporal saliency. Int. J. Comput. Sci. Issues **10**(3), 79–84 (2013)

34. Xia, H., Song, S., He, L.: A modified Gaussian mixture background model via spatiotemporal distribution with shadow detection. Sig. Image Video Process. **2**(10), 343–350 (2016)

35. Zang, Q., Klette, R.: Evaluation of an adaptive composite gaussian model in video surveillance. In: Petkov, N., Westenberg, M.A. (eds.) CAIP 2003. LNCS, vol. 2756, pp. 165–172. Springer, Heidelberg (2003). https://doi.org/10.1007/978-3-540-45179-2_21

36. Zhou, L., Yang, Z., Yuan, Q., Zhou, Z., Hu, D.: Salient region detection via integrating diffusion-based compactness and local contrast. Proc. IEEE Trans. Image Process. **11**, 3308–3320 (2015)

37. Zivkovic, Z.: Improved adaptive Gaussian mixture model for background subtraction. Proc. IEEE Int. Conf. Pattern Recognit. **2**, 28–31 (2004)

Understanding Plane Geometry Problems by Integrating Relations Extracted from Text and Diagram

Wenbin Gan[(✉)], Xinguo Yu, Chao Sun, Bin He, and Mingshu Wang

National Engineering Research Center for E-learning,
Central China Normal University, Wuhan, China
wenbingan@mails.ccnu.edu.cn

Abstract. Understanding problems is a critical and hard step for solving plane geometry problems. This paper presents a method for understanding plane geometry problems by integrating the information from text and diagram two modalities. Then high-confidence geometric relations are extracted for problem understanding through integrating the information separately extracted from text and diagram. And this paper also presents a function that can visually encode the extracted relations into the diagram to interactively present the visual effects of problem understanding results. The geometric relations are mined from the diagram after visual primitives are detected. The syntax-semantics (S^2) model method is adopted to extract geometric relations from the text. And an integration process is used to couple the information from text and diagram to obtain the high-confidence geometric relations. The experimental results show that the proposed method can mine geometric relations in high accuracy and it can understand some problems that cannot be understood by using text only or by using diagram only.

Keywords: Plane geometry problem understanding
Geometric relation extraction · S^2 model · Visually presentation
Textual information extraction · Visual information extraction

1 Introduction

Automatically solving math problems is a long-standing research problem in AI [2,6,12] and it is a core technology in building intelligent educational systems to tutor learners. In this paper we focus on the understanding of plane geometry problems in which the question text is accompanied with a diagram (an example problem is shown in Fig. 1), which is a critical step of automatically solving geometry problems.

Generally, diagram and text are used complementary as effective means to state the problems clearly in geometry discipline. In some geometry problems, the diagram contains the necessary information to solve the problem which are omitted in the question text for avoiding repetition. On the other hand, the text

© Springer International Publishing AG, part of Springer Nature 2018
M. Paul et al. (Eds.): PSIVT 2017, LNCS 10749, pp. 366–381, 2018.
https://doi.org/10.1007/978-3-319-75786-5_30

contains some decidable information that are ambiguous in a diagram because of imprecise scale. For the fully understanding of a geometry problem, it is necessary to propose the mechanism of integrating the information from both text and diagram.

This paper presents a novel method for understanding plane geometry problems by integrating the information from text and diagram. Then it uses LI-Geo, a learner-initiating geometry system, to interactively present the visual effects of the extracted relations to help learners understand the given geometry problems. The proposed problem understanding method identifies visual primitives from diagram and mines basic and derived geometric relations among the primitives, and uses an S^2 model matching method to extract the textual entities and the geometric relations in the problem text. By integrating the visual information and the textual information, coreferences are established between the visual primitives and textual entities that refer to the same object, and some high-confidence geometric relations are found and visually encoded into the diagram to interactively present the visual effects of problem understanding results. Experimental results show that the proposed method has high accuracy in mining geometric relations from both diagram and text and it can understand some problems that cannot be understood by using text or diagram only. A user study also validate the usability of the proposed method in helping people understand geometry problems.

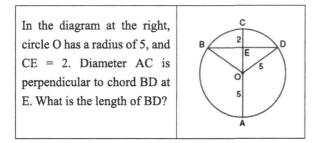

In the diagram at the right, circle O has a radius of 5, and CE = 2. Diameter AC is perpendicular to chord BD at E. What is the length of BD?

Fig. 1. A geometry problem where the question text is accompanied by a diagram.

2   Related Work

A majority of previous work in automatic problem understanding address two problems of diagram understanding and text understanding in isolation [10,11]. For the understanding of the diagram in a geometry problem, a common approach is to detect the basic geometric primitives, mainly points, lines, circles, triangles, rectangles and so on. Hough Transform is a popular method for detecting lines and circles. Triangle and rectangle can be detected in a bottom-up manner where lines are linked together to form the big primitives [11]. Zhang and Fu [16] proposed a method using Hough transform and corner detection algorithm to recognize and understand geometry diagram. The understanding is mainly focus on the finding of vertexes and lines, and their specific coordinate information. Seo et al. [11] proposed a method named G-ALIGNER for diagram understanding in geometry questions that discovers visual elements by maximizing agreement between textual and visual data. The use of textual information to assist in identifying the visual primitives improves the accuracy of primitive detection compared with hough-based method. In the higher-level understanding of the geometry diagram, some meaningful geometric information and properties implied in visual data are extracted from the geometry diagram. Chen et al. [1] proposed a method using geometric features retrieved from the diagram to find the underlying geometry theorem behind the diagram. It detects basic geometric primitives and mines basic geometric relations, then forms a undirected graph by representing the primitives as nodes and the relations as edges. A graph matching method is used to find the underlying theorems in the database. Liu et al. [7] propose a structure analysis method to better understand the spatial relationships of geometry diagram and describe a diagram in a series of features, such as local and global geometric attributes and spatial layout structure. These feature information can well represent the diagram. These works differ from our method in that they perform geometry understanding without considering the textual information. Moreover, these diagram analysis methods are insufficient for the geometry problems in which the diagrams label the values of line length or angle.

For the understanding of geometric textual information described in a problem, Guo et al. [4] proposed an algorithm to understand plane geometry proof problems in natural language (NL). This algorithm uses 196 sentence templates to transform the problems in NL into the problems described in the restricted geometric propositions. Regular expression matching is used to match a simple sentence with predefined relation patterns and get the contained relations. Mukherjee and Garain [9] developed another algorithm for formal representation of plane geometry proof problems. It used a knowledge base called GeometryNet to interpret the geometric meaning of an input text into diagram descriptions. Specifically, it decomposed the extracted entities into atomic entities by consulting the concepts in GeometryNet and used connector to link the entities to form a parse graph and then a translator is designed to translate the parse graph into structured summary of relation representation. Wong et al. [14] developed a system for understanding plane geometry proof problems and making conjectures. It represents each geometry relation as a relation frame consisting of several slots and predesigns a set of rules containing sentence templates for matching input sentences. It records the values of the attributes in the relation frame that are instantiated when a sentence is matched against a template. These works differ from our method because they perform geometry problem understanding by only considering the textual information, hence some information only present in the diagram cannot be obtained.

This paper is related to early work on understanding by integration of text and diagram [10–13]. Nakamura et al. [10] proposed a framework for semantic understanding of a diagram by utilizing textual information. However, it assumes that the visual primitives in the diagrams are manually identified. Seo et al. [12] proposed a geometry solving system named GEOS, which understands geometry problems by combining text and diagram interpretation. This method uses the textual information to assist in identifying the visual primitives and extracts geometric relations by using statistical learning method. The combination of relations from two media improves the performance of problem solving, which also verifies the feasibility of proposed method by integrating textual and visual information in understanding plane geometry problems. However, the statistical learning method used in the text parsing is highly dependent on number of training examples, and since it is hard to obtain a large number of plane geometry problems and learning from a few examples makes it challenging for understanding a broader scope of plane geometry problems. In contrast to this method, we propose a method that also performs geometry problem understanding on the coordinated intake of information from both the text and the diagram but differs from it, the visual information and text information are obtained in isolation and a integration procedure is conducted subsequently to integrate both information. The primitives in the diagram are detected using a hierarchical detection algorithm and the relations (mainly quantity relations and spatial relations) are extracted and represented in the first order logic (FOL) like symbolic description. And an S^2 model matching method is proposed to extract the relations in the text in high performance. Moreover, coreferences are built to align the visual primitives to their corresponding textual mentions, and high-confidence geometric relations are visually encoded into the diagram to interactively present the problem understanding results.

3   Overview of the Proposed Method

This section gives an overview of the proposed method of geometry problem understanding coupling textual and visual information. Before giving the problem formulation, some related concepts are first presented.

Definition 1: A geometric primitive is a visual element detected from a diagram. Four types of basic elements are used to form most of the diagrams in plane geometry, namely points, lines, circles and labels. All the primitives extracted from a diagram form a set $P = \{P_1, P_2, \ldots, P_m\}$.

Definition 2: An entity mention is a word or phrase that indicates a primitive in the diagram. All the entity mentions extracted from the text form a set $E = \{E_1, E_2, \ldots, E_n\}$.

Definition 3: An atomic proposition is a geometric relation by applying a predicate to a sequence of arguments (e.g., $isParallel(AB, CD)$). All the atomic propositions extracted from the text form a set $R_T = \{R_T^1, R_T^2, \ldots, R_T^i | R_T^i = predicate\langle E_1, \ldots, E_a \rangle, a = 1, 2 \ or \ 3\}$ and the atomic propositions extracted from the diagram form a set $R_D = \{R_D^1, R_D^2, \ldots, R_D^j | R_D^j = predicate\langle P_1, \ldots, P_b \rangle, b = 1, 2 \ or \ 3\}$.

These atomic propositions are represented in the form of first order logic (FOL). Three kinds of atomic propositions exist in the geometry problems. They are unary, binary and ternary propositions, which contains different numbers of arguments (see Sect. 5.3). These propositions belong to two categories, namely position relation and quantity relation. For example, *parallel(AB, CD)* is a position relation and *equalAngle (angle(ABC)*, 15°) is a quantity relation.

Given a geometry problem with text T and diagram D, the objective of understanding the problem is to extract the geometric propositions to represent the problem. It can be considered as two subtasks:

1. Extract a set of atomic propositions $R_T = \{R_T^1, R_T^2, \ldots, R_T^i\}$ from text T, and a set of atomic propositions $R_D = \{R_D^1, R_D^2, \ldots, R_D^j\}$ from diagram D.
2. Select a subset of atomic propositions from R_T and R_D to form a high-confidence relation set $\hat{R} = \{R_1, R_2, \ldots, R_l | R_l \in R_T \bigvee R_l \in R_D\}$ and ensure that the high-confidence relations in $\hat{R}$ are compatible with both the text and the diagram.

To achieve these two subtasks, this paper presents a geometry problem understanding method taking the powerful paradigm of coupling the intake from both visual and textual information. Specifically, it consists of three steps, namely visual information extraction, textual information extraction, and the integration process to understand across two media, as shown in Fig. 2. To extract the visual information, geometric primitives are detected using computer vision technologies and geometric relations are mined by examining their corresponding algebraic relations using numeric verification. For extracting the textual information, a syntax-semantics (S^2) model method is proposed to extract geometric relations from the text and form a set of atomic propositions. The integration process is used to fuse both visual and textual information and make mutual corroboration to obtain a set of high-confidence geometric relations which are both compatible with the text and the diagram.

To visually present the problem understanding result and provide the educational value for tutoring learners, we reactivate the visual primitives that have already been represented in the diagram and align them with the corresponding entity mentions in the text. In other words, to build the coreferences between the visual primitives and textual entities that refer to the same object. Moreover, the high-confidence geometric relations are also visually encoded into the diagram.

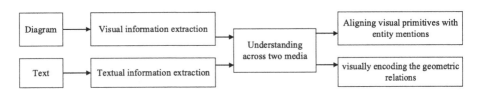

Fig. 2. The framework of the proposed method in understanding plane geometry problem.

4   Visual Information Extraction

This section is to present the extraction of visual information from the diagram. The visual information consists of geometric primitives and the various geometric relations among them. Extracting these information mainly consists of two procedures, namely geometric primitives detecting and geometric relation mining.

Given a diagram D, the geometric primitives detecting is to identify a set of primitives $P = \{P_1, P_2, \ldots, P_m\}$ from the diagram, and the procedure of geometric relation mining finds the geometric relations among the set P and obtain a set of atomic propositions $R_D = \{R_D^1, R_D^2, \ldots, R_D^j\}$. The techniques of these two procedures are presented in the following subsections.

4.1   Geometric Primitives Detecting

Detecting geometric primitives from a diagram is a computer vision problem [8]. However, the extreme lack of both textural and color features in the diagram makes it different from the images typically studied in computer vision [7]. Hence the middle-level elements in the diagram such as the primitives turn out to play a significant role in extracting the visual information.

A geometric object recognition algorithm in [1] is adopted to detect the primitives. We promote the performance of this algorithm by using a hierarchical strategy, which first applies the connected component analysis method to segment the diagram into the body part and label part and then recognizes circles, recognizes lines, collects points of interest and recognizes labels from these two parts successively. The nearest neighbour principle is adopted to assign the recognized labels to the nearest geometric objects. Eventually a set C of circles, a set L of lines, a set I of points and a set B of labels contained in the diagram D can be obtained.

It is worth noting that the detected primitives are the basic primitives including points, lines, circles and labels, some geometric shapes such as triangles, parallelograms and trapezoids are not detected. The reason is that the complicated layout and the overlap of lines and circles in the diagram may produce many such geometric shapes and directly detecting them greatly deteriorates the diagram understanding efficiency. Moreover, some of them are not used in the problem. Hence we defer the detection of such shapes in the alignment process (see Sect. 7) by combining the entity mentions identified in the text and assembling basic primitives to form such geometric shapes.

The structure of a diagram is mainly depicted via the geometric relations among the primitives in the diagram. Hence the geometric relations indicated in the diagram should be mined based on the information of detected geometric primitives.

4.2   Geometric Relation Mining

Geometric relation mining plays an important role in understanding a diagram. By analyzing the geometry diagrams, eight basic geometric relations and four

Table 1. The basic geometric relations

Representation	Meaning	Representation	Meaning
pointOnLine(p, l)	point p lies on line l	equalDistance(AB,CD)	$\parallel AB \parallel = \parallel CD \parallel$
pointOnCircle(p, c)	point p lies on circle c	equalAngle(ABC,DEF)	$\angle ABC = \angle DEF$
parallel(l_1, l_2)	line l_1 is parallel to line l_2	lcTangent(l, c)	line l is tangent to circle c
perpendicular(l_1, l_2)	line l_1 is perpendicular to line l_2	ccTangent(c_1, c_2)	circle c_1 is tangent to circle c_2

Table 2. The derived geometric relations

Relation representation	Meaning	Deriving rule
midPoint(C, AB)	point C is the midpoint of line AB	equalDistance(AC, BC) $\wedge$ pointOnLine(C,AB)
collinear(p_1, p_2, p_3)	p_1, p_2, p_3 are colinear	pointOnLine(p_1,l) $\wedge$ pointOnLine(p_2,l)$\wedge$ pointOnLine(p_3,l)
intersect(p, l_1, l_2)	p is the intersection of line l_1 and line l_2	pointOnLine(p, l_1) $\wedge$ pointOnLine(p, l_2)
angleBisect(DB, ABC)	line DB bisect angle ABC	equalAngle(ABD,CBD)

derived geometric relations are proposed, as shown in Tables 1 and 2. The eight basic geometric relations can be used to describe most features of position and quantity of geometric primitives. The four derived geometric relations are derived from the basic geometric relations and they can describe higher level features of the diagram. All these geometric relations are represented as atomic propositions.

Given the set I of points, the set L of lines, and the set C of circles of a diagram with the set B of labels, geometric relation mining is to find a set $R_D = \{R_D^1, R_D^2, \ldots, R_D^j\}$ composed of basic geometric relations and the derived geometric relations. In general, a geometric relation can be certificated to be true if and only if its corresponding algebraic equality holds. Hence Numerical verification is used to examine the corresponding algebraic relations to obtain the basic geometric relations. For instance, to obtain the pointOnLine relations, we test each pair of point $p \in I$ and line $l \in L$ and calculate the $distance(p, l)$. If the value is less than a threshold[1], then add the geometric relation $pointOnLine(p, l)$ to the set R_D. By using this method, the eight basic geometric relations in Table 1 are obtained. After obtaining the basic geometric relations, we use the deriving rules shown in Table 2 to derive a series of relations and add them to the set R_D.

---

[1] Eight threshold parameters are used to specify tolerances to mine the eight basic relations. These values are acquired empirically by making experiments on a set of test diagrams with fixed size and then are automatically adjusted according to the size of given diagram.

5   Textual Information Extraction

This section is to present the extraction of textual information from the problem text. The textual information consists of entity mentions and the various geometric relations among them. The entity mentions are extracted using natural language analysis and then a syntax-semantics (S^2) model method is proposed to extract geometric relations among these entity mentions from the text.

An algorithm is proposed using geometry S^2 models to extract the geometric relations. It mainly consists of three steps, namely parsing and annotation, geometrical entity identification, and atomic proposition extraction, as depicted in Algorithm 1. The techniques of three steps of Algorithm 1 will be presented in the following subsections.

Algorithm 1. Extracting textual information from problem text

---

Input: The text T of a plane geometry problem described in natural language.
Output: a set E of entity mentions and a set of atomic propositions R_T.
Step 1:(Parsing and Annotation) Uniform the problem text; Parse the problem text into phrases and annotate each phrases with POS;
Step 2:(Element Identification) Identify geometric relation words and entity mentions in each sentence, recognize the type of the extracted mentions and add the extracted entity mentions to E. All the results of extraction and recognition for a sentence form an annotation set F;
Step 3:(Relation extraction) Use the S^2 model to extract the relation of each sentence according to its annotation set F and form a set of atomic propositions R_T.

5.1   Parsing and Annotation

The goal of annotating the text of a plane geometry problem is to transform the problem text into a new form by doing parsing and annotation. ICTCLAS [15] is used to parse the text into phrases and to annotate these phrases with POS (part-of-speech) labels. A prepared geometric dictionary is used as the user dictionary of ICTCLAS to improve the accuracy of annotation.

5.2   Geometry Element Detection

Geometric relation words and entity mentions are important components of geometric relations. After annotation, these entity mentions are annotated with special categories of POS labels, which can be used to assist the extraction of entity mentions. A geometric entity representation is a duple $e = (w, t)$ in which w is a phrase, t is the geometry type of w. Geometric relation words are extracted using keywords matching. A geometric relation representation is a duple $J = (v, o)$ in which o is a representative relation word and v is the variant list of o. This paper have identified 48 kinds of geometric relations widely used in plane geometry problems.

5.3   Atomic Geometry Relation Extraction

Atomic geometry relation extraction is the key step of extracting textual information from problem text in Algorithm 1. To understand the techniques of this
step, the preparation of list of atomic propositions and relation extraction procedure are presented, respectively.

Preparation of List of atomic propositions: The geometry relations in
plane geometry can be divided into three types of unary, binary and ternary
relations. Table 3 gives the examples of these three types of geometry relations.
Each such relation corresponds to an atomic proposition so that there are 48
atomic propositions. Atomic propositions can be written in the form of first
order predicate logic, abbreviated as FOL.

Table 3. Explanation of three types of geometry relations.

	Element representation	Semantics	FOL	#
Unary	(equilateral triangle, ABC, triangle)	ABC is an equilateral triangle	eqTriangle(ABC)	17
Binary	(parallel, AB, CD, line, line)	line AB is parallel to CD	parallel(AB, CD)	22
Ternary	(intersects, AB, CD, E, line, line, point)	line AB intersects CD at point E	Intersect(E,AB,CD)	9

Definition 4: An S^2 model for plane geometry problems is defined as a triple
$N = (J, E, F)$, where J represents geometric relation representation, $E = \{e_1, e_2, e_3\}$ is the set of the involved elements, and F is the atomic proposi-
tions in FOL. Let $\Pi = \{N_i = (J_i, E_i, F_i) | i = 1, 2, \ldots, n\}$ denote all the prepared
S^2 models. It is also called as a pool of S^2 models of plane geometry.

The pool of 48 S^2 models are used to extract all the atomic relations in the
problem text as described in Procedure I.

Procedure I: Extraction of geometry relations using the S^2 models

The input of this procedure is a set of simple sentences of text T. Each sentence S is
annotated with its geometric entity mentions μ and geometry relation representation
ν. The output is the contained atomic propositions in each sentence, denoted as R_T.
Load S^2 models $\Pi = \{N_i = (J_i, E_i, F_i) | i = 1, 2, \ldots, n\}$;
Initialize R_T as empty;
While TRUE
    Pick a simple sentence from the sentence set
    For i from 1 to n do
        If matching J_i with ν is FALSE continue;
        If matching E_i with μ is FALSE continue;
        Put the instantiated F_i of N_i into Δ;
    If all sentences are processed break While loop;

The S^2 model matching method can generate quite high-confidence geometric
relations from the text. However, for some complex sentences containing many

geometric relations, the relations extracted may not fully reliable. Considering the sentence "AD and BC are produced to meet MN at E and F respectively". Here, "AD, BC" and "E, F" are coordinate structures, and the intersect relation is indicated. It is difficult to directly use the Procedure I to obtain the right geometric relations because of the over-numbered geometric elements. Hence, for such cases, we over-generate the geometric relations to obtain all the possible ones from the sentence and defer the validation in the integration process.

6   Integration Process

This section presents the integration process of visual and textual information. Since the imprecision of diagram and the diverse statement of problem text, the intermediate results of visual and textual information are not fully reliable. Hence it is necessary to integrate both visual and textual information and make mutual corroboration to obtain a set of high-confidence geometric relations.

Given the textual relation set R_T and the visual relation set R_D, the integration process is to find a high-confidence relation set

$$\hat{R} = \{R_1, R_2, \ldots, R_i\}, where \ R_i \in R_D \bigvee R_i \in R_T. \tag{1}$$

Generally, the diagram often contains some important geometric relations that are not presented in the text. We call these relations as high-confidence visual relations. Hence, the visual relation set R_D is divided into two sets, namely the high-confidence visual relation set R_Δ and the general visual relation set R_d.

$$R_D = R_\Delta \bigcup R_d \tag{2}$$

By analyzing the relations commonly appeared in the diagram,

$$R_\Delta = \{pointOnLine, \ pointOnCircle, \ collinear, \ intersect, \ equalDistance(line, number),$$
$$equalAngle(angle, \ number)\}.$$

For example, the relation $EqualDistance(OD,5)$ in R_D in Fig. 1 represents the equal relation between a line and a number label. Such relations are confidently extracted from the diagram and form a high-confidence visual relation set R_Δ. All the relations in R_Δ should be added into $\hat{R}$.

Moreover, by using the visual information is not able to check the correctness of some geometric relations extracted from the text. Since the scale in the diagram are different from the text, the corresponding relations cannot be obtained from the diagram. We call these relations as high-confidence textual relations. Hence, the textual relation set R_T is divided into two sets, namely the high-confidence textual relation set R_Ω and the general textual relation set R_t.

$$R_T = R_\Omega \bigcup R_t \tag{3}$$

By analyzing the relations commonly appeared in the text,

$$R_\Omega = \{congruentTriangle, \ similarTriangle, \ equalDistance(line, number),$$
$$equalAngle(angle, \ number)\}.$$

These relations are correct to a large extent, therefore we directly add them into $\hat{R}$.

Therefore, the integration process in Eq. (1) is equal to find the set

$$\hat{R} = \{R_1, R_2, \ldots, R_i\} \bigcup R_\Delta \bigcup R_\Omega, where \ R_i \in R_d \bigcap R_t, R_\Delta \subset R_D, R_\Omega \subset R_T. \tag{4}$$

For each general textual relation $R_j \in R_t$ from the text, we check whether it is also in the general visual relation set R_d. If it satisfies the text and the diagram simultaneously, we add it into $\hat{R}$, otherwise it is regarded as incorrect relation and is discarded.

Based on the above discussion, the procedure of integrating the relations extracted from diagram and text is described in Procedure II.

Procedure II: Integration of relations extracted from diagram and text

The input of this procedure is a set R_T of textual relations and a set R_D of visual relations. The output is a set $\hat{R}$ of high-confidence relations.

(i) $R_\Omega, R_t \leftarrow R_T$: divide the textual relation set R_T into two sets R_Ω, R_t;
(ii) $R_\Delta, R_d \leftarrow R_D$: divide the visual relation set R_D into two sets R_Δ, R_d;
(iii) Initialize $\hat{R}$ as empty;

$\hat{R} = \hat{R} \bigcup R_\Delta \bigcup R_\Omega$;

For each $R_j \in R_t$

If $R_j \in R_d$ then $\hat{R} = \hat{R} \bigcup R_j$;

return $\hat{R}$.

7   Alignment and Visually Presentation

To interactively present the problem understanding result, this section presents the alignment of geometric entities and geometric primitives and visually encoded the high-confidence geometric relations into the diagram.

The relation set $\hat{R}$ (obtained in the Sect. 6) contains all the geometric entities occurred in the problem and their geometric relations. Hence we extract all the entities in $\hat{R}$ and form an entity set E without repeated elements. The geometric primitives (detected in Sect. 4.1) form a set F^2. A matrix $W \in \{0, 1\}^{|E| \times |F|}$ is built to record the alignment. $W_{i,j}$ identifies whether the i_{th} geometric entities E_i is aligned with the j_{th} geometric primitive F_j. This alignment is built by mapping the name of the geometric entities with the label of the corresponding primitives in the diagram. For example, the entity OB is mapped with a line $l_3 := line(O, B)$ in Fig. 1.

---

[2] It is worth noting that the geometric primitives detected in Sect. 4.1 include the points, lines and circles and labels without some complex geometric shapes such as triangles, squares, parallelograms and trapezoids. To tackle this situation, we detect them only when they occurs in the entity set E, and use bottom-up method to combine the basic primitives into the geometric shapes. For example, $\triangle ABC$ is detected by assembling three lines AB, AC and BC. All these detected shapes are also added into the set F.

For tutoring purpose in helping learners understand the problem, we also visually encode the geometric relations into the diagram. When the problem text goes on with mouse clicks, the related geometry elements and their relations in the diagram are highlighted and animated with various visually dynamic effects. This makes the understanding of diagram more vividly visualized and intuitive.

8   Experimental Results

This section is to evaluate the proposed method on understanding plane geometry problems. It first describes the setting for the experiments. Then it presents the results of the proposed method in mining geometric relations. To also better understand the performance on helping learners in geometry problem understanding, a user study is conducted.

8.1   Experimental Setup

Dataset: The datasets consist of the dataset used in [11] named as GeoE100, which contains the 100 plane geometry problems in English and the dataset prepared in this paper named as GeoC50, which contains 50 plane geometry problems in Chinese. These 50 problems are compiled from the test datasets used in [3,5]. Every question has a textual description accompanied by a diagram. We manually annotate all the primitives in the diagram and the entity mentions in the text and build all the alignments between them. Moreover, for each problem we manually understand the problem and prepare a set of geometric relations as its groundtruth, which are required for finding the solutions. Table 4 gives the statistics of the problems and the groundtruth of GeoE100 and GeoC50. In GeoC50, the problem texts are much longer and the diagrams are more complicated than the problems in GeoE100.

Table 4. Statistics on the problems and the groundtruth of GeoE100 and GeoC50.

		Primitives[a]	Entity	V-relations	T-relations	VT-relations
GeoE100	Total	1015	482	821	436	648
	Average	10.2	4.8	8.2	4.4	6.5
GeoC50	Total	707	617	896	329	615
	Average	14.1	12.3	17.9	6.6	12.3

[a]The primitives here include the points, lines, circles and labels

Evaluation measure: Two tasks are evaluated in this experiment. Firstly, mining the geometric relations by integrating the textual and visual information. Secondly, testing the usability of the proposed method.

For the first task, we compare the mined relations with groundtruth relations by measuring them using precision, recall and F_1. For the second task, a user study is conducted to test the usability of the method in helping people understand geometry problems and to obtain feedbacks.

8.2   Results

Mining geometric relations. To study the performance of mining geometric relations by integrating textual and visual information, we compare the relation extracting results on all the test problems in GeoE100 and GeoC50 with ground truth relations. As shown in Table 5, precision is the number of correctly extracted relations divided by total number of extracted relations, recall is the number of correctly extracted relations divided by the number of relations in ground truth. The visual relations (V-relation) extracted from the diagram achieves 0.90 in F_1 score. The entity mentions identified from the text obtain 100% in precision and recall, and the textual relation (T-relation) mined from the text achieves 0.92 in F_1 score. This validates that the S^2 models can extract geometric relations from problem texts both in Chinese and English. By integrating the textual and visual information (D-T integration), it achieves precision of 0.94 at the recall of 0.97 and 0.95 in F_1 score in finding the high-confidence relations (HC-relation). These results show the effectiveness of integrating both textual and visual information to understand geometry problems. And they also show that the proposed method can understand problems that cannot be understood by using text or diagram only.

Table 5. The performance of mining geometric relations on the test problems.

		P	R	F_1
Diagram	V-relation	0.86	0.95	0.90
Text	Entity	1	1	1
	T-relation	0.89	0.96	0.92
D-T integration	HC-relation	0.94	0.97	0.95

User study. We built a learner-initiating interactive geometry system named LI-Geo (Fig. 3). A user study is conducted to test the usability of the system in helping people understand geometry problems. In LI-Geo, there are three separate areas for problem text presentation, diagram showing and geometric relation display. When click on the content in any of the three areas, the corresponding content in the other two will be activated and the dynamic visual effect will be presented in the diagram.

The test task was to understand the geometry problems provided by us and did not require any knowledge beyond senior school, so we recruited 12 graduate students who possessed the required geometry knowledge. we provided each subject 10 plane geometry problems with diagrams, and each subject was asked to select and understand 4 problems in LI-Geo. After trying the LI-Geo system, each subject was asked to answer a post-test questionnaire to grade the primitive detection accuracy, entity extraction accuracy, high-confidence relation extraction accuracy, the visual presentation, comfort of interaction, helpfulness in understanding problems, enjoyment of the tool, all in a 7-level Likert scale (1-very bad, 7-very good).

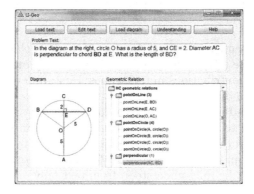

Fig. 3. The user interface of LI-Geo.

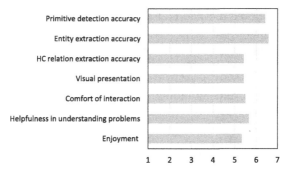

Fig. 4. Users' feedback of using LI-Geo.

Figure 4 exhibits the results of users' feedback. As shown, the primitive detection accuracy, entity extraction accuracy, high-confidence relation extraction accuracy and the visual presentation are all received good feedback from subjects. In addition, the subjects think it is comfortable and enjoyment to use the system and the system helps users in understanding geometry problems.

Discussion. The user study highlights the usefulness of the learner-initiating problem understanding tool. By using the interaction, the given and the goal of a problem and the geometric relations between the primitives (entities) will be better understood. By analyzing the geometric relations obtained by the system, an interesting finding is that some critical information for solving the problem but is not present in the text is obtained. For example, to solve the problem in Fig. 1, one has to know that *pointOnLine(O, AC)*, *collinear(O, E, C)* and *equalDistance(OC, 5)*. Hence the proposed problem understanding method by integrating textual and visual information will facilitate the automated solving of problems. However, this research is ongoing, and how to use the problem understanding method in the task of geometry problem solving and how to use it to tutor learners are our future work.

9 Conclusion

This paper has presented a method for understanding plane geometry problem by integrating the information separately extracted from text and diagram. This paper has four contributions in techniques. First, it developed a method to extract relations from diagram. This method uses numerical verification to mine geometric relations after detecting the visual primitives. Second, it proposed an S^2 model method to extract relations from the problem text. Third, it proposed a new method for understanding geometry problems by integrating textual and visual information. This method can understand a batch of plane geometry problems that cannot be fully understood from text only or from diagram only. Fourth, it developed a procedure to encode the extracted relations into the corresponding positions in the diagram. This procedure makes the understanding of plane geometry problems visualized and intuitive. The experimental results showed that the proposed method had a good performance. This work validates that coupling vision and NLP to process multi-model information helps improve textual or visual interpretations.

In the future, we want to extend the research in multiple directions. First, it is the good future job to develop the improved automatic solvers based on the method of problem understanding. Second, we plan to extend the method to understand geometry problems with hand-drawn input geometry diagrams. Third, we plan to apply the method that couple supplementary explanation extracted from multi-modality into understanding the problems from other subjects.

Acknowledgments. This work is supported by the Open Projects Program of National Laboratory of Pattern Recognition (No. 201600008) and the self-determined research funds of CCNU from the colleges' basic research and operation of MOE (No. ccnu16JYKX005).

References

1. Chen, X., Song, D., Wang, D.: Automated generation of geometric theorems from images of diagrams. Ann. Math. Artif. Intell. **74**(3–4), 333–358 (2015)
2. Chou, S.C., Gao, X.S., Zhang, J.Z.: Machine Proofs in Geometry: Automated Production of Readable Proofs for Geometry Theorems. World Scientific, Singapore (1994)
3. Ge, Q.: Research of automated geometry reasoning and its application with constrained conditions. Ph.D. thesis, Central China Normal University (2011)
4. Guo, H.Y., Liu, Q.T., Chen, M., Huang, H., Ge, Q.: Research for facing the natural language of the geometry drawing. Comput. Sci. **39**(6A), 503–506 (2012)
5. Jiang, J.: iGeo: a theorem prover of the intelligent geometry software. Ph.D. thesis, Chengdu Computer Application Research Institute of Chinese Academy of Sciences (2006)
6. Jiang, J., Zhang, J.: A review and prospect of readable machine proofs for geometry theorems. J. Syst. Sci. Complex. **25**(4), 802–820 (2012)

7. Liu, L., Lu, X., Fu, S., Qu, J., Gao, L., Tang, Z.: Plane geometry figure retrieval based on bilayer geometric attributed graph matching. In: ICPR, pp. 309–314. IEEE (2014)

8. Montalvo, F.: Diagram understanding: the intersection of computer vision and graphics. Massachusetts Institute of Technology (1985)

9. Mukherjee, A., Garain, U.: Understanding of natural language text for diagram drawing. In: 13th International Conference on Artificial Intelligence and Soft Computing (2009)

10. Nakamura, Y., Furukawa, R., Nagao, M.: Diagram understanding utilizing natural language text. In: ICDAR, pp. 614–618. IEEE (1993)

11. Seo, M.J., Hajishirzi, H., Farhadi, A., Etzioni, O.: Diagram understanding in geometry questions. In: 28th AAAI Conference on Artificial Intelligence, pp. 2831–2838 (2014)

12. Seo, M.J., Hajishirzi, H., Farhadi, A., Etzioni, O., Malcolm, C.: Solving geometry problems: combining text and diagram interpretation. In: EMNLP, pp. 1466–1476 (2015)

13. Srihari, R.K.: Computational models for integrating linguistic and visual information: a survey. Artif. Intell. Rev. **8**(5-6), 349–369 (1994)

14. Wong, W.K., Huang, C.W., et al.: A computer-assisted environment for understanding geometry theorem proving problems and making conjectures. Int. J. Intell. Inf. Database Syst. **3**(3), 231–245 (2009)

15. Zhang, H.P., Liu, Q.: ICTCLAS. Institute of Computing Technology, Chinese Academy of Sciences (2002). http://www.ict.ac.cn/freeware/003_ictclas.asp

16. Zhang, X., Fu, H.: Recognizing and understanding of plane geometry. J. Comput. Appl. **35**, 280–283, 341 (2015)

Lane Detection Based on Road Module and Extended Kalman Filter

Jinsheng Xiao[1,2](✉) ⓘ, Li Luo[1], Yuan Yao[3], Wentao Zou[1],
and Reinhard Klette[4] ⓘ

[1] School of Electronic Information, Wuhan University, Wuhan, China
xiaojs@whu.edu.cn
[2] Collaborative Innovation Center of Geospatial Technology, Wuhan, China
[3] College of Physical Science and Technology, Central China Normal University,
Wuhan, China
[4] School of Engineering, Computer, and Mathematical Sciences,
Auckland University of Technology, Auckland, New Zealand
reinhard.klette@aut.ac.nz

Abstract. Lane detection is already a basic component in modern vehicle control systems, with satisfying accuracy on labeled roads. There are still occasional problems of low accuracy and robustness in cases of challenging lighting, shadows, or in cases that road marking is missing. The paper proposes a new algorithm combining a model of road structure with an extended Kalman filter. Lane borders are detected by an adaptive edge detection operator based on scan lines. A new parameter space is defined to adjust the algorithm to the current lane model. All candidate lanes are extracted by voting of edge points. Road boundaries are obtained by considering various constraints. A new driveway model is specified according to roadway geometry and vehicle dynamics. The estimation of parameters is expanded for also covering driveway information. Coordinates of lane border points are tracked and estimated using an extended Kalman filter. Special attention is paid to enhancing stability and robustness of the algorithm. Results indicate that the proposed algorithm is robust under various lighting conditions and road scenarios; it is also of low computational complexity.

1 Introduction

Advanced driver assistance systems are gradually being incorporated into vehicles. Such a system can either alert the driver in dangerous situations, or take on an active part in the driving process. The systems are expected to become more and more complex towards full autonomy during the next decade. The perception problems are the main bottleneck in the development of such systems.

One of the perception problems is road and lane detection, tracking, and analysis, and another one is obstacle detection [1–3]. We consider the first one in this paper. The main perceptual cues for human driving include road color and texture, road boundaries, and lane markings. Autonomous vehicles are expected to share the road with human drivers, at least for some time, and will therefore

© Springer International Publishing AG, part of Springer Nature 2018
M. Paul et al. (Eds.): PSIVT 2017, LNCS 10749, pp. 382–395, 2018.
https://doi.org/10.1007/978-3-319-75786-5_31

most likely continue to rely on the same perceptual cues that human drivers do. It is unrealistic to expect the huge investments required to construct and maintain special infrastructure for autonomous vehicles only. Road and lane perception via traditional cues remains the most likely scenario for autonomous driving; see, for example, [1,3,4].

The road and lane detection task can be broken down into five functional modules. They are image pre-processing, feature extraction, road/lane model fitting, temporal integration, and image-to-world correspondence; see [1,5,6]. Yu and Jain [7] proposed in 1997 a method based on multi-resolution Hough transform to detect lane boundaries. The geometric information of the lane was used to limit the parameter range of the Hough transform. Hough-transform based methods are still in use today for well-marked highway driving. Lee [8] proposed a lane departure warning system to estimate the subsequent direction of a lane through an *edge distribution function* (EDF) and direction changes of vehicle movement. The EDF failed on roads with curved and dashed lanes. Kang and Jung [9] estimated the initial position of a road boundary based on edge direction and amplitude of the lane based on assuming a flat road surface.

The analysis of connected components and an energy density function in dynamic programming are used to obtain the best location of a lane. Wang et al. [10] provided an initial position for a B-snake model in 2004. The lane detection problem can be changed into the problem of control points to determine a spline curve following a road model. In 2010, Zhou and Jiang[11] estimated the parameters from the main direction and the edge direction, and the best lane model was selected by a Gabor filter. In 2012, Mechat [12] detected a lane using a support vector machine (SVM) based method; the model of the lane was defined by a Catmull-Rom curve, and the standard Kalman filter was adopted to estimate and track the parameters of control points. Kortli et al. [13] established a region of interest (ROI) in road images, used a Gauss filter for data pre-processing, and then applied the Canny edge detector to enhance lane boundaries; a method was proposed to extract lane boundaries based on color information and image segmentation by using a histogram threshold, Hough transform; the current vehicle position was obtained. Shin et al. [14] extended a particle-filter-based approach for lane detection, also addressing challenging road situations. Lee et al. [15] proposed a real-time lane detection and tracking algorithm using filters (e.g. a Kalman filter) for an embedded lane departure warning system (LDWS). Lane detection modules provide currently already stable results in general, but their performance under special (i.e. challenging) conditions is still a research topic; those conditions might be defined by strong sunlight, hard to identify lanes (e.g. missing lane marks, confusing marks on the road, or cars parked along a road), shadows caused by trees or other objects, sidewalks, zebra crossings, or text logos on the road.

In view of this, we propose a lane detection algorithm by combining a road structure model with an extended Kalman filter. Considering the characteristics of the lane and according to the roadway geometry and vehicle dynamics, a new lane model is proposed which enhances the stability and anti-jamming of the lane-detection system. The parameter space is defined to accommodate the algorithm for the lane model. Due to algorithmic developments in the area of Hough transform [16], there is good progress to improve the processing speed. The extended Kalman filter is used to estimate and track the lane, which is the major factor for improved accuracy in the proposed lane detection. The effectiveness and robustness of the algorithm are demonstrated in this paper.

The paper is structured as follows. Section 2 reports about the used lane (or road) and vehicle model. Section 3 describes our combination of road model and of an extended Kalman filter. Section 4 informs about our experiments and the performed evaluation. Section 5 concludes.

2   Processing in the Basic Layer

In this paper, estimated parameters for lane detection are related to lane shape and the pose of the *ego-vehicle* (i.e. the vehicle where the lane-detector operates in). These parameters involve lane width, lane curvature, and the motion of the ego-vehicle (described, e.g., by the pitch angle or horizontal angle).

2.1   Algorithm Outline

Figure 1 shows the flowchart of our lane detection algorithm. Parameter estimation is divided into two parts. The first part is the *pose* (i.e. position and viewing

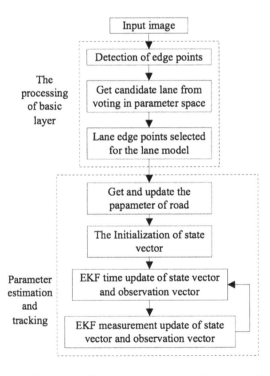

Fig. 1. Schematic diagram of lane detection algorithm

direction) of the camera and the road environment information obtained from the in-vehicle camera. The second part estimates the parameters of the road using the road lane information. The flowchart of our algorithm, presented in this paper, begins with reading a frame of the recorded video sequence. The adaptive edge detection operator, based on scan line processing, is used to extract the edge points from the R channel of the image. We select a region of interest in the algorithm. The image pixel coordinate system is mapped to the road plane coordinate system. Edge points are voted in a customized parameter space to obtain candidate lines. We collect geometrical characteristics and estimate spatial continuity of the lane. The information of the lane in the image pixel coordinate system, and the lane road plane coordinate system is used to exclude non-lane lines. Inner boundary points and an extended Kalman filter are combined to estimate and update lane model parameters.

2.2   Detection of Edge Points

Due to the perspective effect of the camera, visible information differs for different ranges in the image of the road plane. We divide the regions of interest into several areas. A preset area is selected according to the image coordinates which are converted using the vanishing point coordinates and the real coordinates. The customized edge-detection operator is based on scan-line processing for reducing the amount of computations. An image row forms a scanning line. If the number of calculated scan lines is greater than the maximum value, the scan lines are set under the real world coordinates with the same distance of each line. These lines are translated into the image pixel coordinate system. A set of scan lines is shown in Fig. 2, left. By scanning through each pixel in a selected scan line, the edge strength of each pixel is calculated by the following equation. $E(i)$ is the edge strength of a pixel in the scanning line, $I(i)$ represents

Fig. 2. *Left*: a set of scan lines. *Right*: examples of detected edge points; input image is as shown on the left

the image value of the i-th pixel, and L_i defines the neighborhood of the pixel at i:

$$E(i) = - \sum_{k=-L_i}^{-1} I(i+k) + \sum_{k=1}^{L_i} I(i+k) \qquad (1)$$

Our method is not using the same neighborhood for all the pixels; the pixel neighborhood parameter L_i, also called the *scale* here, is chosen adaptively for edge detection; it may change based on the position of the pixel in the image.

We consider the perspective effect of the lane in the road image. The length that each pixel represents in world coordinates on a scanning line is computed after coordinate conversion. The width of the lane is used to be divided by the proportion for each scan line. Then, the pixels can be identified which are needed to compute the edge strength. Pixels which have a maximum or minimum value of edge strength are *edge points*. This customized edge detection operator can greatly reduce the processing time. Edge detection results are shown in Fig. 2, right. The figure shows that the operator can detect edge points in all the lanes; accuracy and efficiency can be called "very good" in general.

2.3   Obtain Candidate Lane from Voting in Parameter Space

After edge points are detected, they need to be aggregated into a candidate lane. The amount of computations for the traditional Hough transform [17] is large but can be reduced [16]. Aiming at the lane model, the parameter space is defined conveniently for our algorithm. The edge points are voting in the parameter space. A diagram of the customized parameter space is shown in Fig. 3. The parameter space is spanned by two parameters p and q. The lane in the region of interest is defined by $x = p + y(q/d)$. Parameter p represents the position of the line on the x axis; parameter q identifies the slope, i.e. the lateral position. The flowchart of our voting algorithm includes three parts:

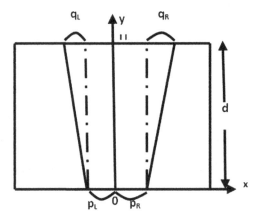

Fig. 3. Parameter space

1. The coordinates of edge points are transformed. The edge points obtained from the edge detection are in the image pixel coordinate system. The edge points need to be converted to the world coordinate system, in which the perspective effect is removed.
2. All the edge points in the selected area are traversed by parameter q. The corresponding p was obtained through the look-up table. The accumulator increases by 1. q is translated from the tilt angle of the lanes. q is discretized and the range of value is $[-88°, 88°]$. p is discretized and the range of value is $[-5\,m, 5\,m]$ in the world coordinate system.
3. Different p,q denote different lines. From the mapping relationship of the parameter space, the larger the value of the accumulator of p, q, there are more edge points in the lane which are represented by this parameter. All possible candidate lines are identified by searching for the maximum value.

The wrong candidate lines are parallel to the right lane boundary in many cases. After searching for all local maximum value, it needs to check whether any pair of candidate line is crossed. If a pair of candidate lines is crossed, the line in which has a smaller value in the parameter space will be discarded. The judgment for determining cross-line is as follows:

$$(p_A - p_B) \cdot (p_B - p_A + q_B - q_A) \geq 0 \qquad (2)$$

The candidate lines can be gotten by the voting algorithm in the parameter space. The geometrical characteristics and spatial continuity of the lane are still needed to exclude the unwanted points and unwanted lanes. The dual information of lane in the image pixel coordinates system and the lane road plane coordinate system is useful too. The final candidate lanes are shown in Fig. 4 left, which detect the current two lanes accurately.

The lane edge points need to be selected for the lane model after the above steps. All the points should be selected, but only ten points are selected if the total number of edge points is greater than ten. The ten points are selected by same distances. The selected points are shown in Fig. 4 right. The perspective

Fig. 4. *Left*: candidates of lane boundary lines. *Right*: selected boundary points

effect in the road line image should be considered in the selection of boundary points which can ensure the reasonableness and accuracy of the lane tracking and estimating in the later.

3   Combining Lane Model and Extended Kalman Filter

Vehicle shaking, light changing and vehicle interference, all can lead to the jitter of the collected images. One or several frames cannot identify the lane lines due to the reasons of broken lane, dirty road, shadows, and so on. The filter algorithm is used to track the lane, which can greatly improve the ability of stability and anti-jamming for the system [18]. Therefore, the information of road structure model is combined with extended Kalman filter. The extended Kalman filter is used to track after the lane lines were detected, which greatly improved the accuracy of lane identification. The effectiveness and robustness of the algorithm are ensured too.

3.1   Lane Model

The lane model is built according to the roadway geometry and vehicle dynamics [19,20]. The road boundary model is defined as follows:

$$x_{t,k}(z) = \frac{1}{2}kW_t + e_t + \theta_t z + \frac{1}{2}c_{0,t}z^2 + \frac{1}{6}c_{1,t}z^3 \tag{3}$$

$x_{t,k}(z)$ is the position for the point of lane boundary which has a distance of z from the vehicle at time t. k denotes the left or right side of the lane with $k = -1$ or $k = 1$. e_t is the lateral offset between the center of the vehicle and the center of the lane. θ_t is the yaw angle between driving direction and the lane. $c_{0,t}$, $c_{1,t}$ are the curvature and the change rate of curvature. φ_t is the pitch angle between the optical axis and the plane of the road plane. The estimated parameters are described as follows:

$$x(t) = \left(\dot{\theta}_t, \theta_t, \dot{e}_t, e_t, c_{1,t}, c_{0,t}, \varphi_t, W_t\right) \tag{4}$$

The "·" on the letters in the formula expresses the change rate of corresponding parameters. Compared with the models [19,20], the model in this paper increases two new estimated parameters, that is, the change rate of the yaw angle $\dot{\theta}_t$ and the lateral offset $\dot{e}_t$. The tracking estimation parameters of lane information increase, the stability, anti-jamming and detection rate of the lane detection system can be corresponding improved.

3.2   Parameter Estimation

When the candidate lanes have been detected preliminarily, they are tracked and estimated by Kalman filter. The traditional Kalman filter is useful when the state equation and measurement equation of system are both linear system. The system noise and measurement noise are consistent with the gaussian distribution. The parameters can be estimated by the principle of minimum mean square error. But the state equation and measurement equation of the lane model in this paper are nonlinear. The traditional Kalman filter is not practicable in this system. So the nonlinear system should be approximated by a linear problem. The Taylor series expansion is the most commonly used linearization method, which ignores the higher order term. So the Kalman filter is replaced by the extended Kalman filtering (EKF) [21]. The update processing of extended Kalman filter is shown as following:

The process has a state vector $x \in \mathbb{R}^n$. It is now governed by the non-linear stochastic difference equation:

$$\begin{cases} x(t) = f(x(t-1), u(t-1), w(t-1)) \\ y(t) = h(x(t), v(t)) \end{cases} \tag{5}$$

where the random variables $w(\cdot)$ and $v(\cdot)$ represent the process and measurement noise with zero-mean. The $u(t-1)$ is the driving function. The time update of state vector and the observation vector for extended Kalman filter are as following:

$$\begin{cases} \hat{x}_p(t) = f(\hat{x}(t-1), u(t-1), 0) \\ P_p(t) = A(t)P(t-1)A(t)^\top + W(t)Q(t-1)W(t)^\top \end{cases} \tag{6}$$

where $\hat{x}_p(t)$ is the priori state estimate at time t. $\hat{x}(t)$ is the posteriori state estimate at time t. $A(t)$ and $W(t)$ are the process Jacobians at time t. Where $P_p(t)$ is the priori estimate error covariance. $P(t)$ is the posteriori estimate error covariance. $Q(t)$ is the process noise covariance. The Kalman gain in the update of measurement is shown as following:

$$K(t) = [P_p(t)H(t)^\top] [H(t)P_p(t)H(t)^\top + V(t)R(t)V(t)^\top]^{-1} \tag{7}$$

where $H(t)$ and $V(t)$ are the measurement Jacobians at time t. $R(t)$ is the measurement noise covariance. The covariance matrix of posteriori estimation error in the measurement update is shown as:

$$P(t) = P_p(t) - K(t)H(t)P_p(t) \tag{8}$$

The updated estimation of observation vector in the measurement update is the following expression:

$$\hat{x}(t) = \hat{x}_p(t) + K(t) [y(t) - h(\hat{x}_p(t), 0)] \tag{9}$$

According to the change of traffic variables and vehicle dynamics, the system matrix can be obtained as follows [19]:

$$A(t) = \begin{pmatrix} 1 & 0 & 0 & 0 & 0 & 0 & 0 & 0 \\ \Delta t & 1 & 0 & 0 & \frac{\Delta t^2 \cdot V^2}{2} & 0 & 0 & 0 \\ 0 & 0 & 1 & 0 & \Delta t^2 \cdot V^3 & 0 & 0 & 0 \\ 0 & 0 & \Delta t & 1 & 0 & 0 & 0 & 0 \\ 0 & 0 & 0 & 0 & 1 & 0 & 0 & 0 \\ 0 & 0 & 0 & 0 & \Delta t \cdot V & 1 & 0 & 0 \\ 0 & 0 & 0 & 0 & 0 & 0 & 1 & 0 \\ 0 & 0 & 0 & 0 & 0 & 0 & 0 & 1 \end{pmatrix} \tag{10}$$

where V is the vehicle's speed. The observation vector is set as x_{road}. Because the estimation points which are selected to estimate parameters are image pixels, the points need to be converted:

$$\begin{cases} y_{img} = -f \dfrac{h}{z_{road}} - f \cdot \varphi_t \\[2mm] x_{img} = f \dfrac{x_{road}}{z_{road}} \end{cases} \tag{11}$$

In keeping with road plane, x_{img} is image's ordinate and y_{img} is abscissa. The Jacobian matrix for the partial derivatives of h respect to x is defined as follows:

$$H_{[i,j]} = \frac{\partial h_{[i]}}{\partial x_{[j]}} (\hat{x}_k, 0)$$

$$= \left(\frac{\partial x_{img}}{\partial x[0]}, \frac{\partial x_{img}}{\partial x[1]}, \frac{\partial x_{img}}{\partial x[2]}, \frac{\partial x_{img}}{\partial x[3]}, \frac{\partial x_{img}}{\partial x[4]}, \frac{\partial x_{img}}{\partial x[5]}, \frac{\partial x_{img}}{\partial x[6]}, \frac{\partial x_{img}}{\partial x[7]} \right) \tag{12}$$

So, from (11) there are:

$$\begin{cases} \dfrac{\partial x_{img}}{\partial x[i]} = \dfrac{f}{z_{road}} \cdot \dfrac{\partial x_{road}}{\partial x[i]}, & i = 0, 1, ..., 5, 7 \\[3mm] \dfrac{\partial x_{img}}{\partial x[6]} = \dfrac{\partial x_{img}}{\partial z_{road}} \cdot \dfrac{\partial z_{road}}{\partial x[6]} \end{cases} \tag{13}$$

From (3), we obtain that

$$x_{road} = \frac{1}{2} k W_t + e_t + \theta_t z_{road} + \frac{1}{2} c_{0,t} z_{road}^2 + \frac{1}{6} c_{1,t} z_{road}^3 \tag{14}$$

Note the definition of $x(t)$ in (4), we have $x(t) = \left(\dot{\theta}_t, \theta_t, \dot{e}_t, e_t, c_{1,t}, c_{0,t}, \varphi_t, W_t \right)$, so:

$$\left(\frac{\partial x_{road}}{\partial x[0]}, \frac{\partial x_{road}}{\partial x[1]}, \frac{\partial x_{road}}{\partial x[2]}, \frac{\partial x_{road}}{\partial x[3]}, \frac{\partial x_{road}}{\partial x[4]}, \frac{\partial x_{road}}{\partial x[5]}, \cdots, \frac{\partial x_{road}}{\partial x[7]} \right) \tag{15}$$

$$= \left(0, z_{road}, 0, 1, \frac{1}{6} z_{road}^3, \frac{1}{2} z_{road}^2, \cdots, \frac{1}{2} k \right)$$

with

$$\frac{\partial x_{road}}{\partial z_{road}} = \theta_t + c_{0,t} z_{road} + \frac{1}{2} c_{1,t} z_{road}^2 \tag{16}$$

So, from Eqs. (11), (14), and (16) we have that

$$\frac{\partial x_{img}}{\partial z_{road}} = \frac{f}{z_{road}^2} \cdot \left(z_{road} \cdot \frac{\partial x_{road}}{\partial z_{road}} - x_{road} \right)$$

$$= \frac{f}{z_{road}^2} \cdot \left(\frac{1}{2} c_{0,t} z_{road}^2 + \frac{1}{3} c_{1,t} z_{road}^3 - \frac{1}{2} k W_t - e_t \right) \tag{17}$$

According to the relationship between angle and ordinate in image, from (11) it can be gotten that $z_{road} = \frac{-f \cdot h}{y_{img} + f \cdot \phi_t}$. Note that $x[6]$ is ϕ_t in (4), so:

$$\frac{\partial z_{road}}{\partial x[6]} = \frac{\partial z_{road}}{\partial \phi_t} = \frac{f^2 \cdot h}{(y_{img} + f \cdot \phi_t)^2} \tag{18}$$

Then

$$H_{[i,j]} = \left(0, f, 0, \frac{f}{z_{road}}, \frac{f \cdot z_{road}^2}{6}, \frac{f \cdot z_{road}}{2}, \frac{\partial x_{img}}{\partial z_{road}} \frac{\partial z_{road}}{\partial x[6]}, \frac{k \cdot f}{2 \cdot z_{road}} \right) \tag{19}$$

The 7th item in the Jacobian matrix H can be obtained by the above formula. The parameters of lane model can be expressed by the state vector and the covariance matrix of estimation error. The abscissas of the lane boundary points in the original input image selected from the above steps, are gotten by the extended Kalman filter to conduct iterative estimation. If the extracted lane candidate boundary points include the noise introduced by observation, but not include wrong identification points, then the unit of standard deviation for noise is pixel. If the value of the variance for estimation error is σ^2, then the maximum change of each parameter is 3σ. Assuming that the standard deviation of x_{img} is σ, the search area of candidate points is $(x_{img} - 3\sigma, y_{img}) \sim (x_{img} + 3\sigma, y_{img})$ for the next time. The selection of lane curvature can be narrowed down, too.

4   Experiments and Analysis

The numerous experiments were implemented to verify the validity of the proposed algorithm with the programming development environment VS2005 on the platform of Intel Core i5-3470 K processor at 3.2 GHz 4 GB cache. The operating system is Windows XP. The algorithm is based on monocular vision, and the road images obtained via an industrial camera: Basler pia1900-32 gm/gc. The focal length is 8 mm. The maximum frame rate of image is 32 frames per second. The size of image is $1,920 \times 1,080$ in pixels. Images obtained from camera are transferred to the computer through a Gigabit Ethernet port.

To verify the effectiveness and robustness of the proposed algorithm, the road video data captured from Erdos in Inner Mongolia is selected to test. These data

Table 1. Detection efficiency for RANSAC and proposed algorithm

Video index	Total number of frames	Number of correctly detected frames		Recognition rate	
		Proposed algorithm	RANSAC algorithm	Proposed algorithm	RANSAC algorithm
1	4060	4028	3947	99.21%	97.22%
2	3660	3610	3519	98.63%	96.15%
3	3120	3101	3017	99.39%	96.70%
4	3540	3509	3368	99.12%	95.14%

include a variety of road conditions, such as trees shadow, pedestrian, vehicle interference, strong light and shadow, curve and so on. Test results of four video sequences are shown as example. The comparison algorithm is RANSAC algorithm based on template [3]. Table 1 is the statistics result for the lane detection, which include the total number of the test frames and the recognition rate. From the data in Table 1, the recognition rate of the proposed algorithm in this paper is 2% to 4% higher than the RANSAC algorithm. The algorithm has good stability and high recognition rate up to 99.39%. The proposed algorithm in this paper has good accuracy and robustness for the structural road environment. The state equation and measurement equation of the lane model here are nonlinear, which are not suitable for the traditional Kalman filter. So the nonlinear system should be approximated by a linear problem. The extended Kalman Filter is used to estimate and track the road lane, which improved the accuracy of the lane detection. Due to the extended Kalman filter, the detection result is very stable and the problems of jitter and low fitting precision in traditional algorithm are missed.

Next, it is necessary to discuss the robustness of the lane detection algorithm under different road environment. The comparative analysis of lane detection effect for complex road environment are shown in Figs. 5, 6, 7 and 8. It includes lane-changing, curve, zebra crossing, strong light and shadow trees, vehicles, etc.

Fig. 5. Detection results for RANSAC. *Left to right*: lane-changing, curve, zebra crossing

Fig. 6. Detection results of the proposed method. *Left to right*: lane-changing, curve, zebra crossing

Fig. 7. Detection results of RANSAC. *Left to right*: vehicle, strong light, shadow

In Fig. 5, the RANSAC algorithm has mistaken identification during changing lanes, while the proposed algorithm solves the problem well in Fig. 6. The RANSAC algorithm has the problem of instability and inaccuracy fitting in curve lane, while the proposed algorithm still has high stability and robustness. In the case of closing to the zebra crossing, the RANSAC algorithm makes a mistake in detection, but the proposed algorithm has a better result.

In Fig. 7 the length of right lane detected by RANSAC algorithm is greatly reduced because of the vehicle, while the detection result of the proposed algorithm is still very accurate in Fig. 8, although there are lots of mistaken edge points. With the strong light, the RANSAC algorithm detected the right lane only, while both lanes are detected by the proposed algorithm. RANSAC algorithm can detect the left lane correctly which has less shadow, but it is unable to identify right lane with serious shadow. The proposed algorithm can accurately detect it with high robustness.

Fig. 8. Detection results for the proposed method. *Left to right*: vehicle, strong light, shadow

From the comparison of detection results above in various complex road conditions, such as lane-changing, curve, the zebra crossing, strong light, shadow trees and vehicles, etc. The efficient and stability of the proposed algorithm are higher than the RANSAC algorithm. The proposed algorithm in this paper can accurately identify the lane for various special road conditions. At the same time, it can achieve real-time processing speed (20 frames per second), which has higher recognition rate and reliability compared with RANSAC algorithm.

Of course, the proposed algorithm also has some shortcomings. For example, in Fig. 9, when the vehicle changes the lane and there are long interference lines which are parallel to the lanes at the same time, there will be a mistaken detection. Further research will be needed later.

Fig. 9. False detection results for the proposed method

5   Conclusions

The paper proposes a new lane detection algorithm based on monocular vision. The algorithm uses the structure of the lane, roadway geometry, and vehicle dynamics; those components have not been fully combined before by traditional methods. A new driveway model is introduced with an increased number of parameters of driveway information to be evaluated. A customized parameter space, which is suitable for the proposed algorithm, is established. The traditional Hough transform is improved in the proposed algorithm for improved processing speed. The combination of the lane model with an extended Kalman filter for lane detection guarantees effectively the stability of the algorithm. This also enhances accuracy for lane fitting. Experiments show that the algorithm has good recognition rates and robustness in various challenging lane environments. The algorithm does not yet provide high confidence levels for some of the challenging lane detection situations. This requires further studies.

Acknowledgement. This work is supported by National Natural Science Foundation of China (Grant No. 61471272), Natural Science Foundation of Hubei Province, China (Grant No. 2016CFB499).

References

1. Hillel, A.B., Lerner, R., Levi, D., Raz, G.: Recent progress in road and lane detection: a survey. Mach. Vis. Appl. **25**(3), 727–745 (2014)
2. Huang, A.S., Moore, D., Antone, M., Olson, E., Teller, S.: Finding multiple lanes in urban road networks with vision and LIDAR. Auton. Robots **26**, 103–122 (2009)
3. Aly, M.: Real time detection of lane markers in urban streets. In: Proceedings of IEEE Intelligent Vehicles Symposium, pp. 7–12 (2008)
4. Xiao, J.-S., Cheng, X., Li, B.-J., et al.: Lane detection algorithm based on beamlet transformation and k-means clustering. J. Sichuan Univ. (Eng. Sci. Ed.) **47**(4), 98–103 (2015). (in Chinese)
5. Meng, L.-X., Sun, F.-C., Shao, Y.: Survey on road image interpretation based on monocular vision. J. Comput. Appl. **30**(6), 1552–1555 (2010). (in Chinese)
6. Xu, H.-R., Wang, X.-D., Fang, Q.: Structure road detection algorithm based on B-spline curve model. Acta Automatica Sinica **37**(3), 270–275 (2011). (in Chinese)
7. Yu, B., Jain, A.K.: Lane boundary detection using a multiresolution Hough transform. In: Proceedings of IEEE International Conference on Image Processing, pp. 748–751 (1997)
8. Lee, J.W.: A machine vision system for lane departure detection. Comput. Vis. Image Underst. **86**(1), 52–78 (2002)
9. Kang, D.J., Jung, M.H.: Road lane segmentation using dynamic programming for active safety vehicles. Pattern Recogn. Lett. **24**, 3177–3185 (2003)
10. Wang, Y., Teoh, E., Shen, D.: Lane detection and tracking using B-Snake. Image Vis. Comput. **22**, 269–280 (2004)
11. Zhou, S., Jiang, Y.: A novel lane detection based on geometrical model and Gabor filter. In: Proceedings of IEEE Intelligent Vehicles Symposium, pp. 59–64 (2010)
12. Mechat, N., Saadia, N., M'Sirdi, N.K., Djelal, N.: Lane detection and tracking by monocular vision system in road vehicle. In: Proceedings of IEEE International Conference on Image, Signal Processing, pp. 1276–1282 (2012)
13. Kortli, Y., Marzougui, M., Atri, M.: Efficient implementation of a real-time lane departure warning system. In: Proceedings of IEEE International Conference on Image Processing Applications Systems, pp. 1–6 (2016)
14. Shin, B., Tao, J., Klette, R.: A superparticle filter for lane detection. Pattern Recogn. **48**, 3333–3345 (2014)
15. Lee, D., Shin, J., Jung, J., et al.: Real-time lane detection and tracking system using simple filter and Kalman filter. In: Proceedings of IEEE International Conference Ubiquitous Future Networks, pp. 275–277 (2017)
16. Xu, Z., Sin, B., Klette, R.: Closed form line-segment extraction using the Hough transform. Pattern Recogn. **48**, 4012–4023 (2015)
17. Hough, P.V.C.: Method and means for recognizing complex patterns. US Patent, pp. 77–79 (1962)
18. Xiao, J., Liu, T., Zhang, Y., et al.: Multi-focus image fusion based on depth extraction with inhomogeneous diffusion equation. Signal Process. **125**, 171–186 (2016)
19. Dickmanns, E.D., Mysliwetz, B.D.: Recursive 3D road and relative ego-state recognition. IEEE Trans. Pattern Anal. Mach. Intell. **14**(2), 199–213 (1992)
20. Watanabe, A., Naito, T., Ninomiya, Y.: Lane detection with roadside structure using on board monocular camera. In: Proceedings of IEEE Intelligent Vehicles Symposium, pp. 191–196 (2009)
21. Welch, G., Bishop, G.: An introduction to the Kalman filter. UNC, Chapel Hill, TR (2006)

Gaussian Noise Detection and Adaptive Non-local Means Filter

Peng Chen[1], Shiqian Wu[1(✉)], Hongping Fang[2], Bin Chen[2], and Wei Wang[1]

[1] Key Laboratory of Metallurgical Equipment and Control Technology,
Ministry of Education, Wuhan, China
shiqian.wu@wust.edu.cn
[2] School of Information Science and Technology,
Wuhan University of Science and Technology, Wuhan 430081, China

Abstract. In this paper, a noise adaptive non-local means (NA-NLM) filter is presented to remove additive Gaussian noise from the corrupted images. Firstly, a novel pixel-wise Gaussian noise detection is proposed via eigen features of local Hessian matrix, and a metric is introduced to measure noise strength. Then, image denoising is performed by adaptive NLM filter according to the pixel-wise noise strength, i.e., the NLM filter varies adaptively with the size selections of the search window and similar patches. Experiments carried on Tampere Image Database (TID) demonstrate that the proposed method outperforms the state-of-the-art methods in terms of the peak signal-to-noise ratio (PSNR), structural similarity (SSIM) and subjective visual assessment.

1 Introduction

Denoising has been one of the fundamental problems in image processing. Unavoidable noise yielded in image acquisition presents unwanted information which degrades image quality. It is well known that the long-standing issue comes from the fact, i.e., while the noise is removed, the image details are smoothed simultaneously, referring the paper [1–3] for more details. As edges are of critical importance to the visual appearance of images, one significant work in this area is to achieve edge-preserving image denoising [4]. Among these works, the anisotropic diffusion filter (ADF) [5], the bilateral filter (BF) [6], the non-local means (NLM) method [7] and the guided image filter (GIF) [8] are typical methods, which provide state-of-the-art denoising performances.

While developing different edge-preserving denoising methods, we found that very few researchers consider the adaptation of denoising methods. The existing methods use the same parameters to process whole image regardless of noise strength and distribution. To our best knowledge, the only works are to detect impulse (salt-and-pepper) noise [9–13], and then adaptive filtering strategy is employed to preserve sharp structure during denoising process. It was indicated in [2] that the knowledge of noise is crucial for image denoising. But noise detection or estimation is very challenging due to the two reasons: (1) The noise model

© Springer International Publishing AG, part of Springer Nature 2018
M. Paul et al. (Eds.): PSIVT 2017, LNCS 10749, pp. 396–405, 2018.
https://doi.org/10.1007/978-3-319-75786-5_32

varies from one image to another; (2) Generally, the noise is not independent, for example, the noise may be signal dependent or scale dependent. However, we argue that the denoising performance by using a priori noise information must be better than the blind methods, even the noise information is not exactly obtained.

Inspired by the above argument, we propose to detect Gaussian noise, which is widely used in image processing, in this paper. Specifically, a novel metric for measuring noise strength in each pixel is proposed based on eigen information of local Hessian matrix. Then an adaptive NLM filter is employed to process each pixel based on its noise strength. To our knowledge, we have not yet found the similar work.

This paper is organized as follows: Sect. 2 presents the Gaussian noise detection and noise measurement. An adaptive NLM filter, which varies denoising capability by changing search windows as well as similar patches, is introduced in Sect. 3. Experimental results on the TID database are performed in Sect. 4, followed by conclusion drawn in Sect. 5.

2   Gaussian Noise Detection

Suppose a linear degradation function is adopted to model the degradation operation, which includes an additive noise term [14]:

$$g(x, y) = f(x, y) + n(x, y) \tag{1}$$

where f is the original image, g is the observed image and n is i.i.d. zero mean Gaussian noise with variance σ^2. It is known that the Gaussian noise is distributed in the whole image, i.e., every pixel in the degraded image is corrupted to some extent. The problem is to estimate the pixel-oriented noise strength.

With the intention of acquiring the noise strength in each pixel, a patch centered at the underlying pixel is adopted. The image local behavior at a point x_0 can be expressed as follows [15]:

$$g(x_0 + \delta x_0) \approx g(x_0) + \delta x_0^T \nabla_0 + \delta x_0^T H_0 \delta x_0 \tag{2}$$

In this expansion, the image structure is approximated up to second order. ∇_0 and H_0 are the gradient vector and Hessian matrix of the image calculated in x_0. As a two-dimensional signal, the Hessian matrix of an image is denoted as:

$$H_g = \begin{bmatrix} g_{xx} & g_{xy} \\ g_{yx} & g_{yy} \end{bmatrix} \tag{3}$$

To compute these differential operators of g in a well-posed fashion, the concepts of linear scale space theory [16,17] are used. In this framework, convolution with derivatives of Gaussian denotes the differential operator:

$$\frac{\partial^2}{\partial_x \partial_y} g(x, y) = g(x, y) \bigotimes \frac{\partial^2}{\partial_x \partial_y} G(x, y, s) \tag{4}$$

where the two-dimensional Gaussian $G(x, y, s)$ is defined as:

$$G(x, y, s) = \frac{1}{2\pi s^2} e^{-\frac{x^2+y^2}{2s^2}} \tag{5}$$

where s is standard deviation.

The principal directions of image can be extracted according to analyzing the eigenvalues of the Hessian matrix, which include the directions of largest and smallest curvature. The maximal and minimal eigenvalues represent largest and smallest curvature respectively, which implies that, the larger eigenvalue indicates great intensity changes, and the smaller one shows slight intensity changes.

The eigenvalues of the Hessian matrix of g at location x can be expressed as [18]:

$$\lambda_{1,2}g(x) = \frac{\varDelta g(x) \pm \sqrt{(\overline{\varDelta}g(x))^2 + (\Gamma g(x))^2}}{2} \tag{6}$$

where the associated differential operators are defined as follows: $\varDelta = \partial_{xx} + \partial_{yy}$, $\overline{\varDelta} = \partial_{xx} - \partial_{yy}$, $\Gamma = 2\partial_{xy}$.

Let λ_k denote the eigenvalue with the k-th smallest magnitude ($|\lambda_1| \leq |\lambda_2|$). Under this assumption, we can summarize the relations between the eigenvalues of the Hessian for the detection of different structures. While the noise strength at one pixel is strong, the two eigenvalues of this point will be large simultaneously. In addition, if a pixel belongs to an image edge, it will be signaled by λ_1 being small and λ_2 of a large magnitude. Moreover, the pixel with small noise strength will be represented by two small eigenvalues. According to above analysis, the Frobenius matrix norm is used to quantify these properties since it can be expressed by the eigenvalues simply when the matrix is real and symmetric. Therefore, we define the following two measures for noise strength:

$$R = \frac{|\lambda_1|}{|\lambda_2|} \tag{7}$$

$$S = \|H\|_F = \sqrt{\sum_{k=1,2} \lambda_k^2} \tag{8}$$

While the noise strength is heavy at the point, the measures R and S will be both large because the two eigenvalues are both large as well. On the contrary, with the light noise strength, the two measures will become smaller since λ_1 will be small. According to above analysis, we propose the following metric for noise detection:

$$M = R(1 - exp(-S)) \tag{9}$$

In this expression, the noise strength is estimated by the features R and S according to different criteria. These different criteria are combined through their product to ensure that the accuracy of noise detection is maximal only if all these criteria are fulfilled.

3   Adaptive Non-local Means Filter

Assuming that the noise has been estimated by equation (9), the next task is to propose an adaptive method for image denoising based on noise strength. In this work, the NLM filter is employed due to its excellent performance, and a noise-adaptive NLM (NA-NLM) filter is developed to restore the original values.

For a noisy image, the corresponding NLM output NL_{xy} at location (x, y) is computed as [7]:

$$NL_{xy} = \frac{\sum\limits_{(k,l)\in\Omega_{x,y}} S_{x,y,k,l} g(k,l)}{\sum\limits_{(k,l)\in\Omega_{x,y}} S_{x,y,k,l}} \tag{10}$$

where $\Omega_{x,y}$ is the pixels set within the $L_s \times L_s$ search window centered at (x, y). The weight $S_{x,y,k,l}$ depends on the similarity between the pixels (x, y) and (k, l) which is the arbitrary pixel in the search window. It is easily known that obtaining the weight $S_{x,y,k,l}$ accurately is the key to recover the noise pixel. In the traditional NLM filter, $S_{x,y,k,l}$ is defined as the exponential function of the Gaussian weighted Euclidean distance between two $L_p \times L_p$ similar windows $N_{x,y}$ and $N_{k,l}$ centered at the two pixels (x, y) and (k, l) as follows:

$$s_{x,y,k,l} = exp(-\|N_{x,y} - N_{k,l}\|_{2,a}^2/h^2) \tag{11}$$

where $a > 0$ is the standard deviation of the Gaussian kernel. h is the parameter controlling the filtering degree.

Obviously, the pixels in the search window are totally used to calculate the denoising result. However, when the weighted Euclidean distances calculated by highly dissimilar image patches are quite large, the positive weights computed by the exponential function will make the output inaccurate. To avoid this problem, the weights of these image patches are set to zero in our method. Thus, after the correction, the weights are ultimately determined as:

$$S_{x,y,k,l} = \left\{ \begin{array}{ll} exp(-\|N_{x,y} - N_{k,l}\|_{2,a}^2/h^2)\,, & \|N_{x,y} - N_{k,l}\|_{2,a}^2 \leq T \\ 0 & ,otherwise \end{array} \right\} \tag{12}$$

where T is the threshold to choose the similar patches, which is proportional to the noise variance σ^2. Based on experiments, we defined $T = \mu\sigma^2 + \theta$, where μ and σ are constant coefficients.

Moreover, it can be seen that in the process of calculating the weights, the traditional NLM filter fixed the search window of $L_s \times L_s$ pixels and the similar window of $L_p \times L_p$ pixels. However, it is difficult to pick out similar image patches precisely using the globally fixed search and similar windows for the whole image while the noise strength varies. Moreover, the wrong patches are included to compute the weights. For instance, in regions where the noise strength is large, the big similar windows in which the noise accounts for a great proportion cannot accurately represent the original image information. Thus the dissimilar patches will be searched for the weights. On the contrary, if the similar windows are relatively small, the ratio between signal and noise will increase, undoubtedly, in the process of calculating weights more similar image patches will be included. As for the similar windows, it is easily understand that small search windows are required to ensure accurate search in heavy noise area. In order to enhance the ability of searching true similar patches, L_s and L_p will be adaptively determined based on the noise detection function M. Simulations on a broad variety of gray-level images show that L_s and L_p should decrease with the increasing noise strength. Based on the extensive simulations, L_s and L_p are chosen as

$$L_s = 2\alpha \cos(M) + 1 \tag{13}$$

$$L_p = 2\beta \cos(M) + 1 \tag{14}$$

where α and β are the predefined constant.

Fig. 1. Test images in TID database

4   Experimental Results

In this section, we demonstrate the validity of the proposed algorithm by using the Tampere Image Database (TID) [19] as shown in Fig. 1. The TID consists 25 images in size of 384×512.

Firstly, the noise strength in our method is appreciated by its visual image, and the noise image is also provided as a referential criteria. Figures 2 and 3 show the original image, the noisy image, original noise image and noise strength estimation of image 6 with $\sigma = 30$ and image 16 with $\sigma = 10$.

Apparently the noise strength estimation image is consistent with the original noise image in term of variance tendency. In the following experiments, the predefined parameters are selected as below: $\mu = 4.23$, $\theta = 147.5$, α and β equal to 10 and 3 respectively, and h is fixed to $10 * \sigma$, as recommended in [1,6].

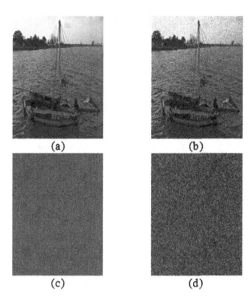

Fig. 2. Noise strength with image 6: (a) original image (b) noisy image ($\sigma = 30$) (c) original noise image (d) noise strength estimation image

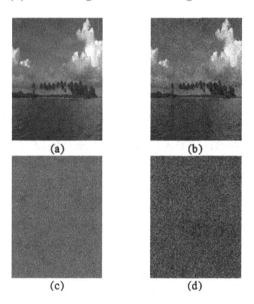

Fig. 3. Noise strength with image 16: (a) original image (b) noisy image ($\sigma = 30$) (c) original noise image (d) noise strength estimation image

To test the performance of the proposed method, each test image is corrupted by additive Gaussian noise in different standard deviations $\sigma \in \{5, 10, 15...40\}$. The denoising performance is evaluated in terms of the peak signal-to-noise ratio (PSNR), the structural similarity (SSIM) [20] and subjective visual assessment.

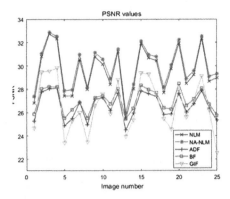

Fig. 4. PSNR results by different methods ($\sigma = 20$)

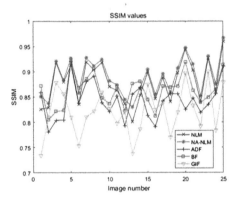

Fig. 5. SSIM results by different methods ($\sigma = 20$)

Figures 4 and 5 demonstrate the PSNRs and SSIMs of the proposed method in comparison with the conventional NLM method, the anisotropic diffusion filter, the bilateral filter and the guided image filter when Gaussian noise with standard deviation $\sigma = 20$ are injected into the 25 test images. It is shown that the proposed method achieves better results than the other filters for almost all test images. Only in image 13 and 14, the anisotropic diffusion filter and the bilateral filter have higher SSIM values, however, our method represent an advantage in PSNR.

Then 8 levels of noise ranged from $\sigma = 5$ to $\sigma = 40$ are injected into the 25 test images. Figures 6 and 7 show the average PSNRs and SSIMs at different levels over 25 images. It is indicated from the PSNR viewpoint, that the proposed method is more effective than the other methods when the test image is less noisy. However, the Fig. 7 implies that the proposed method is more effective than the other methods when the test image is more noisy.

Anyway, results show that the NA-NLM produces higher PSNR and SSIM than the NLM method for every image in any noise level. The results also implies that the denoising performance benefits from obtaining the noise information and accordingly the adaptive strategy.

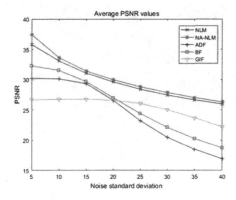

Fig. 6. Average PSNR test on TID database

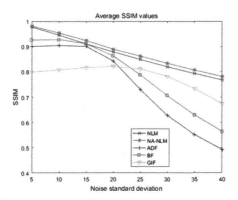

Fig. 7. Average SSIM test on TID database

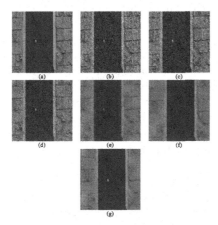

Fig. 8. Visual comparison with enlarged image 1: (a) original image, (b) noisy image ($\sigma = 30$), (c) ADF, (d) BF, (e) GIF, (f) NLM, (g) NA-NLM

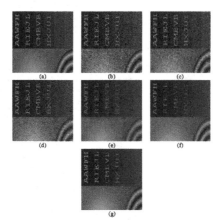

Fig. 9. Visual comparison with enlarged image 25: (a) original image, (b) noisy image ($\sigma = 30$), (c) ADF, (d) BF, (e) GIF, (f) NLM, (g) NA-NLM

Figures 8 and 9 show enlarged portions of two original images, the noisy images with $\sigma = 30$, the corresponding reconstructed images with ADF, BF, GIF, NLM, and our NA-NLM method. The results show that the denoising performances by the NA-NLM are better than those by the other methods. Especially, the visual qualities by the NA-NLM are much better than those by the other methods because the processed images by the NA-NLM keep more details, as shown the white ball in Fig. 8 and the letters in Fig. 9.

5   Conclusions

Image denoising has been a long-standing problem in image processing. The challenge comes from the fact: while noise is reduced, image details are smoothed simultaneously. In order to achieve good trade-off between noise reduction and image structure preserving, we argue that noise detection is very crucial. In this paper, a novel pixel-wise Gaussian noise detection is proposed and a metric for noise measurement is developed via eigen features of local Hessian matrix. The noise information is used to adaptively determine the NLM denoising capability by varying sizes of search window and similarity patch. Experimental results demonstrate that the priori information of noise is very useful to determine right noise deduction without removing image structure. The proposed method is superior to the compared filters in terms of both subjective test and objective measurement.

As the precise estimate of noise information in our algorithm is not accomplished, ongoing further researches will consider a better noise strength expression for significant improvement in image denoising.

Acknowledgements. This work was supported by the National Natural Science Foundation of China under Grant 61371190.

References

1. Buades, A., Coll, B., Morel Song, J.M.: A review of image denoising algorithms, with a new one. SIAM J. Multiscale Model. Simul. **4**(2), 490–530 (2005)
2. Lebrun, M., Colom, M., Buades, A., Morel, J.M.: Secrets of image denoising cuisine. Acta Numerica **21**(1), 475–576 (2012)
3. Milanfar, P.: A tour of modern image filtering: new insights and methods, both practical and theoretical. IEEE Signal Process. Mag. **30**(1), 106–128 (2013)
4. Jain, P., Tyagi, V.: A survey of edge-preserving image denoising methods. Inf. Syst. Front. **18**(1), 159–170 (2016)
5. Perona, P., Malik, J.: Scale-space and edge detection using anisotropic diffusion. IEEE Trans. Pattern Anal. Mach. Intell. **12**(7), 629–639 (2002)
6. Tomasi, C., Manduchi, R.: Bilateral filtering for gray and color images. In: The Sixth IEEE International Conference on Computer Vision, pp. 839–846. IEEE Computer Society, Washington, DC (1998)
7. Buades, A., Coll, B., Morel, J.M.: A non-local algorithm for image denoising. In: The 2005 IEEE Computer Society Conference on Computer Vision and Pattern Recognition, vol. 2, pp. 60–65. IEEE Computer Society, Washington, DC (2005)
8. He, K., Sun, J., Tang, X.: Guided image filtering. IEEE Trans. Pattern Anal. Mach. Intell. **35**(6), 1397–1409 (2013)
9. Chan, R.H., Ho, C.W., Nikolova, M.: Salt-and-pepper noise removal by median-type noise detectors and detail-preserving regularization. IEEE Trans. Image Process. **14**(10), 1479–1485 (2005)
10. Ng, P.E., Ma, K.K.: A switching median filter with boundary discriminative noise detection for extremely corrupted images. IEEE Trans. Image Process. **15**(6), 1506–1516 (2006)
11. Dong, Y., Chan, R.H., Xu, S.: A detection statistic for random-valued impulse noise. IEEE Trans. Image Process. **16**(4), 1112–1120 (2007)
12. Zhang, X., Xiong, Y.: Impulse noise removal using directional difference based noise de-tector and adaptive weighted mean filter. IEEE Signal Process. Lett. **16**(4), 295–298 (2009)
13. Bai, T., Tan, J.: Automatic detection and removal of high-density impulse noises. IET Image Process. **9**(2), 162–172 (2015)
14. Gonzalez, R.C., Woods, R.E.: Digital Image Processing, 3rd edn. Prentice Hall, Upper Saddle River (2008)
15. Frangi, A.F., Niessen, W.J., Vincken, K.L., Viergever, M.A.: Multiscale vessel enhancement filtering. In: Wells, W.M., Colchester, A., Delp, S. (eds.) MICCAI 1998. LNCS, vol. 1496, pp. 130–137. Springer, Heidelberg (1998). https://doi.org/10.1007/BFb0056195
16. Florack, L.M., ter Haar Romeny, B.M., Koenderink, J.J., Viergever, M.A.: Scale and the differential structure of images. Image Vis. Comput. **10**(6), 376–388 (1992)
17. Koenderink, J.J.: The structure of images. Biol. Cybern. **50**(5), 363–370 (1984)
18. Lefkimmiatis, S., Bourquard, A., Unser, M.: Hessian-based norm regularization for image restoration with biomedical applications. IEEE Trans. Image Process. **21**(3), 983–995 (2012)
19. Tampere Image Database 2008 (TID 2008). http://www.ponomarenko.info/tid2008.htm
20. Wang, Z., Bovik, A.C., Sheikh, H.R., Simoncelli, E.P.: Image quality assessment: from error visibility to structural similarity. IEEE Trans. Image Process. **13**(4), 600–612 (2004)

Uncertainty Model for
Template Feature Matching

Hongmou Zhang$^{(\boxtimes)}$, Denis Grießbach, Jürgen Wohlfeil, and Anko Börner

German Aerospace Center, Rutherfordstraße 2, 12489 Berlin, Germany
`Hongmou.Zhang@dlr.de`

Abstract. Using visual odometry and inertial measurements, indoor and outdoor positioning systems can perform an accurate self-localization in unknown, unstructured environments where absolute positioning systems (e.g. GNSS) are unavailable. However, the achievable accuracy is highly affected by the residuals of calibration, the quality of the noise model, etc. Only if these unavoidable uncertainties of sensors and data processing can be taken into account and be handled via error propagation, which allows to propagate them through the entire system. The central filter (e.g. Kalman filter) of the system can then make use of the enhanced statistical model and use the propagated errors to calculate the optimal result. In this paper, we focus on the uncertaintiy calculation of the elementary part of the optical navigation, the template feature matcher. First of all, we propose a method to model the image noise. Then we use Taylor's theorem to extend two very popular and efficient template feature matchers sum-of-absolute-differences (SAD) and normalized-cross-correlation (NCC) to get sub-pixel matching results. Based on the proposed noise model and the extended matcher, we propagate the image noise to the uncertainties of sub-pixel matching results. Although the SAD and NCC are used, the image noise model can be easily combined with other feature matchers. We evaluate our method by an Integrated Positioning System (IPS) which is developed by German Aerospace Center. The experimental results show that our method can improve the quality of the measured trajectory. Moreover, it increases the robustness of the system.

Keywords: Uncertainty model · Image noise model
Template matching · Propagation of uncertainty · Sub-pixel matching

1 Introduction

Uncertainty occurs in almost every element of a computer vision system. For example, the measurements of sensors contain noise, their calibration is affected with errors, etc. In order to archive high accuracy, the uncertainty of each element should be taken into account in computer vision systems. Only if the uncertainties are propagated correctly through the whole system, the central

© Springer International Publishing AG, part of Springer Nature 2018
M. Paul et al. (Eds.): PSIVT 2017, LNCS 10749, pp. 406–420, 2018.
https://doi.org/10.1007/978-3-319-75786-5_33

filter (e.g. Kalman filter) of the system can make use of them to calculate the optimal result by a statistical model.

In this paper, we focus on the uncertainty of the image (i.e. image noise) and the uncertainty of the sub-pixel template feature matching. We propose an image noise model which can be used for real-time processing. On the other hand, the noise model can be combined with our proposed sub-pixel matching algorithm to calculate the uncertainty of template matching without a significant computational overhead. Particular uncertainty calculation methods are presented for the SAD and NCC matcher. However, it can easily be ported to other template feature matching algorithms.

Feature extraction and feature matching are elementary parts in many computer vision applications, such as optical navigation system (e.g. SLAM [4,20,24], IPS [10,11]). In these applications, features are extracted from one image by a feature extractor (e.g. FAST, AGAST [23,26,32]). A feature matcher (e.g. SAD, NCC, KLT [12,21,28]) matches the features to another image. The image noise affects the matching result and therefore influences the performance of the whole system. Many researches focus on the problem of feature uncertainties [15,16,27,31].

In [31] the authors present a framework to calculate the uncertainty of scale invariant features (SIFT) [19] and speeded up robust features (SURF) [3]. In that paper, the uncertainty of features are depend on the scale and the neighborhood. The results of the experiments show that the proposed method improves the performance for bundle adjustment. However, due to the complexity of calculating SIFT features, this method possibly may not be used for real-time computer applications, especially, for mobile platforms.

In [16] the authors proposed a method for involving the uncertainty of features into a homography and fundamental matrix calculation. The paper shows that in most of the cases the results can be improved by considering the covariances of the features. However, because of lacking a noise model, the method can only get rough uncertainties of features.

In our method, we assume that the covariance for the feature extraction step is zero, because the template feature matcher gets pixel by pixel matching results. Therefore the uncertainties of feature extraction can be omitted and the noise in both images impacts the feature matching step. By combined with our proposed image noise model, the template feature matcher provides matching results and covariance matrices with values propagated from image noise. This approach simplifies the calculation and enables real-time processing without losing accuracy. As shown in Sect. 4, the uncertainty can be used to identify and eliminate features with high uncertainties, usually indicating mismatched features. The most important benefit is that the uncertainty of the matching can be involved in further calculations, e.g. triangulation, ego-motion calculation of the system, etc. The propagation of the uncertainties through the whole calculation chain to the central filter significantly increases the stability and the quality of the results.

This paper is organized as follows: In Sect. 2 an introduction to our image noise model is given. Such a model can be used to calculate the uncertainties of sub-pixel matching results as well as for further processing. In Sect. 3 a sub-pixel template matching algorithm and a method to propagate uncertainties from image noise to sub-pixel matching results are described. Experimental results are presented in Sect. 4, and Sect. 5 concludes the paper.

2   Image Noise Model

Even though it varies between cameras and scenes, image noise is always present in images taken with digital cameras. There are two major sources of noise. Firstly, fixed pattern noise is caused by different light sensitivities (photo response non-uniformity - PRNU [2]) and signal offsets (dark signal non-uniformity - DSNU [8]) of the pixels of an image sensor. This noise does not change over short time and is usually corrected by the camera itself. Secondly, dynamic noise changes from image to image even without a change of the input signal. It is mainly caused by the read-out electronics (read-out noise [25]), but also by the stochastic nature of the incoming photons (photon noise). This is just a simple model, more accurate one's can be applied if needed.

To control the impact of image noise to image processing, it can be taken into account as the uncertainty of an image. Such uncertainties can be handled via propagation of uncertainties, which allows to propagate them through the entire computer vision system. In order to achive this goal, the mathematical model of the image noise must be known. There are many noise models proposed in computer vision community, e.g. [5]. However, they either do not quantify the noise (e.g. Salt and Pepper Noise [14]) or are built as common probability models (e.g. Gaussian Noise [9]), which do not take into account the variation of different camera systems.

In this paper, we propose a method to build an image noise model which is suitable for real-time processing. We assume that the parameters of that noise model are different for each camera so that the model building step can be done by camera calibration step. During the calibration, by taking a batch of M frames (e.g. 100) in a short time (less than 1 min) from a fixed scene, M almost identical images are received. The mean value and standard deviation of all pixels are calculated for all values measured during the M frames. Hence:

$$\text{Mean}(i,j) = \frac{1}{M} \sum_{m=1}^{M} g(i,j)_m \tag{1}$$

where $g(i,j)_m$ is the locale gray value at coordinate (i,j) for the frame m. The standard deviation of this input vector can be easily calculated. The relation between all mean values and standard deviations can be displayed in a graph, which is done in Fig. 1 for a set of sample images. The standard deviations can be seen as a function of the corresponding mean values. It is obvious that the standard deviation grows according to the mean gray value. This reveals the

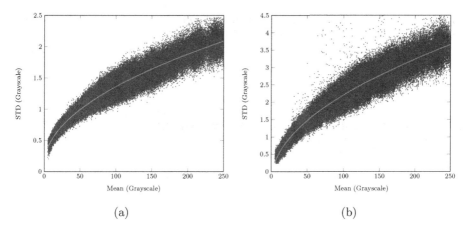

(a)   (b)

Fig. 1. In the left: pixels mean and the corresponding standard deviation are shown by blue points. The red curve is the fitted model based on our proposed noise equation, with $G = 58.1224$ and $N_E = 0.3166$. In the right: by comparison with left side, the input signal of camera is amplified by $10\,\mathrm{dB}$, from decibel equation $G_{dB} = 20log_{10}(V/V_0)$, the ratio between G in (a) and (b) is 3.162. The fitted new noise model is $G = 18.1069$ and $N_E = 0.6453$, the ratio between two G is 3.21, it is very close to the theory value. The camera is Prosilica GC1380H. (Color figure online)

relation between pixel noise and the gray value of the pixel. On the other hand, because of electronic noise, the standard deviation should be greater than zero even for dark pixels. Based on this, we propose a noise model for each pixel.

$$\text{Noise} = \sqrt{N_E^2 + I/G} \qquad (2)$$

N_E^2 is the variance of electronic noise of camera in gray scale values, the second part is from shot noise (Shot noise $= \sqrt{signal}$ [13]), here I is the gray value of the pixel and G is a gain parameter. Next, a Gauss–Newton algorithm is used to estimate the model with the mean values and standard deviations from the calibration images, fitting the curve (2) to the data. Equation (3) shows the Gauss–Newton algorithm.

$$\beta^{(s+1)} = \beta^{(s)} - (J_r^{\mathsf{T}} J_r)^{-1} J_r^{\mathsf{T}} r(\beta^{(s)}) \qquad (3)$$

The Gauss–Newton algorithm iteratively calculates the results. In Eq. 3, β is the vector of variables to calculate (in our case N_E and G), the superscript s indicate the sth iteration value. J_r is the Jacobian matrix of a residual function $r(\beta)$, where

$$r(\beta) = y - f(I, \beta)$$
$$J_r = \frac{\partial r(\beta)}{\partial \beta} \qquad (4)$$

In our case y is the calculated standard deviation of the gray values of the image set, and the $f(I, \beta)$ is the proposed noise model (Eq. (2)). Starting with an initial $\beta^{(0)}$, the Gauss–Newton algorithm can get a convergent β (Fig. 1) after several iterations. More details can be found at [22]. Knowing the parameters G and N_E makes the noise model available. This noise information can be used in the further processing, e.g. to model the uncertainty of template matching introduced in Sect. 3.2.

3   Error Model for Template Sub-pixel Matching Algorithm

Once the image noise model is known, it can be involved into data processing chain to get the uncertainty information. In this section, we focus on the uncertainty of feature matching result based on proposed noise model. The calculated uncertainty of matching result can be easily propagated to further calculation.

The SAD and NCC template feature matchers [1,6] are extensively used in stereo feature matching, feature tracking, etc. Therefore in this paper, these two feature matchers are used. Moreover, we extend them by Taylor's theorem to get sub-pixel level matching results. Sub-pixel matching algorithm is a well-researched topic in computer vision community, many sub-pixel matching algorithms are proposed [17,21,30]. Besides, descriptor based feature extraction algorithm [3,18,19] can get sub-pixel matching result as well. All of these methods can get good sub-pixel matching results. However, these methods need iteration calculation, image pyramid, difference of Gaussian, brute-force search respectively, which are too "heavy" for low computational resource platform. Our method is derived from polynomial interpolation which is faster and easy to implement and can get acceptable results, on the other hand, the uncertainty of matching result can be calculated by combination with our noise model.

3.1   Template Sub-pixel Matching Algorithm

The sub-pixel matching algorithm includes three steps. At first, the common SAD/NCC template feature matcher is used to match the features, the details are shown below. For each extracted feature on the first image, a 5×5 pixel region around it is taken as a template. Then the template is shifted over the second image pixel by pixel. For each position, the SAD/NCC value between the template and covered area in the second image is calculated. The search area in the second image is limited by some conditions (e.g. epipolar line). The position in the second image with the lowest SAD value or the highest NCC value is the matched feature. This step outputs the matching results with pixel-level coordinates.

Secondly, in case that the search area in the first step does not cover all the 3×3 pixel neighbor positions around the matched feature (e.g. epipolar line case), the SAD/NCC values for these positions need to be calculated by the same template. Then a 3×3 SAD/NCC matrix $\boldsymbol{A}$ can be picked up, as shown in Fig. 2.

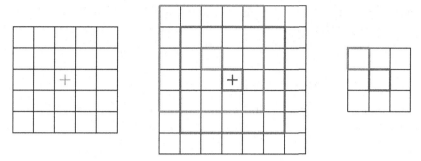

(a) Template from first image   (b) Search area on the second image   (c) SAD/NCC matrix A

Fig. 2. In (a), a 5×5 template is taken from first image, the green cross represents the feature position. In (b), part of search area on the second image is shown, the blue cross indicates the matched feature position, the SAD/NCC value between the template and the covered area (red part) is stored in the central entry of matrix A in figure (c). By sliding the template center around the 3×3 neighbor area of the matched feature in (b) (as indicated by different colors), all the values in the matrix A can be calculated. The template and all the 7×7 pixels in figure (b) are needed for the propagation of uncertainties step which is described in Sect. 3.2. (Color figure online)

In the third step, the values of matrix A can be seen as a surface in 3D space with the central element located in a valley (SAD) or on a hill (NCC). Using a two-dimensional interpolation of the values allows to get a more precise position of the surface's extremum: the sub-pixel position of the matched feature. Two-dimensional interpolation follows the second-order Taylor series in Sect. 3.1.

$$f(x + \delta x, y + \delta y) \approx$$
$$f(x,y) + \left[\frac{\partial f}{\partial x} \delta x + \frac{\partial f}{\partial y} \delta y \right] + \frac{1}{2} \left[\frac{\partial^2 f}{\partial x^2} (\delta x)^2 + 2 \frac{\partial^2 f}{\partial x \partial y} \delta x \delta y + \frac{\partial^2 f}{\partial y^2} (\delta y)^2 \right] \quad (5)$$

In Sect. 3.1, $f(x,y)$ is the matrix A, where x and y are the feature coordinates. If the feature coordinate is expressed in vector form $x = \begin{bmatrix} x & y \end{bmatrix}^{\mathsf{T}}$, then the equation can be written as:

$$f(x + \delta x) \approx f(x) + \left(\frac{df}{dx} \right)^{\mathsf{T}} \delta x + \frac{1}{2} \delta x^{\mathsf{T}} \frac{d^2 f}{dx^2} \delta x \quad (6)$$

The local extremum is calculated by Eq. (7)

$$\frac{\partial f(x)}{\partial x} = 0 \quad (7)$$

this leads to:

$$\delta \hat{x} = - \left(\frac{d^2 f}{dx^2} \right)^{-1} \frac{df}{dx} \quad (8)$$

Equation (8) outputs two real numbers, taken as an offset for the feature coordinate x and y. Adding these two values to the feature pixel level coordinate will get the sub-pixel coordinate of the feature.

3.2   Propagation of Uncertainty of the SAD Feature Matcher

In this subsection, the proposed image noise model is applied to the SAD sub-pixel matching algorithm. The aim is to have an uncertainty model of the matching procedure. The equation of SAD is shown as follows.

$$\text{SAD}(u,v) = \sum_{i,j} |\boldsymbol{S}(u+i, v+j) - \boldsymbol{T}(i,j)| \tag{9}$$

$\boldsymbol{S}(u+i, v+j)$ is the search area in the second image, $\boldsymbol{T}$ is the template from the first image. For each matched feature pair, the SAD propagation of uncertainties algorithm includes two parts. The first part propagates the image noise to the uncertainty of the 3×3 matrix $\boldsymbol{A}$. The second part handles the uncertainty of $\boldsymbol{A}$ and finally gets the uncertainty of the sub-pixel matching result.

Part 1: From the linear propagation of uncertainties theory [7] it is known that in order to propagate the uncertainty; a matrix $\boldsymbol{F}$ which can linearize the SAD calculation must be known.

$$\boldsymbol{a} = \boldsymbol{F}\boldsymbol{v} \tag{10}$$

Referring to Fig. 2, the 9×1 vector $\boldsymbol{a}$ of Eq. (10) is the reformatted 3×3 matrix $\boldsymbol{A}$. The vector $\boldsymbol{v}$ includes all the pixel values from the template and the 7×7 search area on the second image. The method for specifying $\boldsymbol{F}$ is described in the following.

The template from the first image is reformatted, from a 5×5 matrix $\boldsymbol{V}_f$ into a 25×1 vector $\boldsymbol{v}_f$. The corresponding 7×7 area $\boldsymbol{V}_s$ (see Fig. 2) in the second image is reformatted into a 49×1 vector $\boldsymbol{v}_s$.

By concatenation of these two vectors, a 74×1 vector $\boldsymbol{v} = [\boldsymbol{v}_s \ \ \boldsymbol{v}_f]^{\mathsf{T}}$ (see Fig. 3) is defined and used for further calculations. Furthermore, a 9×74 matrix $\boldsymbol{F}$ (see Fig. 3) is built. In the first, $\boldsymbol{F}$ is set to be a zero matrix (i.e. all of the entries equals zero). Then, some entries of $\boldsymbol{F}$ are calculated as follows:

$$\boldsymbol{F}_s[(i+m-1+7(j+n-2)), (m+3(n-1))]$$
$$= \text{sgn}[\boldsymbol{V}_s(i+m-1, j+n-1), \boldsymbol{V}_f(i,j)]$$
$$\boldsymbol{F}_f[(i+5(j-1)), (m+3(n-1))] \tag{11}$$
$$= -\text{sgn}[\boldsymbol{V}_s(i+m-1, j+n-1), \boldsymbol{V}_f(i,j)]$$
$$\text{with } 1 \le i,j \le 5, \quad 1 \le m,n \le 3$$

where $\boldsymbol{V}_f(i,j)$ indicates the entry which is located in the ith column and j^{th} row in matrix $\boldsymbol{V}_f$.

The 9×49 matrix $\boldsymbol{F}_s$ is the left part of $\boldsymbol{F}$ and the 9×25 matrix $\boldsymbol{F}_f$ is the right part, as shown in Fig. 3. Parameters m and n are shift coordinates of

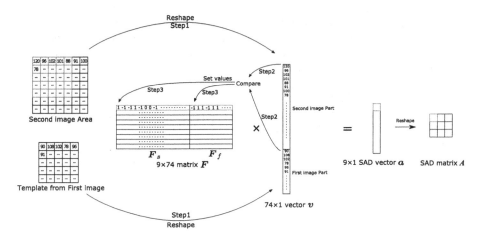

Fig. 3. First-image and second-image areas are reformatted first, forming a 74×1 vector $\boldsymbol{v}$. Next, values in $\boldsymbol{F}$ are calculated by Eq. (12). Finally, SAD vector $\boldsymbol{a}$ equals $\boldsymbol{Fv}$. The 3×3 matrix $\boldsymbol{A}$ is obtained by reformatting $\boldsymbol{a}$; this matrix is identical to the results of the original SAD algorithm. The red part of the second-image area shows the area considered for the calculation of the first SAD value. The red part in $\boldsymbol{F}$ reflects the relationship between the first-image area and the red part of the second-image area. (Color figure online)

the template $\boldsymbol{V}_f$ over the search area $\boldsymbol{V}_s$ in horizontal direction and vertical direction, respectively.

For example, the blue area in Fig. 2(b) indicates the shift coordinate $(1, 1)$, and the red area indicates $(2, 2)$. The sign function sgn is defined as follows:

$$\mathrm{sgn}(x, y) := \begin{cases} -1 & \text{if } x < y \\ 1 & \text{if } x > y \end{cases} \tag{12}$$

The template $\boldsymbol{V}_f$ can only cover a part of search area $\boldsymbol{V}_s$, for each (m, n); some entries in $\boldsymbol{F}_s$ remain unchanged as 0. Therefore, the values in $\boldsymbol{F}$ are from the set $\{-1, 0, +1\}$. Finally, we obtain a dynamically changing matrix $\boldsymbol{F}$, as the values of $\boldsymbol{F}$ are different for different features. These steps guarantee that the vector $\boldsymbol{a}$ in Eq. (10) is always identical to the standard absolute calculation results.

Once we know the matrix $\boldsymbol{F}$, the SAD algorithm becomes a linear calculation. From our proposed noise model, the noise vector $\boldsymbol{v}_n$ of all pixels in $\boldsymbol{v}$ can be calculated. Assuming, that the noise level between each pixel is uncorrelated, a 74×74 covariance matrix $\boldsymbol{\Sigma}_v$ is defined. Its diagonal elements are v_n^2, and the others are 0. The covariance of $\boldsymbol{a}$ can be calculated as:

$$\boldsymbol{\Sigma}_a = \boldsymbol{F}\boldsymbol{\Sigma}_v\boldsymbol{F}^\mathsf{T} \tag{13}$$

Hence, $\boldsymbol{\Sigma}_a$ is the 9×9 covariance matrix of $\boldsymbol{a}$.

Part 2: the task of the second part is the propagation of uncertainties from Σ_a to the final sub-pixel calculation results. From Eqs. (6) and (8), the sub-pixel calculation step is a non-linear function. The Jacobian matrix of Eq. (8) is calculated. First of all, Eq. (8) can be written as:

$$\delta\hat{x} = \begin{bmatrix} -(\partial yy \partial x - \partial xy \partial y)/(\partial xx \partial yy - \partial xy \partial xy) \\ -(\partial xx \partial y - \partial xy \partial x)/(\partial xx \partial yy - \partial xy \partial xy) \end{bmatrix} \tag{14}$$

where

$$\partial x = \frac{a_{23} - a_{21}}{2} \qquad \partial xx = a_{23} + a_{21} - 2a_{22}$$

$$\partial y = \frac{a_{32} - a_{12}}{2} \qquad \partial yy = a_{32} + a_{12} - 2a_{22} \tag{15}$$

$$\partial xy = \frac{a_{33} - a_{31} - a_{13} + a_{11}}{4}$$

a_{ij} is the element of matrix A located in row i and column j. The Jacobian matrix is calculated as:

$$J = \begin{bmatrix} \frac{\partial\hat{x}}{\partial a_{11}} & \frac{\partial\hat{x}}{\partial a_{12}} & \cdots & \frac{\partial\hat{x}}{\partial a_{33}} \end{bmatrix} \tag{16}$$

J is a 2×9 matrix, so the last step of calculation is:

$$\Sigma_{\delta\hat{x}} = J\Sigma_a J^\mathsf{T} \tag{17}$$

$\Sigma_{\delta\hat{x}}$ is a 2×2 covariance matrix, the diagonal elements are the variance values of the matched sub-pixel coordinate, and the off-diagonal entries are the covariance values of the sub-pixel coordinates. This matrix finally includes the uncertainty information propagated from the image noise to the SAD sub-pixel matching result and can be used for further processing.

3.3   Propagation of Uncertainty of the NCC Feature Matcher

The normalized cross correlation (NCC) template matching algorithm is very similar to the SAD algorithm, NCC uses the Eq. (18) to calculate the normalized cross correlation between the templates from both images.

$$\text{NCC}(u, v) = \frac{1}{n} \sum_{i,j} \frac{(S(u + i, v + j) - \bar{S})(T(i,j) - \bar{T})}{\sigma_S \sigma_T} \tag{18}$$

In the equation, $S(u + i, v + j)$ is the search area in the second image, T is the template from the first image, where $n = i \cdot j$ and $\bar{S}$, $\bar{T}$ are the means of the template and the search area. The standard deviation of S and T are represented by the symbols σ_S, σ_T. Because of the non-linear nature of NCC, the error propagation for the 3×3 NCC matrix A needs to be done by a Jacobian matrix. Considering an example, the template size is the same as in Fig. 3. Hence, the Jacobian matrix is calculated as follows:

$$
\boldsymbol{J}_{ncc} = \frac{\partial f}{\partial p} =
\begin{bmatrix}
\dfrac{\partial f_1}{\partial p_{r1}} & \dfrac{\partial f_1}{\partial p_{r2}} & \cdots & \dfrac{\partial f_1}{\partial p_{l25}} \\
\vdots & \vdots & \ddots & \vdots \\
\dfrac{\partial f_9}{\partial p_{r1}} & \dfrac{\partial f_9}{\partial p_{r2}} & \cdots & \dfrac{\partial f_9}{\partial p_{l25}}
\end{bmatrix}
\tag{19}
$$

f is the common NCC equation given in Eq. (18), p_{ln} are the pixel values from the first image template and p_{rn} are the pixel values in the 7×7 search area in the second image. f_1 maps the template and the search area to the first entry of the 3×3 NCC matrix and so on. The usage of the 9×74 matrix $\boldsymbol{J}_{ncc}$ is same to the usage of $\boldsymbol{F}$ in Sect. 3.2. After the calculation of the covariance matrix $\boldsymbol{\Sigma}_a$, the remaining steps are identical with part 2 in Sect. 3.2. To avoid numerical errors, we recommend to use the Matlab symbolic calculation to get the final format of $\boldsymbol{J}_{ncc}$.

4   Experiment Results

To check the quality of the proposed method, we designed three experiments. Without loss of generality, the first experiment quantitatively verifies the proposed algorithm. The second one is a general feature matching test, and the third experiment checks the proposed method on an optical navigation system IPS [11], which was developed at the German Aerospace Center (DLR).

The first test is designed to verify the uncertainties propagation. The testing method is similar to a Monte Carlo test. The difference is that we do not generate artificial noise and add to image. Instead, we take a set of images, these images include noise from the camera system. The details of the test are described below.

The first step is similar to the noise model calculation step: The stereo camera system takes 100 image pairs from a fixed scene in a short time. The image contents are almost the same, but affected by noise from the camera system. Next, a feature extractor detects features from the first left image, then a sub-pixel template matcher matches the features to the first right image (without uncertainties propagation step). This step is repeated for all of the image pairs, but the feature extraction step is skipped. Instead, the coordinates of features in the first left image are used. As features are located in the same coordinate during 100 frames, there are 100 different stereo matching results, the standard deviation of the resulting sub-pixel offset is calculated and drawn as a curve in Fig. 4. Now these empirical results can be used to compare them with the propagated uncertainty which is calculated in the next step.

In the second step, only the first image pair is needed. We apply the sub-pixel template matcher and involve the propagation of uncertainties step in the first image pair. This way we get the uncertainties of matched features which are propagated from image noise. The Fig. 4 indicates that the noise model and

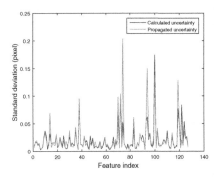 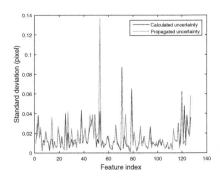

Fig. 4. The left graph shows the sub-pixel uncertainty of x coordinate, the blue curve is the uncertainty of features sub-pixel coordinate calculated from 100 images, and the red curve shows the propagated uncertainty based on our proposed method. The right graph shows the sub-pixel uncertainty of y coordinate. These two graphs show the strong correlation between real uncertainties and propagated uncertainties. (Color figure online)

propagation of uncertainties algorithm shows an accurate reflection of the real uncertainties of the matching results.

The second experiment check the performance of the proposed algorithm on stereo feature matching problem. First, the sub-pixel matching algorithm works on a stereo camera system. The noise model of the camera system is already calculated using our method. Figure 5 shows the images from left and right camera respectively. We use the AGAST [23] feature extractor to get features from the left image, and a SAD template matcher to match the features to the right image under epipolar line constraint. The green and orange crosses on the left image are the features successfully matched to the right image by a common SAD template matcher, and the yellow and cyan crosses symbolize mismatches. However, the orange crosses are the features filtered out by our proposed sub-pixel matching algorithm because of their high uncertainty (higher than 0.4 pixel). And in fact the orange features in Fig. 5 (near the cupboard and the white computer monitor) actually cannot be seen from the right camera's perspective. However, the common template matcher wrongly matches them to the right image (not drawn). Finally, the crosses on the left and right image are the features successfully matched after the sub-pixel matching step. This test shows that with the propagated uncertainty it is possible to filter for mismatched features, proving the correctness of the proposed algorithm from another perspective. The algorithm also improves the robustness of the system by filtering the mismatched features.

The last test based on an optical navigation project. The test platform is IPS. IPS was developed for real-time vision-aided inertial navigation [10,11], especially for an environment where GNSS is not available. The IPS is a Kalman filter based optical navigation system, in the previous version, the normal NCC and SAD feature matcher are used for stereo matching and tracking respectively.

Fig. 5. Image pair from a stereo camera system, the crosses are the features. The orange and green crosses on the left image symbolize the successfully matched features by a normal template matcher, the yellow and cyan crosses are features where matching failed. The orange crosses are filtered out by the proposed SAD sub-pixel matching algorithm with error propagation. (Color figure online)

The matching results are integral pixels. On the other hand, because lacking noise model, we cannot get uncertainties of matching results. However in order to use Kalman filter, the uncertainties information must be provided, therefore in the previous version, only a rough uncertainty of matching result (e.g. quantization error $(\frac{1}{12})$ [29]) are given. These problems can be solved by our proposed method. This experiment shows the comparison of measured trajectory in previous IPS version and the IPS combined with our noise model and sub-pixel algorithm.

For test purposes, a dataset is recorded by walking with the IPS through a realistic scene with a length of about 410 m. Such a physical run is called a session. We recorded eight sessions in total. Because the lack of ground truth, the start and end position of the loop are exactly the same. As the system does only consider the motion information extracted from two consecutive image pairs, and it does not recognize that it has been in a place before, the performance of the system can be measured by the error between the known start position and the calculated end position. As a RANSAC algorithm is used for optical navigation, the calculated positions have a random component. This is why each session is processed (offline) 50 times to calculate the root-mean-square (RMS) of trajectory errors as a final result. More details about the test procedure can be found in [32].

The IPS gets state of the art results, the trajectory error is about 0.1% of the traveled distance. In this instance, usually it is hard to get improvement. However, as Table 1 shows, the accuracy of the measurement is increased about 12% by our method. On the other hand, the new algorithm also leads to a better standard deviation, the improvement of standard deviation is about 44%, which means an improvement of the robustness of the system.

Table 1. The 8 sessions trajectory errors. The RMS is the root-mean-square of errors of 50 runs, and STD is the standard deviation. The results show the sub-pixel matching algorithm decrease not only the trajectory errors but also the standard deviation. New IPS is the IPS combined with proposed methods.

	Session:	1	2	3	4	5	6	7	8
Previous IPS	RMS(m)	0.68	0.25	0.62	0.29	0.52	0.49	0.39	0.44
	STD(m)	0.044	0.047	0.048	0.048	0.038	0.044	0.044	0.045
New IPS	RMS(m)	0.55	0.24	0.43	0.09	0.53	0.54	0.28	0.42
	STD(m)	0.016	0.023	0.026	0.018	0.016	0.019	0.017	0.023

5 Conclusion

In this paper, we propose a method to model the image noise, this noise model can be retrieved during normal camera calibration step. Based on the noise model, uncertainties propagation for sub-pixel matching algorithms is described. The proposed image noise model and the method to get uncertainty of sub-pixel matching results can be widely used in many computer vision applications. The performance of the proposed methods is evaluated by a full system test. The experimental results show that the noise model is actually able to reflect the uncertainty of sub-pixel matching results. An additional test shows that the uncertainty calculation can even be utilized as a mismatched filter without any computational overhead. The last test concentrates on the performance of the new algorithm combined with an optical navigation system. The result proves that the proposed method decreases the trajectory errors and standard deviation of errors simultaneously. The test shows our method can get significantly better results without much effort. In our future work, we will implement the uncertainties propagation method for other sub-pixel matching algorithms.

References

1. Alsaade, F.: Fast and accurate template matching algorithm based on image pyramid and sum of absolute difference similarity measure. Res. J. Inf. Technol. **4**(4), 204–211 (2012)
2. Amerini, I., Caldelli, R., Cappellini, V., Picchioni, F., Piva, A.: Estimate of PRNU noise based on different noise models for source camera identification. IJDCF **2**(2), 21–33 (2010)
3. Bay, H., Tuytelaars, T., Van Gool, L.: SURF: speeded up robust features. In: Leonardis, A., Bischof, H., Pinz, A. (eds.) ECCV 2006. LNCS, vol. 3951, pp. 404–417. Springer, Heidelberg (2006). https://doi.org/10.1007/11744023_32
4. Bloesch, M., Omari, S., Hutter, M., Siegwart, R.: Robust visual inertial odometry using a direct EKF-based approach. In: Intelligent Robots and Systems (2015)
5. Boyat, A.K., Joshi, B.K.: A review paper: noise models in digital image processing. Sig. Image Process.: Int. J. **6**(2), 63–75 (2015)
6. Brunelli, R.: Template Matching Techniques in Computer Vision: Theory and Practice. Wiley, Hoboken (2009)

7. Clifford, A.: Multivariate Error Analysis: A Handbook of Error Propagation and Calculation in Many-Parameter Systems. Wiley, Hoboken (1973)
8. Evtikhiev, N.N., Starikov, S.N., Cheryomkhin, P.A., Krasnov, V.V.: Measurement of noises and modulation transfer function of cameras used in optical-digital correlators. International Society for Optics and Photonics (2012)
9. Gonzalez, R.C., Woods, R.E.: Digital Image Processing, 3rd edn. Prentice-Hall, Inc., Upper Saddle River (2006)
10. Grießbach, D.: Stereo-vision-aided inertial navigation. Ph.D. thesis, Freie Universitt Berlin (2014)
11. Grießbach, D., Baumbach, D., Zuev, S.: Stereo-vision-aided inertial navigation for unknown indoor and outdoor environments. In: 2014 IPIN (2014)
12. Haralick, R., Shapiro, L.: Computer and Robot Vision, vol. 2. Addison-Wesley Publishing Company, Boston (1993)
13. Holst, G.C.: CCD Arrays, Cameras, and Displays, 2nd edn. Society of Photo Optical, Bellingham (1998)
14. Jayaraman: Digital Image Processing, 1st edn. Mc Graw Hill India, New Delhi (2009)
15. Kanatani, K.I.: Uncertainty modeling and model selection for geometric inference. IEEE Trans. Pattern Anal. Mach. Intell. **26**(10), 1307–1319 (2004)
16. Kanazawa, Y., Kanatani, K.: Do we really have to consider covariance matrices for image features? Electron. Commun. Jpn. **86**, 1–10 (2003)
17. Kim, K.B., Kim, J.S., Choi, J.S.: Fourier based image registration for sub-pixel using pyramid edge detection and line fitting. In: Intelligent Networks and Intelligent Systems. IEEE (2008)
18. Leutenegger, S., Chli, M., Siegwart, R.Y.: BRISK: binary robust invariant scalable keypoints. In: ICCV. IEEE (2011)
19. Lowe, D.G.: Distinctive image features from scale-invariant keypoints. Int. J. Comput. Vis. **60**(2), 91–110 (2004)
20. Lowry, S., Sunderhauf, N., Newman, P., Leonard, J.J., Cox, D., Corke, P., Milford, M.J.: Visual place recognition: a survey. IEEE Trans. Robot. **32**(1), 1–19 (2016)
21. Lucas, B.D., Kanade, T.: An iterative image registration technique with an application to stereo vision. In: Proceedings of the 7th International Joint Conference on Artificial Intelligence, IJCAI 1981, vol. 2 (1981)
22. Madsen, K., Nielsen, H.B., Tingleff, O.: Methods for Non-linear Least Squares Problems (1999)
23. Mair, E., Hager, G.D., Burschka, D., Suppa, M., Hirzinger, G.: Adaptive and generic corner detection based on the accelerated segment test. In: Daniilidis, K., Maragos, P., Paragios, N. (eds.) ECCV 2010. LNCS, vol. 6312, pp. 183–196. Springer, Heidelberg (2010). https://doi.org/10.1007/978-3-642-15552-9_14
24. Mourikis, A.I., Roumeliotis, S.I.: A multi-state constraint Kalman filter for vision-aided inertial navigation. In: Proceedings IEEE ICRA (2007)
25. Nakamura, J.: Image Sensors and Signal Processing for Digital Still Cameras. Optical Science and Engineering. CRC Press, Boca Raton (2016)
26. Rosten, E., Porter, R., Drummond, T.: Faster and better: a machine learning approach to corner detection. Pattern Anal. Mach. Intell. **32**(1), 105–119 (2010)
27. Sheorey, S., Keshavamurthy, S., Yu, H., Nguyen, H., Taylor, C.N.: Uncertainty estimation for KLT tracking. In: Jawahar, C.V., Shan, S. (eds.) ACCV 2014. LNCS, vol. 9009, pp. 475–487. Springer, Cham (2015). https://doi.org/10.1007/978-3-319-16631-5_35
28. Shi, J., Tomasi, C.: Good features to track. In: CVPR (1994)

29. Stein, S., Jones, J.: Modern Communication Principles: With Application to Digital Signaling. McGraw-Hill, New York City (1967)
30. Thevenaz, P., Ruttimann, U.E., Unser, M.: A pyramid approach to subpixel registration based on intensity. IEEE Trans. Image Process. **7**(1), 27–41 (1998)
31. Zeisl, B., Georgel, P.F., Schweiger, F., Steinbach, E.G., Navab, N., Munich, G.: Estimation of location uncertainty for scale invariant features points. In: BMVC (2009)
32. Zhang, H., Wohlfeil, J., Grießbach, D.: Extension and evaluation of the AGAST feature detector. In: XXIII ISPRS Congress Annals 2016, vol. 3, pp. 133–137 (2016)

Age Estimation with Local Ternary Directional Patterns

Raphael Angulu[1]([✉])(iD), Jules R. Tapamo[2], and Aderemi O. Adewumi[1]

[1] School of Mathematics, Statistics and Computer Science,
University of KwaZulu-Natal, Durban 4000, South Africa
anguluraphael@gmail.com, adewumia@ukzn.ac.za
[2] School of Engineering, University of KwaZulu-Natal, Durban 4041, South Africa
tapamoj@ukzn.ac.za

Abstract. Local texture descriptors have gained significant momentum in pattern recognition community due to their robustness compared to holistic descriptors. Local ternary patterns and its variants use a static threshold to derive textural code in order to improve Local Binary Patterns robustness to noise. It is not easy to select an optimum threshold in local ternary patterns and its variants for all images in a dataset or all experimental datasets. Local directional patterns uses directional responses to encode image gradient. Apart from considering only k significant responses, local directional patterns does not include central pixel in determining image gradient. Disregarding central pixel and $8 - k$ responses could result in lose of significant discriminative information. In this paper, we propose local ternary directional patterns that combines local ternary patterns and local directional patterns in determining image gradient. In local ternary directional patterns, the threshold is determined by the neighboring pixels and both significant, less significant responses and central pixel are considered in calculating image gradient. Evaluation of local ternary directional patterns on FG-NET dataset shows its robustness in local texture description compared to local directional pattern and local ternary pattern.

Keywords: Age estimation · Local binary patterns
Local directional patterns · Local ternary directional patterns

1 Introduction

Performance of any pattern recognition system is dependent on informative and discriminative power of the extracted features [26,32]. Effectiveness in extraction of discriminative features is a vital consideration in pattern recognition [30]. There are two broad categories of face image representation techniques; holistic and local. Holistic face representation techniques like Principal Component Analysis (PCA) [27] and Linear Discriminant Analysis (LDA) [4] have been proved successful for various pattern recognition application domains. Limitation of such holistic features is that they often fail in small sample size problems. Local face

© Springer International Publishing AG, part of Springer Nature 2018
M. Paul et al. (Eds.): PSIVT 2017, LNCS 10749, pp. 421–434, 2018.
https://doi.org/10.1007/978-3-319-75786-5_34

descriptors include Local Binary Patterns (LBP) [16–18], Local Directional Patterns (LDP) [9], local ternary patterns (LTP) [25], Gabor wavelets [7], speeded-up robust features (SURF) [3], scale-invariant feature transform (SIFT) [14], histogram of oriented gradient (HOG) [6] among others. A good image representation technique should encode more between-class discriminative information with low intra-class variations.

Local texture descriptors have gained popularity in computer vision and pattern recognition research community due to their robustness to illumination and pose variations. Penev and Atick [21] proposed a second-order statistical technique called local feature analysis (LFA). LFA uses a set of local-topological fields for local feature extraction. Gabor wavelet [7] filters texture and wrinkle features using a sinusoidal plane at different orientations, frequencies and scales. Its ability to encode spatial information of an object makes it suitable for local feature extraction [30]. Gabor wavelets have frequency and orientation selectivity witnessed in visual cortex of mammals. This has led to Gabor wavelets intensive use in extraction of bio-inspired features (BIF). Local binary patterns [16,17] is a first-order local texture descriptor that has been applied successfully to various pattern recognition problems like face recognition [2], facial expression analysis [31] and age estimation. LBP is not robust to noise [9,10] and the first-order information it encodes fails to capture detailed information from a given image [30]. LTP improves LBP robustness to noise by using a threshold to filter out possible noise before encoding texture features. Although LTP improves performance of LBP, still it does not capture detailed information of the image. LDP [9,10] represents an image by encoding directional responses at each pixel. The top k significant responses are used to derive LDP code of the reference pixel. LDP only considers top k responses and ignores the remaining $(8-k)$ responses. In LDP, a significant response denotes the presence of an edge and consequently less significant response denotes the absence of an edge an this ought to be captured. Absence of edge signifies a relatively constant surface. Encoding this across the image could help in tracking invariant features that could help improve recognition accuracies.

This paper proposes local ternary directional patterns (LTDP) operator for texture description. For every pixel in an image, LTDP considers directional responses to eight directions for encoding image gradient. The probability of a response appearing is calculated based on the absolute value of the responses. The threshold τ used to generate LTDP code is adaptive to the local region of the image being encoded. This makes LTDP operator not only adaptive but also appropriate for all images in a dataset or all experimental datasets since the threshold is dynamic.

The rest of the paper is organized as follows. Section 2 presents a review of operators related to LTDP. Section 3 discusses details of how LTDP operator encodes image texture while Sect. 4 outlines the experiments done to illustrate robustness of LTDP operator. Section 5 is devoted to results and discussion of LTDP performance in age estimation and Sect. 6 concludes the study and gives some recommendations.

2   Related Work

2.1   Local Binary Patterns

Texture features have been extensively used in age estimation techniques [20]. LBP is a texture description technique that can detect microstructure patterns like spots, edges, lines and flat areas on the skin [16]. LBP is used to describe texture for face recognition, gender classification, age estimation, face detection, face and facial component tracking. Gunay and Nabiyev [8] used LBP to characterize texture features for age estimation. They reported accuracy of 80% on FERET [19] dataset using nearest neighbor classifier and 80–90% accuracy on FERET and PIE datasets using AdaBoost classifier [29]. Figure 1 shows sample 3×3 LBP operation.

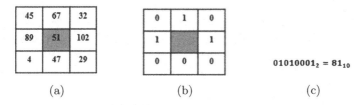

(a)   (b)   (c)

Fig. 1. LBP operation with P = 8 R = 1. (a) Sample image region (b) Thresholding (c) Resultant LBP code.

LBP code is created using the function $LBP_{P,R}$ defined as

$$LBP_{P,R}(x_c, y_c) = \sum_{n=0}^{N-1} 2^n \tau(g_n - g_c) \tag{1}$$

where the thresholding function τ is defined as

$$\tau(x) = \begin{cases} 1 & \text{if } x \geq 0 \\ 0 & \text{otherwise} \end{cases} \tag{2}$$

N is the number of neighboring pixels, R is distance of each neighboring pixel from center pixel, g_c is gray-value of center pixel, g_n for $n = 0, 1, 2, \ldots N - 1$ correspond to gray value of neighboring pixel on circular symmetric neighborhood of distance $R > 0$. Concatenating all 8 bits gives a binary code of (x_c, y_c). The resulting binary code is converted to decimal representation and allocated to central pixel as its LBP code. A histogram of LBP-encoded image $f(x, y)$ is used to represent micro-pattern structures like spots, edges, corners and flat regions. This histogram is encoded as

$$H_i = \sum_{x,y} I(f(x, y), i), i = 0, 1, 2 \ldots, 2^p - 1 \tag{3}$$

where p denotes number of patterns that can be encoded by the LBP operator and I is defined as

$$I(a,b) = \begin{cases} 1, & \text{if } a = b \\ 0 & \text{otherwise} \end{cases} \tag{4}$$

Ojala et al. [17] found that when using 8 neighbors and radius 1, 90% of all patterns are made up uniform patterns. The original LBP operator had limitation in capturing dominant features with large scale structures. The operator was latter extended to capture texture features with neighborhood of different radii [17]. Neighborhood is defined by a set of sampling pixels distributed evenly around the pixel to be labeled. Bilinear interpolation of points that fall outside the neighborhood is done to allow any radii and any number of sampling pixels.

Uniform patterns may represent microstructures as line, spot, edge or flat area. Ojala et al. [16] further categorized LBP codes as uniform and non-uniform patterns. LBP pattern with utmost two bitwise transition from 0 to 1 or 1 to 0 is categorized as a uniform pattern. For instance, $00000000, 00010000$ and 11011111 patterns are uniform while $01010000, 11100101$, and 10101001 are non-uniform patterns. In order to extract rotational invariant features using LBP, the generated LBP code is circularly rotated until its minimum value is obtained [15].

Extended LBP operator could capture more texture features on an image but still it could not preserve spatial information about these features. Ahonen et al. [1] proposed a technique of dividing a face image into n cells. Histograms are generated for each cell then concatenated to a single spatial histogram. Spatial histogram preserves both spatial and texture description of an image. Image texture features are finally represented by histogram of LBP codes. LBP histogram contains detailed texture descriptor for all structures on the face image like spots, lines, edges and flat areas.

2.2 Local Ternary Patterns

Local Binary Pattern is sensitive to illumination and noise. LTP [25] seeks to improve robustness of image features in a fairly uniform region. LTP extends LBP to a 3-value code by comparing pixel values of the neighboring pixels with a preset threshold value ξ. The code 0 is assigned to values within $\pm\xi$, 1 is assigned to values above ξ while -1 is assigned to values below ξ. The thresholding function is defined as

$$f(x_i, x_c, \xi) = \begin{cases} 1 & \text{if } x_i \geq x_c + \xi \\ 0 & \text{if } |x_c - x_i| < \xi \\ -1 & \text{if } x_i \leq x_c - \xi \end{cases} \tag{5}$$

where ξ is a preset threshold, x_c is the value of the central pixel and x_i for $i = 0, 1, 2 \ldots 7$ are the neighboring pixels of x_c. Although this extension makes

LTP robust to noise and encode more patterns, it is not easy to practically select an optimum τ for all images in a dataset or for all datasets and the resultant code is not invariant to pixel value transformations. LTP can encode 3^8 patterns. LTP codes are divided into positive and negative parts and a histogram is generated for each part. These histograms are concatenated and used as feature descriptor for pattern recognition. Figure 2 shows LTP codes for a 3×3 sample image region.

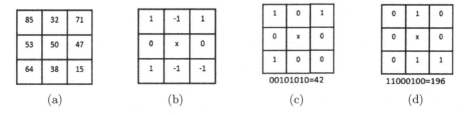

Fig. 2. LTP code with $\xi = \pm 5$ and corresponding positive and negative LBP codes. (a) Original image (b) LTP code ($\xi = \pm 5$) (c) Negative LBP code. (d) Positive LBP code.

2.3 Local Directional Patterns

LBP [18] was found to be unstable to image noise and variations in illumination. Jabid et al. [9] proposed LDP which is robust to image noise and non-monotonic variations in illumination. Figure 3 shows robustness of LDP operator to noise compared to LBP.

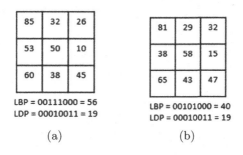

Fig. 3. Robustness of LDP compared to LBP. (a) Original image (b) Noisy image.

Local Directional Patterns compute 8-bit binary code for each pixel in the image by comparing edge response of each pixel in different orientations instead of comparing raw pixel intensities as LBP. Kirsch [11], Prewitt [23] and Sobel [24] are some of edge detectors that can be used [22]. Kirsch edge detector has gained popularity because it detects 8-directional edge responses more accurately compared to others [12].

Kirsch Edge Detector. Kirsch operator is a first-order derivative edge detector that gets image gradients by convolving 3×3 image regions with a set of masks. Kirsch defines a nonlinear edge detector technique as [22]:-

$$P(x,y) = \max \left\{ 1, \max_{k=0}^{7} \left[|5S_k - 3T_k| \right] \right\} \tag{6}$$

where

$$S_k = P_k + P_{k+1} + P_{k+2}$$

and

$$T_k = P_{k+3} + P_{k+4} + P_{k+5} + P_{k+6} + P_{k+7}$$

where $P(x,y)$ is the Kirsch gradient, a in P_a is evaluated as $a\%8$ and P_k $[k = 0,1,2\ldots,7]$ are eight neighboring pixels of $P(x,y)$ as shown in Fig. 4.

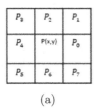   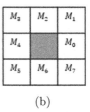

(a)   (b)

Fig. 4. (a) Eight neighbors of pixel $p(x,y)$ (b) corresponding Kirsch mask

The Kirsch gradient in a particular direction is found by convolving 3×3 image region with the respective mask M_k. Figure 5 shows Kirsch Masks (kernels) for 8 directions.

Given a pixel $P(i,j)$ in an image, 8-directional responses are computed by convolving the neighboring pixels, 3×3 image region, with each of the Kirsch masks. For each pixel, there will be 8 directional response values. Presence of an edge or a corner will show high (absolute) response values in that particular direction. The interest of LDP is to determine k significant directional responses and set their corresponding bit-value to 1 and set the rest of $8 - k$ bits to 0. The resulting 8-bit binary string is converted to decimal and assigned to the $P(i,j)$ pixel. This process is repeated for all pixels in the image to obtain LDP representation of the image. Figure 6 shows process of encoding an image using LDP operator.

Given an image region as shown in Fig. 3(a), Kirsch masks application responses are obtained by convolving 3×3 image region with each of the Kirsch masks shown in Fig. 5. The absolute values of the directional responses are arranged in descending order. The LDP_k code is then calculated as

$$LDP_k = \sum_{i=0}^{i=7} \tau (m_i - m_k) \times 2^i \tag{7}$$

where m_k is the kth significant directional response, and τ is defined in (2).

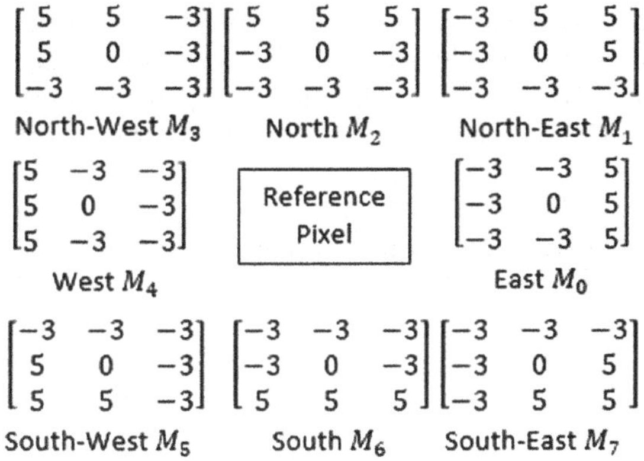

$$\begin{bmatrix} 5 & 5 & -3 \\ 5 & 0 & -3 \\ -3 & -3 & -3 \end{bmatrix} \begin{bmatrix} 5 & 5 & 5 \\ -3 & 0 & -3 \\ -3 & -3 & -3 \end{bmatrix} \begin{bmatrix} -3 & 5 & 5 \\ -3 & 0 & 5 \\ -3 & -3 & -3 \end{bmatrix}$$

North-West M_3 North M_2 North-East M_1

$$\begin{bmatrix} 5 & -3 & -3 \\ 5 & 0 & -3 \\ 5 & -3 & -3 \end{bmatrix} \quad \boxed{\text{Reference Pixel}} \quad \begin{bmatrix} -3 & -3 & 5 \\ -3 & 0 & 5 \\ -3 & -3 & 5 \end{bmatrix}$$

West M_4 East M_0

$$\begin{bmatrix} -3 & -3 & -3 \\ 5 & 0 & -3 \\ 5 & 5 & -3 \end{bmatrix} \begin{bmatrix} -3 & -3 & -3 \\ -3 & 0 & -3 \\ 5 & 5 & 5 \end{bmatrix} \begin{bmatrix} -3 & -3 & -3 \\ -3 & 0 & 5 \\ -3 & 5 & 5 \end{bmatrix}$$

South-West M_5 South M_6 South-East M_7

Fig. 5. Kirsch Masks in eight directions

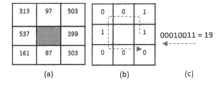

(a)   (b)   (c)

Fig. 6. Process of encoding an image with LDP operator with $k = 3$ (a) Result of convolving each pixel in Fig. 3(a) with 8 Kirsch masks in Fig. 5(b) Pick top $k = 3$ significant responses, set there corresponding bit to 1 and the rest to 0 (c) Resultant LDP code.

For $k = 3$, LDP operator generates $C_3^8 = \frac{8!}{3! \times (8-3)!} = 56$ distinct patterns in the LDP encoded image. A histogram $H(i)$ with C_k^8 bins can be used to represent the input image of size $M \times N$ as:-

$$H_i = \sum_{m=0}^{M-1} \sum_{n=0}^{N-1} I\left(LDP_k\left(m, n\right), i\right) \tag{8}$$

where I is defined in (4) and $0 \le i \le C_k^8$. The resultant histogram has dimensions $1 \times C_k^8$ and is used to represent the image. The resultant feature has spots, corners, edges and texture information about the image [10]. The limitation of LDP with $k = 3$ is that it uses responses of at most 3 directions out of the possible 8 directions. These directional responses could possibly be one sided as South-East, East and North-East. The eight directional responses could be paired as in [12] and guarantee that each directional response will be used to determine the image gradient.

3   Local Ternary Directional Patterns

LTP uses a static user defined threshold ξ for all images in a dataset or for all experimental datasets making it not invariant to pixel value transformations.

It is not practically easy to select an optimum value for ξ in real application domains. The value of ξ should be adaptive to different image conditions and datasets. LDP only considers top k directional responses and disregards the rest of $8 - k$ responses in encoding image gradient. Furthermore, LDP does not consider current reference pixel when calculating the image gradient. The presence of an edge is depicted by sharp difference between a pixel and its neighbors [22]. LDP *encodes image gradient* without considering the central pixel thereby "capturing" an image edge even where there is non. This results into possible lost of discriminative information. In this section, we propose LTDP operator that considers central reference pixel and all directional responses in encoding image gradient. LTDP operator uses an adaptive ξ that depends on the directional responses of the image region.

Local Ternary Directional Patterns compute eight directional responses using Kirsch masks. Given a 3×3 image region, LTDP first determines the differences in pixel intensities between central pixel and its neighboring pixels. The absolute magnitude of the difference is set as the edge difference of the respective pixel as

$$P_{i,j} = |P_{i,j} - P_c| \tag{9}$$

where $P_{i,j}$ is the pixel value at index (i, j) and P_c is the pixel value of the central pixel. Figure 7 shows an example of calculating differential directional responses.

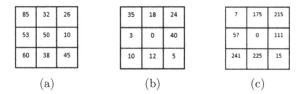

(a)   (b)   (c)

Fig. 7. Differential LDP responses. (a) Image region (b) Differential values (c) Differential directional LDP responses

Responses are then normalized before being used to generate LTDP code. Min-max normalization is done as

$$x_i^{norm} = \frac{x_i - min}{max - min} \tag{10}$$

where x_i is the absolute value of respective responses for $i = 1, 2, \ldots 7$, min and max are minimum and maximum responses respectively and x_i^{norm} is the normalized value of x_i. The normalized responses are in the range of 0.0 and 1.0 which signify the probability of an edge from the central reference pixel stretching towards respective direction.

Threshold ξ is set to ± 0.1667 deviation from 0.50 value. The value 0.5 is selected as offset reference value for ξ because it shows equal chance of there being an edge or not. The value of ξ is chosen to ensure the probability space is divided into 3 equal segments, one for each ternary bit. If the normalized response value is greater or equal to $0.5 + \xi$, its corresponding bit is set to $+1$, if the normalized response value is less or equal to $0.5 - \xi$, its corresponding bit is set to -1, and the corresponding bit is set to 0 if the normalized response is between $0.5 - \xi$ and $0.5 + \xi$ as

$$f(x_i) = \begin{cases} 1 & \text{if} \quad x_i^{norm} \geq 0.50 + \xi \\ 0 & \text{if} \quad 0.50 - \xi < x_i^{norm} < 0.50 + \xi \\ -1 & \text{if} \quad x_i^{norm} \leq 0.50 - \xi \end{cases} \tag{11}$$

Figure 8 shows the process of encoding an image with the proposed LTDP operator.

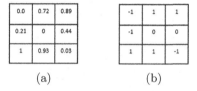

(a)   (b)

Fig. 8. Process of encoding an image with LTDP operator. (a) Normalization of responses in Fig. 7c (b) Assigning LTDP code at $\xi = 0.5 \pm 0.1667$.

The presence of an edge towards a particular direction is signified by not only significant differential directional response towards that direction but also significant differential directional response of one of its neighboring direction. A differential directional response is significant if its value d is greater than $\bar{m} = 0.5 \times m + \xi$ where m is the maximum differential directional response of the local region. Differential directional responses closer to $\bar{m}$ are coded as being invariant relative to central pixel hence there corresponding bit set to 0. The differential directional response further away below $\bar{m} = 0.5 \times m - \xi$ are coded as having a negative image gradient hence there corresponding bit set to -1 and those further away above $\bar{m}$ are coded as having positive image gradient hence there corresponding bit set to 1. Each LTDP is split into its corresponding negative and positive segments as shown in Fig. 9.

These codes are converted to decimal and assigned to corresponding central pixel of positive and negative LTDP encoded images respectively. A histogram is generated for for both negative and positive LTDP encoded images as

$$H_i = \sum_{x,y} I(f(x,y), i), i = 0, 1, 2 \ldots, 2^p - 1 \tag{12}$$

where p is the number of patterns that can be encoded by the LDP operator (positive and negative) and I is defined in (4).

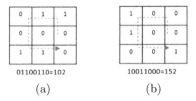

(a)   (b)

Fig. 9. Resultant LDP codes from the LTDP code. (a) Positive LDP code (b) Negative LDP code.

The resultant positive and negative histograms are concatenated and used as LTDP feature for pattern recognition. The histograms can be trimmed down by taking only uniform patterns into respective bins and put the rest of non-uniform patterns into one bin. A pattern is uniform if it contains utmost 2 transitions from 0 to 1 or vice versa. For *n-bit* patterns, the total number of uniform patterns is

$$P_U = n(n-1) + 2 \tag{13}$$

where n is the number of bits used to represent the patterns. LTDP generates $8(8-1)+2 = 58$ uniform patterns for both negative and positive LTDP encoded images. The resultant histogram could have 59 bins with 58 bins storing uniform patterns while the 59th bin storing all non-uniform patterns. These two histograms are concatenated to form final LTDP feature vector.

4 Experiments

Experiments are performed on FG-NET aging dataset to evaluate performance of LTP, LDP and LTDP operators in age estimation. Hybrid approach that consists of between-group classification followed by within-group regression is adopted. Multilayer Perceptron (MLP) [5] Artificial Neural Network (ANN) is used to classify an input image into age group before using SVR regressor for exact age estimation within each age-group. We use SVR-RBF since it can model complex aging patterns for large age ranges [28].

4.1 Dataset

FG-NET aging dataset was used to evaluate age estimation using LTDP. FG-NET has 1002 images of 82 subjects aged between 0 and 69 years. Images have wide variation in illumination, color and expression. Some images have poor quality since they were scanned.

4.2 Feature Extraction

Face region was detected from an input image using Haar-cascade face detection classifier [13]. The face is then cropped, converted to gray scale and resized to

120×120 pixels. The gray scale face image is smoothened using Gaussian filter. The face is then encoded using LTDP operator. Figure 10 shows image encoded with LTDP, LTP and LDP operators.

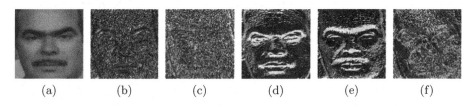

(a)   (b)   (c)   (d)   (e)   (f)

Fig. 10. Image encoded with LTDP, LTP and LDP operators. (a) Input image (b) Resultant positive LTDP image (c) Resultant negative LTDP image (d) Resultant positive LTP image $\xi = \pm 3$ (e) Resultant negative LTP image $\xi = \pm 3$ (f) Resultant LDP image $k = 3$

A histogram is generated for each of these images. The positive and negative histograms are concatenated and used as a feature vector for age estimation. The dimensionality of the resultant feature vector is reduced using LDA.

4.3   Validation and Evaluation Protocol

We use Leave-One-Person-Out (LOPO) validation protocol to evaluate LTP, LDP and LTDP based age estimation techniques. In LOPO, in each iteration, images of one person are left out to be used as test images while images of the rest of the subjects are used to learn a model. Two commonly used measures of age estimation technique performance are; Cumulative Score (CS) and Mean Absolute Error (MAE). MAE is average of absolute errors between estimated age and actual age defined as

$$MAE = \frac{1}{N} \sum_{i=1}^{N} |a_i - \bar{a}_i| \tag{14}$$

where N is size of the test set, a_i is ground truth age of image i, and $\bar{a}_i$ is the estimated age of image i. CS is formulated as

$$CS(x) = \frac{N_{e \leq x}}{N} \times 100\% \tag{15}$$

where $N_{e \leq x}$ are images on which LBP, LDP and SOR-LDP age estimation techniques make an absolute error of less than x years error tolerance and N is size of test set. Our error tolerance x was 5 years.

5   Results and Discussion

FG-NET aging dataset is split into 7 age-groups of 10 years. The first age-group is 0–9 years and last age-group is 60–69 years. Table 1 shows MAE error achieved in each group for LTDP, LDP and LTP operators.

Table 1. Age-group MAE (years) comparison using LTDP, LDP and LTP

Group	Images	LTDP [Proposed]	LDP [10]	LTP [25]
0–9	371	2.72	2.83	2.94
10–19	339	3.26	3.47	3.71
20–29	144	3.41	4.20	4.04
30–39	70	7.58	8.74	8.98
40–49	46	13.65	14.60	15.30
50–59	15	19.84	20.59	21.02
60–69	8	30.37	31.61	31.88
Total	**1002**	**4.35**	**5.12**	**5.74**
CS		**78.3%**	**76.6%**	**73.4%**

As shown in Table 1, LTDP achieved MAE of 2.72 years in age-group 0–9 compared to 2.83 and 2.94 achieved by LDP and LTP respectively. In age-group 10–19, LTDP achieved MAE of 3.26 compared to 3.47 achieved by LDP and 3.71 achieved by LTP in the same age-group. With 144 images in age-group 20–29, LTDP achieved MAE of 3.41 years compared to 4.20 and 4.04 achieved by LDP and LTP respectively. Performance of all three operators deteriorates drastically as from age-group 30–39 due to drastic decrease in number of images per group. Nevertheless, LTDP performed better than LDP and LTP in age-group 30–39 by achieving MAE of 7.58 years compared to 8.74 achieved by LDP and 8.98 achieved by LTP. The performance is poorest in age-group 60–69 because the dataset used has only 8 images in this age-group, which are not sufficient to learn any aging pattern. LTDP achieved overall MAE of 4.35 which is superior relative to 5.12 achieved by LDP and 5.74 achieved by LTP.

It is evident from the experiments that LTDP encodes more discriminative local texture features compared to LDP and LTP. LTDP improves age estimation accuracies by MAE of 0.77 compared to LDP and by 1.42 compared to LTP. The accuracy of LTDP could be attributed to involvement of central pixel as well considering all eight directional responses in calculating image gradient. This shows that all the responses as well as central pixel are vital in achieving age discriminative local texture features.

6   Conclusion and Recommendation

LTDP is proposed for local texture feature extraction. The magnitude of the neighboring pixels is determined by the difference of their values and the central reference pixel. Kirsch masks are applied to these difference in pixel values to obtain directional responses. The directional responses are min-max normalized to obtain the probability of an edge stretching towards a particular direction. Applying a threshold to this probability space, LTDP code is found and used to obtain positive and negative LDP images. Histograms of positive and negative

LDP images are concatenated to obtain texture feature for pattern recognition. Experimental results on FG-NET aging dataset show that LTDP outperforms LTP and LDP in age estimation. Further research is required to make the threshold used in LTDP more adaptive to local image region for effective extraction of more discriminative features.

References

1. Ahonen, T., Hadid, A., Pietikäinen, M.: Face recognition with local binary patterns. In: Pajdla, T., Matas, J. (eds.) ECCV 2004. LNCS, vol. 3021, pp. 469–481. Springer, Heidelberg (2004). https://doi.org/10.1007/978-3-540-24670-1_36
2. Ahonen, T., Hadid, A., Pietikainen, M.: Face description with local binary patterns: application to face recognition. IEEE Trans. Pattern Anal. Mach. Intell. **20**, 2037–2041 (2006)
3. Bay, H., Tuytelaars, T., Van Gool, L.: SURF: speeded up robust features. In: Leonardis, A., Bischof, H., Pinz, A. (eds.) ECCV 2006. LNCS, vol. 3951, pp. 404–417. Springer, Heidelberg (2006). https://doi.org/10.1007/11744023_32
4. Belhumeour, P.N., Hespanda, J.P., Kriegman, D.J.: Eigenfaces vs. Fisherfaces: recognition using class specific linear projection. IEEE Trans. Pattern Anal. Mach. Intell. **19**, 711–720 (1997)
5. Bishop, C.M.: Pattern Recognition and Machine Learning. Springer, New York (2007)
6. Dalal, N., Triggs, B.: Histograms of oriented gradients for human detection. In: Proceedings of IEEE Computer Society Conference on Computer Vision and Pattern Recognition (CVPR), vol. 1, pp. 886–893 (2005)
7. Gabor, D.: Theory of communication. J. Inst. Electr. Eng. **93**, 429–457 (1946)
8. Gunay, A., Nabiyev, V.V.: Automatic age classification with LBP. In: 2008 23rd International Symposium on Computer and Information Sciences, ISCIS 2008, pp. 1–4. IEEE (2008)
9. Jabid, T., Kabir, M., Chae, O.: Local directional pattern (LDP) for face recognition. In: 2010 Digest of Technical Papers International Conference on Consumer Electronics (ICCE). IEEE, January 2010
10. Jabid, T., Kabir, M.H., Chae, O.: Gender classification using local directional pattern (LDP). In: 2010 20th International Conference on Pattern Recognition. IEEE, August 2010
11. Kirsch, R.A.: Computer determination of the constituent structure of biological images. Comput. Biomed. Res. **4**(3), 315–328 (1971)
12. Lee, S.W.: Off-line recognition of totally unconstrained handwritten numerals using multilayer cluster neural network. IEEE Trans. Pattern Anal. Mach. Intell. **18**(6), 648–652 (1996)
13. Lienhart, R.: Stump-based 20 x 20 gentle adaboost frontal face detector. Intel Corporation (2000)
14. Lowe, D.G.: Distinctive image features from scale-invariant keypoints. Int. J. Comput. Vis. **60**, 91–110 (2004)
15. Maenpaa, T., Pietikainen, M.: Texture analysis with local binary patterns. In: Handbook of Pattern Recognition and Computer Vision. World Scientific (2005)
16. Ojala, T., Pietikainen, M., Harwood, D.: A comparative study of texture measures with classification based on featured distribution. Pattern Recogn. **29**, 51–59 (1996)

17. Ojala, T., Pietikainen, M., Maenpaa, T.: Multiresolution gray-scale and rotation invariant texture classification with local binary patterns. IEEE Trans. Pattern Anal. Mach. Intell. **24**, 971–987 (2002)
18. Ojala, T., Pietikäinen, M., Mäenpää, T.: A generalized local binary pattern operator for multiresolution gray scale and rotation invariant texture classification. In: Singh, S., Murshed, N., Kropatsch, W. (eds.) ICAPR 2001. LNCS, vol. 2013, pp. 399–408. Springer, Heidelberg (2001). https://doi.org/10.1007/3-540-44732-6_41
19. Phillips, J.P., Moon, H., Rizvi, S.A., Rauss, P.J.: The feret evaluation methodology for face recognition algorithms. IEEE Trans. Pattern Anal. Mach. Intell. **22**, 1090–1104 (2000)
20. Panis, G., Lanitis, A., Tsapatsoulis, N., Cootes, T.F.: Overview ofreserach on facial ageing using the FG-NET ageing database. IET Biom. **5**, 37–46 (2016)
21. Penev, P.S., Atick, J.J.: Local feature analysis: a general statistical theory for object representation. Netw.: Comput. Neural Syst. **7**(3), 477–500 (1996)
22. Pratt, W.K.: Digital Image Processing. Wiley, New York (1978)
23. Prewitt, J.M.S.: Object enhancement and extraction. In: Picture Processing and Psychopictorics. Academic Press (1970)
24. Sobel, I., Feldman, G.: A 3 x 3 isotropic gradient operator for image processing. Presented at the Stanford Artificial Intelligence Project (SAIL) (1968)
25. Tan, X., Triggs, B.: Enhanced local texture feature sets for face recognition under difficult lighting conditions. IEEE Trans. Image Process. **19**, 1635–1650 (2010)
26. Turaga, P., Chellappa, R., Subrahmanian, V., Udrea, O.: Machine recognition of human activities: a survey. IEEE Trans. Circ. Syst. Video Technol. **18**(11), 1473–1488 (2008)
27. Turk, M., Pentland, A.: Eigenfaces for recognition. J. Cogn. Neurosci. **3**(1), 71–86 (1991)
28. Vapnik, V.: Statistical Learning Theory. Wiley, New York (1998)
29. Yang, Z., Ai, H.: Demographic classification with local binary patterns. In: Proceedings of International Conference on Biometrics, pp. 464–473 (2007)
30. Zhang, B., Gao, Y., Zhao, S., Liu, J.: Local derivative pattern versus local binary pattern: face recognition with high-order local pattern descriptor. IEEE Trans. Image Process. **19**(2), 533–544 (2010)
31. Zhao, G., Pietikainen, M.: Dynamic texture recognition using local binary patterns with an application to facial expressions. IEEE Trans. Pattern Anal. Mach. Intell. **29**(6), 915–928 (2007)
32. Zhao, W., Chellappa, R., Phillips, P.J., Rosenfeld, A.: Face recognition. ACM Comput. Surv. **35**(4), 399–458 (2003)

Computer Vision and Applications

Predicting Turn-Taking by Compact Gazing Transition Patterns in Multiparty Conversation

Li Tian[1(✉)], Qi Jia[2], and Zhen Zhu[1]

[1] Foshan University, Foshan, China
14790314@qq.com
[2] South China University of Technology, Guangzhou, China

Abstract. Gaze behavior plays an important role for analyzing turn-taking in multiparty conversation. In this study, we propose a general and powerful model for predicting turn-taking by analyzing gaze transition patterns in four-participant conversation. We propose gaze labels of different speaker's and listener's gaze movements and then code every gaze transition pattern to a two-label pattern. After that, we analyze the gaze transition patterns by quantitative analysis to confirm their effectiveness. Finally, we build up a prediction model for predicting turn-taking based on these gaze transition patterns. Experiments demonstrate that the prediction results obtained by our model are superior to the state-of-the-art.

Keywords: Multiparty conversation · Gaze behavior analysis
Turn-taking · Nonverbal behaviors · Gaze transition pattern

1 Introduction

Face-to-face conversation is an essential form of communications in our daily life. Analyzing human conversation scenes has been acknowledged as an emerging research field which interests both computer science and human science researchers [20]. Comparing to dyadic conversation, multiparty conversation is more common and complex and researches on it have been growing in recent years. Turn-taking is one of the most important aspects seen in conversation analysis [24]. It is a transitional mechanism in the organization of conversation which comes into play as speaker's change. It is taken for granting one person speaks at a time and people have to take the turn of speaking. A speaking turn is automatically taken by a person who know when and how to do it appropriately. Therefore, turn-taking should be viewed as a kind of communication skills which people naturally acquire along with the acquisition of language competence and sociability.

On the other hand, in face-to-face conversations, people exchange information not only by verbal messages but also by nonverbal behaviors, such as eye gaze, head and body gestures, facial expression, and prosody. Among those nonverbal

© Springer International Publishing AG, part of Springer Nature 2018
M. Paul et al. (Eds.): PSIVT 2017, LNCS 10749, pp. 437–447, 2018.
https://doi.org/10.1007/978-3-319-75786-5_35

behaviors, gaze is the most useful one for predicting turn-taking [5,13,14,24]. In spoken dialog system or human-computer interaction systems, predicting where the turn-taking (speaker change) occurs is especially important.

In this study, we focus on the relationship between gaze behaviors and turn-taking. We propose a prediction model for predicting turn-taking based on analyzing gaze transition patterns in multiparty conversations. We treat each gaze transition using the concept of the n-gram model: turn-taking occurrence doesn't depend on the sequence of whole gaze transition movement events, but only depend on the present n gaze movement states of all participants. Thus, We define meaningful gaze labels of speaker's and listener's gaze movements and then model a gaze transition pattern to a two-label pattern. After that, we analyze those meaningful gaze transition patterns using a corpus of four-participant conversations. The corpus is a multimodal corpus that we collected, includes gaze behaviors and the total time of it is 240 min. Finally, we build up a probabilistic prediction model for predicting turn-taking based on those meaningful gaze transition patterns in multiparty conversation. We compare our models with Ishii's models [12], which uses much more gaze transition patterns. The evaluation results demonstrate that the prediction results obtained by our models are better than Ishii's which are considered as the state-of-the-art in this field.

The rest of our paper is organized as follows. We begin by reviewing related work in Sect. 2. Then, we introduce our multiparty conversation corpus in details in Sect. 3. Next, we discuss the prediction model of turn-taking by analyzing gaze transition pattern and set up different experiments to show the effectiveness of our model in Sect. 4. Finally, we conclude the paper and mention future work in the last section.

2   Related Work

Researches on analyzing multiparty conversation have been studied in both human science and computer science for years.

Various facets of turn-taking in conversation analysis have been studied in the psycholinguistics, sociolinguistics and conversational analysis communities for years. Sacks, Schegoloff and Jefferson first proposed a basic model for the organization of turns in conversation [24]. They focused on the notions of turn constructional units, separated by transition relevance places (TRPs) where speaker changes may happen. Based on Sacks' model, subsequent researches began to reveal the importance of nonverbal behaviors including gaze, gesture, and other nonverbal communication channels in regulating turn-taking in interaction. For instance, Duncan [5] focused on the role of nonverbal behaviors in turn-taking, and proposed that turn-taking is mediated by both verbal and nonverbal cues. Wiemann and Mark [19] surveyed a number of previous studies on turn-taking and performed a quantitative analysis of turn-taking cues in dyadic conversations. Goodwin [8] also discussed various aspects of the relationship between turn-taking and attention. Among different nonverbal behaviors, gaze shows a strong relationship to turn-taking. Kendon [14] suggested that speaker's gaze is a "turn-yielding cue", which means if a speaker gazes at a listener at the end of an utterance, it is possible that the speaker will yield the turn to the listener. He also mentioned that mutual gaze is important in turn-taking. Jokinen et al. [13] also reported a similar results in multiparty settings.

Related work in computer science field mainly concentrate on conversation scene analysis [7,9,16,21,22] and spoken dialog systems [1,3,23,26–28]. These researches aim to provide the automatic description of conversation scenes from the multimodal nonverbal behaviors of participants, which are captured with cameras and microphones or develop more comprehensive computational models and architectures for managing turn-taking in both dyadic and multiparty settings. Prediction of turn-taking is a key factor for these researches. Methods of predicting turn-taking in multiparty conversations can be divided into two groups: one uses speech processing [6,17,18,25] and the other uses nonverbal behaviors such as gaze [2,12,15] and other behaviors [2,4,11,15]. In this study, we focus on the prediction of turn-taking.

3   Multiparty Conversation Corpus

Because turn-taking behaviors of persons engaged in equal relationships, for example, those between classmates, friends and colleagues, are desired in conversation analysis, all conversation participants are 20–30 years old college students. Our corpus contains 16 natural 4-participant conversations by 8 groups (4 Chinese college student groups and 4 Japanese college student groups) with two different conversation topics: one is "What class is good class?" and the other is "How did you spend your spring holidays?". Each conversation is 15 min and the total time of the corpus is 240 min.

3.1   Recording Multiparty Conversation

We use camera arrays and microphones to record multiparty conversations in our corpus. Figure 1 shows the camera layout and a sample scene of recording multiparty conversations. We use two video cameras to record the whole scene of conversation to obtain the nonverbal behaviors including gaze, head movement, gesture, and other body movements. We also set up four web cameras facing four participants in the centering table to get all participants' facial expressions for further researches on other nonverbal behaviors in the future. A voice recorder is also used to obtain the voice data of all the conversations. The frame rate of all videos is 30 Hz in our corpus.

3.2   Annotation

We use EUDICO Linguistic Annotator tool (ELAN)[1] to make annotations in our corpus. It is an annotation tool that allows you to create, edit, visualize

---

[1] http://www.mpi.nl/corpus/html/elan/.

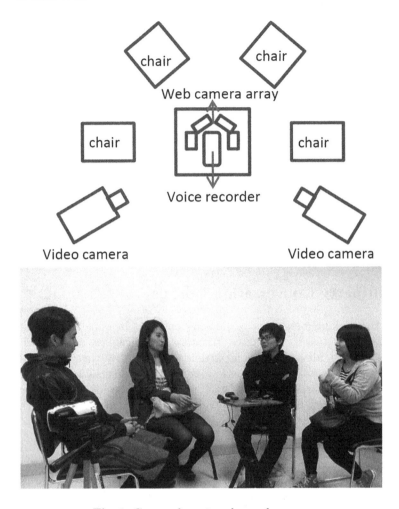

Fig. 1. Camera layout and sample scene.

and search annotations for video and audio data. Inter-pausal units (IPUs) were automatically identified by making reference to the time stamps in the word-segmented transcriptions. A stretch of speech followed by a pause longer than 200 ms were recognized as an IPU in this study. Then, we remove back-channel feedbacks from detected IPUs by skilled human annotators to get the IPU candidates. Finally, we obtained 2285 IPUs including 549 turn-taking and 1736 turn-keeping candidates for the whole corpus. Moreover, nine different gaze labels will be defined and all labels are marked by human in our corpus.

3.3 Coding Gaze Transition Pattern

Because gaze transition is important for predicting turn-taking, we focus on the gaze transition patterns which are coded as a sequence of gaze direction shifts in an examining time interval. We consider gaze directions to other participants (speaker or listener) and mutual gaze in the definitions of labels here. For easy understanding and comparison, we use the same symbols as in [12] and define nine gaze labels including:

S: The listener gazes at the current speaker without mutual gaze (the current speaker doesn't gaze at the listener).

S_M: The Listener gazes at the current speaker with mutual gaze (the current speaker also gazes at the listener).

$L(L_1, L_2, L_3)$: The participant gaze at a listener without mutual gaze. L_1, L_2, and L_3 present different listeners.

$L_M(L_{1M}, L_{2M}, L_{3M})$: The participant gaze at a listener with mutual gaze. L_{1M}, L_{2M}, and L_{3M} denote different listeners.

X: The participant doesn't gaze at other participants but gazes at other places.

We found that gazing at which listener is not important in turn-taking prediction, so we merge L_1, L_2, L_3 into L and L_{1M}, L_{2M}, L_{3M} into L_M in this study. The number of labels can be reduced from 9 to 5 by the emergence, and the number of gaze transition patterns can be reduced much more. The experiment will show that the mergence helps to improve the performance of the prediction models.

The examining time interval for gaze transition is 1200 ms including 1000 ms before and 200 ms after the time when the current IPU is over in this study. We analyze the gazing transitions in this interval and treat the contiguous gaze behavior sequence using the concept of n-gram model. Notice that, unlike in [12], we consider only two gaze labels in modelling the transition patterns. If more than two gaze label obtained in the time interval, we take the last two gaze labels before and after the time when current IPU is over. If only one gaze behavior occurs in the examining time interval, we treat it as two repeating gaze labels before and after the time when current IPU is over. That means our model is based on the concept of 2-gram model and all coded transition patterns are two-label patterns.

We give a labelling sample in Fig. 2 to show how to construct gaze transition patterns by our model and Ishii's [12]. $P1 - P4$ means four different participants in the conversation. As shown in the figure, $P1$ is always gazing at other places in the examining time interval. $P2$ gazes at $P4$ after making eye contact with $P1$. $P3$ doesn't gaze at any participant but looks at other places after looking at $P1$. $P4$ gazes at $P2$ and then $P3$ after gazing at other places. Table 1 shows the coding results by our model and Ishii's. We can see that the transition patterns of $P3$ are the same. For transition patterns of $P1$, our pattern is repeating as $X - X$ because we use two-label patterns. For transition pattern of $P2$, because we merged different listeners' gaze labels, our pattern is $S_M - L_M$. Finally, our transition pattern of $P4$ is $L_M - L$ but $X - L_{1M} - L_2$ obtained in Ishii's work because only last two gaze labels are taken into account in our model.

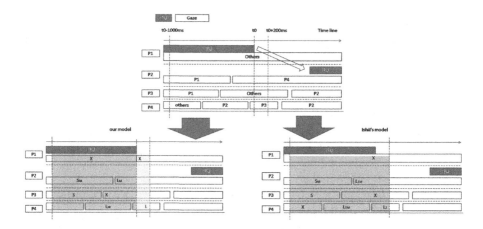

Fig. 2. Labelling process of our and Ishii's models.

Table 1. Coding transition patterns using gaze labels.

	P1	P2	P3	P4
Ishii	X	$S_M - L_{1M}$	$S - X$	$X - L_{1M} - L_2$
Our	$X - X$	$S_M - L_M$	$S - X$	$L_M - L$

4   Prediction Model of Turn-Taking

We will analyze speaker's and listener's gaze transition patterns occur at the time of turn-taking and turn-keeping appear. Then, we will introduce the proposed prediction model based on the analysis and finally evaluate the performance of our model.

4.1   Gaze Transition Patterns and Turn-Taking

If frequent gaze transition patterns in turn-taking are different from those in turn-keeping, the patterns are useful for constructing prediction model of turn-taking. In prediction of turn-taking, we use emerged five gaze labels as defined previously for prediction.

First, we analyze the relation between speaker's gaze transition pattern and turn-taking. Because label S and S_M don't appear in speaker's gaze transition, we totally have nine patterns in this case. The occurrence numbers and frequencies of nine transition patterns of speaker are shown in Fig. 3. We then make a chi square test on the frequencies and use p value, which is defined as the probability that the deviation of the observed from that expected is due to chance alone, to determine if a gaze transition is significantly different in turn-keeping or turn-taking [10]. If $p < 0.01$, the gaze transition is considered to be significantly different and favoured for our prediction model. Here, p values of three

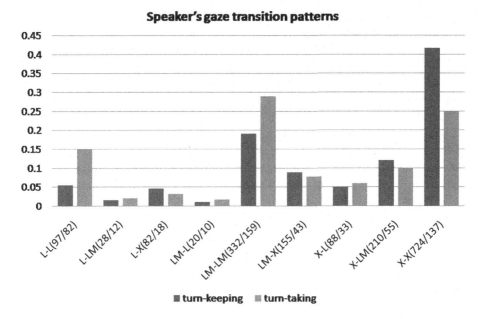

Fig. 3. Occurrences and frequencies of speaker's gaze transition patterns.

patterns $X - X$, $L - L$ and $L_M - L_M$ are smaller than 0.01. We can understand the following things from the results:

1. The frequency of turn-keeping is significantly higher than turn-taking when $X - X$ pattern occurs. That means if a speaker keeps looking at other places, the probability of occurrence of turn-keeping is higher than turn-taking.
2. The frequency of turn-taking is significantly higher than turn-keeping when $L - L$ or $L_M - L_M$ pattern occurs. That means if a speaker is continually looking at a listener with or without mutual gaze, the probability of occurrence of turn-taking is higher than turn-keeping.

Similarly, we analyze the relationship between listener's gaze transition patterns and turn-taking. We have 25 different gaze transition patterns and then calculate the occurrence numbers and frequencies of them. We merge 13 patterns whose frequency of turn-keeping or turn-taking is less than 1% into a new pattern class named as *Others* here. The occurrence numbers and frequencies of different 13 transition patterns of speaker are shown in Fig. 4. As in analysis of speaker's patterns, we also make a chi square test on the result and use p value to determine if a gaze transition is different in turn-keeping and turn-taking. If $p < 0.01$, the gaze transition is considered to be significantly different in turn-keeping and turn-keeping. Here, p values of $S - S$, $S_M - S_M$, $X - S$, $X - S_M$, and *Others* are smaller than 0.01, we can obtain the following conclusions from the results:

1. The frequency of turn-keeping is significantly higher than turn-taking when $S-S$ or S_M-S_M pattern occurs. That means if a listener is continually gazing

at the listener with or without mutual gaze, the probability of occurrence of turn-keeping is higher than turn-taking.

2. The frequency of turn-taking is significantly higher than turn-keeping when $X - S$, or $X - S_M$, or $Others$ pattern occurs. That means if a listener looked at other places and then started to look at the speaker with or without mutual gaze, the probability of occurrence of turn-taking is higher than turn-keeping. Because $Others$ includes too many patters, we don't discuss it here.

Comparing to patterns obtained in work [12], the number of our patterns is less but our patterns are more useful. From the conclusions above, our patterns is more convincable according to many conclusions about the turn-taking and gaze behaviors in human science as mentioned previously. It will be shown that the prediction model based on our patterns perform better than those in work [12] which is considered as the state-of-art in this field.

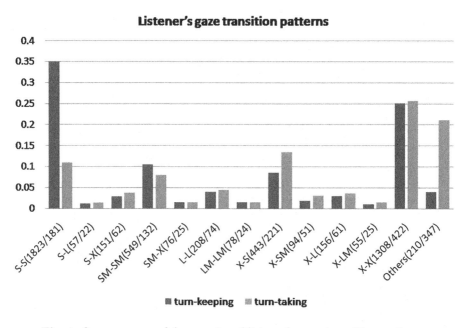

Fig. 4. Occurrences and frequencies of listener's gaze transition patterns.

4.2 Prediction Model

We construct the prediction model of turn-taking using the frequencies of speaker's and listener's gaze transition patterns obtained previously. In particular, we assume each participant's gaze transition pattern is independent and a Naive Bayes classifier is defined as

$$P(y \mid x_S, x_{L_1}, x_{L_2}, x_{L_3}) \propto P(x_S \mid y) \cdot \prod_{i=1}^{3} P(x_{L_i}) \cdot P(y) \tag{1}$$

for prediction. Here, $y = 1$, $y = 0$, and x_S denote the turn-taking, turn-keeping and speaker's gaze transition pattern, respectively; x_{L_i} means listener L_i's gaze transition pattern($i \in 1, 2, 3$). $P(y = 1)$, and $P(y = 0)$ are defined as the occurrence probabilities of turn-taking and turn-keeping, respectively; $P(x_S \mid y = 1)$, and $P(x_S \mid y = 0)$ indicate the conditional probabilities of speaker's gaze transition pattern in turn-taking case and listener's gaze transition pattern in turn-keeping case, respectively; $P(x_{L_i} \mid y = 1)$, and $P(x_{L_i} \mid y = 0)$ are the conditional probabilities of speaker's gaze transition pattern in turn-keeping case and listener's gaze transition pattern in turn-taking case, respectively; For an IPU to be predicted, we calculate $P(y = 1 \mid x_S, xL_1, xL_2, xL_3)$ and $P(y = 0 \mid x_S, xL_1, xL_2, xL_3)$; if $P(y = 1 \mid x_S, xL_1, xL_2, xL_3) > P(y = 0 \mid x_S, xL_1, xL_2, xL_3)$, the prediction result will be turn-taking; otherwise, it will be turn-keeping.

4.3   Evaluation Experiment

We will evaluate the performances of our prediction model and compare it to Ishii's model [12]. We divide corpus data of eight groups into a training set including seven groups and a validation set including the rest one group. We then carry leave-one-out cross-validation and the average prediction result are calculated as the final prediction result. Here, we estimate precision, recall and F-measure and the results are shown in Table 2. We can see that our model obtains better performance than Ishii's model. The improvement of F-measure is from 0.484 to 0.537 and from 0.764 to 0.815 in turn-taking and turn-keeping by using our model. Because we use the same naive Bayes classifier as in Ishii's model, the improvement is considered from our proposed gaze transition patterns and coding method. Moreover, because the number of our gaze transition patterns and coded patterns are smaller than Ishii's, our model could save much time on annotation and coding process.

Table 2. Prediction performances by different models.

	Turn-keeping			Turn-taking		
	Precision	Recall	F-measure	Precision	Recall	F-measure
Ishii's model	0.776	0.752	0.764	0.491	0.477	0.484
Our model	0.820	0.810	0.815	0.542	0.533	0.537

5   Conclusions and Future Work

We presented a prediction model for turn-taking by analyzing gaze transition patterns in multiparty conversations in this study. We treated the gaze transition using the concept of 2-gram model and defined compact labels for coding gaze transition patterns. The prediction models based on the patterns are also convincible. Compared with the state-of-the-art, our model show its superiorities in prediction of turn-taking. Moreover, our models are compact and need less time on annotation and coding process. Future work will aim at extending our model to predictions of next speaker and the time when the speaker begin to speak, integrating more nonverbal behaviors, and exploring real applications in human-machine interaction using our model.

References

1. Bohus, D., Horvitz, E.: Decisions about turns in multiparty conversation: from perception to action. In: Proceedings of International Conference on Multimodal Interfaces, pp. 153–160 (2011)
2. Chen, L., Harper, M.P.: Multimodal floor control shift detection. In: Proceedings of International Conference on Multimodal Interfaces, pp. 15–22 (2009)
3. Dan, B., Horvitz, E.: Multiparty turn taking in situated dialog: study, lessons, and directions. In: Proceedings of Annual Meeting of the Special Interest Group in Discourse and Dialogue, pp. 98–109 (2011)
4. Dielmann, A., Garau, G., Bourlard, H.: Floor holder detection and end of speaker turn prediction in meetings. In: International Conference on Speech and Language Processing, Interspeech (2010)
5. Duncan, S.: Some signals and rules for taking speaking turns in conversations. J. Pers. Soc. Psychol. **23**(2), 283–292 (1972)
6. Ferrer, L., Shriberg, E., Stolcke, A.: Is the speaker done yet? faster and more accurate end-of-utterance detection using prosody. In: Proceedings of ICSLP, p. 2002 (2002)
7. Gatica-Perez, D.: Analyzing group interactions in conversations: a review. In: 2006 IEEE International Conference on Multisensor Fusion and Integration for Intelligent Systems, pp. 41–46 (2006)
8. Goodwin, C.: Restarts, pauses, and the achievement of a state of mutual gaze at turn beginning. Sociol. Inq. **50**, 272–302 (1980)
9. Gorga, S., Otsuka, K.: Conversation scene analysis based on dynamic Bayesian network and image-based gaze detection. In: Proceedings of International Conference on Multimodal Interfaces (2010)
10. Haberman, S.J.: The analysis of residuals in cross-classified tables. Biometrics **29**, 205–220 (1973)
11. Ishii, R., Kumano, S., Otsuka, K.: Predicting next speaker based on head movement in multi-party meetings. In: 2015 IEEE International Conference on Acoustics, Speech and Signal Processing (ICASSP) (2015)
12. Ishii, R., Otsuka, K., Kumano, S., Matsuda, M., Yamato, J.: Predicting next speaker and timing from gaze transition patterns in multi-party meetings, pp. 79–86 (2013). http://dl.acm.org/citation.cfm?id=2522848
13. Jokinen, K., Harada, K., Nishida, M., Yamamoto, S.: Turn-alignment using eye-gaze and speech in conversational interaction. In: Annual Conference of the International Speech Communication Association, pp. 2018–2021 (2010)
14. Kendon, A.: Some functions of gaze-direction in social interaction. Acta Psychologica **26**(1), 22–63 (1967)
15. de Kok, I., Heylen, D.: Multimodal end-of-turn prediction in multi-party meetings. In: Proceedings of the 2009 International Conference on Multimodal Interfaces, ICMI-MLMI 2009. ACM, New York, pp. 91–98 (2009). http://doi.acm.org/10.1145/1647314.1647332

16. Kumano, S., Otsuka, K., Dan, M., Yamato, J.: Recognizing communicative facial expressions for discovering interpersonal emotions in group meetings. In: Proceedings International Conference on Multimodal Interaction, pp. 99–106 (2009)
17. Laskowski, K., Edlund, J., Heldner, M.: A single-port non-parametric model of turn-taking in multi-party conversation. In: 1988 International Conference on Acoustics, Speech, and Signal Processing, 1988. ICASSP-88, pp. 5600–5603 (2011)
18. Levow, G.A.: Turn-taking in mandarin dialogue: interactions of tone and intonation. In: Proceedings of the SIGHAN Workshop (2005)
19. Wiemann, J.M., Mark, L.K.: Turn-taking in conversations. J. Commun. **25**(2), 75–92 (1975)
20. Otsuka, K.: Conversational scene analysis. IEEE Sig. Process. Mag. **28**, 127–131 (2011)
21. Otsuka, K., Araki, S., Ishizuka, K., Fujimoto, M., Heinrich, M., Yamato, J.: A realtime multimodal system for analyzing group meetings by combining face pose tracking and speaker diarization. In: Proceedings of International Conference on Multimodal Interfaces, pp. 257–264 (2008)
22. Otsuka, K., Takemae, Y., Yamato, J.: A probabilistic inference of multiparty-conversation structure based on Markov-switching models of gaze patterns, head directions, and utterances. In: Proceedings of Internetional Conference on Multimodal Interfaces, pp. 191–198 (2005)
23. Raux, A., Eskenazi, M.: A finite-state turn-taking model for spoken dialog systems. In: Proceedings of Human Language Technologies: The 2009 Annual Conference of the North American Chapter of the Association for Computational Linguistics, pp. 629–637 (2009)
24. Sacks, H., Jefferson, G.: A simplest systematics for the organization of turn-taking for conversation. Language **50**(4), 696–735 (1974)
25. Schlangen, D.: From reaction to prediction experiments with computational models of turn-taking. In: Proceedings of Interspeech 2006, Panel on Prosody of Dialogue Acts and Turn-Taking (2006)
26. Thrisson, K.R.: Natural turn-taking needs no manual: computational theory and model, from perception to action. In: Granström, B., House, D., Karlsson, I. (eds.) Multimodality in Language and Speech Systems. Text, Speech and Language Technology, vol. 19. Springer, Dordrecht (2002). https://doi.org/10.1007/978-94-017-2367-1_8
27. Traum, D., Rickel, J.: Embodied agents for multi-party dialogue in immersive virtual worlds. In: Proceedings of the First International Joint Conference on Autonomous Agents and Multiagent Systems: Part 2, pp. 766–773 (2002)
28. Traum, D.R.: A computational theory of grounding in natural language conversation (1994)

Intelligent Assistant for People with Low Vision Abilities

Oleksandr Bogdan$^{(\boxtimes)}$, Oleg Yurchenko$^{(\boxtimes)}$, Oleksandr Bailo$^{(\boxtimes)}$,
Francois Rameau, Donggeun Yoo, and In So Kweon

RCV Lab, Electrical Engineering, KAIST, Daejeon, Republic of Korea
{alex.v.bogdan,oleg145,iskweon77}@kaist.ac.kr,
{obailo,frameau,dgyoo}@rcv.kaist.ac.kr

Abstract. This paper proposes a wearable system for visually impaired people that can be utilized to obtain an extensive feedback about their surrounding environment. Our system consists of a stereo camera and smartglasses, communicating with a smartphone that is used as an intermediary computational device. Furthermore, the system is connected to a server where all the expensive computations are executed. The whole setup is capable of detecting obstacles in the nearest surrounding, recognizing faces and facial expressions, reading texts, providing a generic description and question answering of a particular input image. In addition, we propose a novel depth question answering system to estimate object size as well as objects relative position in an unconstrained environment in near real-time and in a fully automatic way requiring only stereo image pair and voice request as an input. We have conducted a series of experiments to evaluate the feasibility and practicality of the proposed system which shows promising results to assist visually impaired people.

Keywords: Visually impaired people · Wearable device · Mobility
Recognition · Guidance

1 Introduction

According to World Health Organization [8], there are 285 million of people with visual disabilities. Among them, around 246 million have low vision and 39 million are blind. Additionally, 43% of visually impaired people have uncorrected refractive errors (*i.e.* near-sightedness and far-sightedness), which accounts for 105 million people worldwide.

Among the large list of daily life problems encountered by visually impaired people, three major ones can be distinguished: text comprehension, mobility, and social interaction. Reading a text is reported to be the most common problem among people with low vision. Around 66% of people with bad eyesight complain about difficulties with reading [2], which makes it the leading problem. Furthermore, blind people struggle to recognize their surroundings [15]. As a

© Springer International Publishing AG, part of Springer Nature 2018
M. Paul et al. (Eds.): PSIVT 2017, LNCS 10749, pp. 448–462, 2018.
https://doi.org/10.1007/978-3-319-75786-5_36

consequence, a large portion of people with poor vision complains about performing normal in-home activities and their low mobility (15.1% and 16.3%, respectively) [2]. Additionally, around 10% of visually impaired people claim that they do not recognize faces, thus, having problems with social engagement. Moreover, understanding other people's emotion is a challenge. Aforementioned problems pose a difficulty for visually impaired people to work efficiently since most of the jobs require a relevant level of eyesight.

To overcome the mentioned challenges, we propose a portable system which gives information about the surroundings (*i.e.* image captioning and visual question answering), performs obstacle detection, recognizes people and their emotions, reads a text, and implements an automatic size measuring module for the objects of interest. To sum up, the contributions of this work are the following:

- Intelligent system for people with low vision abilities.
- Distributed system structure allowing near real-time performance.
- Depth question answering algorithm to measure objects size automatically.
- All the relevant codes to reproduce the system are made available[1].

This paper is organized as follows. In the next Section, we provide an extensive literature review of recent research works and existing systems developed for visually impaired people. The proposed methodology and existing modules overview explanation are introduced in the Sect. 3. Finally, a large number of experiments is proposed in Sect. 4 followed by a brief conclusion (Sect. 5).

2   Related Works

In this section, we report the existing research works and developed systems that aim to improve the life of visually impaired people. We mostly focus on recent works (*i.e.* starting from 2012) which rely on deep learning.

In recent years, mobile solutions for visually impaired people have gained in popularity. A good example of such work is smartphone based obstacle detection [12,26] which aims to increase the mobility of sightless people. The main emphasis of these works is to detect and classify obstacles in front of the user. In a different work proposed by Wang *et al.* [17], a wearable system that consists of a depth camera and an embedded computer is utilized to provide situational awareness for blind or visually impaired people. The system performs obstacle detection and notifies the user about empty chairs and benches nearby. Additionally, Mattoccia *et al.* [28] have proposed a system that is built upon usage of 3D glasses for object detection. The authors use 3D sensor installed on glasses frames to obtain a depth map of the environment for performing obstacle detection. Since it is commonly reported that visually impaired people have difficulties with face recognition, Neto *et al.* [21] have proposed a solution which relies on Microsoft Kinect as a wearable device. The key point of this work is to help users to distinguish people by specific sounds associated with them. In addition, this sound is virtualized at the direction of the corresponding person.

---

[1] https://github.com/BAILOOL/Assistant-for-People-with-Low-Vision.

In addition to academic research laboratories, several companies have tried to simplify the life of visually impaired people by introducing relevant systems. For example, Microsoft Cognitive Services [4] has developed a system that includes a headset of Pivothead SMART glasses and a host application that transfers pictures from glasses to a smartphone. A Cognitive Services API is utilized to detect faces and facial expressions and to determine the gender and age of the person. This system also performs image captioning (i.e. the description of the photo) and text recognition. On the other hand, NVIDIA has proposed a system called Horus [3,7] that incorporates headset with cameras and pocket-computer powered by NVIDIA Tegra K1 for GPU-accelerated computer vision. They use deep learning techniques to recognize faces and objects, read a text, and perform image captioning. Another important part of the system is the obstacle avoidance using a stereo camera built in Horus. All the commands are given through a controller pad embedded in a pocket computer, while the output is given in a speech format through speakers on the handset. Finally, there exists a smartphone application called Be My Eyes [1] that is created to associate visually impaired user with a sighted volunteer through a video connection. Using this application sighted helpers provide an aid for people with visual disabilities in everyday activities. Even though this type of interaction remains helpful, the technological solution can provide far more satisfying time performance.

Generally, it is observed that the recent research works have concentrated on solving particular problems rather than on creating a unified system that will include all modules crucial for blind people. In this paper, we propose a multipurpose system that incorporates all these modules that solve the most important problems for blind or visually impaired people.

3   Methodology

In this section, we provide a detailed description of the system and available modules. Firstly, in Subsect. 3.1, we briefly describe the proposed system from hardware and software point of view. Subsequently, specific implementation details about every introduced modules are covered in Subsects. 3.2–3.8.

3.1   Detailed Overview of the Proposed System

The proposed system pipeline is composed of three consecutive steps: sending the request to a smartphone application, transferring the data to a server, and receiving the output back to a smartphone application. The pipeline of this process is shown in Fig. 1. Our system can process two different types of images. Namely, monocular images acquired from a Sony SmartEyeGlasses and stereo images obtained from a ZED Stereo Camera. The image acquisition is followed by a user voice request. These two inputs are collected by smartglasses' host application (i.e. smartphone) and are sent to the server. Finally, the server produces relevant outputs that are converted to text format and transferred back

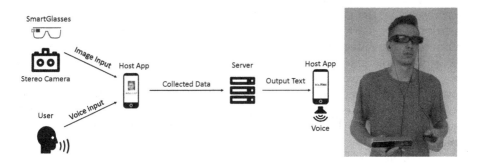

Fig. 1. Server-application interaction architecture of the proposed system.

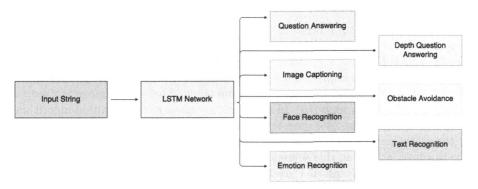

Fig. 2. Modules architecture on the server.

to a smartphone application that displays the text on the screen and produces the voice output that is delivered through the speaker or earphones.

To reduce the computational time, a cloud server is responsible for the main computational load. Our cloud server accepts an image (*e.g.* single or stereo image) as well as a user request as a text. The user request can be given in a form of a question or a command which is translated to a string using [30]. Then, this string is forwarded through a Long Short-Term Memory (LSTM) [27] network that classifies which module is the most appropriate to solve the requested task. After that, the collected image is used as an input for a selected module. Finally, the selected module generates a specific output which is sent back to the user (Fig. 2).

3.2   User Input Classification

One of the main contributions of this paper is the way we distribute the different tasks to the proper modules. This distribution is crucial in terms of usability since it allows the user to create unique requests for the system rather than operating with a set of predefined questions made beforehand. Therefore, the goal of our input classification module is to robustly understand which module is asked to be activated by the user's request. Therefore, in order to perform the sentence classification, we have utilized LSTM network. This decision is motivated by the ability of this architecture to save long-term dependencies throughout learning. The network consists of two LSTM layers and one fully connected layer followed by a softmax. To avoid overfitting, we have utilized two dropout layers: one between LSTM layers and one between LSTM and fully connected layers. The network is fed with sentence representation vectors that we have obtained with fasttext [24]. This architecture is able to achieve a high level of accuracy to robustly classify user requests. The details about prepared dataset as well as training schemes are reported in Subsect. 4.1.

3.3   Depth Question Answering

In order to be able to apprehend the size of the surrounding objects, we have developed a fully automatic size measuring system for a smartphone that works in near real-time. The basic idea is that once the stereo image of the scene is obtained, a user can simply request the system to take the desired measurements of the object of interest through voice commands. The stereo image is used to obtain a dense depth map [10]. In a meantime, the object recognition algorithm proposed by Liu *et al.* [35] detects and recognizes the objects in the left image of the stereo pair. Finally, given the user request as a string, we try to retrieve the words of interest in this sentence. For this purpose, we retrieve all the nouns of the input using Stanford Parser [6] and check their statistical similarity to the label of recognized objects in the image by relying on word2vec [33]. The objects whose labels are matched with the retrieved words of interest from the user request with a similarity over 50% are kept while the rest are removed from further consideration. The overview of the proposed module is shown in Fig. 3.

Given a potentially noisy depth map of the scene and the location (*i.e.* bounding box) of the object of interest, the distance to the object can be estimated by averaging the depth values of the pixels that belong to a recognized class within the bounding box. In order to retrieve those pixels we utilize FCNs [20] which provide a relatively precise segmentation mask with near real-time performance. Then, we select the middle point on each side of the bounding box (left, right, top, bottom) and obtain the 3D positions of these points by assuming that the object lies on a single plane. This approximation remains relatively accurate in most scenarios. Thereafter, the *Euclidian* distances between these extremum 3D points are used to estimate the height and width of the object.

It is worth mentioning that there are several works that aim to measure the size of objects in an unconstrained environment such as Google Tango Project [14]. However, in Project Tango, a user is required to manually select points (boundary selection) on the object of interest. On the other hand, our system mitigates this constraint and proposes a fully automatic measuring device that can be appropriated for blind or visually impaired people.

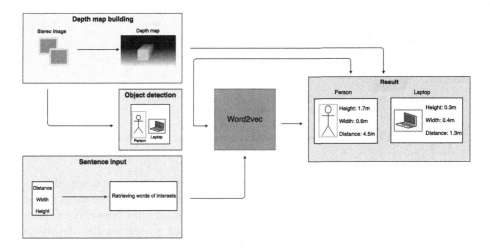

Fig. 3. Depth question answering algorithm pipeline.

3.4 Obstacle Avoidance

Navigation and obstacle avoidance is one of the main problems for people with visual impairment. Our system focuses on detection and timely notifications of possible obstacles observed in front of a user. The algorithm is based on depth map estimation using a stereo camera. First, the pair of images is fed to an algorithm proposed by Geiger *et al.* [10]. However, due to the algorithm simplicity, the obtained disparity map is noisy which might result in a wrong obstacle detection. Therefore, in order to smooth out noisy responses, we apply a median blur filter on the disparity map. Further, in order to improve the robustness of this module, we select the 100 closest points to the user (from depth map) and average them to obtain the position of a probable obstacle. If the calculated value is smaller than one meter, we estimate a relative location of the obstacle. Specifically, the module outputs whether there is an obstacle on the left, right, or front relative to a user. The proposed system works in real time with a processing speed of about 1 fps.

3.5 Emotion Recognition

People without eyesight disabilities perceive other people's emotions by their facial expression and change in intonation. Since it is impossible for visually impaired to perceive facial expression, we propose to include an emotion recognition module to our system. For this purpose, we have used a relatively shallow convolutional neural network shown in Fig. 4. This network has been designed in order to avoid overfitting since available datasets are relatively small. Our network contains three convolutional layers, two max-pooling layers, and three fully connected layers followed by ReLU.

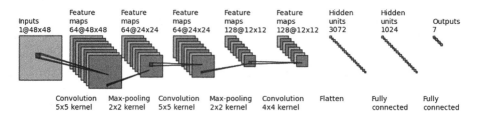

Fig. 4. A shallow CNN used for emotion recognition.

In order to recognize a particular emotion, our method requires cropped faces fed into it. Therefore, prior to emotion recognition, we detect all the faces in the input image. The performance of face detection algorithm influences the accuracy of the whole emotion module. To robustly detect faces we rely on the algorithm proposed by Huaizu and Miller [19] which in essence is Faster RCNN [29].

3.6   Face Recognition

Recognizing friends or a familiar person is a very challenging task for visually impaired people. We tackle the problem from the perspective of facial recognition and perform the following procedures in order to robustly recognize a particular face. The first step to robustly recognize faces is to locate and crop each face on a given image. For this purpose, we utilize a face detection algorithm described in Subsect. 3.5. Subsequently, each detected face is frontalized (aligned) using the algorithm proposed by Hassner *et al.* [31]. This algorithm uses facial landmarks to align detected face with a defined 3D facial model. Then, rectified face is fed to FaceNet [16] which produces 128-dimensional feature vector. There are numbers of different ways to perform a comparison of face vector embeddings. However, under the assumption that each user has a relatively small number of friends (less than few hundreds), L2 norm comparison is expected to be fast and perform efficiently enough for a real-time application. Specifically, we compare the extracted face vector with existing entries in our database.

3.7   Image Captioning and Visual Question Answering

The image captioning module provides a broad description of the photo including the objects that are in the image and their interaction. The urge for such module arises from the need of visually impaired people to get a general feedback about their surroundings. For this purpose, we utilize the Show and Tell algorithm [23] which is a type of encoder-decoder neural network. At the first stage of processing the image, the network encodes it into a fixed-length vector representation which is subsequently decoded into natural language. The encoder network is the state of the art deep convolutional neural network for object detection and recognition. In this work, we have used Inception v3 model described in [13]. LSTM network represents the decoder. On the other hand, to help visually impaired people to orient in their surrounding environment, we have integrated a visual question answering module into our system. The module is built using state-of-art architecture proposed by Fukui *et al.* [9]. First, the model preprocesses the given question and image using LSTM and ResNet512 followed by a multimodal compact (MCB) bilinear pooling and visual attention techniques. Then, visual and text features are transformed to a single 16,000-D vector by feeding them to MCB pooling. Finally, treating the last part of architecture as a multi-class classification, the model retrieves most probable answers.

3.8   Text Recognition

The final module that is present in our system is text recognition. This module implements Optical Character Recognition (OCR) algorithm described by Barber *et al.* [34]. In order to distinguish individual characters, shape's features are used. For this purpose, we have utilized the pytesseract [5] OCR implementation. Despite being relatively fast, this algorithm is only applicable to a black text written on a light background.

4   Experiments

In this section, we report our experimental results only for user input classification, depth question answering, and emotion recognition. Thereafter, we provide an extensive evaluation of the whole system and its time performance.

4.1   User Input Classification

In order to train the network, we have prepared a dataset composed of 590 questions aiming to robustly differentiate between existing modules given a user request. The dataset has been prepared manually under human control. Originally, we have created 460 questions, which we have extended further by performing a data augmentation. Specifically, we change the order of words in a sentence until the meaning of the sentence is still recognizable. This technique makes our algorithm to be more robust and allows to classify better grammatically incorrect sentences. In fact, this way of data augmentation can improve the performance of any training process that includes LSTM network.

Since LSTM network requires an input being a vector, we have utilized fasttext [24] to obtain a text representation in a form of 300-dimensional vector. Considering the input size, we have limited it to a sentence of twenty words maximum. Furthermore, if a number of words in a certain sentence is less than 20, we fill empty entries with zeros. Therefore, the input shape for this network is 20×300 where the row value stands for words and columns represent each word features. In order to precise the module that has to be executed on the user request, we have utilized two LSTM layers with output space of 32-dimensions for the first layer and 16 for the second one, followed by one fully convolutional layer with a softmax. During the training, we have used Adam optimizer with an initial rate of 0.001 and a batch size of 256. Dropout ratio is set to 0.3. Training data constitutes 80%, validation set comprises 10%, and testing - 10% of the dataset. Upon testing, the network has reached a testing accuracy of 96.2%.

4.2   Depth Question Answering

In order to evaluate this module, we have selected about 50 images with various objects of interests. Then we have applied the algorithm to retrieve the information about the size of the objects. The reported average absolute error of measurements is within 15%.

Representative results are shown in Fig. 5. For these particular images the predicted and real values are reported in Table 1. While our method provides relatively accurate measurements, there are obvious cases when the method fails. First of all, the measurement strongly depends on a tightness of the bounding box around the object of interest. In most of the cases, the bounding box is larger than the real object, resulting in overestimated values for width of the Scooter in Table 1. Secondly, another error comes from the fact that we assume that the object lies on a plane which in some scenarios might not be the case.

Fig. 5. Visual results of depth question answering module. The value of the top side of the bounding box represents distance, left - height, and bottom - width.

Table 1. Comparison of predicted vs real measurements values for several objects.

	Scooter		Bicycle		Chair	
	Predicted	Real	Predicted	Real	Predicted	Real
Distance	3.7 m	3.5 m	4.4 m	4.5 m	7.6 m	8.0 m
Height	1.2 m	1.2 m	1.1 m	1.0 m	0.9 m	0.8 m
Width	1.1 m	0.6 m	0.8 m	0.5 m	0.8 m	0.6 m

4.3   Emotion Recognition

In order to train this module we have utilized three distinct datasets: Radboud [22], Cohn-Kanade [25,32], and FER-2013 [18]. By combining these datasets we make the training data more diversified. Moreover, the Radboud dataset includes five different angles of face rotation for each emotion, thus, our algorithm can perform better in a real-case scenario. Altogether, these datasets contain 27100 images. Then, we have performed image mirroring as data augmentation method resulting in doubling the number of images (54200 in total). This combined dataset is divided into training (60%), validation (20%), and testing (20%) in a way that an original image and a mirrored one appear in the same set. During the training, we apply Adam optimizer with the initial learning rate of 0.0001 and a batch size of 2000 images where each grayscale image has a size of 48 × 48p. The dropout ratio is set to 0.5. The training is run for 120 epochs.

Table 2. The confusion matrix for emotion recognition.

	Disgusted	Happy	Surprised	Neutral	Angry	Fearful	Sad
Disgusted	**93.0**	0.1	0.0	1.6	1.1	0.5	0.7
Happy	0.8	**91.1**	2.5	5.7	5.5	4.6	6.2
Surprised	0.2	2.0	**88.6**	1.6	1.1	6.8	2.1
Neutral	1.4	2.7	2.1	**75.7**	8.3	8.5	17.8
Angry	2.9	1.4	1.5	4.7	**72.7**	8.5	8.6
Fearful	0.8	0.8	3.5	3.4	4.4	**65.1**	5.6
Sad	1.0	1.9	1.9	7.4	6.8	6.1	**59.1**

The evaluation results on the testing dataset are presented as confusion matrix in Table 2. In this matrix, the cell at the ith row and jth column represents the percentage of ith emotion being recognized as jth emotion. It can be clearly observed that in our case, the best recognized facial expressions are disgust, happiness, and astonishment. Generally, these emotions are easily distinguishable among themselves making them easy to be recognized by the network. On the other hand, emotions such as sadness and fear might look similar to each other and to anger, making them challenging to be recognized. As a result, our network struggles to derive discriminative features to robustly identify these two emotions. Overall, we have reached 78.4% of accuracy on a testing set.

4.4   Overall Evaluation of the System

The crucial characteristic of our system is its usability. To be able to serve efficiently the time cost of using the system has to be relatively low. To estimate the average executing time of modules we sent 20 requests to each of them and collected the response time. Table 3 illustrates the average time needed to get a response from each module in the proposed system. Firstly, we have checked the response time only for the algorithms themselves, apart from the application. This time is, in fact, an execution time of each algorithm. The biggest response times are observed for the Question Answering and for Face Recognition since the networks used for them have a high time cost of usage. Secondly, we measured the response time of each module when requested from the application. In fact, that is the time between the user input is uploaded to the server and the time the response appears on the screen of a smartphone. The time gap between the algorithm and the application responses is different for each module because it depends on the size of generated output sentence.

Table 3. Time performance evaluation of each module of the system.

	Algorithm response	Application response
Question answering	2.29 s	3.03 s
Image captioning	0.84 s	1.58 s
Emotion recognition	0.29 s	0.85 s
Face recognition	1.29 s	1.56 s
Text recognition	0.56 s	2.36 s
Obstacle detection	0.54 s	1.07 s
Depth question answering	1.03 s	1.58 s

Furthermore, to test the applicability of the system we have conducted a survey that included answers from 25 sighted people. In order to put them in similar conditions as visually impaired people, we have shown each volunteer four blurred pictures where the scene can hardly be recognized on a computer display. The images are selected from the dataset of 20 pictures in a way that people have to send a request to each module to understand what is happening in the images. For instance, each set of four images contains a picture with a text in it for participants to evaluate Text Recognition module. An example of the utilized images can be observed in Fig. 6. We have allowed the participants to ask three questions per image in order to understand the scene using our system only. For each image, we have given them a context of the situation to

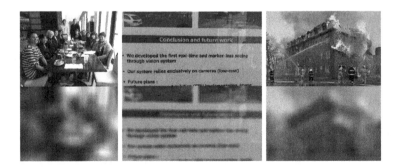

Fig. 6. Sample images used in the survey. First row shows original image, while the second row represents the blurred images that are shown to a respondent.

help them ask relevant questions. However, all the questions have been made by volunteers and have been created in a way that they can obtain as much information as possible from the answer. For instance, for the image with people sitting around the table in Fig. 6 participants frequently asked about what people are doing there and about the number of people in the image. Thereafter, we have shown them original images and have asked them to evaluate our system on a 10-band scale considering the answers they have received back from the system. Our survey (see Table 4) consists of the following criteria: user input classification (UIC) accuracy (denoted as UIC Accuracy); how informative is the content of the answer (Contents); person's satisfaction (Satisfaction); how good is overall system performance (Performance); time efficiency of the system (Time Efficiency). Important to notice that this survey covered all modules except for obstacles detection and depth question answering since these experiments require walking with the stereo camera. In this case, experimenting with blindfolded sighted people produce biased results according to Postma *et al.* [11].

Table 4. Survey results about the performance of the proposed system. The scores in this table are the average scores of all collected samples.

	UIC accuracy	Contents	Satisfaction	Overall performance	Time efficiency
Question answering	9.20	8.01	7.77	7.99	9.41
Image captioning	9.00	7.76	7.79	7.86	9.33
Emotion recognition	9.52	8.00	7.79	8.02	9.50
Face recognition	9.46	8.41	8.17	8.29	8.05
Text recognition	9.33	7.29	6.71	7.29	9.05

The obtained results reveal that people are noticeably satisfied with the working speed of our system and with the user input classification accuracy. Overall, respondents feel positive about the whole system, although their level of satisfaction is relatively lower due to inaccuracies that have occurred in the system response. These inaccuracies include answers lacking the information or the incorrect ones. However, the results also indicate that the content of the answers is considered to be informative. Thus, the content is scored slightly higher than the satisfaction. Moreover, our survey demonstrates that the Face Recognition module outperforms other modules in terms of people's satisfaction. In contrast, during the user study the Text Recognition module has shown the worst performance since the technology we use (see Sect. 3.8) has comparatively low accuracy and stability. It is worth mentioning that the Image Captioning module is the second worst module by the contents and satisfaction. It is explained by the fact that this module sometimes omits the information that can be useful for visually impaired people. For instance, it might ignore an obstacle in front of the user, but explain the actions of people nearby.

5   Conclusion

In this work, we proposed a complete system that targets major challenges of blind or visually impaired people. The system is composed of smartglasses with integrated camera and microphone, a stereo camera, a smartphone that is connected with smartglasses through a host application, and a server that serves the purpose of a computational unit. Our system is capable of detecting obstacles in the nearest surrounding, providing an estimation of the size of objects of interest, recognizing faces and facial expressions, reading the text, providing the generic description and question answering of a particular input image. We conducted series of experiments which proved the applicability and usability of our system for blind or visually impaired people.

Although each module of our system was implemented efficiently, the image transfer speed from Sony SmartEyeGlasses to host smartphone is relatively slow making it unpractical for the real-time application. Therefore, as a future work, we want to explore alternative devices as well as to improve the user interface for a comfortable usage. Another major improvement that can be done is to include background working function, *i.e.*, allow to send the request in advance in order to avoid uncomfortable situations. For example, asking for a person's name in front of this person or sending any voice request in a crowded area.

Acknowledgements. We would like to thank KAIST Research Promotion Team for funding this work through URP program. The fourth author was supported by the KRF Program through the NRF funded by the Ministry of Science and ICT (2015H1D3A1066564).

References

1. Be My Eyes. http://bemyeyes.com/
2. Common problems of people with low vision. http://www.allaboutvision.com/lowvision/helping.htm
3. Horus wearable device. https://horus.tech
4. Microsoft cognitive services. https://azure.microsoft.com/en-us/services/cognitive-services/?v=17.25b#vision
5. Pytesseract. https://pypi.python.org/pypi/pytesseract
6. Stanford parser. http://nlp.stanford.edu:8080/parser/
7. Wearable device to assist visually impaired people. https://blogs.nvidia.com/blog/2016/10/27/wearable-device-for-blind-visually-impaired/
8. World Health Organization. http://www.who.int/mediacentre/factsheets/fs282/en/
9. Fukui, A., Park, D.H., Yang, D., Rohrbach, A., Darrell, T., Rohrbach, M.: Multimodal compact bilinear pooling for visual question answering and visual grounding. arXiv:1606.01847 (2016)
10. Geiger, A., Roser, M., Urtasun, R.: Efficient large-scale stereo matching. In: Kimmel, R., Klette, R., Sugimoto, A. (eds.) ACCV 2010. LNCS, vol. 6492, pp. 25–38. Springer, Heidelberg (2011). https://doi.org/10.1007/978-3-642-19315-6_3

11. Postma, A., Zuidhoek, S., Noordzij, M., Kappers, A.: Differences between early-blind, late-blind, and blindfolded-sighted people in haptic spatial-configuration learning and resulting memory traces. Perception **36**(8), 1253–1265 (2007)
12. Mustapha, B., Zayegh, A., Begg, R.K.: Wireless obstacle detection system for the elderly and visually impaired people. In: ICSIMA (2013)
13. Szegedy, C., Vanhoucke, V., Ioffe, S., Shlens, J., Wojna, Z.: Rethinking the inception architecture for computer vision. In: CVPR (2016)
14. Keralia, D., Vyas, K.K., Deulkar, K.: Google project tango–a convenient 3D modeling device. Int. J. Curr. Eng. Technol. **4**, 3139–3142 (2014)
15. Brady, E., Morris, M.R., Zhong, Y., White, S., Bigham, J.P.: Visual challenges in the everyday lives of blind people. In: SIGCHI (2013)
16. Schroff, F., Kalenichenko, D., Philbin, J.: FaceNet: a unified embedding for face recognition and clustering. In: CVPR (2015)
17. Wang, H., Katzschmann, R., Teng, S., Araki, B., Giarré, L., Rus, D.: Enabling independent navigation for visually impaired people through a wearable vision-based feedback system. In: ICRA (2017)
18. Goodfellow, I.J., et al.: Challenges in representation learning: a report on three machine learning contests. In: Lee, M., Hirose, A., Hou, Z.-G., Kil, R.M. (eds.) ICONIP 2013. LNCS, vol. 8228, pp. 117–124. Springer, Heidelberg (2013). https://doi.org/10.1007/978-3-642-42051-1_16
19. Huaizu, J., Miller, E.: Face detection with the faster R-CNN. CoRR, abs/1606.03473 (2016)
20. Long, J., Shelhamer, E., Darrell, T.: Fully convolutional networks for semantic segmentation. In: CVPR (2015)
21. Neto, L.B., Grijalva, F., Maike, V., Martini, L., Florencio, D., Baranauskas, M., Rocha, A., Goldenstein, S.: A kinect-based wearable face recognition system to aid visually impaired users. Trans. Hum.-Mach. Syst. **47**, 52–64 (2017)
22. Langner, O., Dotsch, R., Bijlstra, G., Wigboldus, D., Hawk, S., Van Knippenberg, A.D.: Presentation and validation of the radboud faces database. Cogn. Emot. **24**(8), 1377–1388 (2010)
23. Vinyals, O., Toshev, A., Bengio, S., Erhan, D.: Show and tell: lessons learned from the 2015 MSCOCO image captioning challenge. IEEE Trans. Pattern Anal. Mach. Intell. (TPAMI) **39**(4), 652–663 (2017)
24. Bojanowski, P., Grave, E., Joulin, A., Mikolov, T.: Enriching word vectors with subword information. arXiv:1607.04606 (2016)
25. Lucey, P., Cohn, J., Kanade, T., Saragih, J., Ambadar, Z., Matthews, I.: The extended Cohn-Kanade dataset (CK+): a complete dataset for action unit and emotion-specified expression. In: CVPR Workshops (2010)
26. Tapu, R., Mocanu, B., Bursuc, A., Zaharia, T.: A smartphone-based obstacle detection and classification system for assisting visually impaired people. In: ICCV Workshops (2013)
27. Hochreiter, S., Schmidhuber, J.: Long short-term memory. Neural Comput. **9**(8), 1735–1780 (1997)
28. Mattoccia, S., Macrì, P.: 3D glasses as mobility aid for visually impaired people. In: Agapito, L., Bronstein, M.M., Rother, C. (eds.) ECCV 2014. LNCS, vol. 8927, pp. 539–554. Springer, Cham (2015). https://doi.org/10.1007/978-3-319-16199-0_38
29. Ren, S., He, K., Girshick, R., Sun, J.: Faster R-CNN: towards real-time object detection with region proposal networks. In: NIPS (2015)
30. Creamer, T., Jaiswal, P., Pavlovski, C.: Voice-to-text reduction for real time IM/chat/SMS. US Patent App. 10/603,495 (2003)

31. Hassner, T., Harel, S., Paz, E., Enbar, R.: Effective face frontalization in unconstrained images. In: CVPR (2015)
32. Kanade, T., Cohn, J., Tian, Y.: Comprehensive database for facial expression analysis. In: FG (2000)
33. Mikolov, T., Chen, K., Corrado, G., Dean, J.: Efficient estimation of word representations in vector space. arXiv:1301.3781 (2013)
34. Barber, W., Cipolla, T., Mundy, J.: Optical character recognition. US Patent 4,339,745 (1982)
35. Liu, W., Anguelov, D., Erhan, D., Szegedy, C., Reed, S., Fu, C.-Y., Berg, A.C.: SSD: single shot multibox detector. In: Leibe, B., Matas, J., Sebe, N., Welling, M. (eds.) ECCV 2016. LNCS, vol. 9905, pp. 21–37. Springer, Cham (2016). https:// doi.org/10.1007/978-3-319-46448-0_2

Using Facial Expression Recognition for Crowd Monitoring

Ross Philip Holder and Jules-Raymond Tapamo[(✉)]

School of Engineering, University of KwaZulu-Natal, Durban 4041, South Africa
tapamoj@ukzn.ac.za

Abstract. In recent years, Crowd Monitoring techniques have attracted emerging interest in the field of computer vision due to their ability to monitor groups of people in crowded areas, where conventional image processing methods would not suffice. Existing Crowd Monitoring techniques focus heavily on analyzing a crowd as a single entity, usually in terms of their density and movement pattern. While these techniques are well suited for the task of identifying dangerous and emergency situations, they are very limited when it comes to identifying emotion within a crowd. In this work, we propose a novel Crowd Monitoring algorithm based on estimating crowd emotion using Facial Expression Recognition (FER). By isolating different types of emotion within a crowd, we aim to predict the mood of a crowd even in scenes of non-panic. To validate the effectiveness of the proposed algorithm, a series of cross-validation tests are performed using a novel Crowd Emotion dataset with known ground-truth emotions. The results show that the algorithm presented is able to accurately and efficiently predict multiple classes of crowd emotion even in non-panic situations where movement and density information may be incomplete.

1 Introduction

Crowd Monitoring is a topic of emerging interest in the field of computer vision and was born largely from the desire to monitor the nature of groups of individuals in crowded areas, where conventional image processing methods would not suffice [31]. Areas where Crowd Monitoring systems are commonly deployed include airport terminals, sports stadiums, and other public facilities that attract large crowds of people. Crowd Monitoring can be used to aid law enforcement in recognizing and identifying crowds that may cause public disorder. Examples include identifying disorderly crowds of sports fans that may have gathered after a football match, or a group of disgruntled protesters that have taken to the street. With the advent of social media platforms, such as Twitter, small gatherings can often gather momentum very quickly, evolving into large crowds that can be difficult to control [5]. This necessitates the need for advances in Crowd Monitoring techniques.

Facial Expression Recognition (FER) [18, 21, 23] is a technique used to extract and classify emotion from an individual's facial expression. It is widely accepted

© Springer International Publishing AG, part of Springer Nature 2018
M. Paul et al. (Eds.): PSIVT 2017, LNCS 10749, pp. 463–476, 2018.
https://doi.org/10.1007/978-3-319-75786-5_37

that there are seven universally recognizable emotions as first identified by Ekman [12], namely: joy, surprise, anger, fear, disgust, sadness and neutral emotion. In this work we use FER to extract and classify emotion from individuals in a crowded environment. The individual emotions can be combined to estimate the emotion of the crowd.

Due to the difficulty associated with extracting individuals from a crowd, most Crowd Monitoring techniques focus heavily on analyzing crowds as a single entity. Many different holistic based [2,3,6,10,30] and object-level based [7,8,24, 32] methods of Crowd Monitoring have been proposed in current literature, such as analyzing crowd movement patterns, flow and density. While these approaches are well suited for the task of identifying emergency situations, such as a large group of people exiting a building at once or a crowd gathering around a fight, they are very limited when it comes to identifying the nature or mood of a crowd outside of scenes of panic. A system that is able to autonomously identify the mood of a crowd in real-time dynamic environments is required.

There is potential for aggressive crowds, fueled by their sense of superiority in numbers [9], to vandalize and loot property while endangering the lives of innocent bystanders. By identifying the mood of a crowd in real-time, the system can help to alert officials to potentially aggressive and disorderly crowds so that necessary measures, such as additional policing units, can be deployed to prevent further aggression and violence. In areas where policing units are limited, the system allows officials to concentrate available units on crowds of interest; maximizing their resources and efficiency. The system uses emotion to represent the mood of the crowd. Crowd emotion can be estimated at object-level using FER.

2 Materials and Methods

This section presents methodology for estimating the overall emotion of a crowd. Firstly, the popular Viola and Jones face detection algorithm is used to detect and extract unobscured faces from individuals in the crowd. Next, a robust and efficient method of FER is used together with a machine learning algorithm to extract and classify each facial expression as one of seven universally accepted emotions [12]. Finally, the emotion of the crowd is estimated by isolating groups of similar emotion based on their relative size and weighting.

2.1 Face Detection

The Viola and Jones [28] face detection algorithm, which uses a boosted cascade of classifiers to rapidly detect faces, has been shown to be extremely effective at identifying faces in uncontrolled backgrounds with great accuracy [17] compared to other existing face detection techniques. In our work, the Viola and Jones method was selected for face detection due to its combination of speed and accuracy. The Viola and Jones face detection algorithm consists of three main steps: (1) Computing the integral image, (2) Learning classifiers using Adaboost, and (3) Combining the classifiers in a cascade structure.

2.1.1   Computing the Integral Image

Images are classified using simple features as opposed to pixel intensities. The simple features used are reminiscent of Haar Basis functions and consist of two, three and four rectangle features. Because the set of rectangle features can be very large, the images are first represented by an integral image. The integral image at location (x, y) represents the sum of the pixels above and to the left of (x, y), inclusive:

$$ii(x, y) = \sum_{x\prime \le x, y\prime \le y} i(x\prime, y\prime) \tag{1}$$

where $ii(x, y)$ is the integral image and $i(x, y)$ is the original image. By using the integral image, the time taken to compute the rectangular feature set at any scale or location is greatly reduced because any rectangular sum can be computed using just four array references.

2.1.2   Learning Classifiers Using Adaboost

The number of rectangle features associated with each image sub-window is far greater than the number of pixels. To ensure fast classification, only a small subset of these features are combined to form an effective classifier. Adaboost [13] is used in such a way that each weak learning algorithm selects only a single rectangle feature which best separates the positive and negative examples. For each of these features, the optimal threshold classification function is computed such that the minimum number of examples are misclassified. A weak classifier $h_j(x)$ is thus represented by:

$$h_j(x) = \begin{cases} 1, \text{ if } p_j f_j(x) < p_j \theta_j \\ 0, \text{ otherwise} \end{cases} \tag{2}$$

where f_j is a feature, θ_j is the threshold, p_j is a parity indicating the direction of the inequality and x is a 24×24 pixel sub-window of an image.

2.1.3   Combining the Classifiers in a Cascade Structure

To speed-up the classification process, successively more complex classifiers are combined in a cascade structure. Each stage in the cascade is constructed by training a classifier using Adaboost with the threshold adjusted to minimize false negatives. By using a cascade of classifiers, sub-windows that are not of interest can be quickly discarded in the early stages so that increased computation is spent only on more promising face-like regions in the later stages; greatly increasing the overall computational efficiency of classification.

2.2   Facial Expression Recognition (FER)

FER consists mainly of three important steps [21]: (1) Pre-processing of facial images, (2) Facial feature extraction, and (3) Expression classification. Due to the wide variety of individuals that can be found in a crowd; an accurate, efficient and robust method of FER is required for the purposes of Crowd Monitoring. In this work, the detected faces are pre-processed to remove non-discriminative expression regions of the face and Gradient Local Ternary Pattern (GLTP) [1] is applied for facial feature extraction. A Support Vector Machine (SVM) [16] is used for feature classification. Each detected facial expression in the crowd is classified as one of seven universally accepted emotions [12].

2.3   Computing the Distance Between Faces

Before we can find groups of individuals situated close together in the crowd, we first need to determine the distance between neighbouring faces. Each face is treated as a node, where the vertex of the node is represented by the top left point of the region of interest (ROI) representing the face. As in [11], a fully-connected undirected graph is used to link every node's vertex with one another, where the distance between any two nodes is represented by the weight of the connecting edge. We say the resulting graph is fully-connected because each node is connected to every other node present, and undirected because there is only one unique edge between each pair of nodes (direction does not matter). As such, for N nodes we have a total of $(N \times (N - 1))/2$ edges; where the distance between nodes i and j is found using the Euclidean norm as:

$$\text{Distance}_{i,j} = \sqrt{(x_i - x_j)^2 + (y_i - y_j)^2} \tag{3}$$

where (x_i, y_i) represents the vertex of node i and (x_j, y_j) represents the vertex of node j. The graph can be represented by an $N \times N$ adjacency matrix (Adj_Mat), where $\text{Adj\_Mat}_{i,j} = \text{Distance}_{i,j}$. The weight of each edge is the Euclidean distance between the nodes. The fully-connected undirected graph for a crowd of 20 people is shown in Fig. 1.

Fig. 1. Fully-connected undirected graph for a crowd of 20 people

2.4   Computing the Closest Neighbours of Each Face

A Minimum Spanning Tree (MST) is used to represent each face's closest neighbours as suggested in [11]. A spanning tree of a graph G is a tree, where every edge in the tree belongs to G and, that includes every node of G. The cost of a spanning tree is represented by the sum of the weights of all edges in the tree. A MST is a spanning tree where the cost is a minimum. Numerous approaches have been suggested for finding a MST. The two most popular approaches are Kruskal's algorithm and Prim's algorithm [27]. In this work, Prim's algorithm was used to find the MST. Starting with an empty MST, for each step of Prim's algorithm, we consider a group of edges that connects the set of nodes already included in the MST with the set of nodes not yet included. The edge with minimum weight is selected and the node is added to the MST. The procedure is repeated until all nodes have been included in the MST. The MST for the fully-connected undirected graph of the crowd given in Fig. 1 is shown in Fig. 2. In a MST there is a total of $N - 1$ edges.

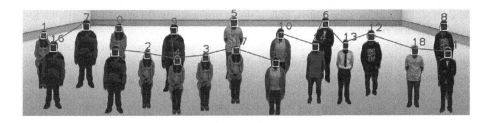

Fig. 2. Minimum spanning tree for a crowd of 20 people

2.5   Estimating Crowd Emotion from Groups of Similar Emotion

The predicted emotion of each face and the MST can be used to identify groups of individuals who are expressing similar emotion and who are situated close together in the crowd. These groups of individuals can be represented by chains of emotion, where the length of each chain is represented by the number of individuals in the chain. The overall emotion of the crowd can then be estimated by finding the largest chain of emotion with the greatest weighting. This approach is more accurate at estimating crowd emotion compared to more simplistic methods such as finding the predominant individual emotion in the crowd. The size of each emotion chain in relation to the crowd is compared to a set threshold value, *thresh*, which represents the minimum size required for the chain to be considered large enough to influence the overall crowd emotion. Each prototypic emotion is assigned a weighting representing its importance. In our work, all emotions are assigned an equal weighting with the exception of neutral emotion which is assigned a lower weighting. This is because neutral emotion does not provide much information about the emotional state of the individuals within the crowd. The overall crowd emotion is predicted as the emotion belonging to the chain that meets the following requirements:

1. The size of the chain in relation to the crowd is greater than or equal to a threshold, *thresh*.

2. The emotion of the chain has the greatest possible weighting out of the chains that meet requirement (1).
3. The size of the chain is the largest out of the chains that meet requirements (1) and (2).

If no chain meets the above requirements; the emotion of the crowd is considered to be mixed. Because individuals in a crowd can take on the emotion of the people around them, it is possible that even a relatively small group of individuals expressing one emotion can influence the emotion of the individuals around them who in turn can influence the individuals around them. This chain reaction is known as the Domino effect and can potentially lead to crowds getting out of control. Our proposed crowd emotion estimation technique aims to identify sufficiently large groups of individuals expressing similar emotion in the crowd, such as anger, before it is able to spread any further. This allows for early detection of potentially problematic crowds.

Consider the crowd given in Fig. 2. The emotion chains for the crowd are illustrated in Fig. 3, where the values above each node represent the node number and predicted FER emotion label of the node. There are a total of 2 unique emotion chains in the crowd; one with emotion label 0 (anger) and another with emotion label 4 (neutral). In this work, the required threshold is set to $thresh = 30\%$ (this value is considered optimal since negative groups of emotion in the crowd can be detected early while false detections are kept to a minimum). The size of both chains are greater than the required threshold. The anger chain has a greater weighting than the neutral chain and because there are no other emotion chains with an equivalent or greater weighting, the overall emotion of the crowd is predicted to be anger.

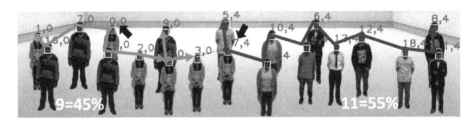

Fig. 3. Finding chains of emotion in the crowd

3   Experimental Setup

In this section, the dataset and procedure used for testing our proposed algorithm are presented.

3.1   Crowd Emotion Dataset

Existing Crowd Monitoring datasets [14, 20, 22, 26, 29] are unsuitable for extracting facial expressions and do not provide known ground-truth emotion labels.

We thus propose the creation of a novel Crowd Emotion dataset with known ground-truth emotion labels. Images from the Extended Cohan-Kanade (CK+) [19] facial expression dataset are pre-processed and placed together in an empty environment to simulate crowd images. The images represent a crowd under optimal conditions with no facial obscurities present. Each crowd image consists of 2 groups of 10 subjects. To produce a ground-truth emotion, subjects in one group are placed so that they are expressing random emotions, none of which exceed the threshold value, while the subjects in the remaining group are placed so that they are expressing the ground-truth emotion. A generated crowd image with ground-truth emotion anger is shown in Fig. 4.

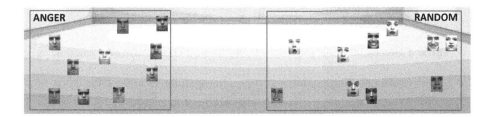

Fig. 4. Generated crowd image with ground-truth emotion anger

3.2 Testing Procedure

To find the average recognition accuracy of our proposed algorithm, we implement a 10-fold cross-validation testing procedure using pre-processed facial images from the CK+ dataset. The images are randomized and divided into 10 roughly equally-sized segments. For each fold, 9 of the segments are used for training the classifier while the remaining segment is used to generate crowd images for testing. This ensures that none of the subjects used for training the classifier are included in the crowd image under test. This process is repeated for the remaining 9 folds and the average recognition accuracy is calculated across all 10 folds.

We define 8 (joy, surprise, anger, fear, disgust, sadness, neutral, mixed), 7 (excludes neutral), and 2 (emotions are grouped into positive and negative) classes of crowd emotion for testing. For 8 & 7 classes of crowd emotion, 3 crowd images are generated for each class per fold, resulting in a total of 240 crowd images for 8 classes and 210 crowd images for 7 classes. For 2 classes of crowd emotion, 12 positive emotion and 12 negative emotion crowd images are generated per fold, resulting in a total of 240 crowd images tested.

4   Results and Discussion

In this section, results are reported on the proposed Crowd Emotion dataset for the algorithm presented.

4.1 Recognition Accuracy

The recognition accuracies achieved for 8, 7, and 2 classes of crowd emotion are summarized in Table 1. An average recognition accuracy of 64.6% was achieved for 8 classes of crowd emotion. Examining the crowd emotion confusion matrix shown in Table 2, we find that joy, neutral and mixed crowd emotions exhibited a high degree of recognition accuracy. On the contrary, anger and sadness emotions exhibited a very poor degree of recognition accuracy. These findings share a direct correlation with the chosen method of FER, which achieved an average recognition accuracy of 85.4% on the crowd images. The confusion matrix for FER is given in Table 3 and shows that out of the 7 facial emotions on test, anger and sadness emotions achieved the lowest recognition accuracies; being confused to a great extent with neutral emotion.

Table 1. Recognition accuracy (%) for 8, 7 and 2 classes of crowd emotion

Classes of crowd emotion	Recognition accuracy (%)
8 class	64.6 ± 2.1
7 class	81.3 ± 1.6
2 class (with neutral emotion)	72.4 ± 2.5
2 class (without neutral emotion)	94.8 ± 1.1

Table 2. Crowd confusion matrix (%) for 8 classes of crowd emotion

	Joy	Sur	Ang	Fear	Dis	Sad	Neu	Mixed
Joy	**97**	0	0	0	0	0	3	0
Sur	0	**62**	0	0	0	0	37	1
Ang	0	0	**5.7**	0	0	0	91.6	2.7
Fear	0	0	0	**58.3**	0	0	38	3.7
Dis	0	0	0	0	**66.3**	0	32	1.7
Sad	0	0	0	0	0	**29**	67	4
Neu	0	0	0	0	0	0	**100**	0
Mixed	0	0	0	0	0	0	1.7	**98.3**

An average recognition accuracy of 81.3% was achieved for 7 classes of crowd emotion. This shows a 16.7% improvement compared to when neutral emotion was included. Examining the crowd emotion confusion matrix in Table 4, we note that while all emotion classes displayed an improvement in recognition accuracy compared to 8 class testing, in particular, anger and sadness emotions experienced the largest improvement; having increased more than threefold. This is

Table 3. FER confusion matrix (%) for 8 classes of crowd emotion

	Joy	Sur	Ang	Fear	Dis	Sad	Neu
Joy	**98.8**	0	0.1	0	0	0	1.1
Sur	1.3	**92.3**	0.3	0.2	1.6	0.1	4.2
Ang	0	3.6	**51.3**	0.7	3.1	1.6	39.7
Fear	1.3	3.2	0.3	**85.1**	0	3.9	6.2
Dis	3	0.5	0.1	0.1	**87.9**	0	8.4
Sad	0	1.2	0.1	0.3	0	**71.5**	26.9
Neu	0.2	1	0.3	0.7	0.5	1.1	**96.2**

Average: 85.4%

supported by the FER confusion matrix given in Table 5, where anger and sadness emotions experienced the most significant increase in recognition accuracy out of the 6 facial emotions on test. With neutral emotion excluded, the average FER recognition accuracy improved by 7.6% from 85.4% to 93%. Further examination of both 7 class and 8 class FER confusion matrices shows that pleasing emotions such as joy and surprise tend to exhibit higher recognition accuracies compared to other displeasing emotions such as anger, fear and disgust, which often get confused between one another. This is evident in Table 5, where anger and fear is confused with disgust and sadness.

Table 4. Crowd confusion matrix (%) for 7 classes of crowd emotion

	Joy	Sur	Ang	Fear	Dis	Sad	Mixed
Joy	**98.3**	0	0	0	0	0	1.7
Sur	0	**79**	0	0	0.3	0	20.7
Ang	0	0	**51.7**	0	0	0	48.3
Fear	0	0	0	**64.3**	0	0	35.7
Dis	0	0	0	0	**85.3**	0	14.7
Sad	0	0	0	0	0	**91.3**	8.7
Mixed	0.3	0	0	0	0.3	0	**99.4**

We reduce the 8 and 7 classes of crowd emotion into just 2 classes - positive and negative. Emotions that can be considered pleasing are grouped into the positive class while emotions that can be considered displeasing are grouped into the negative class. For what was previously 7 classes of crowd emotion, we group joy and surprise into the positive class while anger, fear, disgust and sadness are grouped into the negative class. For what was previously 8 classes of crowd emotion, we consider neutral emotion to be non-negative and place it in

Table 5. FER confusion matrix (%) for 7 classes of crowd emotion

	Joy	Sur	Ang	Fear	Dis	Sad
Joy	**99.5**	0	0.4	0	0.1	0
Sur	1.1	**95.5**	0.6	0.6	2.1	0.1
Ang	0	7	**83**	1	4.4	4.6
Fear	1.7	3	0.9	**86.2**	0.1	8.1
Dis	3.2	0.8	1.7	0	**94.2**	0.1
Sad	0.1	2.3	1.3	0.2	0.1	**96**

Average: 93.0%

the positive emotion class. Crowd's of mixed emotion are also considered non-negative and thus classified as positive. We repeat our cross-validation testing on the reduced class set for 2 given scenarios: (1) neutral emotion is included as part of the positive emotion class and (2) neutral emotion is excluded.

An average recognition accuracy of (1) 72.4% (neutral emotion included) and (2) 94.8% (neutral emotion excluded) was achieved for 2 classes of crowd emotion. These results show an improvement in accuracy of 7.8% compared to 8-class testing and 13.5% compared to 7-class testing. We note that by excluding neutral emotion from 2 class testing, recognition accuracy improved by 22.4% compared to when it was included. This significant increase in recognition accuracy due to the exclusion of neutral emotion is consistent with our findings during 7 class testing, where we also noted a significant increase in accuracy compared to 8 class testing. The crowd emotion confusion matrices for 2 classes of crowd emotion are given in Tables 6 and 7. In both cases, all crowd images with positive emotion were correctly predicted; demonstrating that positive emotions may be more easily recognized compared to negative emotions. For the first case, with neutral emotion included, more than half of the negative emotion crowd images on test were misclassified. Some negative emotions, such as anger and sadness, would have been misclassified as neutral emotion causing those crowd images to be incorrectly classified as having positive emotion. For the second case, with neutral emotion excluded, the number of crowd images with negative emotion that were correctly predicted was much higher; resulting in the largest average recognition accuracy achieved on test. Overall, these findings show that greater accuracies can be achieved by combining multiple emotions of a similar type to form a reduced class set, while maintaining the ability to discern negative crowd emotion from positive crowd emotion.

Table 6. Crowd confusion matrix (%) for 2 classes of crowd emotion (with neutral)

	Positive	Negative
Positive	**100**	0
Negative	55.2	**44.8**

Table 7. Crowd confusion matrix (%) for 2 classes of crowd emotion (without neutral)

	Positive	Negative
Positive	**100**	0
Negative	10.2	**89.8**

4.2 Efficiency

To test the performance of our proposed algorithm, we vary the size of crowd while measuring the average time taken to predict the emotion of each crowd image on a Core 2 Duo, with a clock-speed of 2.0 GHz and 3 GB of RAM. The individuals placed in the crowd are selected at random and the results are given in Fig. 5. The results show a linear relationship between crowd size and prediction runtime. We note that for small crowds of 1 to 20 people, prediction takes less than 1 s. On the other hand, for larger crowds of 200 to 220 people, it takes in the region of 12 to 13 s for each prediction. Overall the algorithm shows potential for real-time application.

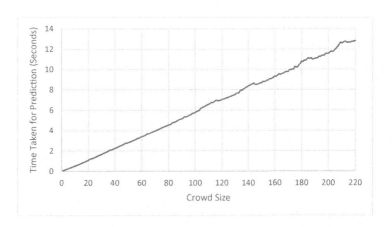

Fig. 5. The effect of varying crowd size on prediction runtime

4.3 Comparison to Results in Literature

We compare our proposed algorithm to existing Crowd Monitoring techniques aimed at emotion detection in crowds. Although a direct comparison cannot be made due to differences in the datasets and the testing procedures used, we outline any advantages and disadvantages between methods and where possible compare accuracies. In [25], it was proposed that emotion-based classification of a crowd could be used to better predict crowd behaviour. The authors created a novel crowd behaviour dataset consisting of video sequences for 5 types of crowd behaviour annotated with 6 emotion labels (disgust was excluded) based on the motion of the crowd. Using dense trajectory and SVM classification, emotion descriptions were extracted for each video sequence and mapped to a crowd behaviour. The authors reported a recognition accuracy of 43.9% using a leave-one-out testing procedure (which typically gives higher accuracies), 20.7% lower than our 8 class results, although the dataset used in their work was considerably more difficult. Although the authors work represents a novel approach to Crowd Monitoring through the use of crowd emotion, it requires obtaining video sequences of crowds around the apex of their behaviour to be truly effective, which is a complex real-world task. The method is also highly dependent on the type of crowd sequences supplied during the training stage and thus may not work in all environments. In comparison, our proposed method focuses only on 2D static images, which is far more computationally efficient for practical real-world applications. By relying solely on facial expressions for emotion classification, our method should not be greatly effected by changing environments or scenery within the crowd (apart from illumination variation and noise).

In [4], a dynamic probabilistic clustering technique was proposed to model a crowd's response to different events. A simulation model to produce evacuation and panic situations was implemented to test the proposed method. Crowd emotion was classified as either positive or negative based on the clustering together (herding) of individuals within the crowd in response to panic situations. The authors report that a recognition accuracy of 88.6% for correctly detecting positive emotion and 85.8% for correctly detecting negative emotion was achieved using a Receiver Operating Curve (ROC) obtained from 50 simulations. If we were to take the average of these values, we find that the method achieved an average recognition accuracy of 87.2% for both classes of emotion. Ignoring any discrepancies due to differences in testing procedures, we note that the overall accuracy achieved is in the same region (>85%) as that of our 2 class test results without neutral emotion. However, the authors proposed method is only able to discern positive and negative emotion from panic/evacuation situations; which, depending on how the emotion is defined, may not be a true reflection of negative emotion. While this method is limited to panic and evacuation events, our proposed method can be implemented during multiple types of events for the detection of multiple types of emotion.

5   Conclusion

In this paper, we confirmed, via extensive testing on a novel Crowd Emotion dataset with ground-truth emotion, that our proposed Crowd Monitoring algorithm is able to correctly classify a crowd emotion with multiple classes. We found that by excluding neutral emotion and grouping emotions to form a reduced class set, high recognition accuracies were able to be achieved. When testing the performance of our proposed method, it was shown that real-time application is possible. In a comparison with existing methods of Crowd Monitoring in current literature, we found that our proposed algorithm offers a viable alternative to existing techniques. In future work, an improved method of GLTP [15] may be used to further enhance accuracy and efficiency of the algorithm. Implementing a multiple array camera setup to track faces in 3-Dimensional space will also help to alleviate current limitations with facial obscurities in densely populated crowds.

References

1. Ahmed, F., Hossain, E.: Automated facial expression recognition using gradient-based ternary texture patterns. Chin. J. Eng. **2013**, 1–8 (2013)
2. Ali, S., Shah, M.: A lagrangian particle dynamics approach for crowd flow segmentation and stability analysis. In: IEEE Conference on Computer Vision and Pattern Recognition, pp. 1–6 (2007)
3. Andrade, E.L., Blunsden, S., Fisher, R.B.: Modelling crowd scenes for event detection. In: 18th International Conference on Pattern Recognition, pp. 175–178 (2006)
4. Baig, M.W., Barakova, E.I., Marcenaro, L., Rauterberg, M., Regazzoni, C.S.: Crowd emotion detection using dynamic probabilistic models. In: del Pobil, A.P., Chinellato, E., Martinez-Martin, E., Hallam, J., Cervera, E., Morales, A. (eds.) SAB 2014. LNCS (LNAI), vol. 8575, pp. 328–337. Springer, Cham (2014). https://doi.org/10.1007/978-3-319-08864-8_32
5. Barry, E.: Protests in Moldova Explode, with a Call to Arms on Twitter. The New York Times, p. A1, 7 April 2009
6. Boghossian, B.A., Velastin, S.A.: Motion-based machine vision techniques for the management of large crowds. In: The 6th IEEE International Conference on Electronics, Circuits and Systems, vol. 2, pp. 961–964 (1999)
7. Brostow, G.J., Cipolla, R.: Unsupervised Bayesian detection of independent motion in crowds. In: Computer Society Conference on Computer Vision and Pattern Recognition, pp. 594–601 (2006)
8. Cheriyadat, A.M., Radke, R.: Detecting dominant motions in dense crowds. IEEE J. Sel. Topics Sig. Process. **2**(4), 568–581 (2008)
9. Cikara, M., Jenkins, A.C., Dufour, N., Saxe, R.: Reduced self-referential neural response during intergroup competition predicts competitor harm. NeuroImage **96**, 36–43 (2014)
10. Davies, A.C., Yin, J.H., Velastin, S.A.: Crowd monitoring using image processing. Electron. Commun. Eng. J. **7**(1), 37–47 (1995)
11. Dhall, A.: Context based facial expression analysis in the wild. In: 2013 Humaine Association Conference on Affective Computing and Intelligent Interaction (ACII), September 2013
12. Ekman, P.: Strong evidence for universals in facial expressions: a reply to russell's mistaken critique. Psychol. Bull. **115**(2), 268–287 (1994)
13. Freund, Y., Schapire, R.E.: A decision-theoretic generalization of on-line learning and an application to boosting. J. Comput. Syst. Sci. **55**, 119–139 (1997)
14. Hassner, T., Itcher, Y., Kliper-Gross, O.: Violent flows: real-time detection of violent crowd behavior. In: 3rd IEEE International Workshop on Socially Intelligent Surveillance and Monitoring (SISM) at the IEEE Conference on Computer Vision and Pattern Recognition (CVPR), Rhode Island, June 2012
15. Holder, R.P., Tapamo, J.R.: Improved gradient local ternary patterns for facial expression recognition. EURASIP J. Image Video Process. **2017**(1), 42 (2017). https://doi.org/10.1186/s13640-017-0190-5
16. Hsu, C.W., Lin, C.J.: A comparison on methods for multiclass support vector machines. IEEE Trans. Neural Netw. **13**(2), 415–425 (2002)

17. Khryashchev, V., Ganin, A., Golubev, M., Shmaglit, L.: Audience analysis system on the basis of face detection, tracking and classification techniques. In: Proceedings of the International MultiConference of Engineers and Computer Scientists, vol. 1, Hong Kong, March 2013

18. Kumari, J., Rajesh, R., Pooja, K.M.: Facial expression recognition: a survey. In: Second International Symposium on Computer Vision and the Internet, vol. 58, pp. 486–491 (2015)

19. Lucey, P., Cohn, J.F., Kanade, T., Saragih, J., Ambadar, Z., Matthews, I.: The extended cohn-kanade dataset (ck+): a complete expression dataset for action unit and emotion-specified expression. In: Proceedings of the Third International Workshop on CVPR for Human Communicative Behavior Analysis, San Francisco, CA, USA, pp. 94–101. IEEE (2010)

20. Mahadevan, V., Li, W., Bhalodia, V., Vasconcelos, N.: Anomaly detection in crowded scenes. In: IEEE Computer Vision and Pattern Recognition (2010)

21. Mahto, S., Yadav, Y.: A survey on various facial expression recognition techniques. Int. J. Adv. Res. Electr. Electron. Instrum. Eng. **3**(11), 13028–13031 (2014)

22. Mehran, R., Oyama, A., Shah, M.: Abnormal crowd behavior detection using social force model. In: IEEE Computer Vision and Pattern Recognition (2009)

23. Mishra, S., Dhole, A.: A survey on facial expression recognition techniques. Int. J. Sci. Res. (IJSR) **4**(4), 1247–1250 (2015)

24. Rabaud, V., Belongie, S.: Counting crowded moving objects. In: Computer Society Conference on Computer Vision and Pattern Recognition, pp. 705–711 (2006)

25. Rabiee, H.R., Haddadnia, J., Mousavi, H., Nabi, M., Murino, V., Sebe, N.: Emotion-based crowd representation for abnormality detection, pp. 1–7. CoRR abs/1607.07646 (2016)

26. Solmaz, B., Moore, B.E., Shah, M.: Identifying behaviors in crowd scenes using stability analysis for dynamical systems. IEEE Trans. Pattern Anal. Mach. Intell. **34**(10), 2064–2070 (2012)

27. Tarjan, R.E.: Minimum spanning trees. In: Data Structures and Network Algorithms, CBMS-NSF Regional Conference Series in Applied Mathematics, vol. 44, chap. 6, pp. 72–77. Bell Laboratories, Murray Hill (1983)

28. Viola, P., Jones, M.: Rapid object detection using a boosted cascade of simple features. In: Proceedings of the 2001 IEEE Computer Society Conference on Computer Vision and Pattern Recognition, Kauai, HI, USA, pp. 511–518. IEEE (2001)

29. Wang, X., Ma, X., Grimson, W.E.L.: Unsupervised activity perception in crowded and complicated scenes using hierarchical Bayesian models. IEEE Trans. Pattern Anal. Mach. Intell. **31**(3), 539–555 (2009)

30. Wu, X., Liang, G., Lee, K.K., Xu, Y.: Crowd density estimation using texture analysis and learning, pp. 214–219 (2006)

31. Zhan, B., Monekosso, D.N., Remagnino, P., Velastin, S.A., Xu, L.Q.: Crowd analysis: a survey. Mach. Vis. Appl. **19**(5), 345–357 (2008)

32. Zhang, D., Tong, C., Lu, Y., Liu, Z.: Dominant motions detection in dense crowds based on particle video. Int. J. Digit. Content Technol. Appl. (JDCTA) **6**(10), 294–301 (2012)

Block-Wise Gaze Estimation Based on Binocular Images

Xuemei Wu[1], Jing Li[2], Qiang Wu[1], Jiande Sun[3(✉)], and Hua Yan[4]

[1] School of Information Science and Engineering, Shandong University,
Jinan, China
Wuxue1991sdu@163.com, wuqiang@sdu.edu.cn
[2] School of Mechanical and Electrical Engineering,
Shandong Management University, Jinan, China
lijingjdsun@hotmail.com
[3] School of Information Science and Engineering, Shandong Normal University,
Jinan, China
jiandesun@hotmail.com
[4] School of Computer Science and Technology,
Shandong University of Finance and Economics, Jinan, China
huayan73@hotmail.com

Abstract. Appearance-based gaze estimation methods have been proved to be highly effective. Different from the previous methods that estimate gaze direction based on left or right eye image separately, we propose a binocular-image based gaze estimation method. Considering the challenges in estimating the precise gaze points via regression models, we estimate the block-wise gaze position by classifying the binocular images via convolutional neural network (CNN) in the proposed method. We divide the screen of the desktop computer into 2×3 and 6×9 blocks respectively, label the binocular images with their corresponding gazed block positions, train a convolutional neural network model to classify the eye images according to their labels, and estimate the gazed block through the CNN-based classification. The experimental results demonstrate that the proposed gaze estimation method based on binocular images can reach higher accuracy than those based on monocular images. And the proposed method shows its great potential in practical touch screen-based applications.

Keywords: Gaze estimation · Gaze block · Appearance-based
Eye image · Convolutional neural network (CNN)

1 Introduction

Gaze-based interaction has been a highlight in the field of Human-Computer Interaction. As the fundamental technology of gazed-based interaction, gaze estimation attracted lots of researches in recent years. So far, there are mainly two kinds of gaze estimation methods, i.e., model-based [1–8] and appearance-based methods [10–18].

Most of the model-based gaze estimation methods are usually based on cameras with high resolution and infrared (IR) lights [5, 6]. These methods established the

© Springer International Publishing AG, part of Springer Nature 2018
M. Paul et al. (Eds.): PSIVT 2017, LNCS 10749, pp. 477–487, 2018.
https://doi.org/10.1007/978-3-319-75786-5_38

eyeball geometry referring to the location of pupil center and the reflections of the IR lights on the cornea, and estimated the gaze points according to the location relationship between the IR lights and the cameras [7, 8]. Most of the model-based gaze estimation methods can reach high accuracy, but most of them needed calibration process for individual user before estimation, which destroys the naturality of HCI and degrades the quality of experience.

Different from the model-based gaze estimation methods, the appearance-based gaze estimation methods are data-driven methods. They estimate the gaze point based on the mapping between gaze points and the related eye images or their features, which is obtained based on the training eye images labelled with their corresponding gaze directions. Compared to the model-based methods, the appearance-based methods don't need any calibration, and have low hardware requirements, which make these methods promising in practical applications. Lu et al. [9, 10] divided an eye image into sub-regions and adopt intensity feature vector as the extracted feature. Sugano et al. [11] proposed an appearance-based gaze estimation using visual saliency. When referring to the gaze estimation methods, the most commonly used mapping functions include Gaussian Bayesian regression [12], adaptive clustering [13], random forest regression [14, 15], neural network [16–18], and so on. Most of the above methods estimate the exact gaze points via regression model. And referring to the performance announced in previous researches, the accuracy of appearance-based methods is much lower that of model-based ones in estimating the exact gaze point, even with the support of deep learning and large amounts of training data.

In practical interaction applications, the button-based touch interface is almost the most popular way. Given this interaction consideration and the challenge in estimating the exact gaze point, we propose a novel appearance-based gaze estimation method. Our contributions in this paper are:

(1) We estimate the gaze blocks, not the exact positions of fixation points. During button-based touch interactions, the user usually tends to touch the center of the button, though any touch on any position of the button can trigger the operation. It is the same that the user usually tends to gaze the center of the button, when he tries to trigger the button via gazing. It means that all of the gaze falling into one button can be classified as the gaze which can trigger this button. Therefore, we can broaden the gaze estimation task from point-wise estimation to block-wise estimation taking account of the practical interaction applications.

(2) We take the mapping between the eye images and gaze blocks as a classification task, which is implemented by CNN-based classification. Because all the gazes falling into the same button can trigger the button, these gazes can be considered in the same class in the case of button-based interaction, and the corresponding accuracy can be relaxed to the size of the button. The classification-base estimation can balance the requirements of practical applications and difficulty in accurate estimation.

(3) We use the binocular images as the training data because the binocular images can provide more information of head pose and relative position between two eyes than monocular images, which are considered useful for accurate gaze estimation. It is different from most of the existing methods, which use left or right eye

images independently, or use left or right eye images separately and fuse them finally. In addition, different user have their own dominant eyes, the estimation accuracy on monocular images of dominant eye will be higher than that on the non-dominant eye. And the estimation based on binocular images can achieve accurate and robust results.

We perform block-wise gaze estimation on the 6- and 54-block levels with our collected data and MPII dataset. The experiments verify the outperformance of the proposed method in gaze block estimation.

2 Proposed Method

2.1 Framework

As mentioned above, this paper is dedicated to the appearance-based gaze estimation method via CNN. Figure 1 shows the basic framework of our binocular data-driven method. Just like the most appearance-based method, the learning-based gaze estimation method first requires a large amount of data for model training. For this purpose, we established our binocular dataset as detailed below. After the data collection, we take the binocular images as the input of CNN.

2.2 Binocular Image Collection

There are many existing human eye datasets, which can be available publicly. However, most existing datasets provide only monocular data and most of them are designed for regression problems. Unlike these datasets, we build our own dataset as in Sect Data Collection, label all eye images with their corresponding block, and take the eye images with the same label as the same category.

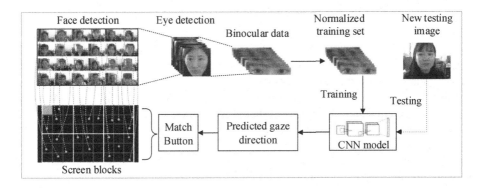

Fig. 1. Framework of the proposed gaze estimation method.

Data Collection. Our experimental images are captured from a single web camera, the Logic C270, with the resolution of 640 × 480, and one normal 19-in screen with the aspect ratio 16:9. The screen blocks are as shown in Fig. 1. We first divide the screen into 2 × 3 blocks as shown in thick lines and each block is further divided into 3 × 3 small blocks as shown in thin lines according to our screen ratio. The subjects are asked to sit about 60 cm away from screen with their heads free and this can ensure that one centimeter on screen is approximately equal to one degree in gaze direction. The big blocks are with the size of 12.75 × 12.75 cm and the corresponding 6-class classification can achieve the accuracy of ±6.38°. The small blocks are with the size of 4.25 × 4.25 cm and the corresponding 54-class classification can achieve the accuracy of ±2.13°.

We provide a simple way for data collecting. Each subject is asked to gaze the center of the blocks on the screen. And the center of the block is taken as the ground truths of fixation points falling in this block. The gazes that fixate any point in each block are classified the same category in our method. Totally 56 groups of eye videos are collected from 22 subjects aged in 20–30 range, and each video lasted about 4 min with 15 fps. In order to prevent the fixation fatigue, we set a two-second rest between every two fixation points.

Binocular Images. Figure 1 shows the acquisition of binocular data. We adopted the face and eye detection method in [19]. Given a fixation video of a subject, we first detected the face of the first frame by Haar-like features [20]. And then, we detected all remaining images by matching with the detected face from the first frame. For the obtained human face area, we used the empirical theory namely the general positions of the two eyes in the face area to obtain each eye's center. The precise locations of the two eyes center can be further determined based on the human face. The binocular rectangle can be obtained by setting the threshold. All extracted binocular images contain both left and right eyes and are normalized to the fixed size of 40 × 184 according to the average size of the eye image samples. We randomly selected the 151200 training images and 30240 testing images to train the CNN model. The eye images in training set and testing set remain mutually disjoint.

2.3 Gaze Estimation Using CNN

Although many appearance-based gaze estimation methods based on regression models have been proposed, it is difficult to achieve high accuracy because it is a really hard task to estimate the exact gaze position. Our proposed block-wise classification-based gaze estimation method relax the estimation from one point to a block, which reduce the difficulty of training a learning-based model. Besides, the estimation of the gaze blocks is exactly suitable for the touch-based interaction.

Considering the good performance of the CNN model used in [21] for image classification in ImageNet competition, we fine tune the parameters of this network to suit our input image. Figure 2 illustrates the deep structure of our CNN model. The network contains three convolutional layers followed by max pooling layers, and two fully connected layers which connect the extracted features into multidimensional vector. The last layer determines the final category that the input image belongs to by calculating the probability of each class. The category with the highest probability is just the one which the input image belongs to. The cuboids in Fig. 2 represent the convolutional layers, and max pooling layers. The length, width, and height of the cuboid

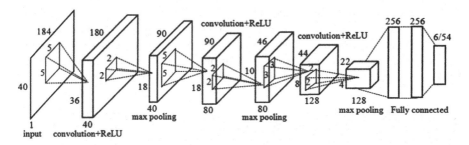

Fig. 2. The structure of deep convolutional neural network.

denote the number of feature maps, and the size of each map. The size of the convolution kernel is illustrated by small squares in each cuboid. Two fully connected layers are represented by rectangular bar with the dimension of 256 and the final layer represents the number of classes. In this paper, we give two classification criteria namely 6-class classifications and 54-class classifications which denote two different block size.

2.4 CNN-Based Classification

We choose the RGB images as the input as the color information in the CNN is useful to improve the accuracy. We define x_i^{l-1} as the ith feature map of the $l-1$th layer, M as the number of feature maps of this layer. So, the output of the lth convolutional layer can be expressed as:

$$x_j^l = Relu(\sum_{i \in M} x_i^{l-1} * k_{ij}^l + b_j^l) \tag{1}$$

Where k_{ij}^l is the convolution kernel, b_j^l is the bias, and the "$*$" represents the convolution operator. The previous feature maps are convoluted with different convolution kernels and shifted by a bias, followed by the activation function. Then, the result can form one of the feature maps in the convolutional layer.

The output of the current sub-sampling layer can be expressed as:

$$x_j^l = f(\beta_j^l \cdot down(x_j^{l-1}) + b_j^l) \tag{2}$$

Where $down(\cdot)$ represent the max-pooling operation. Pooling results are multiplied with a gain coefficient β and shifted by a bias followed by the activation function f.

We set Rectified Linear Units (ReLU) as the activation function and add Local Response Normalization (LRN) layer between the convolutional and the pooling layers to improve the performance. We adopt the dropout layer to prevent over-fitting.

The convolution layers, the pooling layers and the activation functions are used to map the original input into the hidden feature space. After the feature extracted, we use the fully connected layers to realize the classification. The last two fully connected layers are realized by inner product operation. In our network, a 256-dimension feature vector is generated. In the final classification operator, the probability values belonging to different classes are calculated and the category corresponding to the highest probability value is the category which the input image belongs to. When the test image goes through the trained network, the outputs of three pooling layers in CNN are shown in Fig. 3. The images indicate that the contour of input image is gradually blurred and the deep features are gradually extracted as the network grows deeper.

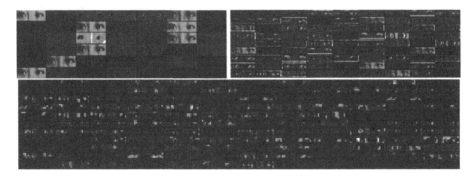

Fig. 3. Output of different pooling layers in CNN. Output of the 1st pooling layer (40 × 18 × 90) (top left), output of the 2nd pooling layer (80 × 10 × 46) (top right), output of the 3rd pooling layer (128 × 4 × 22) (bottom).

3   Experiments and Evaluations

3.1   Gaze Estimation Performance

In this section, we present the results of our proposed binocular image based method. Just as mentioned above, we randomly choose the training set and the testing set with a 5:1 sample number ratio, and the two sets are completely disjoint without any overlap. We choose the binocular data, left eyes and right eyes as the training data of the network respectively. All of the experiments are repeated in both 6-classes and 54-classes scenario. For binocular data, the proposed method can reach the average accuracy with 98.52% for the 6-class classification and 90.97% for the 54-class classification. For left eyes only, the accuracy can reach 93.31% for 6-class classification and 80.89% for 54-class classification. And for right eyes only, the accuracy can reach 92.74% for 6-class classification and 79.42% for 54-class classification. The experimental results of average classification accuracy are shown in Fig. 4. The rising curves indicate accuracy change with iterations for different type of input. It can be seen that the accuracy improvement of binocular images is about 5% in 6 block case and about 10% in 54 block case, which means the binocular images is helpful in accurate gaze estimation.

We also give the confusion matrix to display the classification performance of each category in Fig. 5. The horizontal axis of the confusion matrix represents the real category, and the vertical axis represents the predicted classification. So, the diagonal in confusion matrix indicates the probability of the correct classification. We can find that the proposed binocular data-driven method can get high classification accuracy in each category.

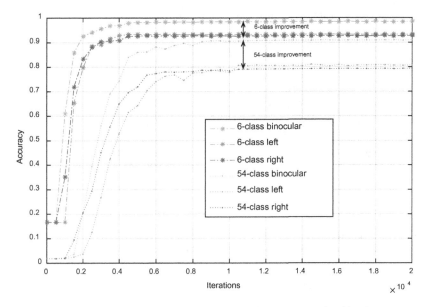

Fig. 4. Experimental results of both 6-class and 54-class average classification accuracy.

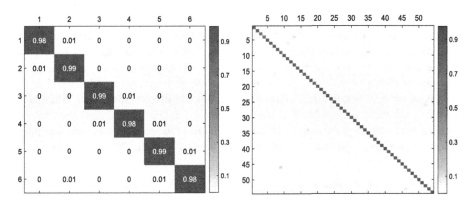

Fig. 5. The confusion matrix for 6-class classification (left) and confusion matrix for 54-class classification (right).

3.2 Comparison with MPIIGaze Dataset

In this section, we discuss our classification method based on MPIIGaze dataset in [18]. This dataset offered eye images and the corresponding gaze direction. In order to meet the needs of our experiment, we first turn the three-dimensional coordinates of fixation points into angular coordinates, and then we map the coordinates into the corresponding blocks on a screen, which is same as the one used in our data collection. The human eyes are labeled according to these corresponding mapping blocks. We select 33000 left eye samples and 33000 right eye samples from the MPIIGaze dataset. The

Table 1. Comarison with the MPIIGaze dataset.

Datasets	Estimation accuracy (%)	
	6-class	54-class
Ours	98.52	90.97
MPIIGaze [18]	75.64	39.18

estimation accuracy results when using both our dataset and the MPIIGaze dataset are shown in Table 1. In [18], the lowest error is about 6° and the mean error is about 10.3°. We have already described the range of degree of our blocks in Sect. 2.2. From Table 1, we can see that the accuracy of gaze estimation can mostly reach about 6.38°, and some can reach about 2.13°. It demonstrates that our proposed method outperforms the method in [18] on their MPIIGaze dataset. The experimental results may also indicate that the datasets based on regression methods are not suited for the block-based classification, and it is necessary to build the specific dataset for the button based gaze interaction.

3.3   Cross-Subject Performance

A practical network should have a wide range of adaptability to the new subjects. So, we test the cross-subject performance for our trained CNN. We randomly selected 4 subjects marked as n1–n4 out of the 22 subjects and tested the classification accuracy of the samples from the 4 subjects in our trained CNN. The experimental results for both 6-class and 54-class classification are shown in Table 2. It can be seen that there are significant differences between subjects, and the performance in 54-class classification is worse than that in 6-class classification. The possible reason for the differences between subjects can be related to the diversity of human eyes. And the general characteristics extracted through CNN can only be used to represent the common parts between individuals. As our dataset contains few individual (22 individuals), it is

Table 2. Investigation on cross-subject gaze block estimation.

Test subjects		Estimation accuracy (%)	
		6-class	54-class
Ours	n1	85.86	49.69
	n2	82.72	46.96
	n3	80.04	46.54
	n4	87.56	31.88
MPIIGaze [18]	s1	69.28	15.21
	s2	52.18	14.82
	s3	51.54	15.97
	s4	48.50	12.95

difficult to cover all appearance of users, and the performance could be better when the training set cover more individuals. The poor accuracy for 54-class classification may be that the block size of 54-class classification is much smaller than 6-class classification, so the classification accuracy becomes worse compared to 6-class classification. We also give the comparison with MPIIGaze dataset for the cross-subject evaluation in Table 2. We also randomly select 4 subjects marked as s1–s4 from the 15 subjects of MPIIGaze dataset as the validation set and set the eye samples from the other 11 subjects as the training set for classification based on our CNN model.

3.4 Comparison with Other Methods

We compare our binocular data-driven method with other appearance-based methods based on our dataset. George and Routray [22] proposed a real-time eye gaze direction classification method using CNN. They adopted the similar classification method with us, but they trained two networks for left and right eyes independently and got the final category by combining the two scores. They finally get 86.81% recognition rate for 7-class classification in the Eye Chimera dataset [23]. Our proposed method finally achieves 9.39% accuracy improvement for 6-class classification and 36.39% accuracy improvement for 54-class classification over the method in [22]. Zhang et al. [18] trained a regression network to estimate the fixation points. In order to unify the comparison pattern, we estimated the fixation point positions using their method and mapped the fixation points to our screen blocks. The mapping results are very poor as their best performance of mean error in [18] is 10.5° for cross-dataset evaluation. The comparison results in Table 3 show that our classification method has higher accuracy in both monocular and binocular data. And the binocular data can improve the classification performance effectively.

Table 3. Comarison with other methods.

Methods		Estimation accuracy (%)	
		6-class	54-class
Method in [18]		23.80	\
Method in [22]		89.13	54.84
Ours	Right eye	92.74	79.42
	Left eye	93.31	80.89
	Binocular image	98.52	90.97

4 Conclusion

In this paper, we proposed a binocular-image-based gaze estimation method, which estimates the gaze block by using CNN classification. Through the mapping relationship between eyes appearance, gaze estimation and the screen blocks, we estimated a new gaze estimation pattern based on classification. Different from the previous gaze estimation methods, we have achieved the twofold improvement on both accuracy and stability by the block based classification and the information provided by binocular images. For the future work, we will continue to enrich and release our dataset with more subjects and more situations to improve the performance for cross-subjects.

Acknowledgements. This work is supported by Key Research and Development Foundation of Shandong Province (2016GGX101009), Natural Science Foundation of Shandong Province (ZR2014FM012), and Scientific Research and Development Foundation of Shandong Provincial Education Department (J15LN60). We acknowledge the support of NVIDIA Corporation with the donation of the TITAN X GPU used for this research.

References

1. Morimoto, C.H., Mimica, M.R.M.: Eye gaze tracking techniques for interactive applications. Comput. Vis. Image Underst. **98**(1), 4–24 (2005)
2. Yang, C., et al.: A gray difference-based pre-processing for gaze tracking. In: 10th International Conference Proceedings on Signal Processing Proceedings, Beijing, China, pp. 1293–1296. IEEE Computer Society (2010)
3. Shih, S.-W., Liu, J.: A novel approach to 3-D gaze tracking using stereo cameras. Trans. Syst. Man Cybern. **34**(1), 234–245 (2004)
4. Cheung, Y., Peng, Q.: Eye gaze tracking with a web camera in a desktop environment. IEEE Trans. Hum.-Mach. Syst. **45**(4), 419–430 (2015)
5. Morimoto, C.H., Amir, A., Flickner, M.: Detecting eye position and gaze from a single camera and 2 light sources. In: 16th International Conference Proceedings on Pattern Recognition, Washington, DC, USA, p. 40314. IEEE Computer Society (2002)
6. Coutinho, F.L., Morimoto, C.H.: Free head motion eye gaze tracking using a single camera and multiple light sources. In: 19th Brazilian Symposium Proceedings on Computer Graphics and Image Processing, Manaus, Brazil, pp. 171–178. IEEE Computer Society (2006)
7. Guestrin, E.D., Eizenman, M.: General theory of remote gaze estimation using the pupil center and corneal reflections. IEEE Trans. Bio-Med. Eng. **53**(6), 1124–1133 (2006)
8. Niu, C., Sun, J., Li, J., Yan, H.: A calibration simplified method for gaze interaction based on using experience. In: 2015 International Workshop Proceedings on Multimedia Signal Processing, Xiamen, China, pp. 1–5. IEEE Computer Society (2015)
9. Lu, F., Sugano, Y., Okabe, T., Sato, Y.: Adaptive linear regression for appearance-based gaze estimation. IEEE Trans. Pattern Anal. Mach. Intell. **36**(10), 2033–2046 (2014)
10. Lu, F., Sugano, Y., Okabe, T., Sato, T.: Inferring human gaze from appearance via adaptive linear regression. In: 2011 International Conference Proceedings on Computer Vision Processing, Washington, DC, USA, pp. 153–160. IEEE Computer Society (2011)
11. Sugano, Y., Matsushita, Y., Sato, Y.: Appearance-based gaze estimation using visual saliency. IEEE Trans. Pattern Anal. Mach. Intell. **35**(2), 329–341 (2013)
12. Ye, N., Tao, X., Dong, L., Ge, N.: Mouse calibration aided real-time gaze estimation based on boost Gaussian Bayesian learning. In: 2016 International Conference Proceedings on Image Processing, Phoenix, AZ, USA, pp. 2797–2801. IEEE Computer Society (2016)
13. Sugano, Y., Matsushita, Y., Sato, Y., Koike, H.: Appearance-based gaze estimation with online calibration from mouse operations. IEEE Trans. Hum.-Mach. Syst. **45**(6), 750–760 (2015)

14. Wang, Y., Shen, T., Yuan, G., Bian, J., Xianping, F.: Appearance based gaze estimation using deep features and random forest regression. Knowl.-Based Syst. 1(10), 293–301 (2016)
15. Sugano, Y., Matsushita, Y., Sato, Y.: Learning-by-synthesis for appearance-based 3D gaze estimation. In: 2014 IEEE Conference Proceedings on Computer Vision and Pattern Recognition, Washington, DC, USA, pp. 1821–1828. IEEE Computer Society (2014)
16. Krafka, K., et al.: Eye tracking for everyone. In: 2016 IEEE Conference Proceedings on Computer Vision and Pattern Recognition, Las Vegas, NV, USA, pp. 2176–2184. IEEE Computer Society (2016)
17. Baluja, S., Pomerleau, D.: Non-intrusive gaze tracking using artificial neural networks. Technical report. Carnegie Mellon University, Pittsburgh, PA, USA (1994)
18. Zhang, X., Sugano, Y., Fritz, M.: Andreas bulling: appearance-based gaze estimation in the wild. In: 2015 IEEE Conference Proceedings on Computer Vision and Pattern Recognition, Boston, MA, USA, pp. 4511–4520 (2015)
19. Baggio, D.L., et al.: Mastering OpenCV with Practical Computer Vision Projects, 1st edn. Packt, Birmingham (2012)
20. Lienhart, R., Maydt, J.: An extended set of Haar-like features for rapid object detection. In: 2002 International Conference Proceedings on Image Processing, Rochester, New York, USA, pp. I-900–I-903 (2002)
21. Krizhevsky, A., Sutskever, I., Hinton, G.E.: ImageNet classification with deep convolutional neural networks. In: Pereira, F., Burges, C.J.C., Bottou, L., Weinberger, K.Q. (eds.) 25th International Conference Proceedings on Neural Information Processing Systems 2012, pp. 1097–1105. Curran Associates Inc., USA (2012)
22. George, A., Routray, A.: Real-time eye gaze direction classification using convolutional neural network. In: 2016 International Conference Proceedings on Signal Processing and Communications Processing, Bangalore, India, pp. 1–5 (2016)
23. Florea, L., Florea, C., Vrânceanu, R., Vertan, C.: Can your eyes tell me how you think? A gaze directed estimation of the mental activity. In: Proceedings of the 2013 British Machine Vision Conference, Bristol, UK, pp. 60–61. BMVA Press (2013)

Integrated Multi-scale Event Verification in an Augmented Foreground Motion Space

Qin Gu[1,2(✉)], Jianyu Yang[1], Wei Qi Yan[2], and Reinhard Klette[2]

[1] University of Electronic Science and Technology of China,
Chengdu 611731, Sichuan, People's Republic of China
guqin.uestc@outlook.com
[2] Auckland University of Technology, Auckland 1010, New Zealand

Abstract. Moving event verification plays an important role in intelligent traffic supervision systems. We propose a novel event-verification framework using a deep convolutional neural network (CNN) in a proposed augmented foreground-motion space. First, we use a Gaussian mixture model for extracting foreground targets and generate multi-scaled regions to speed-up object or behaviour detection in high-resolution input video frames. Second, we use an augmented foreground motion space to reduce (in a group of adjacent frames) the given video data, motion, and scale information. A CNN-based deep neural network is organised for joint object detection and behaviour verification. The contribution of this paper is to propose a solution for multi-scale event verification. We verify the performance of multi-scale event verification for three typical events via real complex road-intersection surveillance videos.

Keywords: Deep learning · Event verification
Convolutional neural network · Gaussian mixture model

1 Introduction

Vision-based intelligent surveillance is an active field due to its high credibility and relatively low costs [8]. Moving event verification plays an important role in intelligent traffic supervision systems, especially for traffic-violation monitoring and recording. The majority of related algorithms are divided into two main categories.

In the first category, the whole frame, possibly also including time-adjacent frames, is used to obtain a conclusive verification result of the current scene. These coarse scene-understanding frameworks have been widely used for the analysis of abnormal events, such as traffic-accident detection.

In the second category, there is a wide diversity of research focusing on object-centric event descriptions. Here, two steps are implemented in traditional

© Springer International Publishing AG, part of Springer Nature 2018
M. Paul et al. (Eds.): PSIVT 2017, LNCS 10749, pp. 488–500, 2018.
https://doi.org/10.1007/978-3-319-75786-5_39

event-verification frameworks, being object detection (recognition), and object behaviour analysis (recognition) in an interval of time.

In this paper, we focus on the second category and combine moving object detection as well as event verification with a convolutional neural network in a novel compressed feature space. Motion information is compressed into a 3-dimensional (3D) augmented foreground motion space for event representation. Then, a deep regional convolutional neural network is used for object-oriented event verification. We list the contributions of this paper:

1. an augmented foreground motion space for event feature representation,
2. a fast Gaussian mixture model (GMM) based region proposal method for automatically generating a group of regions of interest for real-time traffic event recognition, and
3. a particular deep convolutional neural network (CNN), trained for integrated object detection and behaviour recognition in video data.

The remainder of this paper is organized as follows. Section 2 presents related work. Section 3 details the specification of an augmented foreground motion space for feature representation and compression. A joint CNN framework for object detection and event verification is given in Sect. 4. Section 5 shows experimental results for verifying the proposed method. Section 6 concludes.

2   Related Work

There is already a considerable diversity of existing work in traffic-event detection and verification.

Scene-oriented approaches are used for abnormal event detection [16,19] in videos; this has been tackled directly without locating any moving objects. A conclusive classification (i.e., normal or abnormal) is video-frame-based.

To obtain a precise description for an event, we use two steps which include moving object detection and behaviour understanding, to verify an object-based traffic event.

First, it is beneficial to detect objects of interest and extract the spatial location for further object-based event verification. The GMM is used in [24] for vehicle detection in complex urban traffic scenes. We show that GMM is also of benefit for time-efficient multi-object detection and tracking while this algorithm alone can only be used to extract foreground regions and generate coarse hypotheses.

Template-related algorithms have also been proposed for object detection and event hypothesis generation. A robust object-detection framework can be based on Haar-like features and the use of a cascade AdaBoost classifier [21]. This is verified to be an effective and fast method for rigid and one-class object detection. Deformable part models (DPMs) [5] are proposed for vehicle verification by using a support vector machine (SVM) and histogram-of-gradient (HOG) features. The active basis model [22] has also been widely employed for vehicle detection [10,15] in traffic surveillance. With the assistance of a shared skeleton method, it can be easily trained with a considerable detection performance.

Recently, deep learning [13] achieves remarkable advances to solve these problems. It dramatically develops the performance of frame-wise object detection and recognition [6,12,18]. However, it is also time consuming to detect, track, and understand the objects, frame by frame, using a deep neural network.

Second, object tracking methods [7,17,23] reconstruct the moving path of the detected object for further moving pattern matching. These tracking-based behaviour understanding algorithms are able to represent various moving patterns, but they highly rely on continuous and accurate detection results. Subsequently, hidden Markov models (HMM) [1], Bayesian approaches [3], or 3D models [9] can also be used to understand the trajectory of moving targets.

On the other hand, we can directly use a recurrent neural network (RNN) and long-short-term memory (LSTM) mechanisms [2] to construct a system for spatial-temporal event recognition and verification. However, we need a large number of labeled samples for each possible event category to train such a network.

Different to existing work, our contribution in this paper is an integrated framework for real-time and multi-class event recognition for road intersections. Motion detection and event recognition are conducted with a deep convolutional neural network for a proposed augmented foreground motion space.

3   Feature Representation

This section presents our event feature representation method using an *augmented foreground motion space*. See Fig. 1 for an outline. It is subject to the following considerations:

Simplified Data Dimension. In our application, it is time-consuming to detect multi-class events in series of high resolution and colour frames. Hence, an event representation with simplified data dimensions is greatly beneficial for speed-up. We verified that it is more significant to include motion information of objects in multiple frames than colour information.

High Information Density. Usually, traditional multi-frame image processing methods (e.g. *background subtraction*, or *optical flow*) result in some information loss compared to the given images. We expect to have a simplified event representation method which is still close to ensuring completeness of information for subsequent object detection, objet tracking, and behaviour recognition, after multi-frame compression.

Effectiveness. Considering the real-world applications, the feature representation method should be effective for fast regional proposals, accurate event recognition for different kinds of objects, and an adaption for multi-scale objects.

A common RGB colour image I has pixel values $u(x, y) = (I_R, I_G, I_B)$, where $0 \leq I_R, I_G, I_B \leq G_{\max}$ [11]; coordinates x and y define the pixel locations in an

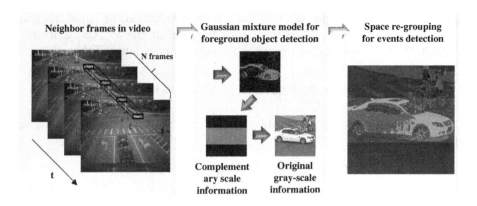

Fig. 1. Framework of the proposed method. *Left:* Generation of a group of region proposals for moving objects. *Middle:* The procedure for feature representation merges original gray-scale images, foreground object detection results, and scale information for compressing the motion information of multiple frames via space re-grouping. *Right:* Further processing of an extracted region for joint event detection and recognition.

image. Value $G_{\max}$ usually equals $2^8 - 1$, or $2^{16} - 1$. For video analysis, we extend this to a 4D video V which has pixel values $v(x, y) = (I_R, I_G, I_B, t)$, where t corresponds to the time slot of a frame in a video.

In this paper, we represent pixel descriptors also in another 3D value space M; we set the value of each pixel as $M(x, y) = (M_U, M_V, M_S)$ where M_U, M_V, and M_S are the proposed 3D features at a pixel location (x, y) with respect to a short video sequence. M_U belongs to the *original image space* for the considered time slot t, M_V is the *complementary foreground space* information of this pixel location during this short video sequence, and M_S refers to the *complementary relative scale space* feature; for details see below.

The Original Image Space. The first value M_U at position (x, y) is the original gray level $\alpha I_R + \beta I_G + \gamma I_B$ of the current frame. It is used to preserve the local skeleton and texture features for object classification. In this paper, for convenience, we use $\alpha = \beta = \gamma = \frac{1}{3}$.

Complementary Foreground Region. To record motion information for a short sequence of adjacent frames, we use the second value M_V for specifying the foreground space. Using GMM, the pixel value at position (x, y) is described by $\{X_1,...,X_t\} = \{I(x, y, i) : 1 \le i \le t\}$. Here, $I(x, y, t)$ corresponds to the intensity value at position (x, y) at time t. All the pixels are represented by K ($3 \le K \le 5$) states, and each state can be approximated using a Gaussian distribution:

$$p(X_t) = \sum_{k=1}^{K} \omega_{k,t} \cdot \Gamma(X_t \,|\, \mu_{k,t}, \Sigma_{k,t})$$

where $\omega_{k,t}$ is the weight of kth Gaussian distribution at time t, and $\Gamma(X_t | \mu_{k,t}, \Sigma_{k,t})$ is the probability density function of the kth Gaussian distribution. By $\mu_{k,t}$ and $\Sigma_{k,t}$ we denote the mean and covariance. Thus,

$$\Gamma(X_t | \mu_{k,t}, \Sigma_{k,t}) = \frac{1}{\sqrt{2\pi \cdot |\Sigma_k|}} \exp\left[-\frac{1}{2}(\mathbf{x}_t - \mu_k)^\top \Sigma_k^{-1}(\mathbf{x}_t - \mu_k)\right]$$

A comparison between pixel value X_t and the Gaussian cluster is given as follows for matching:

$$X_t \in \Gamma(X_t | \mu_{k,t}, \Sigma_{k,t}), \text{ if } |X_t - \mu_{k,t}| < 2.5 \cdot \sigma_{k,t}$$

where $\sigma_{k,t}$ is the variance of the kth cluster. Let T be an indicative function,

$$T(\alpha) = \begin{cases} 1 & \text{if } \alpha \text{ is true} \\ 0 & \text{otherwise} \end{cases} \tag{1}$$

Then, an updating process of weights is implemented by

$$\omega_{k,t} = (1 - \varepsilon)\omega_{k,t-1} + \varepsilon \cdot T(X_{t-1} \in \Gamma(X_{t-1} | \mu_{k,t-1}, \Sigma_{k,t-1}))$$

where ε is the updating learning rate of the video. Further updating, for a matched k^{th} cluster, is implemented by

$$\mu_{k,t} = (1 - \delta)\mu_{k,t-1} + \delta X_t$$

$$\sigma_{k,t}{}^2 = (1 - \delta)\sigma_{k,t-1}{}^2 + \delta(X_t - \mu_{k,t-1})^T (X_t - \mu_{k,t-1})$$

$$\delta = \varepsilon \cdot \Gamma(X_t | \mu_{k,t-1}, \Sigma_{k,t-1})$$

The first H distributions are taken as a model for the background, with

$$H = \arg\min_l \left(\sum_{k=1}^{l} \omega_{k,t} \geq \tau\right)$$

for a threshold $\tau > 0$. H corresponds to the minimum number of distributions to construct the model of the background. Pixel value M_V in the second layer equals

$$M_V = \frac{G_{max}}{2} \cdot T(X_t \notin H)$$

where $T(\cdot)$ is still the indicative function as defined above.

In this layer, we try to include the dynamic motion information which refers to a micro-event related to object motion. As the initial region proposal is given by GMM, feature re-organization will only take very little time.

Complementary Relative Scale Space. As we expect to detect all the multi-scale targets and events in a wide supervising range, we need to handle objects at different scales. For example, for a hypothesis "a human" we search for a vertical rectangle, and for "a forward-looking vehicle" we search for a square.

We identify each proposed region hypothesis with a rectangle, and then with a square of minimum size, denoted by $S \in \mathbb{R}^{k \times k}$, for $k = \max(w, h)$. Here, S is the proposed region for further event verification, and w and h refer to width and height of the detected foreground hypothesis. Then, in the third layer of the proposed pixel value representation space, we compress the scale information into

$$M_S = \frac{G_{\max}}{2} \cdot T((x, y) \notin S \,|\, S_o)$$

where (x, y) is the position of the current pixel, S is the generated square hypothesis region (i.e. a square block of *complementary scale information*; see Fig. 1), and S_o is the original multi-scale hypothesis region (i.e. the gray area in the square block of the complementary scale information in Fig. 1).

4 Deep CNN for Micro-Event Detection and Verification

This section explains our framework for event verification. The proposed method consists of two phases. The first phase addresses the region proposal process. Each hypothetical motion region is extracted via this phase for further processing (aimed at verification). In the second phase, we train a deep convolution neural network to solve the problem of integrated object detection and event verification.

Region Proposal. Aiming at reducing the time-complexity of event verification, we avoid scanning each pixel or generating a large number of hypotheses with methods like selective search [20] in such large sized frames. As we only focus on events in the supervised region corresponding to moving targets in the video, the proposed method in this paper relies on GMM for the region proposal. The region proposal process is illustrated in Fig. 2.

Fig. 2. *Left to right:* Illustration of the process of region proposal formation using GMM.

A detected (i.e. proposed) region is resized into $227 \times 227 \times 3$ for further deep feature extraction and classification.

Network Layer Overview. In this paper, we use a convolutional layer, a max pooling layer, rectified linear units (ReLUs), and fully connected (FC) layers to construct our traffic event verification network.

Input data pass through all the organised layers to generate the final verification outputs. In the convolution layers, a group of kernels is used to filter the input such as to produce feature maps for deeper feature extraction. The function of the pooling layer is to calculate the overall response of a neighbour area in a feature map, which is one of the outputs of the convolution layer. Being aware of the problem of over-fitting, dropout layers are proposed for training optimisation. Finally, by using the softmax optimisation method, a multi-class identification result is given with an FC layer.

Network Architecture. We use a pre-trained model from the ImageNet Dataset [12]. During the training stage, over a million URLs of images have been used to obtain parameters for this network, and the whole architecture used in this paper is as shown in Fig. 3. At the end of this pre-trained network, the layers are designed to classify 1,000 objects.

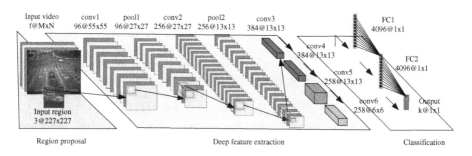

Fig. 3. Framework of the proposed micro-event verification using a deep CNN.

The detailed architecture of the deep neural network, adopted in this paper, consists of five convolution layers, seven ReLU layers, three max-pooling layers, and three FC layers. We generally divided this network into three main parts. First, the proposed region of interest is resized into $227 \times 227 \times 3$. In deep feature extraction, there are five main layers.The first convolutional layer has 96 kernels (all of size $11 \times 11 \times 3$).

After the convolution process with stride [4,4] and padding [0,0] and ReLU activity, we perform a normalisation with 5 channels per element. Then, a 3×3 max-pooling is used with stride [2,2] and padding [0,0]. Similarly, the second main layer of Part 2 consists of one convolutional layer sized 256@5 $\times$ 5 $\times$ 48 with stride [1,1] and padding [0,0], ReLu activity, cross channel normalisation, and the same max-pooling as before. The third, fourth and fifth main layers all encompass one convolution layer (384@3 $\times$ 3 $\times$ 256, 384@3 $\times$ 3 $\times$ 192, or 384@3 $\times$ 3 $\times$ 192, respectively), and one ReLU activity layer.

After an additional max-pooling layer with stride [2,2] and padding [0,0], we extract a deep feature sized $1 \times 4,096$. There are three FC layers and two ReLU layers in the third part for multi-class classification.

Learning Details. Even though there is a big difference between the image in the ImageNet dataset for pre-training and the actually re-organised event representation in the augmented foreground motion space, it is still available to use the pre-trained network for further transfer learning. The reasons are:

The re-organised event representation in the augmented foreground motion space has three dimensions for each pixel. This is the same for the original colour image in the ImageNet dataset.

According to the examples of the event representation in the augmented foreground motion space, the skeleton of objects has been contained in the original image space. Information in this space can be easily learned from the pre-trained network.

Information in two other spaces (i.e. complementary foreground region and complementary relative scale space) also conclude relative edge and texture features for the original image. As a result, we can use a fine-tuning technology to abstract from the representation in these two augmented foreground motion spaces, respectively.

With such a deep convolutional neural network architecture, we use transfer learning technology to rebuild our own (event detection and verification) deep classifier for traffic scenes based on supervised learning. In this paper, we keep the architecture with the learned weights except for the last five layers. As we choose several events as our target, we segment the deep convolution neural network into two stages. The first 16 layers are taken for deep feature extraction, and the last 7 layers in our simulation are for classification.

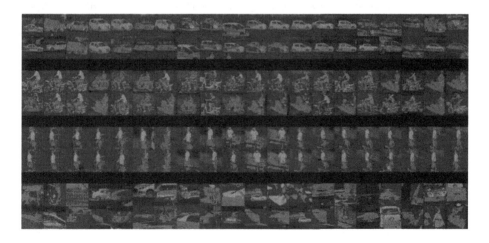

Fig. 4. Samples with some micro events in the augmented foreground motion space.

Totally, 3,622 event samples (see Fig. 4) are extracted and labeled manually from a video for further training for some special events such as vehicle horizontal traversal, motorcycle horizontal traversal, a motorcycle or pedestrian vertical traversal. The final seven layers are reorganized for event verification. First, we use an FC layer with 64 nodes, followed by an ReLU layer. Third, another FC layer with four nodes is given. The softmax optimisation process provides the final classification output.

Specifically, at the training stage, the batch size is set to be equal 128 in this paper, and the learning rate is set to be equal 0.0001 to fine-tune the network. There are 20 cycles being run at this training stage, each epoch means one complete pass through the training data. This training process costs 2,410.27 s with the assistance of a GPU in the used computer.

5   Experiments

The experimental report is divided into three segments. Detailed information of the dataset is given at the beginning. Then, we compare the performance of event localisation for different methods. Finally, we present the performance of event verification for extensive data recorded at a real traffic intersection using the proposed method.

Datasets. To evaluate the proposed method, we collect a dataset from downtown road intersections with a camera located about 8 meters over the road surface. Our videos record top or rear views of vehicles moving below the camera level. It is also possible to observe in the recorded data vehicles, motorcycles, and pedestrians on the other side of the intersection. We use four videos to evaluate the proposed method of moving object detection and behaviour verification. The videos were recorded at a frequency of 25 frames per second.

For event localisation, event descriptions of three time intervals of traffic videos are listed in Table 1. Each dataset contains 500 frames. The resolution of each frame is $2,592 \times 2,048$. We use each 10 adjacent frames to construct an event validation unit. The initial 5 frames are used for foreground region extraction and region proposals. Then, the last 5 frames are used for integrated object detection and behaviour verification.

Table 1. Validation datasets for traffic target detection and tracking, and event supervision.

	Resolution	Frames	Frames showing Event 1	Frames showing Event 2	Frames showing Event 3
Dataset 1	$2,592 \times 2,048$	500	48	44	35
Dataset 2	$2,592 \times 2,048$	500	107	129	27
Dataset 3	$2,592 \times 2,048$	500	68	50	-

Event Localisation. Normally, robust object detection and tracking are necessary for event localisation. In this paper, we compare the proposed integrated method and the traditional object detection method in a traffic scene at the intersection. In order to identify vehicle movements showing Event 1, we extract two hundred frames from the datasets and locate moving vehicles with the *active basis model* of [10], the *deformable part model* of [4], and our proposed method.

The active basis model performs well for rear-view vehicles, but it is difficult to train it for accurate vehicle event localisation in case of other viewing-angles. The deformable part based model is very accurate for detecting objects with a rigid structure, but it costs too much time to tackle one frame for one kind of targets even when using a cascade speed-up technology. Besides, we even need to cope with whole frames several times to extract different objects. The method proposed by us shows comparable results but proves to be much more time-efficient for extract multiple moving objects of interest. A further validation of verification accuracy is given in the next section.

Event Recognition. In this paper, we consider three types of significant events at a traffic intersection as examples, briefly identified as (i) vehicle horizontal traversal (i.e. left-to-right or right-to-left), (ii) motorcycle or bicycle horizontal traversal, or (iii) a motorcycle, bicycle, or pedestrian vertical traversal (i.e. top-down or bottom-up). We call those (i) Event 1, (ii) Event 2, and (iii) Event 3. Note that they may occur concurrently. They have been manually labeled, frame by frame, for having ground truth available. The total number of frames, showing each event, is given in Table 1.

Based on automatic detection and behaviour verification results, the performance of the proposed method is verified by using measures *Recall*, *Precision*, and a false-positive rate C_{FR}, defined as follows:

$$Recall = \frac{\text{detected events 1, 2, or 3}}{\text{total number of events 1, 2, or 3}}$$

$$Precision = \frac{\text{detected events 1, 2, or 3}}{\text{detected events 1, 2, or 3 + false positives (per event)}}$$

$$C_{FR} = \frac{\text{false positives (per frame)}}{\text{total number of frames}}$$

Table 2. Comparisons of event localisation (object detection), computational costs, and available detection classes.

	Detection rate	Processing speed	Categories for verification
Active basis model	54%	0.51 fps	Vehicle
Deformable part model	94%	0.03 fps	Vehicle
Proposed method	91%	2.00 fps	Vehicle, motorcycle, and pedestrian

By using the proposed event verification framework, each moving object of interest showing a specific behaviour is detected, frame by frame. The performance is given in Table 2, and also illustrated in Fig. 5.

The entire algorithm is implemented in Matlab 2016a and CUDA in OS Windows 10 with 12 GB RAM and a GTX960M GPU processor. Processing is on average at 4.3 fps (Table 3).

Fig. 5. Event verification at a road intersection. Three events are detected, recognized and labelled by a red rectangle (Event 1), a yellow rectangle (Event 2), and a green rectangle (Event 3). An object is detected when it moves; this generates an event to be classified; static objects are not labelled. (Color figure online)

Table 3. Performance of event verification in complex traffic scenes.

	Verification performance of Event 1		Verification performance of Event 2		Verification performance of Event 3		Comprehensive false alarm
	Recall	Precise	Recall	Precise	Recall	Precise	CFR
Dataset 1	91.6%	99.3%	95.5%	98.3%	82.9%	100.0%	1.8%
	(44/48)	(408/411)	(42/44)	(356/362)	(29/35)	(243/243)	(9/500)
Dataset 2	92.5%	99.9%	89.1%	99.7%	88.9%	84.8%	9.6%
	(99/107)	(1033/1034)	(115/129)	(1060/1063)	(24/27)	(228/272)	(48/500)
Dataset 3	88.2%	93.2%	80.00%	98.7%	-	-	10.8%
	(60/68)	(616/661)	(40/50)	(710/719)	-	-	(54/500)

6   Conclusions

This paper presents a novel integrated object-oriented event verification framework using a deep convolutional neural network. A new feature representation space is proposed to compress multi-frame and multi-object motion information into one colour image, which proved to be very helpful for integrated detection, tracking and behaviour understanding.

Considering the limited number of training samples from road-intersection traffic scenes, we initialised the neural network with a pre-trained ImageNet network. The experiments show that the proposed method outperforms previous work on multi-class object event localisation either in accuracy or in run-time. The accuracy of event classification has been improved as demonstrated for real data.

Acknowledgement. The experimental work was partially supported by Shandong Provincial Key Laboratory of Automotive Electronics and Technology, Institute of Automation, Shandong Academy of Sciences.

References

1. Bashir, F.I., Khokhar, A.A., Schonfeld, D.: Object trajectory-based activity classification and recognition using hidden Markov models. IEEE Trans. Image Process. **16**(7), 1912–1919 (2007)
2. Baccouche, M., Mamalet, F., Wolf, C., Garcia, C., Baskurt, A.: Action classification in soccer videos with long short-term memory recurrent neural networks. In: Diamantaras, K., Duch, W., Iliadis, L.S. (eds.) ICANN 2010. LNCS, vol. 6353, pp. 154–159. Springer, Heidelberg (2010). https://doi.org/10.1007/978-3-642-15822-3_20
3. Dore, A., Regazzoni, C.: Interaction analysis with a Bayesian trajectory model. IEEE Trans. Intell. Syst. **16**(7), 1912–1919 (2007)
4. Felzenszwalb, P.F., Girshick, R.B., McAllester, D.: Cascade object detection with deformable part models. In: Proceedings of IEEE Conference on Computer Vision, Pattern Recognition, pp. 2241–2248 (2010)
5. Felzenszwalb, P.F., Girshick, R.B., McAllester, D., Ramanan, D.: Object detection with discriminatively trained part-based models. IEEE Trans. Pattern Anal. Mach. Intell. **32**(9), 1627–1645 (2010)
6. Girshick, R.: Fast R-CNN. In: Proceedings of IEEE International Conference on Computer Vision, pp. 1440–1448 (2015)
7. Gupte, S.O., Masoud, O., Martin, R.F.K., Papanikolopoulos, N.P.: Detection and classification of vehicles. IEEE Trans. Intell. Transp. Syst. **3**(1), 37–47 (2002)
8. Hu, W., Tan, T., Wang, L., Maybank, S.: A survey on visual surveillance of object motion and behaviours. IEEE Trans. Syst. Man Cybern. Part C **34**(3), 334–352 (2004)
9. Hu, W., Xiao, X., Xie, D., Tan, T., Maybank, S.: Traffic accident prediction using 3D model-based vehicle tracking. IEEE Trans. Veh. Technol. **53**(3), 677–694 (2004)
10. Kamkar, S., Safabakhsh, R.: Vehicle detection, counting and classification in various conditions. IET Intel. Transp. Syst. **10**(6), 406–413 (2016)
11. Klette, R.: Concise Computer Vision. Springer, London (2014). https://doi.org/10.1007/978-1-4471-6320-6
12. Krizhevsky, A., Sutskever, I., and Hinton, G.E.: ImageNet classification with deep convolutional neural networks. In: Proceedings of Advances Neural Information Processing Systems, pp. 1097–1105 (2012)
13. LeCun, Y., Bengio, Y., Hinton, G.: Deep learning. Nature **521**(7553), 436–444 (2015)

14. Li, Y., Li, B., Tian, B., Yao, Q.: Vehicle detection based on the and-or graph for congested traffic conditions. IEEE Trans. Intell. Transp. Syst. **14**(2), 984–993 (2013)
15. Li, Y., Li, B., Tian, B., Yao, Q.: Vehicle detection based on the deformable hybrid image template. In: Proceedings of IEEE International Conference on Vehicular Electronics Safety, pp. 114–118 (2013)
16. Li, Y., Liu, W., Huang, Q.: Traffic anomaly detection based on image descriptor in videos. Multimedia Tools Appl. **75**(5), 2487–2505 (2016)
17. Niknejad, H.T., Takeuchi, A., Mita, S., McAllester, D.: On-road multivehicle tracking using deformable object model and particle filter with improved likelihood estimation. IEEE Trans. Intell. Transp. Syst. **12**(2), 748–758 (2012)
18. Ren, S., He, K., Girshick, R., Sun, J.: Faster R-CNN: towards real-time object detection with region proposal networks. In: Proceedings of Advances Neural Information Processing Systems, pp. 91–99 (2015)
19. Sabokrou, M., Fayyaz, M., Fathy, M., Klette, R.: Deep-cascade: cascading 3D deep neural networks for fast anomaly detection and localization in crowded scenes. IEEE Trans. Image Process. **26**(4), 1992–2004 (2017). ieeexplore.ieee.org/document/7858798/
20. Uijlings, J.R.R., Van De Sande, K.E.A., Gevers, T., Smeulders, A.W.M.: Selective search for object recognition. Int. J. Comput. Vis. **104**(2), 154–171 (2013)
21. Viola, P., Jones, M.: Robust real-time face detection Int. J. Comput. Vis. **57**, 137–154 (2004)
22. Wu, Y.N., Si, Z., Gong, H., Zhu, S.-C.: Learning active basis model for object detection and recognition. Int. J. Comput. Vis. **90**(2), 198–235 (2010)
23. Xu, Y., Yu, G., Wu, X., Wang, Y., Ma, Y.: An enhanced Viola-Jones vehicle detection method from unmanned aerial vehicles imagery. IEEE Trans. Intell. Transp. Syst. **18**(7), 1845–1856 (2016). ieeexplore.ieee.org/document/7726065/
24. Zhang, Y., et al.: Vehicles detection in complex urban traffic scenes using Gaussian mixture model with confidence measurement. IET Intel. Transp. Syst. **10**(6), 445–452 (2016)

Author Index

Printed in the United States
By Bookmasters